Exam 70-643: *TS: Configuring Windows Server® 2008 Applications Infrastructure*

Objective	Chapter	Lesson
Deploying Servers		
Deploy images by using Windows Deployment Services.	1	1, 2
Configure Microsoft Windows activation.	1	4
Configure Windows Server Hyper-V and virtual machines.	1	3
Configure high availability.	2	2
Configure storage.	2	1
Configuring Terminal Services		
Configure Windows Server 2008 Terminal Services RemoteApp (TS RemoteApp).	4	3
Configure Terminal Services Gateway.	4	2
Configure Terminal Services load balancing.	3	2
Configure and monitor Terminal Services resources.	4	1
Configure Terminal Services licensing.	3	1, 2
Configure Terminal Services client connections.	4	1
Configure Terminal Services server options.	3	2
Configuring a Web Services Infrastructure		
Configure Web applications.	5, 6	Chapter 5, Lessons 1, 2 Chapter 6, Lesson 1
Manage Web sites.	5, 6	Chapter 5, Lesson 2 Chapter 6, Lesson 2
Configure a File Transfer Protocol (FTP) server.	7	1
Configure Simple Mail Transfer Protocol (SMTP).	7	2
Manage Internet Information Services (IIS).	5	2
Configure SSL security.	6	1
Configure Web site authentication and permissions.	6	1, 2
Configuring Network Application Services		
Configure Windows Media server.	8	1
Configure Digital Rights Management (DRM).	8	1
Configure Microsoft Windows SharePoint Services server options.	9	1
Configure Windows SharePoint Services e-mail integration.	9	1

Note: Exam objectives are subject to change at any time without prior notice and at Microsoft's sole discretion. Please visit the Microsoft Learning Certification Web site (*www.microsoft.com/learning/mcp/*) for the most current listing of exam objectives.

Microsoft

MCTS Self-Paced Training Kit (Exam 70-643): Configuring Windows Server® 2008 Applications Infrastructure

J.C. Mackin and
Anil Desai

PUBLISHED BY
Microsoft Press
A Division of Microsoft Corporation
One Microsoft Way
Redmond, Washington 98052-6399

Library of Congress Control Number: 2008920566

Printed and bound in the United States of America.

1 2 3 4 5 6 7 8 9   QWT   3 2 1 0 9 8

Distributed in Canada by H.B. Fenn and Company Ltd.

A CIP catalogue record for this book is available from the British Library.

Microsoft Press books are available through booksellers and distributors worldwide. For further information about international editions, contact your local Microsoft Corporation office or contact Microsoft Press International directly at fax (425) 936-7329. Visit our Web site at www.microsoft.com/mspress. Send comments to tkinput@microsoft.com.

Microsoft, Microsoft Press, Active Directory, ActiveX, Aero, BitLocker, Excel, Internet Explorer, MSDN, MS-DOS, Outlook, RemoteApp, SharePoint, SQL Server, Visio, Visual Basic, Visual Studio, Win32, Windows, Windows Live, Windows Media, Windows NT, Windows PowerShell, Windows Server, and Windows Vista are either registered trademarks or trademarks of Microsoft Corporation in the United States and/or other countries. Other product and company names mentioned herein may be the trademarks of their respective owners.

The example companies, organizations, products, domain names, e-mail addresses, logos, people, places, and events depicted herein are fictitious. No association with any real company, organization, product, domain name, e-mail address, logo, person, place, or event is intended or should be inferred.

This book expresses the author's views and opinions. The information contained in this book is provided without any express, statutory, or implied warranties. Neither the authors, Microsoft Corporation, nor its resellers, or distributors will be held liable for any damages caused or alleged to be caused either directly or indirectly by this book.

Acquisitions Editor: Ken Jones
Developmental Editor: Laura Sackerman
Project Editor: Maria Gargiulo
Editorial Production: nSight, Inc.
Technical Reviewer: Bob Hogan
Cover: Tom Draper Design

Body Part No. X14-37563
Section No. X14-54819

About the Authors

J.C. Mackin

J.C. Mackin (MCITP, MCTS, MCSE, MCDST, MCT) is a writer, editor, consultant, and trainer who has been working with Microsoft networks for more than a decade. Books he has previously authored or co-authored include *MCSA/MCSE Self-Paced Training Kit (Exam 70-291): Implementing, Managing, and Maintaining a Microsoft Windows Server 2003 Network Infrastructure; MCITP Self-Paced Training Kit (Exam 70-443): Designing a Database Server Infrastructure Using Microsoft SQL Server 2005;* and *MCITP Self-Paced Training Kit (Exam 70-622): Supporting and Troubleshooting Applications on a Windows Vista Client for Enterprise Support Technicians.* He also holds a master's degree in telecommunications and network management.

When not working with computers, J.C. can be found with a panoramic camera photographing medieval villages in Italy or France.

Anil Desai

Anil Desai (MCITP, MCSE, MCSD) is an independent consultant based in Austin, Texas. He specializes in evaluating, implementing, and managing IT solutions. He has worked extensively with Microsoft server products and the Microsoft .NET development platform and has more than 12 years of IT experience. Anil is a Microsoft MVP (Windows Server – Management Infrastructure).

Anil is the author of numerous technical books focusing on Microsoft certifications, the Windows Server platform, virtualization, Active Directory, Microsoft SQL Server, and IT management topics. He has made dozens of conference presentations at national events and is a contributor to several online and print magazines. In his spare time, he enjoys cycling, playing guitar and drums, and playing games on his Xbox 360. For more information, please see *http://AnilDesai.net.*

Contents at a Glance

Table of Contents

What do you think of this book? We want to hear from you!

Microsoft is interested in hearing your feedback so we can continually improve our books and learning resources for you. To participate in a brief online survey, please visit:

www.microsoft.com/learning/booksurvey/

What do you think of this book? We want to hear from you!

Microsoft is interested in hearing your feedback so we can continually improve our books and learning resources for you. To participate in a brief online survey, please visit:

www.microsoft.com/learning/booksurvey/

Introduction

This training kit is designed for information technology (IT) professionals who support or plan to support Windows Server 2008 networks and who also plan to take the Microsoft Certified Technology Specialist (MCTS) 70-643 exam. It is assumed that before you begin using this kit, you have a solid, foundation-level understanding of Microsoft Windows client and server operating systems and common Internet technologies.

The material covered in this training kit and on the 70-643 exam relates to the technologies in a Windows Server 2008 network that support distributed access to Web content, media, operating systems, and applications.

By using this training kit, you will learn how to do the following:

- Deploy Windows servers and clients across a network by using Windows Deployment Services and the Windows Automated Installation Kit (WAIK)
- Configure Hyper-V and other Windows virtualization technologies
- Configure high-availability storage solutions for servers
- Configure and manage Terminal Services in Windows Server 2008
- Configure and manage Internet Information Services 7.0
- Configure Windows Media Services
- Configure Windows SharePoint Services

Find additional content online   As new or updated material that complements your book becomes available, it will be posted on the Microsoft Press Online Windows Server and Client Web site. Based on the final build of Windows Server 2008, the type of material you might find includes updates to book content, articles, links to companion content, errata, sample chapters, and more. This Web site will be available soon at *www.microsoft.com/learning/books/online/serverclient* and will be updated periodically.

Hardware Requirements (Virtual PC)

To minimize the time and expense of configuring physical computers for this training kit, it's recommended that you use Virtual PC 2007 or later, which you can download for free at *http://www.microsoft.com/downloads*. You can use other virtualization software instead, such as Virtual Server 2005 R2 or Hyper-V, but the practice setup instructions in the book assume that you are using Virtual PC. If you are not using virtualization software, see the section that follows for physical hardware requirements.

If you choose to use virtualization software, you need only one physical computer to perform the exercises in this book. That physical host computer must meet the following minimum hardware requirements:

- 1-GHz processor
- 2.0 GB of RAM or more (recommended if you are using Windows Vista or Windows Server 2008 as the host operating system in a virtual environment)
- 80 GB of available hard disk space
- DVD-ROM drive
- Internet connectivity

Hardware Requirements (Physical)

If you choose to use physical computers instead of virtualization software, use the following list to meet the minimum hardware requirements of the practice exercises in this book:

- Three personal computers, each with a 1-GHz processor, 512 MB of RAM, network card, video card, and DVD-ROM drive.
- The following storage requirements:
  - ❑ Computer 1 (Server1) must have one attached hard disk with a storage capacity of at least 20 GB.
  - ❑ Computer 2 (Server2) must have at least two and preferably three attached hard disks. Each hard disk should have a storage capacity of at least 15 GB.
  - ❑ Computer 3 (Core1) must have one attached hard disk with a storage capacity of at least 5 GB.
  - ❑ All hard disks must be freshly formatted. (No software should be installed.)
- All three computers must be physically connected to each other and to the Internet.
- The network adapter on Computer 2 (Server2) must be PXE-boot compatible.
- If your network does not already include an Internet gateway, Computer 1 (Server1) needs a second network adapter so that it can act as the Internet gateway for the other two computers.
- The test network that includes these computers should be isolated from your production network. (For example, your test network cannot already include a DHCP server that automatically assigns addresses to computers.)

Software Requirements

The following software is required to complete the practice exercises:

- If you are using Virtual PC 2007 or later to create the practice exercises in a virtual environment, the physical host computer must already be running a Windows operating system and have network drivers installed. At the time of this writing, Virtual PC 2007 is officially supported on Windows Vista Business, Windows Vista Enterprise, Windows Vista Ultimate, Windows XP Professional, and Windows XP Tablet PC Edition. You can check the Virtual PC Web site at *http://www.microsoft.com/windows/products/winfamily/virtualpc/default.mspx* for updated information about which operating systems can run Virtual PC.

- Windows Server 2008. You can download an evaluation edition of Windows Server 2008 at the Microsoft Download Center at *http://www.microsoft.com/downloads*. Note that you must use a 32-bit version of Windows Server 2008 within Virtual PC.

- The Windows Automated Installation Toolkit (WAIK). You can download the WAIK at the Microsoft Download Center at *http://www.microsoft.com/downloads*.

- If you are *not* using virtualization software, you need software that allows you to handle .iso and .img files. This software needs to perform either or both of the following functions:
  - ❏ Burn .iso and .img files to CDs or DVDs. (This solution also requires CD/DVD recording hardware.)
  - ❏ Mount .iso and .img files as virtual CD or DVD drives on your computer.

Practice Setup Instructions

You need to prepare three computers for the exercises in this training kit. The following instructions assume you have installed Virtual PC 2007 or later on a host computer that meets the minimum hardware requirements specified in the "Hardware Requirements (Virtual PC)" section of this introduction. If you choose to use other virtualization software or physical computers in place of Virtual PC, you can use the following instructions to determine the general setup requirements of the practice, but you will need to adjust the step-by-step instructions accordingly.

IMPORTANT   Download required software

Before you begin preparing the practice computers, you must have a copy of Windows Server 2008 (either as an .iso file or as a DVD) and the Windows Automated Installation Kit (either as an .img file or as a DVD).

The practice setup occurs in four phases. In the first phase, you create the three virtual machines. Figure 1 shows the virtual hardware configuration of the virtual machines as they appear after this first phase.

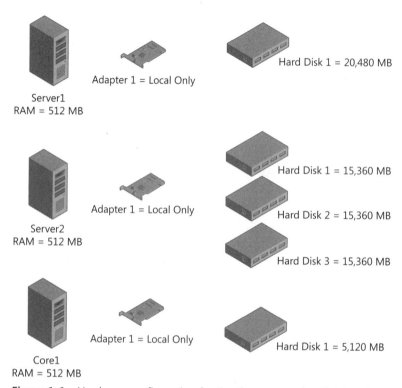

Server1
RAM = 512 MB

Adapter 1 = Local Only

Hard Disk 1 = 20,480 MB

Server2
RAM = 512 MB

Adapter 1 = Local Only

Hard Disk 1 = 15,360 MB

Hard Disk 2 = 15,360 MB

Hard Disk 3 = 15,360 MB

Core1
RAM = 512 MB

Adapter 1 = Local Only

Hard Disk 1 = 5,120 MB

Figure 1-1   Hardware configuration for the three computers in Virtual PC

In the second phase of the practice setup, you configure the software for the Server1 and Core1 machines. (No software configuration is necessary for Server2 because this computer must be left clean as a virtual bare-metal machine.)

The third phase of practice setup describes the configuration necessary to provide an Internet connection for all three computers. By performing these steps, you add a second virtual network adapter to Server1 and configure Network Address Translation (NAT) across its two adapters, as shown in Figure 2.

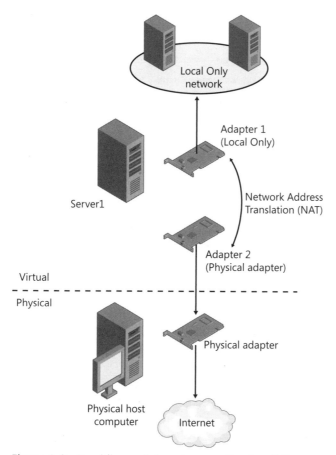

Figure 1-2   Providing an Internet connection for all three computers in Virtual PC

In the fourth and final phase of the practice setup, you activate the Server1 and Core1 servers over the Internet.

Phase 1: Create the Virtual Machines

Perform the following steps to create the virtual machines for this training kit.

Create the Server1 Virtual Machine

In the Virtual PC console, click the New button to launch the New Virtual Machine Wizard, and then specify the following settings:

- Options: Create a Virtual Machine
- Name and location: Server1

   (The default location is used if you specify only a name for this setting.)

- Operating System: Windows Server 2003 (Windows Server 2008 if available)

   At the time of this writing, Virtual PC 2007 does not offer the option to specify Windows Server 2008 as the operating system. When this option does become available, choose Windows Server 2008.

- RAM: 512 MB

   If you choose Windows Server 2003 as the operating system, Virtual PC recommends 256 MB of RAM. In this case, select the option to adjust the recommended RAM and enter 512 instead.

- Hard disk size: 20,480 MB

Configure the Network Adapter in Virtual PC   After you have created a new (empty) virtual machine named Server1 in Virtual PC, use the Virtual PC console to open the settings of the Server1 machine. Then, configure Adapter 1 to connect to the Local Only network, as shown in Figure 3. Do not add a second adapter yet.

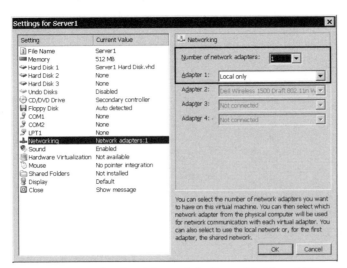

Figure 1-3   Configuring Adapter 1 for Server1 in Virtual PC

Create the Core1 Virtual Machine

Use the New Virtual Machine Wizard to create a second virtual machine. Configure all settings identically to those of the Server1 machine (including the network adapter) except in the following two cases:

- Name and location: Core1
- Hard disk size: 5120 MB

Create the Server2 Virtual Machine

Use the New Virtual Machine Wizard to create the final virtual machine. Configure all settings identically to those of the Server1 machine (including the network adapter) except in the following two cases:

- Name and location: Server2
- Hard disk size: 15360 MB

IMPORTANT   **In Hyper-V, use a legacy adapter for Server2**

If you are creating your servers in Hyper-V instead of Virtual PC, be sure to configure the network adapter on Server2 as a legacy adapter. Otherwise, the adapter will not be PXE-compatible. This feature is required for the deployment of Windows Server 2008 that is performed on Server2 in the exercises found at the end of Chapter 1, Lesson 2, "Configuring Windows Deployment Services."

Configure the second and third hard disks for Server2   Use the Virtual PC console to open the settings for the Server2 virtual machine. In the Settings For Server2 dialog box, select Hard Disk 2 in the left pane, and then click the Virtual Disk Wizard button. Use the Virtual Disk Wizard to create a virtual hard disk with a name and location of your choice. Choose the option for a Dynamically Expanding disk, and then specify the size as 15360 MB. After the virtual disk is created, in the Settings For Server2 dialog box, select the Virtual Hard Disk File option and browse to select the new virtual hard disk you have just created.

Finally, use the same process to create and attach a 15360 MB virtual hard disk for Server2's Hard Disk 3.

After you have added the two additional virtual hard disks, the settings for Server2 should indicate a VHD file for all three hard disks, as shown in Figure 4.

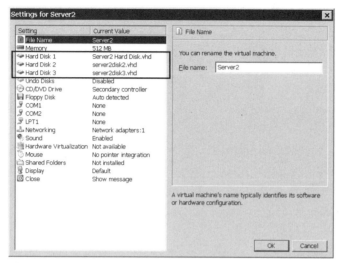

Figure 1-4   The Server2 virtual machine should have three attached virtual hard disks

Phase 2: Configure the Operating Systems on Server1 and Core1

Use the following instructions to configure the Server1 and Core1 computers.

Configure Server1

Server1 will be used as a DHCP server, DNS server, and Active Directory domain controller for the contoso.com domain. Server1 also needs to have the WAIK installed. Perform the following steps to meet the configuration requirements for the server.

1. In Virtual PC 2007, start the new Server1 virtual machine. Then, use the CD menu to attach the Windows Server 2008 DVD or ISO image to the virtual machine, as shown in Figure 5. (Note that you can use the *Capture ISO Image* command to capture either an ISO file or an IMG file.)

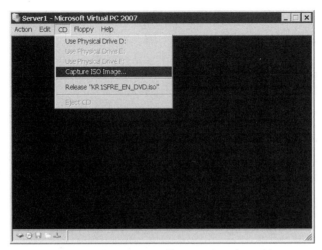

Figure 1-5   Attaching an ISO file to a virtual machine

2. Perform a default installation of Windows Server 2008. Use the following guidelines:

   ❑ If desired, choose a language and keyboard corresponding to your region.

   ❑ Do not enter a product key at this time.

   ❑ Choose Windows Server 2008 Standard (Full Installation) or Windows Server 2008 Enterprise (Full Installation).

   ❑ Install Windows in the default location (Disk 0 Unallocated Space).

   ❑ Use a strong password of your choice when logging on as Administrator for the first time.

   ❑ After you log on as Administrator, use the Initial Configuration Tasks window to make the following configuration changes.

3. Configure the Local Area Connection on Server1. You can perform this step by using either the Initial Configuration Tasks window or a command prompt.

   In the Initial Configuration Tasks window, click Configure Networking, open the properties of the Local Area Connection, and then configure the properties of Internet Protocol version 4 (TCP/IPv4) with the following options and values:

   ❑ Select Use The Following IP Address

      ● IP Address: 192.168.10.1

      ● Subnet Mask: 255.255.255.0

      ● Default Gateway: leave blank

❑ Select Use The Following DNS Server Addresses
  ● Preferred DNS server: 192.168.10.1
  ● Alternate DNS server: leave blank

To configure these same IP settings at a command prompt, type the following two commands in succession:

```
netsh interface ipv4 set address "local area connection" static 192.168.10.1
255.255.255.0
netsh interface ipv4 set dns "local area connection" static 192.168.10.1
```

Configure the computer name. You can perform this step by using either the Initial Configuration Tasks window or a command prompt.

In Initial Configuration Tasks, click Provide Computer Name And Domain. Then, click the Change button and specify the computer name as Server1. Do not specify a domain at this time.

To set the computer name at the command prompt, type the following command:

```
netdom renamecomputer %computername% /newname:Server1 /reboot
```

4. Use the Run box from the Start menu to run Dcpromo and configure Server1 as a domain controller in a new Active Directory domain named contoso.com. Specify the following options in the Active Directory Domain Services Installation Wizard:

❑ Create a New Domain In A New Forest.

❑ FQDN Of The Forest Root: **contoso.com.**

❑ Forest Functional Level: Windows Server 2008.

❑ Additional Domain Controller Options: DNS Server (Default).

❑ If you are warned that the computer has a dynamically assigned IP address, click Yes.

❑ If you are warned that a delegation for this DNS server cannot be created, click Yes.

❑ Locations for database, log files, and Sysvol: Leave defaults.

❑ Directory Services Restore Mode Administrator Password: Any strong password of your choice.

5. After the Active Directory Domain Services Installation Wizard completes, restart Server1 immediately, and then log on to the contoso.com domain from Server1 as CONTOSO\Administrator.

IMPORTANT How do you log on to a computer in Virtual PC?

Note that in Virtual PC, you must use the Right Alt+Del command to enter the keystroke Ctrl+Alt+Del. You also have the option of choosing Ctrl+Alt+Del from the Action menu.

---

6. Add the DHCP Server role. In the Initial Configuration Tasks window, click Add Roles. Use the Add Roles Wizard to add the DHCP Server role with the following options:

   ❑ Network Connection Bindings: Default. (Leave 192.168.10.1 checked.)
   ❑ IPv4 DNS Server Settings:
      ● Parent Domain: **contoso.com**.
      ● Preferred DNS Server IPv4 Address: **192.168.10.1**.
      ● Alternate DNS Server IPv4 Address: Leave blank.
   ❑ WINS Server Settings: WINS is not required.
   ❑ Add a DHCP scope with the following specifications:
      ● Scope Name: **Contoso.com**.
      ● Starting IP Address: **192.168.10.2**.
      ● Ending IP Address: **192.168.10.10**.
      ● Subnet Mask: **255.255.255.0**.
      ● Default Gateway: **192.168.10.1**. (This assumes an Internet access configuration as described in Phase 3 of the practice setup instructions.)
      ● Subnet Type: Wired.
      ● Activate This Scope: Leave checked.
      ● DHCPv6 Stateless Mode: Leave default.
      ● IPv6 DNS Server Settings: Leave default.
      ● Authorize DHCP Server: Leave default.

7. Create and name three domain administrator accounts. To do so, use the following step-by-step instructions.

   a. In the Active Directory Users And Computers administrative tool, expand the *contoso.com* node in the console tree, and then select the Users folder.

   b. Right-click the Users folder, point to New on the shortcut menu, and then click User.

   c. In the New Object – User dialog box, type the name **ContosoAdmin1** in the Full Name and User Logon Name text boxes, and then click Next.

   d. Enter a password of your choice, click Next, and then click Finish.

   e. In the Active Directory Users And Computers console, locate the ContosoAdmin1 account you have just created in the details pane. Right-click the account, and then click Add To A Group from the shortcut menu.

   f. In the Select Groups dialog box, type **domain admins**, and then press Enter. In the Active Directory Domain Services message box, click OK.

    g. Create two additional domain administrator accounts named ContosoAdmin2 and ContosoAdmin3, respectively, using steps b through f.

    h. If desired, create an additional domain administrator account with your name.

8. Enable File Sharing on Server1. Open Network and Sharing Center by right-clicking on the Network icon in the Notification area and clicking Network And Sharing Center. In the Sharing And Discovery area, select the option to turn on file sharing.

9. Install the Windows Automated Installation Kit (WAIK) using the WAIK DVD or IMG file you have downloaded from the Microsoft Download Center. To do so, use the following step-by-step instructions.

    a. Mount the WAIK DVD or .img file as a DVD drive in Virtual PC by using the *Capture ISO Image* command from the CD menu.

    b. In the Welcome To Windows Automated Installation Kit window, use the .NET Framework Setup and MSXML 6.0 Setup links to install these components if necessary.

    If either of these components is already installed on the local machine, you will not be given an Install option.

    c. Use the Windows AIK Setup link to install the WAIK.

10. Install Virtual Machine Additions on Server1.

    From the Action menu, select Install Or Update Virtual Machine Additions. Follow the prompts to install Virtual Machine Additions on Server1. Restart the computer and log back on as CONTOSO\Administrator.

Configure Core1

Core1 will act as a member server in the contoso.com domain. Use the following instructions to configure the Core1 server.

1. Attach the Windows Server 2008 ISO file or DVD to the Core1 virtual machine, and then perform a default installation of Windows Server 2008 Server Core. Use the following guidelines:

    ❑ If desired, choose a language and keyboard corresponding to your region.

    ❑ Do not enter a product key at this time.

    ❑ Choose Windows Server 2008 Standard (Server Core Installation) or Windows Server 2008 Enterprise (Server Core Installation).

    ❑ Install Windows in the default location (Disk 0 Unallocated Space).

❑ To log on for the first time, click the Other User tile, and then specify a User Name Of Administrator *with a blank password*.

You will immediately be prompted to change the password.

2. Verify the IP configuration. At the command prompt, type **ipconfig /all** to ensure that Core1 has received an IP configuration from Server1.

3. Configure the Core1 computer name and domain membership. At the command prompt, type the following command:

```
netdom renamecomputer %computername% /newname:Core1
```

4. To join Core1 to the Contoso.com domain, type the following command:

```
netdom join %computername% /domain:Contoso.com /userd:ContosoAdmin1 /passwordd:*
```

5. Then, type the password associated with the domain user (ContosoAdmin1) when prompted.

NOTE **Note the spelling**

Note the repetition of the letter "d" used in the passwordd switch in the Netdom command.

---

6. Finally, restart Core1 by typing the following command:

```
shutdown /r /t 0
```

Phase 3: Configure Internet Access for the Contoso.com Network

In this phase, you add to Server1 a second adapter that is bound to a physical network adapter on the physical host machine. You then configure network address translation (NAT) on Server1.

Add and Configure a Second Virtual Adapter on Server1

Complete the following steps to add and configure a second virtual adapter on Server1.

1. Shut down Server1. Use the Virtual PC Console to open Server1 settings.

2. In the Settings For Server1 dialog box, set the number of network adapters to 2. For Adapter 2, choose the network adapter that corresponds to the physical adapter connected to the Internet on the host machine.

The physical adapter should already have its own IP address and be able to communicate with the Internet. An example such a configuration is shown in Figure 6.

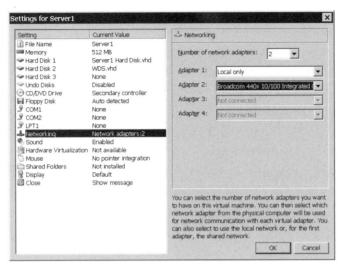

Figure 1-6   Configuring the second adapter on Server1

3. Start and log on to Server1.

4. In Server Manager, click Add Roles. Use the following information to complete the Add Roles Wizard:

    ❏   Select Server Roles: Network Policy and Access Services

    ❏   Select Role Services: Routing and Remote Access Services (Do not select any other role services at this time.)

Configure NAT on Server1

Use the following step-by-step instructions to configure NAT on Server1.

1. Open the Routing And Remote Access administrative tool.

2. In the Routing And Remote Access console tree, right-click the Server1 node, and then click Configure And Enable Routing And Remote Access.

3. Specify the following settings in the Routing And Remote Access Server Setup Wizard:

    ❏   On the Configuration page, click Network Address Translation (NAT).

    ❏   On the NAT Internet Connection page, select Local Area Connection 2 as the public interface to connect to the Internet.

4. In Server Manager, select the Server Manager node. In the Security Information area, click Configure IE ESC. Select the option to turn IE ESC off for Administrators.

5. Open Internet Explorer and select Internet Options from the Tools menu. Set the home page to an Internet-based Web page of your choice.

6. Verify Internet connectivity in Internet Explorer by clicking the Home icon.

Phase 4: Activate the Servers (Recommended)

Perform the following steps if you have product keys for both Server1 and Core1.

1. Activate Server1. Open the System Control Panel and select the option to change the product key. Type the product key when prompted and click Next.

    Windows will automatically activate over the Internet.

2. Activate Core1 by using the following step-by-step procedure:

    a. Log on to contoso.com from Core1 as a domain administrator, and then type the following command, where *productkey* is your product key (with dashes):

    ```
    slmgr -ipk productkey
    ```

    b. When you receive a message indicating that the product key was installed successfully, type the following command:

    ```
    slmgr -ato
    ```

    c. After you receive a message indicating that the product has been activated successfully, you can shut down Core1 by typing the following command:

    ```
    shutdown /s /t 0
    ```

Using the CD and DVD

A companion CD is included with this training kit. The companion CD contains the following:

■ **Practice tests** You can reinforce your understanding of how to configure Windows Server 2008 by using electronic practice tests you customize to meet your needs from the pool of Lesson Review questions in this book. Alternatively, you can practice for the 70-643 certification exam by using tests created from a pool of over 200 realistic exam questions, which give you many practice exams to ensure that you are prepared.

■ **Webcasts** To supplement your learning, the CD includes Microsoft-sponsored Webcasts from experts. These Webcasts are lectures and demonstrations that provide additional information about subjects covered in the book.

■ **An eBook** An electronic version (eBook) of this book is included for when you do not want to carry the printed book with you. The eBook is in Portable Document Format (PDF), and you can view it by using Adobe Acrobat or Adobe Reader.

■ **Sample chapters**   Sample chapters from other Microsoft Press titles on Windows Server 2008. These chapters are in PDF, as well.

> **Digital Content for Digital Book Readers:** If you bought a digital-only edition of this book, you can enjoy select content from the print edition's companion CD. Visit *http://download.microsoft.com /download/F/3/3/F335F2B1-2AA4-46D2-BA69-A495540B19FA/9780735625112_OCC.exe* to get your downloadable content. This content is always up-to-date and available to all readers.

How to Install the Practice Tests

To install the practice test software from the companion CD to your hard disk, do the following:

1. Insert the companion CD into your CD drive and accept the license agreement.

   A CD menu appears.

   NOTE If the CD menu does not appear

   If the CD menu or the license agreement does not appear, AutoRun might be disabled on your computer. Refer to the Readme.txt file on the CD-ROM for alternate installation instructions.

2. Click Practice Tests and follow the instructions on the screen.

How to Use the Practice Tests

To start the practice test software, follow these steps.

1. Click Start\All Programs\Microsoft Press Training Kit Exam Prep.

   A window appears that shows all the Microsoft Press training kit exam prep suites installed on your computer.

2. Double-click the lesson review or practice test you want to use.

   NOTE Lesson reviews vs. practice tests

   Select the (70-643) TS: Windows Server 2008 Applications Infrastructure, Configuring lesson review to use the questions from the "Lesson Review" sections of this book. Select the (70-643) TS: Windows Server 2008 Applications Infrastructure, Configuring practice test to use a pool of 200 questions similar to those that appear on the 70-643 certification exam.

Lesson Review Options

When you start a lesson review, the Custom Mode dialog box appears so that you can configure your test. You can click OK to accept the defaults, or you can customize the number of questions you want, how the practice test software works, which exam objectives you want the questions to relate to, and whether you want your lesson review to be timed. If you are retaking a test, you can select whether you want to see all the questions again or only the questions you missed or did not answer.

After you click OK, your lesson review starts.

- To take the test, answer the questions and use the Next and Previous buttons to move from question to question.
- After you answer an individual question, if you want to see which answers are correct—along with an explanation of each correct answer—click Explanation.
- If you prefer to wait until the end of the test to see how you did, answer all the questions, and then click Score Test. You will see a summary of the exam objectives you chose and the percentage of questions you got right overall and per objective. You can print a copy of your test, review your answers, or retake the test.

Practice Test Options

When you start a practice test, you choose whether to take the test in Certification Mode, Study Mode, or Custom Mode.

- **Certification Mode**   Closely resembles the experience of taking a certification exam. The test has a set number of questions. It is timed, and you cannot pause and restart the timer.
- **Study Mode**   Creates an untimed test in which you can review the correct answers and the explanations after you answer each question.
- **Custom Mode**   Gives you full control over the test options so that you can customize them as you like.

In all modes the user interface when you are taking the test is basically the same but with different options enabled or disabled, depending on the mode. The main options are discussed in the previous section, "Lesson Review Options."

When you review your answer to an individual practice test question, a "References" section is provided that lists where in the training kit you can find the information that relates to that question and provides links to other sources of information. After you click Test Results to score your entire practice test, you can click the Learning Plan tab to see a list of references for every objective.

How to Uninstall the Practice Tests

To uninstall the practice test software for a training kit, use the Add Or Remove Programs option (Windows XP) or the Programs And Features option (Windows Vista) in Windows Control Panel.

Microsoft Certified Professional Program

The Microsoft certifications provide the best method to prove your command of current Microsoft products and technologies. The exams and corresponding certifications are developed to validate your mastery of critical competencies as you design and develop, or implement and support, solutions with Microsoft products and technologies. Computer professionals who become Microsoft certified are recognized as experts and are sought after industry-wide. Certification brings a variety of benefits to the individual and to employers and organizations.

MORE INFO All the Microsoft certifications

For a full list of Microsoft certifications, go to *http://www.microsoft.com/learning/mcp/default.asp.*

Technical Support

Every effort has been made to ensure the accuracy of this book and the contents of the companion CD. If you have comments, questions, or ideas regarding this book or the companion CD, please send them to Microsoft Press by using either of the following methods:

- E-mail: tkinput@microsoft.com
- Postal mail at:

   Microsoft Press
   Attn: *MCTS Self-Paced Training Kit (Exam 70-643): Configuring Windows Server 2008 Applications Infrastructure,* Editor
   One Microsoft Way
   Redmond, WA 98052-6399

For additional support information regarding this book and the CD-ROM (including answers to commonly asked questions about installation and use), visit the Microsoft Press Technical Support Web site at *http://www.microsoft.com/learning/support/books.* To connect directly to the Microsoft Knowledge Base and enter a query, visit *http://support.microsoft.com/search.* For support information regarding Microsoft software, connect to *http://support.microsoft.com.*

Chapter 1

Implementing and Configuring a Windows Deployment Infrastructure

For years before the arrival of Windows Vista and Windows Server 2008, the process of deploying Windows in large networks remained virtually unchanged. This latest generation of Windows operating systems, however, has introduced a number of new deployment technologies (such as ImageX and Windows Deployment Services) along with new deployment considerations (such as virtual machines and Windows activation infrastructure). Consequently, there is now much to learn about the seemingly elementary topic of Windows deployment, even for experienced Windows administrators. This chapter introduces you to the many new deployment technologies and concepts that you need to understand for the 70-643 exam.

For more in-depth information about deployment that goes beyond what you need to know for the exam, consult the appendix at the back of this training kit.

Exam objectives in this chapter:
- Deploying Servers
  - ❑ Deploy images by using Windows Deployment Services.
  - ❑ Configure Microsoft Windows activation.
  - ❑ Configure Windows Server Hyper-V and virtual machines.

Lessons in this chapter:

Before You Begin

To complete the lessons in this chapter, you must have:

- A domain controller named Server1.contoso.com with at least 3 GB of free space on any partition or volume.
- A computer or virtual machine with no operating system installed and at least 512 MB of RAM. (This bare-metal computer will be used for Server2.)
- Downloaded the Windows Automated Installation Kit (Windows AIK) from the Microsoft Download Center (*http://www.microsoft.com/download*) and installed the Windows AIK on Server1.

Real World

JC Mackin

Should we begin with the fact that all Windows installations are now image-based? Or should we start by naming some of the new tools that you need to learn—such as ImageX, Windows PE, Windows System Image Manager, and Windows Deployment Services—which are all used to support deploying these new Windows images? Or maybe we should talk first about the fact that, since those handy corporate versions of Windows are things of the past, you now need to learn how to activate massive numbers of computers after deployment. And by the way, before deploying any servers or clients, you should definitely decide whether it's best to deploy them on a physical or virtual hardware platform.

Talk about an overhaul! Deployment might in fact be the single biggest change between Windows Server 2008 and earlier versions of Windows Server. If you're new to Windows administration, consider yourself lucky. In this particular area, you are now on an even playing field with the seasoned pros. If, however, you're a seasoned pro, take heart. Once you do learn these new technologies, they will make Windows deployment easier than it ever has been before.

Lesson 1: Deploying Windows in a Windows Server 2008 Environment

To deploy an operating system means to make that operating system ready for use, typically on many computers in a corporate network. In a network made up of clients running Windows Vista and servers running Windows Server 2008, you can deploy new clients and servers in a number of ways, and all these methods—including basic installation—are based on imaging technology. To deploy Windows images, you can use the installation media (DVD), Windows imaging tools such as ImageX and Microsoft System Center Configuration Manager 2007, or the Windows Deployment Services server role built into Windows Server 2008.

> **After this lesson, you will be able to:**
> - Understand the tools that can help you manage, edit, and deploy Windows images.
> - Understand the various methods you can use to deploy Windows Vista and Windows Server 2008.
> - Create a Windows PE CD.
>
> **Estimated lesson time: 50 minutes**

Windows Deployment Fundamentals

Beginning with Windows Vista and continuing with Windows Server 2008, Microsoft has introduced a new process for installing and deploying Windows. This change is reflected in new technologies and tools that support the new Windows imaging format, which is based on the WIM file.

What Is a WIM File?

A Windows Imaging Format (WIM) file contains one or more disk images in the WIM format. These images are file-based, which means that they are composed of collections of volume files and are not merely sector-based snapshots of disk data, as is common with many other disk imaging applications. The main advantage of file-based images over sector-based images is that you can modify them before, during, and after deployment.

Besides storing file data, WIM files include XML-based metadata describing the files and directories that make up each image. This metadata includes access control lists (ACLs), short/long file names, attributes, and other information used to restore an imaged volume.Figure 1-1 shows the metadata associated with a specific WIM file.

```
GUID:        <63961e63-415e-4074-845a-aac3bd6334df>
Image Count: 1
Compression: LZX
Part Number: 1/1
Boot Index:  1
Attributes:  0x8
             Relative path junction

Available Image Choices:
------------------------
<WIM>
  <TOTALBYTES>164001377</TOTALBYTES>
  <IMAGE INDEX="1">
    <NAME>Microsoft Windows Vista PE (X86)</NAME>
    <DESCRIPTION>Microsoft Windows Vista PE (X86)</DESCRIPTION>
    <WINDOWS>
      <ARCH>0</ARCH>
      <PRODUCTNAME>Microsoft« Windows« Operating System</PRODUCTNAME>
      <PRODUCTTYPE>WinNT</PRODUCTTYPE>
      <PRODUCTSUITE></PRODUCTSUITE>
      <LANGUAGES>
        <LANGUAGE>en-US</LANGUAGE>
        <DEFAULT>en-US</DEFAULT>
      </LANGUAGES>
      <VERSION>
        <MAJOR>6</MAJOR>
        <MINOR>0</MINOR>
        <BUILD>6000</BUILD>
        <SPBUILD>16386</SPBUILD>
      </VERSION>
      <SYSTEMROOT>WINDOWS</SYSTEMROOT>
    </WINDOWS>
    <DIRCOUNT>2070</DIRCOUNT>
    <FILECOUNT>8291</FILECOUNT>
    <TOTALBYTES>702583225</TOTALBYTES>
    <CREATIONTIME>
      <HIGHPART>0x01C6FE9D</HIGHPART>
      <LOWPART>0x88C3DFFD</LOWPART>
    </CREATIONTIME>
    <LASTMODIFICATIONTIME>
      <HIGHPART>0x01C6FE9D</HIGHPART>
      <LOWPART>0x89174FF8</LOWPART>
    </LASTMODIFICATIONTIME>
  </IMAGE>
</WIM>
```

Figure 1-1   Viewing WIM file information

NOTE   Install.wim

The base images of Windows Server 2008 stored on the Windows product DVD are contained in the file Install.wim.

WIM files offer a number of additional Windows deployment advantages, including the following:

- Because the WIM image format is hardware-agnostic, you need only one image to support many hardware configurations or hardware abstraction layers (HALs). (Separate images, however, are needed for x86 and 64-bit operating systems.)
- WIM files enable you to customize images by scripts or automate them by answer files upon installation.
- The WIM image format enables you to modify the contents of an image offline. You can add or delete certain operating system components, updates, and drivers without creating a new image.
- WIM files need to keep only one copy of disk files common to all the images stored in the file. This feature dramatically reduces the amount of storage space required to accommodate multiple images.
- You can start a computer from a disk image contained in a WIM file by marking an image as bootable.

- The WIM image format allows for nondestructive deployment. This means that you can leave data on the volume to which you apply the image because the application of the image does not erase the disk's existing contents.

- A WIM file image uses only as much space as the files that comprise it. Therefore, you can use WIM files to capture data on a volume with empty space and then migrate the data to a smaller volume.

- A WIM file can span multiple CDs or DVDs.

- WIM files support two types of compression—Xpress (fast) and LZX (high)—in addition to no compression (fastest).

Windows Automated Installation Kit Tools

You can download the Windows Automated Installation Kit (AIK) from the Microsoft Download Center at *http://www.microsoft.com/downloads*. The Windows AIK provides both corporate administrators and original equipment manufacturers (OEMs) with a set of tools and documentation for performing unattended installs of Windows Server 2008, Windows Vista, and some earlier versions of Microsoft Windows, including Windows XP and Windows Server 2003.

The Windows AIK includes several important deployment tools, including the following:

- **Windows Preinstallation Environment (Windows PE) 2.0**   Windows Preinstallation Environment (PE) 2.0, also known as WinPE, is a bootable and lightweight version of Windows that you can use to start a computer from a removable medium such as a CD or USB key or from a network source. Although the main purpose of Windows PE is to provide an environment from which to capture or apply a Windows image, you can also use it to troubleshoot or recover an installed operating system. In general, you can think of Windows PE as a replacement for bootable MS-DOS disks, but unlike the 16-bit MS-DOS that requires its own set of drivers, the 32-bit and 64-bit Windows PE operating system versions both take advantage of the drivers used in Windows Vista and Windows Server 2008.

NOTE   A lightweight version of Windows

Although installations of Windows PE vary in size, a typical installation requires about 100 MB of RAM. Because of its size, Windows PE cannot be run from a floppy disk and must be run from a CD, DVD, USB key, or a network source.

Windows PE can run many familiar (typically, command-line) programs and even communicate over IP networks. If you boot a computer from a typical Windows PE disk, a command prompt will appear from which you can run built-in tools and other programs you have made available through customization.

NOTE Windows Setup and Windows PE

Windows PE provides the basis for all Windows Vista and Windows Server 2008 installations. Whenever you boot from the product DVD and run the Setup program, Windows PE is actually running in the background.

Although Windows PE starts from the CD drive, Windows PE 2.0 does not actually run from the CD when it is fully booted. Windows PE 2.0 instead creates a RAM disk (a portion of RAM used as a drive), loads the operating system into that drive, and then runs from that RAM disk. This RAM disk is assigned the drive letter X.

NOTE Replacing the CD in Windows PE

Because Windows PE loads into and runs from a RAM disk, you can remove the Windows PE CD and insert a second CD to access additional required drivers or software. The X:\Windows\System32 folder contains many programs and utilities you can execute in Windows PE. Although most of these tools are also used in the full version of Windows Vista, some tools are specific to Windows PE.

- **ImageX** ImageX is a command-line tool you can use to capture, modify, and apply WIM images for deployment. The main function of ImageX is to enable you to capture a volume to a WIM file image and apply a WIM file image to a volume. For example, to capture an image, you can boot into Windows PE and use the command *Imagex.exe /capture* path*wimfilename.wim "Image_Name"*. To apply an image to a volume, use *Imagex /apply* path*wimfilename.wim 1*. (In this case, the value 1 indicates the index number of the image within the file wimfilename.wim.) Another important feature of ImageX is that it enables you to mount a WIM file image in the Windows file system so that you can modify the contents of that image. For example, you can mount an operating system image to add device drivers and then unmount it so that it is once again ready to be applied to a volume

- **Windows SIM** Windows System Image Manager (SIM) is the tool used to create unattended Windows Setup answer files. In Windows Vista and Windows Server 2008, answer files are XML-based documents used during Windows setup to supply information needed by the Windows installation. For example, you can use Windows SIM to create an answer file that partitions and formats a disk before installing Windows or that changes the default setting for the Internet Explorer home page. By modifying settings in the answer file, you can also use Windows SIM to install third-party applications, device drivers, language packs, and other updates.

NOTE   Windows SIM vs. Setup Manager

As a means to create answer files for unattended installations, Windows SIM replaces the Setup Manager tool used with previous versions of Windows.

Windows SIM uses catalog (.clg) files along with Windows images (WIM files) to display the available components and packages that can be added to an unattended answer file. Catalog files and WIM files contain configurable settings that you can modify once the component or package is added to an answer file.

NOTE   Catalog (.clg) files

You need to re-create the catalog file associated with a Windows image whenever you update a WIM file image.

Figure 1-2 shows the Windows SIM tool.

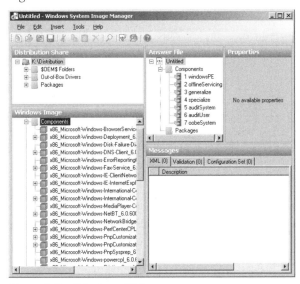

Figure 1-2   Windows SIM

Exam Tip   You need to know the function of Windows PE, ImageX, and Windows SIM for the 70-643 exam.

Sysprep

Sysprep is a tool found in the *%SystemRoot%*\System32\Syseprep folder of a Windows Vista or Windows Server 2008 installation. The purpose of Sysprep is to generalize a model computer installation image so that it can be used on many other computers. Sysprep achieves this generalization by removing only those settings of the model installation that should not be shared by other computers—settings such as the computer name, its domain membership, the time zone, the product key, the security identifier (SID), and various other user and machine settings. When you run Sysprep on an installation of Windows, a Sysprep image is generated and the installation is said to be Sysprepped.

After you run Sysprep, the computer shuts down. The Sysprepped installation then resides on the hard disk, ready to be captured by ImageX or Windows Deployment Services into a WIM file and deployed to other computers.

Of course, the settings removed by Sysprep need to be replaced on each computer that uses the Sysprepped image. Some of these settings (such as the computer SID) are automatically regenerated when the installation boots for the first time after Sysprep has run. Other settings might be provided by an answer file you configure in advance and supply when the Sysprepped image first boots. All remaining settings needed by the system are provided by the user in an interactive wizard that appears during the first boot after Sysprep is run.

Windows Deployment Methods

Deployment technologies in a Windows Server 2008 network are used to deploy both Windows clients and Windows servers. The following section discusses deployment methods, therefore, that relate to both Windows Vista and Windows Server 2008.

Windows Vista and Windows Server 2008 are typically deployed in one of four ways: by means of the product DVD, WIM files stored on a network share, Windows Deployment Services, or System Center Configuration Manager 2007. Each of these four methods offers an increasing level of automation, but each method also requires an increasing amount of resources, expertise, and preparation. The most suitable method for you to use depends on the resources you have available, the size of your organization, and the number of deployments you need to make.

Booting from a DVD

The simplest method to deploy Windows onto new hardware is to use the Windows product DVD. If you supply an answer file named Autounattend.xml at the root of an accessible Universal Serial Bus (USB) Flash Device (UFD) drive or floppy disk when you begin Setup, you can automate the process and eliminate the need for end-user interaction. This deployment method is most suitable when no high-bandwidth connection to the destination computer is available (as might be the case with a branch office), when you are deploying Windows to a small number of computers, and when no IT personnel are available at the site of the target computer. Compared to other automated forms of deployment, this deployment method also requires the least amount of technical preparation, resources, and expertise at both source and destination sites.

However, deploying Windows by means of the product DVD does have significant limitations. First, it requires more interaction on the part of nontechnical end users than is ideal for operating system installations. If the target computer does not have a floppy disk drive or if you have distributed the Autounattend.xml through a network connection, the required user interaction is significant; the user must place the answer file at the root of a UFD or floppy disk and boot the computer with that disk and the product DVD loaded. A second limitation of the media distribution method is that it does not allow for any additional drivers or updates (called configuration sets) to be installed as part of Setup without significant technical expertise at the site of the end user. Finally, one last limitation of this deployment method is that physical media need to be distributed to every target computer. Installation can occur simultaneously only on as many computers as product DVDs you have available.

Using Windows AIK Tools and a Network Share Distribution

You can deploy Windows Vista and Windows Server 2008 to computers from a network share in one of two ways: by using the Setup program or by applying a WIM file image. In the first method, the contents of the Windows product media are stored on the network share. You can then either keep the default version of Install.wim or replace it (and associated catalog files) with an image of your own custom-configured master installation. Setup is then launched from the command prompt in Windows PE on the local computer. To specify an answer file, use the /unattend switch. For example, if you have mapped a drive Y to the network share containing the installation files and saved an answer file named deploy_unattend.xml in the same share, you could boot the local computer by means of Windows PE and type the following:
Y:\setup.exe /unattend:deploy_unattend.xml

The second way to deploy Windows by means of a network share is to store on that share the captured WIM file image of a Sysprepped master installation. In this case, you can even keep an answer file inside the installation in the following location: *%SystemRoot%*\Panther\Unattend. (The name of the answer file must be Unattend.xml or Autounattend.xml.) Then, on the target computer, you can apply the Windows image by means of Windows PE and ImageX. For example, if you have mapped a drive Y to the network share containing the WIM file images, you would boot the local computer by means of Windows PE and type the following:
Imagex /apply Y:\myimage.wim 1 c:

Deploying Windows through a network share is a suitable solution when sufficient bandwidth exists to copy very large files across the network, when you need to deploy only a small number (between five and 20) of computers, and when the network environment does not include an Active Directory directory service domain or the System Center Configuration Manager 2007 network management application.

The main disadvantage of this method is that it is not completely automated. Instead, it requires someone at the site of the target computer with the technical expertise to boot into Windows PE and run appropriate commands at the command prompt. Unlike Windows Deployment Services (WDS), this solution does not automatically find the source files on the network and provide a menu of operating systems to download. Unlike System Center Configuration Manager 2007, this solution does not allow an administrator to deploy operating systems automatically to remote locations.

Besides this lack of automation, a second disadvantage of network share deployment is that it is not a managed solution. There is no central tool from which to manage and modify the Windows images stored at the network source. As a result, network share deployments are typically scalable only to network sizes of 20 or fewer computers.

Windows Deployment Services

Unlike the network share deployment scenario, WDS enables an end user without any technical expertise to boot a computer with no operating system and simply select, from a menu, a Windows image to install. The target computer is able to find the WDS server and download this operating system menu from it by means of the Pre-boot eXecution Environment (PXE) boot process. PXE is a technology that takes advantage of Dynamic Host Configuration Protocol (DHCP) to locate a WDS server during a computer's boot phase.

NOTE   PXE-boot computers

For a WDS client computer to find a WDS server, the client computer needs to have a PXE–boot compatible network card.

WDS is a far more scalable and manageable solution than is simply storing WIM files on a network. However, in almost all installations (in which the Deployment Server role service is installed), WDS does have the following fairly extensive infrastructure requirements:

- **Active Directory** A Windows Deployment Services server must be either a member of an Active Directory domain or a domain controller for an Active Directory domain. The Active Directory domain and forest versions are irrelevant; all domain and forest configurations support Windows Deployment Services.

■ **Dynamic Host Configuration Protocol** You must have a working DHCP server with an active scope on the network because Windows Deployment Services uses PXE, which in turn uses DHCP. The DHCP server does not have to be on the Windows Deployment Services server, but it (or a DHCP Relay Agent) does need to be on the same subnet as the client.

■ **Domain Name System** A working Domain Name System (DNS) server on the network is required to run Windows Deployment Services. The DNS server does not have to be running on the Windows Deployment Services server.

■ **NTFS volume** The server running Windows Deployment Services requires an NTFS file system volume for the image store.

■ **A high-speed, persistent connection between the WDS servers and the target computers** Such a connection is necessary because of the size of the images being distributed to the target computers. In addition, these servers should be on adjacent subnets to the target computers to ensure high-speed connectivity.

Aside from the extensive infrastructure requirements of WDS, another limitation of this deployment solution is that it requires end-user participation. The administrator cannot simply choose to push an operating system to any desktop in the organization.

As a result of these limitations, WDS does not scale well to the largest corporate networks with multiple Active Directory domains, IP subnets, or physical sites.

NOTE WDS outside of Active Directory

Besides the Deployment Server role service, the Windows Deployment Services role also includes the Transport Server role service. The Transport Server role service enables the transmission of any files or folders (such as operating system images, data files, or an MP3 archive) to remote clients by using multicast IP addressing. When used without the Deployment Server, Transport Server does not require an Active Directory infrastructure or DHCP, but it is a far more complicated method for deploying an operating system. Unlike the Deployment Server role service, it does not respond to PXE requests. It is also managed and used only through the Wdsutil.exe command-line tool. Outside of Active Directory domains, you will most likely find deploying Windows Vista and Windows Server 2008 easier by using network shares with the Windows AIK tools.

Quick Check

■ What are the server and infrastructure requirements for WDS?

Quick Check Answer

■ Windows Server 2008 with WDS installed, Active Directory, DNS, DHCP, an NTFS volume, and a persistent high-speed connection.

System Center Configuration Manager 2007

When used in conjunction with the other deployment methods, System Center Configuration Manager 2007 enables you to create a fully managed deployment solution for large organizations. Unlike other deployment options, System Center Configuration Manager 2007 allows for a completely unattended operating system deployment to remote computers.

System Center Configuration Manager 2007 assists with the many tasks involved when you apply automated procedures to multiple servers and client computers, tasks such as:

- Selecting computers that have the hardware necessary for a given operating system and that you are ready to support.
- Distributing the operating system source files to all sites, including remote sites and sites without technical support staff.
- Monitoring the distribution to all sites.
- Providing the appropriate user rights for the upgrade.
- Automatically initiating the installation of software packages, with the possibility of having users control the timing.
- Resolving problems related to the distributions or installations.
- Reporting on the rate and success of deployment.
- Verifying that all computers in your organization have received the standardized operating system configuration.

Deploying Windows Vista or Windows Server 2008 with System Center Configuration Manager 2007 requires a high-speed, persistent connection between the servers and target computers used in the deployment process. Such a connection is necessary because of the large size of the images being distributed to the target computers.

Among the disadvantages of System Center Configuration Manager 2007 is, first, that unlike the other deployment methods mentioned, it is a separate product requiring a purchase beyond that of Windows Server 2008. In addition, installing and configuring a System Center Configuration Manager 2007 infrastructure requires significant technical expertise. A third disadvantage of System Center Configuration Manager 2007 is that, unlike WDS, you can't use it to deploy an operating system to a bare-metal system. The target computer requires the System Center Configuration Manager 2007 client software. (Because of this last limitation, in fact, System Center Configuration Manager 2007 is typically used in conjunction with WDS and not as a replacement for it.)

PRACTICE Creating a Windows PE CD

In this practice, you will create a bootable Windows PE CD from which you can capture or apply native Windows images. This practice requires you to have installed the Windows AIK on the C drive on Server1.

▶ **Exercise Create a Windows PE CD**

In this exercise, you will create a WinPE CD with which you can later boot a computer and use tools such as ImageX.

1. On Server1, launch Windows PE Tools Command Prompt from the Windows AIK program group.

2. In Windows PE Tools Command Prompt, type the line below that corresponds to the CPU architecture of the computer or computers on which you will use the Windows PE CD:

    ```
    Copype.cmd x86 C:\WinPE_x86
    Copype.cmd amd64 C:\WinPE_amd64
    Copype.cmd ia64 C:\WinPE_ia64
    ```

    The Copype.cmd script creates a new directory with the name specified in the command. After you run this command, the new directory will contain, among other files and folders, a directory named ISO. This ISO directory is important because it contains the eventual contents of the WinPE CD. For this reason, you need to copy any tools (such as the ImageX utility) that you want to include on the WinPE CD to the ISO directory. You copy these tools in the next step.

3. In Windows PE Tools Command Prompt, type the line below that corresponds to the CPU architecture of the computer or computers on which you will use the Windows PE CD:

    ```
    Copy "C:\Program files\Windows AIK\Tools\x86\imagex.exe" C:\WinPE_x86\ISO
    Copy "C:\Program files\Windows AIK\Tools\amd64\imagex.exe" C:\WinPE_amd64\ISO
    Copy "C:\Program files\Windows AIK\Tools\ia64\imagex.exe" C:\WinPE_ia64\ISO
    ```

4. In Notepad, create an empty file named Wimscript.ini and save it to the new WinPE_x86 \ISO, WinPE_amd64\ISO, or WinPE_ia64\ISO folder as appropriate.

5. Enter the following text into Wimscript.ini, and then save the file again.

    ```
    [ExclusionList]
    ntfs.log
    hiberfil.sys
    pagefile.sys
    "System Volume Information"
    RECYCLER
    Windows\CSC

    [CompressionExclusionList]
    *.mp3
    *.zip
    ```

```
*.cab\WINDOWS\inf\
*.pnf
```

The [ExclusionList] section in the Wimscript.ini file specifies which files should not be captured when you are performing an image capture by using the ImageX tool. The [CompressExclusionList] section of Wimscript.ini specifies which files or file types should not be compressed when you are compressing an image by using the ImageX tool.

6. In Windows PE Tools Command Prompt, type the line below that corresponds to the CPU architecture of the computer or computers on which you will use the Windows PE CD:

```
Oscdimg -n -bc:\WinPE_x86\etfsboot.com c:\WinPE_x86\ISO
c:\WinPE_x86\WinPE_x86.iso

Oscdimg -n -bc:\WinPE_amd64\etfsboot.com c:\WinPE_x86\ISO
c:\WinPE_amd64\WinPE_amd64.iso

Oscdimg -n -bc:\WinPE_ia64\etfsboot.com c:\WinPE_ia64\ISO
c:\WinPE_x86\WinPE_ia64.iso
```

The Oscidmg command makes an .iso file of the specified ISO directory. The –b switch makes the eventual Windows PE CD bootable by specifying the location of the boot sector file, etfsboot.com. Note that there is no space after the –b switch. (The *c* that follows the switch is the drive letter in the path to etfsboot.com.) Finally, the –n switch in Oscdimg enables long file names in the .iso file.

7. (Optional) Using software of your choice, burn the new .iso file to a CD (or mount the .iso in a virtual CD drive).

Lesson Summary

- In a network made up of clients running Windows Vista and servers running Windows Server 2008, you can deploy new clients and servers in a number of ways, and all these methods—including basic installation—are based on WIM files.

- A WIM file is a file containing one or more disk images in the native Windows imaging format. WIM files are file-based and, therefore, can be modified before, during, and after deployment.

- The Windows AIK is an ISO file you can download from the Microsoft Web site; it includes several important deployment tools, including Windows PE, ImageX, and Windows SIM.

- Sysprep is a tool found in the *%SystemRoot%*\System32\Sysprep folder of a Windows Vista or Windows Server 2008 installation. The purpose of Sysprep is to generalize a model computer installation image so that it can be used on many other computers.
- You can deploy Windows from a DVD by using a network share with Windows AIK tools or by using Windows Deployment Services.

Lesson Review

The following question is intended to reinforce key information presented in this lesson. The question is also available on the companion CD if you prefer to review it in electronic form.

NOTE Answers

The answer to this question and an explanation of why each answer choice is correct or incorrect are located in the "Answers" section at the end of the book.

1. Which of the following tools can be used to reseal a master installation to prepare it for having its image captured for use in image-based deployment?

    A. Windows PE

    B. Imagex

    C. Sysprep

    D. Windows SIM

Lesson 2: Configuring Windows Deployment Services

Windows Deployment Services (WDS) is a suite of components that represents the most recent version of Remote Installation Services (RIS), a deployment technology first included as part of Windows 2000 Server. Windows Server 2008 includes a WDS server role you can add to servers by using Server Manager, and WDS provides a server-based, image-based deployment technology suitable for mid-sized companies that need to automate the deployment of workstations, servers, or both.

The Windows Server 2008 version of WDS includes new features such as an improved management interface, a scriptable command-line tool called Wdsutil.exe, support for the new Windows imaging (.wim) format, and improvements to make large network deployments more bandwidth efficient.

After this lesson, you will be able to:
- Deploy Windows images by using Windows Deployment Services.

Estimated lesson time: 120 minutes

Introducing Windows Deployment Services

WDS is a server-based technology for deploying Windows images onto bare-metal computers. The WDS server is used to store Windows images, and bare-metal clients locate the WDS server during the boot phase by using either remote client boot disks or PXE, a DHCP-based technology used by most network cards. You can also use WDS to manage and customize images, which makes WDS a good choice for organizations that have high-volume deployment needs that require a lot of customization.

Comparing WDS to Windows AIK Tools

WDS provides a graphical user interface that eliminates the need to use some Windows AIK tools directly. For example, you can use WDS (instead of ImageX) to capture and deploy images onto computers. However, familiarity with the Windows AIK tools increases the power of WDS. You can use Windows SIM, for instance, to create answer files you can then use to automate your WDS deployments.

Performing automated Windows deployment by using the Windows AIK requires a large degree of manual configuration and customization. Alternatively, WDS provides an easy-to-use management console that simplifies many of these configuration and customization tasks; also, by using the Wdsutil command-line tool, you can automate many WDS tasks by scripting them. Finally, as a server-based solution, WDS makes it easy to manage large numbers of customized boot and install images. Windows AIK by comparison provides no native framework for managing such images—you need to create and maintain this framework manually.

Advantages of WDS

WDS has several advantages that can make it the ideal choice for a deployment solution for many organizations. First, as a server-based solution, WDS makes it easier to centralize and manage all aspects of the deployment process, including capturing, customizing, maintaining, updating, and installing images. Such centralization helps reduce the complexity of the deployment process and can, therefore, also help reduce cost and effort in such deployments. Second, the Windows Server 2008 version of WDS supports deploying any of the following operating systems: Windows Server 2008, Windows Vista, Windows Server 2003, and Windows XP. This means that if you have a mixed environment containing both current and earlier Windows platforms, you need only one deployment infrastructure to maintain them. Third, the Windows Server 2008 version of WDS includes enhancements to the Trivial File Transfer Protocol (TFTP) and multicast support that enable very large environments to deploy Windows without overwhelming ordinary network usage.

Understanding WDS Infrastructure Components

Before you deploy the Windows Deployment Services server role in your environment, you must take steps to prepare your environment. These steps differ, depending on which WDS role service you are deploying. During installation of the Windows Deployment Services server role, you have a choice of two role services:

- **Deployment Server** This role service provides the full functionality of WDS and enables you to create and customize images and deploy them remotely onto bare-metal systems. If you choose to deploy this role service, you must first have deployed Active Directory Domain Services (AD DS), a DNS server, and a DHCP server on your network.

- **Transport Server** This role service provides only a subset of WDS functionality and can be used to create custom solutions using standalone deployment servers and multicast addressing. You do not require AD DS, a DNS server, or a DHCP server to support this role service.

    Although the Transport Server role service has fewer infrastructure requirements than the Deployment Server role service does, the Transport Server role service is intended for advanced scenarios and requires special customization to function as a deployment solution. This chapter, therefore, focuses only on using the Deployment Server role service of WDS for deploying Windows.

MORE INFO **Locating your DHCP server**

It's possible to install everything—Active Directory together with your DNS, DHCP, and WDS servers—on a single computer instead of deploying the WDS role on a separate computer. If you do so, however, you will have to choose a special option when prompted during WDS installation. For information about configuring this option with the Wdsutil utility, see the "Performing Initial Server Configuration Using Wdsutil" section later in this lesson.

- **Server components** These are located on the WDS server itself and include an image repository that contains boot images, install images, and other files needed for remote installation over a network; a PXE server to enable the remote computer to boot remotely with no operating system; a TFTP server to enable the remote computer to download and install an operating system image from the image repository; a networking layer that includes support for multicasting image files over the network; and a diagnostic component that ties into the Windows Eventing infrastructure of Windows Server 2008.

- **Client components** These include a graphical user interface that runs within Windows PE and enables a user to select the operating system image to be installed on the remote computer. Once the selection is made, the client components then request and download the appropriate image from the image repository on the WDS server.

- **Management components** These include the Windows Deployment Services console found in the Administrative Tools program group, the Wdsutil command-line utility, and other tools.

Figure 1-3 illustrates in simplified form the WDS architecture.

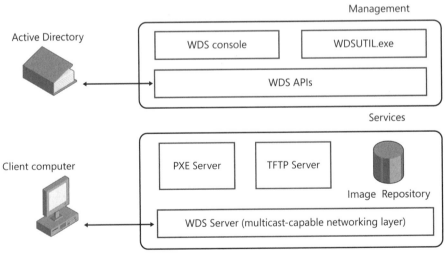

Figure 1-3 Architecture of Windows Deployment Services

Installing WDS

The simplest way of installing the WDS role is to use the Add Roles Wizard. To launch this wizard from Server Manager, right-click the Roles node, and then select Add Roles. If the Before You Begin page appears, click Next. When the Select Server Roles page appears, select the Windows Deployment Services option and click Next (Figure 1-4).

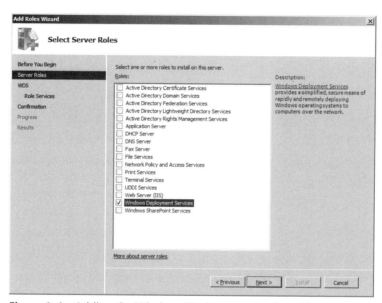

Figure 1-4   Adding the Windows Deployment Services role

The Overview Of Windows Deployment Services page appears next. This page provides a brief overview of what WDS is about and includes links to further information on installing, configuring, and managing the role.

Clicking Next brings up the Select Role Services page (Figure 1-5). This is where you can specify whether your WDS server will function as a deployment server or a transport server. If you choose the Deployment Server option, you must also select Transport Server because the former role depends upon the latter for its operation.

To finish the wizard, click Next, review the changes that will be made on your server, and then click Install to begin the installation.

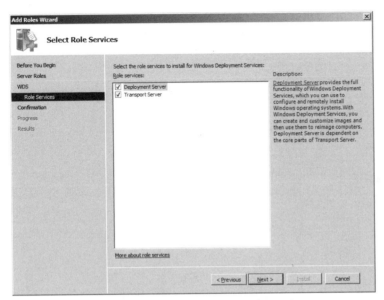

Figure 1-5   Installing the Deployment Server role service

Configuring WDS

Before you can use WDS, you must configure it. The following sections describe some of the more common WDS configuration tasks, including performing initial server configuration, adding a default boot image, adding a default install image, and configuring the boot menu.

Performing Initial Server Configuration

The initial configuration of your WDS can be performed by using either a wizard or the command line. Configuring your server does several things. First, it creates the image store where your boot and install images will be stored. By default, the wizard suggests the location *%SystemDrive%*\RemoteInstall as an image store location (Figure 1-6), but for performance reasons, you might want to use a different partition on a dedicated hard drive for this purpose. The only requirements, however, for your image store location is that the partition be formatted using NTFS and has sufficient free space to hold your images.

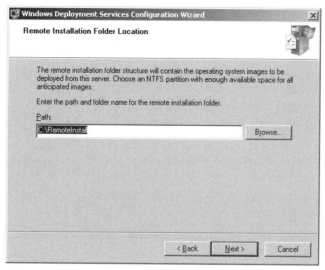

Figure 1-6   Configuring image store location

The second thing that happens during initial server configuration is that you must configure the answer policy for your server. This means you specify the kind of client computers to which your WDS server will respond (Figure 1-7).

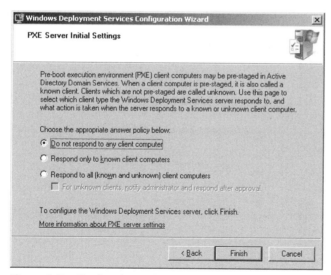

Figure 1-7   Configuring PXE Server initial settings

Depending on how you configure your server, it might respond to:

- **Do Not Respond To Any Client Computers** Leaving WDS in this state means that no installations will be performed. You can think of this as parking your WDS server until it is needed.
- **Respond Only To Known Client Computers** A known client computer is one whose computer account has been pre-staged in Active Directory. Configuring WDS this way will prevent your WDS server from responding to installation requests from unstaged and rogue systems.
- **Respond To All (Known And Unknown) Client Computers** An unknown computer is one whose computer account has not been pre-staged, so selecting this configuration option means that your WDS server will respond to any client system that makes an installation request.

The final action that happens during initial server configuration is that the image store is created on the WDS server. The image store consists of several subfolders that are used for storing different kinds of images on your server.

To perform the initial configuration of your WDS server, open the Windows Deployment Services console from the Administrative Tools program group, right-click the node representing your server, and select Configure Server (Figure 1-8). This launches the Windows Deployment Services Configuration Wizard, and you simply follow the steps in this wizard to complete the configuration of your server.

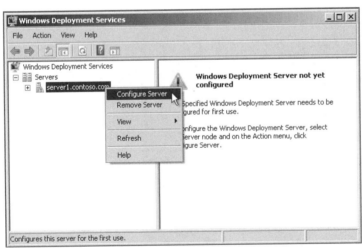

Figure 1-8 Windows Deployment Services needing configuration

Performing Initial Server Configuration Using Wdsutil   You can also perform initial configuration of your WDS server by using the Wdsutil command-line utility. Two steps are involved in doing this. First, use the following command to create your image store:

`wdsutil /Initialize-Server /reminst:path\foldername`

Then use the following command to configure the answer policy for your server. (The specific policy being configured here is to allow your server to respond to all client computers, both known and unknown.)

`wdsutil /Set-Server /AnswerClients:all`

Finally, if your WDS computer is also your DHCP server, then you need to perform the following task at this point:

`wdsutil /Set-Server /UseDHCPPorts:no /DHCPoption60:yes`

This step sets two separate but related options. The first option (/UseDHCPPorts:no) disables the use of DHCP ports by WDS. Both DHCP and WDS listen on port 67 by default. However, when WDS and DHCP exist on the same computer, WDS does not need to use this DHCP port, and doing so would cause a conflict. Therefore, WDS must be configured not to use the port. The second option (/DHCPoption60:yes) adds DHCP option tag 60 to the local DHCP server leases. This tag uses the DHCPOffer packet to inform DHCP client computers that there is a PXE server listening on the network.

Note that you need to run this last command only if you are using Wdsutil to perform your initial server configuration. If you are using the Windows Deployment Services console instead to configure your server, this step is handled easily through the configuration wizard.

Quick Check

1. What setting should you configure on your WDS server if you don't want PXE-enabled client computers to try to connect to your server automatically and download an image?
2. What setting should you configure on your WDS server if you plan on pre-staging your client computer accounts in Active Directory?

Quick Check Answers

1. Select the Do Not Respond To Any Client Computers option on the PXE Response Settings tab of your WDS server Properties sheet.
2. Select the Respond Only To Known Client Computers option on the PXE Response Settings tab of your WDS server Properties sheet.

Adding the Default Boot Image

The simplest way of using WDS to deploy Windows is to use the default boot image included in the \sources folder on your Windows Server 2008 product DVD. A *boot image* is a relatively small Windows image (.wim) file you can use to boot a bare-metal client computer to begin the deployment of an operating system to the computer. By contrast, an *install image* is an image of the Windows Vista or Windows Server 2008 operating system itself that you plan on deploying on the client computer. The \sources folder on your Windows Vista and Windows Server 2008 product DVDs each contain two images: a default boot image (Boot.wim) and a default install image (Install.wim). You can use the default boot image to boot client computers to start the deployment process, which in turn can then use the default install image to install Windows on these computers. Alternatively, you can customize either or both of these images as needed.

To add the default boot image to the image store on your WDS server, right-click the Boot Images folder under your server node and select Add Boot Image. This launches the Add Image Wizard (Figure 1-9), and you follow the steps of the wizard to add the Boot.wim file from your product DVD to your image store.

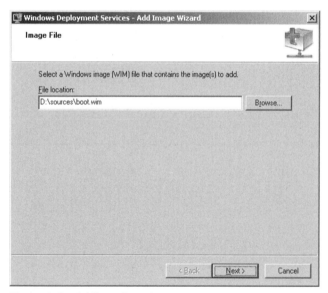

Figure 1-9   Adding a boot image

IMPORTANT   Use the right boot image!

You must use the boot image from a Windows Server 2008 DVD or a Windows Vista integrated with Service Pack 1 DVD if you want to take advantage of advanced WDS features such as multi-casting that are not supported by versions of WDS prior to Windows Server 2008. If you use the boot image from a Windows Vista RTM DVD instead, then your WDS deployment infrastructure will not support the enhanced features included in the Windows Server 2008 version of WDS.

Adding the Default Boot Image Using Wdsutil   You can also use the Wdsutil command-line utility to add the default boot image from your Windows Server 2008 DVD to your image store. To do this, use the following command:

```
wdsutil /Add-Image /ImageFile:DVD_drive_letter\sources\Boot.wim
/ImageType:boot
```

Adding the Default Install Image

Again, the simplest way of using WDS is to use the default install image included in the \sources folder on your Windows Server 2008 product DVD. Once you've added this image (Install.wim) and the default boot image (Boot.wim), you can start using WDS to boot remote computers and install Windows on them, although in a real-world environment, you would want to customize your images first and then create answer files to ensure that your deployment meets your organization's needs.

To add the default install image to the image store on your server, right-click the Boot Images folder under your server node and select Add Install Image. This launches the Add Image Wizard, and the first thing you're prompted to do is create or specify the image group that will contain your image. An image group is a mechanism for storing Windows images in the image repository of WDS. File resources are shared across an image group and are single-instanced, which makes image groups more storage-efficient than storing images individually on your server. WDS suggests a default image group name of ImageGroup1, but you can customize this as desired and create as many image groups as you need to manage your images. (See Figure 1-10.)

After you've specified the image group, you are prompted to select which install images you want to add to your image store. Depending on your product media, different images might be displayed here. For example, Figure 1-11 shows an Install.wim file that contains images for six Windows Server 2008 images (three editions with two installation options—full or Server Core—for each edition).

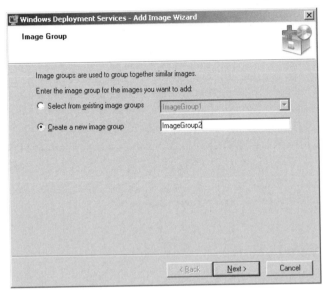

Figure 1-10   Creating an image group

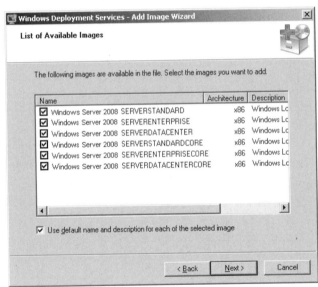

Figure 1-11   Choosing which install images to add to your image store

For example, if you purchased a product key to install Windows Server 2008 Enterprise Edition, you would leave the second and fifth check boxes selected in the preceding figure and clear the others. This would result in only two install images being added to your image store:

one for a full installation of Enterprise Edition and one for the Server Core installation option of Enterprise Edition. If, however, you choose to add all the install images to your server, your image store will look like Figure 1-12.

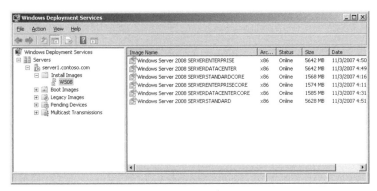

Figure 1-12   Image store with two install images

You can also configure who can access the images in an image group by right-clicking the image group in the Windows Deployment Services console and selecting Security. This displays the Security tab of the image group Properties dialog box, where you can configure the ACL for your image group and the images it contains.

Adding the Install Boot Image Using Wdsutil   You can also use the Wdsutil command-line utility to add the default install image from your Windows Server 2008 DVD to a particular image group in your image store. To do this, use the following command:

```
wdsutil /Add-Image /ImageFile:DVD_drive_letter\sources\Boot.wim
/ImageType:install /ImageGroup:name
```

Other Configuration Tasks

Another configuration task you need to perform is to configure the boot menu. When a PXE-enabled computer that has no operating system boots, it contacts the PXE server on your WDS server, obtains an IP address, and downloads the WDS client. The WDS client then displays a boot menu, which presents a list of operating systems that can be installed on the system. This boot menu can include different versions of Windows, different editions of the same Windows version, different install options (Full or Server Core) of the same edition, or different architecture types (x86 or x64) you can choose from to install on the system. The WDS boot menu uses the same Boot Configuration Data (BCD) menu structure used by Windows Vista and Windows Server 2008.

The boot menu will be displayed only if there is more than one supported boot image on your WDS server. In other words, if you add only the default boot image to your server, no boot menu will be displayed on the client. Boot menus also cannot display more than 13 boot images because of limitations in the number of characters that can be displayed in the system loader boot menu. One reason to add several boot images to your server is to provide different functions to clients through each image. For example, you can use one boot image to launch Windows Setup to install Windows in unattended mode, another boot image to launch the WDS Image Capture Wizard so you can capture the image of a master computer to use as an install image for future installations, and a third boot image to repartition and reformat a system's hard drives to support BitLocker Drive Encryption before installing Windows on them.

Once you've added several boot images to your WDS server, you can then use the Bcdedit.exe command to modify the boot menu behavior by editing the Default.bcd file. This file is found in the *Path*\RemoteInstall\Boot*architecture* folder on your server. (The RemoteInstall folder is found on the NTFS partition you choose during WDS configuration.) For help on using this command, type **bcdedit /?** at a command prompt.

Finally, there are a number of settings you can configure for the WDS server itself. To configure these server-level settings using the Windows Deployment Services console, right-click your server node, select Properties, and then select the tabs you want to configure (Figure 1-13).

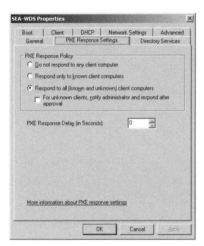

Figure 1-13   Configuring server settings

The following section describes the configuration options available on each of the eight server-level properties tabs.

- **General** Displays server name, mode, and location of the remote installation folder where images are stored.

- **PXE Response settings** Specifies the response policy for the server or which types of computers (known or unknown) can download and install images from the server. Also specifies the PXE boot delay in seconds (zero by default).

- **Directory Services** Specifies the name of the computer account and the location where this account will be stored in Active Directory for each computer that uses WDS to install from. To prevent a computer account from being created, use the Client tab.

- **Boot** Specifies the default network boot program and image for each architecture type (x86, x64, or IA64). The Pxeboot.com network boot program is the default for x86 and x64 computers. It presents clients with the prompt for F12 and continues with WDS-assisted installation only if F12 is pressed. A common alternative selection to Pxeboot.com is the Pxeboot.n12 network program. This network boot program immediately brings the PXE client into the WDS-assisted installation without requiring a user to press F12. A second alternative is Abortpxe.com. This network boot program ensures that client computers able to boot from a second boot device specified in the BIOS are allowed to do so; it prevents the PXE boot process from launching unnecessarily and unintentionally.

- **Client** Used to enable and configure unattended installation of the WDS client software.

- **DHCP** You need to configure this tab only if you have a DHCP server running on your WDS server. When a DHCP server is running locally, you need to configure WDS not to listen on port 67, and you need to configure this local DHCP server with Option Tag 60. Configuring these options essentially delegates certain responsibilities to the DHCP server that the WDS server would normally perform on its own, thereby avoiding a conflict.

- **Network Settings** Specifies IP address and port ranges and the bandwidth of your network (from 10 Mbps to 1 Gbps) or a custom bandwidth. Also used to configure a multicast address range when performing multicast deployments.

- **Advanced** Used to authorize your WDS server in DHCP and to either specify a domain controller and global catalog or allow WDS to discover them on its own.

Note that you can also use the Wdsutil utility to configure most of these server-level settings. For help on how to use Wdsutil, type **wdsutil /?** at a command prompt.

MORE INFO   Configuring server settings

For detailed information concerning each WDS server setting, select Help Topics from the Help menu option of the Windows Deployment Services console.

Capturing Images with WDS

Once you have WDS installed and configured, the next step is to create and customize the boot and install images you will use later to install Windows onto destination (also known as client) computers, which are bare-metal systems. Remember that WDS can be used to deploy both Windows Vista and Windows Server 2008 (and earlier operating systems if you upgraded your server from the Windows Server 2003 version of WDS), so these procedures can be used for deploying both client and server computers. For purposes of illustration, however, the focus here is on deploying computers running Windows Server 2008 by using WDS.

A boot image boots the client computer to begin the process of installing Windows. Boot images contain Windows PE and the WDS client, and they display a boot menu on the client computer that enables you to select which operating system image you want to install on the computer. Boot images can be added to the image store in WDS, and they can be customized. Another thing you can do with boot images is use them as a basis for creating two special types of boot images: capture images and discovery images.

A *capture image* is a special boot image that you use to boot a master computer. (Recall that a master computer is a system that has a master installation installed on it—a customized installation of Windows that you plan to duplicate on one or more destination computers.) To use a capture image, you first prepare your master installation by configuring Windows, installing applications, and performing any other customizations needed. Then, you sysprep your master computer to remove any machine-specific information from your master installation. After sysprep shuts the computer down, you reboot the system, using the capture image, which launches a wizard that captures an install image from the computer and saves it as a .wim file to a location you specify. Once you've captured an image of your master installation like this, you can then add the image to your image store as a new install image that you can then deploy to your destination computers by using WDS.

A *discover image* is a boot image you can use to deploy an install image onto a computer that is not PXE enabled. Discover images can be useful in a number of scenarios. For example, you can use a discover image to deploy Windows to an older computer system that does not support PXE booting by creating the discover image, saving it to bootable media (CD or DVD media or a USB flash drive), and then booting the client computer using the media to start the installation process. Alternatively, you might use discover images in an environment where PXE is not allowed for policy reasons. You can also use discover images in an environment where you have multiple WDS servers and configure each discovery image to connect to a different WDS server for initiating deployment.

Creating a Capture Image

To create a new capture image, begin with the default boot image found in the Boot Images folder of the Windows Deployment Services console. Right-click the default boot image and select Create Capture Boot Image to launch the Create Capture Image Wizard. On the first page of this wizard, you specify a name and description for your capture image, and you specify a name and location for the capture image (Figure 1-14). The location should be a folder on a local hard drive on your WDS server.

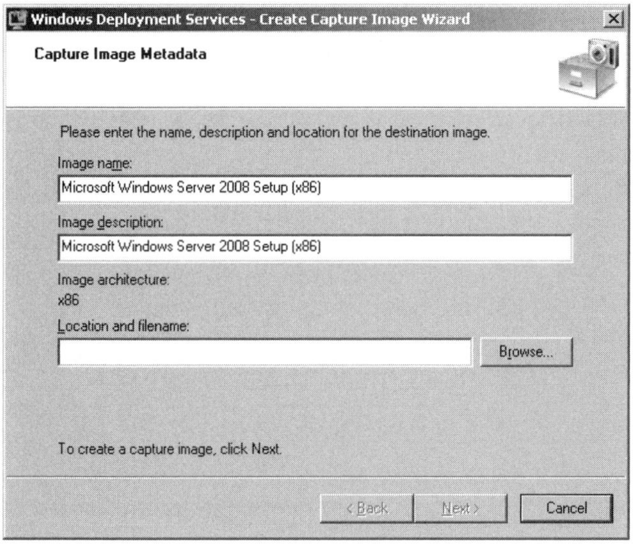

Figure 1-14   Creating a capture boot image

Clicking Next causes the Create Capture Image Wizard to extract the image from the source file (the default boot image) and capture it to the destination .wim file you specified. Once this is completed, you can then right-click the Boot Images folder, select Add Boot Image, and add your new capture image to the image store. (See Figure 1-15.)

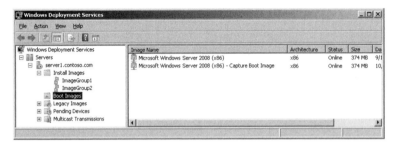

Figure 1-15   Default and capture boot images

Creating a Discover Image

Creating a discover image needs a little more configuration than creating a capture image does. To create a new discover image, right-click the default boot image as before, but this time, select Create Discover Boot Image. The first page of this wizard requires you to specify a name and description for the image and a filename and local path for storing it as well as the fully qual-ified domain name (FQDN) of the WDS server the capture image will connect the client with (Figure 1-16). Clicking Next causes the wizard to extract the image from the source file and capture it to the destination .wim file you specified, and then you can add the new discover image to the image store as before. If you need to create boot media (CD or DVD media or a USB flash drive) with this image, you can use the Oscdimg tool in the Windows AIK to do this. (Using Oscdimg was demonstrated in Exercise 1, "Create a Windows PE CD," in the Lesson 1 practice earlier in this chapter.)

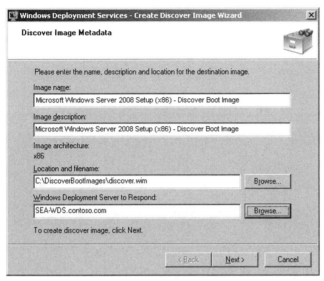

Figure 1-16 Creating a discover boot image

Deploying Images with WDS

Once you have configured your WDS server, added boot images, captured an install image from a customized master installation, and added this install image to your store, you are ready to begin deploying Windows to your client computers. To do this, your client computers must have at least 512 MB of RAM (so they can load and run Windows PE boot images in RAM disk), and they must have their BIOS configured so that PXE is first in the boot order (unless you are booting them from media using bootable discover images).

You can use WDS to deploy images both manually and in automated fashion by using answer files. Manual deployment requires the least preparation on your part but needs the most attention at the client end. Automated deployment requires using the Windows SIM to create an answer file.

Manually Deploying an Image with WDS

To deploy an install image manually to a client computer, start by turning on the client computer, and then press F12 when prompted to do so. The Windows Boot menu appears at this point, and you select the boot image you want to use to boot the system and begin the installation. (See Figure 1-17.)

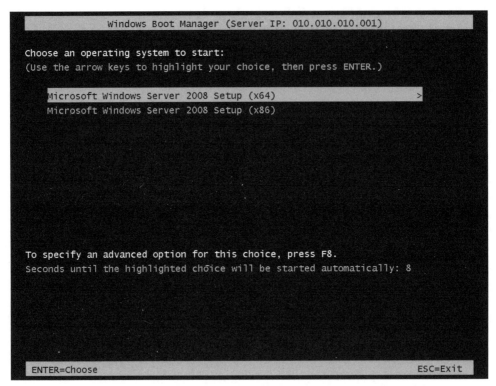

Figure 1-17 Selecting a boot image during manual deployment

After the boot image has been downloaded from the TFTP server, the client computer boots into Windows PE, and you are prompted to choose the locale you want Windows Setup to run in (Figure 1-18).

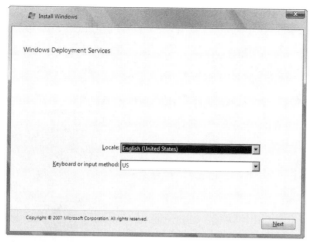

Figure 1-18   Selecting a locale for Setup

When you are prompted to do so, enter your domain Administrator credentials to connect the client computer to the image store on your WDS server. Once a connection has been established, a list of install images you can install will be displayed. Select the customized image you captured from your master installation (Figure 1-19).

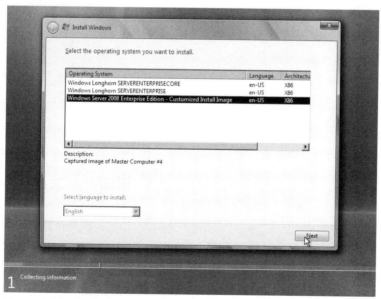

Figure 1-19   Choosing an image to install

When you click Next, you are prompted to select a drive to install Windows on, and after this has been done, the server will initiate a session with the client computer, and the customized install image will be downloaded and installed onto your client computer. Once this process has been completed, the destination computer will reboot and Setup will finish its work.

Understanding What Happens During Deployment

It's worthwhile to understand what's going on during the preceding deployment scenario to provide a good foundation for troubleshooting issues when something goes wrong. Here's a quick summary of what's happening at the network level when a PXE-enabled client computer connects to a WDS server to download and install an image:

1. The client computer broadcasts a DHCP discover message to locate a DHCP server.
2. The DHCP server responds with a DHCP offer message offering an IP address to the client.
3. The client sends a DHCP request message requesting to lease the IP address contained in the previous DHCP offer message.
4. The DHCP server responds with a DHCP acknowledgment message indicating that the client has successfully leased the address.
5. The client broadcasts a second DHCP request message to locate a PXE server (that is, the WDS server).
6. The PXE server responds with a DHCP reply message that contains the ServerHostName (the WDS server name) and BootFileName (pxeboot.com for a manual install initiated by pressing F12 on the client).
7. The client now uses TFTP to download the boot file from the TFTP server (that is, the WDS server). This involves a lot of UDP traffic.
8. Once the boot file is downloaded, the client then downloads the Windows Boot Manager Bootmgr.exe, using TFTP.
9. Once this is done, the client displays the boot loader menu from which you choose your boot image.
10. The boot image is then downloaded from the server, using TFTP, and then loaded into memory.
11. At this point, Windows PE is now running in a RAM disk, and once you've selected the install image you want to install on your computer and specified any other information needed, the server will use Server Message Block (SMB) to download the install image, so it can be applied to your computer.

PRACTICE Configuring Windows Deployment Services

In this practice, you will install and configure the Windows Deployment Services role on Server1. You will then use WDS to deploy Windows Server 2008 on Server2. For this practice, you will need at least 3GB of free space on an NTFS partition on Server1. Server2 must be a PXE-boot compatible computer, located on the same physical or virtual network as Server1, that has no operating system installed. (Note that virtual machines in Virtual PC 2007 meet this PXE requirement. Also note that in Virtual PC, you should ensure that both virtual machines are connected to the Local Only network.)

▶ **Exercise 1 Add the Windows Deployment Server Role**

In this exercise, you install the Windows Deployment Services role on Server1.

1. Log on to Server1 as a domain administrator, and then open Server Manager.
2. In the Server Manager console tree, select the Roles node, and then, in the details pane, click Add Roles.

    The Add Roles Wizard appears.
3. On the Before You Begin page, click Next.
4. On the Select Server Roles page, select Windows Deployment Services, and then click Next.
5. On the Overview Of Windows Deployment Services page, read all the text on the page and click Next.
6. On the Select Role Services page, verify that both role services are selected, and then click Next.
7. On the Confirm Installation Selection page, click Install.
8. On the Installation Results page, click Close.
9. Close Server Manager and proceed to Exercise 2.

▶ **Exercise 2 Perform Initial Server Configuration**

In this exercise, you will configure your WDS server by creating a RemoteInstall folder for your image store and by configuring the PXE boot settings for your server.

1. While you are logged on to Server1 as a domain administrator, launch Windows Deployment Services from the Administrative Tools program group.
2. Expand the console tree until the local server node appears beneath the Servers node.
3. Right-click the local server node, and then click Configure Server.

    The Windows Deployment Services Configuration Wizard launches, displaying the Welcome page.

4. On the Welcome page of the Windows Deployment Services Configuration Wizard, read all the text on the page, and then click Next.

5. On the Remote Installation Folder Location page, read all the text on the page.

6. In the Path text box, change the default path as necessary to specify an NTFS partition with 3 GB of free space or more. It is preferable (but not necessary) to choose a drive other than the Windows system volume. Leave the default folder name of RemoteInstall.

7. On the Remote Installation Folder Location page, click Next.

8. If a warning message appears indicating that the volume you selected is also the Windows system volume, click Yes to continue.

9. On the DHCP Option 60 page, read all the text on the page.

10. On the DHCP Option 60 page, select both check boxes, and then click Next.

11. On the PXE Server Initial Settings page, read all the text on the page.

12. On the PXE Server Initial Settings page, select the Respond Only To Known Client Computers option, and then click Finish.

▶ **Exercise 3 Add the Default Boot and Install Images**

In this exercise, you will add the default boot image and the default install image from your Windows Server 2008 DVD media to your image store.

1. While you are logged on to Server1 as a domain administrator, open the Windows Deployment Services console if it is not already open.

2. In the Windows Deployment Services console tree, expand the local server node under Servers until the various folders contained in the server's image store are displayed.

3. Insert your Windows Server 2008 DVD into the DVD drive of your WDS server. If the AutoPlay dialog box opens up, close it. Alternatively, you can mount a Windows Server 2008 ISO file.

4. Right-click the Boot Images folder and select Add Boot Image.
   The Windows Deployment Services - Add Image Wizard launches.

5. On the Image File page, click Browse and browse the file system to select the Boot.wim file in the \Sources folder on your product DVD. Then, click Open to begin adding the default boot image Boot.wim from your Windows Server 2008 product DVD to the image store on your WDS server.

6. On the Image File page, click Next.

7. On the Image Metadata page, accept the default image name and description for your boot image, and then click Next.

8. On the Summary page of the wizard, read all the text, and then click Next.

The Take Progress page appears while the boot image from your product DVD is added to your image store. This may take a number of minutes to complete.

9. When the image is successfully added to your server, click Finish.

   Now that you have added your default boot image to WDS, you will add your default install image from your product DVD.

10. In the WDS console, right-click the Install Images node, and then select Add Install Image.

    The Image Group page of the Windows Deployment Services - Add Image Wizard appears, prompting you to create a new image group on your server.

11. Accept the default name for this image group, and then click Next.

12. On the Image File page, browse to locate the default install image Install.wim on your product DVD. Then, open the image to begin adding it to your image store.

13. On the Image File page, click Next.

14. On the List Of Available Images page, review the images available. Deselect all images except for SERVERSTANDARD or SERVERENTERPRISE, and then click Next.

15. On the Summary page, review the information provided on the page, and then click Next.

    The Task Progress page appears while the images are added to the store. This process can take 15 minutes or more.

16. When the image is successfully added to your server, click Finish.

▶ **Exercise 4 Pre-Stage the Client Computer in the Contoso Domain**

In this exercise, you will pre-stage the Server2 computer by adding its account to Active Directory and entering a 32-byte value associated with its MAC address. This procedure is necessary because you have configured Windows Deployment Services only to respond to known client computers.

To perform this exercise, Server2 must be a new virtual machine or other computer that is PXE-boot compatible. No operating system or other software should be installed on Server2, and you should remove any floppy disk or bootable CDs from the local drives.

1. Obtain the MAC address of Server2. To do this, start Server2. If you see the 12-character client MAC address displayed within a few seconds of startup, write this number down, shut down the computer, and then skip to step 3. (In Virtual PC, you can use the *Pause* command on the Action menu to give you time to write down the address if necessary.)

   If you do not see the MAC address displayed, proceed to step 2 to enable PXE boot in the BIOS.

2. Restart Server2 and immediately select the option to enter the Setup program to modify the BIOS. (In Virtual PC, this option is the Delete key.) Use the BIOS Setup program to ensure that PXE is available as the first boot device for Server2, and then exit the BIOS Setup program (saving changes). Restart Server2, and then go back to step 1.

3. Log on to Server1 as a domain administrator. Then, open Active Directory Users And Computers from the Administrative Tools program group.

4. In the Active Directory Users And Computers console tree, expand the Contoso.com node.

5. In the console tree, right-click the Computers container, select New, and then click Computer.

    The New Object - Computer page appears.

6. In the Computer Name text box, type **Server2**, and then click Next.

    The Managed page appears.

7. On the Managed page, read all the text on the page, and then select This Is A Managed Computer.

8. In the Computer's Unique ID (GUID/UUID) text box, type 20 zeroes followed by the 12-character MAC address of Server2. For example, if the MAC address of Server2 is 00 03 FF 9F B5 36, then you should type **0000000000000000000003FF9FB536**.

9. On the Managed page, click Next.

10. On the Host Server page, read all the text on the page, and then, leaving the default selection, click Next.

11. On the New Object - Computer page, click Finish.

▶ **Exercise 5 Deploy Windows Server 2008 Through WDS**

In this exercise, you will deploy Windows Server 2008 to Server2. To perform this exercise, you must ensure that Server2 is located in the same broadcast domain (physical subnet or virtual network) as Server1. If you are using Virtual PC, you can achieve this by configuring the Networking Settings for Server2 so that Adapter #1 is set to Local Only.

1. Start Server2.

    After a few moments, the PXE boot process begins, and the local DHCP client immediately seeks and obtains an IP address for Server2. After an address is obtained, you are prompted to press F12 to begin a network service boot.

2. Press F12 on Server2. You will have only a few seconds to perform this step. If you miss the opportunity, reset Server2 and try again.

    You will see a message indicating that Windows is loading files as the boot image is loaded from Server1. This process can take 5 minutes or longer.

After the boot image is loaded, a graphical user interface appears, and then the Windows Deployment Services page of the Install Windows Wizard appears.

3. On the Windows Deployment Services page, choose an appropriate locale and keyboard for your region, and then click Next.

    You are prompted to enter credentials for the domain.

4. Type the username and password corresponding to a domain administrator in the Contoso.com domain, and then click OK. Be sure to enter the username in the format contoso\username.

5. On the Select The Operating System You Want To Install page, choose Windows Server 2008 SERVERSTANDARD or Windows Server 2008 SERVERENTERPRISE, and then click Next.

6. On the Where Do You Want To Install Windows page, ensure that Disk 0 is selected, and then click Next.

    Windows installation begins. This process can take 30 minutes or more, during which time the server reboots.

7. When the Set Up Windows page appears, select the appropriate options for your country or region, time and currency, and keyboard layout, and then click Next.

8. If the Type Your Product Key For Activation page appears, type in a product key if available, and then click Next.

9. On the Please Read The License Terms page, review the license terms, click the I Accept The License Terms check box, and then click Next.

10. When the Thank You message appears, click Start.

11. When prompted, press Ctrl + Alt + Del to log on. (In Virtual PC, press Right Alt + Del.)

12. Click the Other User tile.

13. Type the credentials of a domain administrator in the Contoso.com domain, and then press Enter.

    A desktop appears, and then the Initial Configuration Tasks window appears.

14. Take a few moments to review the computer information displayed on the Initial Configuration Tasks page.

    The full computer name is listed as Server2.contoso.com, and the domain is listed as contoso.com.

15. Click Set Time Zone to adjust the time zone if necessary.

16. In Control Panel, open Network and Sharing Center, and then use this tool to enable both Network Discovery and File Sharing on Server2.

17. If you are using Virtual PC, use the Action menu to install Virtual Machine Additions (VMA) on Server2 at this time.

When you select the option to install VMA, a virtual CD (.iso file) is attached to the local virtual machine, and the autoplay feature opens a new window in which you are given an opportunity to run Setup.exe from the CD and install VMA.

18. If you are using Virtual PC, click Finish after VMA Setup completes.

19. Shut down Server2, and then shut down Server1.

Lesson Summary

- Windows Deployment Services is a server-based technology for deploying Windows images onto bare-metal computers.

- When a PXE-enabled computer that has no operating system boots, it contacts the PXE server on your WDS server, obtains an IP address, and downloads the WDS client. The WDS client then displays a boot menu, which presents a list of operating systems that can be installed on the system.

- A *boot image* is a Windows image (.wim) file you can use to boot a bare-metal client computer to begin the deployment of an operating system to the computer. When deploying images with WDS, you can use the default boot image from the \sources folder on the Windows Server 2008 DVD.

- An *install image* is an image of the Windows Vista or Windows Server 2008 operating system itself that you plan on deploying onto the client computer. The simplest way of using WDS is to deploy the default install image included in the \sources folder on your Windows Server 2008 product DVD.

- A *capture image* is a special boot image that you use to boot a master computer and upload an image to a WDS server.

- A *discover image* is a boot image you can use to deploy an install image onto a computer that is not PXE enabled.

Lesson Review

The following questions are intended to reinforce key information presented in this lesson. The questions are also available on the companion CD if you prefer to review them in electronic form.

NOTE   Answers

Answers to these questions and explanations of why each answer choice is correct or incorrect are located in the "Answers" section at the end of the book.

---

1. Which of the following is not a component of Windows Deployment Services?
    A. Image store
    B. Trivial File Transfer Protocol (TFTP) server
    C. Windows System Image Manager (Windows SIM)
    D. Pre-boot eXecution Environment (PXE) server

2. You want to use WDS to deploy Windows Vista RTM to 50 PXE-enabled client computers. You have, therefore, installed the WDS role and performed the following configuration tasks:
    A. Created a *Path*\RemoteInstall folder on a disk volume formatted using FAT32.
    B. Configured the PXE Server Initial Settings to allow both known and unknown client computers.
    C. Added the Boot.wim file from the *Path*\Sources folder of your Windows Vista RTM media to your image store.
    D. Added the Install.wim file from the *Path*\Sources folder of your Windows Vista RTM media to your image store.

3. When you try to use WDS, you find it doesn't work as expected. In particular, your image store doesn't work, and you can't take advantage of the enhancements found in the new Windows Server 2008 version of WDS. Why? (Choose all that apply.)
    A. Your *Path*\RemoteInstall folder must be on an NTFS volume.
    B. The PXE Server Initial Settings should allow only known clients.
    C. You must use the Boot.wim file from either Windows Server 2008 or Windows Vista integrated with Service Pack 1 media if you want to take advantage of the enhancements found in the new Windows Server 2008 version of WDS.
    D. You must use the Install.wim file from either Windows Server 2008 or Windows Vista integrated with Service Pack 1 media if you want to take advantage of the enhancements found in the new Windows Server 2008 version of WDS.

Lesson 3: Deploying Virtual Machines

Computer virtualization enables you to emulate physical computers in software. Through computer virtualization software such as Microsoft Virtual PC, Virtual Server, and Hyper-V, you can run multiple operating systems as self-contained computers on a single physical server. This technology is becoming widespread because of the advantages it offers as a means to consolidate physical computers, to support older operating systems on newer hardware, and to facilitate testing and server management.

After this lesson, you will be able to:

■ Understand the benefits of computer virtualization.

■ Understand the feature differences among all three Microsoft virtualization technologies.

Estimated lesson time: 50 minutes

What Are Virtual Machines?

A virtual machine (VM) is a software emulation of a physical computer. With VMs, you can run several operating systems simultaneously on a single physical computer, as shown in Figure 1-20.

Figure 1-20   Several VMs running on a Windows desktop

Virtualization software works by providing a software environment for an operating system that is indistinguishable from that of a physical computer. The operating system running in the virtualized environment is known as the *guest*, and the operating system on which the virtualization software is running is known as the *host*. Within the host operating system or on top of a hardware virtualization layer, each guest VM runs its own operating system with its own installed applications, as shown in Figure 1-21.

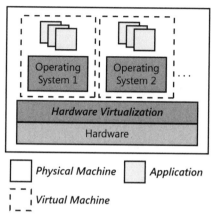

Figure 1-21   An illustration of hardware virtualization

Why Use Virtual Machines?

You can deploy VMs or migrate physical servers to VMs to provide the following functions or benefits:

- **Consolidate production servers**   Virtualization is most commonly used to consolidate the workloads from a large number of underutilized physical servers onto a smaller number of physical servers. In enterprise networks, the hardware utilization rates for physical servers can often be as low as 5 or 10 percent of server capacity. By migrating physical servers to a virtual environment, efficiency increases, and the costs associated with powering, cooling, and maintaining the physical servers are reduced. Physical space is also saved, which is a critical factor in many data centers.

- **Support older applications and operating systems**   Virtual machines are often used to host applications requiring an earlier operating system such as Windows NT. By hosting the operating system and application in a virtual environment, you no longer have to dedicate an entire physical server for this purpose.

- **Software test and development**   VMs can easily be isolated from (or integrated with) a corporate network, and they can quickly be repurposed. Some virtualization software even allows VLAN tagging, enabling the use of virtual networks with multiple subnets. Because of this flexibility, you can use VMs to test and model operating systems, applications, or security.

- **Maximize server uptime**   With virtualization, you can isolate applications in their own machines and prevent one application from affecting the performance of another in a production environment. For example, if a VM hosting one application crashes, no other server applications will be affected. Another way that virtualization improves server uptime is by reducing or eliminating hardware conflicts. Virtual machines with their generic hardware drivers provide a stable environment for applications; as a result, applications tend to function reliably in a virtual environment.

- **Efficient server management and maintenance**   By using management tools such as Microsoft System Center Virtual Machine Manager, you can manage VMs remotely and even migrate a VM from one physical server to another with minimal downtime. These features simplify management and allow you the flexibility of adjusting server workloads in response to current demands.

Microsoft provides three computer virtualization solutions: Virtual PC, Virtual Server, and Hyper-V. These solutions each provide overlapping but distinct sets of features that are designed to be used in different scenarios, as explained in the following section.

Virtual PC 2007

Like all virtualization solutions, Virtual PC 2007 enables you to run multiple operating systems on a single computer. Virtual PC, however, is designed for simplified management. In Virtual PC, each VM appears in its own resizable window on the desktop, as shown in Figure 1-22.

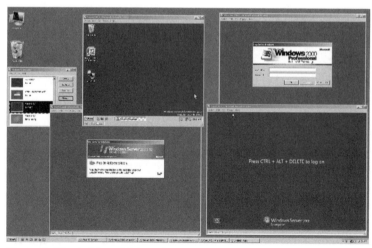

Figure 1-22   In Virtual PC, each VM appears on the desktop in a resizable window

You can easily configure the settings for each VM by selecting it in the Virtual PC Console and then clicking Settings, as shown in Figure 1-23.

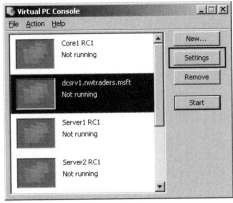

Figure 1-23 Virtual PC Console enables simplified administration

The following list describes the features and limitations of Virtual PC 2007.

- **Virtual hard disk file support** Virtual PC 2007 uses virtual hard disk (VHD) files as the local hard disks for VMs. These VHDs are also used in Virtual Server and Hyper-V, so VMs can easily be migrated from solution to solution.
- **Host-only 64-bit support** Microsoft provides a 64-bit version of Virtual PC 2007 that enables the software to run natively on 64-bit operating systems. However, you cannot run a 64-bit VM within Virtual PC. Only 32-bit guest systems are available, even on 64-bit hosts.
- **Supported hosts** You can install and run Virtual PC on the following operating systems:
    - ❑ Windows Server 2008
    - ❑ Windows Vista
    - ❑ Windows Server 2003
    - ❑ Windows XP Professional
    - ❑ Windows XP Tablet
- **Supported guests** You can run any of the following operating systems within VMs in Virtual PC:
    - ❑ Windows Server 2008
    - ❑ Windows Vista
    - ❑ Windows Server 2003
    - ❑ Windows XP Professional

❑ Windows 2000

❑ Windows 98 Second Edition

❑ OS/2

The following operating systems also run in Virtual PC, but they are no longer officially supported by Microsoft:

❑ MS-DOS 6.22

❑ Windows 95

❑ Windows 98

❑ Windows Millennium Edition (Windows Me)

❑ Windows NT 4.0 Workstation

■ **Single CPU support on guest**   In Virtual PC, each guest is assigned one single-core
CPU, regardless of whether the host system contains a multicore processor or multiple
processors.

■ **Virtual networking**   In Virtual PC, you can assign each guest up to four network adapters. For each virtual adapter, you can configure one of the following options:

❑ Not Connected

When this option is selected, networking is not available in the virtual machine.
This option is recommended when the physical computer is not on a network or
if you do not plan to access the Internet from a virtual machine.

❑ Local Only

This option provides networking support between virtual machines only. This
means that the virtual machine will not have access to any network resources on
the host operating system, but the other VMs connected to this local network will
share a virtual broadcast domain.

❑ Shared Networking (NAT)

This option is available for only the first virtual adapter in the VM. When this
option is selected, the VM is connected to a private network created by Virtual PC.
The network includes a virtual DHCP server and a virtual network address translation (NAT) server. The virtual machine is then able to access most TCP/IP-based
resources that the host operating system can access.

❑ (Specific Host Physical Adapter)

When this option is selected, the virtual machine is connected directly to the currently selected network connection of the host operating system. The virtual
machine will appear and behave like a separate physical computer on the same network. If the network uses a DHCP server, an IP address is assigned dynamically to

the virtual machine. Similarly, if the network uses static IP addresses, you must manually configure the virtual machine to use a compatible static IP address.

IMPORTANT   **Limited virtual networking in Virtual PC**

A key limitation of Virtual PC is that it provides only one virtual broadcast domain among guest VMs. In other words, you cannot create multiple virtual networks to test communication among isolated groups of VMs.

■ **Connection to host (share)**   In Virtual PC, you can connect to the host operating system only by configuring a network drive that is mapped to a folder on the host. You can configure this with the Shared Folder option, shown in Figure 1-24.

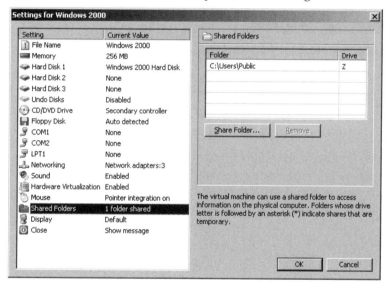

Figure 1-24   In Virtual PC, you connect to the host operating system through network drives

■ **Hardware-assisted virtualization**   If the processor on the physical host includes a virtualization-enhancing technology such as Intel-VT or AMD-V, Virtual PC 2007 can take advantage of that technology to improve the performance of the virtual machine.

This option, which is enabled by default, is shown in Figure 1-25.

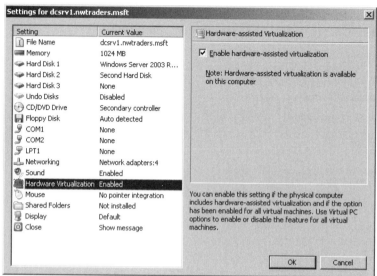

Figure 1-25   Virtual PC supports hardware-assisted virtualization

- **PXE boot**   The virtual network adapters in Virtual PC 2007 are PXE enabled by default. This technology enables a bare-metal computer to obtain a DHCP address and download an operating system from the network. (PXE boot is demonstrated in the Lesson 2, "Configuring Windows Deployment Services," practice, "Configuring Windows Deployment Services.")
- **Virtual Machine Additions**   To optimize the performance of any virtual machine in Virtual PC, you must install VM Additions. Installing VM Additions provides greatly improved overall performance, improved mouse cursor tracking and control, and other enhancements.

Because of the features and limitations of Virtual PC, it is recommended for supporting earlier desktop applications, for application testing, and for training.

Virtual Server 2005 R2 SP1

Virtual Server is different from Virtual PC in that it provides more advanced capabilities to support the requirements of enterprise server applications and administration.

The following list describes the additional features offered in Virtual Server beyond those available in Virtual PC:

- **Expanded guest operating system support**   Beyond the operating systems supported in Virtual PC, Virtual Server also enables you to run the following operating systems as a guest:
    - ❑ Red Hat Linux
    - ❑ SuSE Linux
    - ❑ Solaris
    - ❑ Windows NT Server SP6a
- **Failover clustering support**   Virtual Server provides simple two-node failover from one virtual machine to another. You can use this feature for testing and development only; it is not supported for use in a production environment.
- **Network load balancing (NLB) support**   For testing environments, Virtual Server supports virtualized NLB farms.
- **Multiprocessor support**   When the host machine has a multicore CPU or multiple CPUs, you can assign one core or processor to a VM in Virtual Server. You cannot assign more than one core or CPU to a guest VM. For example, on a 32-processor host computer, you could allocate your CPU capacity so that 31 simultaneously running VMs would each use up to one CPU, leaving a CPU free for the host operating system.
- **Expanded virtual networking support**   With Virtual Server, you can create an unlimited number of virtual networks (broadcast domains), each with its own virtual DHCP server. You can also configure DNS and WINS servers, IP addresses, and IP address lease time.
- **SCSI support**   Virtual Server supports virtual SCSI drives up to 2 terabytes in size.
- **Remote management capabilities**   You can administer Virtual Server remotely by using the Web-based Administration Web site. You can also access and administer virtual machines remotely by using Virtual Machine Remote Control (VMRC).
- **Facilitated physical-to-virtual (P2V) conversion**   The Virtual Server 2005 Migration Toolkit (VSMT) is a free, downloadable tool used with Virtual Server 2005. VSMT simplifies the migration of a complete operating system, along with its installed applications, from a physical server to a virtual environment in Virtual Server 2005.

MORE INFO   Watch a P2V Demo Online

To perform a P2V migration, you can also use Virtual Machine Manager 2007. To see a demonstration of a P2V migration in Virtual Machine Manager, view the "Physical to Virtual Machine Migration" demo at *mms://wm.microsoft.com/ms/systemcenter/scvmm/demo/vmm_intro_03.wmv*.

The advanced features of Virtual Server make it a good solution for consolidating servers, for hosting network applications, for testing complex networking scenarios, and for supporting Linux and Solaris in a virtual environment.

Hyper-V

Hyper-V is virtualization technology and Windows Server 2008 server role scheduled to be made available 180 days after the release of Windows Server 2008. Unlike Virtual PC and Virtual Server, Hyper-V is a *hypervisor* technology. A hypervisor is a thin layer of software that runs on top of the hardware and beneath the parent operating system. When a hypervisor is installed, the parent and guest (or child) operating systems are installed in separate partitions and have equal access to the hardware. This architecture is illustrated in Figure 1-26.

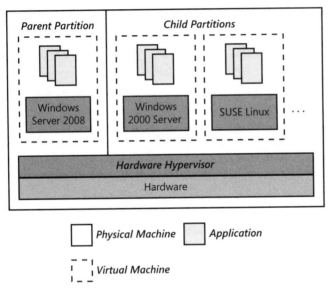

Figure 1-26 Hyper-V runs beneath all installed operating systems

In Windows Server 2008, Hyper-V is managed through the Hyper-V Manager administration tool. This tool is shown in Figure 1-27.

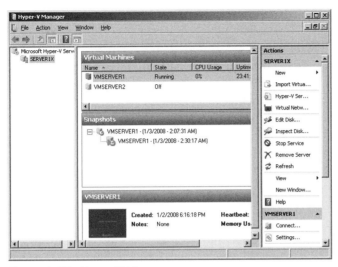

Figure 1-27   Hyper-V Manager

Compared to Virtual PC and Virtual Server, Hyper-V offers significant improvements in performance, scalability, and manageability. The following list describes some of the specific features and benefits Hyper-V offers beyond those available in Virtual PC or Virtual Server:

- **64-bit guest support**   Hyper-V supports 64-bit operating systems in guest (child) VMs.
- **Multicore and multiprocessor guest support**   On a Hyper-V enabled server, each guest VM can be assigned up to four processors.
- **Increased memory support for guests**   In Virtual PC and Virtual Server, you can assign a maximum of 3.6 GB of RAM per VM. In Hyper-V, you can assign up to 32 GB of RAM per VM.
- **Improved performance**   The hypervisor technology, as well as the support for multiple CPUs and increased memory, results in much improved performance for VMs in the Hyper-V environment.
- **Virtual machine snapshots**   Hyper-V provides the ability to take snapshots of a running virtual machine, so you can easily revert to a previous state and facilitate backups.
- **Enhanced NLB support**   Hyper-V includes new virtual switch capabilities. This means that virtual machines can be easily configured to run with NLB to balance load across virtual machines on different servers.

■ **Integration Components**   Integration Components (ICs) in Hyper-V serve the same role that VM Additions do in Virtual PC and Virtual Server: they greatly improve performance and help integrate a virtual machine with the physical hardware and parent operating system. When you create a virtual machine in Hyper-V, unlike with VM additions, the ICs *are automatically preinstalled* with Windows guest operating systems. However, in some cases, you must install the ICs manually. For example, if you want to migrate a VM from Virtual PC or Virtual Server to Hyper-V, you must first remove VM Additions before the migration, and then install the ICs manually after the migration. You also have to install the ICs manually to support virtual machines running non-Windows operating systems.

Exam Tip   Know these Hyper-V features for the 70-643 exam.

Quick Check

■ What is a hypervisor?

Quick Check Answer

■ A hypervisor is a thin layer of software that runs beneath the parent operating system and that grants both parent and child operating systems equal access to the hardware. A hypervisor essentially turns all locally installed operating systems into virtual machines.

Hyper-V Hardware and Software Requirements

Hyper-V has strict hardware requirements that relate to the processor. Specifically, Hyper-V requires an x64-based processor that includes both hardware-assisted virtualization (AMD-V or Intel VT) and hardware data execution protection. (On AMD systems, the data execution protection feature is called the No Execute or NX bit. On Intel systems, this feature is called the Execute Disable or XD bit.) In addition, these features must be enabled in the BIOS. (By default, they are often disabled.)

The software requirements of Hyper-V are an x64 version of Windows Server 2008 Standard Edition, Enterprise Edition, or Datacenter Edition. Hyper-V can run on a server core installation as well as on the full installation of Windows Server 2008.

Exam Tip   Be sure to know the hardware and software requirements for Hyper-V.

Use the following procedure to install Hyper-V on a full installation (as opposed to a Server Core installation) of Windows Server 2008.

▶ **Install Hyper-V**

1. Ensure that your system meets the hardware requirements for Hyper-V and that both hardware-assisted virtualization and data execution protection have been enabled prior to installation. If BIOS reconfiguration changes were made to enable these hardware features, you must complete a full power-cycle before proceeding.

2. In Server Manager, add the Hyper-V role. To do this, click Add Roles under Roles Summary, and then select Hyper-V in the Add Roles Wizard, as shown in Figure 1-28.

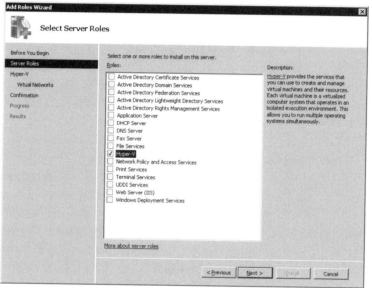

Figure 1-28   Adding the Hyper-V role

3. Follow the on-screen instructions to complete the Add Roles Wizard.

4. At the end of the Add Roles Wizard, you must restart the system for the Hyper-V role to be enabled.

5. Upon restart, log on with the same account used to install the Hyper-V role.

6. Confirm the installation of the Hyper-V role by expanding the Roles node in Server Manager, selecting the Hyper-V node, and verifying that the Hyper-V services are running, as shown in Figure 1-29.

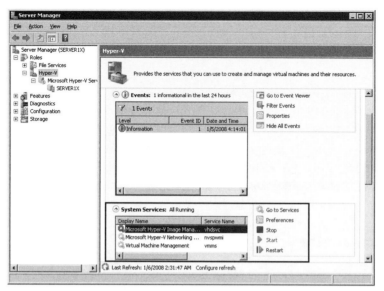

Figure 1-29   Hyper-V services

NOTE   Hyper-V servers should be dedicated to that role

It is recommended that no other Windows Server 2008 role be enabled on the host system if the Hyper-V role is enabled on the system.

Use the following procedure to enable Hyper-V on a Server Core installation of Windows Server 2008.

▶ **Enable Hyper-V on a Server Core Installation**

1. Type **start /w ocsetup Microsoft-Hyper-V** to enable the Hyper-V role.

2. . Restart when prompted.

IMPORTANT   To Manage Hyper-V installed on a Server Core installation, you must remotely connect to the server by using Hyper-V Manager on a different system.

Once you have installed Hyper-V, you can begin to create virtual machines. Use the following procedure to do so.

▶ **Create a Virtual Machine in Hyper-V**

1. Open Hyper-V Manager from the Administrative Tools program group.

2. From the Action pane, click New, and then click Virtual Machine.

3. Proceed through the pages of the wizard to specify the custom settings you want to make. You can click Next to move through each page of the wizard, or you can click the name of a page in the left pane to move directly to that page.

4. After you have finished configuring the virtual machine, click Finish.

Virtual Disk Types in Hyper-V

Like Virtual PC and Virtual Server, Hyper-V uses .vhd files for virtual hard disks. These virtual hard disks appear in three varieties: dynamically expanding, fixed, and differencing.

- **Dynamically expanding** Dynamically expanding virtual hard disks provide storage capacity as needed to store data. The size of the .vhd file is small when the disk is created and grows as data is added to the disk. The size of the .vhd file does not shrink automatically when data is deleted from the virtual hard disk. However, you can compact the disk to decrease the file size after data is deleted by using the Edit Virtual Hard Disk Wizard.

- **Fixed** Fixed virtual hard disks provide storage capacity by using a .vhd file that is the size specified for the virtual hard disk when the disk is created. The size of the .vhd file remains fixed regardless of the amount of data stored. However, you can use the Edit Virtual Hard Disk Wizard to increase the size of the virtual hard disk, which increases the size of the .vhd file.

- **Differencing** A differencing virtual hard disk is a virtual hard disk associated with another virtual hard disk in a parent–child relationship. The differencing disk is the child, and the associated virtual disk is the parent. The parent disk can be any type of virtual hard disk. The differencing disk (the child) stores a record of all changes made to the parent disk and provides a way to save changes without altering the parent disk. In other words, by using differencing disks, you ensure that changes are made, by default, to the differencing disks and not to the original virtual hard disk. You can, however, elect to merge changes from the differencing disk to the original virtual hard disk when it is appropriate to do so.

You can also use many differencing disks that share a single parent. This method saves storage space if you need to have multiple virtual hard disks based on a single image.

Exam Tip   Be sure to understand the three virtual hard disk types for the 70-643 exam.

Configuring Virtual Networks in Hyper-V

Hyper-V enables you to create complex virtual networks with multiple interconnected subnets or broadcast domains. You can create any of three network types: external, internal, and private.

- **External**   An external virtual network binds to the physical network adapter so that virtual machines can access a physical network. For example, if there is a DHCP server on the physical network, virtual machines connected to an external network will receive a DHCP address from that network server.

    When you add the Hyper-V server role, you are given the opportunity to create an external network for each hardware network adapter connected to the computer.

- **Internal**   An internal virtual network can connect all the virtual machines with the local physical computer. This type of virtual network cannot provide access to a physical network connection.

- **Private**   A private virtual network can be used only to connect virtual machines to each other running on the local physical computer. It cannot be used to connect to the local physical computer itself.

Creating New Virtual Networks

After you install the Hyper-V server role, you might want to create additional virtual networks. To do so, in Hyper-V Manager, click Virtual Network Manager in the Actions pane. Then, in the Virtual Network Manager window, select the type of virtual network you want to create and click Add, as shown in Figure 1-30.

Afterward, when you create a new virtual machine by using the New Virtual Machine Wizard, you are given an opportunity to connect the new machine to any virtual networks you have already created, as shown in Figure 1-31.

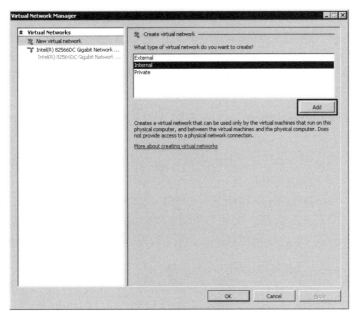

Figure 1-30   Creating a new virtual network

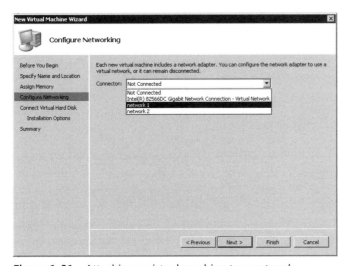

Figure 1-31   Attaching a virtual machine to a network

Assigning Virtual Machines to Virtual LANs

Typically, if you wanted to isolate a group of virtual machines from other virtual machines hosted on a physical computer, you would assign those virtual machines to a single and distinct virtual network. However, you can also isolate a group of virtual machines by assigning the VMs to the same virtual LAN (VLAN) within a given virtual network.

For example, you might want to divide an internal virtual network named InternalA into two subnets and assign a DHCP server to each subnet. By assigning separate VLAN IDs to each portion of the network, you can then assign one DHCP server to each VLAN and distribute clients between these VLANs. Clients within each VLAN would then respond to the DHCP server on their own VLAN only. In this way, VLAN IDs enable you to simulate separate physical networks within a single virtual network.

To assign a virtual machine to a VLAN, first open the settings of the virtual machine by right-clicking the VM in Hyper-V Manager and then clicking Settings, as shown in Figure 1-32.

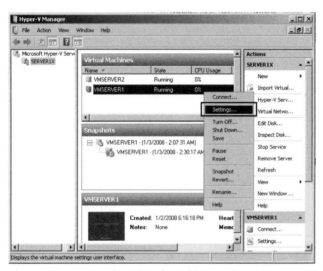

Figure 1-32   Accessing virtual machine settings in Hyper-V Manager

Then, in the Settings window that opens, select the network adapter and the option to enable LAN identification, as shown in Figure 1-33. Finally, choose a VLAN ID. Each VLAN ID essentially represents a subnet within the chosen virtual network. When virtual LAN identification is enabled on a particular VM, other virtual machines can directly communicate with that VM only when they are assigned the same network and VLAN ID.

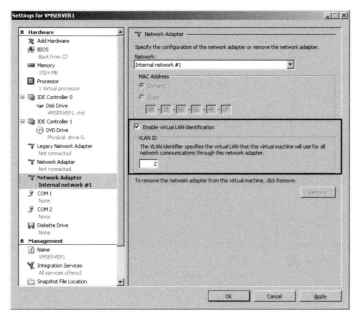

Figure 1-33   Accessing a virtual machine to a VLAN

Exam Tip   You need to understand the basics of Hyper-V virtual networks (including VLANs) for the 70-643 exam.

Lesson Summary

■ A virtual machine is a software emulation of a physical computer. Virtual machines are used (among other reasons) to help consolidate physical servers, support earlier applications and operating systems, and assist in testing and development.

■ Microsoft provides three separate computer virtualization solutions: Virtual PC, Virtual Server, and Hyper-V. These solutions each provide overlapping but distinct sets of features.

■ Installing VM Additions in a virtual machine greatly improves the performance of that machine.

■ Hyper-V is a *hypervisor* technology, which is a thin layer of software that runs on top of the hardware and beneath the parent operating system. Unlike Virtual PC and Virtual Server, Hyper-V supports 64-bit guest operating systems as well as multicore and multi-processor guests.

Lesson Review

The following questions are intended to reinforce key information presented in this lesson. The questions are also available on the companion CD if you prefer to review them in electronic form.

NOTE   Answers

Answers to these questions and explanations of why each answer choice is correct or incorrect are located in the "Answers" section at the end of the book.

---

1. Which of the following is a feature only of Hyper-V and not of Virtual PC or Virtual Server?
   - A. Network load balancing support
   - B. On multiprocessor hosts, the ability to assign a host processor to a virtual machine
   - C. 64-bit host support
   - D. 64-bit guest support.
2. Which of the following tools can you use to help you perform physical-to-virtual conversions of servers?
   - A. Virtual PC
   - B. Virtual Server
   - C. Hyper-V
   - D. Virtual Server Migration Toolkit

Lesson 4: Implementing a Windows Activation Infrastructure

A volume license key is a product key used to validate multiple copies of software, usually in large networks. With Windows XP and Windows Server 2003, volume license keys needed to be entered during installation, but these installations didn't need to be activated. This older volume license activation policy, however, has changed with Windows Vista and Windows Server 2008 in that even these volume-license deployments of operating systems need to be activated within 30 days of installation. Activation, as a result, now needs to be considered an integral part of corporate deployment.

The new options, procedures, and technologies used to activate volume-license editions of Windows Vista or Windows Server 2008 are known collectively as Volume Activation 2.0. This lesson describes the options and procedures that form Volume Activation 2.0.

After this lesson, you will be able to:
- Describe the difference between MAK and KMS licensing.
- Describe the scenarios in which MAK or KMS licensing is preferable.
- Install and configure a KMS host.

Estimated lesson time: 50 minutes

Product Activation Types

There are three basic types of product activations for Windows Vista and Windows Server 2008: OEM, retail, and volume. OEM activation is the BIOS-bound, out-of-the-box activation that is performed automatically on computers preinstalled with an operating system. Retail activation is what you must perform if you purchase Windows Vista or Windows Server 2008 through a software retailer. These purchases include a retail license key that typically applies to one computer only. After entering this retail license key, you can activate the software online or over the telephone.

Volume activation is more complex. It provides customers with the following two types of keys, including three methods of activation.

- Multiple Activation Key (MAK)
    - MAK independent activation
    - MAK proxy activation
- Key Management Service (KMS) Key
    - KMS activation

NOTE   How do you purchase a volume license key?

To obtain a volume license key for a Microsoft product, go to *http://www.microsoft.com/licensing* to learn about the various volume license programs and to locate an authorized reseller. Note that for Windows Vista and Windows Server 2008, you must purchase a minimum of five licenses to be eligible for volume licensing.

All customers are free to purchase and use a MAK, but a KMS key can be used only by organizations that can activate 25 physical computers (for Windows Vista) or five physical computers (for Windows Server 2008). These keys and activation methods are described in the following sections.

Implementing MAK Activation

MAKs are typically used in environments with fewer than 25 computers. With MAK activation, you use a product key to activate a specific number of Windows installations. This product key does not need to be entered during installation because, as with all versions of Windows Vista and Windows Server 2008, you have a 30-day grace period to enter the product key and activate Windows. The Windows activation is then valid until there is a significant hardware change on the computer.

In general, there are two ways to activate computers by using a MAK.

- **MAK independent activation**   In independent activation, two steps are required. First, you must enter the MAK on each computer to be activated. You can perform this step during operating system installation or afterward. After installation, you can enter the key on the client locally by using the Change Product Key Wizard or remotely by connecting to the computer over the network with the Volume Activation Management Tool (VAMT).

MORE INFO   Where can you obtain the VAMT?

The VAMT can be downloaded from the Microsoft Download Center at *http://www.microsoft.com/download*.

After you enter the MAK, you can then activate each computer either by using the VAMT or the telephone, as illustrated in Figure 1-34.

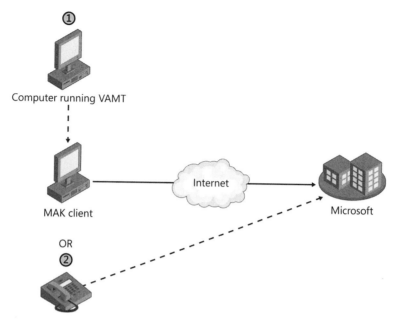

Figure 1-34   You can perform MAK independent activation by using the VAMT on another computer

In general, you can think of independent activation as the method to use to activate MAK clients that have an Internet connection or to activate by telephone a very small number (1–3) of computers that are not connected to the Internet.

IMPORTANT   Activating Server Core

To activate a Server Core installation of Windows Server 2008 with a MAK or retail key, use the *Slmgr* command to perform the following two steps.

First, if you have not entered the key during Windows setup, type the following command at the prompt, where **product key** is your product key (including the four dashes in the key):

slmgr -ipk *product key*

(If you already entered the product key during Windows Setup, you can skip this first step.)

Then, type the following command to perform the actual activation:

slmgr -ato

You can also use *Slmgr* command to activate a remote installation. For more information, type **slmgr** at a command prompt.

- **MAK proxy activation** Activating clients by telephone is a time-consuming process. If you have a fair number (4–24) of computers on your network that are isolated from the Internet, it would not be desirable or practical to activate them all in this fashion. MAK proxy activation provides a simpler method to activate such groups of computers that have no Internet access.

  With MAK proxy activation, on a computer that can connect to the isolated computers, you use the VAMT to collect the Installation IDs (IIDs) of those computers and to save those IIDs in an XML file. Then, on a computer that has Internet access, you again use the VAMT to connect to Microsoft and obtain the Confirmation IDs (CIDs) associated with those IIDs. (If necessary, you can manually move the XML file from one computer to another to complete this process.) Those CIDs are then saved to the same XML file. Finally, you again use VAMT to connect to the isolated computers and use the updated XML file to activate them.

The MAK proxy activation procedure is illustrated in Figure 1-35.

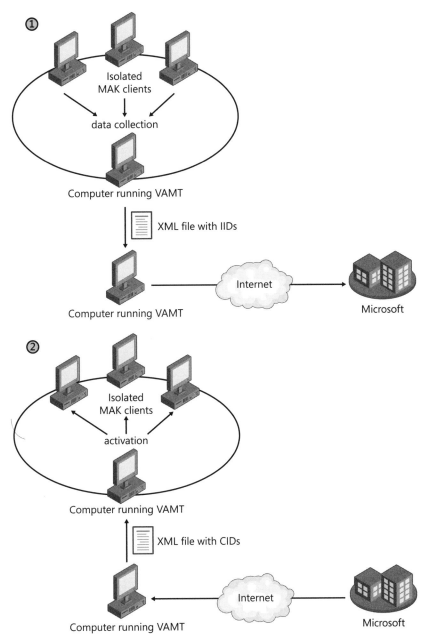

Figure 1-35   In MAK proxy activation, activation is performed with the aid of an XML file

Advantages and Disadvantages of MAK Licensing

When you need to activate a relatively small number of computers, MAK licensing is easy. It requires no infrastructure to be set up. You can use the VAMT to facilitate the process, but you also have the familiar option to enter the product key and activate locally as you would with any retail key. In addition, once you activate a MAK Windows installation, that installation remains forever activated unless the local hardware changes significantly.

However, if you have a large number of clients to activate, MAK licensing would be difficult from an administrative point of view. Typing in product keys 250 to 2,000 times, keeping track of the number of times each key has been activated, and then keeping track of the computers that have been activated would be a time-consuming process.

For such large networks, it would be preferable to have an option for activation that did not require you to enter any product key on the local computer and on which activation for clients was performed automatically without user intervention. That option is available in KMS licensing.

Implementing KMS Activation

KMS licensing enables clients in a large network to be activated automatically without contacting Microsoft. In a KMS infrastructure, there is only one key on the network—the KMS key—and that key is installed on a single computer, known as the KMS host. Of all the computers on the network, only this KMS host activates directly with Microsoft, and this step is performed only once. Beyond the initial activation, a KMS host never again needs to communicate with the Microsoft Activation servers.

Computers running volume license editions of Windows Vista and Windows Server 2008 (KMS clients) automatically attempt to activate by connecting to a KMS host machine. Clients not yet activated will attempt to connect with the KMS host every two hours. Once activated, KMS clients must reactive periodically; this is an essential difference between KMS activation and other forms of activation. KMS clients must in fact renew their activation at least once every 180 days (or 210 days if you include the grace period). Activated KMS clients will attempt to reconnect to the KMS host every seven days and, if successful, will renew the full 180-day activation life span. If clients are unable to contact a KMS server after the 180-day activation life span ends, they have an additional 30-day grace period to complete activation or re-activation. Clients not activated within this time period will go into Reduced Functionality Mode (RFM).

Figure 1-36 depicts a basic KMS infrastructure.

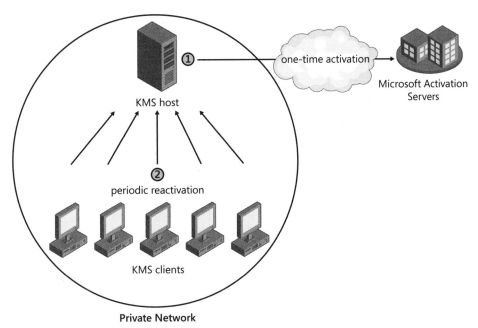

Figure 1-36   KMS clients activated periodically by contacting a KMS host on your network

Minimum KMS Client Numbers (Thresholds)

KMS activation requires a minimum number of physical (as opposed to virtual) computers to connect to the KMS host before activation can occur. This minimum number is known as the KMS activation threshold. This nonconfigurable threshold helps ensure that the delegated activation service is used only in an enterprise environment and serves as a piracy protection mechanism.

The KMS host counts activation requests and responds to each valid request with the count of how many systems have contacted the KMS host in the past 30 days. If the count meets or exceeds the KMS activation threshold, that KMS client will self-activate.

The threshold for Windows Server 2008 and Windows Vista differs and is calculated in the following manner:

■   For a Windows Server 2008 client to activate successfully, at least five physical KMS client computers must request activation on the KMS host. These client requests can originate from computers running Windows Server 2008 or Windows Vista.

- For a Windows Vista client to activate, at least 25 physical KMS client machines must request activation on the KMS host. These client requests can originate from computers running Windows Vista or Windows Server 2008.

Note that virtual machines do not contribute to the count, but once the threshold is met, they can be activated through the KMS host. Note also that the KMS host itself does not contribute to the count.

KMS Host Discovery

For KMS-based activation, clients must be able to locate a KMS host on a network. Clients can locate the KMS host by using one of two methods: *Autodiscovery*, in which a KMS client uses DNS records to locate a local KMS host automatically; or *direct connection*, in which a system administrator specifies the KMS host location and communication port.

- **Autodiscovery** By default, a KMS client discovers a KMS host by querying a DNS server for an SRV record named _vlmcs._TCP. If a client wants to discover a KMS host, therefore, the DNS server with which the client communicates needs to contain an SRV record named _vlmcs._TCP that points to the KMS host.

  The KMS host will automatically attempt to create this SRV record by using dynamic DNS. For KMS autodiscovery to work properly, DNS servers must support both dynamic DNS registrations and SRV resource records. Versions of Microsoft DNS included with Windows 2000 Server, Windows Server 2003, and Windows Server 2008 and BIND DNS versions 8 through 9.4.0 all support this functionality.

  However, if dynamic DNS registration does not work for any reason, the DNS server administrator must create the SRV record manually. The full name of the record should be _vlmcs._TCP.*DNSDomainName*, where *DNSDomainName* is the name of the local DNS domain. The time to live (TTL) for these records should be 60 minutes. The KMS host address and port (1688/TCP) should also be included in each record.

- **Direct connection** You can use the Windows Software Licensing Management Tool script, Slmgr.vbs, located in the *%SystemRoot%*\System32 folder, to specify a KMS host on the client and bypass the autodiscovery process. To configure this type of direct connection, type the following command on the KMS client, where *KMS-host* is the DNS name or IP address of the KMS host:

```
cscript %systemroot%\system32\slmgr.vbs -skms KMS-host
```

Exam Tip For the 70-643 exam, know how to configure SRV records manually on a DNS server as well as how to specify a direct connection to a KMS host.

Installing and Configuring a KMS host

All the tools required for KMS host operation are already included in Windows Vista and Windows Server 2008. You simply need to use the Slmgr.vbs script to first install and then enable the KMS key. After performing those steps, the KMS host can begin servicing activation requests from KMS clients.

To configure a KMS host, perform the following steps on a computer running Windows Vista or Windows Server 2008.

1. Install an enterprise volume license key by running the following command in an elevated command prompt window, where *Key* is the enterprise volume license key:

    cscript **%systemroot%\system32\slmgr.vbs -ipk Key**

2. Activate the KMS host, using the Internet, by running this script:

    cscript **%systemroot%\system32\slmgr.vbs -ato**

3. To activate the KMS by telephone, start the Windows Activation Wizard by running this executable:

    slui.exe

    Click Activate Windows Online Now, and then click Use The Automated Phone System To Activate.

4. Ensure that the KMS port (the default is 1688/TCP) is allowed through all firewalls between the KMS host and KMS client computers.

IMPORTANT   KMS host security

Do not provide unsecured access to KMS hosts over an uncontrolled network such as the Internet. Doing so can lead to exposure to penetration attempts and unauthorized activation by computers outside the organization.

---

5. Make any configuration changes required for the environment.

    By using the Slmgr.vbs script and editing the KMS host's registry, you can customize the configuration of KMS. For example, you can configure KMS to register SRV resource records on multiple DNS domains, not to register with DNS at all, to use nonstandard ports, and even to control client renewal intervals.

Advantages and Disadvantages of KMS Licensing

KMS licensing is generally preferable to MAK licensing because it requires no user intervention. The KMS host automatically registers its address in DNS, and the KMS client then automatically uses DNS to locate the KMS host.

The disadvantages of KMS licensing are its significant infrastructure requirements. First, the KMS client threshold requires at least 25 KMS clients for Windows Vista and five KMS clients for Windows Server 2008. In addition, all KMS clients must be able to connect to a KMS host at least once every 180 days. In contrast, MAK licensing has no such requirements; once a MAK client is activated, it is activated forever unless the hardware is significantly changed.

Because of the diverse topology of large, multisite networks, many large organizations need both MAK and KMS licensing.

Activation Infrastructure Example

Because KMS activation is preferable to MAK activation, the general rule for designing an activation infrastructure for large organizations is simply to use KMS licensing wherever possible and to use MAK everywhere else. This principle is illustrated in Figure 1-37, which shows a private network with four sites.

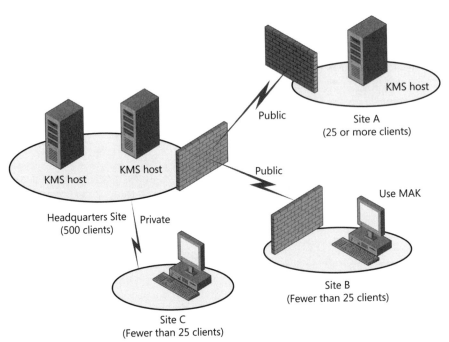

Figure 1-37   Multisite networks typically need both KMS and MAK licensing

This figure shows a private network with four sites. At the Headquarters site, 500 clients are sufficient to support KMS licensing, so KMS activation is used. (The two servers shown in the diagram can be used either to support activation for two separate DNS domains or merely to balance the request load between two servers.) At Site A, the 25 or more clients are enough to support a local KMS host, so a local KMS host is used. At Site B, there are not enough clients to support a local KMS host. In addition, the clients at the site are not able to connect to a KMS host elsewhere on the private network. In such a case, KMS licensing is not an option, so MAK licensing should be used instead. At Site C, there are not enough clients to support a local KMS host, but the clients at the site are able to connect to a KMS host at the Headquarters site. In this case, KMS licensing is the best option.

Quick Check

- Why would you ever need to create SRV records to help activation?

Quick Check Answer

- KMS clients query for an SRV record in DNS to discover the address of a KMS host. If the local KMS host has not automatically created this SRV record on the DNS server, you have to create the record manually.

PRACTICE Activating Windows Server 2008

In this practice, you will use the Change Product Key Wizard to activate Server2 on the Internet.

▶ **Exercise Activate Server2**

In this exercise, you use the System Control Panel to activate Server2. Before beginning this exercise, you must ensure that Server2 can connect to the Internet.

1. Log on to Contoso.com from Server2 as a domain administrator.
2. In Control Panel, click System And Maintenance, and then click System.
3. In the Windows Activation area of the System window, click 30 Day(s) To Activate. Activate Windows Now.

    The Activate Windows Now page of the Windows Activation Wizard appears.
4. Click Activate Windows Online Now.
5. If you are prompted to enter a product key, type the key in the space provided, and then click Next.

    The Windows Activation Wizard indicates that activation was successful, and a Windows Activation message box appears, informing you that you need to restart your computer.
6. Click Close to close the Windows Activation message box.

7. Click Close to close the Windows Activation Wizard.

8. Shut down Server2.

Lesson Summary

- The volume license activation policy has changed with Windows Vista and Windows Server 2008 in that these operating systems need to be activated within 30 days of installation.

- For Windows Vista and Windows Server 2008, two types of volume licenses are available: Multiple Access Key (MAK) licenses and Key Management Service (KMS) licenses. Each of these licenses is associated with a different method of activation.

- MAKs are typically used in environments with fewer than 25 computers. With MAK activation, you use a product key to activate a specific number of Windows installations.

- KMS licensing enables clients in a large network to be activated automatically without contacting Microsoft. In a KMS infrastructure, there is only one key in the network—the KMS key—and that key is installed on a single computer known as the KMS host. Computers running volume license editions of Windows Vista and Windows Server 2008 (KMS clients) automatically attempt to activate by connecting to a KMS host machine.

Lesson Review

The following questions are intended to reinforce key information presented in this lesson. The questions are also available on the companion CD if you prefer to review them in electronic form.

NOTE Answers

Answers to these questions and explanations of why each answer choice is correct or incorrect are located in the "Answers" section at the end of the book.

---

1. You are an administrator for a corporate network. At a branch office, you want to deploy Windows Vista to 21 client computers and Windows Server 2008 to four servers. For which operating systems is the branch office eligible for KMS licensing?

   A. Windows Vista

   B. Windows Server 2008

   C. Both Windows Vista and Windows Server 2008

   D. Neither Windows Vista nor Windows Server 2008

2. Which of the following is the most efficient way to activate 15 volume-license computers
    running Windows Vista on a research subnet that has no Internet access?

    A. MAK-independent activation

    B. MAK proxy activation

    C. KMS host activation

    D. Retail key activation

Chapter Review

To further practice and reinforce the skills you learned in this chapter, you can:

- Review the chapter summary.
- Review the list of key terms introduced in this chapter.
- Complete the case scenarios. These scenarios set up a real-world situations involving the topics of this chapter and asks you to create solutions.
- Complete the suggested practices.
- Take a practice test.

Chapter Summary

- You can deploy Windows Vista and Windows Server 2008 by using the product DVD, by using tools included in the Windows Automated Installation Kit (AIK), or by using Windows Deployment Services (WDS). All methods to deploy Windows Vista and Windows Server 2008 are based on a new native Windows imaging WIM format. WIM files (.wim) contain file-based (as opposed to sector-based) images that can be modified before, during, and after deployment.
- You can use WDS to deploy Windows Vista or Windows Server 2008 to bare-metal computers. With WDS, a PXE-enabled computer contacts the WDS server and downloads a menu of available operating systems. An end-user can then choose an operating system to install from this menu.
- A virtual machine is an emulation of a physical computer that can be used in server consolidation, testing, and hosting earlier applications. Microsoft provides three virtualization solutions (Virtual PC, Virtual Server, and Hyper-V), each of which is suitable in different environments.
- Hyper-V is a server role in Windows Server 2008 that installs a hypervisor beneath the parent operating system. Hyper-V gives parent and guest systems equal access to the hardware.
- Even volume license versions of Windows Vista and Windows Server 2008 need to be activated. There are two volume licensing options: Multiple Access Key (MAK) licensing and Key Management Service (KMS) licensing. MAK licensing is for environments of fewer than 25 computers. KMS licensing provides larger networks with a more automated solution for activation.

Key Terms

Do you know what these key terms mean? You can check your answers by looking up the terms in the glossary at the end of the book.

- boot image
- capture image
- discover image
- guest (child) operating system
- host (parent) operating system
- hypervisor
- install image
- Key Management Service (KMS)
- Multiple Acess Key (MAK)
- WIM file

Case Scenarios

In the following case scenarios, you will apply what you've learned in this chapter. You can find answers to these questions in the "Answers" section at the end of this book.

Case Scenario 1: Deploying Servers

You are a network administrator for Contoso.com. You have been assigned to design a deployment solution for a rollout of 200 installations of Windows Vista and 25 installations of Windows Server 2008.

1. Management requests the ability to deploy operating systems remotely from a central location. Which deployment solution should you use to meet this requirement?

2. You have only 20 available servers on which to deploy Windows Server 2008. Ten other servers in the company are being used to host Windows NT and Linux applications, and the utilization rates of those servers average 15 percent of capacity. Given this scenario, how can you use virtualization to reduce the costs associated with deploying Windows Server 2008?

Case Scenario 2: Creating an Activation Infrastructure

You work in IT support for Northwind Traders, and you are a part of the deployment team. Northwind Traders is planning to deploy 500 installations of Windows Vista and 50 installations of Windows Server 2008. You have been asked to design the activation infrastructure for the new operating systems.

Northwind Traders includes three sites. At the Headquarters site in New York, you plan to deploy 400 Windows Vista clients and 43 installations of Windows Server 2008. Among its 400 clients, Headquarters includes an isolated research network of 20 Windows Vista clients. The research network has no connection to the Internet or to the rest of the Nwtraders.com network.

The second Northwind Traders site is located in Binghamton, NY. This branch office network includes 80 Windows Vista clients and five servers running Windows Server 2008. The Binghamton office network is connected to the Headquarters network by a virtual private network (VPN).

The third site is located in Syracuse, NY. This branch office network is composed of 20 Windows Vista clients and two servers running Windows Server 2008. There is no VPN network connection from the Syracuse site to either of the other two company network sites.

1. How should you design the activation infrastructure for the Headquarters site?
2. How should you design the activation infrastructure for the Binghamton site?
3. How should you design the activation infrastructure for the Syracuse site?

Suggested Practices

To help you successfully master the exam objectives presented in this chapter, complete the following tasks.

Deploy Images by Using Windows Deployment Services

Use these practices to solidify your understanding of WDS deployment.

- **Practice 1** Create and customize an installation of Windows Vista that includes Microsoft Office and any other software you need in your daily work. Then, use the Sysprep utility to generalize the installation and prepare it for imaging. Use a capture image to turn the Sysprepped installation into a WIM file, upload the new image to WDS, and then deploy the image to a PXE-enabled client.

■ **Practice 2**   Watch the Webcast entitled "Overview of Windows Deployment Services" by Chris Henley, available on the companion CD in the Webcasts folder. Alternatively, you can find this Webcast by visiting *http://msevents.microsoft.com* and searching for event ID 1032322748.

Configure Windows Activation

This webcast will help reinforce concepts related to KMS and MAK licensing.

■ **Practice**   Watch the Webcast entitled "Windows Vista Volume Activation 2.0" by Thomas Lindeman, available on the companion CD in the Webcasts folder. Alternatively, you can find this Webcast by visiting *http://msevents.microsoft.com* and searching for event ID 1032318045.

Configure Hyper-V and Virtual Machines

As with any technology, Hyper-V is best understood by working with it hands-on. If you have a computer that meets the hardware requirements for Hyper-V, perform the first practice. In either case, you should watch the webcasts in the second practice.

■ **Practice 1**   On a 64-bit computer that meets the hardware requirements for Hyper-V, install Windows Server 2008, and then add the Hyper-V server role. Then, install your choice of operating system on a child partition.

■ **Practice 2**   Watch the Webcast entitled "Hyper-V Tour.wmv" by Keith Combs, available on the companion CD in the Webcasts folder. Alternatively, you can find this Webcast by visiting *http://blogs.technet.com/keithcombs/archive/2007/09/13/windows-server-2008-screencast-virtualization-10-minute-tour.aspx*.

Watch the Webcast entitled "SCVMM-15 Minute Tour.wmv" by Keith Combs, available on the companion CD in the Webcasts folder. Alternatively, you can find this Webcast by visiting *http://blogs.technet.com/keithcombs/archive/2007/09/06/everything-you-need-to-know-about-scvmm-in-15-minutes.aspx*.

Take a Practice Test

The practice tests on this book's companion CD offer many options. For example, you can test yourself on just one exam objective, or you can test yourself on all the 70-643 certification exam content. You can set up the test so that it closely simulates the experience of taking a certification exam, or you can set it up in study mode so that you can look at the correct answers and explanations after you answer each question.

MORE INFO   **Practice tests**

For details about all the practice test options available, see the "How to Use the Practice Tests" section in this book's introduction.

Chapter 2
Configuring Server Storage and Clusters

Storage area networks (SANs), host bus adapters (HBAs), and logical unit numbers (LUNs) were once the sole domain of storage specialists, far removed from the expertise of your average Microsoft Windows administrator. However, the arrival of new technologies such as the Windows Virtual Disk service and iSCSI, along with the increasingly complex realities of enterprise storage, has brought these once-specialized topics into the realm of Windows Server 2008 administration. To be an effective Windows server administrator today, you still need to know the difference between the various RAID levels, but you also need to know quite a bit more about server storage technologies.

This chapter introduces you to the basics of disk management in Windows Server 2008, along with more advanced storage technologies such as SANs. The chapter then builds upon this storage information to introduce the various clustering technologies available in Windows Server 2008.

Exam objectives in this chapter:
- Deploying Servers
  - Configure storage.
  - Configure high availability.

Lessons in this chapter:

Before You Begin

To complete the lessons in this chapter, you must have:

■ A computer named Server2 that is running Windows Server 2008. Beyond the disk on which the operating system is installed, Server2 must be physically equipped with one and preferably two additional hard disks. Both additional disks must have a storage capacity that is equal to or greater than the operating system disk. (The use of Microsoft Virtual PC or Server is recommended as a way to meet these hardware requirements.)

■ A basic understanding of Windows administration.

Lesson 1: Configuring Server Storage

A variety of server storage solutions is available for corporate networks, and Windows Server 2008 connects to these technologies in new ways. This lesson introduces you to the major server storage types and the tools built into Windows Server 2008 that can be used to manage them.

> **After this lesson, you will be able to:**
> - Understand the basic features of direct-attached storage, network-attached storage, and storage-area networks.
> - Know the function of the Virtual Disk service.
> - Understand the features of simple, spanned, striped, mirrored, and RAID-5 volumes.
> - Use the Disk Management console to create the various volume types.
>
> **Estimated lesson time: 80 minutes**

Understanding Server Storage Technologies

As the demand for server storage has grown, so too has the number of new storage technologies. Over the years, the range of server storage options has broadened from simple direct-attached storage (DAS) to network-attached storage (NAS) and, most recently, to Fibre Channel (FC) and iSCSI SANs.

Direct-Attached Storage

DAS is storage attached to one server only. An example of a DAS solution is a set of internal hard disks within a server or a rack-mounted RAID that is connected to a server through a SCSI or FC controller. The main feature of DAS is that it provides a single server with fast, *block-based* data access to storage directly through an internal or external bus. (Block-based, as opposed to file-based, means that data is moved in unformatted blocks rather than in formatted files.) DAS is an affordable solution for servers that need good performance and do not need enormous amounts of storage. For example, DAS is often suitable for infrastructure servers such as DNS, WINS and DHCP servers, and domain controllers. File servers and Web servers can also run well on a server with DAS.

The main limitation of DAS is that it is directly accessible from a single server only, which leads to inefficient storage management. For example, Figure 2-1 shows a LAN in which all storage is attached directly to servers. Despite the fact that the Web and App2 servers have excess storage, there is no easy way for these resources to be redeployed to either the Mail or App1 server, which need more storage space.

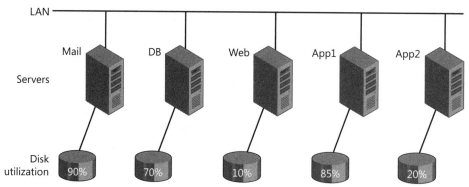

Figure 2-1   A network with only a DAS solution

Managing DAS in Windows Server 2008   The main tool used for managing DAS in Windows is the Disk Management console. This tool, which you can access in Server Manager, enables you to partition disks and format volume sets. You can also use the Diskpart.exe command-line utility to perform the same functions available in Disk Management and perform additional functions as well.

Network-Attached Storage

NAS is self-contained storage that other servers and clients can easily access over the network. A NAS device or appliance is a preconfigured server that runs an operating system specifically designed for handling file services. The main advantage of NAS is that it is simple to implement and can provide a large amount of storage space to clients and servers on a LAN. The downside of NAS is that, because your servers and clients access a NAS device over the LAN as opposed to over a local bus, access to data is slower and file-based as opposed to block-based. NAS performance is, therefore, almost always slower than that of DAS.

Because of its features and limitations, NAS is often a good fit for file servers, Web servers, and other servers that don't need extremely fast access to data.

Figure 2-2 shows a network in which clients use a NAS appliance as a file server.

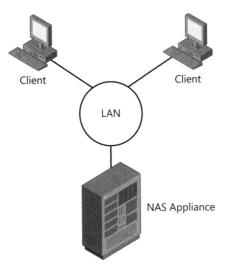

Figure 2-2   A LAN with a NAS appliance

Managing NAS   NAS appliances come with their own management tools, which are typically Web based.

Storage-Area Networks

SANs are high-performance networks dedicated to delivering block data between servers and storage subsystems. From the point of view of the operating system, SAN storage appears as if it were installed locally. The most important characteristic that distinguishes a SAN from DAS is that in a SAN, the storage is not restricted to one server but is, in fact, available to any of a number of servers. (SAN storage can be moved from server to server, but outside of clustered file system environments, it is not accessible by more than one server at a time.)

NOTE   SAN vs. DAS

Although DAS data transfer rates are typically faster than those of a SAN, the performance gap between DAS and SAN technologies is constantly shrinking. Despite the bus speed advantage offered by DAS, SANs are still considered preferable because the advantage SANs offer of shared storage outweighs the shortcoming of slightly lower access speeds.

A SAN is made up of special devices, including HBAs on the host servers, switches that help route storage traffic, disk storage subsystems, and tape libraries. These hardware devices that connect servers and storage in a SAN are called the SAN *fabric*. All these devices are then interconnected by fiber or copper. Once connected to the fabric, the available storage is divided up into virtual partitions called logical unit numbers (LUNs), which then appear to servers as local disks.

SANs are designed to enable centralization of storage resources while eliminating the distance and connectivity limitations posed by DAS. For example, parallel SCSI bus architecture limits DAS to 16 devices at a maximum (including the controller) distance of 25 meters. Fibre Channel SANs extend this distance limitation to 10 km or more and enable an essentially unlimited number of devices to attach to the network. These advantages enable SANs to separate storage from individual servers and to pool unlimited storage on a network where that storage can be shared.

SANs are a good solution for servers that require fast access to very large amounts of data (especially block-based data). Such servers can include mail servers, backup servers, streaming media servers, application servers, and database servers. The use of SANs also allows for efficient long distance data replication, which is typically part of a disaster recovery (DR) solution.

Figure 2-3 illustrates a simple SAN.

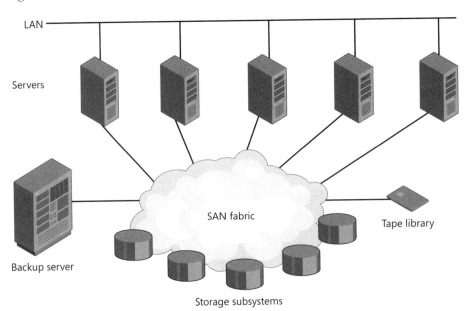

Figure 2-3   A sample storage-area network (SAN)

SANs generally occur in two varieties: Fibre Channel and iSCSI.

Fibre Channel SANs   Fibre Channel (FC) delivers high-performance block input/output (I/O) to storage devices. Based on serial SCSI, FC is the oldest and most widely adopted SAN interconnect technology. Unlike parallel SCSI devices, FC devices do not need to arbitrate (or contend) for a shared bus. FC instead uses special switches to transmit information between multiple servers and storage devices at the same time.

The main advantage of FC is that it is the most widely implemented SAN technology and has, at least until recently, offered the best performance. The disadvantages of FC technology are the cost of its hardware and the complexity of its implementation. Fibre Channel network components include server HBAs, cabling, and switches. All these components are specialized for FC, lack interoperability among vendors, are relatively expensive, and require special expertise.

iSCSI SANs   Internet SCSI (iSCSI) is an industry standard developed to enable transmission of SCSI block commands over an Ethernet network by using the TCP/IP protocol. Servers communicate with iSCSI devices through a locally installed software agent known as an *iSCSI initiator*. The iSCSI initiator executes requests and receives responses from an *iSCSI target*, which itself can be the end node storage device or an intermediary device such as a switch. For iSCSI fabrics, the network also includes one or more Internet Storage Name Service (iSNS) servers that, much like DNS servers on a LAN, provide discoverability and zoning of SAN resources.

By relying on TCP/IP, iSCSI SANs take advantage of networking devices and expertise that are widely available, a fact that makes iSCSI SANs generally simpler and less expensive to implement than FC SANs.

Aside from lower cost and greater ease of implementation, other advantages of iSCSI over FC include:

- **Connectivity over long distances**   Organizations distributed over wide areas might have a series of unlinked "SAN islands" that the current FC connectivity limitation of 10 km cannot bridge. (There are new means of extending Fibre Channel connectivity up to several hundred kilometers, but these methods are both complex and costly.) In contrast, iSCSI can connect SANs in distant offices by using in-place metropolitan area networks (MANs) and (wide-area networks) WANs.
- **Built-in security**   No security measures are built into the Fibre Channel protocol. Instead, security is implemented primarily through limiting physical access to the SAN. In contrast to FC, the Microsoft implementation of the iSCSI protocol provides security for devices on the network by using the Challenge Handshake Authentication Protocol (CHAP) for authentication and the Internet Protocol security (IPSec) standard for encryption. Because these methods of securing communications already exist in Windows networks, they can be readily extended from LANs to SANs.

NOTE   **iSCSI SAN fabric**

An iSCSI SAN can use dedicated devices for its fabric, or it can rely on an organization's existing LAN, MAN, or WAN infrastructure. For both security and performance, a dedicated iSCSI network separating network traffic from storage traffic is recommended.

The main disadvantage of an iSCSI SAN is that, unless it is built with dedicated (and expensive) 10-GB Ethernet cabling and switches, the I/O transfer of iSCSI is slower than an FC-based SAN can deliver. And if indeed you do choose to use 10-GB equipment for your iSCSI SAN instead of the much more common choice of gigabit Ethernet, the high cost of such a 10-GB solution would eliminate the price advantage of iSCSI relative to FC.

Exam Tip   Vocabulary terms you should understand for the exam include *LUNs, HBA, iSCSI initiator, iSCSI target, SAN fabric,* and *iSNS.*

Managing SANs   Windows Server 2008 includes the Virtual Disk service (VDS), an application programming interface (API) that enables FC and iSCSI SAN hardware vendors to expose disk subsystems and SAN hardware to administrative tools in Windows. When vendor hardware includes the VDS hardware provider, you can manage that hardware within Windows Server 2008 by using tools such as Disk Management, Storage Manager for SANs (SMfS), Storage Explorer, iSCSI Initiator, or the command-line tool DiskRAID.exe.

- **SMfS**   SMfS is available in Windows Server 2008 as a feature that you can add through the Add Features Wizard. You can use SMfS to manage SANs by provisioning disks, creating LUNs, and assigning LUNs to different servers in the SAN.

  Figure 2-4 shows the SMfS console.

- **Storage Explorer**   Storage Explorer is available by default in Windows Server 2008 through the Administrative Tools program group. You can use Storage Explorer to display detailed information about servers connected to the SAN as well as about fabric components such as HBAs, FC switches, and iSCSI initiators and targets. You can also use Storage Explorer to perform administrative tasks on an iSCSI fabric.

- **iSCSI Initiator**   The iSCSI Initiator tool is available by default in Windows Server 2008 through the Administrative Tools program group. This tool enables you to configure security, discovery, and other features of the local server connections to iSCSI targets.

- **DiskRAID**   DiskRAID is a command-line tool that enables you to manage LUNs in a VDS-enabled hardware RAID.

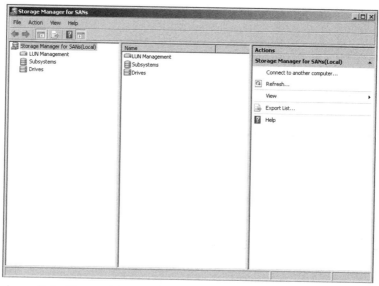

Figure 2-4   Storage Manager for SANs

Exam Tip   For the 70-643 exam, you need to understand the importance of VDS and its relation-ship to the tools just described.

Managing Disks, Volumes, and Partitions in Windows Server 2008

The main tool you can use to manage disks, volumes, and partitions in Windows Server 2008 is Disk Management. With Disk Management, you can initialize disks, bring disks online or offline, create volumes within disks, format volumes, change disk partition styles, extend and shrink volumes, and create fault-tolerant disk sets.

To access Disk Management, you can type **Diskmgmt.msc** in the Run box, select Disk Man-agement beneath the Storage node in Server Manager, or select the Disk Management node in the Computer Management console (accessible through Administrative Tools).

Disk Management is shown in Figure 2-5.

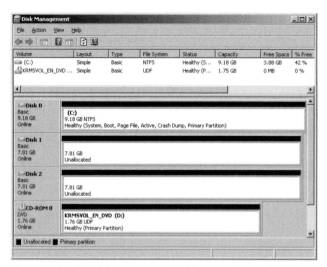

Figure 2-5 Disk Management in Windows Server 2008

Understanding Basic and Dynamic Disks

Disk Management enables you to manage both basic and dynamic disks.

By default, all disks are basic disks. A basic disk is a physical disk that contains primary partitions, extended partitions, or logical drives. The number of partitions you can create on a basic disk depends on the disk's *partition style*. On disks that use the master boot record (MBR) partition style, you can create up to four primary partitions per basic disk, or you can create up to three primary partitions and one extended partition. Within the one extended partition, you can then create unlimited logical drives. On basic disks that use the GUID partition table (GPT) partition style, you can create up to 128 primary partitions. Because GPT disks do not limit you to four partitions, you do not need to create extended partitions or logical drives. GPT disks are recommended for disks larger than 2 terabytes (TB) and for disks on 64-bit systems.

NOTE Partition styles

Partition styles refer to the most elemental disk structure visible to the operating system. Partition styles do not affect file formats within partitions such as NTFS or FAT32. Basic and dynamic disks can occur on either partition style.

Dynamic disks provide advanced features that basic disks do not, features such as the ability to create an unlimited number of volumes, volumes that span multiple disks (spanned and striped volumes), and fault-tolerant volumes (mirrored and RAID-5 volumes). There are five types of dynamic volumes: simple, spanned, striped, mirrored, and RAID-5.

In previous versions of Windows, you needed to convert a basic disk to a dynamic disk before you could create any of these volume types. When you use Disk Management in Windows Server 2008 to create any of these volume types, however, basic disks are automatically converted to dynamic during the process. As a result, the question of whether a disk is basic or dynamic has become less important from an administrative point of view. Despite this development, it is still important to know for dual-boot configurations that many earlier versions of Windows (such as Windows NT, Windows 98, and Windows ME) cannot access dynamic disks. Also relevant for dual-boot configurations is the fact that dynamic disks are compatible only with Windows operating systems.

Exam Tip   Even though basic disks are automatically converted to dynamic when necessary, you still need to know which volume types require dynamic disks for the 70-643 exam.

Creating Volumes

You can use Disk Management or the Diskpart command-line utility to create the following volume types in Windows Server 2008.

- **Simple or basic volumes**   Simple volumes are basic drives that are not fault tolerant. A simple volume can consist of a single region on a disk or multiple regions that are on the same disk and linked together.

    To create a simple volume in Disk Management, right-click unallocated space on a disk, and then click New Simple Volume, as shown in Figure 2-6. (This process is identical whether you are creating the volume on a basic or dynamic disk, even though on a basic disk, the new volume is technically called a partition or basic volume.) You might need to right-click the disk and select Online first.

    To create a simple volume by using the Diskpart utility, use the utility to select the disk and then, on a dynamic disk, type the command **create volume simple**. To create a new volume (partition) on a basic disk, type **create partition**. You can use **create volume ?** or **create partition ?** to learn the specific syntax associated with these commands.

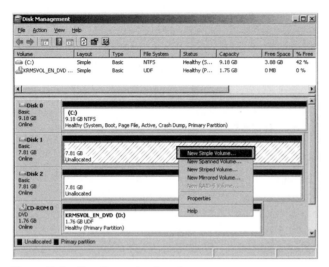

Figure 2-6   Creating a simple volume

- **Spanned volumes**   A spanned volume is a dynamic volume consisting of disk space on more than one physical disk. If a simple volume is not a system volume or boot volume, you can extend it across additional disks to create a spanned volume, or you can create a new volume as a spanned volume by using unallocated space on more than one disk.

  To create a new spanned volume, in Disk Management, right-click unallocated space on one of the disks where you want to create the spanned volume, and then click New Spanned Volume. This step opens the New Spanned Volume Wizard, in which you can add space to the spanned volume from the disks available.

  Figure 2-7 shows a spanned volume, assigned drive letter E. Notice how the drive uses space from Disk 1 and Disk 2 but appears as only a single volume with a capacity of 7.32 GB.

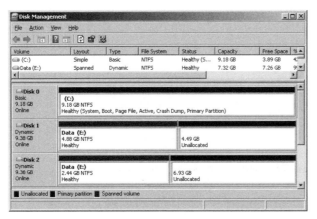

Figure 2-7   A spanned volume in Disk Management

■ **Striped volumes**   A striped volume, which is also known as RAID 0, is a dynamic volume that stores data in stripes across two or more physical disks. Striped volumes offer the best performance of all the volumes that are available in Windows, but they do not provide fault tolerance. If a disk in a striped volume fails, the data in the entire volume is lost. Figure 2-8 shows how data in a striped volume is written across a set of disks.

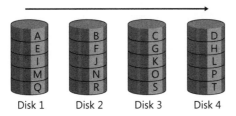

Figure 2-8   A RAID 0 or striped volume stripes data across disks

When should you use a striped volume? A striped volume is the best storage solution for temporary data that does not need fault tolerance but does require high performance. Examples of such temporary data include page files and Temp folders. To create a new striped volume in Disk Management, right-click unallocated space on a disk, and then click New Striped Volume.

A striped volume in Disk Management is shown in Figure 2-9. Notice how the volume uses 1.46 GB of space from both Disk 1 and Disk 2 and appears as a single volume E with a total capacity of 2.93 GB. Note also how the volume is being used to store temporary data (the Page File).

NOTE   RAID disks

As with all RAID solutions, a striped volume is built with disks of equal size.

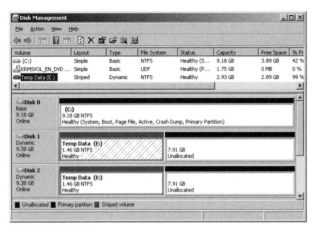

Figure 2-9   A RAID 0 or striped volume in Disk Management

■ **Mirrored volumes**   Also known as a RAID 1, a mirrored volume is a fault-tolerant volume that provides data redundancy by using two copies, or mirrors, of the same volume. All data written to the mirrored volume is written to both volumes, which are located on separate physical disks. If one of the physical disks fails, the data on the failed disk becomes unavailable, but the system continues to operate using the unaffected disk.

Figure 2-10 illustrates how data is stored on a mirrored volume. Because data is duplicated, no data is lost if either disk fails.

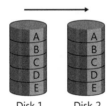

Figure 2-10   A RAID 1 or mirrored volume copies all data onto a second disk

NOTE   **Triple mirroring and beyond**

Although mirrored volumes configured in Windows Server 2008 are limited to two disks, mirrors created through third-party solutions can be created out of three disks or more. In a triple mirror configuration, for example, the contents of one disk are duplicated on two additional disks. Multiple mirrors degrade write performance but improve fault tolerance. They are good solutions for mission-critical data.

As a fault tolerant solution, a mirrored volume has advantages and disadvantages. One advantage of a mirrored volume is that it offers very good read performance as well as fairly good write performance. In addition, mirroring requires only two disks, and almost any volume can be mirrored, including the system and boot volumes. The disadvantage of a mirrored volume is that it requires 50 percent of a disk's total storage capacity to be reserved for fault tolerance. Overall, if you need a fault tolerant storage solution, a mirror is a good choice if you have only two disks; if you need good read and write performance; or if you need to provide fault tolerance for the system volume, the boot volume, or other mission-critical data.

To create a mirrored volume, you can either add a mirror to an existing volume or create a new mirrored volume. To add a mirror to an existing volume in Disk Management, right-click the existing volume, and then click Add Mirror, as shown in Figure 2-11.

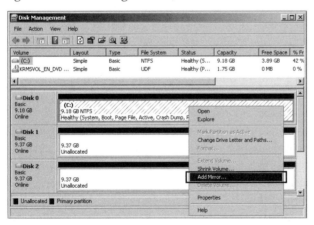

Figure 2-11   Adding a mirror to the System partition

To create a new mirrored volume in Disk Management, right-click unallocated space on a disk, and then click New Mirrored Volume. A new mirrored volume is shown in Figure 2-12. Notice how the drive uses 5.86 GB of space from both Disk 1 and Disk 2 and appears as a single volume E with a total capacity of 5.86 GB.

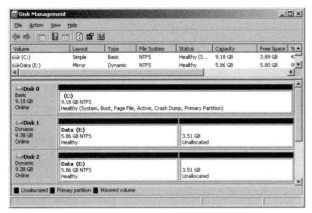

Figure 2-12   A RAID 1 or mirrored volume

■ **Raid-5 volumes**   A RAID-5 volume is a fault tolerant volume that combines areas of free space from at least three physical hard disks into one logical volume. RAID-5 volumes stripe data along with *parity* (evenness or oddness) information across a set of disks. When a single disk fails, Windows Server 2008 uses this parity information to re-create the data on the failed disk. RAID-5 volumes can accept the loss of only a single disk in the set.

Exam Tip   On the 70-643 exam, you might see a RAID-5 volume referred to as a *striped volume with parity*.

Figure 2-13 shows a RAID-5 volume made up of four disks. Data written to the volume is striped across these disks from left to right. For each stripe across the set of disks, one disk is used to hold parity information about the evenness or oddness of the other data in the stripe. In the simplified example shown in Figure 2-13, parity is set to 1 when the sum of the values in the stripe is odd, and parity is set to 0 when the sum of the remaining values is even. Using this parity information along with other disk data, if any one (and only one) disk fails, Windows can reconstruct the complete contents of that failed disk. The data of the failed drive can be re-created in real time as users request it. The party information can also be re-created live on a new disk once the failed disk has been replaced.

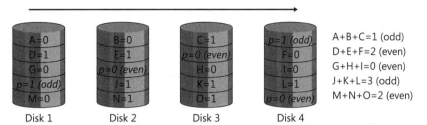

Figure 2-13   A RAID-5 volume calculates parity (evenness or oddness) for fault tolerance

The space approximately equivalent of one disk is always used for fault tolerance in a RAID-5 volume. For example, if you create a RAID-5 out of four 120-GB disks, the total storage space available in that RAID-5 is 360 GB.

When should you use a RAID-5 volume? A RAID-5 volume is characterized by very good read performance, relatively poor write performance, and optimal use of storage space in a fault tolerant solution. Therefore, consider using a RAID-5 volume when good write performance is not a priority or when you need a fault tolerant storage solution that makes the best use of available storage. Note also that you cannot assign the system or boot partition to a RAID-5 volume created in Windows Server 2008.

NOTE   Software and hardware RAIDs

A RAID-5 volume created in Disk Management is an example of a software RAID because the RAID is created by the operating system. Some vendors, however, sell disk enclosures that include their own built-in RAID setup utility. If you configure a RAID-5 with this vendor software, the storage appears to Windows Server 2008 as a single local volume. A RAID configuration such as this, which is transparent to the operating system, is known as a hardware RAID. Although software RAID has lower performance than hardware RAID does, software RAID is inexpensive and easy to configure because it has no special hardware requirements other than multiple disks. If cost is more important than performance, software RAID is an appropriate solution.

To create a RAID-5 volume in Disk Management, right-click unallocated space on one of the dynamic disks on which you want to create the RAID-5 volume, and then click New RAID-5 Volume. Then, follow the instructions in the New RAID-5 Volume Wizard.

To create a RAID-5 volume by using the Diskpart utility, use the command **create volume raid**. You can use the **help create volume raid** command to learn the exact syntax.

Real World

JC Mackin

Although you cannot create them in Windows, the RAID levels known as RAID 0+1 and RAID 1+0 are becoming increasingly common in the real world. A RAID 0+1 (or 01) is a *mirror of stripes*, essentially twin copies of a striped volume. This type of RAID is constructed by creating RAID 0 sets and then mirroring them. A RAID 1+0 (or 10), alternatively, is a *stripe of mirrors* in which the data is striped across multiple mirrored sets. You construct this type of RAID by first creating a series of mirror sets and then building a RAID 0 set across the mirror sets.

Both of these solutions allocate 50 percent of the disks for fault tolerance, and both offer excellent read and write performance. RAID 1+0, however, offers a better chance for recoverability if more than one disk fails.

Note also that the naming conventions for these two RAID levels are not firmly established. Some companies (including Microsoft) might refer to both RAID 01 and 10 generally as 0+1. If you need to clarify your requirements to vendors, you are better off specifying either a *mirror of stripes* or a *stripe of mirrors*.

Exam Tip   For the 70-643 exam, make sure you understand RAID levels and the different volume types.

Extending a Volume

You can add more space to existing simple or spanned volumes by extending them into unallocated space on the same disk or on a different disk. To extend a volume, it must either be formatted with the NTFS file system or unformatted. To extend a volume in Disk Management, right-click the simple or spanned volume you want to extend, and then click Extend Volume.

NOTE   **Extending boot and system volumes**

You cannot extend a boot or system volume onto another disk.

Shrinking a Volume

You can decrease the space used by simple or spanned volumes by shrinking them into contiguous free space at the end of the volume. For example, if you need to increase the amount of unallocated space on a disk to make room for a new partition or volume, you can attempt to shrink the existing volumes on the disk. When you shrink a partition, any ordinary files are automatically relocated on the disk to create the new unallocated space. There is no need to reformat the disk to shrink the partition.

The amount of space you can gain from shrinking a volume varies greatly. In general, the greater the percentage of unused space on the volume and the fewer the bad clusters, the more you will be able to shrink the volume. If, however, the number of bad clusters detected by dynamic bad-cluster remapping is too great, you will not be able to shrink the volume at all. If this occurs, consider moving the data and replacing the disk.

CAUTION **Do not shrink raw partitions that contain data**

If a partition is not formatted with a file system but still contains data (such as a database file), shrinking the partition can actually destroy the data.

To shrink a volume in Disk Management, right-click the simple or spanned volume that you want to shrink, and then click Shrink Volume, as shown in Figure 2-14.

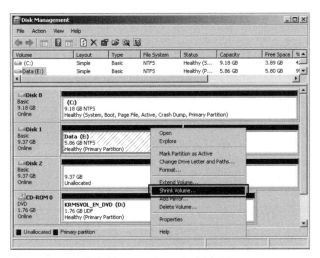

Figure 2-14   Shrinking a volume in Disk Management

Exam Tip   Shrinking is a feature that is new in Windows Server 2008. Expect to see a question on this topic on the 70-643 exam.

Configuring a Mount Point

A mount point is a folder in a volume that acts as a pointer to the root directory of another volume. For example, if you need to make more storage space available to the system or boot disk, you can create a new volume on another disk and then mount that volume in a folder in the system volume.

This arrangement is illustrated in Figure 2-15. In this scenario, the original disk capacity of the C drive is 9.18 GB. By mounting a 3.51-GB volume in a folder named MountedVolume in C, you are able to access more disk space through C even though you have not changed the capacity of the disk.

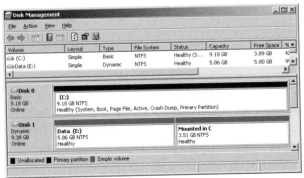

Figure 2-15   A new volume mounted in the system volume

You can create a mount point in Disk Management by creating a new volume and then choosing the option to mount the volume in an empty NTFS folder, as shown in Figure 2-16.

NOTE   **Extending the system or boot volume**

Because you cannot extend a system volume onto another disk, mount points are the only way you can make more space available to the system volume without replacing hardware.

You can also create a mount point for an existing volume by right-clicking the volume and then selecting Change Drive Letter And Paths. In the Change Drive Letter And Paths dialog box, click Change, and then choose the option to mount the volume in an empty NFTS folder.

Exam Tip   You need to understand mount points for the 70-643 exam.

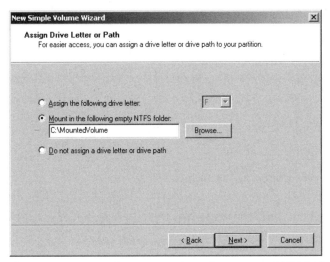

Figure 2-16   Mounting a new volume in an empty NTFS folder

Quick Check

1. Can you extend a mirrored volume?
2. True or False: You cannot use a hardware RAID-5 volume as the system or boot volume in Windows Server 2008.

Quick Check Answers

1. No
2. False. A hardware RAID-5 volume would be transparent to Windows Server 2008. The limitation for RAID-5 volumes affects what you can configure from within the Windows operating system. You cannot add the system or boot partition to a software RAID-5 volume, and you cannot install an operating system on a RAID-5 volume that you create in Windows. (Note also that installing an operating system on a hardware RAID-5 volume, though possible, is discouraged because of the poor write performance associated with RAID-5.)

PRACTICE Working with Disk Sets

In this practice, you will create various volume types in Disk Management.

NOTE   How many disks do you need for these exercises?

Exercises 1–3 require Server2 to have one unpartitioned disk (Disk 1) whose storage capacity is at least as large as the disk (Disk 0) on which the operating system is installed. Exercises 4–6 require two empty disks (Disk 1 and Disk 2) in addition to Disk 0. Note that you can easily create new disks in Virtual PC or Server.

▶ **Exercise 1 Work with Disks and Simple Volumes**

In this exercise, which you perform on Server2, you will create simple volumes on Disk 1 while switching first between dynamic and basic disks and then between MBR and GPT disks.

1. Log on to Contoso.com from Server2 as a domain administrator.

2. In the Run box, type **diskmgmt.msc**, and then press Enter.

3. In Disk Management, in the top pane, ensure that only the C volume is visible. If necessary, back up data, and then delete all other volumes.

    In the bottom pane of Disk Management, at least two disks should be displayed: Disk 0, Disk 1, and (optionally) Disk 2.

4. Right-click the unallocated space on Disk 1, and then click New Simple Volume.
    The New Simple Volume Wizard opens.

5. On the Welcome page of the New Simple Volume Wizard, click Next.

6. On the Specify Volume Size page, read all the text on the page, and then click Next.

7. In the Assign Drive Letter Or Path page, read all the text on the page, and then click Next.

8. On the Format Partition page, read all the text on the page, select the Perform A Quick Format option, and then click Next.

9. In the Completing The New Simple Volume Wizard, click Finish.
    After the creation and formatting are complete, the new volume appears in Disk Management.

10. In Disk Management, in the bottom pane, right-click the Disk 1 tile, and then click Convert To Dynamic Disk.

11. In the Convert To Dynamic Disk dialog box, verify that Disk 1 is selected, and then click OK.

12. In the Disks To Convert Dialog box, click Convert.

13. In the Disk Management dialog box, read all the text, and then click Yes.

14. After several moments, the new volume changes from blue to green.

15. Right-click the Disk 1 tile, and then answer the following questions:

    Can you convert Disk 1 back to a basic disk?

    Answer: No, because the option is grayed out.

    Can you convert Disk 1 to the GPT partition style?

    Answer: No, again because the disk contains volumes, so the option is unavailable.

16. Right-click the new volume you have created on Disk 1, and then click Delete Volume. Click Yes when prompted to confirm.

17. After the volume has deleted, answer the following question:

    Is Disk 1 now listed as Basic or Dynamic?

    Answer: Basic. By default, disks with no volumes are basic.

18. Right-click Disk 1 and choose the option to convert Disk 1 to a dynamic disk. Then, after the conversion has completed, right-click Disk 1 to convert it back to a basic disk.

    Note that when a disk contains no volumes, you can convert freely between basic and dynamic disks. However, when a disk contains volumes, you can convert only from basic to dynamic.

19. Right-click Disk 1, and then click Convert To GPT Disk.

20. After a few moments, right-click Disk 1 again, and then click Convert To MBR Disk.

    Note that when a disk contains no volumes, you can convert a disk freely between MBR and GPT partition styles. However, you cannot convert the partition style of a disk when it contains any volumes.

21. Leave Disk Management open and proceed to Exercise 2.

▶ **Exercise 2 Create Mount Points**

In this exercise, which you perform on Server2, you will mount two volumes as folders in volume C.

1. While you are logged on to Contoso.com from Server2 as a domain administrator, in the root of volume C, create two new folders named **MountVol1** and **MountVol2**, respectively.

2. In Disk Management, right-click the unallocated space in Disk 1, and then click New Simple Volume.

3. On the Welcome To The New Simple Volume Wizard page, click Next.

4. On the Specify Volume Size page, in the Simple Volume Size In MB text box, type a value that represents approximately half of the available space. For example, if 10,000 MB are available, type 5,000, and then click Next.

5. On the Assign Drive Letter Or Path page, select Mount In The Following Empty NTFS Folder. Then, type **C:\MountVol1** in the associated text box (or use the Browse button to select that folder), and then click Next.

6. On the Format Partition page, in the Volume Label text box, replace the text "New Volume" by typing **Mounted in C**.

7. On the Format Partition page, select Perform A Quick Format, and then click Next.

8. On the Completing the New Simple Volume Wizard page, click Finish.

   After a few moments, the new volume appears in Disk Management. Notice how it is not assigned a drive letter but that it is labeled Mounted In C.

9. In the Start menu, select Computer.

   In the Computer window, only the C drive is visible. You cannot directly access the new drive you have just created.

10. Open the C drive.

    In the C drive, the MountVol1 folder is marked by a special icon. It is also associated with a large size, even though the volume is empty.

11. Open the properties of MountVol1.

    In the MountVol1 Properties dialog box, the type is listed as Mounted Volume.

12. In the MountVol1 Properties dialog box, click the Properties button.

    The Mounted In C (C:\MountVol1) Properties dialog box opens. The dialog box displays the same information that you would find in the properties sheet of a volume.

13. Click OK to close the Mounted In C (C:\MountVol1) Properties dialog box, and then click OK to close the MountVol1 Properties dialog box.

14. In Disk Management, create a new simple volume on Disk 1 by using the same process as described in Exercise 1. Use all the remaining space on Disk 1 for the new volume and do *not* select the option to mount the volume in an NTFS folder. Choose a name of Mounted In C (2) for the volume and choose the option to perform a quick format.

    After the new volume is created, it appears in Disk Management. Notice that it is assigned a drive letter such as E.

15. In Disk Management, right-click the Mounted In C (2) volume, and then click Change Drive Letter And Paths.

16. In the Change Drive Letter And Paths dialog box, click Remove, and then click Yes to confirm.

    You can mount an existing volume only if you first remove any drive letter associated with it.

17. In Disk Management, right-click the Mounted In C (2) volume again, and again click Change Drive Letter And Paths.

18. In the Change Drive Letter And Paths dialog box, click Add.

19. In the Add Drive Letter Or Path dialog box, click Mount In The Following Empty NTFS Folder, and then type or browse to C:\MountVol2.

20. In the Add Drive Letter or Path dialog box, click OK.

21. Click Start, and then Computer to verify that Mounted In C (2) has been configured as a mount point in the folder named MountVol2 in the C drive.

22. In Disk Management, delete both the Mounted In C and the Mounted In C (2) volumes. Verify that only unallocated space remains on Disk 1.

23. Close all windows except for Disk Management, and then proceed to Exercise 3.

▶ **Exercise 3 Add and Break a Mirror**

In this exercise, which you perform on Server2, you will use Disk 1 to add a mirror for volume C.

1. While you are still logged on to Contoso.com from Server2 as a domain administrator, in Disk Management, right-click the C volume (in either the top or bottom pane), and then click Add Mirror.

2. In the Add Mirror dialog box, select Disk 1, and then click Add Mirror.

3. In the Disk Management dialog box, read all the text, and then click Yes.

     A new volume is created on Disk 1, and then, after both Disk 0 and Disk 1 are converted to dynamic disks, the new volume on Disk 1 is also assigned the drive letter C. Then, the status of the twin volumes is shown to be Resynching while the mirror is created. This process of resynching varies, depending on the size of the volumes.

4. After the mirror volume has finished resynching, take a few moments to browse Disk Management, noting the single volume listed in the top pane and the capacity of the drive.

5. On Disk 1, right-click volume C. Use the options available on the shortcut menu to answer the following questions:

     Which option on the shortcut menu should you choose if you want to turn the mirrored volume into two separate volumes?

     Answer: Break Mirrored Volume. You should choose this option when one of the disks fails or becomes corrupted.

     Which option on the shortcut menu should you choose if you want to delete the mirror on Disk 1 immediately?

     Answer: Remove Mirror.

6. On the shortcut menu, click Remove Mirror.

7. In the Remove Mirror dialog box, select Disk 1, and then click Remove Mirror.

8. In the Data Management dialog box, click Yes to confirm.

     In Disk Management, Disk 1 once again appears as a basic disk with only unallocated space.

9. Leave Disk Management open and proceed to Exercise 4.

▶ **Exercise 4 Create a Spanned Volume**

In this exercise, you will create a spanned volume on Disk 1 and Disk 2. Note that you need two unpartitioned dynamic disks for this exercise.

1. In Disk Management, right-click the unallocated space in Disk 1, and then click Create New Spanned Volume.

2. The New Spanned Volume Wizard opens.

3. On the Welcome To The New Spanned Volume Wizard page, read all the text on the page, and then click Next.

4. On the Select Disks page, verify that only Disk 1 is visible in the Selected area.

5. In the Select The Amount Of Space In MB text box, type an amount that is equal to approximately half of the available space. For example, if the default number in the box is 10,000, replace that amount by typing **5,000**.

6. On the Select Disks page, select Disk 2, which is shown in the Available area, and then click the Add button to move Disk 2 to the Selected area.

7. In the Selected area, click to select Disk 2.

8. In the Select The Amount Of Space In MB text box, type an amount that is equal to approximately 25 percent of the available space. For example, if the default number in the box is 10,000, replace that amount by typing **2,500**.

9. On the Select Disks page, click Next.

10. On the Assign Drive Letter Or Path page, click Next.

11. On the Format Volume page, in the Volume Label text box, replace the text by typing **Spanned Volume**.

12. On the Format Volume page, click the Perform A Quick Format check box, and then click Next.

13. On the Completing The New Spanned Volume Wizard page, click Finish.

14. If the Disk Management dialog box appears, read the text, and then click Yes.

    After the creation and formatting complete, the new spanned volume appears in Disk Management. The new volume spans disks 1 and 2.

15. Spend a few moments browsing the information related to the new volume in Disk Management. Note, for example, the capacity of the volume and the fact that it is assigned a single drive letter.

16. Leave Disk Management open and proceed to Exercise 5.

▶ **Exercise 5 Create a Striped Volume**

In this exercise, you will create a new striped volume in the remaining space on Disk 1 and Disk 2.

1. While you are logged on to Contoso.com from Server2 as a domain administrator, in Disk Management, right-click the unallocated space in Disk 1, and then click New Striped Volume.

   The New Striped Volume Wizard appears.

2. On the Welcome page of the New Striped Volume Wizard, click Next.

3. On the Select Disks page, note that only Disk 1 appears in the Selected area.

4. On the Select Disks page, select Disk 2 in the Available area, and then click the Add button to move Disk 2 to the Selected area.

   Notice that the amount of space associated with Disk 1 and Disk 2 is identical. In a striped volume, all member disks must be the same size.

5. On the Select Disks page, click Next.

6. On the Assign Drive Letter Or Path page, click Next.

7. On the Format Volume page, in the Volume Label text box, replace the text by typing **Striped Volume**.

8. On the Format Volume page, select the Perform A Quick Format check box, and then click Next.

9. On the Completing The New Striped Volume Wizard page, click Finish.

   After the creation and formatting complete, the new striped volume appears in Disk Management.

10. Spend a few moments browsing the information related to the new striped volume in Disk Management. Note, for example, the capacity of the volume and the fact that it is assigned a single drive letter.

11. Leave Disk Management open and proceed to Exercise 6.

▶ **Exercise 6 Shrink and Extend a Volume**

In this exercise, you will shrink the spanned volume you created in Exercise 5. Then, after deleting the striped volume you created in the same exercise, you will extend the spanned volume into the available space on Disk 1.

1. While you are still logged on to Contoso.com from Server2 as a domain administrator, in Disk Management, right-click the Spanned Volume on Disk 2, and then click Shrink Volume.

   The Querying Shrink Space box appears, and then the Shrink [Drive Letter] dialog box appears.

2. In the Shrink dialog box, read all the text.

   Note that in the Enter The Amount Of Space To Shrink In MB text box, the default amount provided is equal to the maximum amount that you can shrink the drive.

3. Click the Shrink button to shrink the volume the maximum allowable amount.

   After several moments, the spanned volume appears in its newer, smaller size. The volume now might or might not be limited to Disk 1.

4. In Disk Management, right-click the striped volume (not the spanned volume), and then click Delete Volume.

5. In the Delete Striped Volume dialog box, read the text, and then click Yes to confirm.

   After the volume is deleted, new unallocated space appears on Disk 1.

6. Right-click the spanned volume on Disk 1, and then click Extend Volume.

   The Extend Volume Wizard opens.

7. On the Welcome To The Extend Volume Wizard page, read the text, and then click Next.

8. On the Select Disk page, verify that only Disk 1 is shown in the Selected area.

9. On the Select Disk page, leave the default (full) amount of space to expand on Disk 1, and then click Next.

10. On the Completing the Extend Volume Wizard page, click Finish.

    After a few moments, the volume appears in Disk Management, occupying all the space on Disk 1. If the volume is confined to Disk 1, it is now designated as a simple volume. If some portion remains on Disk 2, it is still designated as a spanned volume.

11. Right-click the volume on Disk 1, click Delete Volume, and then click Yes to confirm the deletion.

    After a few moments, Disk Management shows that Disk 1 and Disk 2 have returned to their original state.

12. Log off Server2.

Lesson Summary

- In general, disk storage occurs in three varieties: direct-attached storage (DAS), network-attached storage (NAS), and storage-area networks (SANs). Both DAS and SANs provide block-based access to data storage, and NAS provides file-based access. SANs provide the additional benefit of shared storage that you can easily move from server to server.

- When vendor disk storage subsystems include a hardware provider for Virtual Disk Service (VDS), you can manage that hardware within Windows Server 2008 by using tools such as Disk Management, Storage Manager for SANs (SMfS), Storage Explorer, iSCSI Initiator, or the command-line tool DiskRAID.exe.

- Disk Management is the main tool you can use for managing disks and volumes in Windows Server 2008. Disk Management enables you to create simple, spanned, striped, mirrored, and RAID-5 volumes.

- Using Disk Management, you can extend or shrink a simple or spanned volume.

- Using Disk Management, you can configure a volume as a mount point in another volume.

Lesson Review

The following questions are intended to reinforce key information presented in this lesson. The questions are also available on the companion CD if you prefer to review them in electronic form.

NOTE Answers

Answers to these questions and explanations of why each answer choice is correct or incorrect are located in the "Answers" section at the end of the book.

---

1. You work as a network administrator, and your responsibilities include managing server storage. You have been asked to purchase a new disk subsystem for your company's storage-area network (SAN). You are in the process of testing hardware solutions before making purchases, and you attach a new disk subsystem to the network. You want to provision the new disks and create new logical unit numbers (LUNs) to assign to a server named Server1. You open Storage Manager for SANs, but you can't see the new hardware. However, you can connect to the new hardware by using the software provided by the vendor. You want to be able to manage the new disk subsystem you purchase by using Storage Manager for SANs. What should you do?

    A. In Disk Management, choose the Rescan Disks option.

    B. Choose a disk subsystem from a vendor that has a Virtual Disk Service hardware provider.

    C. On Server1, configure iSCSI Initiator to specify the new hardware as a favorite target.

    D. Use Storage Explorer to configure Server1 as an iSNS server.

2. You work as an IT support specialist. Your job responsibilities include managing server storage. You are designing storage for a new application server. The application makes heavy use of temporary storage, and you want to allocate three 20-GB disk drives to that storage. If excellent read and write performance is a high priority, and you also want to use as much available space as possible, which of the following volume types should you create?

    A. Simple volume

    B. Spanned volume

    C. Mirrored volume

    D. Striped volume

    E. RAID-5 volume

Lesson 2: Configuring Server Clusters

In enterprise networks, groups of independent servers are often used to provide a common set of services. Different physical computers, for example, can be used to answer requests directed at a common Web site or database server. Although these server groups are often referred to generally as *clusters*, cluster types can serve very different purposes. This lesson describes the load balancing and high-availability server clusters you can configure in Windows Server 2008.

After this lesson, you will be able to:
- Understand the features and limitations of DNS round-robin.
- Understand the main function and features of Network Load Balancing clusters.
- Know the basic steps to configure a Network Load Balancing cluster.
- Understand the main function and features of failover clusters.
- Understand the requirements for creating a failover cluster.

Estimated lesson time: 50 minutes

Server Cluster Fundamentals

In Windows Server 2008, you can configure three types of server groups for load balancing, scalability, and high availability. First, a *round-robin distribution group* is a set of computers that uses DNS to provide basic load balancing with minimal configuration requirements. Next, a *Network Load Balancing (NLB) cluster* (also called an *NLB farm*) is a group of servers used not only to provide load balancing but also to increase scalability. Finally, a *failover cluster* can be used to increase the availability of an application or service in the event of a server failure.

NOTE   What is load balancing?

Load balancing is a means of distributing incoming connection requests to two or more servers in a manner that is transparent to users. Load balancing can be implemented with hardware, software, or a combination of both.

Round-Robin Distribution

Round-robin DNS is a simple method for distributing a workload among multiple servers. In round-robin, a DNS server is configured with more than one record to resolve another server's name to an IP address. When clients query the DNS server to resolve the name (find the address) of the other server, the DNS server responds by cycling through the records one at a time and by pointing each successive client to a different address and different machine.

For example, suppose that a DNS server authoritative for the DNS domain contoso.com is configured with two separate resource records, each resolving the name *web.contoso.com* by pointing to a different server, as shown in Figure 2-17. When the first client (Client1) queries the DNS server to resolve the web.contoso.com name, the DNS server answers by pointing the client to the server named websrv1 located at the 192.168.3.11 address. This is the information associated with the first DNS record matching "web." When the next client, Client2, queries the DNS server to resolve the same name (web.contoso.com), the DNS server answers the query with the information provided in the second record matching "web." This second record points to a server name websrv2, which is located at the 192.168.3.12 address. If a third client then queries the DNS server for the same name, the server will respond with information in the first record again.

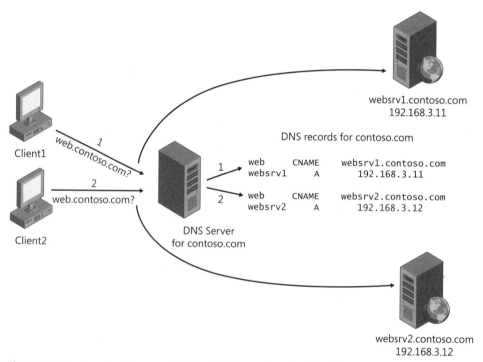

Figure 2-17 Round-robin uses DNS to distribute the client load between two or more servers

The purpose of DNS round-robin is to load balance client requests among servers. Its main advantage is that it is very easy to configure. Round-robin DNS is enabled by default in most DNS servers, so to configure this simple sort of load balancing, you only need to create the appropriate DNS records on the DNS server.

However, there are serious limitations to round-robin as a load balancing mechanism. The biggest drawback is that if one of the target servers goes down, the DNS server does not respond to this event, and it will keep directing clients to the inactive server until a network administrator removes the DNS record from the DNS server. Another drawback is that every record is given equal weight, regardless of whether one target server is more powerful than another or a given server is already busy. A final drawback is that round-robin does not always function as expected. Because DNS clients cache query responses from servers, a DNS client by default will keep connecting to the same target server as long as the cached response stays active.

Network Load Balancing

An installable feature of Windows Server 2008, NLB transparently distributes client requests among servers in an NLB cluster by using virtual IP addresses and a shared name. From the perspective of the client, the NLB cluster appears to be a single server. NLB is a fully distributed solution in that it does not use a centralized dispatcher.

In a common scenario, NLB is used to create a *Web farm*—a group of computers working to support a Web site or set of Web sites. However, NLB can also be used to create a terminal server farm, a VPN server farm, or an ISA Server firewall cluster. Figure 2-18 shows a basic configuration of an NLB Web farm located behind an NLB firewall cluster.

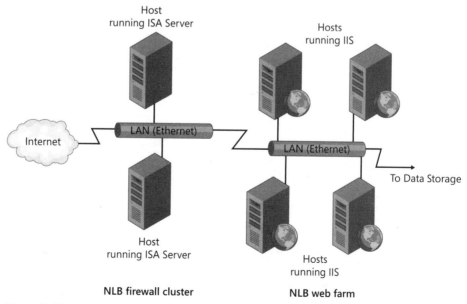

Figure 2-18   Basic diagram for two connected NLB clusters

As a load balancing mechanism, NLB provides significant advantages over round-robin DNS. First of all, in contrast to round-robin DNS, NLB automatically detects servers that have been disconnected from the NLB cluster and then redistributes client requests to the remaining live hosts. This feature prevents clients from sending requests to the failed servers. Another difference between NLB and round-robin DNS is that in NLB, you have the option to specify a load percentage that each host will handle. Clients are then statistically distributed among hosts so that each server receives its percentage of incoming requests.

Beyond load balancing, NLB also supports scalability. As the demand for a network service such as a Web site grows, more servers can be added to the farm with only a minimal increase in administrative overhead.

Failover Clustering

A failover cluster is a group of two or more computers used to prevent downtime for selected applications and services. The clustered servers (called nodes) are connected by physical cables to each other and to shared disk storage. If one of the cluster nodes fails, another node begins to take over service for the lost node in a process known as failover. As a result of failover, users connecting to the server experience minimal disruption in service.

Servers in a failover cluster can function in a variety of roles, including the roles of file server, print server, mail server, or database server, and they can provide high availability for a variety of other services and applications.

In most cases, the failover cluster includes a shared storage unit that is physically connected to all the servers in the cluster, although any given volume in the storage is accessed by only one server at a time.

Figure 2-19 illustrates the process of failover in a basic, two-node failover cluster.

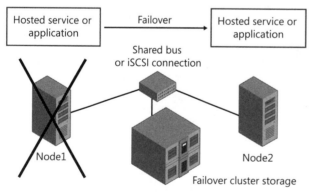

Figure 2-19   In a failover cluster, when one server fails, another takes over, using the same storage

In a failover cluster, storage volumes or LUNs that are exposed to the nodes in a cluster must not be exposed to other servers, including servers in another cluster. Figure 2-20 illustrates this concept by showing two two-node failover clusters dividing up storage on a SAN.

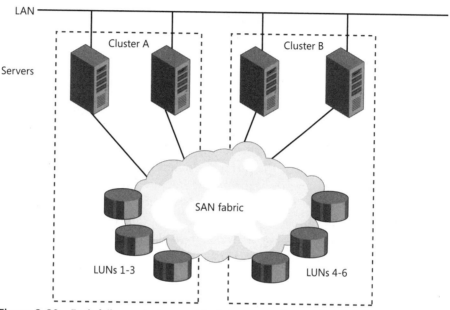

Figure 2-20   Each failover cluster must isolate storage from other servers

Configuring an NLB Cluster

Creating an NLB cluster is a relatively simple process. To begin, install Windows Server 2008 on two servers and then, on both servers, configure the service or application (such as IIS) that you want to provide to clients. Be sure to create identical configurations because you want the client experience to be identical regardless of which server users are connected to.

The next step in configuring an NLB cluster is to install the Network Load Balancing feature on all servers that you want to join the NLB cluster. For this step, simply open Server Manager, and then click Add Features. In the Add Features Wizard, select Network Load Balancing, click Next, and then follow the prompts to install.

The final step in creating an NLB cluster is to use Network Load Balancing Manager to configure the cluster. This procedure is outlined in the following section.

▶ **To create an NLB cluster**

1. Launch Network Load Balancing Manager from Administrative Tools. (You can also open Network Load Balancing Manager by typing **Nlbmgr.exe** from a command prompt.)

2. In the Network Load Balancing Manager console tree, right-click Network Load Balancing Clusters, and then click New Cluster.

3. Connect to the host that is to be a part of the new cluster. In Host, enter the name of the host, and then click Connect.

4. Select the interface you want to use with the cluster, and then click Next. (The interface hosts the virtual IP address and receives the client traffic to load balance.)

5. On the Host Parameters page, select a value in the Priority (Unique host identifier) drop-down list. This parameter specifies a unique ID for each host. The host with the lowest numerical priority among the current members of the cluster handles all the cluster's network traffic not covered by a port rule. You can override these priorities or provide load balancing for specific ranges of ports by specifying rules on the Port rules tab of the Network Load Balancing Properties dialog box.

6. On the Host Parameters page, verify that the dedicated IP address from the chosen interface is visible in the list. If not, use the Add button to add the address, and then click Next to continue.

7. On the Cluster IP Addresses page, click Add to enter the cluster IP address shared by every host in the cluster. NLB adds this IP address to the TCP/IP stack on the selected interface of all hosts chosen to be part of the cluster. Click Next to continue.

NOTE   Use only static addresses

NLB doesn't support Dynamic Host Configuration Protocol (DHCP). NLB disables DHCP on each interface it configures, so the IP addresses must be static.

---

8. On the Cluster Parameters page, in the Cluster IP Configuration area, verify appropriate values for IP address and subnet mask, and then type a full Internet name (Fully Qualified Domain Name) for the cluster.

   Note that for IPv6 addresses, a subnet mask is not needed. Note also that a full Internet name is not needed when using NLB with Terminal Services.

9. On the Cluster Parameters page, in the Cluster Operation Mode area, click Unicast to specify that a unicast media access control (MAC) address should be used for cluster operations. In unicast mode, the MAC address of the cluster is assigned to the network adapter of the computer, and the built-in MAC address of the network adapter is not

used. It is recommended that you accept the unicast default settings. Click Next to continue.

10. On the Port Rules page, click Edit to modify the default port rules. Configure the rules as follows:

    ❑ In the Port Range area, specify a range corresponding to the service you want to provide in the NLB cluster. For example, for Web services, type **80 to 80** so that the new rule applies only to HTTP traffic. For Terminal Services, type **3389 to 3389** so that the new rule applies only to RDP traffic.

    ❑ In the Protocols area, select TCP or UDP, as needed, as the specific TCP/IP protocol the port rule should cover. Only the network traffic for the specified protocol is affected by the rule. Traffic not affected by the port rule is handled by the default host.

    ❑ In the Filtering mode area, select Multiple Host if you want multiple hosts in the cluster to handle network traffic for the port rule. Choose Single Host if you want a single host to handle the network traffic for the port rule.

    ❑ In Affinity (which applies only for the Multiple host filtering mode), select None if you want multiple connections from the same client IP address to be handled by different cluster hosts (no client affinity). Leave the Single option if you want NLB to direct multiple requests from the same client IP address to the same cluster host. Select Network if you want NLB to direct multiple requests from the local subnet to the same cluster host.

11. After you add the port rule, click Finish to create the cluster.

    To add more hosts to the cluster, right-click the new cluster, and then click Add Host To Cluster. Configure the host parameters (including host priority and dedicated IP addresses) for the additional hosts by following the same instructions that you used to configure the initial host. Because you are adding hosts to an already configured cluster, all the cluster-wide parameters remain the same.

Creating a Failover Cluster

Creating a failover cluster is a multistep process. The first step is to configure the physical hardware for the cluster. Then, you need to install the Failover Clustering feature and run the Failover Cluster Validation Tool, which ensures that the hardware and software prerequisites for the cluster are met. Next, once the configuration has been validated by the tool, create the cluster by running the Create Cluster Wizard. Finally, to configure the behavior of the cluster and to define the availability of selected services, you need to run the High Availability Wizard.

Preparing Failover Cluster Hardware

Failover clusters have fairly elaborate hardware requirements. To configure the hardware, review the following list of requirements for the servers, network adapters, cabling, controllers, and storage:

- **Servers**   Use a set of matching computers that consist of the same or similar components (recommended).

- **Network adapters and cabling**   The network hardware, like other components in the failover cluster solution, must be compatible with Windows Server 2008. If you use iSCSI, each network adapter must be dedicated to either network communication or iSCSI, not both.

  In the network infrastructure that connects your cluster nodes, avoid having single points of failure. There are multiple ways of accomplishing this. You can connect your cluster nodes by multiple, distinct networks. Alternatively, you can connect your cluster nodes with one network constructed with teamed network adapters, redundant switches, redundant routers, or similar hardware that removes single points of failure.

- **Device controllers or appropriate adapters for the storage**   If you are using serial attached SCSI or FC in all clustered servers, the mass-storage device controllers that are dedicated to the cluster storage should be identical. They should also use the same firmware version. If you are using iSCSI, each clustered server must have one or more network adapters or HBAs that are dedicated to the cluster storage. The network you use for iSCSI cannot be used for network communication. In all clustered servers, the network adapters you use to connect to the iSCSI storage target should be identical. It is also recommended that you use Gigabit Ethernet or higher. (Note also that for iSCSI, you cannot use teamed network adapters.)

- **Shared storage compatible with Windows Server 2008**   For a two-node failover cluster, the storage should contain at least two separate volumes (LUNs), configured at the hardware level.

  The first volume will function as the *witness disk*, a volume that holds a copy of the cluster configuration database. Witness disks, known as *quorum disks* in Microsoft Windows Server 2003, are used in many but not all cluster configurations.

  The second volume will contain the files that are being shared to users. Storage requirements include the following:

  - To use the native disk support included in failover clustering, use basic disks, not dynamic disks.

  - It is recommended that you format the storage partitions with NTFS. (For the witness disk, the partition must be NTFS.)

When deploying a storage area network (SAN) with a failover cluster, be sure to confirm with manufacturers and vendors that the storage, including all drivers, firmware, and software used for the storage, are compatible with failover clusters in Windows Server 2008.

After you have met the hardware requirements and connected the cluster servers to storage, you can then install the Failover Cluster feature.

NOTE   What is the quorum configuration?

The quorum configuration in a failover cluster determines the number of failures that the cluster can sustain before the cluster stops running. In Windows Server 2008, you can choose from among four quorum configurations. The first option is the Node Majority quorum configuration, which is recommended for clusters with an odd number of nodes. In node majority, the failover cluster runs as long as a majority of the nodes are running. The second option is the Node and Disk Majority quorum configuration, which is recommended for clusters with an even number of nodes. In node and disk majority, the failover cluster uses a witness disk as a tiebreaker node, and the failover cluster then runs as long as a majority of these nodes are online and available. The third option is the Node And File Share Majority quorum configuration. In node and file share majority, which is recommended for clusters that have an even number of nodes and that lack access to a witness disk, a witness file share is used as a tiebreaker node, and the failover cluster then runs as long as a majority of these nodes are online and available. The fourth and final option is the No Majority: Disk Only quorum configuration. In this configuration, which is generally not recommended, the failover cluster remains as long as a single node and its storage remain online.

Quick Check

1. What is a witness disk?
2. What is the quorum configuration of a failover cluster?

Quick Check Answers

1. A witness disk is a shared volume used in many failover clusters that contains a copy of the cluster configuration database.
2. The quorum configuration is what determines the number of node failures that a failover cluster can sustain before the cluster should stop running.

Exam Tip   On the 70-643 exam, you might see basic questions about quorum configurations, witness disks, or witness file shares.

Installing the Failover Clustering Feature

Before creating a failover cluster, you have to install the Failover Clustering feature on all nodes in the cluster.

To install the Failover Clustering feature, begin by clicking Add Features in Server Manager. In the Add Features Wizard, select the Failover Clustering check box. Click Next, and then follow the prompts to install the feature.

Once the feature is installed on all nodes, you are ready to validate the hardware and software configuration.

Validating the Cluster Configuration

Before you create a new cluster, use the Validate A Configuration Wizard to ensure that your nodes meet the hardware and software prerequisites for a failover cluster.

To run the Validate A Configuration Wizard, first open Failover Cluster Management Administrative Tools program group. In Failover Cluster Management, click Validate A Configuration in the Management area or the Actions pane, as shown in Figure 2-21.

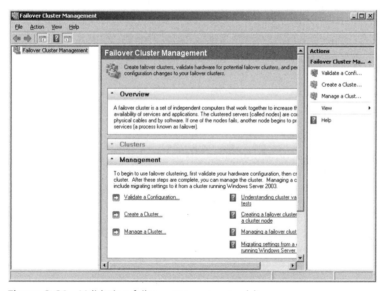

Figure 2-21   Validating failover server prerequisites

After the wizard completes, make any configuration changes if necessary, and then rerun the test until the configuration is successfully validated. After the cluster prerequisites have been validated, you can use the Create Cluster Wizard to create the cluster.

Running the Create Cluster Wizard

The next step in creating a cluster is to run the Create Cluster Wizard. The Create Cluster Wizard installs the software foundation for the cluster, converts the attached storage into cluster disks, and creates a computer account in Active Directory for the cluster. To launch this tool, in Failover Cluster Management, click Create A Cluster in the Management area or Actions pane.

In the Create Cluster Wizard, simply enter the names of the cluster nodes when prompted. The wizard then enables you to name and assign an IP address for the cluster, after which the cluster is created.

After the wizard completes, you need to configure the services or applications for which you wish to provide failover. To perform this aspect of the configuration, run the High Availability Wizard.

Running the High Availability Wizard

The High Availability Wizard configures failover service for a particular service or application. To launch the High Availability Wizard, in Failover Cluster Management, click Configure A Service Or Application in the Action pane or Configure area.

To complete the High Availability Wizard, perform the following steps:

1. On the Before You Begin page, review the text, and then click Next.
2. On the Select Service Or Application page, select the service or application for which you want to provide failover service (high availability), and then click Next.
3. Follow the instructions in the wizard to specify required details about the chosen service. For example, for the File Server service, you would need to specify the following:
   - ❏ A name for the clustered file server
   - ❏ Any IP address information that is not automatically supplied by your DHCP settings—for example, a static IPv4 address for this clustered file server
   - ❏ The storage volume or volumes that the clustered file server should use
4. After the wizard runs and the Summary page appears, to view a report of the tasks the wizard performed, click View Report.
5. To close the wizard, click Finish.

Testing the Failover Cluster

After you complete the wizard, test the failover cluster in Failover Cluster Management. In the console tree, make sure Services and Applications is expanded, and then select the service you have just added with the High Availability Wizard. Right-click the clustered service, click Move

This Service Or Application To Another Node, and then click the available choice of node. You can observe the status changes in the center pane of the snap-in as the clustered service instance is moved. If the service moves successfully, the failover is functional.

PRACTICE Exploring Failover Clustering

In this practice, you watch a webcast demonstrating how to create a failover cluster in Windows Server 2008.

▶ **Exercise 1 Watch a Screencast about Failover Clustering**

To perform this exercise, watch the 17-minute screencast titled "How to Create a Failover Cluster in Windows Server 2008" by Jose Barreto. You can find this file by browsing to the Webcasts folder on the companion CD. This is also available for viewing at *https://www.livemeeting.com/ cc/microsoft/view?id=FailoverClustering&pw=josebda*.

Lesson Summary

- You can configure groups of servers in Windows Server 2008 to provide load balancing, scalability, or high availability for a particular service or application. These server groups are often called clusters and can be used for very different purposes. Typically, clusters are transparent and appear as a single server to clients.

- Round-robin DNS is a basic method of balancing requests for a single server between two or more servers. Round-robin is easy to configure but has significant limitations such as the lack of awareness of server status.

- Network Load Balancing (NLB) is an installable feature of Windows Server 2008. Like round-robin, NLB transparently distributes client requests for a single server between two or more servers. However, NLB overcomes the limitations of round-robin DNS by providing advanced features such as the ability to redirect requests away from a downed or busy server automatically. NLB is often used to create Web farms, which are NLB clusters used to answer requests for a Web site or set of Web sites.

- Failover Clustering is an installable feature of Windows Server 2008. A failover cluster is a group of computers used to prevent downtime for selected applications and services. Servers (or nodes) in a failover cluster are connected to each other and to shared storage. Failover clusters have fairly elaborate hardware requirements, and you should be sure to review these requirements before making purchasing decisions.

Lesson Review

The following questions are intended to reinforce key information presented in this lesson. The questions are also available on the companion CD if you prefer to review them in electronic form.

NOTE Answers

Answers to these questions and explanations of why each answer choice is correct or incorrect are located in the "Answers" section at the end of the book.

---

1. You work as a network administrator for Tailspintoys.com. Your job responsibilities include supporting company servers. The Tailspintoys.com network hosts a Web server that runs on a single server named Websrv1. Recently, traffic to the Web site has been increasing, and the performance of the Web server has been deteriorating. Traffic to the Web site is expected to continue to increase over the next five to eight years. You want a solution that can solve the performance problems of the Web server and meet the increasing workload requirements for the Web site for the next five to eight years. What should you do?

    A. Migrate the Web site to a more powerful server.

    B. Use NLB to create a Web farm to support the Web site.

    C. Use failover clustering to support the Web site with multiple servers in a cluster.

    D. Add a second Web server, and then use DNS round-robin to distribute Web requests between the two servers. Add more servers as necessary.

2. You are configuring a failover cluster for a database server. You are assigning four nodes to the cluster. All nodes have access to a SAN, and adequate storage is available. Which of the following options should you choose for your quorum configuration?

    1. Node Majority

    2. Node And Disk Majority

    3. Node And File Share Majority

    4. No Majority: Disk Only

Chapter Review

To further practice and reinforce the skills you learned in this chapter, you can perform the following tasks:

- Review the chapter summary.
- Review the list of key terms introduced in this chapter.
- Complete the case scenario. This scenario sets up a real-world situation involving the topics of this chapter and asks you to create solutions.
- Complete the suggested practices.
- Take a practice test.

Chapter Summary

- Servers require block-based access to data to run operating systems and applications. Usually, direct-attached storage is used for this purpose. This type of storage includes all internally installed hard disks as well as externally attached storage.
- Windows Server 2008 includes the Virtual Disk Service (VDS) API, which exposes compatible storage subsystems to Windows Server 2008 administration tools such as Storage Manager for SANs.
- You can use Disk Management in Windows Server 2008 to create simple volumes, spanned volumes, striped volumes, mirrored volumes, and RAID-5 volumes. You can also choose to extend or shrink existing volumes.
- Network Load Balancing (NLB) is used to balance a workload among multiple servers. Clients connect to an NLB cluster by specifying a virtual computer name and virtual IP address. An available server in the NLB cluster then answers the request.
- Failover clustering is a solution used to minimize server downtime. In a failover cluster, cluster servers or nodes share the same storage. When one server fails, another server takes over for the failed server.

Key Terms

Do you know what these key terms mean? You can check your answers by looking up the terms in the glossary at the end of the book.

- block-based
- cluster
- iSCSI initiator

- iSCSI target
- parity
- partition style
- quorum configuration
- round-robin DNS
- SAN fabric
- Web farm
- witness disk

Case Scenarios

In the following case scenario, you will apply what you've learned in this chapter. You can find answers to these questions in the "Answers" section at the end of this book.

Case Scenario 1: Designing Storage

You are an IT support specialist for Woodgrove Bank. Your manager informs you that the bank has decided to create a SAN for shared storage among its servers, and you have been asked to research SAN technology options. Migration of chosen servers to SAN storage will occur in approximately one year.

The primary goals for the future SAN are to provide flexible storage and extremely low latency for database servers. Other goals are to take advantage of the existing networking expertise of the IT staff as much as possible and to facilitate as much administration of the SAN as possible through the Windows Server 2008 interface. No one currently employed on the IT staff has any expertise working with SANs.

1. Given the storage needs of the organization, which connection technology should you choose for the SAN?
2. Which element should you seek in vendor solutions that will enable you to meet the administrative goals of the SAN?

Case Scenario 2: Designing High Availability

You are a server administrator for Trey Research. Recently, Trey Research purchased a line-of-business application named App1 that is to be used heavily by all 500 employees throughout the day. App1 is a Web-based application that connects to a back-end database.

You and other members of the IT staff are currently designing the servers to host App1 and its database. In general, the design team foresees two separate servers or clusters, one to host IIS and App1 and the second to host the database. All servers must run Windows Server 2008. The goals for the server design are to minimize downtime and provide the best possible performance for both the application and the database. In addition, the solution must use a single database that is always internally consistent. All tables must always be visible to App1.

Within the design team, you have been tasked with researching cluster solutions for the Web application server and database server.

Which clustering technology built into Windows Server 2008 is most suitable for the Web application server and why?

 Which clustering technology built into Windows Server 2008 is most suitable for the database server and why?

Suggested Practices

To help you successfully master the exam objectives presented in this chapter, complete the following tasks.

Configure Storage

If you have access to a system with three extra disks, virtual or physical, then you should perform all three practices. If you do not have access to such a system, then watch the webcasts noted in Practice 2 and Practice 3. Although Practice 2 was recorded for Windows Server 2003 R2, it introduces many concepts and tools that are relevant for Windows Server 2008, so watching it is highly recommended.

- **Practice 1**   On a Windows Server 2008 system, create a RAID-5 volume. Save data to the volume. Bring one of the disks offline, and then attempt to access the data.
- **Practice 2**   Watch the Webcast "Build a Simple SAN with Windows Server 2003 R2 and Intelligent iSCSI Storage" by Tres Hill. You can find this on the companion CD or by searching for event ID 1032289955 at *http://msevents.microsoft.com*.
- **Practice 3**   Watch the Webcast "Reducing IT Overhead with Windows Server 2008 Storage Features" by Dave Lalor. You can find this on the companion CD or by searching for event ID 1032347804 at *http://msevents.microsoft.com*.

Configure High Availability

Perform at least the first two practices. If you can use virtual machine software or two physical servers, perform Practice 3.

- **Practice 1** Watch the "Load Balancing" screencast by Orin Thomas, available at *mms:// wm.microsoft.com/ms/windowsserversystem/compare/screencasts/Load_balancing _Windows.wmv*. This five-minute screencast demonstrates creating an NLB cluster in Windows Server 2003.

- **Practice 2** Go to *http://msevents.microsoft.com* and search for event ID 1032345932. Register for and perform the virtual lab named "TechNet Virtual Lab: Windows Server 2008 Enterprise Failover Clustering Lab."

- **Practice 3** Install Windows Server 2008 on two servers, and then add the Network Load Balancing feature on both servers. Create an NLB cluster, and then add both servers to the cluster.

Take a Practice Test

The practice tests on this book's companion CD offer many options. For example, you can test yourself on just one exam objective, or you can test yourself on all the 70-643 certification exam content. You can set up the test so that it closely simulates the experience of taking a certification exam, or you can set it up in study mode so that you can look at the correct answers and explanations after you answer each question.

MORE INFO   Practice tests

For details about all the practice test options available, see the "How to Use the Practice Tests" section in this book's introduction.

Chapter 3

Installing and Configuring Terminal Services

If you think of an application infrastructure as a set of technologies that helps deliver applications to remote users, then Terminal Services has to be considered one of its very central components. Terminal Services is, in fact, a technology that enables remote users to establish interactive sessions—both desktop sessions and application sessions—on a computer running Windows Server 2008.

The central role of Terminal Services is reflected on the 70-643 exam. With the many features, tools, and functions associated with Terminal Services, there's a fair amount to learn about this topic both for real-world administration and for the test. For this reason, the content is divided into two chapters. This chapter covers the deployment and configuration of the core Terminal Services role. In the next chapter, we will discuss the many complementary components that make up a Terminal Services infrastructure.

Exam objectives in this chapter:
- Configuring Terminal Services
    - ❏ Configure Terminal Services server options.
    - ❏ Configure Terminal Services licensing.
    - ❏ Configure Terminal Services load balancing.

Lessons in this chapter:

Before You Begin

To complete the lessons in this chapter, you must have:

- A computer running Windows Server 2008 named Server1 that is a domain controller in a domain named Contoso.com.
- A computer running Windows Server 2008 named Server2 that is a member server in the Contoso.com domain.
- A Server Core installation of Windows Server 2008 named Core1 that is a member server in the Contoso.com domain.

Real World

JC Mackin

The most important thing to know about Terminal Services in Windows Server 2008 is that it includes some radically new and important features beyond those offered in Remote Desktop or in any previous version of Windows Server. The RemoteApp feature, to begin with, enables you to run a remote program on another computer as if that program were installed locally. Another feature, Terminal Services Web Access (TS Web Access), provides a Web page from which you can launch these same remote applications, and Terminal Services Gateway (TS Gateway), for its part, gives your organization an attractive alternative to virtual private networks (VPNs) by allowing authorized users to connect from the Internet to any desired desktop on your internal network.

In the past, such functionality was available only through third-party applications. Now that these powerful features are built into Windows Server 2008, more organizations will start to take advantage of them. As a Windows support technician, you might have dismissed Terminal Services in the past as a feature that you didn't really have to understand too well, but the role of Terminal Services is now certain to grow.

Terminal Services is moving closer to the core of essential, real-world support technologies that you absolutely must know and understand. Given this, it's time to start looking very closely at this feature if you haven't already.

Lesson 1: Deploying a Terminal Server

The decision to deploy Terminal Services is complicated by the fact that Windows Server 2008 already includes a technology—Remote Desktop—that essentially performs the same function as Terminal Services. For this reason, before you deploy Terminal Services, it is important to understand the features this server role offers beyond those of Remote Desktop.

This lesson describes the features unique to the Terminal Services role and then describes the steps necessary to install and deploy a terminal server.

After this lesson, you will be able to:

- Understand the basic features and function of Terminal Services.
- Compare and contrast Terminal Services with the built-in Remote Desktop feature of Windows.
- Install the Terminal Services role on a full installation and a server core installation of Windows Server 2008.
- Describe client licensing options for a terminal server.
- Prepare a terminal server for deployment.

Estimated lesson time: 40 minutes

Understanding Terminal Services

Terminal Services enables remote users to establish interactive desktops or application sessions on a computer running Windows Server 2008. During a Terminal Services session, Terminal Services clients offload virtually the entire processing load for that session to the terminal server. This functionality offered by Terminal Services thus enables an organization to distribute the resources of a central server among many users or clients. For example, Terminal Services is often used to offer a single installation of an application to many users throughout an organization. This option can be especially useful for companies deploying line-of-business (LOB) applications and other programs responsible for tracking inventory.

Figure 3-1 illustrates how a terminal server can make a central application available to remote clients.

Terminal Server

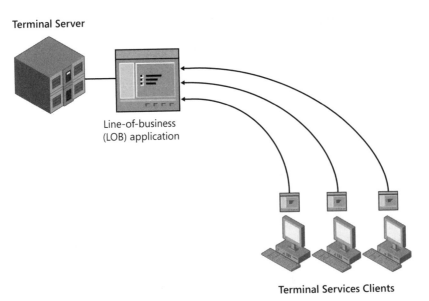

Line-of-business
(LOB) application

Terminal Services Clients

Figure 3-1   Using terminal servers to deploy an application

Comparing Terminal Services and Remote Desktop

Microsoft Windows XP, Windows Vista, Windows Server 2003, and Windows Server 2008 all include a feature called Remote Desktop, which, like Terminal Services, enables users to establish an interactive desktop session on a remote computer. Remote Desktop and Terminal Services are in fact closely related. First, both technologies use the same client software, named Remote Desktop Connection (also called Terminal Services Client or Mstsc.exe). This client software is built into all versions of Windows since Windows XP can be installed on virtually any Windows-based or non-Windows–based computer. From the remote user's perspective, then, the procedure of connecting to a terminal server is identical to connecting to a remote desktop. Second, the server component of both features is also essentially the same. Both Terminal Services and Remote Desktop rely on the same service, called the Terminal Services service. Finally, both Remote Desktop and Terminal Services establish sessions by means of the same protocol, called Remote Desktop Protocol (RDP), and through the same TCP port, 3389.

Despite these similarities, the differences between Remote Desktop and Terminal Services are significant in that Terminal Services offers much greater scalability and a number of important additional features. For example, on a computer running Windows Server 2008 on which Remote Desktop is enabled, only two users can be connected concurrently to an active desktop session (including any active local user console session). However, no such limitation exists for a server on which Terminal Services has been installed and configured.

NOTE Connections vs. sessions

Strictly speaking, what is the difference between a Terminal Services connection and session? A Terminal Services connection is merely an open Remote Desktop Connection window displaying a desktop on a remote computer. A Terminal Services session, however, is a continuous period during which a user is logged on to a remote computer. If you closed a Remote Desktop Connection window without logging off from a remote computer, the connection would end, but (provided that the server settings allow it) the session would continue. If you then reconnected to the remote server, you would find the same session in progress with the open programs and files exactly as you had left them. The *console session*, as you might guess from its name, is not a Terminal Services session at all. It is instead the particular desktop session that is active at the physical computer.

Terminal Services in Windows Server 2008 also includes the following additional features beyond those available in Remote Desktop:

- **Multiuser capability**   Terminal Services includes two modes: Execute mode (for the normal running of applications) and Install mode (for installing programs). When you install an application on a terminal server in Install mode, settings are written to the Registry or to .ini files in a way that supports multiple users. Unlike Terminal Services, the Remote Desktop feature in Windows does not include an Install mode or provide multiuser support for applications.

- **RemoteApp**   In Windows Server 2008, the RemoteApp component of Terminal Services enables you to deploy an application remotely to users as if the application were running on the end user's local computer. Instead of providing the entire desktop of the remote terminal server within a resizable window, RemoteApp enables a remote application to be integrated with the user's own desktop. The application deployed through Terminal Services thus runs in its own resizable window with its own entry in the taskbar.

- **TS Web Access**   TS Web Access enables you to make applications hosted on a remote terminal server available to users through a Web browser. When TS Web Access is configured, users visit a Web site (either from the Internet or from the organization's intranet) and view a list of all the applications available through RemoteApp. To start one of the listed applications, users simply click the program icon on the Web page.

- **TS Session Broker**   By using Network Load Balancing (NLB) or DNS round-robin distribution, you can deploy a number of terminal servers in a farm that, from the perspective of remote users, emulates a single server. A terminal server farm is the best way to support many users, and to enhance the functionality of such a farm, you can use the Terminal Services Session Broker (TS Session Broker) role service. The TS Session Broker component ensures that clients connecting to a terminal server farm can reconnect to disconnected sessions.

- **TS Gateway**   TS Gateway enables authorized users on the Internet to connect to remote desktops and terminal servers located on a private corporate network. TS Gateway provides security for these connections by tunneling each RDP session inside an encrypted Hypertext Transfer Protocol Secure (HTTPS) session. By providing authorized users broad access to internal computers over an encrypted connection, TS Gateway can eliminate the need for a VPN in many cases.

Advantages of Remote Desktop

The main advantage of Remote Desktop, compared to Terminal Services, is that its functionality is built into Windows Server 2008 and does not require the purchase of any Terminal Services client access licenses (TS CALs). If you don't purchase any TS CALs for Terminal Services, the feature will stop working after 120 days. After this period, Terminal Services functionality will revert to that of Remote Desktop.

Another advantage of Remote Desktop, compared to Terminal Services, is that the feature is very easy to implement. Whereas enabling Terminal Services requires installing and configuring a new server role, enabling Remote Desktop requires you to select only a single option in the System Properties dialog box.

NOTE   Remote Desktop vs. Remote Desktop for Administration

In Windows Server 2003 and Windows Server 2008, the built-in Remote Desktop feature is often referred to as Remote Desktop for Administration (RDA). The difference between RDA and the Remote Desktop feature in Windows XP and Windows Vista is that RDA in Windows Server 2008 enables two active desktop sessions to the RDA-enabled server: either two remote sessions, or one remote session and one console session. Windows XP and Windows Vista, however, do not allow concurrent desktop sessions. Only one Remote Desktop user can connect at a time and, when a remote user does connect, any locally logged-on user must first be logged off.

Exam Tip   In Windows Server 2008, the Remote Desktop feature typically is used for remote administration, and Terminal Services is used to host applications. However, the main difference between these two features is scale, and the purposes of their implementations do overlap. You can use the Remote Desktop feature to connect to a seldom-used application just as you can administer a server remotely on which Terminal Services has been installed. Remember also that the core client and server components of these technologies are shared, so do not be surprised if you hear the terms used interchangeably.

Enabling Remote Desktop

By default, Windows Server 2008 does not accept connections from any Remote Desktop clients. To enable the Remote Desktop feature in Windows Server 2008, use the Remote tab of the System Properties dialog box. To access this tab, you can open System located in Control

Panel and then click the Remote Settings link, or you can type **control sysdm.cpl** in the Run box and then, after the System Properties dialog box opens, click the Remote tab.

On the Remote tab, if you want to require a high standard of security from RDP connections, select the option to require Network Level Authentication (NLA), as shown in Figure 3-2. This selection will enable connections only from Remote Desktop Connection clients running Windows Vista or later. Alternatively, you can select the option to allow connections from computers running any version of Remote Desktop.

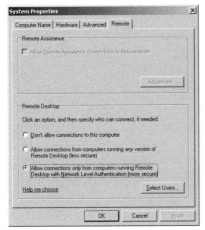

Figure 3-2   Enabling the Remote Desktop feature on Windows Server 2008

In Windows Server 2008, when you use the System Properties dialog box to allow Remote Desktop connections, a Windows Firewall exception for RDP traffic is created automatically. Therefore, you do not have to create the exception manually to allow connections from Remote Desktop clients.

NOTE   What is Network Level Authentication?

NLA is a feature of Remote Desktop Protocol 6.0 that ensures that user authentication occurs before a Remote Desktop connection is fully established between two computers. With earlier versions of RDP, a user could enter a username and password for authentication only after a Log On To Windows screen from the remote computer appeared in the Remote Desktop session. Because every attempt to authenticate a session demanded relatively significant resources from the server, this behavior in earlier versions of RDP made Remote Desktop–enabled and Terminal Services–enabled computers susceptible to denial-of-service attacks.

Also important to know is that, by default, Remote Desktop Connection 6.0 (also known as Terminal Services Client 6.0 or mstsc.exe) does not support NLA on computers running Windows XP. However, this version of the Remote Desktop client can be made to support NLA on Windows XP SP2 if you download and install the Terminal Services Client 6.0 update for Windows XP (KB925876), available on the Microsoft Web site.

Enabling Remote Desktop on a Server Core Installation

A Server Core installation of Windows Server 2008 does not support the full Terminal Services role. However, you can enable the Remote Desktop feature on a Server Core installation by using the Server Core Registry Editor script, Scregedit.wsf. Scregedit.wsf provides a simplified way of configuring the most commonly used features in a Server Core installation of Windows Server 2008.

IMPORTANT   Where can you find Scregedit.wsf?

Scregedit.wsf is located in the *%SystemRoot%*\System32 folder of every Server Core installation.

To use the Scregedit.wsf script to enable Remote Desktop, use Cscript.exe to invoke the script, and then pass the /AR switch a value of 0, which allows Remote Desktop connections. (By default, the /AR value is set to 1, which disables Remote Desktop connections.) The full command to enable Remote Desktop is shown here:

```
Cscript.exe C:\Windows\System32\Scregedit.wsf /AR 0
```

By default, enabling Remote Desktop on the Server Core installation in this way configures the server to accept Remote Desktop connections only from clients running Windows Vista or later. To enable the server to accept Remote Desktop connections from earlier versions of RDP, you need to relax the security requirements of the server by using the Scregedit.wsf script with the /CS switch and a value of 0, as shown:

```
Cscript.exe C:\Windows\System32\Scregedit.wsf /CS 0
```

NOTE   Connecting to a Server Core through Remote Desktop

When you connect to a Server Core installation by means of Remote Desktop, you receive the same interface that you would receive as if you were seated locally at the server. A Remote Desktop connection to a computer running Windows Server 2008 Server Core, in other words, does not provide you with access to any additional graphical tools to manage the server.

Exam Tip   For the 70-643 exam, you need to know how to enable Remote Desktop on a Server Core installation of Windows Server 2008 and how to allow connections from RDP clients earlier than RDP 6.0. Also, do not be surprised if the exam refers to this process as "enabling Terminal Services" or "enabling Terminal Services for remote administration."

Installing Terminal Services

Unlike Remote Desktop, the full implementation of Terminal Services requires you to add the Terminal Services server role. As with any server role, the simplest way to install Terminal Services on a full installation of Windows Server 2008 is to click Add Roles in Server Manager.

Clicking Add Roles launches the Add Roles Wizard. On the Select Server Roles page, select the Terminal Services check box, as shown in Figure 3-3.

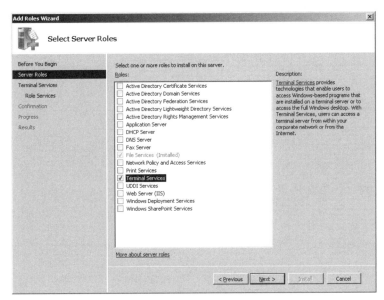

Figure 3-3   Adding the Terminal Services role

Click Next on the Add Roles Wizard page to open the Terminal Services page. This page provides a brief explanation of the Terminal Services role. Then, click Next on the Terminal Services page to open the Select Role Services page.

Selecting Role Services

On the Select Role Services page of the Add Roles Wizard, you can select any of the following five role services associated with the Terminal Services role:

- **Terminal Server**   This role service provides the basic functionality of Terminal Services, including the RemoteApp feature.
- **TS Licensing**   You need to install this role service only if you have purchased Terminal Services client access licenses (TS CALs) and can activate a license server. Terminal Services has a 120-day grace period: if you have not purchased any TS CALs and installed them on a Terminal Services license server, Terminal Services will stop functioning after this many days. (For information about how to install and configure Terminal Services Licensing (TS Licensing) Terminal Services, see Lesson 2, "Configuring Terminal Services," of this chapter.)
- **TS Session Broker**   Install and configure this role service when you plan to implement Terminal Services in a server farm. As mentioned in the "Comparing Terminal Services and Remote Desktop" section earlier in this lesson, this role service enhances the functionality of the server farm by ensuring that clients are able to reconnect to disconnected sessions.
- **TS Gateway**   Install this role service if you want to make a number of terminal servers accessible to authorized external clients beyond a firewall or Network Address Translation (NAT) device.
- **TS Web Access**   Install this role service if you want to make applications deployed through Terminal Services available to clients through a Web page.

The Select Role Services page is shown in Figure 3-4.

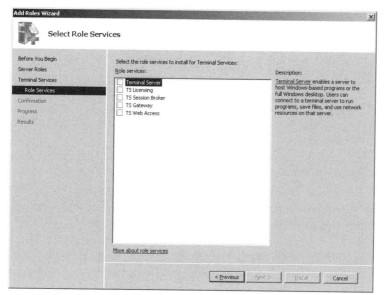

Figure 3-4   Adding the Terminal Services role services

The following sections describe the process of installing the Terminal Services role services.

Uninstalling Applications

After you select the Terminal Services role service, the Add Roles Wizard reminds you that any applications that you want to deploy to users through Terminal Services should be installed after you add the Terminal Services role. If you have already installed any applications you want to deploy, you should uninstall and reinstall them later (in Terminal Services Install mode) if you want them to be available to multiple users. This reminder is shown in Figure 3-5.

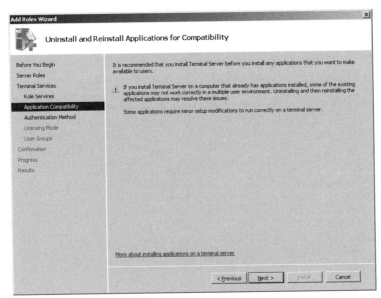

Figure 3-5   Reminder to reinstall TS applications

Specifying NLA Settings

Next, you have to specify whether the terminal server will accept connections only from clients that can perform NLA. When you select this requirement, shown in Figure 3-6, Remote Desktop connections will be blocked from computers with operating systems earlier than Windows Vista.

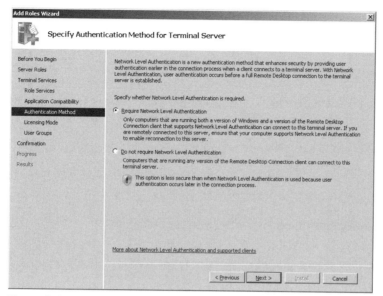

Figure 3-6   Setting NLA/client version requirements

Specifying Client Access License Types

The Add Roles Wizard then gives you the option to specify the TS CAL types you have purchased. Two types of CALs for Terminal Services are available:

- **TS Per Device CALs**   TS Per Device CALs are permanent CALs assigned to any computer or device that connects to Terminal Services more than once. When the Per Device licensing mode is used and a client computer or device connects to a terminal server for the first time, the client computer or device is issued a temporary license by default. When a client computer or device connects to a terminal server for the second time, if the license server is activated and if enough TS Per Device CALs are available, the license server issues the client computer or device a permanent TS Per Device CAL.

- **TS Per User CALs**   TS Per User CALs give users the right to access Terminal Services from any number of devices. TS Per User CALs are not assigned to specific users. If you opt for per user licensing, you simply need to make sure that you have purchased enough licenses for all the users in your organization.

Exam Tip   Windows Server 2008 includes automatic per-device and per-user license tracking to help you determine how many TS licenses are currently in use. Windows Server 2003 only included per-device license tracking.

In deciding which of these two CALs to purchase for your organization, consider several factors. First, consider the number of devices and users in your organization. In general, it's financially preferable to choose per device CALs if you anticipate having fewer devices than users over the life of the terminal server and to choose per user licensing if you anticipate fewer users than devices. Another factor to consider is how often your users travel and connect from different computers. Per user licensing is often preferable when a small number of users tend to connect from many different sites, such as from customer networks.

If you have not yet decided which TS CALs to purchase, you can select the Configure Later option, as shown in Figure 3-7. You then have 120 days to purchase TS CALs and to install these licenses on a locally activated license server. After this grace period, Terminal Services stops functioning.

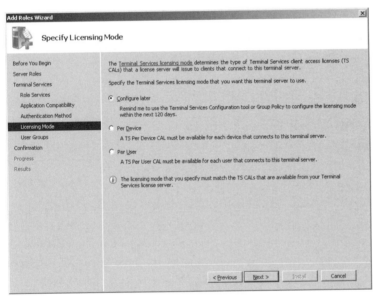

Figure 3-7   Specifying a licensing mode

Exam Tip   For the 70-643 exam, you definitely need to know the difference between the client access license modes.

Authorizing Users

The last configuration step is to choose the users and groups you want to allow access through Terminal Services. The Remote Desktop Users built-in local group automatically is granted the user right to connect to the local computer through Terminal Services, and the Add Roles Wizard here simply provides a fast way of adding accounts to this Remote Desktop Users group. By default, local administrators are already members of the Remote Desktop Users group, as shown in Figure 3-8.

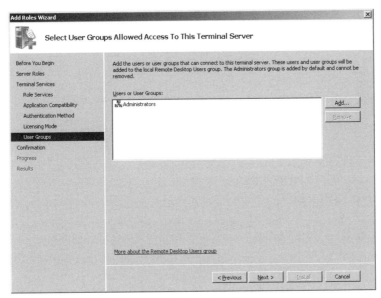

Figure 3-8 Authorizing users for Terminal Services

After this last step, you simply need to confirm your selections and begin the Terminal Services installation, as shown in Figure 3-9.

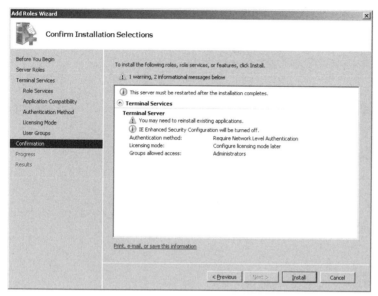

Figure 3-9   Confirming Terminal Services installation options

Staging the Terminal Server

Staging a server refers to the process of preparing it in advance of deployment. In the case of a terminal server, staging a computer involves installing and configuring all the components on the server that you want to make available to Terminal Services clients. At a minimum, this process includes installing appropriate server features and applications.

Installing Windows Server 2008 Built-in Features

Server Manager enables you not only to add server roles but also to install any of 36 Windows Server 2008 features. Features are smaller Windows components that enable specific functionality in the operating system. To prepare a terminal server for deployment, you need to know which of these Windows Server 2008 features you want to make available to clients connecting to the terminal server.

Because the only features available to remote users are those that you install on the terminal server, you need to review client needs and the functionality offered by each feature. For example, if you want Windows Media Player or Windows Aero to be made available to clients connecting to Terminal Services, you have to install the Desktop Experience feature on the computer running Terminal Services.

To install a feature, click Add Features in Server Manager to launch the Add Features Wizard. Figure 3-10 shows a partial list of the features made available by the Add Features Wizard.

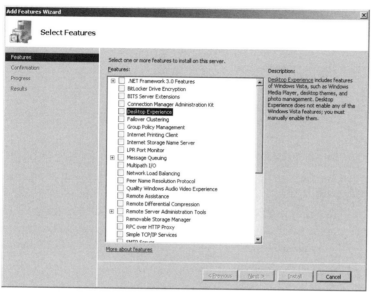

Figure 3-10   The Add Features Wizard

A list follows of some example Windows Server 2008 features that you might need to make available to Terminal Services clients. Successful deployment of Terminal Services requires you to understand these features and to review them during the server staging process.

- **Desktop Experience**   This feature installs Windows Media Player 11, desktop themes, and the photo gallery. It also makes the Windows Aero graphical features available, although these features must be enabled manually by each user.

- **Quality Windows Audio Video Experience**   This feature enables high-quality performance for streaming media over IP networks.

- **Network Load Balancing**   The NLB feature enables you to join a server to an NLB cluster or NLB server farm.

- **Windows Server Backup Features**   You can install the Windows Server Backup Features to enable administrators to perform backups as part of remote maintenance of the computer running the terminal server.

- **Windows PowerShell**   Windows PowerShell is a command-line environment and administrative scripting language built into Windows Server 2008. You can install the Windows PowerShell feature to enable remote administration of the computer running Terminal Services by using Windows PowerShell.

- **Group Policy Management**   Group Policy Management is a console that facilitates administration of Group Policy. You can install this feature if you anticipate that administrators will use the server to manage Group Policy remotely.
- **Windows System Resource Manager**   Windows System Resource Manager (WSRM) enables you to manage the resources of a server so that the workload is spread equitably among roles.

Exam Tip   Be sure to review server features for the 70-643 exam. Although it's a good idea to review all features, pay special attention to those just listed.

Installing Terminal Services Applications

Terminal Services is often used to deploy a single installation of an application to many users. Deploying an application in this way is frequently the best option for data-entry programs designed to run on a single server or for those tied to a locally installed database. However, you might also want to deploy an application through Terminal Services to reduce associated licensing fees, to offload processing from client computers, or simply to facilitate user productivity within a Terminal Services session.

After you have decided which applications to make available to remote users through Terminal Services, you need to install these applications in a way that makes them available to multiple users. To do this, you must install the applications while Terminal Services is in Install mode. You can install programs in Install mode by using an MSI installer program, by using the Install Application on Terminal Server program in Control Panel, or by using the *Change user/install* or *Chgusr/install* command. For more information about using Install mode, see Chapter 4, "Configuring and Managing a Terminal Services Infrastructure."

Quick Check

1. Which server feature should you install on a terminal server if you want users to be able to play audio and video in Terminal Services sessions?
2. On a computer running Windows Server 2008 that has the Remote Desktop feature enabled, what is the maximum number of concurrent active user sessions (including remote and console sessions) that can be hosted?

Quick Check Answers

1. Desktop Experience
2. Two

PRACTICE **Installing a Terminal Server**

In this practice, you will install Terminal Services on a full installation of Windows Server 2008 and then enable the Remote Desktop feature on a server core installation.

▶ **Exercise 1 Install the Terminal Services Role**

In this exercise, you will install the Terminal Services server role on Server2.

1. As a domain administrator, log on to Contoso.com from Server2.
2. In Server Manager, select the Roles node in the console tree, and then click Add Roles in the details pane.
    If the Before You Begin page is displayed, click Next.
3. On the Select Server Roles page of the Add Roles Wizard, select the Terminal Services check box, and then click Next.
4. On the Terminal Services page, read all the text on the page, and then click Next.
5. On the Select Role Services page, select the Terminal Server check box, and then click Next.
6. On the Uninstall And Reinstall Applications For Compatibility page, read all the text on the page, and then click Next.
7. On the Specify Authentication Method For Terminal Services page, read all the text on the page, select Require Network Level Authentication, and then click Next.
8. On the Specify Licensing Mode page, read all the text on the page, leave the default selection of Configure Later, and then click Next.
9. On the Select User Groups Allowed Access To This Terminal Server page, read all the text on the page, and then click Next.
10. On the Confirm Installation Selections page, read all the text on the page, and then click Install.
11. After the installation is complete, read all the text on the Installation Results page, and then click Close.
12. In the Add Roles Wizard dialog box, click Yes to restart the server.
13. After the server reboots, log back on to Contoso.com from Server2 by using the same domain administrator account.

IMPORTANT **Always log back on with the same account**

In Windows Server 2008, whenever you add or remove a server role, you are prompted to restart the server. You must immediately log back on with the same user account to complete the procedure.

After several moments, the Resume Configuration Wizard appears.

When the Installation Results page appears, click Close.

14. In Control Panel, open Windows Firewall.

15. Click the Allow A Program Through Windows Firewall option.

16. On the Exceptions tab of the Windows Firewall Settings dialog box, verify that the Remote Desktop and Terminal Services check boxes are checked, and then click OK.

17. Close all open windows, and then proceed to Exercise 2.

▶ **Exercise 2 Test the Terminal Services Connection**

In this exercise, you will test the Terminal Services configuration on Server2 by connecting to it from a Remote Desktop Connection on Server1.

1. Log on to Contoso.com from Server1 as a domain administrator.

2. From the Start menu, select Run.

3. In the Run box, type **mstsc**, and then press Enter.

Exam Tip   You need to know the function of the *Mstsc* command for the 70-643 exam.

The Remote Desktop Connection window opens.

4. In the Computer text box of the Remote Desktop Connection window, type **server2 .contoso.com**, and then press Enter.

The Windows Security window opens.

5. In the Windows Security window, enter the credentials of a domain administrator. Be sure to enter the username in the form **contoso*username*.**

After several moments, a Remote Desktop connection is established to Server2. Within the desktop of Server1, the remote Server2 desktop is designated with a yellowish banner labeled "server2.contoso.com."

6. Using the Start button within the Remote Desktop session to Server2, log off the Remote Desktop connection.

The Remote Desktop window closes.

▶ **Exercise 3 Enable Remote Desktop on a Server Core Installation of Windows Server 2008**

In this exercise, you will enable Remote Desktop on the Core1 computer and then test the configuration.

NOTE Server1 and Server2

Although Server1 is needed for this exercise, Server2 is not. If you are using virtual machines and do not have enough RAM to support all three computers, you can shut down Server2 before beginning this exercise.

---

1. Log on to Contoso.com from Core1 as a domain administrator.
2. At the command prompt, type the following command: **cd C:\Windows\System32**.
3. At the command prompt, type the following command: **cscript scregedit.wsf /AR /v**.

   This command shows the current status of the fDenyTSConnections registry setting. When set to 1, the local computer is configured to deny incoming Remote Desktop connections.
4. Type the following command: **cscript scregedit.wsf /AR 0**.
5. To verify the setting change, type the following command: **cscript scregedit.wsf /AR /v**.

   The output from the command reveals that the fDenyTSConnections registry setting is now set to 0.
6. To ensure that the server will accept connections from RDP clients earlier than 6.0, or from clients native to Windows XP and earlier, type the following command: **cscript scregedit.wsf /CS 0**.
7. To verify the setting, type the following command: **cscript scregedit.wsf /CS /v**.
8. The output from the command reveals that the RDP-Tcp UserAuthentication setting is now set to 0. This setting enables connections from earlier versions of Remote Desktop.

   Type the following command: **netsh firewall show service**.

   This command displays the firewall exceptions that have been created for various services on Core1. In this case, the output verifies that a firewall exception has been created (enabled) for the Remote Desktop service in the Domain profile.
9. Log on as a domain administrator to Contoso.com from Server1.
10. In the Run box, type **mstsc**, and then press Enter.

    The Remote Desktop Connection window opens.
11. In the Computer text box, type **core1.contoso.com**, and then click Connect.
12. In the Windows Security window, enter the username and password of a domain administrator. Be sure to enter the name in this format: contoso*username*.

13. In the Windows Security window, click OK.

    After a few moments, a Remote Desktop connection to Core1 is established. The Remote Desktop connection shows the same Server Core desktop that you can see when you log on to Core1 locally.

14. On Server1, within the Remote Desktop session to Core1, type **logoff** at the command prompt.

    On Server1, the Remote Desktop session closes.

15. On Core1, type **shutdown /p** at the command prompt to shut down the computer.

Lesson Summary

- Terminal Services enables users to establish and interact with a desktop or application session on a remote computer running Terminal Services.

- Terminal Services shares its core functionality with that of Remote Desktop. In terms of its core functionality, the biggest difference between these two features is that when Remote Desktop is enabled, Windows Server 2008 allows only two concurrent desktop sessions (including any local console session). Terminal Services has no such limits.

- In Windows Server 2008, Terminal Services includes many new and important features such as TS Gateway, RemoteApp, and TS Web Access. (These topics are covered in detail in Chapter 4.)

- To install Terminal Services on a computer running Windows Server 2008, add the Terminal Services server role.

- Terminal Services requires client access licenses (CALs) either for all connecting users or for all connecting devices. If you do not purchase and install Terminal Services CALs, Terminal Services will stop working after 120 days.

Lesson Review

The following questions are intended to reinforce key information presented in this lesson. The questions are also available on the companion CD if you prefer to review them in electronic form.

NOTE Answers

Answers to these questions and explanations of why each answer choice is correct or incorrect are located in the "Answers" section at the end of the book.

---

1. You want to enable Remote Desktop on a Server Core installation of Windows Server 2008 and then enable the server to accept connections from clients configured with RDP versions prior to 6.0. Which commands should you use? (Choose two.)

   A. cscript scregedit.wsf /AR 0

   B. cscript scregedit.wsf /AR 1

   C. cscript scregedit.wsf /CS 0

   D. cscript scregedit.wsf /CS 1

2. You are 1 of 75 consultants employed by an IT services company named Contoso.com. As part of your job, you and other team members provide network support for over 150 businesses in your city. Your company is about to implement a business process in which consultants must connect to an application server on the Contoso.com network while working at customer premises. When connected to the application server, consultants provide critical information about each assignment in the field. To connect to the Contoso.com application server, consultants are expected to use Remote Desktop Connection on customer computers running Windows XP or Windows Vista. You have been asked to determine whether your company needs to purchase client access licenses (CALs) for Terminal Services. Which of the following options best suits the needs of your organization?

   A. Use Remote Desktop for Administration on the application server, and purchase per user CALs.

   B. Use Remote Desktop for Administration on the application server, but do not purchase any CALs.

   C. Install Terminal Services on the application server, and purchase per device CALs.

   D. Install Terminal Services on the application server, and purchase per user CALs.

Lesson 2: Configuring Terminal Services

The Terminal Services Configuration console is the main tool used to configure the Terminal Services role. The server options available in this tool primarily affect the user's environment when connecting to the local terminal server. Other options available in this tool, however, relate to server licensing and load balancing features. After describing all the options and features configurable in the Terminal Services Configuration console, this lesson describes supplementary configuration options available in Group Policy for one feature in particular: printer redirection.

After this lesson, you will be able to:
- Configure terminal server options.
- Configure Terminal Services load balancing.
- Install and configure a Terminal Services license server.

Estimated lesson time: 50 minutes

Introducing the Terminal Services Configuration Console

The Terminal Services Configuration (TSC) console is designed to control settings that affect all users connecting to the terminal server or all users connecting through certain connection types. For instance, you can use the TSC console to set the encryption level of all Terminal Services sessions, to configure the graphical resolution of sessions, or to restrict all users to one session. The TSC console is shown in Figure 3-11.

The TSC console provides two general areas for configuration: the connection (RDP-Tcp) properties dialog box and the Edit Terminal Server Settings area. The following sections describe the options available through each of these configuration areas.

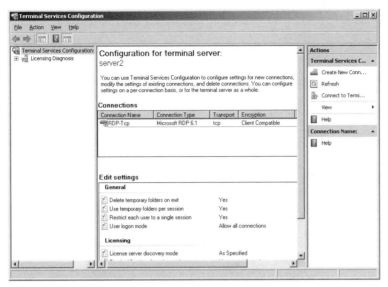

Figure 3-11   The Terminal Services Configuration console

Configuring Connection (RDP-Tcp) Properties

Connection properties are used to customize the behavior of all Terminal Services sessions initiated through certain specific transport protocols (such as RDP over TCP) or through specific network adapters on the terminal server. By default, only one connection (named RDP-Tcp) is available for configuration; the properties configured for this connection apply to RDP sessions through all local network adapters. Beyond this default connection, you can also create new connections that apply to third-party transport protocols or to particular adapters.

For environments using only the built-in functionality offered by Windows Server 2008, the RDP-Tcp connection normally will serve as the only connection, and the RDP-Tcp Properties dialog box provides key configuration options for the entire server.

To open the properties of the RDP-Tcp connection, in the TSC console Connections area, right-click RDP-Tcp, and then click Properties. This procedure opens the RDP-Tcp Properties dialog box, as shown in Figure 3-12.

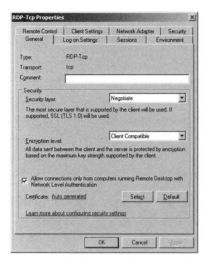

Figure 3-12 RDP-Tcp Properties General tab

The following section explains the configurable options available through each of the eight tabs.

Exam Tip Learn all the settings on the eight RDP-Tcp Properties tabs.

General Tab

The General tab enables you to modify settings in three security areas: security layer, encryption level, and NLA. These three areas are described in the following section.

Security Layer All RDP connections are encrypted automatically. Security layer settings determine the type of encryption used for these Terminal Services connections. Three options for the security level are available: RDP Security Layer, SSL (TLS 1.0), and Negotiate.

- The RDP Security Layer option limits encryption to the native encryption built into Remote Desktop protocol. The advantages of this option are that it requires no additional configuration and that it offers a high standard of performance. Its disadvantage is that it does not provide terminal server authentication for all client types. Although RDP 6.0 can provide server authentication for clients running Windows Vista and later, Terminal Services clients running Windows XP and earlier do not support server authentication. If you want to enable RDP clients running Windows XP to authenticate the terminal server before establishing a connection, you have to configure SSL encryption.

- The SSL (TSL 1.0) option offers two advantages over RDP encryption. First, it offers stronger encryption. Second, it offers the possibility of server authentication for RDP client versions earlier than 6.0. SSL is, therefore, a good option if you need to support terminal server authentication for Windows XP clients. However, this option does have some drawbacks. To begin with, SSL requires a computer certificate for both encryption and authentication. By default, only a self-signed certificate is used, which is equivalent to no authentication. To improve security, you must obtain a valid computer certificate from a trusted certification authority (CA), and you must store this certificate in the computer account certificate store on the terminal server. Another disadvantage of SSL is that its high encryption results in slower performance compared to that of other RDP connections.

- When you choose the Negotiate option, the terminal server will use SSL security only when supported by both the client and the server. Otherwise, native RDP encryption is used. Negotiate is also the default selection.

Encryption Level   The Encryption Level setting on the General tab enables you to define the strength of the encryption algorithm used in RDP connections. The default selection is Client Compatible, which chooses the maximum key strength supported by the client computer. The other available options are FIPS Compliant (highest), High, and Low.

Network Level Authentication   When the Allow Connections Only From Computers Running Remote Desktop With Network Level Authentication setting is enabled, only clients that support NLA will be allowed to connect to the terminal server.

To determine whether a computer is running a version of the Remote Desktop Connection (RDC) client that supports NLA, start the RDC client, click the icon in the upper-left corner of the Remote Desktop Connection dialog box, and then click About. Look for the phrase "Network Level Authentication Supported" in the About Remote Desktop Connection dialog box, shown in Figure 3-13.

Figure 3-13   Verifying NLA support

Logon Settings Tab

The Logon Settings tab, shown in Figure 3-14, enables you to configure all Terminal Services clients to use a single predefined username and password. Sharing credentials in this way enables users to connect to the terminal server without having to supply any credentials. Choosing this option might be suitable for testing environments or for public terminals.

When you select the Always Prompt For Password option, the user must always supply at least a password (if not the username) before connecting.

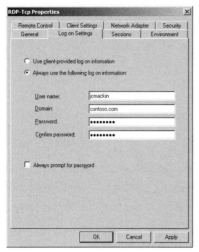

Figure 3-14   Configuring Terminal Services logon settings

Sessions Tab

You can use the Sessions tab to control session timeout settings for the terminal server. Specifically, this tab enables you to choose timeout settings for disconnected sessions, set time limits for active and idle sessions, and define the behavior for disconnections and session limits.

By default, these settings are defined not in this RDP-Tcp Properties dialog box but in each user's domain account properties. To override these user-defined settings, you can click the Override User Settings check box, as shown in Figure 3-15, and then choose options for the following policies:

- **End A Disconnected Session**   This setting determines when (if ever) a user is automatically logged off from a disconnected session.
- **Active Session Limit**   This setting determines how long a user can stay active within a Terminal Services session before automatically being disconnected.

- **Idle Session Limit**   This setting determines how long a user can leave an inactive connection open to a Terminal Services session before automatically being disconnected.
- **When Session Limit Is Reached Or Connection Is Broken**   This setting determines whether a user is logged off automatically when a connection is broken (manually or automatically).

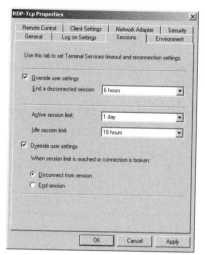

Figure 3-15   Terminal Service timeout and reconnection settings

Environment Tab

This tab enables you to control whether initial programs defined in a user's profile should be allowed to run automatically at the start of a Terminal Services session. It also enables you to specify a program to start for all users connecting to the local terminal server through RDP.

The Environment tab is shown in Figure 3-16.

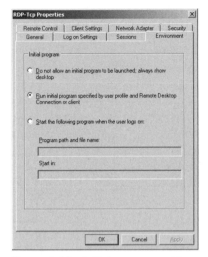

Figure 3-16 Initial program settings

Remote Control Tab

The remote control feature of Terminal Services enables an administrator to see or interact with another user's Terminal Services session. By default, the properties that define the behavior of this feature are set on a per-user basis in each user account's properties dialog box. (These properties define how an administrator can view or control that user's Terminal Services sessions.) The Remote Control tab enables you to control the settings of this feature on a per-server basis instead.

The default settings of a user account enable an administrator to interact with another user's Terminal Services session only if the user provides consent. However, you can use the Environment tab of the RDP-Tcp Properties dialog box to enable administrators to interact with (or merely to view) all user sessions with or without consent. You can also prevent administrators from viewing or interacting with other users' sessions completely.

IMPORTANT   Remote Control works only from remote session

You can use the Remote Control feature only from within an RDP session. If an administrator is logged on to a terminal server locally, the feature is disabled.

The Remote Control tab is shown in Figure 3-17.

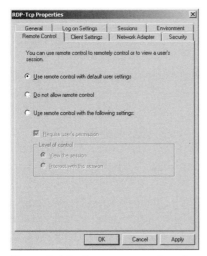

Figure 3-17   Remote control settings

Client Settings Tab

The Client Settings tab, shown in Figure 3-18, enables you to configure redirection of certain user interface features.

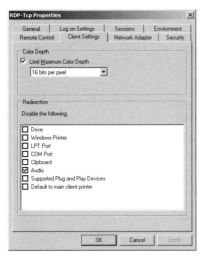

Figure 3-18   The Client Settings tab

In the Color Depth area of the tab, you can define the amount of color detail sent from the Terminal Server to the client. The default setting is 16 bits per pixel, but you can adjust this higher or lower. In general, when you require more bit depth for RDP connections, appearance is improved at the expense of performance.

In the Redirection – Disable The Following area of the tab, you can determine which features should not be redirected to the client. The advantage of disabling redirection is improved performance, but this improvement comes at the expense of the advantages offered by each particular feature that you choose to disable.

- **Drive**   When you select this option, the drives local to the client cannot be included in the Terminal Services connection. (To include the drives, this check box must be cleared, and the Drives option must be selected on the Local Resources tab of the Remote Desktop Connection client.)
- **Windows Printer**   When you select this option, printers local to the client cannot be accessed in the Terminal Services connection. However, a user can still connect to the client printer at the command prompt by using LPT port mapping or COM port mapping.
- **LPT Port**   Selecting this option prevents users from mapping a connection to an LPT printer.
- **COM Port**   Selecting this option blocks a connection from the Terminal Services session to COM devices on the client computer.
- **Clipboard**   This option, when selected, prevents users from cutting or copying data from a Remote Desktop (Terminal Services) session and then pasting that data into the local session on the client computer. Over slow connections, disabling clipboard redirection can prevent screen freezes.
- **Audio**   When enabled, this option prevents the transmission of audio data from the remote desktop to the local client computer. This is the only option that is selected by default.
- **Supported Plug and Play Devices**   This option, when selected, prevents Plug and Play devices local to the client from being redirected to a Terminal Services session.
- **Default to Main Client Printer**   When you select this option, the default printer assigned to the Terminal Services client is prevented from serving as the default printer for the Terminal Services session.

Network Adapter Tab

This tab enables you to restrict the default RDP-Tcp connection to listen for RDP connection attempts on only one particular network adapter. The tab also enables you to set a limit on the number of connections allowed by the terminal server. By default, no limit is set, as shown in Figure 3-19.

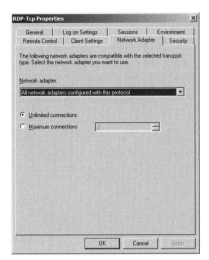

Figure 3-19   The Network Adapter tab

Security Tab

This tab enables you to set user permissions for all RDP connections to the terminal server. It is recommended that you do not use this tab to configure user access to Terminal Services; for that, use the Remote Desktop Users group instead. You should use this tab to determine which users should have administrative control (Full Control) of Terminal Services.

The Security tab is shown in Figure 3-20.

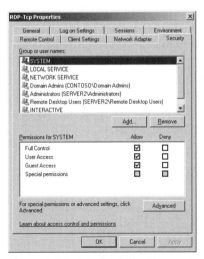

Figure 3-20   The RDP-Tcp Properties Security tab

Configuring Terminal Services Server Properties

Besides the RDP-Tcp Properties tabs, the TSC console offers a second important set of Terminal Services configuration options, available through the Edit Settings area. These settings apply to the entire terminal server only; unlike RDP-Tcp or other connection settings, they cannot be configured to apply merely to one transport protocol or to one particular network adapter.

The Edit Settings area provides a summary of seven terminal server options organized under three categories: General, Licensing, and TS Session Broker. To change these server options, double-click any one of them. This procedure opens a Properties dialog box whose three tabs are also named General, Licensing, and TS Session Broker.

The options available in these three tabs are explained in the following section.

General Tab

The General tab enables you to configure the following features related to user logon sessions:

- **Delete Temporary Folders On Exit**   When this option is enabled, as it is by default, all temporary data is deleted when a user logs off from a Terminal Services session. Deleting temporary data in this way decreases performance but improves privacy because it prevents users from potentially accessing another user's data.

  This setting functions only when the next option, Use Temporary Folders Per Session, is also enabled.

- **Use Temporary Folders Per Session**   Enabled by default, this option ensures that a new folder to store temporary data is created for each user session. When this option is disabled, temporary data is shared among all active sessions. Sharing temporary data among users can improve performance at the expense of user privacy.

- **Restrict Each User To a Single Session**   This option is enabled by default. When enabled, it allows only one logon session to the terminal server per user. For instance, if you are logged on to a server locally with the built-in Administrator account, you cannot log on to the same computer through a Remote Desktop connection by using the same Administrator account until you first log off the server locally.

  By ensuring that you log off one session before beginning another, this default setting prevents possible data loss in the user profile. It also prevents stranded user sessions and, therefore, conserves server resources.

- **User Logon Mode**   The settings in the User Logon Mode area enable you to prevent new users from logging on to the terminal server, for instance, in advance of a maintenance shutdown. The Allow All Connections option is the default setting. To prevent users from connecting to the terminal server indefinitely, you can select the Allow Reconnections, But Prevent New Logons option. To prevent users from connecting to the server only until you reboot the server, you can select the Allow Reconnections, But Prevent New Logons Until The Server Is Restarted option. Note that none of these options forces a session termination. If you need to reboot a server, you might need to end these sessions manually, as described in Chapter 4.

The General tab is shown in Figure 3-21.

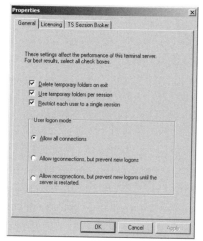

Figure 3-21   User Logon Mode settings

Exam Tip   The three settings available in the User Logon Mode area are new to Windows Server 2008. For this reason, you should expect to see at least one question about these options on the 70-643 exam. Also note that the feature to prevent new logons is sometimes called "Drain Mode."

Licensing Tab

The Licensing tab, shown in Figure 3-22, enables you to configure two features related to terminal server licensing: the licensing mode and the license server discovery mode.

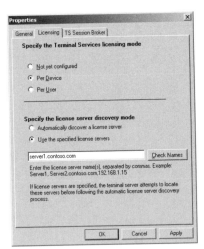

Figure 3-22   Server Options Licensing tab

- **Terminal Services licensing mode**   During the installation of the Terminal Services server role, you can specify the licensing mode of the terminal server or select the option to configure the licensing mode later. To set or reset the licensing mode after installation, select the Server Properties Licensing tab, and then choose the Per Device or Per User option in the Specify The Terminal Services Licensing Mode area.

- **License server discovery mode**   The license server discovery mode is the method by which a terminal server contacts a license server to obtain TS CALs. By default, the discovery mode is set to Automatically Discover A License Server. In the automatic license server discovery process, a terminal server attempts to contact any license servers published in Active Directory services or installed on domain controllers in the local domain. As an alternative to the automatic discovery mode, you can specify the license server manually by selecting the Use The Specified License Servers option and by then typing a license server name or address in the associated text box.

Exam Tip   In Active Directory Users and Computers, you can see a domain local security group called Terminal Server Computers. You can edit the membership of this group to restrict the terminal servers allowed to communicate with license servers in the domain.

TS Session Broker Settings Tab

The TS Session Broker Settings tab, shown in Figure 3-23, is used to configure settings for a member server in a TS Session Broker farm. TS Session Broker can be used to balance the session load among servers in a farm by directing new user sessions to the server in the farm with the fewest sessions. TS Session Broker is also used to ensure that users can reconnect automatically to disconnected sessions on the appropriate farm member server.

NOTE   TS Session Broker and Active Directory

The server on which you install TS Session Broker must be a member of a domain.

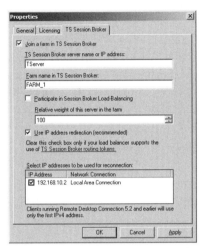

Figure 3-23   Configuring Terminal Services load balancing

To configure a terminal server farm, the first step is to install the TS Session Broker role service on a server that you want to use to track user sessions for the entire farm. This server becomes the TS Session Broker server. Then, you need to add the terminal servers in the farm to the Session Directory Computers local group on the TS Session Broker server. Finally, you have to configure the terminal servers to join the farm by configuring the following desired options on this tab:

- **Join A Farm In TS Session Broker**   Select this check box to add the local server to a farm and to make the remaining options available for configuration.
- **TS Session Broker Server Name Or IP Address**   In this text box, type the name or IP address of the server on which you have installed the TS Session Broker role service.
- **Farm Name In TS Session Broker**   In this text box, you must type the name of the farm that will be shared by all farm members. This name also represents the Domain Name System (DNS) name that clients will use to connect to the terminal server farm. (For this reason, in the appropriate DNS server, be sure to add multiple DNS records that correspond to this farm name and that specify the IP address of each farm member.)

- **Participate In Session Broker Load-Balancing**   Select this check box to configure the local server to participate in the load balancing feature enabled by TS Session Broker.

- **Relative Weight Of This Server In The Farm**   You can use this setting to give powerful servers a larger proportion of user sessions than less powerful servers. For example, if you assign a powerful server a weight of 200 and a less powerful server a weight of 100, the first server will receive twice the number of sessions as the second server.

- **Use IP Address Redirection (Recommended)**   Session Broker can use two methods to redirect a client to a disconnected session: IP address redirection and routing token redirection. IP address redirection is enabled by default and is suitable in most scenarios. This redirection method works when the clients can connect to each terminal server in the farm directly. Clear this check box only if your terminal services clients cannot connect to all terminal servers in the farm and when your network load balancing solution supports TS Session Broker routing tokens.

- **Select IP addresses to be used for reconnection**   Use this section to select the IP address that you want to enable for use in the terminal server farm.

Exam Tip   Remember to disable IP address redirection in TS Session Broker when your network includes a load balancer (usually a hardware load balancer) that supports routing tokens.

Exam Tip   For both the 70-643 exam and the real world, remember that you need to add each farm member to the Session Directory Computers local group on the TS Session Broker server.

IMPORTANT   TS Session Broker and load balancing initial connections

To distribute the initial connections to the server farm, TS Session Broker load balancing must rely on a load balancing solution such as DNS round-robin, Network Load Balancing, or a hardware load balancer.

Configuring Terminal Services Printer Redirection

Printer redirection is a feature that enables the client's printers to be used as printers for a Terminal Services session. Although you can easily modify basic options regarding printer redirection in the Client Settings tab of the RDP-Tcp Properties dialog box, Group Policy contains important additional options concerning this feature.

You can disable or customize the behavior of printer redirection by using Group Policy and the Group Policy Management console. To find printer redirection configuration options in Group Policy, open a Group Policy object (GPO), and navigate to Computer Configuration\Policies

\Administrative Templates\Windows Components\Terminal Services\Terminal Server\Printer Redirection. Within the Printer Redirection folder, you can configure the following five policy settings:

■ **Do Not Set Default Client Printer To Be Default Printer In A Session**   By default, Terminal Services automatically designates the client default printer as the default printer in a Terminal Services session. You can use this policy setting to override this behavior. If you enable this policy setting, the default printer in the Terminal Services session will be designated as the printer specified on the remote computer.

■ **Do Not Allow Client Printer Redirection**   This policy setting essentially disables printer redirection completely. If you enable this policy setting, users cannot redirect print jobs from the remote computer to a local client printer in Terminal Services sessions.

■ **Specify Terminal Server Fallback Printer Driver Behavior**   This policy setting determines the behavior that occurs when the terminal server does not have a printer driver that matches the client's printer. By default, when this occurs, no printer is made available within the Terminal Services session. However, you can use this policy setting to fall back to a Printer Control Language (PCL) printer driver, to a PostScript (PS) printer driver, or to both printer drivers.

■ **Use Terminal Services Easy Printer Driver First**   The Terminal Services Easy Printer driver enables users to print reliably from a terminal server session to the correct printer on their client computer. It also enables users to have a more consistent printing experience between local and remote sessions. By default, the terminal server first tries to use the Terminal Services Easy Printer driver to install all client printers. However, you can use this policy setting to disable the use of the Terminal Services Easy Printer driver.

■ **Redirect Only The Default Client Printer**   By default, all client printers are redirected to Terminal Services sessions. However, if you enable this policy setting, only the default client printer is redirected in Terminal Services sessions.

Exam Tip   Be sure to understand these Group Policy settings for the 70-643 exam.

Quick Check

1. You want to prepare to take a server in a server farm offline. You do not want to force any users off. What should you do?
2. You want to enable audio in Terminal Services connections to a server named TS1. What should you do?

Quick Check Answers
1. In the Terminal Services Configuration console, configure the terminal server properties to allow reconnections but prevent new logons.
2. Clear the Audio check box on the Client Settings tab in RDP-Tcp properties on TS1.

PRACTICE **Installing and Configuring a License Server**

After you have purchased TS CALs from Microsoft or a third-party reseller, you need to install and activate the license server. In this exercise, you will install a Terminal Services license server on Server1. Server1 will thus act as a license server for Server2, on which Terminal Services is already installed.

After installing the license server, you will then open the TS Licensing Manager console to review the procedures for activating a license server and installing TS CALs.

▶ **Exercise 1 Install the TS Licensing Server Role**

In this exercise, you will use the Add Roles Wizard to install a Terminal Services license server on the Contoso.com domain controller.

1. Log on to Contoso.com from Server1 as a domain administrator.
2. Open Server Manager.
3. In the Server Manager console tree, select the Roles node, and then click Add Roles in the details pane.
   The Add Roles Wizard opens.
4. On the Before You Begin page, click Next.
5. On the Select Server Roles page, select the Terminal Services check box, and then click Next.
6. On the Terminal Services page, click Next.
7. On the Select Role Services page, select the TS Licensing check box, and then click Next.
8. On the Configure Discovery Scope For TS Licensing page, read all the text on the page.
   Note that you can configure the license server for the local Active Directory domain or for the entire forest in a multidomain environment. The current Active Directory environment is composed of a single-domain forest.

Exam Tip Be sure to read this page carefully. For the exam, you need to understand the concepts of discovery scopes for TS licensing.

9. On the Configure Discovery Scope For TS Licensing page, leave the default selection of This Domain, and then click Next.

10. On the Confirm Installation Selections page, read all the text on the page, and then click Install.

    When the installation completes, the Installation Results page appears.

11. On the Installation Results page, click Close.

▶ **Exercise 2 Activate a Terminal Services Licensing Server**

In this exercise, you will activate the license server and review the process for installing TS CALs. This process requires Server1 to be connected to the Internet.

1. While you are logged on to Server1 as a domain administrator, open the TS Licensing Manager console by clicking Start, pointing to Administrative Tools, pointing to Terminal Services, and then clicking TS Licensing Manager.

   TS Licensing Manager opens.

   Although TS Licensing Manager is installed automatically on any server on which you have installed the TS Licensing role service, you do not need to manage the licensing server from the server itself. You can also install TS Licensing Manager on any server and connect to the license server remotely.

2. In the TS Licensing Manager console tree, expand the All Servers node, and then select the SERVER1 node. (The node should be marked by a red X at this point because it has not been activated.)

3. Right-click the SERVER1 node, and then click Activate Server.

   The Activate Server Wizard appears.

4. On the Welcome To The Activate Server Wizard page, read all the text on the page, and then click Next.

5. On the Connection Method page, read all the text on the page, and then answer the following question: By default, which is the default Connection Method assigned to the license server?

   Answer: Automatic Connection (Recommended)

6. On the Connection Method page, in the Connection Method drop-down list, select Web Browser.

7. Read the new associated Description and Requirements sections that have been refreshed on the page. The Web Browser connection method is useful when the licensing server does not connect to the Internet. With this option, you need merely to be able to connect from another server to both the licensing server and the Internet.

8. On the Connection Method page, in the Connection Method drop-down list, select Telephone.

9. Read the new associated Description and Requirements sections that have been refreshed on the page. The Telephone connection method is useful when your network is not connected to the Internet.

10. On the Connection Method page, in the Connection Method drop-down list, select Automatic Connection, and then click Next.

    The Activate Server Wizard dialog briefly appears while Server1 contacts the activation server at the Microsoft Clearinghouse. After a moment, the Company Information page appears.

11. On the Company Information page, enter appropriate information in the First Name, Last Name, and Company text boxes. Then, choose your country from the Country Or Region drop-down list.

12. Click Next.

13. Another Company Information page appears. Optionally, you may provide the requested information. Click Next.

    The Activate Server Wizard dialog box appears briefly, and then the Completing The Activate Server Wizard page appears. Note that the Start Install Licenses Wizard Now check box is selected.

14. On the Completing The Activate Server Wizard page, read all the text, and then click Next.

    The Welcome To The Install Licenses Wizard page appears.

15. Leave all windows open and proceed to Exercise 3.

▶ **Exercise 3 Review the Process to Install TS CALs**

Installing client licenses is the last stage of deploying a license server. Even if you do not have any TS CALs to install at this point, it is a good idea to review the pages of the Install Licenses Wizard to gain a better understanding of this deployment process in its entirety.

In this exercise, you will review the process of installing TS CALs in your newly activated server.

1. On the Welcome To The Install Licenses Wizard page, shown in Figure 3-24, read all the text on the page, and then click Next.

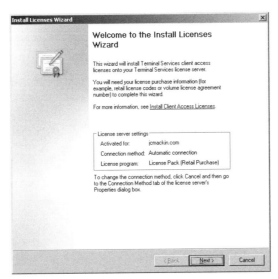

Figure 3-24   The Welcome page of the Install Licenses Wizard

The Install Licenses page briefly appears, and then the License Program page appears. The License Program page is shown in Figure 3-25.

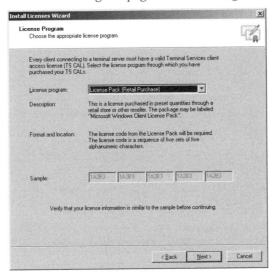

Figure 3-25   The License Program page of the Install Licenses Wizard

2. Read all the text on the License Program page.

3. Review the options from the License Program drop-down list.

4. Take a few moments to explore the various license program options by selecting each option and reading the entire associated text on the page.

5. In the License Program drop-down list, ensure that the default option of License Pack (Retail Purchase) is selected, and then click Next.

    The License Code page appears. The License Code page is shown in Figure 3-26.

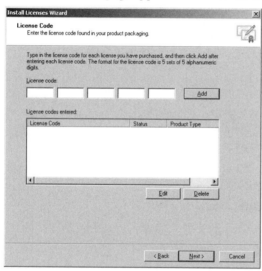

Figure 3-26   The License Code page of the Install Licenses Wizard

6. Read all the text on the page.

    If you have obtained a valid license code, you can perform the remaining steps of the practice. Otherwise, you can click Cancel to close the wizard and then simply read the remaining steps of the practice.

7. In the License Code text boxes, type a valid license code, and then click the Add button.

8. On the License Code page, click Next.

    The Install Licenses Wizard dialog box briefly appears, and then the Completing The Install Licenses Wizard page appears. This page is shown in Figure 3-27.

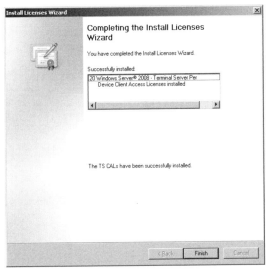

Figure 3-27   The Completing page of the Install Licenses Wizard

9. On the Completing The Install Licenses Wizard page, click Finish.

10. In the TS Licensing Manager console tree, the Server1 node is now designated with a green check mark, as shown in Figure 3-28. The licensing server is now configured.

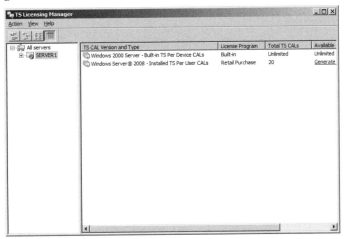

Figure 3-28   Successful deployment of a licensing server

11. Log on to Contoso.com from Server2 as a domain administrator, and then open the Terminal Services Configuration console.

12.   In the Edit Settings – Licensing area, double click the Terminal Services Licensing Mode option.

13.   On the Licensing tab of the Properties dialog box, select either the Per Device or the Per User option, corresponding to the type of TS CALs you have installed on Server1.

14.   In the Specify The License Server Discovery Mode area, select the Use The Specified License Servers option, and then type **Server1.contoso.com** in the associated text box.

15.   Click Check Names to verify the connection to the server.

16.   When you receive a message indicating that the server specified is a valid terminal server license server, click OK.

17.   In the Properties dialog box on Server2, click OK.

In the Terminal Services Configuration console, the Terminal Services Licensing Mode option is now specified as Per Device or Per User.

18.   Close all open windows, and then log off both Server1 and Server2.

Lesson Summary

■   The main tool used for configuring Terminal Services is the Terminal Services Configuration console.

■   You can edit RDP-Tcp properties in the Terminal Services Configuration console to configure Terminal Services session features such as encryption strength, timeout settings, and printer availability.

■   The Terminal Services server properties available in the Terminal Services Configuration console enable you to configure settings related to load balancing, license server discovery, temporary folders, and new logon prevention.

■   Group Policy offers additional control for Terminal Services printer redirection, notably for the option to fall back to a generic printer driver and to redirect only the default client printer.

Lesson Review

The following questions are intended to reinforce key information presented in this lesson. The questions are also available on the companion CD if you prefer to review them in electronic form.

NOTE   Answers

Answers to these questions and explanations of why each answer choice is correct or incorrect are located in the "Answers" section at the end of the book.

1. Your company network has implemented a terminal server farm named TSFARM1. The farm consists of five computers running Windows Server 2008, including a server named TSLB1 on which the TS Session Broker role service is installed. You want to add a sixth computer running Windows Server 2008, named TSLB6, to the farm. After configuring the server with the same hardware and software options as those of the other farm members, you join TSLB6 to the farm by specifying TSLB1 as the TS Session Broker Server and TSFARM1 as the farm name in the TS Session Broker properties on TSLB6. You verify that some users who attempt to connect to the virtual server name TSFARM1 are able to establish Terminal Services sessions on TSLB6, but these users are not able to reconnect to disconnected sessions. You want users connecting to TSLB6 through TSFARM1 to be able to reconnect to disconnected RDP sessions. What should you do?

   A. Add TSLB6 to the Session Directory Computers local group on TSLB6.

   B. Add TSLB6 to the Session Directory Computers local group on TSLB1.

   C. In the DNS server, add a Host (A) record named TSFARM1 that maps to the IP address of TSLB6.

   D. In the DNS server, add a Host (A) record named TSLB6 that maps to the IP address of TSLB6.

2. Your company network consists of a single Active Directory domain named Contoso.com. In the company network, you have deployed Terminal Services on a computer named TS1 that is running Windows Server 2008. Some users who connect to TS1 through RDP complain that they cannot print successfully to their local printers. You want to ensure that TS1 uses a generic PostScript printer driver whenever Terminal Services cannot find an adequate driver for Terminal Services client printers. What should you do?

   A. On the Client Session tab of RDP-Tcp properties on TS1, select the Windows Printer option.

   B. On the Client Session tab of RDP-Tcp properties on TS1, select the Default To Main Client Printer option.

   C. In a Group Policy object (GPO), configure the User Terminal Services Easy Printer Driver First policy setting, and then apply the GPO so that TS1 falls within the scope of the policy.

   D. In a Group Policy object (GPO), configure the Specify Terminal Server Fallback Printer Driver policy setting with the PS option, and then apply the GPO so that TS1 falls within the scope of the policy.

Chapter Review

To further practice and reinforce the skills you learned in this chapter, you can:

- Review the chapter summary.
- Review the list of key terms introduced in this chapter.
- Complete the case scenario. This scenario sets up a real-world situation involving the topics of this chapter and asks you to create solutions.
- Complete the suggested practices.
- Take a practice test.

Chapter Summary

- Terminal Services enables users to establish a desktop or application session on a remote computer. In Windows Server 2008, Terminal Services includes many new and important features such as TS Gateway, RemoteApp, and TS Web Access.
- Terminal Services requires client access licenses (CALs) either for all connecting users or for all connecting devices. If you do not purchase and install Terminal Services CALs, the feature will stop working after 120 days.
- To install Terminal Services on a computer running Windows Server 2008, add the Terminal Services server role.
- The main tool used for configuring Terminal Services is the Terminal Services Configuration (TSC) console. In the TSC console, you can edit RDP-Tcp properties to configure Terminal Services user session features such as encryption strength, timeout settings, and printer availability. You can also edit server properties to configure settings related to load balancing, license server discovery, and new logon prevention.

Key Terms

Do you know what these key terms mean? You can check your answers by looking up the terms in the glossary at the end of the book.

- Network Level Authentication (NLA)
- Printer Redirection
- Remote Desktop for Administration (RDA)
- Remote Desktop Protocol (RDP)
- Terminal Services connection
- Terminal Services session

- Terminal Services client access license (TS CAL)
- TS Session Broker

Case Scenarios

In the following case scenario, you will apply what you've learned in this chapter. You can find answers to these questions in the "Answers" section at the end of this book.

Case Scenario 1: Choosing a TS Licensing Strategy

You work as a network administrator in a large company. Your department has recently implemented two terminal servers, named TS1 and TS2, and you have been tasked with making licensing recommendations for each server.

TS1 is an application server. Although the application is not considered mission critical, as many as five users tend to be connected to it simultaneously. Overall, 20 users need to connect to TS1 at some point during the day. They can connect from any of 50 different computers.

TS2 is a DNS server that occasionally requires remote maintenance and administration. Only administrators connect to TS2.

1. Do you need to install Terminal Services on TS1? Which type of client access licenses would you purchase, if any?

2. Do you need to install Terminal Services on TS2? Which type of client access licenses would you purchase, if any?

Case Scenario 2: Troubleshooting a Terminal Services Installation

You work in IT support for a large company whose network consists of a single Active Directory domain. One of your responsibilities is supporting terminal servers in the Advertising department. Over the course of a week, you encounter the following two problems:

1. You deploy Terminal Services on a new computer running Windows Server 2008 named App3, but you discover that no users running Windows XP can connect to it. What should you do?

2. Users that connect to a terminal server named App1 complain that they cannot always reconnect to a disconnected session. What should you do?

Suggested Practices

To help you successfully master the exam objectives presented in this chapter, complete the following tasks.

Deploy a Terminal Server Farm

In this practice, you create a load balanced terminal server farm.

- **Practice**   Using either virtual or physical computers, join two identical installations of Windows Server 2008 to a domain. Install the Terminal Server role service on both computers but the TS Session Broker role service on just one. Add both computer names to the Session Directory Computers local group on the Session Broker computer. Use the TS Session Broker tab in the Terminal Services Configuration console on both computers to configure the Terminal Services farm. Create Host (A) records for the farm name in DNS, one record for each server IP address. Then, connect to the server farm through from a remote RDP client.

Watch a Webcast

In this practice, you watch a Webcast about Terminal Services in Windows Server 2008.

- **Practice**   Watch the "A Technical Overview of Windows Server 2008 Terminal Services" Webcast by Blain Barton, available on the companion CD in the Webcasts folder. This Webcast is also available online at *http://msevents.microsoft.com*; search for event ID 1032345660.

Take a Practice Test

The practice tests on this book's companion CD offer many options. For example, you can test yourself on just one exam objective, or you can test yourself on all the 70-643 certification exam content. You can set up the test so that it closely simulates the experience of taking a certification exam, or you can set it up in study mode so that you can look at the correct answers and explanations after you answer each question.

MORE INFO   **Practice tests**

For details about all the practice test options available, see the "How to Use the Practice Tests" section in this book's introduction.

Chapter 4

Configuring and Managing a Terminal Services Infrastructure

This chapter moves beyond the topic of deploying a terminal server and discusses how to configure the components that comprise an entire Terminal Services infrastructure—clients, servers, gateways, and applications.

Even more than other Microsoft Windows Server technologies, Terminal Services components are best understood by working with them directly. With this idea in mind, be sure to perform the extensive practices at the end of each lesson to develop the skills you need for both the exam and the real world.

Exam objectives in this chapter:
- Configuring Terminal Services
    - Configure Terminal Services client connections.
    - Configure Terminal Services Gateway.
    - Configure Windows Server 2008 Terminal Services RemoteApp (TS RemoteApp).
    - Configure and monitor Terminal Services resources.

Lessons in this chapter:

Before You Begin

To complete the lessons in this chapter, you must have:

- A computer running Windows Server 2008 named Server1 that is a domain controller in a domain named Contoso.com.
- A computer running Windows Server 2008 named Server2 that is a member server in the Contoso.com domain. On Server2, the Terminal Server role service is installed, but no other role services in the Terminal Services role are installed.
- Three domain administrator accounts, named ContosoAdmin1, ContosoAdmin2, and ContosoAdmin3.

Real World

JC Mackin

Virtualization is a big IT trend these days, and Terminal Services represents a part of this trend by offering what has been called *presentation virtualization*. Anything related to virtualization sounds like a cool thing today, but what's the actual purpose of this technology? What problem is it trying to fix?

Beyond the hype, a real-world benefit of a presentation virtualization is its ability to assist in server consolidation. Recently, many IT departments have started to consolidate their application servers with a view to improving efficiency and lowering costs. Server consolidation is essentially the process of centralizing the resources of many servers onto as few physical servers as possible. Terminal Services is a key component of such an application consolidation strategy because it enables many users to access many applications on a single server.

Lesson 1: Configuring and Managing Terminal Services Clients

A Terminal Services (TS) infrastructure includes many areas for client configuration, areas such as user profiles, client session options, resource allocation, and the TS client program (Mstsc) itself.

This lesson introduces you to tools you can use to administer these and other aspects of TS clients connections.

After this lesson, you will be able to:
- Understand the configuration options available in Remote Desktop Connection.
- Manage connections to Terminal Services.

Estimated lesson time: 50 minutes

Configuring Terminal Services Client Settings

The Terminal Services client, Remote Desktop Connection (RDC), is highly configurable. For example, you can configure the client to display remote desktops with a certain screen resolution or to make certain local drives available in the session. These features can be configured in the client application itself or at the domain level by using a Group Policy Object (GPO).

Configuring Remote Desktop Connection Options

RDC, also known as Mstsc.exe, is the primary client program used to connect to Terminal Services. The other client program is Remote Desktops, which is available as a snap-in through Microsoft Management Console (MMC). Through its options tabs, RDC enables you to customize a Terminal Services connection within the limitations set at the server or in Group Policy.

To explore the configuration options available through RDC, open RDC, and then click the Options button, as shown in Figure 4-1.

Figure 4-1   Accessing RDC options tabs

This step reveals the six RDC options tabs. The following section describes the features you can configure on these RDC options tabs.

- **General**   The General tab, shown in Figure 4-2, enables you to define a target computer and a set of authentication credentials for the connection. It also enables you to save the options defined for the connection in an RDP (Remote Desktop) file.

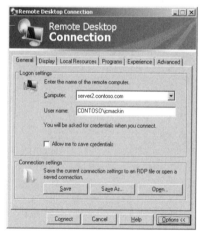

Figure 4-2   RDC General tab

- **Display**   The Display tab, shown in Figure 4-3, enables you to define the screen resolution and color bit depth for the TS client window.

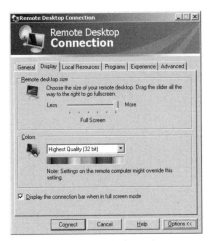

Figure 4-3   RDC Display tab

■ **Local Resources**   The Local Resources tab enables you to choose which local resources (such as the Clipboard, any locally defined printers, and any local drives) should be made available within the TS session. This tab also enables you to determine the behavior of features such as sounds and keystrokes in the TS session.

The Local Resources tab is shown in Figure 4-4.

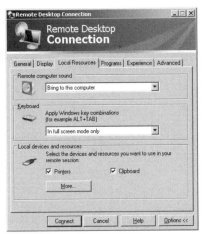

Figure 4-4   RDC Local Resources tab

■ **Programs**   This tab enables you to define any program you want to start automatically when the TS connection begins.

The Programs tab is shown in Figure 4-5.

Figure 4-5   RDC Programs tab

■ **Experience**   The Experience tab, shown in Figure 4-6, enables you to choose which optional graphical user interface (GUI) effects you want to display from the terminal server. For example, the Desktop background and font smoothing features visually enhance the TS session but can also strain network resources and slow TS client performance. Performance settings will be selected automatically, as a suggestion, when you choose a connection type.

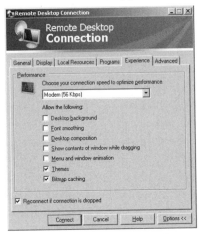

Figure 4-6   RDC Experience tab

■ **Advanced**   The Advanced tab, shown in Figure 4-7, enables you to configure client behavior for the Server Authentication and Terminal Services Gateway (TS Gateway) features. Server Authentication is a feature, native to Windows Vista and Windows Server

2008, through which a terminal server can confirm that its identity is the computer specified by the TS client. On the Advanced tab, you can configure a TS client to warn, block, or enable a connection to a server on which Server Authentication has failed.

The Terminal Services Gateway feature enables a TS client to traverse a corporate firewall and connect to any number of terminal servers in an organization. This feature and its configuration are described in detail in Lesson 2, "Deploying Terminal Services Gateway."

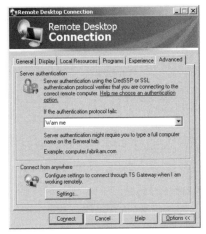

Figure 4-7   RDC Advanced tab

Saving RDP Files

After you have defined the desired options for a TS client in RDC, these settings are saved automatically in the Documents folder to a hidden file named Default.rdp. This file contains the settings used for RDC when you open the program from the Start menu. However, you can also save TS client configuration settings in custom .rdp files by clicking the Save As button on the General tab. These .rdp files can then be used to initiate TS sessions with specific client options (such as server name and authentication information).

Exam Tip   On the 70-643 exam, expect to see a question about saving RDC settings in an .rdp file. Be sure to review the settings on all the RDC options tabs so that you understand the kind of configuration details that can be saved in such a file.

Configuring Terminal Services Clients Through Group Policy

Group Policy enables you to enforce settings centrally on users or computers in an Active Directory environment. As a way to manage many TS clients, you can use a GPO to ensure that Remote Desktop Connection is always configured with the settings you choose. In many cases, this is the most efficient and effective way to manage TS clients.

In the Computer Configuration section of a GPO, you can specify client settings such as whether the passwords should be saved in RDC, whether the client should always be prompted for credentials, how server authentication should be performed, and which resources should be redirected to the TS session. You can explore these settings in a GPO by browsing to Computer Configuration\Policies\Administrative Templates\Windows Components\Terminal Services.

In the User Configuration section of a GPO, you can configure settings related to session time limits, remote control, and the remote session environment. You can explore these settings in a GPO by browsing to User Configuration\Policies\Administrative Templates\Windows Components\Terminal Services.

Single Sign-on   A particularly useful Terminal Services client feature that you can configure in Group Policy is Single Sign-on (SSO). In an Active Directory domain environment, you can use SSO to eliminate the need to enter user credentials when you use RDC to connect to a terminal server. With SSO, instead of prompting for your credentials, RDC automatically uses the credentials of the user currently logged on to the local computer running Microsoft Windows.

To configure SSO, enable the Allow Delegating Saved Credentials policy setting, which you can find in Computer Configuration\Policies\Administrative Templates\System\Credentials Delegation. After enabling the policy, you then need to create in the same policy a server list that specifies the terminal servers that will accept SSO credentials. Add each server name in the form TERMSRV/<Your server name>. To enable all terminal servers within the scope of the policy to accept SSO credentials, you can add the entry TERMSRV/*.

Exam Tip   For the 70-643 exam, you need to understand only that Group Policy provides the best method to enforce a TS or RDC configuration for many users and computers. You do not need to memorize all the configurable options or where to find them. However, it is still a good idea to browse through these options to get a sense of the ones that are enforceable in an Active Directory environment.

Configuring User Profiles for Terminal Services

In general terms, a *user profile* simply refers to the collection of data that comprises a user's individual environment—data including a user's individual files, application settings, and desktop configuration. In more specific terms, a *user profile* also refers to the contents of the personal folder, automatically created by Windows, that bears the name of an individual user. By default, this personal folder is created in the C:\Users folder when a user logs on for the first time to a computer running Windows Vista or Windows Server 2008. It contains subfolders such as Documents, Desktop, and Downloads as well as a personal data file named Ntuser.dat. For example, by default, a user named StefanR will store the data that makes up his personal environment in a folder named C:\Users\StefanR.

In a Terminal Services environment, user profiles are stored on the terminal server by default. This point is important because when many users access the terminal server, profiles are centralized and can consume a large amount of server disk space. If storage space on the terminal server is insufficient, plan to store user data and profiles on a disk that is separate from the operating system installation disk drive. Also consider using disk quotas to limit the amount of space available to each user. (You can configure disk quotas through the properties of the drive on the terminal server where the profiles are stored.)

Exam Tip   For the 70-643 exam, you need to know you can use disk quotas to limit the size of user profiles in Terminal Services.

Another way to manage TS user profiles is to configure users with a Terminal Services–specific roaming user profile that is stored on a central network share. Such a profile is downloaded to the user's TS session whenever and wherever such a session is initiated. This TS-specific roaming user profile can be defined on the Terminal Services Profile tab of a user account's properties, as shown in Figure 4-8. Alternatively, you can use Group Policy to define these TS roaming user profiles. (You can find Terminal Services profile settings in a GPO in Computer Configuration \Policies\Administrative Templates\Windows Components\Terminal Services\Terminal Server\Profiles. The specific policy setting used to configure TS-specific roaming user profiles is named Set Path For TS Roaming User Profile.)

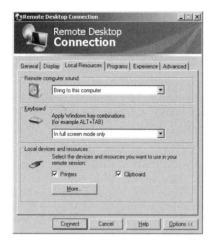

Figure 4-8   Configuring a TS-specific roaming user profile

CAUTION   Roaming user profiles and Terminal Services

Ordinary roaming user profiles are those that follow a user as he or she logs on and off from various computers in a Windows domain. Ordinary roaming user profiles should not be used for Terminal Services sessions because they can lead to unexpected data loss or corruption. If you have configured roaming user profiles in your organization, be sure to implement TS-specific user profiles as well.

Configuring Home Folders

When a user chooses to save a file, the default path points to a location known as the *home folder*. For Terminal Services, the home folder by default is located on the terminal server. However, it is usually helpful to configure the home folder either on the local disk drive or on a network share. Configuring the home folder in this way ensures that users can locate their saved files easily. As with TS-specific roaming user profiles, you can define home folder locations for Terminal Services either in the properties of the user account or in Group Policy. (Home folder settings for Terminal Services can be found in a Group Policy object in Computer Configuration \Policies\Administrative Templates\Windows Components\Terminal Services\Terminal Server\Profiles. The policy setting used to configure home folders is named Set TS User Home Directory.)

Quick Check

1. Where is the default location of the user profile for a TS user?
2. What is the most efficient way of configuring RDC options for many users in your organization?

Quick Check Answers

1. On the terminal server
2. Group Policy

Managing Terminal Services User Connections

Terminal Services Manager (TSM) is the main administrative tool used to manage connections to a terminal server. You can use TSM to view information about users connected to a terminal server, to monitor user sessions, or to perform administrative tasks such as logging users off or disconnecting user sessions.

To open TSM from the Start menu, point to Administrative Tools, point to Terminal Services, and then click Terminal Services Manager. You can also open TSM by typing **tsadmin.msc** in the Start Search or Run boxes on the Start menu.

The next section reviews the main management tasks you can perform in TSM and provides many command-line alternatives for these management tasks. To learn more about using TSM, be sure to perform the exercises at the end of this lesson.

Exam Tip   Although TSM is the main tool used to manage TS user connections, most of the management functions provided also have command-line equivalents. Be sure to learn the GUI *and* command-line versions of all the functions described in this section.

TSM is shown in Figure 4-9.

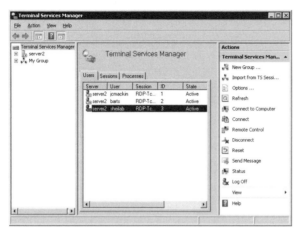

Figure 4-9   The Terminal Services Manager console

TSM provides three tabs from which to view and manage Terminal Services connections: Users, Sessions, and Processes.

- The Users tab displays information about users connected to the terminal server, information such as the currently logged on user accounts, the time of the user's logon to the server, and the session status.

  To display information about user sessions on a terminal server, you can also use the *Query user* or *Quser* command-line commands.

MORE INFO   Use the /? switch for more info

To learn more about any of the command-line tools introduced in this section, simply type the command at the command prompt with the **/?** switch. For example, to learn the syntax for Quser, type **quser /?**.

- The Sessions tab provides information about the sessions connected to the terminal server. Because some sessions are initiated by services or by the operating system, sessions typically outnumber users.

  To display information about sessions on a terminal server, you can also use the *Query session* command.

- The Processes tab displays information about which programs each user is running on the terminal server.

  To display information about processes that are running on the terminal server, you can also use the *Query process* or *Qprocess* command.

Managing User Sessions

To manage user sessions in TSM, simply right-click a user shown on the Users tab, and then select any of the seven command options available on the shortcut menu. Alternatively, you can select a user, and then click an action available on the Actions menu. Both of these options are shown in Figure 4-10.

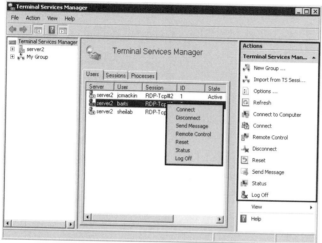

Figure 4-10   The Terminal Services Manager user session commands

The following section describes the seven management options available on the user session shortcut menu, along with their command-line tool equivalents.

- **Connect**   You can use the *Connect* command to reconnect to your own active or disconnected user session. (This scenario is possible only when you have configured the terminal server to accept multiple sessions from the same user.) In addition, if you have been granted the Full Control or Connect special access permission on the server's RDP-Tcp connection (configured in the Terminal Services Configuration console), you can also use this command to connect to the active or disconnected session of another user.

  As an alternative to using TSM to connect to a TS client session, you can also use the *Tscon* command-line command.

IMPORTANT   Using the Connect feature in TSM

You must be connected to the terminal server in a client session to use the Connect feature in TSM. The feature is disabled in TSM when you are logged on locally to the terminal server. (A local logon session is also known as a *console session*.)

- **Disconnect** You can use the *Disconnect* command in the Actions pane or on the shortcut menu to disconnect a user from a session. When you disconnect a user from a session, all the programs and processes running in the session continue to run. Therefore, too many disconnected sessions can drain terminal server resources and slow server performance.

  As an alternative to using TSM to disconnect a TS client session, you can also use the *Tsdiscon* command-line tool.

  Disconnecting another user from a session requires the Full Control or Disconnect special access permission on the server's RDP-Tcp connection.

- **Send Message** The *Send Message* command enables you to send a simple console message to a user connected to a terminal server. Use this command, for example, when you need to warn a user that he or she is about to be disconnected or logged off.

  To send a message to a user on a terminal server, you can also use the *Msg* command-line tool.

  Sending a message to another user in Terminal Services requires the Full Control or Message special access permission on the server's RDP-Tcp connection.

- **Remote Control** The *Remote Control* command enables you to view or control another user's TS client session. (You can configure the behavior of the Remote Control feature in the Terminal Services Configuration console, the Remote Control tab of a user account's properties, or in Group Policy.)

  You can also use the *Shadow* command-line tool to control an active session of another user on a terminal server remotely.

  To control another user's session remotely, you must be assigned the Full Control or Remote Control special access permission on the server's RDP-Tcp connection.

IMPORTANT Using the Remote Control feature in TSM

You must be connected to the terminal server in a client session to use the Remote Control feature in TSM. The feature is disabled in TSM when you are logged on locally to the terminal server in a console session.

- **Reset** Resetting a Terminal Services session deletes that session immediately without saving any session data. Reset a session only when it appears to have stopped responding.

  You can also use the *Rwinsta* or *Reset session* command-line command to reset a user session on a terminal server.

  Resetting another user's TS session requires the Full Control access permission on the server's RDP-Tcp connection.

■ **Status**   When you right-click a user session shown on the Users tab and then select the *Status* command from the shortcut menu, the Status dialog box appears, containing additional status information about the session. This information includes the TS client's IP address, computer name, and total bytes transmitted during the session. Figure 4-11 shows such a status dialog box.

Figure 4-11   The Terminal Services Manager Status dialog box

To view the status of another user's session, you must be granted the Full Control or Query Information special access permission on the server's RDP-Tcp connection.

■ **Log Off**   Logging off a user ends all user processes and then deletes the session from the terminal server. If you want to log off a user, send the user a message first. Otherwise, the user could lose unsaved session data.

Besides using TSM to log off a user, you can also use the *Logoff* command-line command.

To log off another user from a session, you must have the Full Control permission on the server's RDP-Tcp connection.

Ending a TS User Session Process

You can use the Processes tab in TSM to force a particular process in a user session to close. This might be necessary, for example, if a certain application is hanging in a user session and is causing a screen freeze. To end a process for this reason or any other, simply right-click the process in question, and then click End, as shown in Figure 4-12.

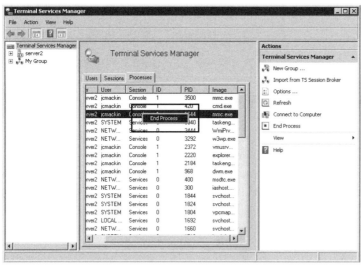

Figure 4-12 Ending a process in a TS user session

To end a process within a terminal services user session, you can also use the *Tskill* command-line command.

Quick Check

- On a terminal server, what is a console session?

Quick Check Answer

- The console session is the session of the locally logged-on user.

Managing Resources in Client Sessions

You can use the Windows Server Resource Manager (WSRM) feature in Windows Server 2008 to ensure that each client connecting to a terminal server is granted equal access to the server's resources. To use WSRM, you must first install it by opening Server Manager, selecting the Features node, and then clicking Add Features. You can then use the Add Features Wizard to select the feature and proceed with the installation. Once the tool is installed, you can access WSRM through Administrative Tools.

WSRM uses Resource Allocation Policies to determine how computer resources are allocated to processes running on the computer. At any given time, only one Resource Allocation Policy is considered the *managing policy* or the policy in effect.

Four Resource Allocation Policies are built into WSRM, and two are specifically designed for computers running Terminal Services:

- **Equal_Per_User**   When this policy is set as the managing policy, available CPU bandwidth is shared equally among users. For example, if two users are running multiple applications that consume 100 percent of the allocated CPU bandwidth, WSRM will lower the priority of processes run by the user who exceeds 50 percent CPU usage. In this policy, the number of terminal services sessions owned by each user is not considered.

- **Equal_Per_Session**   If you implement the Equal_Per_Session resource-allocation policy, each user session (and its associated processes) gets an equal share of the CPU resources on the computer. For example, if two users each own two separate user sessions on a terminal server and consume 100 percent of the allocated CPU bandwidth, WSRM will lower the priority of the processes run in the terminal services session that exceeds 25 percent CPU usage.

In general, you can think of these built-in Resource Allocation Policies in WSRM as a simple means to ensure that no single user or session consumes more than an equal share of the server's available resources. However, you can also use WSRM to create custom Resource Allocation Policies. When you create custom Resource Allocation Policies, you define *Process Matching Criteria* that specify services, processes, or applications on the local server. In the Resource Allocation Policy, you can then allocate a certain amount of CPU or memory resources to those chosen services, processes, or applications.

Exam Tip   You need to understand the Equal_Per_User and Equal_Per_Session Resource Allocation Policies for the 70-643 exam. You also need to understand the general role that Process Matching criteria play in a custom Resource Allocation Policy.

PRACTICE Managing Client Connections

In this practice, you will use the TSM console to view, control, and end Terminal Services user sessions.

▶ Exercise 1 View Terminal Services Sessions

In this exercise, you will use the TSM console to view Terminal Services sessions from within a console (local logon) session. This practice requires the use of three separate domain administrator accounts. In the following steps, these accounts are named ContosoAdmin1, ContosoAdmin2, and ContosoAdmin3, respectively.

1. Log on to Contoso.com from Server2 as ContosoAdmin1.
2. Open Terminal Services Manager by clicking Start, Administrative Tools, and Terminal Services and then clicking Terminal Services Manager.

3. If a Terminal Services Manager message box appears, read all the text, and then click OK.

4. In the console tree, select the Server2 node.

   The details pane within the middle portion of the console is named Manage Terminal Server: server2. This area contains three tabs: Users, Sessions, and Processes.

5. Verify that the Users tab in the center pane is selected, and then answer the following questions.

   How many users are currently connected?

   Answer: One

   What is the session type associated with the listed user(s)?

   Answer: Console

   Is this session type associated with a local or remote user?

   Answer: Local

6. Right-click the user displayed on the Users tab, and then answer the following questions.

   Which commands are available from the shortcut menu?

   Answer: *Disconnect*, *Send Message*, and *Log Off*

   Which commands listed on the shortcut menu are not available?

   Answer: *Connect*, *Remote Control*, *Reset*, and *Status*

   Why are these commands unavailable?

   Answer: *Connect* and *Remote Control* cannot be performed from within a console session. *Reset* and *Status* can be performed only on another user session.

7. Log on to Contoso.com from Server1 as ContosoAdmin2.

8. On Server1, open the Remote Desktop Connection client.

9. In the Computer text box, type **server2.contoso.com**, and then click Connect.

10. In the Windows Security dialog box, enter the credentials of ContosoAdmin2, and then click OK. Be sure to type the user account in the form **contoso\contosoadmin2**.

11. On Server1, minimize the Remote Desktop window.

12. On Server1, open another instance of Remote Desktop Connection.

13. In the Computer text box in Remote Desktop Connection, type **server2.contoso.com**, and then click Connect.

14. In the Windows Security dialog box, click Use Another Account.

15. Use the text boxes to enter the credentials of ContosoAdmin3, and then click OK. Be sure to enter the username in the form **contoso\contosoadmin3**.

16. Return to TSM on Server2. Refresh the Users tab by clicking Refresh in the Actions pane.

17. Answer the following questions:

    How many user sessions are now visible on the Users tab?

    Answer: Three

    What is the session type associated with the ContosoAdmin2 and ContosoAdmin3 sessions?

    Answer: RDP-Tcp

    Which two commands are available for the RDP-Tcp sessions that are not available for the console session?

    Answer: *Reset* and *Status*

    What is the difference between the *Reset* and *Log Off* commands?

    Answer: Both commands disconnect and end a session. However, the *Reset* command deletes a session immediately without logging off the user.

18. Leave all windows open and proceed to Exercise 2.

▶ **Exercise 2 Manage Terminal Services Sessions**

In this exercise, you will manage one Terminal Services session from within another. This practice assumes that you have two active Terminal Services sessions from Server1 to Server2.

1. Return to Server1.

2. In the ContosoAdmin2 Remote Desktop session, open TSM. (You can use the Start menu to help you distinguish between the two Remote Desktop sessions.)

3. Answer the following question: Which is the only user session on the Users tab that is designated by a green arrow pointing upward?

    Answer: The ContosoAdmin2 user session.

4. On Server1, switch to the ContosoAdmin3 Remote Desktop window. If the screen is locked, provide credentials so that you can see the Server2 desktop again.

5. Mark the ContosoAdmin3 desktop in some way so that you can recognize it as belonging to ContosoAdmin3. For example, you can save a Notepad file named ADMIN3 on the desktop.

6. Switch back to the ContosoAdmin2 Remote Desktop window. In TSM, right-click the ContosoAdmin3 user session, and then click Remote Control.

7. In the Remote Control dialog box, read the entire text, and then click OK.

8. Switch to the ContosoAdmin3 Remote Desktop window.

    The Remote Control Request dialog box appears. The dialog box informs you that ContosoAdmin2 is requesting to control your session remotely and asks you whether you accept the request.

9. In the Remote Control Request box, click Yes.

10. Switch back to the ContosoAdmin2 remote desktop session.

    The ContosoAdmin3 desktop is now visible in the ContosoAdmin2 session.

11. From the remote control window, perform any action, such as opening Notepad. ContosoAdmin2 is now able to control the ContosoAdmin3 desktop.

12. Switch to Server2.

13. On the Users tab in TSM, right-click the ContosoAdmin3 session, and then click Log Off.

14. In the Terminal Services Manager dialog box, click OK to confirm the choice.

    The ContosoAdmin3 session is ended. (To see the user session disappear from the list, you might need to click Refresh.)

15. On the Users tab in TSM, right-click the ContosoAdmin2 session, and then click Disconnect.

16. In the Terminal Services Manager dialog box, click OK to confirm the choice.

    The ContosoAdmin2 session state changes from Active to Disconnected. (To see this change, you might need to click Refresh.)

17. Leave all windows open and proceed to Exercise 3.

▶ **Exercise 3 Reconnect to a Disconnected Session**

In this exercise, you will reconnect to a disconnected session. You will then attempt a second connection to the terminal server with the same username and observe the effects.

1. In the TSM console on Server2, click the Sessions tab.

   The Sessions tab shows that the ContosoAdmin2 session is disconnected.

2. Click the Processes tab.

   The Processes tab shows that many processes from the ContosoAdmin2 session are still running.

3. Right-click any of the processes listed.

   The shortcut menu that appears provides the option to end the process. You can perform the same function with the End Process option in the Actions pane on the right side of the TSM console. You can also perform this function with the *Tskill* command-line command.

4. Without choosing to end the process you have selected, switch to Server1.

   The Remote Desktop Disconnected message box has appeared, informing you that the ContosoAdmin2 remote desktop session has ended.

5. In the Remote Desktop Disconnected message dialog box, click OK.

   The Remote Desktop Connection window appears on the desktop.

6. Use the Remote Desktop Connection client and the credentials for ContosoAdmin2 to establish a new connection to Server2 from Server1.

7. Switch to Server2.

8. In the TSM console on Server2, click the Users tab.

   Note that the ContosoAdmin2 session is listed as Active again.

9. Switch to Server1.

10. Minimize the current Remote Desktop window on Server1.

11. Open Remote Desktop Connection by using the Start menu.

12. Use the ContosoAdmin2 credentials to attempt to create a second Terminal Services session to Server2.

13. Investigate all open windows on Server1 and Server2, and then answer the following question: Were you able to establish a second simultaneous Terminal Services session to Server2?

   Answer: No. The second connection attempt merely took over the active user session, and the first connection was deleted.

14. Switch to Server2.

15. Open the Terminal Services Configuration (TSC) console by clicking Start, Administrative Tools, and Terminal Services and then clicking Terminal Services Configuration.

16. In the center pane of the TSC console, under the Edit Settings – General area, double-click the Restrict Each User To A Single Session option.

17. In the Properties dialog box, clear the Restrict Each User To A Single Session check box, and then click OK.

18. If a Terminal Services Configuration error message appears, read the message, and then click OK.

19. Return to Server1 and once again attempt to establish a second Remote Desktop connection to Server2 by using the ContosoAdmin2 credentials.

   The second Remote Desktop connection is established. In the TSM console on Server2, if you click Refresh, you can see that two sessions from ContosoAdmin2 are now listed as Active.

   When you enable simultaneous sessions to a computer running Terminal Services, you leave open the possibility of stranded sessions.

20. On Server2, use TSM to log off the first ContosoAdmin2 session and to reset the second.

21. On Server2, use the TSC console to re-enable the option to restrict each user to a single session.

22. On both Server1 and Server2, close all open windows and log off all users.

Lesson Summary

- You can configure TS client settings at the client by using Remote Desktop Connection options or at the domain level by using a Group Policy object (GPO).

- When users connect to a terminal server, their profiles are stored on the remote server by default. As a result, when many users access the terminal server, profiles can consume a large amount of disk space. To remedy this, you can use disk quotas.

- You can manage a TS user profile by configuring a Terminal Services–specific roaming user profile that is stored on a central network share. This TS-specific roaming user profile can be defined on the Terminal Services Profile tab of a user account's properties or in Group Policy.

- Terminal Services Manager (TSM) is the main administrative tool used to manage connections to a terminal server. You can use TSM to view information about users connected to a terminal server, to monitor user sessions, or to perform administrative tasks such as logging users off or disconnecting user sessions.

- You can use Windows System Resource Manager (WSRM) to allocate a terminal server's resources equally among users or sessions.

Lesson Review

The following questions are intended to reinforce key information presented in this lesson. The questions are also available on the companion CD if you prefer to review them in electronic form.

NOTE   Answers

Answers to these questions and explanations of why each answer choice is correct or incorrect are located in the "Answers" section at the end of the book.

---

1. TS1 is a server running Windows Server 2008 and Terminal Services. Users in your organization connect to the server TS1 to run a line-of-business application. Recently, you have noticed that user profiles are threatening to consume the total disk capacity on TS1. You want users to be able to save their own data, but you also want to prevent profiles from exhausting the total storage capacity of the disk on TS1. What should you do?

    A. Use Group Policy to assign mandatory profiles to users who connect to TS1.

    B. Configure disk quotas for the disk on TS1 on which user profiles are stored.

    C. Use Group Policy to assign Terminal Services roaming user profiles to users who connect to TS1.

    D. Configure disk quotas for the local disk of each user who connects to TS1.

2. TS3 is a server running Windows Server 2008 and Terminal Services. You have the responsibility of supporting users who connect to TS3 to run various applications. Users complain that the application is responding slowly. You use the *quser* command on TS3 and discover that many users have multiple disconnected sessions on the server with idle times of two days or more. You want to reduce the strain on the TS3 by eliminating disconnected sessions that have been idle for more than two days. What should you do?

    A. Use the *Rwinsta* command.

    B. Use the *Tsdicon* command.

    C. Use the *Tskill* command.

    D. Use the *Tscon* command.

Lesson 2: Deploying Terminal Services Gateway

Terminal Services Gateway (TS Gateway) enables authorized users to establish connections to terminal servers located behind a firewall. As simple as this idea sounds, the implications of TS Gateway are surprisingly important. Before, you had to use a virtual private network (VPN) to connect to resources on a private network from the Internet. Now, you can connect to even more resources—including terminal server desktops and published applications—with a technology that is actually easier to implement.

This lesson introduces you to TS Gateway and then describes how to install, configure, and use it.

> **After this lesson, you will be able to:**
> - Understand the function of TS Gateway.
> - Install TS Gateway.
> - Configure TS Gateway.
> - Configure Remote Desktop Connection to use TS Gateway.
>
> **Estimated lesson time: 50 minutes**

Overview of Terminal Services Gateway

TS Gateway is an optional TS component that enables authorized Remote Desktop clients to establish Remote Desktop Protocol (RDP) sessions between the Internet and Terminal Services resources found behind a firewall on a private network. ("Terminal Services resources," in this case, refers both to terminal servers and to computers with Remote Desktop enabled.) As they pass over the Internet, RDP connections to a TS Gateway server are secured and encrypted by the Secure Sockets Layer (SSL) protocol. A key feature of TS Gateway is that it enables RDP traffic to stream through corporate firewalls at TCP port 443, which is normally open for SSL traffic. (By default, RDP traffic communicates over TCP port 3389.)

In a basic TS Gateway deployment, shown in Figure 4-13, a user on a home computer (point 1) connects over the Internet to TS Gateway (point 2) located behind an external corporate firewall.

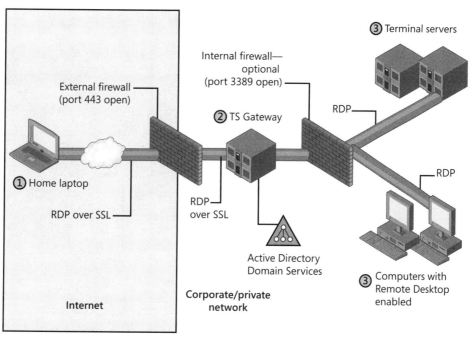

Figure 4-13   Basic TS Gateway scenario

The connection from points 1 to 2 is established by means of the RDP protocol encapsulated in an HTTPS (HTTP over SSL) tunnel. To receive this HTTPS connection in the perimeter network, the TS Gateway server must be running the Internet Information Services (IIS) Web server. After receiving the connection, the TS Gateway server then strips away the HTTPS data and forwards the RDP packets to the destination terminal servers (point 3) located behind a second, internal firewall. In this scenario, if incoming connections are allowed or denied to Active Directory accounts, Active Directory Domain Services must be installed on the TS Gateway.

As an alternative to the basic scenario illustrated in Figure 4-13, you can use Internet Security and Acceleration (ISA) Server instead of a TS Gateway server to serve as the SSL/HTTPS end-point for the incoming TS client connection. In this scenario, illustrated in Figure 4-14, ISA Server (point 2) serves as either an HTTPS-to-HTTPS or an HTTPS-to-HTTP bridge to the TS Gateway server (point 3), and the TS Gateway server then directs the RDP connection to the appropriate internal resource (point 4). This method provides the advantage of protecting Active Directory information within the corporate network.

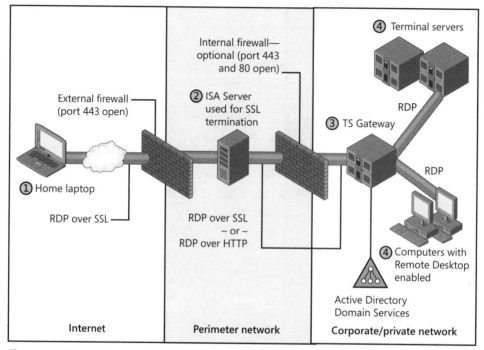

Figure 4-14 TS Gateway with ISA Server used for SSL termination

Exam Tip When you use ISA Server as an HTTPS-to-HTTPS bridge to TS Gateway, remember to export the server certificate used for SSL from the TS Gateway server to the computer running ISA Server and install that certificate on this latter server.

Installing and Configuring a TS Gateway Server

You can install and configure a TS Gateway server first by adding the TS Gateway role service and then by configuring the clients to point to the TS Gateway server. These steps are described in detail in the following section.

Adding the TS Gateway Role Service

When you choose to add the TS Gateway role service by using Server Manager, the Add Role Services Wizard launches. The Add Role Services Wizard then performs two main tasks. First, it automatically installs (if necessary) the prerequisite role services for TS Gateway: the IIS Web server and Network Policy Server (NPS). Second, it guides you through the process of configuring the three component features of TS Gateway that are required for the role service to function: a server certificate for SSL encryption, a TS Connection Authorization Policy (TS CAP), and a TS Resource Authorization Policy (TS RAP).

- **Server Certificate for SSL** TS clients connections to TS Gateway are encrypted by using SSL (also known as Transport Layer Security [TLS]), which requires a server certificate. This server certificate can originate from a trusted third-party certificate authority (CA) or from a trusted local CA (such as Certificate Services). As a less secure alternative suitable for testing environments, the Add Role Services Wizard can also generate a *self-signed* server certificate for use with TS Gateway.

IMPORTANT **The client must trust the server's root certificate**

Every TS client that connects to the TS Gateway server must trust the CA that issued the TS Gateway server's certificate. If neither a trusted third-party CA nor a CA integrated in the client's own Active Directory domain has issued the certificate, you must export and install TS Gateway Server Root Certificate in the Trusted Root Certification Authorities store on the Terminal Services client. You can view this store by using the Certificates snap-in. For a demonstration of this procedure, see the practice section at the end of this lesson.

Figure 4-15 shows the page in the wizard on which you can specify or create a server certificate for SSL encryption.

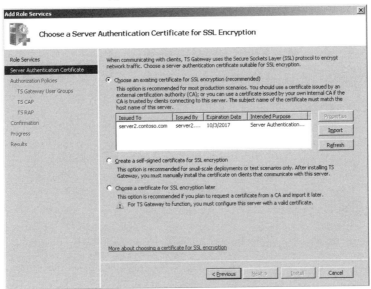

Figure 4-15 Choosing a server certificate for SSL encryption

- **TS CAP** A TS CAP essentially is a policy that specifies which external users or computers can connect to TS Gateway. The Add Role Services Wizard enables you only to create the first and primary TS CAP, but you can create others later by using the administrative console for TS Gateway, TS Gateway Manager.

NOTE **TS Gateway Manager and TS CAPs**

To open TS Gateway Manager, click Start, point to Administrative Tools, point to Terminal Services, and then click TS Gateway Manager.

To create a new TS CAP in TS Gateway Manager, right-click the Connection Authorization Policies folder in the console tree, select Create New Policy in the shortcut menu, and then point to Wizard or Custom, as desired. To modify the properties of an existing TS CAP, right-click an existing TS CAP in the Connection Authorization Policies pane, and then click Properties.

On the Select User Groups That Can Connect Through TS Gateway page of the Add Role Services Wizard, the process of creating the first TS CAP is simplified and enables you to specify users (typically, Active Directory security groups) that are permitted to connect. These same user groups are then made available to the main TS RAP created next by the wizard.

Note that a TS CAP also enables you to choose an authentication method for remote users: Password, Smart Card, or both.

The Select User Groups page is shown in Figure 4-16.

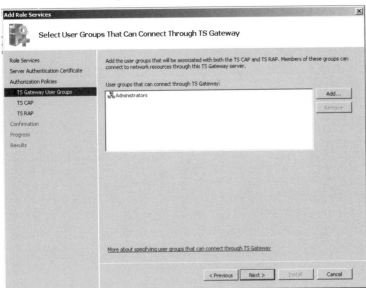

Figure 4-16 Defining groups for a TS CAP and TS RAP

When you use the TS Gateway Manager console to create or modify a TS CAP, you also have the option of specifying the computers for which you want to enable access to TS Gateway. Another configuration choice for a TS CAP, available only in the TS Gateway Manager console, is the option to restrict device redirection. In other words, you can use a TS CAP to prevent certain client devices such as a USB drive from being redirected to the TS user session through TS Gateway.

The properties sheet of a TS CAP, available in the TS Gateway Manager console, is shown in Figure 4-17.

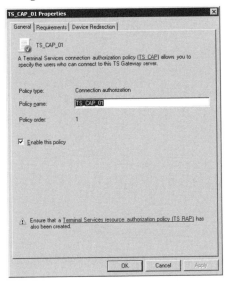

Figure 4-17   Modifying a TS CAP

■ **TS RAP**   A TS RAP is a TS Gateway policy that specifies which users can connect to which Terminal Services resources in an organization. The Add Role Services Wizard enables you to create the first and primary TS RAP, but you can create others later by using the TS Gateway Manager console.

NOTE   TS Gateway Manager and TS RAPs

To create a new TS RAP in TS Gateway Manager, right-click the Resource Authorization Policies folder in the console tree, select Create New Policy in the shortcut menu, and then click Wizard or Custom, as desired. To modify the properties of an existing TS RAP, simply right-click an existing TS RAP in the Resource Authorization Policies pane, and then click Properties.

In the simplified policy created by the Add Role Services Wizard, you determine whether the user group you have selected on the Select User Groups That Can Connect Through

TS Gateway page should be granted access to all terminal servers on the network or merely a subset, defined by an Active Directory security group.

The Create A TS RAP For TS Gateway page of the Add Role Services Wizard is shown in Figure 4-18.

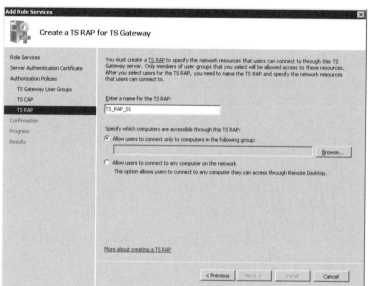

Figure 4-18   Creating a TS RAP in the Add Role Services Wizard

As with a TS CAP, using the TS Gateway Manager console to create or modify a TS RAP presents additional configuration options. For example, when you use the TS Gateway Manager console to create a TS RAP, the computer group to which you enable access can be an Active Directory security group or a *TS Gateway-managed computer group*, as shown in Figure 4-19. This latter group type is used only for TS Gateway and is created only through the TS Gateway Manager console. A second TS RAP configuration choice only available in the TS Gateway Manager console is the option to control the TCP ports through which a TS client may connect to a resource. For example, you can restrict all RDP connections to TCP port 3389 (the standard port for RDP), or you can specify a nonstandard port or set of ports on which the computer group will listen for connections.

Exam Tip   You can use the Monitoring node in TS Gateway Manager to view the user sessions that are currently connecting through the TS Gateway.

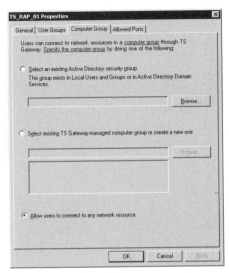

Figure 4-19 Specifying a computer group for an RAP

Configuring Remote Desktop Connection to Use TS Gateway

To use Remote Desktop Connection to initiate connections through TS Gateway, you must first configure RDC to use the gateway. To do so, first open RDC, click the Options button if necessary, and then select the Advanced tab. On the Advanced tab, click the Settings button in the Connect From Anywhere section, as shown in Figure 4-20.

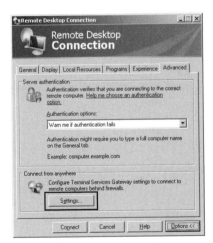

Figure 4-20 Configuring RDC to use TS Gateway, step 1

This procedure opens the Gateway Server Settings dialog box, as shown in Figure 4-21.

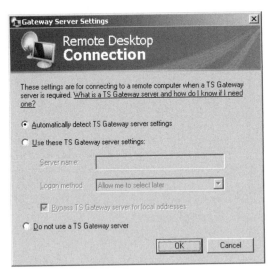

Figure 4-21   Configuring RDC to use TS Gateway, step 2

In the Gateway Server Settings dialog box, select the Use These TS Gateway Server Settings option. Then, specify the TS Gateway server in the Server Name box and an appropriate logon method (password or smart card) in the Logon Method box. To force RDC to use TS Gateway even for computers on your LAN, clear the option to bypass TS Gateway for local addresses.

In the Logon Settings area of the dialog box, you can specify whether the TS Gateway server should pass your credentials along to the target terminal server. By default, this option is selected. However, if you need to enter a different username or password at the remote server, clear this option.

Quick Check

1. Which type of policy authorizes connections from the Internet to TS Gateway?
2. Which type of policy authorizes connections from TS Gateway to internal resources?

Quick Check Answers

1. TS CAPs
2. TS RAPs

PRACTICE Installing and Configuring TS Gateway

In this series of exercises, you install TS Gateway on Server2 and then configure RDC on Server1 to connect to a terminal server through the gateway. Before you can achieve this, you have to install Server2's server certificate on Server1.

▶ **Exercise 1 Add the TS Gateway Role Service**

In this exercise, you will install the TS Gateway role service on Server2.

1. Log on to Contoso.com from Server2 as a domain administrator.
2. Open Server Manager.
3. In the Server Manager console tree, expand Roles, and then select the Terminal Services node.
4. In the details pane, in the Role Services area, click Add Role Services.
   The Add Role Services wizard opens.
5. On the Select Role Services page of the Add Role Services Wizard, select the TS Gateway check box.
   At this point, the Add Role Services dialog box might appear and ask whether you want to add the role services required for TS Gateway.
6. If the Add Role Services dialog box appears, click Add Required Role Services.
7. On the Select Role Services page of the Add Role Services Wizard, click Next.
8. On the Choose A Server Authentication Certificate For SSL Encryption page, read all the text on the page.
   At this point, in a production environment, you would designate a server authentication certificate obtained from a trusted CA. In this test environment, you will specify a self-signed certificate.
9. Select the option to Create A Self-Signed Certificate For SSL Encryption, and then click Next.
10. On the Create Authorization Policies For TS Gateway page, read all the text on the page and then, leaving the default option to Create Authorization Policies now, click Next.
11. On the Select User Groups That Can Communicate Through TS Gateway page, read all the text on the page, and then click Next.
12. On the Create A TS CAP For TS Gateway page, read all the text on the page and then, leaving the Password box checked, click Next.
13. On the Create A TS RAP For TS Gateway page, read all the text on the page, and then select the option to enable users to connect to any computer on the network.
14. Click Next.

15. On the Network Policy And Access Services page, read all the text on the page, and then click Next.

16. On the Select Role Services page, read all the text on the page, and then click Next.

17. On the Web Server (IIS) page, read all the text on the page, and then click Next.

18. On the Select Role Services page, click Next.

19. On the Confirm Installation Selections page, review your installation selections, and then click Install.

   The Installation Progress page appears while the selected role services are installed. After installation, the Installation Results page appears.

20. On the Installation Results page, click Close.

▶ **Exercise 2 Create a Certificates Console to Manage Certificates**

In this exercise, you will create consoles on Server1 and Server2 from which to manage certificates.

1. Log on to Server1 as an administrator.

2. In the Start Search box of the Start menu, type **mmc**, and then press Enter.

3. From the File menu, click Add/Remove Snap-In.

4. In the Add Or Remove Snap-Ins window, click Certificates from the list of available snap-ins, and then click Add.

5. On the Certificates Snap-In page, select Computer Account, and then click Next.

6. On the Select Computer page, click Finish.

7. In the Add Or Remove Snap-Ins window, click OK.

8. Use the File menu to save the menu with the name **Certificates MMC**. Save the console in the default location, the Administrative Tools folder.

9. Repeat steps 1–8 on Server2.

▶ **Exercise 3 Export a Server Certificate**

In this exercise, you will export to the Documents folder a self-signed certificate on Server2. You will then copy the exported certificate to Server1.

1. Open the Certificates MMC console on Server2. If you have saved this console in the Administrative Tools folder, you can find it by clicking Start, All Programs, Administrative Tools, and then Certificates MMC.

2. In the Certificates MMC console tree on Server2, navigate to Certificates (Local Computer)\Personal\Certificates.

   When the Certificates folder is selected, the details pane displays a certificate named Server2.contoso.com. The certificate has been issued by Server2.contoso.com. It is the self-signed certificate that you created in Exercise 1.

3. Right-click the Server2.contoso.com certificate, point to All Tasks on the shortcut menu, and then click Export.

   The Certificate Export Wizard appears.

4. On the welcome page of the wizard, read all the text on the page, and then click Next.

5. On the Export Private Key page, leave the default option not to export the private key, and then click Next.

6. On the Export File Format page, leave the default selection, and then click Next.

7. On the File To Export page, click the Browse button.

8. In the Save As dialog box, give the file the name **Server2cert**, and save the file in the Documents folder.

9. On the File To Export page, click Next.

10. On the Completing The Certificate Export Wizard page, review the name and location of the exported certificate, and then click Finish.

11. The Certificate Export Wizard message box appears, informing you that the export was successful. Click OK.

12. Using any method you choose, copy the Server2cert.cer file from Server2 to Server1, and then proceed to Exercise 4. For instance, you can use a USB flash drive to copy the file and move it physically from Server2 to Server1, or you can share a folder on Server1 and copy the file over the network to that share.

▶ **Exercise 4 Import a Server Certificate**

In this exercise, you will import the certificate you exported from Server2 into the Trusted Root Certification Authorities store on Server1.

1. Open the Certificates MMC console on Server1. If you have saved this console in the Administrative Tools folder, you can find it by clicking Start, All Programs, Administrative Tools, and then Certificates MMC.

2. In the Certificates MMC console tree on Server1, navigate to Certificates (Local Computer) \Trusted Root Certification Authorities\Certificates.

3. Right-click the Certificates folder, point to All Tasks on the shortcut menu, and then click Import.

   The Certificate Import Wizard appears.

4. On the Welcome page of the wizard, read all the text on the page, and then click Next.

5. On the File To Import page, click the Browse button.

   The Open window appears.

6. Using the navigation tree in the window, browse for and select the local copy of Server2cert.cer file that you saved in Exercise 3, and then click Open.

7. On the File To Import page, click Next.

8. On the Certificate Store page, leave the default selection, and then click Next.

9. On the Completing The Certificate Import Wizard page, click Finish.

10. The Certificate Import Wizard message box appears. Click OK.

▶ **Exercise 5 Connect to TS Gateway Through Remote Desktop Connection**

In this exercise, you will configure RDC to connect to the Terminal Services component on Server2 through the TS Gateway component on Server2. You will then test the connection.

1. While you are logged on to Server1 as a domain administrator, open Remote Desktop Connection.

2. In the Remote Desktop Connection window, click the Options button to expand the window.

3. Click the Advanced tab.

4. In the Connect From Anywhere area, click the Settings button.
    The TS Gateway Server Settings dialog box appears.

5. In the Connection Settings area, select Use These TS Gateway Server Settings.
    The option to detect TS Gateway server settings automatically queries Group Policy for the appropriate setting.

6. In the Server Name text box, type **server2.contoso.com**.

7. In the Logon Method drop-down list box, select Ask For Password (NTLM).

8. Clear the Bypass TS Gateway Server For Local Addresses check box.

9. Verify that the Use My TS Gateway Credentials For The Remote Computer check box is selected, and then click OK.

10. In the Remote Desktop Connection window, click the General tab.

11. In the Computer text box, type or select **server2.contoso.com**.

12. In the User Name text box, enter the credentials of a domain administrator.

13. Click Connect.
    The Windows Security dialog box appears.

14. Read all the text in the Windows Security dialog box. Notice that the credentials you supply will be used for TS Gateway and for the remote terminal server.

15. Type the credentials of a domain administrator, and then click OK.

    A Terminal Services connection to Server2 is established through the TS Gateway.

16. Log on to Contoso.com from Server2 with a different domain administrator account than the one you just used to connect through RDC on Server1.

17. On Server2, open TS Gateway Manager by clicking Start, pointing to Administrative Tools, pointing to Terminal Services, and then clicking TS Gateway Manager.

    TS Gateway Manager opens.

18. In the TS Gateway Manager console tree, select SERVER2 (Local)\Monitoring.

    In the center (Monitoring) pane, you can see the connection from Server1 is listed. The connection has been successfully relayed by TS Gateway.

19. On Server1, from the Remote Desktop window, log off Server2.

20. On both Server1 and Server 2, close all open windows and log off.

Lesson Summary

- TS Gateway is a role service that enables authorized remote users to establish RDP connections to terminal servers located behind a corporate firewall.

- TS client communications with TS Gateway are encrypted with SSL and use SSL port 443.

- Typically, the TS Gateway server is located in a perimeter network, and the remote TS clients communicate with it directly. However, you can also use ISA Server to forward client requests to TS Gateway.

- Three components are required for TS Gateway to function: a server certificate for SSL, a TS CAP (which authorizes connections to the gateway), and a TS RAP (which authorizes connections to internal resources).

- The main tool used to manage TS Gateway is TS Gateway Manager.

Lesson Review

The following questions are intended to reinforce key information presented in this lesson. The questions are also available on the companion CD if you prefer to review them in electronic form.

NOTE Answers

Answers to these questions and explanations of why each answer choice is correct or incorrect are located in the "Answers" section at the end of the book.

1. Which TCP port must you leave open in your company's firewall if you want clients to be able to initiate RDP connections to terminal servers through TS Gateway?

   A. 25

   B. 3389

   C. 443

   D. 80

2. Your network includes a TS Gateway server named TSG1. TSG1 has installed a self-signed server certificate that it uses for SSL communications. You want to use a computer running ISA Server as an SSL endpoint for TS Gateway connections. Which of the following steps must you take to ensure that ISA Server can communicate with TS Gateway?

   A. Enable HTTPS-HTTP bridging between ISA Server and TS Gateway.

   B. Open TCP port 443 on the computer running ISA Server.

   C. Export the SSL certificate of ISA Server to TS Gateway.

   D. Export the SSL certificate of TS Gateway to ISA Server.

Lesson 3: Publishing Applications with TS RemoteApp

TS RemoteApp is a technology built into Terminal Services that enables you to *publish* applications—that is, make them available to remote users. In this lesson, you will learn how to use TS RemoteApp to publish applications in three different ways: through Terminal Services Web Access (TS Web Access), through RDP files, and through Windows Installer packages.

After this lesson, you will be able to:
- Understand the TS RemoteApp feature of Terminal Services and the scenarios in which it can be used.
- Install an application on a terminal server so that the application can support multiple users.
- Make an application installed on a Windows Server 2008 terminal server available to remote users through a Web browser.
- Create an RDP file that launches an application installed on a remote Windows Server 2008 terminal server.
- Create a Windows Installer package that creates shortcuts to a RemoteApp application in the user's Start menu and desktop.

Estimated lesson time: 45 minutes

Overview of TS RemoteApp

TS RemoteApp enables programs to run through Terminal Services and appear as if they were running on a user's local computer. Before Windows Server 2008, TS users who needed to run an application on a remote terminal server first needed to establish a desktop session on the server and then launch the application within that desktop session. With TS RemoteApp, the application alone is streamed through RDP to a resizable window on the user's local desktop.

You can deploy a RemoteApp program to users in either of the following ways:

- You can make RemoteApp programs available on a Web site by distributing the RemoteApp programs through the TS Web Access page. This page is located at http:// *servername*/ts or https://*servername*/ts (if the Web server can accept SSL connections). In this scenario, you configure the TS Web Access page to display icons of available RemoteApp programs. Clicking any of these icons launches the RemoteApp program on the user's computer.

- You can distribute RemoteApp programs as RDP files or Windows Installer packages through a file share or through other distribution mechanisms such as Microsoft Systems Management Server 2003, Microsoft System Center Configuration Manager 2007, or Active Directory software distribution. After obtaining the RDP file or installing it through a Windows Installer package, a user launches the program by double-clicking that RDP file, by accessing the program from the Start menu, or by opening a file whose extension is associated with the RemoteApp program.

After launching the RemoteApp program by one of these methods, a user is able to run the program as if it were installed locally. As with any TS session, the terminal server provides virtually all the resources needed to run the RemoteApp program.

NOTE   **TS RemoteApp and user sessions**

When a user runs two RemoteApp programs hosted on the same terminal server, the programs belong to the same TS user session.

TS RemoteApp enables you to take advantage of the resources of a central server and reduce management complexity in the following situations:

- Users need to access programs hosted on your network from remote locations. In this case, you can deploy TS RemoteApp together with TS Gateway so that the remote users can access the programs from the Internet.

- Your network includes old computers that lack the hardware or software resources needed to run a required application.

- Your company has a branch office that lacks the IT personnel needed to support a given application on site.

- Your network includes user desktops with operating system or software conflicts that prevent the installation of a required application.

- You need to support users who do not have assigned computers but who do need to use a particular application consistently.

- You want to reduce costs associated with an application by installing it on only one computer.

Configuring a Server to Host RemoteApp Programs

To prepare a server to host RemoteApp programs, you first need to install the Terminal Services role service on that server. No other role service is necessary because TS RemoteApp is integrated into the main component of Terminal Services.

The next step in configuring a server to host a RemoteApp program is to install the desired applications in a way that will make them available to multiple users. You can achieve this only by installing the program while the terminal server is in Install mode. When Terminal Services is in Install mode, installing an application creates only master copies of the Registry entries or .ini files that are used to store user-specific application data. Only when users later launch the application are these master entries then copied into the users' profiles to store personal settings.

To install an application in Install mode, you have three options:

- You can use a Windows Installer package (MSI) file to install the program. When you install a program by using a Windows Installer package, the program will install in Terminal Server Install mode.

- You can use the Install Application On Terminal Server option in Control Panel to install the program. This option is shown in Figure 4-22.

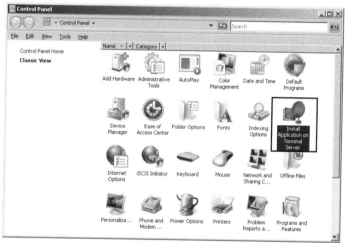

Figure 4-22   Use this Control Panel option to install a program for multiple TS users

- Before you install a program, you can run the *Change user /install* or *Chguser /install* command from the command line. After the program is installed, run the *Change user /execute* or *Chguser /execute* command to exit from Install mode.

Exam Tip   For the 70-643 exam, you need to know the significance of Terminal Services Install mode and all the ways you can install an application in this mode.

Adding Programs for Publication in TS RemoteApp Manager

After you install the required applications in Install mode, you need to add these programs to the RemoteApp Programs list in TS RemoteApp Manager.

NOTE What is TS RemoteApp Manager?

TS RemoteApp Manager is the main administrative console used to deploy, manage, and configure RemoteApp programs. You can open TS RemoteApp Manager by clicking Start, Administrative Tools, Terminal Services, and then TS RemoteApp Manager.

To perform this step, open TS RemoteApp Manager, and then click Add RemoteApp Program in the Actions pane. After you select the program in a simple wizard, the application appears in the RemoteApp Programs list, as shown in Figure 4-23.

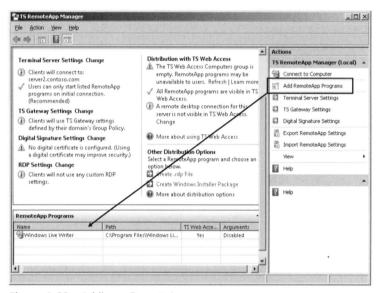

Figure 4-23 Adding a RemoteApp program

Once programs are added to this list, they automatically appear in TS Web Access by default if that component is already installed on the same terminal server. You also can use TS RemoteApp Manager to create RDP files or Windows Installer packages of programs that are already added to the list.

All three of these publishing options are described in more detail in the following sections.

Deploying a RemoteApp Program Through TS Web Access

To make the TS Web Access feature available, you need to install the TS Web Access role service. If you install TS Web Access on the same server as the terminal server hosting the RemoteApp programs, all the programs listed in the RemoteApp Programs list in the TS RemoteApp Manager appear on the TS Web Access page by default.

To access the TS Web Access page, users open Microsoft Internet Explorer and browse to *http://*servername*/ts*. (Alternatively, users can browse to *https://*servername*/ts* if the server has been configured with a server certificate issued by a trusted CA.) The TS Web Access page is shown in Figure 4-24.

Figure 4-24   The TS Web Access page

On the TS Web Access page, users can launch any of the RemoteApp programs by clicking the appropriate icon. In a two-server scenario, TS Web Access and Terminal Services run on separate servers. In this case, you need to take two additional steps to ensure that the TS Web Access page displays RemoteApp programs hosted on the terminal server.

1. On the Configuration tab of the TS Web Access page, you must type the name of the remote terminal server in the Terminal Server Name text box, as shown in Figure 4-25. (To see the Configuration tab, you must connect to the TS Web Access server with the credentials of a user account that is a member of the TS Web Access Administrators local group on the TS Web Access server.)

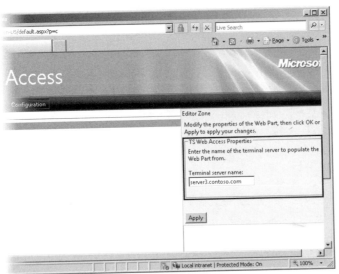

Figure 4-25 Configuring TS Web Access to obtain RemoteApp program information from another server

2. You must add the computer account of the TS Web Access server to the TS Web Access Computers security group on the terminal server.

NOTE **TS Web Access points to one server**

Regardless of whether you implement TS Web Access with one or two servers, the TS Web Access page displays resources that reside on just one terminal server.

Creating an RDP File of a RemoteApp Program for Distribution

You can create an RDP file of any program listed in the RemoteApp Programs list in TS RemoteApp Manager. To do so, simply select the program in the list, and then click Create .RDP File under Other Distribution Options, as shown in Figure 4-26.

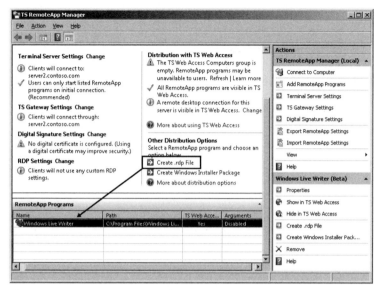

Figure 4-26   Creating an RDP file that points to a RemoteApp program

This procedure launches the RemoteApp Wizard. Before creating an RDP file that points to a remote program, the RemoteApp Wizard enables you to configure certain settings for that RDP file on the Specify Package Settings page. For example, it allows you to specify the TCP port on which the remote terminal server will listen for connection requests. (The standard port is 3389.) The wizard also enables you to require that user connections proceed through a specified TS Gateway server before launching the RemoteApp program. Finally, the wizard enables you to sign the RDP file digitally with a certificate. This signature assures clients that the RDP files have been issued by a trusted publisher.

The Specify Package Settings page is shown in Figure 4-27.

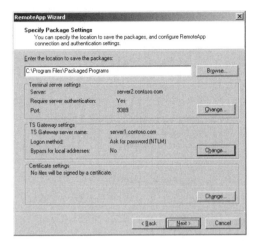

Figure 4-27 Specifying settings for an RDP file

Exam Tip You can configure Group Policy to restrict the use of digitally signed RDP files that you make available on a distribution share. For example, you can allow users logged on only to computers in a particular Organizational Unit (OU) to use the RDP files while explicitly denying the use of the files to other users in the domain. One way to achieve this goal is to *disable* the use of RDP files from valid publishers at the domain level and then *enable* this policy setting for the OU containing the client computers whose users you want to enable to use the files. To find this policy setting, browse to Computer Configuration\Policies\Administrative Templates\Windows Components \Terminal Services\Remote Desktop Connection Client and then select Allow .RDP Files From Valid Publishers And User's Default .RDP Settings.

After you create the RDP file by using the RemoteApp Wizard, you can distribute the file to client computers by using your existing software distribution process, such as Microsoft Systems Management Server (SMS) 2003, Microsoft System Center Configuration Manager 2007, or Group Policy. Alternatively, you can also distribute the file through e-mail or a network share.

Creating a Windows Installer Package of a RemoteApp Program for Distribution

As an alternative to creating RDP files for distribution, you can create and distribute MSI files instead. To perform this task, select the desired RemoteApp program in the RemoteApp program list in TS RemoteApp Manager, and then click Create Windows Installer Package under Other Distribution Options, as shown in Figure 4-28.

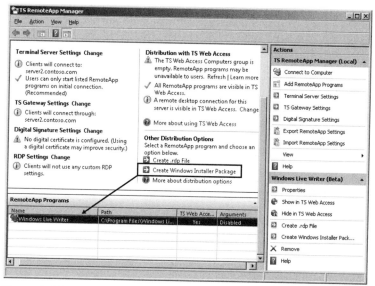

Figure 4-28   Creating a Windows Installer for a RemoteApp program

This step opens the RemoteApp Wizard. As with RDP files, the RemoteApp Wizard includes a Specify Package Settings page on which you can specify a terminal server, a TS Gateway setting, and a digital certificate whenever you create a Windows Installer package.

However, when you create a Windows Installer package, the RemoteApp Wizard also displays a Configure Distribution Package page with a second set of options. First, you can use this page to specify the location of the shortcuts to the RemoteApp program that will be installed. The optional locations are the user's desktop and a Start menu folder with a name of your choice. Second, you can also use the Configure Distribution Package page to configure the RemoteApp program to open every time a file with the associated file extension is opened. (Use this option only when clients do not have locally installed versions of the program.)

Exam Tip   For the 70-643 exam, you need to remember that these two options on the Configure Distribution Package page (shortcuts and file extension associations) are only made available when you create a Windows Installer package of a RemoteApp program.

The Configure Distribution Package page of the RemoteApp Wizard is shown in Figure 4-29.

Figure 4-29   Configuring installation options for a Windows Installer package

As with RDP files, you can distribute Windows Installer packages to clients by using SMS, System Center Configuration Manager, or Group Policy. Alternatively, you can distribute the files through e-mail or a network share.

Exam Tip   One advantage of publishing applications through TS Web Access is that the changes you make to the properties of RemoteApp programs are immediately registered by clients. However, if you have made a RemoteApp program available through RDP or MSI files and want to change its properties so that (for example) clients would now be required to connect to it through TS Gateway, you would need to re-create those files and then redistribute them to users.

Quick Check

1. True or False: You can configure TS Web Access to display RemoteApp programs found on various servers in your organization.

2. Which is the only RemoteApp program deployment option that enables you to install shortcuts to the program in the Start menu?

Quick Check Answers

1. False. TS Web Access displays resources located on a single server.
2. Creating a Windows Installer package (MSI file). You can also deploy MSI files through Group Policy so that the shortcuts in the Start menu are installed automatically.

PRACTICE **Publishing Applications with TS RemoteApp Manager**

In this series of exercises, you will publish an application in three ways. First, you will enable users to launch a remote application by means of a Web page. Second, you will create and distribute an RDP file for the remote application. Finally, you will create and distribute an installer package to allow users to install an RDP file to the remote application.

▶ **Exercise 1 Install the TS Web Access Role Service**

The simplest way to publish a RemoteApp program is through TS Web Access. In this exercise, you will prepare the terminal server for publishing applications through this method by installing the TS Web Access Role Service.

1. Log on to Contoso.com from Server2 as a domain administrator.
2. Open Server Manager.
3. In the Server Manager console tree, expand the Roles node, and then select Terminal Services.
4. In the Role Services area of the details pane, click Add Role Services.

    The Select Role Services page of the Add Role Services Wizard appears.
5. In the list of available role services, select the TS Web Access check box.

    At this point, the Add Role Services dialog box might appear and ask whether you want to add the role services required for TS Web Access.
6. If the Add Role Services dialog box appears, click Add Required Role Services.
7. On the Select Role Services page, click Next.
8. If the Web Server (IIS) page appears, read all the text on the page, and then click Next.
9. If the Select Role Services page appears, read all the text on the page, and then click Next.
10. On the Confirm Installation Selections page, click Install.

    The Installation Progress page appears while the components are being installed. When the installation completes, the Installation Results page appears.
11. On the Installation Results page, click Close.

▶ **Exercise 2 Publish an Application for TS Web Access**

In this exercise, you will add MS Paint to the list of RemoteApp programs in TS RemoteApp Manager.

1. If you have not already done so, log on to Contoso.com from Server2 as a domain administrator.

2. Open TS RemoteApp Manager by clicking Start, Administrative Tools, Terminal Services, and then TS RemoteApp Manager.

3. In TS RemoteApp Manager, in the Actions pane on the right side of the console, click Add RemoteApp Programs.

4. On the welcome page of the RemoteApp Wizard, click Next.

5. On the Choose Programs To Add To The RemoteApp Programs List page, select Paint from the list, and then click Next.

6. On the Review Settings page, click Finish.

   In TS RemoteApp Manager, Paint is now listed in the RemoteApp Programs area. Note that its TS Web Access status is set to Yes.

7. Proceed to Exercise 3.

▶ **Exercise 3 Launch a Remote Application through TS Web Access**

In this exercise, you will run Paint through TS Web Access.

1. Log on to Contoso.com from Server1 as a domain administrator.

2. Open Internet Explorer.

3. From the Tools menu, select Internet Options, and then click the Security tab.

4. On the Security tab of the Internet Options dialog box, select the Local Intranet zone, and then click the Sites button.

5. In the Local Intranet dialog box, add the Web site **https://server2.contoso.com** and **https://server2.contoso.com** to the list of Web sites, and then click Close.

6. In the Internet Options dialog box, click OK.

7. In the Internet Explorer address box, type **https://server2.contoso.com/ts**, and then press Enter.

8. In the Security Alert message box, click OK.

   The TS Web Access page opens. While the RemoteApp Programs tile is selected, a Paint icon appears in the main area of the Web page.

9. Click the Paint icon.

   A RemoteApp Starting window appears, and then a RemoteApp warning message appears.

10. Read all the text in the warning message, and then click Connect.

11. In the Windows Security window, enter the credentials of a domain administrator, and then click OK.

    After a minute, a Paint window opens.

12. From the File menu, click Save.

    The Save As windows appears.

    Answer the following questions: Is the default location for a saved file found on Server1 or Server2? Why?

    Answer: Server2, because the program is actually running on Server2

    In the Save As window, click Cancel, and then close the Paint window.

▶ Exercise 4 Create a Distribution Share

In this exercise, you will create a distribution share with read access for all domain users. The share will be used to distribute RDP files and TS-enabled installer packages.

1. Log on to Contoso.com from Server2 as a domain administrator.

2. Create a folder named **TS Apps** at the root of the C drive.

3. Right-click the TS Apps folder, and then click Share from the shortcut menu.

4. The File Sharing window opens.

5. In the text box provided, type **Domain Users**, and then click Add.

6. Domain Users now appears in the Name list with an associated Permission Level of Reader.

7. Click the Share button.

8. The File Sharing window displays the message that your folder is shared.

9. Click Done.

▶ Exercise 5 Create an RDP File for a Published Application

In this exercise, you will create an RDP file for WordPad and save it to the TS Apps distribution share.

1. While you are logged on to Contoso.com from Server2 as a domain administrator, open TS RemoteApp Manager if it is not already open.

   In TS RemoteApp Manager, in the Actions pane, click Add RemoteApp Programs.

   Use the RemoteApp Wizard to add WordPad to the RemoteApp Programs list, as described in Exercise 2.

   When you have completed the wizard, WordPad appears in the RemoteApp Programs list in TS RemoteApp Manager.

2. Select WordPad in the RemoteApp Programs list and then, in the Other Distribution Options area in TS RemoteApp Manager, click Create .Rdp File.

   The RemoteApp Wizard opens.

3. On the welcome page of the RemoteApp Wizard, click Next.

4. On the Specify Package Settings Page, read all the text on the page, and then click the Browse button.

5. In the Browse For Folder dialog box, locate and select the TS Apps folder in the root of the C drive. Click OK.

6. On the Specify Package Settings page of the RemoteApp Wizard, click Next.

7. On the Review Settings page, click Finish.

8. Proceed to Practice 6.

▶ Exercise 6 Launch a Remote Application with a Local RDP File

In this exercise, you will copy an RDP file from a distribution share to Server1 and then use that RDP file to launch a remote application.

1. If you have not already done so, log on to Contoso.com from Server1 as a domain administrator.

2. In the Start Search box of the Start menu, type **Server2**, and then press Enter.

   A Server2 window opens in Windows Explorer.

3. In the Server2 window, double-click the network share named TS Apps.

4. In the TS Apps share, copy the RDP file named Wordpad to your desktop on Server1.

5. Close all open windows on Server1, and then double-click the Wordpad file on the Server1 desktop.

   The RemoteApp Starting window appears, and then a RemoteApp warning message appears.

6. Read all the text in the warning message, and then click Connect.

7. In the Windows Security prompt, provide the credentials of a domain administrator, and then click OK.

8. After a minute, WordPad opens on Server1.

9. Close all open windows.

▶ Exercise 7 Create a RemoteApp Installer Package for Distribution

In this exercise, which requires an Internet connection, you will download and install Microsoft Office Word Viewer from the Microsoft Download Center and then add it to the RemoteApp Programs list. You will then create an installer package to distribute to users over the network.

> **NOTE Use an alternate program if desired**
>
> In this exercise, Word Viewer is simply used as an example. You can substitute any installable pro-gram for Word Viewer.

1. Log on to Contoso.com from Server2 as a domain administrator.
2. Using Internet Explorer, connect to the Microsoft Download Center at *http://www.microsoft.com/downloads*. On the Microsoft Download Center Web site, search for Word Viewer.
3. Locate and download Microsoft Office Word Viewer from the Microsoft Download Web site.
4. Install Word Viewer on Server2.
5. After the installation has completed, open TS RemoteApp Manager.
6. In TS RemoteApp Manager, in the Actions pane on the right side of the console, click Add RemoteApp Programs.
7. Use the RemoteApp Wizard to add Microsoft Office Word Viewer to the RemoteApp Pro-grams list, as described in Exercise 2.

    After you have completed the wizard, Microsoft Office Word Viewer appears listed in the RemoteApp Programs area of the TS RemoteApp Manager.
8. Select Microsoft Office Word Viewer in the list and then, in the Other Distribution Options area of TS RemoteApp Manager, click Create Windows Installer Package.
9. On the welcome page of the RemoteApp wizard, click Next.
10. On the Specify Package Settings page, read all the text on the page, and then click the Browse button.
11. In the Browse For Folder dialog box, select the TS Apps folder in the root of the C drive, and then click OK.
12. On the Specify Package Settings page, click Next.
13. On the Configure Distribution Package page, read all the text on the page, select the Desktop check box, and then click Next.
14. On the Review Settings page, click Finish.
15. Proceed to Exercise 8.

▶ **Exercise 8 Install a Remote Program**

In this exercise, you will use the installer package created in the last exercise to install Word Viewer as a remote application.

1. If you have not already done so, log on to Contoso.com from Server1 as a domain administrator.

2. In the Start Search box of the Start menu, type **\\Server2**, and then press Enter.

   A Server2 window opens in Windows Explorer.

3. In the Server2 window, double-click the network share named TS Apps.

4. In the TS Apps share, copy the Windows Installer Package (.MSI file) named WORD-VIEW to your desktop on Server1.

5. Close all open windows on Server1, and then double-click the WORDVIEW file on the Server1 desktop.

   When the program finishes installing, a new shortcut to an RDP file appears on the desktop. The shortcut is named Microsoft Office Word Viewer.

6. Double-click the Microsoft Office Word Viewer shortcut.

   A RemoteApp warning message appears.

7. Read all the text in the warning message, and then click Connect.

8. In the Windows Security window, enter the credentials of a domain administrator.

   After several moments, Word Viewer opens, along with an Open dialog box that prompts you to specify a Word file to open.

9. Close all open windows, and then log off both Server1 and Server2.

Lesson Summary

■ TS RemoteApp enables programs to run through Terminal Services and appear as if they were running on a user's local computer. TS RemoteApp is useful in situations in which users need to access applications remotely or simply lack the hardware or software required to run the application in question.

■ A program that is published through TS RemoteApp is known as a RemoteApp Program. There are three ways to publish RemoteApp Programs: through the TS Web Access page, through RDP files, and through Windows Installer packages.

■ When you install an application to be published on a terminal server, you have to make sure that the terminal server is in Install mode. Installing the application while the server is in this mode enables the application to support multiple users.

■ The main tool used to configure and manage RemoteApp programs is TS RemoteApp Manager.

Lesson Review

The following questions are intended to reinforce key information presented in this lesson. The questions are also available on the companion CD if you prefer to review them in electronic form.

NOTE Answers

Answers to these questions and explanations of why each answer choice is correct or incorrect are located in the "Answers" section at the end of the book.

---

1. How can you ensure that an application installed on a computer running Terminal Services can support multiple users?

   A. Use the *Chglogon* command.

   B. Use the *Chguser* command.

   C. Use the *Qappsrv* command.

   D. Use the *Mstsc* command.

2. You have recently created and distributed RDP files for a certain RemoteApp program. However, you find that the application performs poorly and needs to be migrated to a more powerful server. What should you do to ensure that users can connect to the RemoteApp program after it is migrated? (Choose two. Each answer presents a complete solution.)

   A. Create a new TS Web Access site for the new terminal server and publish the application to the new site.

   B. Re-create an RDP file for the RemoteApp program after the migration and distribute the file to users.

   C. Modify the properties of the existing RDP file and re-distribute the file to users.

   D. In TS RemoteApp Manager on the old terminal server, change the Terminal Server settings so that the server name listed is the new terminal server.

Chapter Review

To further practice and reinforce the skills you learned in this chapter, you can perform the following tasks:

- Review the chapter summary.
- Review the list of key terms introduced in this chapter.
- Complete the case scenario. This scenario sets up a real-world situation involving the topics of this chapter and asks you to create solutions.
- Complete the suggested practices.
- Take a practice test.

Chapter Summary

- You can configure TS client properties by choosing options directly in Remote Desktop Connection or by enforcing settings in Group Policy Object (GPO).
- To manage user sessions on a terminal server, use Terminal Services Manager (TSM). TSM can be used to display information about users connected to a terminal server, to monitor user sessions, or to perform administrative tasks such as logging users off or disconnecting user sessions.
- A TS Gateway server enables authorized users to connect to terminal servers located behind a firewall. A TS Gateway server provides confidentiality to TS client sessions by encrypting them with SSL. To configure and manage a TS Gateway server, use TS Gateway Manager.
- TS RemoteApp is a feature that enables you to publish programs running on a terminal server so that they appear to be running on the client instead. You can use TS Remote-App when users need to access applications remotely or simply lack a required level of hardware or software. To configure and manage TS RemoteApp, use TS RemoteApp Manager.
- You can publish RemoteApp programs through TS Web Access, RDP files, or Windows Installer packages.

Key Terms

Do you know what these key terms mean? You can check your answers by looking up the terms in the glossary at the end of the book.

- CA
- certificate
- console session
- home folder
- HTTPS
- Install mode
- publish (an application)
- self-signed certificate
- SSL
- TS CAP
- TS Gateway
- TS RAP
- TS RemoteApp
- TS Web Access
- user profile

Case Scenarios

In the following case scenario, you will apply what you've learned in this chapter. You can find answers to these questions in the "Answers" section at the end of this book.

Case Scenario 1: Managing TS Sessions

You are the administrator of a computer named TS1 that is running Windows Server 2008. TS1 is running Terminal Services and is hosting several applications. Throughout the day, many users are connected to TS1, and you are responsible for managing the user sessions to the server.

1. A user informs you that his TS session on TS1 is frozen. What commands can you use to find his session ID and then end his session?
2. A new user calls to inform you that she is having trouble using an application on TS1. Because she works in another building, you want to be able to show her how to use the application without having to visit her desk. How can you achieve this?

Case Scenario 2: Publishing Applications

Your company has recently configured a server named Server1 to host a line-of-business application named App1. Server1 is running Windows Server 2008 and Terminal Services. You are part of the team that is testing and publishing the application in Windows Server 2008. Your first goal is to publish the application App1 to all users in the domain Contoso.com.

1. After installing App1 on Server1, your team wants to publish App1 to users' desktops. You do not want to have them copy files from a share to run the remote application. Which deployment method or methods would you recommend?

2. You want users to see the application listed in the Start menu and, if users open a file that is associated with App1, you want the remote program to start automatically. How can you achieve this most efficiently?

3. You want to make App1 available to users as a RemoteApp program in remote locations outside of the corporate network. How can you accomplish this? (Assume that your company has a firewall and perimeter network that hosts public servers.)

Suggested Practices

To help you successfully master the exam objectives presented in this chapter, complete the following tasks.

Deploy a Terminal Services Infrastructure

In this practice, you deploy a Terminal Server, a TS Gateway server, and a RemoteApp Program.

- **Practice 1**   Install Windows Server 2008 and Terminal Services on a server in your organization. Install an application on the server while the server is in Install mode, and then add the application to the list of RemoteApp Programs in TS RemoteApp Manager. Install TS Web Access on the same server, and then connect to the TS Web Access page from another computer. Launch the RemoteApp program from the TS Web Access page.

- **Practice 2**   Then, deploy TS Gateway on a second server in your organization. Use TS RemoteApp Manager on the first server to create an RDP file for the same application. Configure the RDP file to specify the new TS Gateway address. Export the TS Gateway server's certificate to a client computer (if necessary), and then use the RDP file on the client computer to launch the RemoteApp program through the gateway.

Watch a Webcast

In this practice, you watch webcasts about Terminal Services in Windows Server 2008.

- **Practice**   Watch the "Windows Server 2008 Terminal Services RemoteApp and Web Access" Webcast by David Hanna, available on the companion CD in the Webcasts folder or by visiting *http://msevents.microsoft.com* and searching for event ID 1032355810.

Perform a Virtual Lab

In this practice, you configure and manage a Terminal Services infrastructure online.

- **Practice 1**   Go to *http://msevents.microsoft.com* and search for event ID 1032345540. Register for and perform the virtual lab named "TechNet Virtual Lab: Managing Terminal Services Gateway and RemoteApps in Windows Server 2008."
- **Practice 2**   Go to *http://msevents.microsoft.com* and search for event ID 1032347559. Register for and perform the virtual lab named "TechNet Virtual Lab: Centralized Application Access with Windows Server 2008."

Take a Practice Test

The practice tests on this book's companion CD offer many options. For example, you can test yourself on just one exam objective, or you can test yourself on all the 70-643 certification exam content. You can set up the test so that it closely simulates the experience of taking a certification exam, or you can set it up in study mode so that you can look at the correct answers and explanations after you answer each question.

MORE INFO   Practice tests

For details about all the practice test options available, see the "How to Use the Practice Tests" section in this book's introduction.

Chapter 5
Installing and Configuring Web Applications

Modern Web sites provide functionality that is on par with the experience found in many locally installed client applications. They provide access to databases in both public and intranet environments and enable users to customize their experience based on specific needs. Web applications or Web services rely upon a variety of standards, protocols, and development technologies.

The Windows Server 2008 operating system includes Internet Information Services (IIS) 7.0, a complete Web services platform that is capable of supporting various types of Web content and applications. IIS 7.0 provides significant enhancements in manageability, scalability, and reliability. It also provides backward compatibility to support the millions of Web sites already hosted on previous versions of IIS.

In this chapter, you'll learn how to install and configure the Web Server (IIS) and Application Server roles in Windows Server 2008. There are numerous features and services that you can enable based on the needs of your environment. This information will help you deploy and configure IIS and its related features in production environments.

Exam objectives in this chapter:
- Configuring a Web Services Infrastructure
  - ❑ Configure Web applications.
  - ❑ Manage Web sites.
  - ❑ Manage Internet Information Services (IIS).

Lessons in this chapter:

Before You Begin

To complete the lessons in this chapter, you must have installed Windows Server 2008 on Server2.contoso.com.

NOTE   Alternative setup

You can perform most of the steps on another computer running Windows Server 2008, but you might need to make some adjustments to the steps. Also, although there are some licensing differences between the different editions of Windows Server 2008, the basic architecture of the Web Server (IIS) role is consistent among them.

Real World

Anil Desai

The success of a server installation is often based on how well its configuration matches the needs of users and developers. If some features are missing, applications will not run as expected. If too many features are enabled, there could be security, compatibility, or performance implications. The goal is to "get it right." This is one area in which communications are important.

In many IT departments, I've seen a significant disconnect between development teams (such as groups of Web developers) and the systems administrators responsible for deploying and supporting the applications that the developers create. Often, the responsibilities of each part of the organization are not clearly defined, and it can become difficult to figure out who is ultimately responsible for the final configuration.

Fortunately, these types of problems can be solved. On the systems administration side, IT staff should try to determine the specific business and technical needs of the Web applications they support. Web developers can do their part by proactively communicating upcoming requirements and potential implications for the configuration of production servers. Writing documentation is helpful for thinking through and communicating the most important points. Finally, it's important to remember end users. Whether these are people who are part of your organization or the public at large, it's important to understand their specific reasons for visiting your Web sites. Marketing input can often help in this area.

Lesson 1: Installing the Web Server (IIS) Role

Although enabling IIS and its related components is usually a simple procedure, the primary challenge lies in understanding the architecture, components, and available features of the platform. In this lesson, you will learn about the modular architecture of IIS and how to configure a computer running Windows Server 2008 as a Web server.

After this lesson, you will be able to:
- Describe the architecture of IIS 7.0, including new features.
- Define the purpose of the Application Server role.
- Describe the purpose of role services related to the Web Server (IIS) role.
- Install the Web Server (IIS) role and add and remove role services.
- Perform command-line installations and automated installations of the Web Server (IIS) role.

Estimated lesson time: 45 minutes

Understanding Web Server Security

IIS 7.0 includes an array of features and options to support different types of Web services and applications. Using the Server Manager utility simplifies the process of installing IIS and its related features and options. As a systems administrator, you will be responsible for deploying IIS based on different needs and requirements. Therefore, it is important to understand the design of IIS before learning methods for installing the Web Server and Application Server roles. This section will provide details about deployment options for the IIS platform.

MORE INFO   Other features of IIS

In addition to supporting Web applications, the IIS platform also provides server components for the File Transfer Protocol (FTP) and the Simple Mail Transfer Protocol (SMTP). This chapter focuses on Web-based applications. For more information about these other features, see Chapter 7, "Configuring FTP and SMTP Services."

Web Standards and Protocols

To understand the purpose and function of the IIS platform, you must first understand the protocols and standards used by Web Applications. Hypertext Transfer Protocol (HTTP) is the primary protocol that communicates with Web services. HTTP is designed to provide a request–response model for communicating among computers across a network. HTTP traffic is accessed by using Transmission Control Protocol/Internet Protocol (TCP/IP)–based network connections. Due to the importance of Web-based traffic, most organizations allow their users to access the Internet by using TCP port 80, the default HTTP port. The HTTP protocol is stateless; that is, it provides no built-in mechanism to keep track of conversations between clients and servers. Each request must include details that identify the requester and any other data that might be required to complete a transaction.

Web standards and protocols also include methods for securing data as it is passed among computers. By default, HTTP traffic is transmitted using a plaintext stream that can be decoded easily. Although this is acceptable when users are accessing public content, many Web sites and applications need to transmit information securely between clients and servers. The most common example is that of a payment-processing site that accepts credit card information over the Internet. The HTTP Secure (HTTPS) protocol is designed to provide support for encryption of HTTP-based traffic. By default, HTTPS connections use TCP port 443 for communications, although any other port can be used as well. The most commonly used encryption mechanisms are Secure Sockets Layer (SSL) and Transport Layer Security (TLS). Other encryption mechanisms can also be used, especially in intranet environments.

Web standards and protocols provide a consistent method of exchanging information among computers. The Hypertext Markup Language (HTML) is the primary specification for Web pages. The tag-based format of HTML pages enables developers to use a variety of technologies to create their content in a way that is accessible by different Web browsers. The development tools can range from text editors such as Microsoft Windows Notepad to full-featured development environments such as the Microsoft Visual Studio platform.

The HTTP and HTML specifications were designed to provide basic communication and presentation services. Modern Web applications include features that enable complex application functionality to be presented using these standards. Web developers can use development platforms such as ASP.NET (a component of the Microsoft .NET Framework) to build active Web sites. These sites can keep track of user sessions and can provide access to databases and other information that is stored within the environment.

MORE INFO **Further details about Internet standards**

For more information about specific Internet and Web-based standards, see the World Wide Web Consortium (W3C) Web site at *http://www.w3.org* and the Internet Engineering Task Force (IETF) Web site at *http://www.ietf.org*. Both sites include the official specifications and descriptions for basic Internet protocols.

Web Server Usage Scenarios

The primary advantage of using Web-based content and applications is accessibility from a broad range of client computers. Unlike standard applications, there is generally no need to install or configure any software on users' computers. Because modern operating systems include or support standards-based Web browsers such as Windows Internet Explorer, most users already have the basic client tools they need to access content. IT staff and software developers can use various technologies to present content and deploy applications to both internal and external users.

The IIS platform has been designed to support a variety of scenarios. Some examples include:

- **Public Web sites**   Many businesses have relatively simple needs for communicating information on the Internet. For example, a small business might want to provide contact information and details about its services on a simple Web site.

- **Online shopping**   The Internet has become a commercial marketplace that enables vendors to display and sell a wide variety of products. Online sites include shopping-cart functionality, order processing, and customer support features.

- **Intranet scenarios**   The Web provides a simple method for all users within an organization to access and present content. Company tasks such as creating expense reports or verifying benefits can often be performed online without the need to contact internal staff.

- **Enterprise applications**   A common challenge with enterprise line-of-business applications is the need to deploy and manage client-side installations. To alleviate some of these problems, many organizations have created internal applications that are designed to be accessed through a Web browser. The applications can range from basic single-function sites to distributed enterprise-wide systems.

- **Internet applications**   Users can access their e-mail and create documents, for example, without installing applications on their computers. Distributed organizations and teams can also take advantage of secure access to corporate applications by using the Internet while traveling or working from remote locations.

- **Extranet scenarios**   Businesses commonly partner with other organizations to obtain services. An extranet scenario is one in which users from outside the organization are able to access information. Security is an important concern, but Web-based applications are a good choice because they provide a standard method by which users can access the information they need.

- **Web hosting**   Many companies have focused on offering the service of hosting Web sites for their customers. These hosting companies tend to run large numbers of Web sites on a single physical server, so ensuring security, performance, and reliability are key concerns.

Most organizations will deploy IIS in several roles within the organization. It is important to note that requirements related to features and options will vary based on the specific needs of each deployment.

Exam Tip   When learning about the many features and options of the IIS platform, it often helps to think of scenarios in which those features can be helpful to meet technical or business requirements. When taking Exam 70-643, expect to see questions that require you to understand specific requirements and find the most appropriate option or feature to meet them.

You'll learn more about the specific features and services that the IIS platform supports later in this lesson.

New Features in IIS

The IIS platform is one of the most popular Web servers in use for both public and private Web sites. IIS 7.0 in Windows Server 2008 includes numerous new features that provide increased performance and functionality in a broad range of areas. The major areas of improvement include:

- **Administration**   One of the primary challenges of working with previous versions of IIS was dealing with a large number of property pages and dialog boxes. IIS 7.0 includes new administration tools that are designed to manage the many available options and settings more effectively. The user interface has been designed to be both powerful and accessible for both Web developers and systems administrators.

- **Security**   By default, the Web Server (IIS) server role is enabled with only a basic set of functionalities. Even the binary files for unused features are not available for access in the standard operating system locations. Systems administrators must enable additional services and features explicitly. This helps reduce the attack surface of IIS while also simplifying manageability. In addition, functionality for automatically detecting common hacking attempts is included with the product itself. (This feature was commonly enabled in the past by installing the URLScan utility.)

- **Diagnostics and troubleshooting**   Because organizations depend on Web services as a mission-critical component of their infrastructure, it's important to detect and resolve any Web-based errors quickly. IIS 7.0 includes new features that make it easier to pinpoint problems and obtain the details necessary to address them.

- **Centralized configuration management**   Many organizations support dozens or even hundreds of IIS installations. To meet scalability and performance requirements, it is often necessary to deploy numerous Web servers that essentially have the same configuration settings. In previous versions of IIS, it was difficult to manage these configurations without connecting to each server. IIS 7.0 provides a simplified method by which administrators can share configuration information across server farms. Further, a consistent set of user accounts, including globally unique identifiers (GUIDs) and permissions, are used for IIS security accounts. This means administrators can depend on specific account names and settings when scripting and automating common processes. IIS 7.0 also includes greatly improved command-line support.

- **Support for delegation** It is often necessary to divide Web server administration tasks for security or management reasons. IIS 7.0 provides the ability to implement granular security configuration permissions to support Web-hosting environments and enterprise-level configurations.

- **Backward compatibility** The vast majority of Web sites and applications that were created for previous versions of IIS will remain compatible with IIS 7.0. In addition, IIS 6.0 management tools are provided for those applications that depend on them.

Overall, IIS 7.0 has been designed to address the most common issues encountered with previous versions of IIS. There are also numerous additional improvements in IIS that you'll learn about as this chapter discusses the various features in depth.

MORE INFO   IIS in Windows Vista

Microsoft first made the IIS 7.0 platform available in the Windows Vista operating system. Because the core architecture of IIS in Windows Vista is similar to that in Windows Server 2008, Web developers can use similar environments on both their development workstations and their production servers. It is important to note that there are some feature and licensing differences between the two platforms. For more information, see the Microsoft Internet Information Services Web site at *http://www.microsoft.com/iis/*.

Understanding IIS Components and Options

The IIS platform has been designed with a modular, component-based architecture. In its simplest configuration, the Web server component provides basic HTTP functionality. IIS includes many components and features that can be used to support different types of content and applications. Most deployments will need only a subset of these features. Therefore, administrators can choose to enable only those components that their Web applications require.

Although the modular approach requires systems administrators to enable explicitly the features that they require, this architecture provides numerous advantages:

- **Enhanced security** Each enabled service or feature potentially can increase the security attack surface on an IIS server. This is a significant concern for publicly accessible servers that might be the targets of malicious attacks of unauthorized access attempts.

For example, a defect or vulnerability in a specific type of IIS extension might be used to perform unauthorized actions on the server. Administrators can reduce these risks greatly by enabling only those features and services that are required by their content and applications.

- **Improved performance** Installing and enabling unnecessary components can use up system resources on the server that is running IIS. By enabling only those features that are required specifically, server resources can be retained for use by other applications. The end result is better performance and scalability.

- **Ability to customize server configurations** As mentioned earlier in this lesson, organizations tend to use IIS in a variety of deployment scenarios. The security and functionality requirements can vary significantly, and a modular architecture enables systems administrators to customize each deployment based on its specific needs. For example, the authentication and security requirements of internal Web servers and Internet-accessible servers often differ. Administrators can enable the required features for each type of server independently.

In this section, you'll learn about components and options that are related to the IIS platform.

MORE INFO   Information from the IIS team

The IIS team at Microsoft has created a Web site that includes tutorials, technical articles, and other details about working with the IIS platform. This is a great resource for in-depth information about the many available features and components. The site includes links to downloads and information about products that work with (or on) the IIS platform. Team members have their own blogs, too, which focus on their specific areas of expertise. The main page is located at *http://www.iis.net*.

Understanding the Application Server Role

One of the primary strengths of the Windows platform is its ability to support a range of application development technologies. Modern applications often rely on extensive communications features. For example, a distributed application might need to create and manage transactions across several different sites and services using a distributed network. Building this type of functionality can be difficult and complicated. Applications developers can save significant time and effort by taking advantage of the features that are already available on their operating system platform.

Windows Server 2008 includes the Application Server role to provide support for a variety of different application development technologies. The Application Server role is based on .NET Framework 3.0 technology and includes support for other communications and presentation features. Although the Application Server role is not specifically dependent on the Web Server

(IIS) role, distributed applications that are built using ASP.NET or Windows Communication Foundation (WCF) will require both roles.

Exam Tip   The Application Server role provides additional functionality on top of ASP.NET support and other services that are available for the Web Server (IIS) role. In general, you should not need to install the Application Server role unless a specific Web application or Web service requires it. Basic ASP.NET applications, for example, will run without the Application Server role enabled on the server.

You can install the Application Server role by using the Add Roles Wizard in Server Manager. When you add the role, you will be given the option of determining which additional role services you plan to enable. The specific features include:

- **Application Server Foundation**   This is a required feature of the Application Server role. It includes support for technology in the .NET Framework 3.0 platform. The primary technology components are the WCF, Windows Presentation Foundation (WPF), and Windows Workflow Foundation (WF).

- **Web Server (IIS) Support**   The Application Server role can be integrated with the Web Server (IIS) role to enable Web applications to access advanced features. When you select this option, the Add Roles Wizard will prompt you to install IIS automatically if it is not already installed.

- **COM+ Network Access**   The Component Object Model (COM) standard provides applications developers with a method for accessing different pieces of application code. COM+ provides the ability to invoke (or access) application code remotely across a network. Distributed applications, such as those that require multiple tiers of functionality, might require this feature.

- **TCP Port Sharing**   A potential management challenge of working in distributed environments is that of supporting many server applications on a single computer. Generally, each application requires its own TCP port for responding to inbound requests. The TCP Port Sharing feature enables multiple applications to share the same port to simplify server and firewall configuration.

- **Windows Process Activation Service Support**   The Windows Process Activation Service (WAS) provides the ability to access application services over the network by using different types of protocols and services. This feature can be used by IIS itself to support additional protocols and communications methods.

- **Distributed Transactions**   Applications that involve distributed transactions require multiple servers and applications to coordinate their activities before changes are made permanent. By using this section, you enable incoming and outgoing remote transactions and support the WS-Atomic Transactions standard for Web Services.

Generally, you should verify requirements with Web application developers to determine which Application Server components (if any) are required.

When done correctly, collecting and communicating Web server requirements can help ensure that systems administrators are aligned with the developers and users that they support. From an IT standpoint, IIS is one of those technology areas that can benefit from input and expertise from all areas of your organization. Be sure to do your homework before diving into the configuration process and you're much more likely to end up with the right IIS configuration.

Understanding IIS 7.0 Role Services

Role services define which specific features and options of the IIS platform are available for use on the local Web server. Once you have installed IIS 7.0 on a computer running Windows Server 2008, you can add components by using Server Manager. When you use Server Manager, you will see a dialog box like the one shown in Figure 5-1.

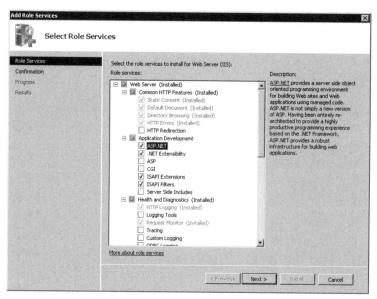

Figure 5-1   Managing Web Server role services in Server Manager

IIS role services are organized into several major areas:

- Common HTTP Features
- Application Development
- Health and Diagnostics
- Security

- Performance
- Management Tools
- FTP Publishing Service

The top level of the hierarchy is the Web Server itself. This item represents the core IIS services that are required by the optional components that are also available for installation. Two other items, Management Tools and the FTP Publishing Service, can be installed independently of the Web Server. Each area contains features and options that are related. Several of the items depend on other role services. If you select an item without first selecting its dependencies, you will be given the option to add the required role services automatically. (See Figure 5-2.)

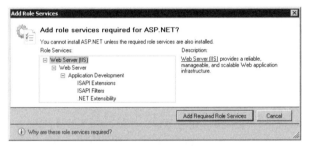

Figure 5-2 Including role dependencies when adding a role service

---

Exam Tip Note that adding a role service makes it available for use by your Web sites and applications. Additional configuration is sometimes required to take advantage of the service. For example, enabling certain authentication options will not make them automatically apply to all your Web sites. When taking Exam 70-643, keep in mind that adding a Web Server role service might be only one step in meeting the complete solution requirements.

Default IIS Role Services

As mentioned earlier, the default configuration includes a limited set of functionality. It is appropriate for installations that serve only limited static content and do not need advanced security or development features. In many cases, you will want to enable additional options.

Table 2-1 lists the role services that are included when you add the Web Server (IIS) server role to the computer.

Table 5-1 Default Role Services in the Web Server (IIS) Server Role

Group/Category	Feature(s)
Common HTTP Features	Static Content Default Document Directory Browsing HTTP Errors
Health and Diagnostics Features	HTTP Logging Request Monitor
Security	Request Filtering
Performance Features	Static Content Compression
Management Tools	IIS Management Console

In the following sections, you'll learn more about the purpose of these and the many optional role services.

Common HTTP Features

The most important function of the Web Server (IIS) role is to serve HTML Web pages by using the HTTP protocol. The components of the Common HTTP Features group that are available to install are:

- **Static Content** This functionality allows for serving static Web pages to clients, using HTTP. The most common content types are static HTML pages and images. Static content files are usually sent directly to users without any server-side processing.

- **Default Document** This feature allows IIS to return a specific file automatically for a Web site when one is not explicitly requested in the URL. For example, if a user attempts to connect to *http://www.contoso.com*, the Web server can be configured to return the default.htm file as a response.

- **Directory Browsing** IIS includes built-in functionality for providing basic directory listings to users. When enabled, directory browsing sends information about the files and folders on a Web site to the client's Web browser. Because users will have the ability to access and download any files to which they have the appropriate permissions, this feature is usually disabled for public Web sites. If the default document feature is enabled and a default document is found, users will not see the directory browsing screen.

- **HTTP Errors** By default, most Web browsers are designed to present an error message automatically to users whenever a problem occurs. For example, if a page cannot be found or if the server is too busy, the Web browser will display this information to the user. To enhance the user experience, IIS can be configured to return custom error pages automatically when these problems occur. The content of the error pages can include contact information for the Web site's administrator or other details about resolving the problem.

■ **HTTP Redirection**   The HTTP protocol supports a method of redirecting a request from one site to another. The Web server can be configured to send an HTTP redirect request automatically to a Web user when a specific site is accessed. Site redirection is useful for situations in which a Web site has been relocated to a different URL or when multiple URLs are designed to access the same content.

Although these Common HTTP Features can be added, the specific behavior of each IIS Web site will be based on its content and configuration settings.

Application Development Features

Although some basic Web sites can meet their requirements by using only static content, it's far more common for production sites to require dynamic Web services and Web application support. IIS has been designed to support a broad array of different features and technologies to support these requirements. The list of Application Development role services includes:

■ **ASP.NET**   ASP.NET is the primary Microsoft Web server development platform. It is based on the .NET Framework and provides a powerful and flexible development framework for handling common Web site design tasks. Features include built-in support for managing access to databases, security and authorization methods, and reliability and scalability features.

■ **.NET Extensibility**   The Microsoft .NET Framework programming platform can be used to make modifications to IIS Web server functionality. This role service enables developers to access the IIS management namespaces and objects for building logic that interacts with Web server requests.

■ **ASP**   Active Server Pages (ASP) technology is the predecessor to the ASP.NET platform. ASP provided a simplified, script-based method of developing Web-based applications. ASP scripts run on the Web server and generate HTML content that is passed back to the user through IIS. Support for ASP is provided primarily for backward compatibility with applications that have not yet been moved to the ASP.NET platform.

■ **CGI**   The Common Gateway Interface (CGI) is a standard that defines how Web servers can pass information to programmatic scripts. It is required by some server-side components, especially those that have been written to run on multiple Web server platforms. Web development languages such as PHP: Hypertext Preprocessor (PHP) rely on CGI support within the Web server. IIS 7.0 includes features that can improve the performance of CGI processing significantly.

■ **ISAPI extensions**   IIS supports an extensibility standard known as the Internet Server Application Programming Interface (ISAPI). By building ISAPI extensions, Web developers can create their own content handlers that can interact with every aspect of the Web request pipeline. The ISAPI standard is designed to provide scalability for supporting many simultaneous requests.

- **ISAPI filters**   ISAPI filters are custom code that developers can create to process specific Web server requests. The logic can receive Web request details and return the appropriate content based on server-side logic. IIS attempts to match Web requests with the most appropriate ISAPI filter for handling that type of content. Enabling this role service allows developers to add custom ISAPI filters to IIS.

- **Server Side Includes**   Web designers can often benefit from having the ability to embed certain common content on all their Web pages. Examples include a site header, navigation elements, and site footers. The Server Side Includes role service enables the Web server to include other pieces of content when generating a Web server request. For security reasons, this feature is disabled by default. However, sites that do not rely on other Web development technologies (such as ASP.NET) might require this capability.

When planning to deploy production Web sites, determine which additional features should be enabled. This information is usually available from the Web application development team or organization.

Health and Diagnostics Features

Although basic Web server functionality can appear simple, there are numerous steps that must be performed during the processing of a typical Web request. Organizations that depend on their Web servers for access to critical information and systems need a method of isolating and troubleshooting any problems that might occur. Role services that are included in the Health and Diagnostics features section are designed to help administrators and developers collect and analyze information about Web requests.

A common challenge with monitoring Web sites is managing the volume of information that is generated. The process of recording in-depth details about all requests can add a significant level of performance overhead to production systems. To help address this issue, IIS 7.0 includes enhanced features for collecting details on specific requests and for configuring which information should be collected. The specific role services are:

- **HTTP Logging**   The most basic form of logging in IIS is to store HTTP request information within text files on the server's file system. HTTP logging enables this functionality, along with a set of default settings for logging requests. Details can be customized by accessing the properties of each Web site. The default location for log files is *%SystemDrive%*\Inetpub\Logs\LogFiles. Figure 5-3 shows a list of fields that can be included in the log files.

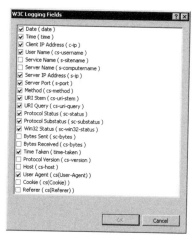

Figure 5-3   Configuring logging options

- **Logging Tools**   Raw HTTP request logs are difficult to view and analyze manually. On busy Web servers, the files can get extremely large quickly. Because the content typically is organized with a single row per request, administrators might need to search through thousands of rows to get the information they need. The Logging Tools role service provides simple utilities for accessing and analyzing log files.

- **Request Monitor**   A common difficulty with diagnosing performance-related issues on a Web server is that of trying to determine which activity is occurring currently. The Request Monitor feature enables administrators to see which requests are executing within the Web server process currently. This can help isolate the potential source of slowdowns or loss of service due to long-running requests or other issues.

- **Tracing**   When an error or performance-related issue occurs on a Web server, it is useful to collect as much information as possible about the problem. Unfortunately, due to performance requirements, it's usually impractical to store details about all requests. Tracing functionality enables IIS to store detailed information for any failed requests. This feature works by keeping information about executing requests in memory just long enough to determine whether it was successful. If it was not, the results can be stored on the Web server for later analysis.

- **Custom Logging**   The HTTP Logging feature provides a default text-based format for storing Web request information. Although this can meet the basic needs for most Web sites and services, organizations can also create their own COM-based modules, using the Custom Logging option. Developers will need to build the logging module and then register it with IIS for it to store data. This approach provides the greatest flexibility in determining which details are important to record.

- **ODBC Logging** Although storing data in a text file is an efficient method of logging requests, it makes the process of analyzing and reporting on Web server performance difficult. The ODBC Logging role service enables applications to store Web request data in any format that is supported by an Open Database Connectivity (ODBC) connection. Examples include relational database servers such as Microsoft SQL Server and file-based formats such as Microsoft Excel. It is important to note, however, that logging to ODBC-based sources can cause significant processing and storage overhead, especially on busy Web servers.

Web administrators often use log analyzer applications to process the text-based log files that store request information. Details can be used to isolate problems (such as erroneous links or missing content) as well as to analyze traffic and the popularity of specific Web pages.

Security Features

Maintaining security for Web sites, Web applications, and Web services is an important concern with all Web servers. Depending on the specific deployment and usage configuration, organizations can enable a wide variety of security mechanisms. The Security role services that are available for IIS include:

- Basic Authentication
- Windows Authentication
- Digest Authentication
- Client Certificate Mapping Authentication
- IIS Client Certificate Mapping Authentication
- URL Authorization
- Request Filtering
- IP and Domain Restrictions

Selecting and implementing these security mechanisms is covered in Chapter 6, "Managing Web Server Security."

Performance Features

Organizations often find that they receive a large volume of activity on their production Web servers, so it is fundamental for all types of Web servers to be able to service a large number of requests in a given amount of time. IIS includes numerous architectural features that help make the servicing of Web requests as efficient as possible. In addition, the Performance role services section includes two additional options:

- **Static Content Compression** The HTTP protocol provides a method by which static Web pages (such as HTML files) can be compressed before they are sent to clients' Web browsers. The Web browser uncompresses the information and renders the Web page. This method can save significant bandwidth with a minimal cost to CPU performance on the client and the server. In addition, IIS has the ability to store frequently accessed static content in memory, further increasing performance and scalability. This feature is enabled by default and will work automatically as long as users' Web browsers support HTTP compression.

- **Dynamic Content Compression** Dynamic content usually results in different information being sent to different users. Because dynamic content often changes for each request that is made to the Web server, the amount of processing overhead for compressing the data can be significant. Dynamic content compression is disabled by default, but it can be added to help reduce bandwidth consumption for Web applications.

In general, bandwidth is more limited than is processing power on modern servers. Therefore, unless an organization has a specific reason to disable it, it is recommended that static content compression remain enabled.

Management Tools

The Management Tools section provides administrators with the ability to determine which programs will be available for working with IIS. By default, only the primary administration tool, the IIS Management Console, is installed along with the Web Server (IIS) role. This tool provides a graphical method of configuring and managing IIS Web services. You can choose to remove the IIS Management Console if you will be managing the server remotely or if your corporate security policy requires it.

The other available Management Tools options include IIS Management Scripts and Tools, which allows for command-line administration of IIS, and the Management Service, which enables you to administer IIS remotely using the IIS Management Console.

An important design goal for IIS 7.0 was to provide support for IIS 6.0–based Web applications. Although many applications can be moved directly to IIS 7.0, several backward-compatibility features are included as role services:

- IIS 6.Management Compatibility
- IIS 6 Metabase Compatibility
- IIS 6 WMI Compatibility
- IIS 6 Scripting Tools
- IIS 6 Management Console

You'll learn more about these features and how you can use them in Lesson 2, "Configuring Internet Information Services."

Installing the Web Server (IIS) Role

Although numerous features and options are available for the Web Server (IIS) role, installing the appropriate options is a simple task. Adding this role is the basis for providing Web server functionality. Components of IIS are also required by several other features and options that are part of Windows Server 2008. You begin the server role process by using the Add Roles Wizard in Server Manager. (See Figure 5-4.)

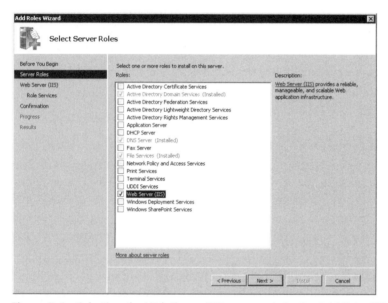

Figure 5-4   Selecting the Web Server (IIS) server role in the Add Roles Wizard

The Add Roles Wizard will evaluate the configuration of the local computer automatically and determine whether any additional role services are required. For example, if the Windows Process Activation Service has not yet been installed, you will be prompted to add it.

The Web Services (IIS) step provides some introductory information about IIS. The note also provides information about installing WSRM to ensure performance if the computer will be servicing multiple roles.

The Select Role Services page enables you to decide which components of IIS will be installed as part of the role setup process. (See Figure 5-5.) The default options provide a minimal set of features for the core Web server role. As described later in this section, you can also add or remove role services after the Web Server (IIS) role has been enabled. Because some role features depend on other features, you might be prompted to add those dependencies when selecting an item.

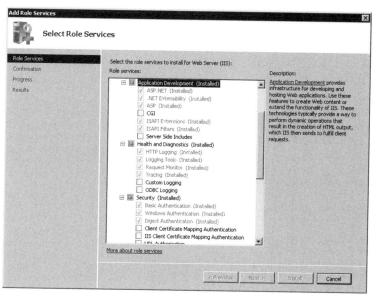

Figure 5-5 Selecting roles services for the Web Server (IIS) role

The Confirm Installation Selections page will provide you with a list of the configuration settings and role services you have chosen. Once you review the list and click Finish, the installation process will begin. Depending on which role services you've selected, the setup process might take significant time, require a reboot of the computer, or both. If a reboot is required, the Add Roles Wizard will resume from its previous ending point after you log on to the server again. Finally, on the Installation Results page (shown in Figure 5-6), you will see a confirmation of which features have been installed and any additional information that should be noted.

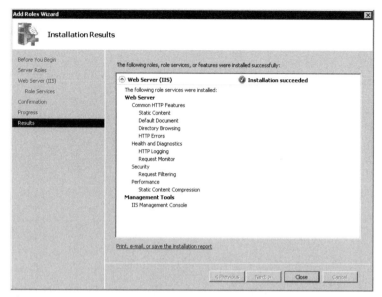

Figure 5-6 Viewing the installation results for adding the Web Server (IIS) server role

Verifying the IIS Installation by Using Server Manager

Once you have installed IIS, there are several ways in which you can verify that the Web Server processes are working properly. The first is by using the Server Manager tool. Expand the Roles section and then click Web Server (IIS) to view the relevant details. This page provides information on any event log items that need attention. In addition, it lists the services that have been installed, along with their current state. (See Figure 5-7.) The specific list of included items will vary based on which role services and dependencies you have installed. The World Wide Web Publishing Service (W3SVC) component is the main process responsible for responding to Web requests.

Server Manager also shows information about which role services have been installed for the Web Server. (See Figure 5-8.) You can use the Add Role Services and Remove Role Services links to make changes to the configuration.

Finally, the Resources And Support section shows recommendations and other detailed information that can be helpful when you first set up IIS and the Web Server role on a computer. You will learn more about these options in Lesson 2. Links are also available to various online resources for learning more about IIS.

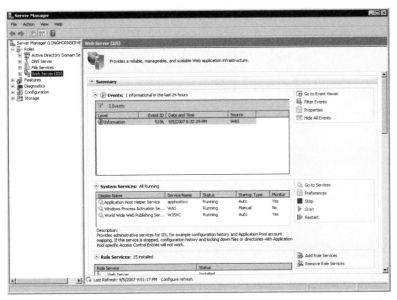

Figure 5-7   Viewing the status of the Web Server (IIS) role in Server Manager

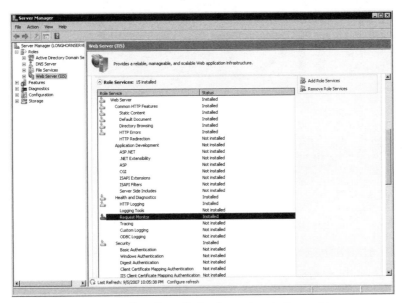

Figure 5-8   Viewing a list of installed role services in Server Manager

Verifying the IIS Installation by Using Internet Explorer

When you add the Web Server (IIS) role to a computer running Windows Server 2008, a default Web site that is configured to respond on HTTP port 80 is created automatically. The default location for this site is the *%SystemDrive%*\Inetpub\wwwroot folder. The default content includes only a simple static HTML page and an image file.

Because the purpose of IIS is to serve Web pages, a good way to verify that it is working properly is to launch a Web browser and connect to the local computer. You can use the built-in local alias by browsing to *http://localhost*, or you can use the local computer's fully qualified name (for example, *http://server1.contoso.com*). Using either method, you should see the default welcome page, as shown in Figure 5-9. When you click a language, the links will take you automatically to the *http://www.iis.net* Web site (assuming that the server has access to the Internet).

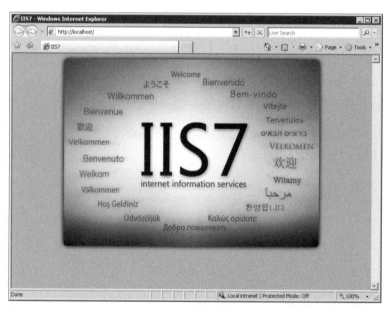

Figure 5-9   Viewing the default IIS Web site

It is also a good idea to attempt to access the IIS Web site from a remote computer. Just open any Web browser and connect to the fully qualified address of the Web server. If you are unable to connect, some of the likely problems are Domain Name System (DNS) name resolution issues or firewall configuration problems.

Managing Role Services

The modular architecture of IIS enables you to add or remove role services quickly and easily after the Web Server (IIS) role has been enabled on a computer running Windows Server 2008. The most common reasons for changing the role service configuration are to support a new type of Web application or Web service. You can also remove unnecessary services if they are no longer needed or the technical requirements have changed. Because the removal or addition of a role service affects the configuration of the entire server, make sure to consider the potential effects on all the Web sites on the server.

To do this, open Server Manager, expand Roles, right-click Web Server (IIS), and choose either Add Role Services or Remove Role Services. The dialog box will show which components are installed. The check mark means that an item (or an item and all its children, if there are any) have been installed. A cleared check box indicates that the item has not been installed. A dimmed box means that some of the role services components have been installed.

When you add or remove role services, you'll receive a confirmation message, and then the process will continue. If a reboot of the computer is required, the configuration process will resume automatically whenever you next log on to the computer.

Using Command-Line and Automated Installation Options

Organizations that rely on IIS often need to deploy many different installations of IIS. Although you can perform the process locally on each server, it is often more efficient to create scripts or commands for performing the necessary steps. There are several methods of performing automated and command-line–based installations.

The ServerManagerCmd.exe utility can be launched to install the Web Server (IIS) server role from the command line. For example, the command *ServerManagerCmd.exe –install Web-Server* will attempt to install the default Web server components. You can use the *ServerManagerCmd.exe –query* command to view which roles and features have been installed on the local computer. (See Figure 5-10.) This can be helpful when you want to collect complete configuration information quickly to determine whether changes are required to support a new Web application. For more information about using this command, type **ServerManagerCmd.exe -?** at a command prompt. You can also use this command to add or remove features such as WSRM.

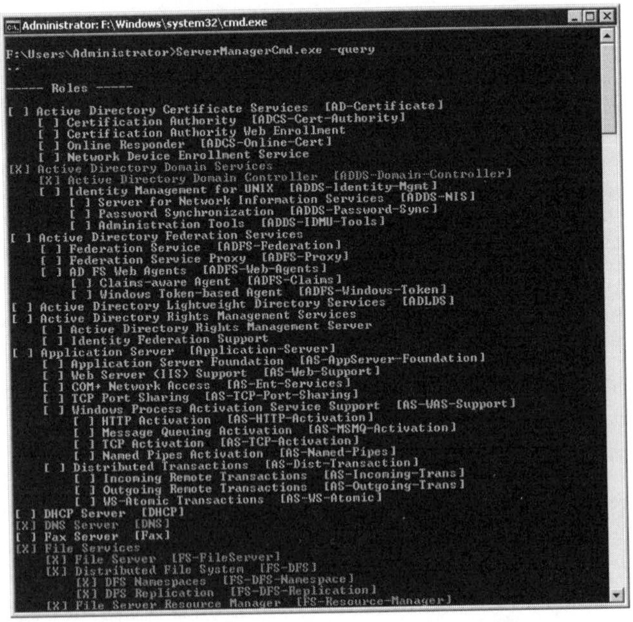

Figure 5-10   Viewing a list of installed role services and features, using *ServerManagerCmd.exe*

Another option for performing a command-line installation of the Web Server (IIS) server role is to use the Windows Package Manager (PkgMgr.exe) utility. Windows Package Manager uses an XML file to store details about which features and options should be included in the IIS installation. For more information about using this utility, type **PkgMgr.exe -?** at a command prompt.

In Lesson 2, you will learn about how to use other commands to configure IIS further by using the command line or from within scripts.

Removing the Web Server (IIS) Role

If you no longer require an installation of Windows Server 2008 to serve as a Web server, you can remove IIS and all its related components by using the Remove Roles command in Server Manager. Keep in mind, however, that many different components and features of the operating system might require the Web Server to be installed. These dependent features either will be removed or the dependent functionality will be made available. Figure 5-11 shows the Confirm Removal Selections page.

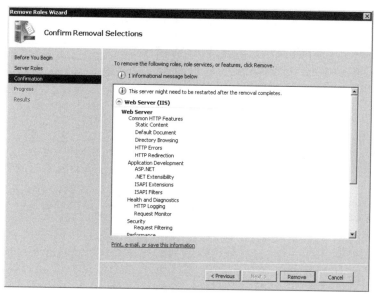

Figure 5-11   Confirming the removal of the Web Server (IIS) role

Depending on which features were installed, it might be necessary to restart the computer during the removal process. If that is necessary, the process will resume automatically whenever a user next logs on to the computer.

Removing the Web Server (IIS) role will remove all the binary files and role services that are associated with the Web server. The basic server configuration, including the list of Web sites and their settings, will be retained if you choose to reinstall the Web server role. Actual Web site content will not be deleted automatically. If you are planning to remove Web services permanently from the server, manually delete any remaining Web pages and data that are no longer required.

Using Windows System Resource Manager

An important consideration for any server is to ensure that critical services are not interrupted when the system is under load. By default, most services in Windows Server 2008 run at an equal priority level. Windows System Resource Manager (WSRM) helps administrators assign priorities to various system processes such as IIS. Although WSRM is not a requirement for running IIS, on busy Web servers or servers that are providing many important services, enabling this feature can be helpful. For example, administrators can create Resource Allocation policies to define CPU and memory limitations to ensure that the system continues to respond well even when under heavy load. (See Figure 5-12.)

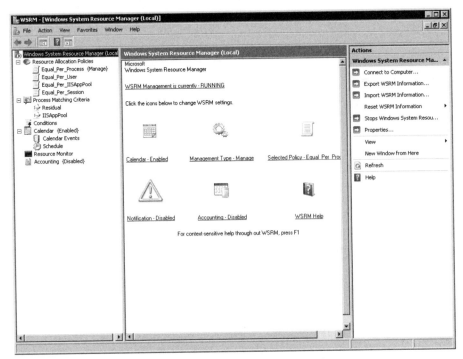

Figure 5-12   The Windows System Resource Manager console

You can add WSRM to a computer running Windows Server 2008 by using Server Manager. Right-click the Server Manager item and select Add Features to start the process. The Add Features Wizard includes an option to add WSRM. For more information about WSRM, in the Start menu Start Search box, type **system resource**, and then press Enter. The help file includes details on creating and managing resource settings.

Quick Check

1. What are two methods by which you can verify a successful installation of the Web Server (IIS) role?
2. When can you add role services to the Web Server (IIS) server role?

> **Quick Check Answers**
> 1. You can use Server Manager to verify that the proper services have been installed and started, and you can use Internet Explorer or another Web browser to verify that the default Web site is responding.
> 2. You can add the role services when you initially add the server role, or you can add them after the Web Server (IIS) role has been enabled.

PRACTICE Installing and Verifying the Web Server (IIS) Role

In this practice, you will perform the steps of installing the Web Server (IIS) server role on the server2.contoso.com server. You must complete Exercise 1 before performing Exercise 2.

▶ **Exercise 1 Install the Web Server Role**

In this exercise, you will perform the steps required to add the Web Server (IIS) server role. You will install the service with only the basic role services that are enabled by default.

1. Log on to server2.contoso.com, using an account that is a member of the local Administrators group.

2. Open Server Manager. Right-click Roles, and select Add Roles to open the Add Roles Wizard. Click Next on the Before You Begin page if it is displayed.

3. On the Select Server Roles page, select the Web Server (IIS) server role. If any required dependencies are detected, choose to add them automatically. Click Next.

4. On the Web Server (IIS) page, read the basic introductory information about IIS. Note that you can use the Additional Information links to learn more about IIS and related components. Click Next.

   On the Select Role Services page, the default selections will include those components that are part of the basic Web Server (IIS) role. Note that you can obtain more information about each item in the list by selecting it and reading the text on the right side of the page. Links to additional information in the help file are available for most items. For the purpose of this exercise, keep only the default options selected, and then click Next. For a list of which options are selected by default, see Table 5-1.

5. On the Confirm Installation Selections page, verify the role service selections that will be included. Optionally, you can choose to print, e-mail, or save the information to keep a record of which components were installed. When you are ready to begin the installation process, click Install.

6. When the installation process has completed, verify the installed roles and services on the Installation Results page. To complete the process, click Close.

7. When finished, close Server Manager.

▶ **Exercise 2   Verify the IIS Installation**

In this exercise, you will verify the installation of the Web Server (IIS) role that you added to server2.contoso.com in Exercise 1. Specifically, you will use both Server Manager and Internet Explorer to ensure that IIS is working properly.

1. Log on to server2.contoso.com, using an account that is a member of the local Administrators group.

2. Open Server Manager. Expand Roles, and then click Web Server (IIS).

   You will see a summary of information about the Web Server role. The Events section will display any important messages that are related to the Web Server (IIS) server role.

3. In the System Services section, verify that the World Wide Web Publishing Service (W3SVC) is started. You will also see the Application Host Helper Service (apphostsvc) and the Windows Process Activation Service (WAS). If either of these services is stopped, click it and choose to start it.

4. In the Role Services section, view a list of the installed items, and verify that all the default options have been installed. (The list of default role services is provided in Table 5-1 in Lesson 1, "Installing the Web Server (IIS) Role.")

5. Close Server Manager and open Internet Explorer. In the Address box, type **http:// localhost**, and then press Enter. You should see the default IIS welcome page.

6. In the Internet Explorer Address box, type the URL **http://server2.contoso.com** and press Enter. You should again see the IIS welcome page. Close Internet Explorer.

7. When you are finished, close Server Manager.

Lesson Summary

- The Web Server (IIS) role is designed to provide access to Web site content, using the HTTP protocol.

- The Application Server role provides support to applications that require features of the .NET Framework 3.0, COM+, and distributed transactions.

- Windows System Resource Manager (WSRM) can be used to assign resource allocation rules to various workloads and services such as IIS.

- IIS 7.0 role services include features for application development, health and diagnostics, security, performance, and management.

- You can use Server Manager to add the Web Server (IIS) server role and to manage role services.
- You can verify the installation of IIS by using Server Manager or by browsing to the default Web site, using Internet Explorer.

Lesson Review

You can use the following questions to test your knowledge of the information in Lesson 1, "Installing the Web Server (IIS) Role." The questions are also available on the companion CD if you prefer to review them in electronic form.

NOTE Answers

Answers to these questions and explanations of why each answer choice is correct or incorrect are located in the "Answers" section at the end of the book.

---

1. You are a systems administrator who is attempting to troubleshoot a problem with accessing a Web site on a computer running Windows Server 2008. In the past, users have been able to access the Web site by using *http://hr.contoso.com*. However, when they attempt to access the site now, they receive the error message "Internet Explorer Cannot Display The Web page." Which of the following steps should you take to resolve the error?

    A. Using Server Manager, add the HTTP Errors server role.

    B. Using Server Manager, verify that the World Wide Web Publishing Service has been started.

    C. Verify the configuration of the users' Web browsers.

    D. Using Server Manager, add the HTTP Logging server role.

    E. Using Server Manager, click Web Server (IIS) in the list of roles, and verify that the IIS Admin Service has been started.

Lesson 2: Configuring Internet Information Services

After you have installed the Web Server (IIS) role, you will likely need to create and manage Web sites and enable specific features that are required by your applications. The details of these tasks will be based on the type of Web services you require and the way in which IIS will be used. Considerations include migrating Web sites from previous versions of IIS and managing multiple sites and applications on the same server. Fortunately, IIS includes several useful management tools and methods for simplifying administration. In this lesson, you'll learn about how to manage Web sites and server settings for the Web Server (IIS) role in Windows Server 2008.

MORE INFO   Securing IIS

One of the most important considerations for production Web servers is that of managing security settings and permissions. This lesson focuses on configuring Web applications and features other than security. For more information about authentication and authorization approaches, see Chapter 6.

> **After this lesson, you will be able to:**
> - Use the IIS Manager utility to connect to and manage server settings for the Web Server role.
> - Create and configure settings for Web sites, including site bindings.
> - Create and manage new Web applications within Web sites.
> - Describe the purpose of application pools and manage application pool settings for Web sites and Web applications.
> - Create and manage virtual directories.
> - Use *AppCmd.exe* to perform common IIS Web server administration tasks.
> - Describe how IIS 7.0 manages configuration settings stored in the Application-Host.config and Web.config files.
> - Provide support for migrating applications from IIS 6.0.
>
> **Estimated lesson time: 60 minutes**

Working with IIS Management Tools

As you learned in Lesson 1, IIS includes many features and options that can be enabled to meet technical and business requirements. The Internet Information Services (IIS) Manager utility is the primary tool you will use to configure and manage Web sites and their related settings. It is installed automatically when you add the Web Server (IIS) server role to a computer running Windows Server 2008 using the default options. You can launch it by selecting

Internet Information Services (IIS) Manager from the Administrative Tools program group. Figure 5-13 shows the user interface.

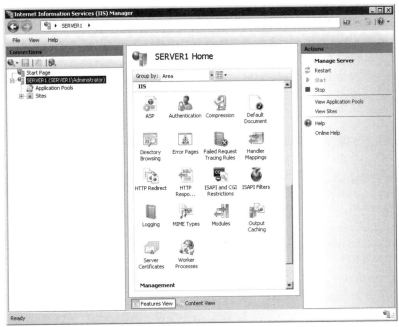

Figure 5-13   Using the IIS Manager console to connect to the local server

By default, IIS Manager will connect to the local server. This will enable you to make configuration changes to the server and other settings for this computer. IIS Manager has been designed to provide a vast array of information, using simple and consistent user interface features. The left pane shows information about the server to which you are connected. You can expand these branches to view information about Web sites and other objects that are hosted on that server. Some items contain additional commands that are available by right-clicking the object name.

Using the Features Views

The center pane of the display provides details and options that are related to the selected item in the left pane. Two main views can be selected at the bottom of the screen. Features View shows a list of all the available settings that can be configured for the selected item. The specific list of items will vary based on which role servers you have added to the server's configuration. The Group By drop-down list enables you to specify how you want the various items to be displayed. The options are:

- **No Grouping**   All items are displayed alphabetically in a single list.
- **Category**   Items are grouped based on their functional areas (for example, Performance and Security).
- **Area**   Items are groups based on the configuration areas that they will affect.

Figure 5-14 shows the items that are displayed when the server item is selected in the left pane and when the Category grouping is selected. In addition to these options, you can display the items by using Details, Icons, Tiles, or List options. The overall layout is similar to that of Windows Explorer. It is designed to organize and display a large number of settings in a way that is easy for systems administrators to understand and manage.

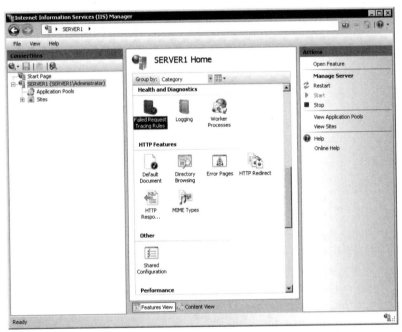

Figure 5-14   Viewing IIS Manager configuration items grouped by category

Double-clicking specific features will load a separate options page that enables you to modify those settings.

Exam Tip Learning about the many features and options that are part of the IIS platform can be daunting, especially if you're not already familiar with Web development and management. Often, a picture can be worth a thousand words (and can help you remember available options and settings when you're taking Exam 70-643). For that reason, there are plenty of screen shots in this lesson. There's no substitute for doing, so a good way to prepare for the exam is simply to access the various properties pages for the many features and role services that are available. Having seen these options can be helpful when deciding how best to meet specific requirements, both on the exam and in the real world.

Using the Content View

Content View is designed to show the files and folders that are part of a Web site. It displays details in a Windows Explorer format and offers the ability to filter and group the list of files. (See Figure 5-15.) Content View is most useful when you are managing site content rather than site settings. It is also similar to default display in the management tools from previous versions of IIS.

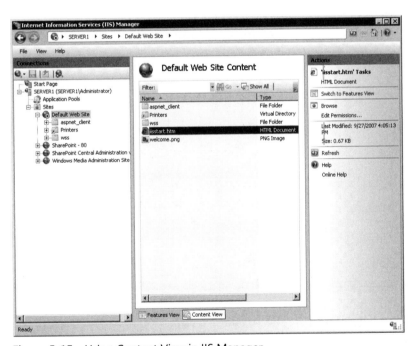

Figure 5-15 Using Content View in IIS Manager

MORE INFO   Transitioning from IIS 6.0

If you're moving to IIS 7.0 after having worked with IIS 6.0, rest assured that all the functionality that you're used to seeing is still here. Roughly speaking, the Features View is a replacement for the properties pages that were available for configuring an IIS 6.0 Web server. Content View shows the information about the files and folders within each selected Web site and directory in a way that is similar to the right-side pane in IIS 6.0. The goal in IIS 7.0 is to organize the presentation of a wide range of options without overwhelming systems administrators.

Using the Actions Pane

The right side of the IIS Manager screen displays the Actions pane. The specific commands that appear here are context-sensitive. For example, when you select a Web site, you will see actions for browsing to the Web site and for stopping, starting, or restarting the Web site. (See Figure 5-16.) Furthermore, when you are changing settings for specific features, generally you will find Accept and Cancel links within the Actions pane.

Figure 5-16   Viewing commands for managing a Web site in the IIS Manager Actions pane

Creating and Configuring Web Sites

Although some Web servers might be responsible primarily for hosting only a single Web site, it is much more common for a single IIS server to host many different Web services and applications. Before you learn about how to administer IIS, it is important to understand how the different Web server components and objects fit together.

Understanding Sites and Site Bindings

Web sites are the top-level containers that provide access to Web content. Every Web site must map to a physical path on the server. Generally, this path will contain the root folder for all content that will be available to users who access the site.

The configuration of the Web site specifies which protocols, ports, and other settings will be used to connect to the Web server. This information is known collectively as a *site binding*. Each site can have multiple bindings, based on the needs of the server. The details that can be specified in a site binding include:

- **Type**   Specifies the protocol that will used to connect to the Web server. The two default options are HTTP and HTTPS.

NOTE Supporting other protocols

One of the benefits of the WAS is that it enables IIS 7.0 to create sites that respond to protocols other than HTTP and HTTPS. For the purpose of taking the exam (and the content in this chapter), you will learn primarily about working with the two most common Web server protocols. When supporting distributed applications, such as those that use the WCF, keep in mind that IIS sites can support direct TCP connections and other methods of communications.

- **IP Address**   The list of IPv4 or IPv6 address(es) on which the server will respond. If the server is configured with more than one IP address, different Web sites can be configured to respond to each. In addition to selecting a specific IP address, administrators can also choose the (All Unassigned) option to allow the Web site to respond to a request on any interface that doesn't have an explicit port and protocol binding.

- **Port**   Specifies the TCP port on which the server will listen and respond. The default port for HTTP connections is port 80. Users who need to access Web sites on alternative ports must specify the port number in their URL. For example, the URL address *http://Server1.contoso.com:5937* will attempt to connect to the Web server named Server1.contoso.com by using the HTTP protocol on TCP port 5937. The standard range for TCP ports is between 1 and 65535. Generally, many of the port numbers under 1024 are reserved for use by specific well-known applications, although there is no technical reason that they cannot be used for hosting a Web site.

- **Host Name**   This text setting allows multiple Web sites to share the same protocol type, IP address, and port number while still allowing users to connect to different Web sites. The method works by interpreting the host header information stored in an HTTP request. Site administrators can configure their DNS settings to allow multiple domain names to point to the same IP address. The domain name information is then used by the Web server to determine to which Web site the user is attempting to connect and to generate the response from the appropriate site.

It is important to remember that the combination of site binding settings must be unique for every Web site hosted on an installation of IIS. For example, no two Web sites can respond using the same protocol, IP address, port, and host name setting. Although it is possible to create multiple sites with the same site bindings, IIS will allow only a single one of these sites to be started at a time.

Managing the Default Web Site

Initially, the Web Server (IIS) role includes a site called Default Web Site. The site is configured to respond to requests, using HTTP (port 80) and HTTPS (port 443). To view a list of the bindings, right-click the Default Web Site in IIS Manager (see Figure 5-17) and select Edit Bindings. (You can also use the Bindings link in the Actions pane to open the same dialog box.)

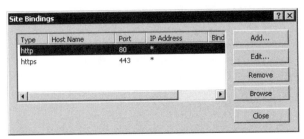

Figure 5-17   Viewing the site bindings for the Default Web Site

When you launch a Web browser and connect to a URL such as *http://server2.contoso.com*, IIS receives the request on HTTP port 80 and returns the content from the appropriate Web site.

To add a new site binding for the Default Web Site, click the Add button in the Site Bindings dialog box. As shown in Figure 5-18, you can specify the protocol type, IP address, and port information along with an optional host name. If you attempt to add a site binding that is already in use, you will be reminded that you must configure a unique binding.

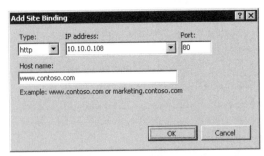

Figure 5-18   Adding a new site binding to the Default Web Site

Adding Web Sites

Start the process of adding a new Web site to IIS by right-clicking the Sites container in IIS Manager and selecting Add Web Site. Figure 5-19 shows the options that are available for the new site.

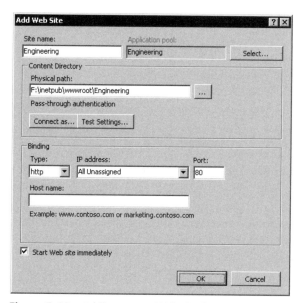

Figure 5-19   Adding a new Web site by using IIS Manager

In addition to specifying the default protocol binding for the site, you will need to provide the site name. This setting is simply a logical name that will not be seen directly by users of the site. By default, IIS Manager will create a new *application pool* with the same name you provide for the Web site. You can also select an existing application pool by clicking the Select button. You will learn more about application pools and their purpose later in this lesson.

The Content Directory section enables you to provide the full physical path to the folder that will be the root of the Web site. The default root location for IIS Web content is *%SystemDrive%* \Inetpub\wwwroot. The initial files for the default Web site are located in this folder. You should create a new folder (either within this path or in another one) to store the content of the new Web site. The Connect As button enables you to specify the security credentials that will be used by IIS to access the content. The default setting is to use Pass-Through Authentication, which means that the security context of the requesting Web user will be used. You will learn more about securing Web site content in Chapter 6.

The final check box enables you to specify whether you want the site to be started immediately after you click the OK button. Again, you will be given a warning if the Web site binding information is already in use. (See Figure 5-20.)

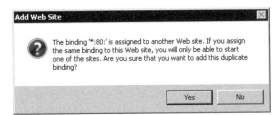

Figure 5-20   Attempting to create a new Web site by using duplicate binding information

Once you click OK to add the Web site, it will appear within the left pane of IIS Manager. Web sites can be started and stopped individually by selecting them and using the commands in the Actions pane or by right-clicking and selecting the Manage Web Site menu. Other details, such as site bindings, can also be modified at any time. This enables you to create, reconfigure, and stop sites individually without affecting other sites on the same server. In addition to the basic site-related settings, there are some configuration settings that are defined at the site level.

Configuring Web Site Limits

Web Site Limits settings place maximum limitations on the amount of bandwidth and the number of connections that can be supported by the Web site. These settings enable systems administrators to ensure that one or more sites on the server do not use excessive network bandwidth or consume too many resources. To configure Web site limits, select the appropriate Web site and click the Limits command in the Actions pane. Figure 5-21 shows the default settings for a new Web site.

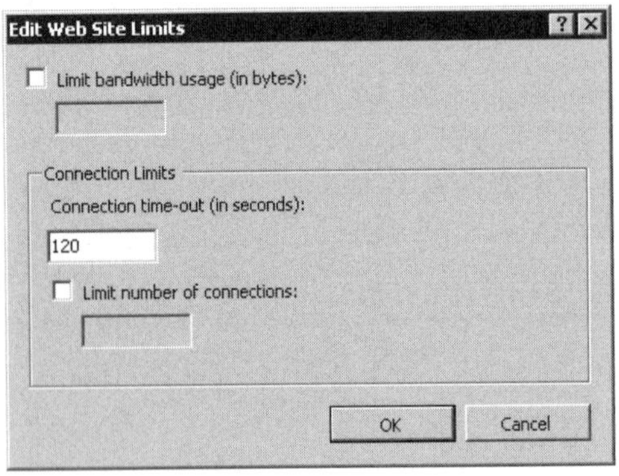

Figure 5-21   Configuring bandwidth usage and user connection limits for a Web site

The Limit Bandwidth Usage option (which is initially disabled) enables you to enter the maximum number of bytes per second that the Web server will support. If this limit is exceeded, the Web server will throttle responses by adding a time delay.

The Connection Limits section refers to the maximum number of user connections that can be active on the site. Each user connection is timed-out automatically if a new request is not received within the specified number of seconds. (The default is 120 seconds, or two minutes.) In addition, you can configure the maximum number of connections allowed for the site. If this number is exceeded, users that attempt to make a new connection will receive an error message stating that the server is too busy to respond.

Configuring Site Logging Settings

Another site-level setting is Logging. You can access these properties by selecting the appropriate Web site and, in the Features View, double-clicking Logging. Figure 5-22 shows the default options for logging.

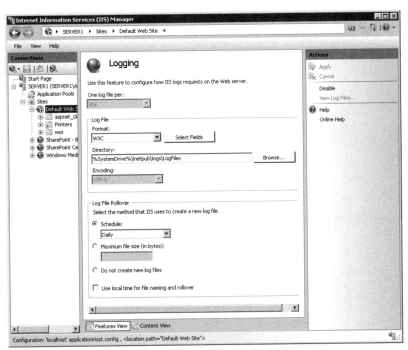

Figure 5-22   Configuring logging settings for a Web site

The specific options that are available will be based on which role services were installed for the Web server. By default, each new site is configured to store text-based log files within the

%SystemDrive%\Inetpub\Logs\LogFiles path on the local server. Each Web site will be assigned its own folder, and each folder will contain one or more log files. You can choose from different log file formats, but the default is the W3C format, which is a standard that can be used to compare log information from different Web server platforms. The Select Fields button enables you to determine which information is stored in the log file. The default field settings are designed to provide a good balance between performance and useful information. Adding fields can affect Web server performance adversely and increase log file size, so add the information that you plan to use in alter analysis only.

On busy Web servers, log files will grow quickly. Because the log files are text-based, it can often be difficult to manage and analyze large files. The Log File Rollover section enables you to specify when IIS will create a new log file. By default, a new log file will be created daily. You can choose a different time interval, or you can specify the maximum size of each log file. There is also an option to use only a single log file. Although it is possible to obtain information by opening the log files in a text viewer such as Notepad, it is much more common to use log analysis utilities to parse the results.

Understanding Web Applications

It is common in many Web server usage scenarios for a single site to provide access to different types of content. Web applications are created within Web sites to point to the physical location of a set of content files. For example, an online news site might include two different Web applications: one for registered users and one for nonregistered users. Each Web application can point to a separate physical folder on the computer so IIS can determine how to process the requests. Web applications can also use other methods to ensure that the same content (such as news stories) is available to both sites.

Creating Web Applications

You can create new Web applications easily by using IIS Manager. Right-click the Web site within which you want to create a Web application and then select Add Application. Figure 5-23 shows the available options. The first setting option is the alias that will be used for the site. This is the name that users will type as part of their URL to connect to the content. For example, if a new Web application with the alias Engineering is created within the default Web site, visitors will use a URL such as *http://server1.contoso.com/Engineering* to access the content. You will learn about application pool setting later in this lesson.

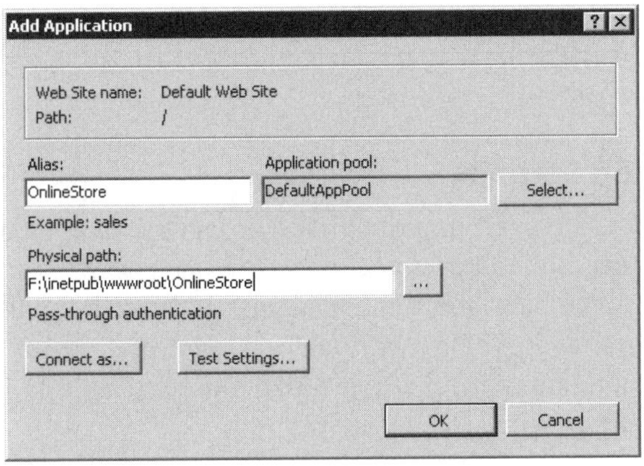

Figure 5-23   Adding a new Web application to a Web site

The Physical Path option enables you to specify the folder in which the content for the Web application will be stored. Generally, the file system location should be unique and unshared with other Web applications. As with the process of creating a site, you will be able to keep the default setting of Pass-Through Authentication or click the Connect As button to specify a username and password to use. The Test Settings button enables you to verify the connection details that you have entered (if any). The Test Connection dialog box as shown in Figure 5-24 details that if you keep the default setting, IIS Manager will be unable to verify the authorization permissions. (You will learn more about authentication and authorization in Chapter 6.) This is because the specific user context is not defined until a user attempts to access the content.

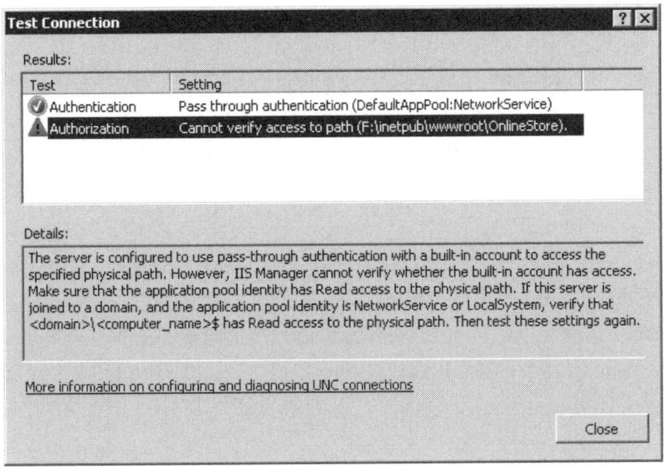

Figure 5-24   Testing physical path connection settings when creating a new Web application

To finish the creation of the Web application, click OK. You will now see a new Web application under the site object in IIS Manager. You can now also modify other settings for the Web application by using the Features View.

Managing Web Application Settings

By default, many of the settings for a new Web application will be inherited automatically from the Web site in which it was created. This enables you to use the same default settings easily for each new site. In most cases, you can also override the settings at the Web application level based on specific needs of the application. To do this, double-click any of the items in the Features view and make the corresponding changes at the Web application level. Most of these settings will override those that are assigned for the parent site.

Working with Application Pools

One of the primary concerns with managing Web servers is the potential for one Web site or application to affect operations of others on the same computer negatively. Issues such as memory leaks or application bugs potentially can cause a loss of service or reduced performance for many different Web applications. Application pools are designed to isolate different sites from each other so that failures and other problems can be contained. Within each application pool, worker processes are actually responsible for completing Web requests. Each application pool contains its own set of worker processes, so it is impossible for problems in one pool to affect processes in another. Application pools can also be started and stopped independently.

By default, IIS includes the Classic .NET AppPool and DefaultAppPool application pools along with an application pool that has the same name as the application itself. Classic .NET AppPool is used to support applications that require Microsoft .NET Framework 2.0, using classic Managed Pipeline Mode (a mode that enables .NET code to use methods of intercepting and responding to requests that are being processed by IIS). DefaultAppPool, as its name implies, is used to support the Default Web Site. It also supports Microsoft .NET Framework 2.0, but it uses the new Integrated Managed Pipeline Mode. You will learn more about pipeline modes later in this lesson.

By default, IIS Manager will create a new application pool when you create a new Web site. The application pool will have the same name as the site. This is the recommended approach because it allows the processes within each Web site to run independently of others. When you create a new Web application, you will have the option of selecting from any of the available application pools.

Creating Application Pools

IIS Manager includes an *Application Pools* object that enables you to manage application pools on the Web server. The default display will show all the application pools that currently exist on the server, along with their current status and settings. (See Figure 5-25.)

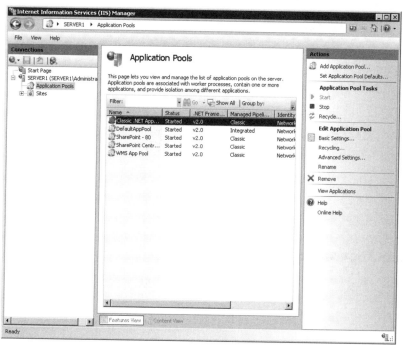

Figure 5-25   Managing application pools in IIS Manager

To create a new application pool, right-click the *Application Pools* object and select Add Application Pool. Figure 5-26 shows the available options. The name option will be used by systems administrators to identify the purpose of the application pool. If you are creating this object to support a specific Web site, include identifying information in the name. The .NET Framework version options will be based on which versions are available on the local computer. By default, the .NET Framework 2.0 and No Managed Code options are offered. The latter option specifies that .NET functionality will not be available for Web applications that are part of the pool.

Figure 5-26 Creating a new application pool

Managed Pipeline Mode specifies the method that will be supported for code that needs to intercept and modify Web request processing. The Classic option supports ASP.NET applications that were written for previous versions of IIS and that depend on integrating with request pipeline events. The Integrated mode provides better performance and functionality for ASP.NET applications and is recommended for those Web applications that do not depend directly on the Classic Managed Pipeline Mode. Finally, you can choose whether you want to start the application pool immediately.

Managing Application Pools

Each application pool present on a Web server can be started and stopped independently. Stopping an application pool will prevent requests from being processed by any applications that are a part of that pool. Users that attempt to access content from these sites will receive an error message stating HTTP Error 503, "Service Unavailable." It is a good idea to verify which applications are using an application pool before you stop it. You can do this by right-clicking one of the application pool items in IIS Manager and selecting View Applications.

Configuring Recycling Settings

An alternative to stopping an application pool is to recycle it using the *Recycle* command in the Actions pane. This command instructs IIS to retire any current worker process automatically after it has executed existing requests. The benefit is that users will not see a disruption to service on their computer, but the worker process will be replaced by a new one as quickly as possible. Recycling application pools is generally done when issues such as memory leaks or resource usage tend to increase significantly over time. Often, the root cause of this problem is a defect or other problem in the application code. The ideal solution is to correct the underlying application problem. However, it is possible at least to address the symptoms by using the *Recycle* command.

In some cases, you might automatically recycle worker processes based on resource usage or at specific times. You can access these options by clicking the Recycling command under Edit Application Pool in the Actions pane. (See Figure 5-27.)

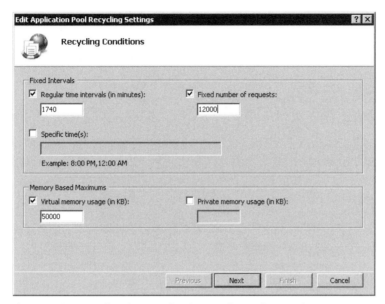

Figure 5-27   Configuring Application Pool recycling settings

The primary options for recycling settings are either Fixed Intervals (which are based on specific times or after a fixed number of requests is processed), or Memory Based Maximums. The most appropriate options will be based on the specific problems you are trying to troubleshoot or avoid. In general, recycling application pools too quickly can reduce performance. However, if a Web application has serious problems, it is preferable to address them through recycling worker processes before users see slowdowns or errors on the Web site.

Keeping track of application pool recycle events is also an important part of ensuring that your Web server and its applications are running as expected. For example, if you set the maximum memory settings, you will likely want to know how often the application pool has been recycled. Figure 5-28 shows the Recycling Events To Log step that enables you to define which events are recorded. To view the Recycling Events To Log page, click Next.

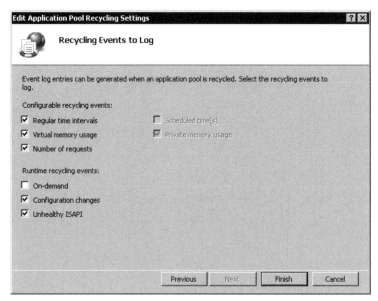

Figure 5-28   Choosing which recycling events should be logged

Configuring Advanced Application Pool Settings

In addition to the basic configuration settings and recycling options for an application pool, systems administrators can configure additional details to control the behavior of worker processes. To access these settings, select an application pool in IIS Manager and click the Advanced Settings link in the Actions pane. (See Figure 5-29.)

The options allow for setting detailed parameters related to CPU and memory resource usage. In general, you should not change these parameters manually unless you are reasonably sure of their intended effects. Some modifications can result in reducing processing speed for the applications that are part of the pool. Others can result in reserving or using too many system resources for a particular pool.

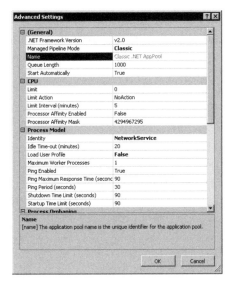

Figure 5-29   Configuring Advanced Settings for an application pool

Working with Virtual Directories

A common requirement within Web sites is to include content from folders that are located outside of the Web site's primary folder structure. For example, multiple Web sites that share the same set of images might need to access a pointer to a single path from which they can all access files. Virtual directories are designed to provide this capability. Virtual directories can be created at either the level of a Web site or within a specific Web application. They include an alias name (which will be used in the requesting URL) and point to a physical file system location path.

Creating a Virtual Directory

The process of creating a virtual directory is similar to that of creating a Web application. In IIS Manager, right-click the appropriate parent Web site or Web application and then select Add Virtual Directory. You will be able to provide an alias for the virtual directory (such as Images), along with security credentials and the physical path to the virtual directory. When a request is received for this alias, IIS will look in the appropriate file system location automatically for the requested content.

Comparing Virtual Directories and Web Applications

Although the settings for a virtual directory are similar to those of a Web application, there are some differences in their usage. Web Applications are generally designed to support executable Web code such as applications built using ASP.NET. They run within an isolated process space, using WAS. The reliance on WAS also enables Web applications to respond using protocols other than HTTP and HTTPS (assuming that other protocols have been installed and configured on the local server).

Virtual directories, on the other hand, are primarily used to point to static content that is stored in an alternate file system location. Both Web applications and virtual directories form a portion of the complete URL that is used to access a Web site. They can also both be nested to provide access to multiple levels of site content. The more appropriate choice will be based on the requirements of the Web application that you plan to support.

MORE INFO   Keeping the configuration simple

Web applications and virtual directories offer a lot of power and flexibility for both Web server administrators and Web developers. In general, try to keep your configurations as simple and intuitive as possible. For example, although both types of objects can be nested within each other, complex nesting can be confusing (especially if some of the objects share the same names). Overall, keep management of the Web site in mind when creating and designing the site structure.

Using Command-Line Management

Performing simple administrator tasks on a few IIS servers is a relatively simple process, using the IIS Manager console. However, when you want to commit the same changes on many different servers, or you want to automate the configuration process by using scripting, command-line utilities can make these tasks more efficient. IIS includes an executable command, AppCmd.exe, which provides a simple way for systems administrators to perform common operational tasks. The actual parameters are designed to map to the structure of IIS Web sites, Web applications, and virtual directories.

The AppCmd.exe file is located within the *%SystemRoot%*\System32\Inetsrv folder. You can get initial help for the utility by running the command with the -/? switch. (See Figure 5-30.) You can use the same switch to get additional details about other commands. The general syntax for the command is:

```
AppCmd.exe Command Object "ObjectName" /parameter:value
```

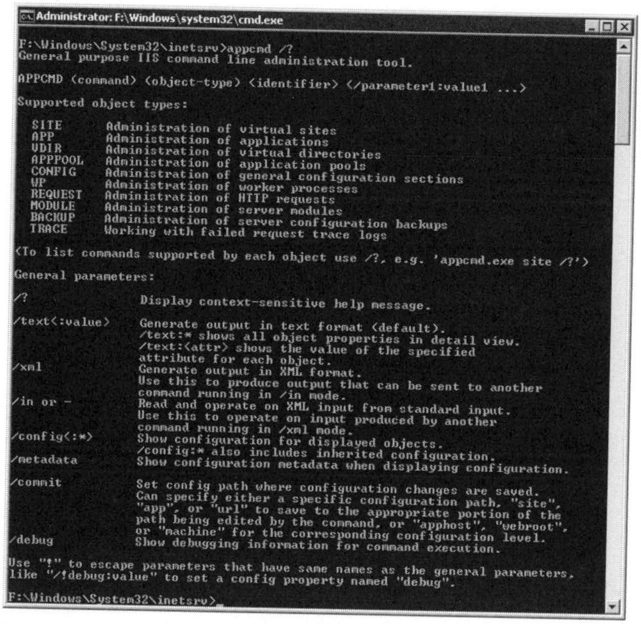

Figure 5-30   Viewing help for the AppCmd.exe utility

Understanding Command Options

AppCmd has been designed to use a simple set of six commands for performing tasks on objects. The list of commands includes:

- **List**   Returns information about the specified object.
- **Add**   Creates a new object of the type that is specified. Details can be added, using parameters and values.
- **Delete**   Deletes the specified object (such as a Web site or Web application).
- **Set**   Changes settings for the object, as specified by the parameters and values.
- **Start / Stop**   Available for objects that support these actions (such as a Web site).

If you want to perform multiple operations (either from a script file or from the command line), you will need to call AppCmd.exe for each operation. This helps keep the syntax of the statements simple and easy to read.

Understanding Objects

In a standard AppCmd statement, you will need to provide an object type and the name of the object that you plan to use. The types of objects supported by AppCmd.exe include the following:

- App (Web Application)
- AppPool (Application Pool)
- Backup (Server configuration backups)
- Config (Server configuration information)
- Module
- Request
- Site (Web Site)
- Trace
- VDir (Virtual Directory)
- WP (Worker Process)

You can get more information about the parameters and values that apply to an object by typing -? after the command.

```
Appcmd site -?
```

Examples of Commands

The process of listing, creating, and managing IIS configuration settings by using AppCmd is generally fairly simple. Table 5-2 provides some examples of common commands and their purpose.

Table 5-2 Sample Commands for AppCmd.exe

Command	Purpose
`AppCmd list site`	Returns a list of Web sites on the local server
`AppCmd add site /name:TestSite01`	Adds a new Web site called TestSite01
`AppCmd add vdir /app.name:"Default Web Site/" /path:/Images /physicalPath:"C:\Inet-pub\wwwroot\images"`	Adds a new virtual directory with the alias Images and points to the specified physical file system location
`AppCmd list request`	Returns a list of currently running Web server requests
`AppCmd list config`	Returns the entire contents of the current Web server configuration in XML format

Exam Tip   When preparing for Exam 70-643, it's not necessary to memorize every command-line option and parameter for utilities such as AppCmd.exe. Instead, focus on the basic syntax and the types of operations that can be performed. There's no better way to become familiar with the commands than by actually performing actions such as creating sites and changing configuration settings. This will help you identify (and rule out) answer choices when you're taking the exam. Generally, if you know what you're trying to accomplish, you should be able to identify the correct command-line option.

Using Windows PowerShell

In addition to using the AppCmd utility, Web server administrators can use the command shell and scripting language, Microsoft Windows PowerShell. Windows Server 2008 includes Windows PowerShell as a feature, but it is not enabled by default. To enable Windows Power-Shell, open Server Manager, right-click Features, and select Add Feature. Select the Windows PowerShell option, and then click Next to finish installing it. Once it has been installed, you can launch it from within the Windows PowerShell 1.0 program group in the Start menu. Windows PowerShell enables you to write and create powerful scripts for performing many common administration operations.

MORE INFO   Learning Windows PowerShell

Although a complete description of how to use PowerShell is beyond the scope of this book (and Exam 70-643), you can find more information about using it to manage IIS by searching for Powershell at *http://www.iis.net*. The Microsoft TechNet Scripting with Windows PowerShell Web site offers tutorials and examples for creating new scripts at *http://www.microsoft.com/technet/scriptcenter/hubs/msh.mspx*.

Automation Using .NET Framework

Many Web developers already have a significant amount of knowledge about working with the .NET Framework. Therefore, it can be helpful for them to manage IIS by using standard .NET code. IIS 7.0 provides two .NET namespaces that can be used to manage IIS configuration settings programmatically. They are:

■ *Microsoft.Web.Administration*   This namespace provides objects and methods that are useful for managing and changing Web server settings. It is focused primarily on performing configuration changes for an IIS Web server.

■ *Microsoft.Web.Management*   Although the default IIS Manager user interface has been designed to provide simple access to the majority of commonly used functionality, some environments might want to create their own management extensions for performing specific tasks. The *Microsoft.Web.Management* namespace includes objects and methods that enable developers to extend the user interface functionality of IIS management tools. These additions can then be configured to run in a standalone environment, or they can be integrated with the built-in IIS Manager utility for easy access.

Understanding how to write applications by using the .NET Framework is beyond the scope of Exam 70-643, but it can be helpful to know that these options are available for automating configuration and management tasks. Additional information about the namespaces mentioned here and others can be found at *http://msdn2.microsoft.com/en-us/library/aa388745.aspx*.

Managing Web Server Configuration Files

Although making configuration settings on one or a few servers is easiest using graphical tools, systems administrators often need to configure many Web servers. In addition to using IIS Manager and related tools for configuring settings, you can also configure your Web server by using XML configuration files. In addition, by storing settings in a single file, you can back up and restore settings to other IIS installations easily. In this section, you'll learn about where Web server and Web site settings are stored.

Understanding ApplicationHost.config

All the configuration settings that have been defined for the local IIS Web server are stored in an XML text file named *ApplicationHost.config*. The default file system location for these files is *%SystemDrive%*\Inetpub\History. Within this base folder is a series of folders, each of which contains a copy of the ApplicationHost.config file. The ApplicationHost Helper Service, a default component that is included when you install the Web Server (IIS) role, automatically makes periodic backups of the configuration of the local Web server. This process automatically creates a new folder and a copy of the ApplicationHost.config file. The schema subfolder contains a file that is used to describe and interpret the specific settings that can be used in the configuration files.

An ApplicationHost.config file can be opened and modified, using a standard text editor (such as Windows Notepad) or by using an XML-aware application (such as Visual Studio). The contents are arranged in a hierarchy that defines the various settings and options that can be configured within IIS. (See Figure 5-31.) Before you make changes directly to a configuration file, be sure to make a backup copy of it. It is fairly easy to introduce changes that can cause errors in IIS.

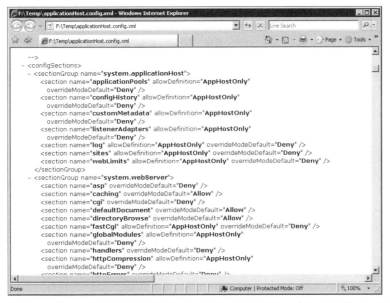

Figure 5-31   Using Internet Explorer to view a portion of the ApplicationHost.config file.

Restoring the ApplicationHost.config File

In the event that you need to revert the configuration of IIS to an earlier state by using the automatic backup files, you can copy over the working config file manually. The active version of the ApplicationHost.config file is in the *%SystemRoot%*\System32\Inetsrv\Config folder. To roll back the configuration of IIS, find the ApplicationHost.config version you want to use and then copy it over the current file. Note that for the changes to be reflected, it might be necessary to restart the Web server and IIS Manager. It is also highly recommended that you copy the current configuration file to a backup location in the event you need to refer to it later.

Understanding Web.config Files

A common problem related to managing Web applications and Web sites is that of retaining settings as sites are moved between servers. In previous versions of IIS, it was often necessary to re-create settings manually to ensure that the site would run properly. IIS 7.0 uses a hierarchical approach to create and manage configuration settings. In addition to the server-level settings that are defined in the ApplicationHost.config file, systems administrators and Web developers can include other settings in Web.config files.

Web.config files can be located within the root folder for a Web site or Web application. These files can contain settings that override the default server-level settings that are included in the ApplicationHost.config file. The format of the files and options is similar. By default, a new Web.config file is created automatically whenever you add a new Web site or a new Web application. The default settings are inherited from the server-level settings unless you specifically change them.

Overall, the hierarchy for configuration files is:

1. Host (ApplicationHost.config)
2. Site (Web.config)
3. Application (Web.config)

Settings in lower-level files can override settings defined in the parent. A useful benefit of this approach is that the configuration information is included automatically when you choose to copy an entire folder of Web content to another server or to another location on the same server.

Exam Tip   When making changes to IIS and Web application configurations, consider which portions of the site structure the modifications should affect. If the goal is to modify all Web sites, consider making the change in the server-level ApplicationHost.config file. Otherwise, making site-level or application-level changes will likely be more appropriate.

Migrating Web Sites and Web Applications

The presence of Web.config files within Web application and Web site folders helps make the process of migrating Web sites to different servers or physical locations simpler. For most applications, all that is required is for all the files within the appropriate folders to be moved or copied to the new location. Then, within IIS Manager, you can re-create any additional Web sites, Web applications, and virtual directories that are required. It is important, however, to test any migrated Web application thoroughly. In some cases, incompatibilities or other issues between server-level and application-level settings can have unintended consequences. Overall, however, the process of moving and copying Web sites is usually fairly simple and straightforward.

Backing Up and Restoring Configuration Data Using AppCmd.exe

An important aspect of Web server administration is ensuring that the configuration of the server is protected against data loss. Because IIS configuration settings are stored automatically in the *%SystemDrive%*\Inetpub\History folder, ensure that this folder is included in file system backup policies. In addition, it's important to back up Web sites and Web applications to ensure that they can be restored quickly in the case of a failure. Often, however, you'll need to create your own configuration backups manually. For example, if you want to transfer configuration data to another IIS installation, or if you want to protect against unwanted changes, it is a good idea to make an on-demand configuration backup.

You can use AppCmd.exe to create a backup of the configuration of IIS and store it to a text file. The utility offers simple capabilities for creating a backup and for restoring from it. The standard command for adding a new backup is:

```
AppCmd add backup "BackupName"
```

BackupName specifies the name of the file that you want to create. You can leave off the name, and an automatic filename that includes a timestamp will be generated. The file will be created in the location in which AppCmd.exe was run, but you can always move or copy the file manually to another location.

You can restore the configuration information from the backup, using the following command:

```
AppCmd restore backup "BackupName"
```

This process restores the configuration of the IIS Web server to the settings that were included in the backup file. If you want to view a list of backups that have been made, you can use the following command:

```
AppCmd list backups
```

You will see a list of all the backup files you have created. Figure 5-32 shows an example of all these backup-related commands at work.

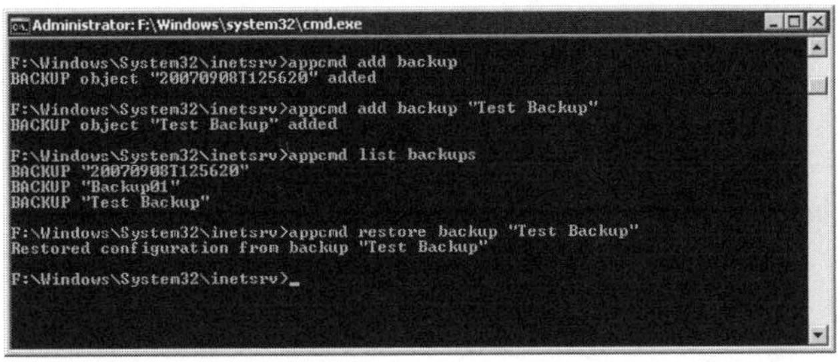

Figure 5-32 Performing IIS configuration backup and restore operations by using *AppCmd.exe*

Using Centralized Configuration for Server Farms

As organizations place a greater reliance on their Web sites and Web-based applications, the ability to improve performance, scalability, and reliability are important goals. With relation to Web servers, a common configuration is known as a *Web server farm*. In this approach, many Web servers are configured to provide access to the same content. Generally, they have the same configuration settings and either store local copies of Web sites and applications or access them from a shared location.

From a systems administration standpoint, managing large groups of Web servers can be challenging. When configuration changes are required, they often have to be committed manually to many computers. Even with the use of automation or scripting, it is possible to overlook one or a few servers. To support the server farm usage scenario better, IIS 7.0 enables you to share centrally stored configuration data with multiple Web servers.

The first step in the process of creating a shared configuration is to export the configuration of a single IIS server. Generally, you will configure this server with all the settings that you want to use on the other servers. Then, using IIS Manager, click the server name and double-click Shared Configuration in the Features View. To generate an export, click the Export Configuration command in the Actions pane. (See Figure 5-33.) You will be able to provide a path into which the configuration files will be stored. To protect sensitive information in the configuration files, you must type and confirm an encryption key password. This password will be required to view the settings in the file. You can also use the Connect As option to provide security credentials if you are planning to store the configuration in a network location.

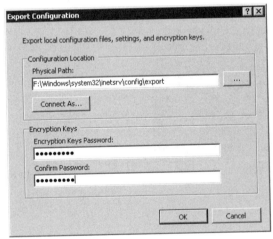

Figure 5-33   Exporting IIS configuration information

The second step of the process is to place the shared configuration file in a location that is accessible to all the Web servers. Usually, the best choice is a shared network folder on a reliable server. Once you know the path to the files, you can use the Shared Configuration feature to enter the details. First, select the Enable Shared Configuration check box. (See Figure 5-34.) This will enable you to specify the Physical Path setting. You can use a local file system location or a Universal Naming Convention (UNC)-based network path (for example, \\Server1\WebConfig). The User Name and Password fields enable you to enter the security credentials that will be used by IIS to connect to the physical path you have specified.

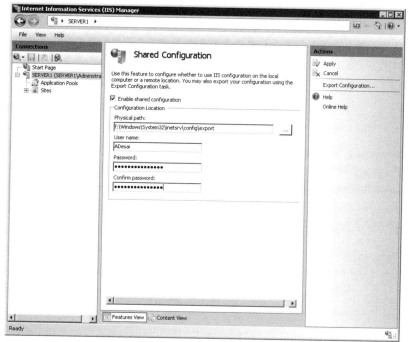

Figure 5-34   Enabling Shared Configuration for an IIS Web server

To save the settings, click the Apply command in the Actions pane. You will be prompted to enter the encryption key password for the configuration files. Once the configuration import is complete, you will be notified that you must restart IIS Manager for it to recognize the configuration changes. You can disable the shared configuration settings later by deselecting the Enable Shared Configuration check box. This returns the Web server to using locally defined configuration settings.

MORE INFO   **Creating production server farms**

The ability to share settings easily among Web servers is helpful for setting up IIS-based Web server farms. However, sharing configuration data is only one part of an overall Web server farm configuration. Other considerations include deploying and synchronizing content updates, handling session state, managing security, implementing load-balancing, and responding to fail-over events. Rest assured, there are many good ways of addressing these challenges. However, always be sure to involve Web developers and systems administrators when designing a scale-out strategy.

Migrating From IIS 6.0

A large number of Web developers have depended on previous versions of IIS to support their Web applications and Web sites. IIS 6.0, the version included with Windows Server 2003, provided several enhancement features and capabilities over previous versions. IIS 7.0 provides even more improvements in functionality, performance, reliability, and management capabilities. However, with these new improvements, preserving backward compatibility with existing applications built for IIS 6.0 was an important goal.

For Web sites and Web applications that rely primarily on static content, the migration process to IIS 7.0 should be fairly easy. Generally, all that is required is for the content to be moved and any associated site-level or application-level settings to be re-created. However, there are additional options and considerations for other types of applications, such as those that were built using ASP.NET or that rely on IIS 6.0 architectural features. In this section, you'll learn about how to migrate Web applications to IIS 7.0.

Upgrading from Windows Server 2003 and IIS 6.0

One approach to moving Web applications to Windows Server 2008 is to perform an in-place upgrade of a computer running Windows Server 2003. The upgrade process automatically makes decisions that will help preserve compatibility with older applications. For example, the majority of role services that are optional with a standard Web Server (IIS) role installation are included automatically. Furthermore, IIS 6.0 management tools and features are available for use. Following an upgrade to Windows Server 2008 and IIS 7.0, verify which installed components are required and remove those that are not. And, as with any migration, thoroughly test the functionality of your Web sites before redeploying them into production.

Another option for upgrading to IIS 7.0 is to migrate Web sites manually by copying the relevant content to a new Windows Server 2008 installation. In this approach, the existing content is transferred to a new server, and Web sites and Web applications must be reconfigured.

Installing IIS 6 Management Compatibility

Some Web sites and Web applications might include application code that relies on the architecture of IIS 6.0 for handling requests. Examples include Web applications that need access to the IIS 6.0 configuration database and compatibility with earlier scripting methods. In addition, some applications might require access to an earlier version of the management console.

By default, backward-compatibility features are not installed automatically for new Web server installations in Windows Server 2008. To provide backward-compatibility, you can use Server Manager to add role services to the Web Server (IIS) role. The available options are:

- **IIS 6 Management Compatibility** This compatibility feature provides support for two scripting and administration features that were included with IIS 6.0: Admin Base Object (ABO) and Active Directory Services Interface (ADSI). Web applications that relied on these technologies will need these features to operate correctly. Additionally, the IIS 6 Management Compatibility role service is required to enable other IIS 6.0 compatibility options.

- **IIS 6 Metabase Compatibility** IIS 6.0 used a configuration database known as the metabase for storing server settings and other details. In IIS 7.0, this has been replaced by new types of XML-based configuration files such as ApplicationHost.config and Web.config files. IIS 6.0 Web applications could use the ability to query the metabase to manage IIS settings. To support these applications, you must enable the IIS 6 Metabase Compatibility role service.

- **IIS 6 WMI Compatibility** Windows Management Instrumentation (WMI) is a programming interface that enables application code to query and manage IIS settings, using scripts or WMI-capable tools. This role service adds compatibility that enables IIS 6.0 WMI–based commands to apply to IIS 7.0 Web servers.

- **IIS 6 Scripting Tools** Web developers and systems administrators can transition IIS 6.0 management scripts to IIS 7.0 by enabling this role service. The IIS 6 Scripting Tools option adds support for using ActiveX Data Objects (ADO) and ADSI.

- **IIS 6 Management Console** For systems administrators who want to manage IIS 6.0 installations remotely, it is possible to install IIS 6 Management Console on Windows Server 2008. This console is capable only of connecting to IIS 6.0 servers, however, and cannot connect to a Windows Server 2008 Web server.

Overall, these tools and features can help ensure that previous versions of applications that relied on IIS 6.0 will continue to function in Windows Server 2008.

Understanding ASP.NET Integration Modes

IIS 7.0 provides enhancements for the ASP.NET development platform. In previous versions of IIS, ASP.NET processing was performed through an ISAPI code module. Although this approach worked well, there were some important limitations. In IIS 7.0, ASP.NET integration has been enhanced by more closely incorporating the process of ASP.NET Web pages with the Web server request pipeline. This new architecture offers several benefits, including greater control over request processing and the ability to use ASP.NET features for types of content other than dynamic Web pages.

All ASP.NET applications can take advantage of the new .NET Integrated Mode pipeline when they are running on IIS 7.0. However, applications that relied on IIS 6.0 architecture for intercepting and modifying requests will need support for the Classic pipeline mode. You can configure the processing mode by changing application pool settings or modifying the configuration of existing application pools. (Both topics were covered earlier in this lesson.)

Quick Check

1. How can you avoid potential performance or resource-related problems for multiple Web sites that are running on the same IIS Web server?
2. How can you back up the configuration of the IIS Web server before you make changes to the configuration?

Quick Check Answers

1. By configuring each Web site to run in a separate application pool, you can minimize the risks of problems with one application conflicting with another.
2. The AppCmd.exe utility provides commands for creating and restoring backups of the IIS configuration.

PRACTICE **Configuring and Managing IIS Settings**

In this practice, you will create Web sites and Web applications on Server2.contoso.com and test the backup and recovery process for configuration settings. The steps in the exercise assume that you have already installed the Web Server (IIS) role on this computer, using the default role services. (For more information about adding the role, see Lesson 1, Exercise 1.) The steps in Exercise 2 require you to complete the steps in Exercise 1 because the new Web site you created will be used for testing the backup and restore processes.

► **Exercise 1 Create Web Sites and Web Applications**

In this exercise, you will use IIS Manager to create a new Web site on the local server. Because the default Web site is already configured to use the standard HTTP and HTTPS ports, you will specify alternate site-binding information. You will also create a new Web application that includes a test Web page to ensure that the server is responding properly.

1. Log on to Server2.contoso.com with local administrative credentials.
2. Before you create a new Web site, you will create content folders within the file system. Using Windows Explorer, navigate to the *%SystemDrive%*\Inetpub\wwwroot path on the computer's system drive.
3. Within the Wwwroot folder, create a new folder called **Contoso**. Within the Contoso folder, create another new folder called **WebApp01**.

   You will use these folders as the physical paths for the Web site and Web application you will create in later steps.
4. Copy the Iisstart.htm and Welcome.png files from the Wwwroot folder to the Contoso folder. Rename the Iisstart.htm file to Default.htm.
5. Within the *%SystemDrive%*\Inetpub\wwwroot\Contoso\WebApp01 folder, create a new text file named Default.htm. Within the text file, enter the following text and then save the file:

   ```
   <html>
   <title>Web Application 01</title>
   <body>
   <h1>Welcome to Web Application 01.<h1>
   </body>
   </html>
   ```
6. Launch Internet Information Services (IIS) Manager from the Administrative Tools program group.
7. If prompted to connect to a server, choose to connect to the local computer.
8. Expand the local computer object and the Sites container to view a list of existing Web sites.

   You will see the default Web site that was installed when the Web Server (IIS) role was added to the computer.
9. To create a new Web site, right-click the Sites container, and click Add Web Site.

   This will open the Add Web Site dialog box.
10. For the name of the new Web site, type **Contoso Test Site**. Note that, by default, a new application pool of the same name is created and selected automatically. For this practice exercise, you will use this new application pool; however, you can choose an existing pool by clicking the Select button.

11. For Physical Path, browse to the *%SystemDrive%*\Inetpub\wwwroot\Contoso folder that you created earlier. Accept the default security setting of Pass-Through Authentication, and then click Test Settings. Note that IIS is able to verify authentication but not authorization because this information will not be known until a user attempts to access the site.

12. Click Close to return to the Add Web Site dialog box.

13. In the Binding section, choose the following settings:
     - ❏ Protocol: **HTTP**
     - ❏ IP Address: **All Unassigned**
     - ❏ Port: **8000**
     - ❏ Host Name: (blank)

14. Verify that the Start Web Site Immediately option is selected, and then click OK to create and start the new Web site automatically.

15. Click the newly created Contoso Test Site object in the left pane of IIS Manager. Note that the Actions pane provides commands for working with the Web site. To verify that the site is configured properly, click the *Browse *:8000 (http)* command. This will launch Internet Explorer automatically and connect to *http://Server2:8000.contoso.com*. You should see the default IIS start page content in the Web browser. When finished, close Internet Explorer.

16. To create a new Web application, right-click the Contoso Test Site item in IIS Manager and select Add Application.

17. For the Alias of the application, type **TestApp**. For the physical path, type or browse to the *%SystemDrive%*\Inetpub\wwwroot\Contoso\WebApp01 physical path. Notice that the DefaultAppPool option is selected for the application pool.

18. Click the Select button to change the application pool to Contoso Test Site. Leave all other settings at their defaults, and then click OK to create the new Web application.

19. In the left pane of IIS Manager, you will see a new Web application called TestApp within the Contoso Test Site object. To verify the content of this application, select the TestApp item, and then click the Content View button at the bottom of the center pane in IIS Manager. You will see the default.htm file that you created earlier.

20. To test the Web application, click the Browse button in the Manage Application section of the Actions pane. This will launch Internet Explorer and connect to *http://Server2:8000 .contoso.com/TestApp/default.htm*. The title bar for the Web browser will read Web Application 01, and the text will display the welcome message you specified in the HTML file. When finished, close Internet Explorer.

21. Close IIS Manager.

▶ **Exercise 2 Back Up and Restore the IIS Configuration**

In this exercise, you will perform the steps required to make a backup of the IIS configuration, using the AppCmd.exe utility. You will then delete the Contoso Web Site object that you created in Exercise 1, using IIS Manager. To restore the Web site configuration, you will again use the AppCmd.exe utility.

1. Log on to Server1.contoso.com with local administrative credentials.

2. Open a new command prompt window by clicking Start and then Run. Type **cmd**.

3. Change the current working directory to the location of AppCmd.exe by typing **cd %SystemRoot%\Windows\System32\Inetsrv**.

4. To create a new backup of the IIS configuration, type the following command at the command prompt:

   ```
   AppCmd add backup "IISBackup01"
   ```

5. To verify that the backup has been created, type the following command:

   ```
   AppCmd list backups
   ```

6. You should see the IISBackup01 item in the list. (If you have made other backups of the configuration, they will also appear in the list.)

7. Leave the command prompt window open, and then launch the Internet Information Services (IIS) Manager console.

   In the next step, you will remove a Web site from the configuration of IIS.

8. Connect to the local server, and expand the Sites object. Right-click the Contoso Test Site object, and select Remove. When prompted, select Yes to confirm the removal. Note that the site and its Web application have been deleted.

9. Return to the command prompt window, and type the following command to restore the IIS configuration from the backup you created earlier:

   ```
   AppCmd restore backup "IISBackup01"
   ```

10. When the command finishes, close the command prompt, and return to the IIS Manager console.

11. To refresh the display, right-click the Sites object, and choose Refresh.

    You will now see the Contoso Test Site object. Note that removing the Web site did not delete any of the content that was stored in the file system, so the site should be available for use. In some cases, it might be necessary to close the IIS Manager console and reload it after the restore process has been performed.

12. When you are finished, close IIS Manager.

Lesson Summary

- IIS Manager provides an integrated graphical user interface for managing IIS-related settings, features, and Web content.

- Web sites have associated site bindings that specify the protocol, IP address, port, and host headers to which a site will respond. Systems administrators can configure bandwidth limitations, user connection limits, and logging settings for each Web site.

- Application pools provide independence and isolation for multiple Web sites and Web applications that are running on the same IIS installation.

- Systems administrators and Web developers can use AppCmd.exe to perform common IIS management tasks from the command line.

- IIS server configuration settings are stored in the ApplicationHost.config file. These settings can be overridden by Web.config files that are located in content folders.

- Windows Server 2008 provides numerous backward-compatibility features for supporting applications built for IIS 6.0 and for managing IIS 6.0 servers.

Lesson Review

You can use the following questions to test your knowledge of the information in Lesson 2, "Configuring Internet Information Services." The questions are also available on the companion CD if you prefer to review them in electronic form.

NOTE Answers

Answers to these questions and explanations of why each answer choice is correct or incorrect are located in the "Answers" section at the end of the book.

---

1. You are a systems administrator responsible for managing a Windows Server 2008 Web server. Currently, there are no Web sites configured on the server. You need to configure the server to host two Web applications: EngineeringApp and SalesApp. Both Web applications must be accessible by using HTTP port 80 without the use of host headers. Also, you must protect against problems in one Web application affecting the performance or reliability of the other Web application. Which two steps should you take to meet these requirements?

   A. Create a single Web site that contains both Web applications.

   B. Create two Web sites, one for each Web application.

   C. Assign both Web applications to the same application pool.

   D. Assign each Web application to its own application pool.

2. You are a systems administrator responsible for managing a Windows Server 2008 Web server. You have not created any manual backups of the IIS configuration. Recently, a Web developer reported that he had accidentally removed two Web sites from the IIS configuration. Both Web sites contained several Web applications. You have verified that the two sites do not appear when you open the IIS Manager console and expand the Sites object. You have also verified that the content for the two Web sites is still present in the C:\WebSites folder. By interviewing other members of the Web development team, you have also ensured that no other changes have been made to the IIS configuration. Which of the following steps should you take to restore the two missing Web sites with their associated settings as quickly as possible?

   A. Manually re-create the two Web sites and then re-create the associated Web applications.

   B. Manually modify the Web server's ApplicationHost.config file and add the Web site and Web application settings.

   C. Restore the IIS configuration, using the AppCmd utility.

   D. Copy an earlier version of the ApplicationHost.config file from the *%SystemDrive%*\Inetpub\wwwroot\History folder over the current active version of Application-Host.config.

Chapter Review

To further practice and reinforce the skills you learned in this chapter, you can perform the following tasks:

- Review the chapter summary.
- Review the list of key terms introduced in this chapter.
- Complete the case scenarios. These scenarios set up real-world situations involving the topics of this chapter and ask you to create a solution.
- Complete the suggested practices.
- Take a practice test.

Chapter Summary

- The Web Server (IIS) role in Windows Server 2008 is designed to support Web sites and Web applications.
- The Web Server (IIS) role offers numerous role services related to security, performance, diagnostics, and backward compatibility.
- The IIS Manager console is the primary method for creating and managing Web sites, Web applications, application pools, and virtual directories.
- IIS can be managed, using the AppCmd.exe command-line utility, Windows PowerShell, and the .NET Framework.
- Windows Server 2008 provides several methods for maintaining backward compatibility with applications built for previous versions of IIS.

Key Terms

Do you know what these key terms mean? You can check your answers by looking up the terms in the glossary at the end of the book.

- AppCmd.exe
- application pools (IIS)
- ApplicationHost.config file
- ASP.NET
- Hypertext Transfer Protocol (HTTP)
- Hypertext Transfer Protocol Secure (HTTPS)
- IIS Manager

- Internet Information Services (IIS)
- Secure Sockets Layer (SSL)
- site bindings
- Transport Layer Security (TLS)
- Web Server (IIS) server role
- Web server farms
- Web.config files
- Windows PowerShell
- Windows System Resource Manager (WSRM)

Case Scenarios

In these case scenarios, you will apply the information you have learned about Web sites and Web applications to meet business and technical requirements.

Case Scenario 1: IIS Web Server Administration

You are a systems administrator responsible for managing five different Web servers for your organization. Each Web server supports multiple Web applications. Your general requirements include ensuring reliability and performance for all Web applications. In addition, you must simplify administration tasks for the servers. The organization requires that no more than four hours of configuration or site content changes can be lost in the event of a hardware failure. A Web developer has stated that she needs to make multiple changes to the IIS settings on one test Web server.

1. How can you simplify the configuration of all the servers, assuming that the settings must be the same for all of them?
2. Which content should you include in the backup process?
3. What are two ways in which you can roll back the server configuration on a test server if an accidental or unwanted modification is made?

Case Scenario 2: Managing Multiple Web Sites

You are a server administrator responsible for managing fifteen Web sites on a single Windows Server 2008 Web server. For security, reliability, and performance reasons, you need to prevent problems in one Web application from causing issues with others. In addition, several different Web applications must be configured to respond on HTTP port 80 and HTTP port 443, using the same public IP address. One of the ASP.NET Web applications was originally designed for IIS 6.0 and takes advantage of advanced request processing features.

1. How can you minimize the risks associated with Web application defects affecting other Web applications on the same server?
2. What configuration settings will enable you to meet the default HTTP and HTTPS connection requirements?
3. What are some methods by which you can support the IIS 6.0 Web application on Windows Server 2008?

Suggested Practices

To help you successfully master the exam objectives presented in this chapter, complete the following tasks.

Manage Web Applications

Perform the following exercises to practice the process of creating and managing Web applications, using IIS Manager and command-line utilities.

- **Practice 1** Web applications often have numerous requirements and features that must be enabled to function properly in IIS. If possible, download sample Web applications and deploy them in IIS, using various settings for application pools and other options. A good starting point for downloading applications based on ASP.NET is the Microsoft ASP.NET Starter Kit site at *http://www.asp.net /downloads/starter-kits/*. In addition, if your organization has any existing Web sites or applications, attempt to install them in a test environment.

- **Practice 2** Once you are familiar with the concepts of using IIS Manager to create and manage Web sites, try performing the same actions by using the command line. Use the AppCmd.exe utility to perform operations such as:
  - ❑ Creating a new Web site, including unique site-binding parameters.
  - ❑ Creating multiple Web applications within the new Web site.
  - ❑ Adding virtual directories that point to file system locations outside of the folder for the default site or Web application.
  - ❑ Backing up and restoring the IIS configuration.
  - ❑ Deleting the test sites and other objects you have created.

If you need to create many sites on several Web servers, you can also combine multiple commands in a batch file to automate the process.

Take a Practice Test

The practice tests on this book's companion CD offer many options. For example, you can test yourself on just one exam objective, or you can test yourself on all the 70-643 certification exam content. You can set up the test so that it closely simulates the experience of taking a certification exam, or you can set it up in study mode so that you can look at the correct answers and explanations after you answer each question.

MORE INFO   Practice tests

For details about all the practice test options available, see the "How to Use the Practice Tests" section in this book's introduction.

Chapter 6
Managing Web Server Security

From a systems administration standpoint, one of the main goals for managing Web servers is to maintain a high standard of security. Security is an important concern in all areas of IT, but it's especially important for information and applications that are readily accessible to large numbers of users. In this chapter, you will learn how to configure security for a Windows Server 2008 Web server.

Lesson 1, "Configuring IIS Security," focuses on securing access to Internet Information Services 7.0 (IIS 7) and the content it contains. You will learn how to configure permissions for remote management and how to increase the security of the server by disabling or removing unneeded features and options. In Lesson 2, "Controlling Access to Web Services," you will learn about ways in which you use authentication and authorization. You will also learn how to increase security through server certificates and IP address restrictions.

Exam objectives in this chapter:
- Configuring a Web Services Infrastructure
  - ❑ Configure Web applications.
  - ❑ Manage Web sites.
  - ❑ Manage Internet Information Services (IIS).
  - ❑ Configure SSL security.
  - ❑ Configure Web site authentication and permissions.

Lessons in this chapter:

Before You Begin

To complete the lessons in this chapter, you should have:

- Installed the Web Server (IIS) server role on Server2.contoso.com, using the default installation options for this server role. If you have created additional Web sites or Web applications in previous exercises, you may leave them configured on this server.
- The ability to create and manage Web sites and Web applications. These topics are covered in Chapter 5, "Installing and Configuring Web Applications."

Real World

Anil Desai

The primary goal for systems administrators who are responsible for managing access to Web Services is to minimize the potential for unauthorized access to and misuse of applications or data. The idea on an "attack surface" is based on the number and ways that the server can be accessed. One of the primary ways to secure a server is by reducing its attack surface. IIS supports Web applications that use a variety of technologies. If certain Web applications do not require a particular technology (for example, support for the Microsoft .NET Framework), you can reduce potential unauthorized access to the system by disabling that feature.

Another major strategy related to Web server security is defense in depth. This technique involves a multilayered security approach. Security options include authentication, authorization, file system permissions, and other settings that provide multiple barriers to access. These security mechanisms work together to ensure that only authorized users have access to the system. Additionally, if one layer of security is incorrectly configured or is compromised, other security settings can help restrict or prevent unauthorized access.

Security settings can often be difficult and complicated to manage, and this reduces security because many systems administrators find it challenging to set up the appropriate permissions. IIS has been designed so that you use a hierarchical arrangement of objects, such as Web sites and Web applications, that helps organize settings and content. For example, you can apply security-related settings at the server level, for specific Web sites, for specific Web applications, or directly on virtual directories, physical files, and folders.

In general, applying permissions at higher levels in the hierarchy simplifies administration. Figure 6-1 shows how objects such as the Web server, Web sites, Web applications, and other items are arranged into nested parent–child relationships. In general, settings placed on higher-level objects (such as for a Web site) will apply automatically to all the lower-level objects (such as multiple Web applications). Administrators can then override settings for specific Web applications, using whatever method is dictated by business or technical requirements. The end result of this configuration strategy is a high level of security with minimal administrative effort.

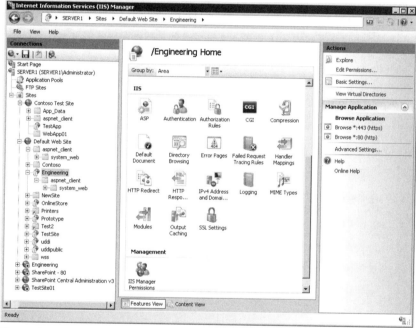

Figure 6-1 Viewing a hierarchy of objects in IIS Manager

Exam Tip Although you might not be asked directly about general security concepts and approaches on Exam 70-643, you should still keep in mind the recommended practices of defense in depth and reducing the attack surface for the Web server. Often, the best solution (and correct answer) for a scenario will be based on applying various security methods in the most appropriate combination.

Lesson 1: Configuring IIS Security

IIS primarily functions as a server for Web services. Due to the importance of securing Web-based content, there are numerous security-related industry standards, which are supported by IIS 7 and with which you should be familiar. In this lesson, you will learn how to configure and manage security for the Web Server (IIS) server role and its associated components. You will first learn how to determine the permissions that administrators will have on Web servers. You will learn ways to extend IIS administration capabilities to other users and Web developers in your organization through remote management and delegation settings. Then, you will learn how to increase security by configuring request handlers and their associated settings to minimize risks related to the execution of unwanted or malicious code or content.

After this lesson, you will be able to:

- Describe the security architecture of IIS, including built-in accounts.
- Enable remote management features for IIS Web servers.
- Configure IIS Manager users, permissions, and feature delegation for distributed administration.
- Manage request handlers and handler mappings to reduce the attack surface of the Web server.

Estimated lesson time: 60 minutes

Understanding IIS 7 Security Accounts

When you add the Web Server (IIS) role to a computer running Windows Server 2008, as discussed in Chapter 5, "Installing and Configuring Web Applications," the process makes numerous changes and additions to the configuration of the server. In earlier versions of IIS, each installation used service accounts that were based on the name of the server. Because the accounts and their security identifiers (SIDs) were different, copying Web content and settings between Web servers required multiple steps.

In IIS 7, a standard account named IUSRS and a local security group called IIS_IUSRS are used on each Windows Server 2008 Web server computer. Passwords for the accounts are managed internally, so administrators do not need to keep track of them.

Exam Tip Web services are programs that enable a server to store, create, and deliver information by using standard protocols and methods such as the Hypertext Transfer Protocol (HTTP). In the context of IIS 7, this includes Web applications and static Web site content that is included in the server configuration. When taking the exam, you should usually think of "Web services" as any of the functionality provided by IIS.

Managing File System Permissions

To implement security, Web server administrators must be able to define which content should be protected. They must also be able to specify which users or groups of users have access to protected content. Permissions settings for Web content are managed through NTFS file system permissions. These permissions can be administered directly, using Windows Explorer, or by right-clicking a specific object in the IIS Manager hierarchy and clicking Edit Permissions. As shown in Figure 6-2, the permissions settings display which users or groups of users have access to the content and which permissions they have. IIS uses these permissions to determine whether credentials are required when attempting to complete a request from a Web client.

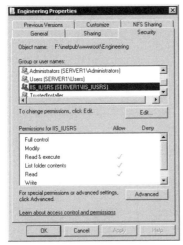

Figure 6-2 Viewing permissions for a folder within the Engineering Web site

Configuring IIS Administration Features

When you add the Web Server (IIS) role to a computer running Windows Server 2008, the default configuration enables only local administration of the server. This enhances security because users of other computers are unable to use IIS Manager to make changes to the server's configuration. Although this is appropriate for small, simple installations, often systems administrators benefit from the ability to use IIS Manager to configure the server remotely.

In many environments, multiple systems administrators manage Web sites and Web applications. In large deployments, it is common to have several administrators responsible for the same Web server. For example, a single IIS server might host several important Web applications, each of which is administered by a different individual or group. In hosting situations—

where an organization provides IIS server access to subscribers—you must enable subscribers to control certain Web content and features. In this case, subscribers act as remote administrators for certain portions of the servers. Remote administration is helpful for both multiple administrators and for management performance from multiple locations.

To allow remote administrators to manage IIS, you must first enable remote management on the server. You can then define and configure IIS Manager users. Feature delegation enables you to specify which actions remote administrators can perform.

Enabling Remote Management

To enable remote management functionality, you first add the IIS Management Service role service to the local server. You can do this by using Server Manager. Right-click the Web Server (IIS) role in the Roles folder, and then select Add Role Services. Add IIS Management Service, which is located in the Management Tools section of the available role services.

The IIS remote management service works by using a standard HTTP or HTTPS connection. Communications are configured to transmit over port 8172 by default. Assuming that traffic is allowed on this port through any firewalls or network security devices, this enables remote administrators to manage their IIS servers over a local network connection or over the Internet.

After you have added the IIS Management Service role service to the Web Server (IIS) role, you can use IIS Manager to enable remote management. To do this, open IIS Manager, and select the Web server object in the left pane. Then, select Management Service from the Management section in the Features view. (See Figure 6-3.)

Initially, the Enable Remote Connections option will be deselected. To enable manager users to connect to IIS over the network, select the Enable Remote Connections option. The Identity Credentials section enables you to specify whether you will allow authentication by using Windows credentials only (the default setting), or if you will also allow IIS Manager credentials.

The Connections portion of the settings enables you to specify on which IP address(es) and port(s) the management service will respond. The default setting is for the service to respond to all available IP addresses on port 8172. If your Web server is configured with multiple network connections or IP addresses, you can increase security by restricting remote access connections to a specific address. The SSL Certificate section enables you to select one of the SSL certificates that has been configured on the local server. You can also configure the path into which remote management requests will be logged. The default is *%SystemDrive%*\Inetpub\Logs\WMSvc.

Finally, the IPv4 Address Restrictions section enables you to increase security by restricting which computers can connect to IIS remotely. As shown in Figure 6-4, you can configure rules based on a specific IPv4 address or based on an address range (which is defined by a combination of an IP address and subnet mask). The Access For Unspecified Clients drop-down list defines whether IP addresses without entries will be allowed or denied. You can then create Allow or Deny entries to define which IP addresses can connect. These options are most useful when you have control over the groups of computers that will be used for administering Web services.

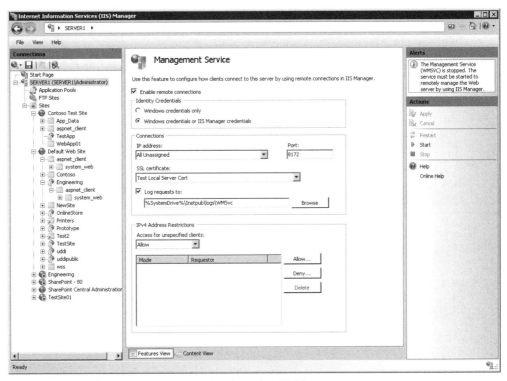

Figure 6-3   Configuring Management Service using IIS Manager

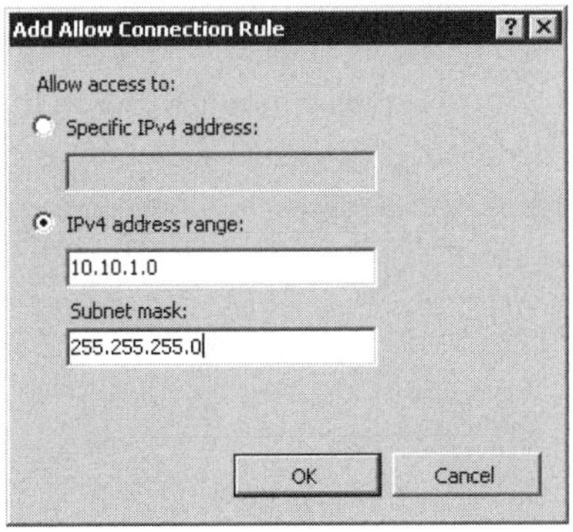

Figure 6-4   Configuring IPv4 address restrictions for Management Service in IIS Manager

Because the management service is stopped by default, you will need to click the *Start* command in the Actions pane to start allowing remote connections. You must stop the management service to make changes to the configuration.

Understanding IIS Manager Users

To connect to a Windows Server 2008 Web server using IIS Manager, users must have the necessary permissions. Users who are logged on to a computer running Windows Server 2008 with administrator credentials automatically will have the necessary permissions to complete all the available tasks on the server. For other types of users, such as remote systems administrators, you must decide how you want to manage permissions.

By default, the Web Server (IIS) role enables permissions to be assigned using Windows Authentication only. This means that all administrators who attempt to manage IIS must have Windows-based credentials and permissions. Windows Authentication is most appropriate for environments in which all the Web server administrators belong to the same domain. Users who are logged on to the domain will not have to supply credentials manually when they connect to a server using IIS Manager, assuming that they have the necessary permissions. Windows Authentication is also useful when you plan to create either local or domain accounts for all the administrators who will need access to IIS Manager.

In some cases, it might be impractical to create local or domain accounts for each of the potential IIS administrators. For example, Web service hosting companies can have hundreds of users who require the ability to manage their servers. In these environments, each user generally can modify specific settings for her or his own Web site. These users should not have access to other users' Web sites and often will be restricted to changing only certain settings. To support these scenarios, you need to enable the Windows Credentials Or IIS Manager Credentials option. When this option is enabled using the Management Service described in the previous section, you will be able to create username and password combinations solely for the purpose of managing IIS. These credentials can then be given to other users and administrators, so they can connect to the Web server without requiring individual Windows accounts for each of the users.

Creating IIS Manager Users

The IIS Manager utility enables you to define which users can connect to and administer Web sites and Web services. To configure these settings:

1. Open IIS Manager, and select a server in the left pane.
2. Click IIS Manager Users in the Management section of the features view. By default, the IIS installation will not contain any locally defined users.

3. To create a new user, first click Open Feature in the Actions pane, and then click the Add User command in the Actions pane. You will be prompted to provide a username and to type and confirm a password. (See Figure 6-5.) These settings are defined locally in IIS, so it is not necessary to use a fully qualified username that is compatible with your domain design.

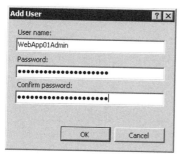

Figure 6-5   Adding an IIS Manager user

In addition to configuring permission through IIS Manager users, you can use group membership settings to determine which users can connect remotely. Users who have permission to log on to the local computer and to use IIS Manager will be able to do so from a remote computer.

Defining IIS Management Permissions

So far, you have learned how to enable remote management and how to specify which users can use IIS Manager to administer a Web server. Next, you will need to decide which permissions remote administrators will have after they connect. In some cases, you might want to enable a remote administrator to have full administrative access to the Web server. In other cases, you will want to restrict access to only specific Web sites or Web applications. You can configure IIS Manager Permissions at the Web site and application levels. However, you cannot configure permissions directly at the server level. This helps ensure that users are given permissions to modify the settings for only the specific Web sites and Web applications to which they need access.

To manage permissions, select a Web site or Web application, and then click IIS Manager Permissions in the Management section of the Features View. By default, new IIS Manager users are not given permissions to connect to a specific Web site or Web application. To enable a new user to connect at the selected level, first click Open Feature in the Actions pane, and then click the Allow User command in the Actions pane. You will be given the opportunity to specify a Windows user or an IIS Manager user (if IIS Manager credentials are accepted), as shown in Figure 6-6. If you are using the Windows option, you can select an existing user or group that is defined either in the domain (if the server is a member of a domain) or locally.

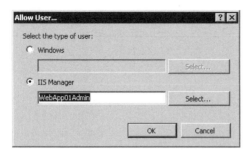

Figure 6-6   Allowing a user to administer a Web site

When users connect to IIS remotely, they will be able to access only those Web sites and Web applications on which they have been allowed. By default, permissions from higher-level objects are inherited automatically by lower-level objects. You can also choose the Deny User command in the Actions pane to prevent access explicitly to specific levels.

To simplify administration of many users, two commands are available when managing permissions for a Web site. Show All Users will provide a list of all the users available on the IIS installation. Show Only Site Users will restrict the display to only users who have access to the site.

Configuring Feature Delegation

The ability to define users and permissions enables you to manage administration based on site content structure. However, it is also important to determine which features users can view and configure. For example, you might want a Web server administrator to connect to the Default Web Site, but you do not want her to be able to change Authentication settings. Delegation is the process by which an administrator can determine which features of IIS a user can view and change.

Default settings for feature delegation initially are defined at the server level in IIS. To access these settings using IIS Manager, select the Web server object in the left pane, and then double-click Feature Delegation in the Management section of the Features View, as shown in Figure 6-7.

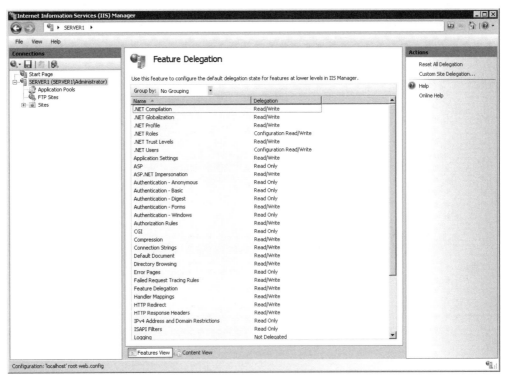

Figure 6-7   Viewing Feature Delegation settings for an IIS Web server

The list of items available for delegation will include all the features that have been added through the Web Server (IIS) server role and enabled role services. To change the setting for a feature, select it from the list and use the commands in the Set Feature Delegation section of the Actions pane. Most features have options of Read Only or Read/Write. In addition, some items have a Configuration Read/Write or Configuration Read Only setting. These settings enable Web developers to specify settings in their configuration files or to manage them based on database settings. The Not Delegated setting means that the feature has not been enabled for delegation at lower levels and is not available for configuration. You can also use the Delegation option in the Group By drop-down list to determine quickly how all the settings have been configured, as shown in Figure 6-8.

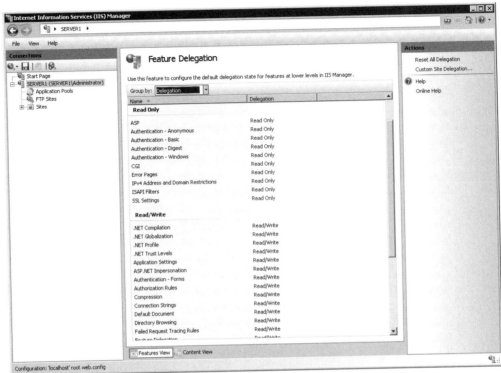

Figure 6-8   Viewing Feature Delegation configuration grouped by the delegation setting

The settings that you define at the server level automatically apply to all child Web sites and applications by default. In some cases, you will want to restrict feature delegation at the site level. To do this, click the Custom Site Delegation command in the Actions pane. This will bring up the Custom Site Delegation screen, as shown in Figure 6-9, which will enable you to select specific sites to which you want delegation settings to apply.

The Copy Delegation command enables you to copy the currently selected settings to one or more Web sites on the server. You can also use the Reset To Inherited and Reset All Delegation commands in the Actions pane to change groups of settings quickly to earlier values. You use feature delegation settings to determine which parts of the system configuration will be available when remote users connect to the server using IIS Manager.

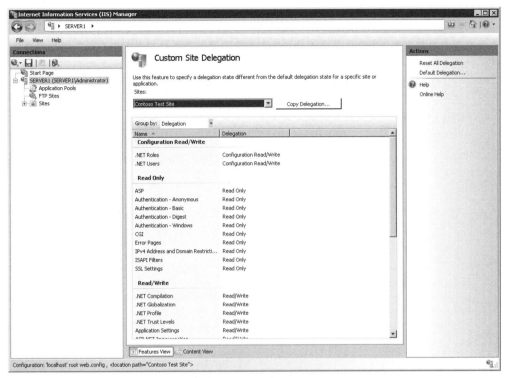

Figure 6-9   Specifying Custom Site Delegation settings

NOTE   When implementing remote management security, keep in mind the specific administration requirements. Some settings, such as IIS Manager Users and Feature Delegation, can be configured only at the level of the Web server. That makes these settings applicable to all the lower-level objects. IIS Manager Permissions, alternatively, can be configured for specific Web sites and Web applications. This enables you to implement granular security for those users who should have access only to limited portions of the Web server.

Connecting to a Remote Server Using IIS Manager

After you have enabled remote management and configured the appropriate permissions and settings, remote users will be able to connect to the server by using the IIS Manager console. To verify the configuration from either the local computer or from a remote computer that has the IIS Manager console installed, you can use the Start Page item in IIS Manager or the File menu to connect to IIS. As shown in Figure 6-10, remote users will be able to connect to the server at one of several different levels. The available commands include:

- Connect To A Server
- Connect To A Site
- Connect To An Application

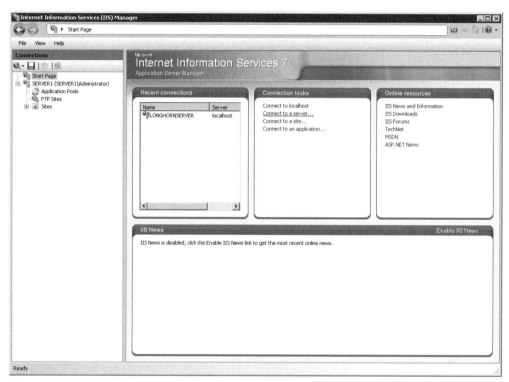

Figure 6-10 Connecting to a remote installation of IIS

MORE INFO Downloading the IIS Manager console

Users of Microsoft Windows Server 2003, Microsoft Windows XP, and Windows Vista can download a copy of the IIS Manager console to install on their own computers. To find the download, visit *http://www.iis.net/downloads* and search for Internet Information Services (IIS) 7.0 Manager. After remote users install the program, they can connect to installations of Windows Server 2008 that include the Web Server (IIS) server role and for which remote management is enabled.

Figure 6-11 shows the options available for connecting directly to a Web application. Remote administrators will be prompted to provide credentials (including a User Name and Password) to make the connection. If the connection is successful, remote administrators will see a new object in the left pane of the IIS Manager. These administrators also can name or rename these connections to keep track of multiple connections.

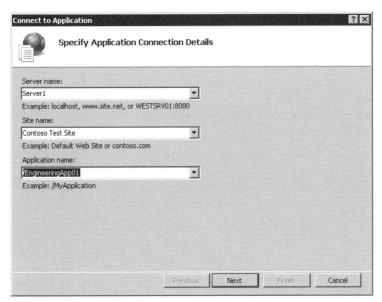

Figure 6-11   Creating a connection to a Web application

The specific items available for management will be based on feature delegation settings. Although the same icons might appear, remote administrators will be unable to make or save configuration changes for particular items. For most settings, they will be able to access the configuration page that shows the details, but the controls themselves will be disabled. Therefore, they will be unable to make and save changes. Figure 6-12 shows an example.

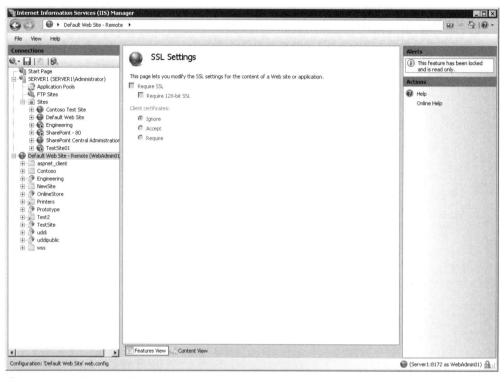

Figure 6-12   Viewing SSL options that are disabled due to feature delegation settings

Managing Request Handlers

To provide support for various Web application technologies, the architecture of IIS allows for enabling and disabling request handlers. Request handlers are programs that can process Web requests and generate responses that are then returned to clients. Web servers and Web applications can be configured with their own sets of request handlers, based on the types of content that must be supported. For example, a Web application might be configured to support static content (such as HTML) as well as ASP.NET Web pages.

The primary benefit is that Web developers can choose the technologies that are most useful for their tasks. However, there is a drawback from a security standpoint. When IIS is configured with multiple request handlers, the security attack surface is increased. A vulnerability in any of the enabled request handlers can result in unauthorized access or related issues. Therefore, it is recommended that systems administrators enable only those request handlers that they plan to use. In this section, you'll learn how to enable and disable request handlers.

Real World

Anil Desai

Web developers and systems administrators tend to grant far too many permissions on their Web servers. Their motivation is simple: it's just easier to provide complete access for all features and settings. That way, it's unlikely that you'll miss some strange requirement. Often, systems administrators don't understand the complexities of Web application security, and Web developers don't appreciate the importance of minimizing the attack surface of production Web servers. The end result is security that is less than ideal, and increased risk of unauthorized access. So what's the solution?

The most important aspect of determining ideal security settings is communication. Server administrators should ask Web application developers for a list of specific requirements for applications running in production. A pre-production checklist that includes details about intended users, required IIS handlers, authentication requirements, and code access security requirements is a good start. Web developers should understand the importance of minimizing exposure of services and of reducing execution permissions for their applications. To ensure that these goals are being met, both teams can develop tests that validate the configuration from functional and security standpoints.

Overall, Web developers and Web server administrators tend to have different technical backgrounds and areas of expertise. This is a positive difference as long as both groups understand the benefits of implementing production server security.

Understanding Handler Mappings

When the Web server receives a request, IIS uses the definition of handler mappings to determine which request handler to use. A handler mapping includes the following information:

- **Verb** HTTP requests include verbs that define the type of request being made. The two most common verbs are GET, which is used to obtain information from the Web server, and POST, which can also include information sent from the client browser to the Web server.

- **Request extension** Web servers commonly return a wide array of content types. The most common types of information are standard HTML pages and images such as .jpg and .gif files. IIS can use the file extension information from the HTTP request to determine which type of content must be processed. For example, the default file extension for ASP.NET Web pages is .aspx. Requests for .aspx pages are mapped automatically to the ASP.NET request handler. Most Web development platforms have their own conventions for extensions. It is also possible to create new extensions and provide the appropriate mappings for them.

■ **Handler information**   The handler mapping includes details related to the specific request handler that IIS should call based on the verb and request extension. This information can be provided in different ways, including a full path to an executable or as the name of a program that is designed to handle the request.

In addition to specific handler mappings based on these settings, IIS provides the ability to return content by using a default handler. The StaticFile handler mapping is configured to respond to requests that do not map to an existing file. The specific response will be based on the settings for the Web application. If a default document is specified for the Web application or virtual directory, that document will be returned if a file is not specified in the URL. For example, a request to *http://Server1.contoso.com/TestSite* will result automatically in the return of the default.htm document (if one exists).

If a default document does not exist or the feature is disabled, the StaticFile handler checks whether directory browsing is enabled. If it is, a listing of the contents of the folder is returned to the requester. Finally, if neither of these methods is able to complete the request, the user will receive an error stating that the request is forbidden. The complete error message is HTTP Error 403.14, The Web Server Is Configured To Not List The Contents Of This Directory. (See Figure 6-13.)

NOTE   Local vs. remote error messages

For security purposes, IIS is configured to provide one type of error message to Web users who access the server from the local computer, and another type of error message to users who access it remotely. This is done to maintain security: potentially sensitive information is not exposed to remote Web browser users, but useful troubleshooting information is still provided to systems administrators and Web developers.

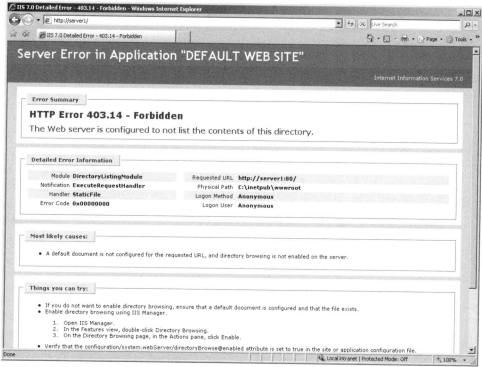

Figure 6-13   A detailed Request Not Found error page

Configuring Handler Mappings

When you add the Web Server (IIS) role to Windows Server 2008, a default set of handler mappings are defined for the Web server and for the default Web site. New Web sites and Web applications are also configured with a default set of handler mappings. In addition, when you add role services to the Web Server (IIS) role, additional handler mappings might be added automatically to the configuration.

You can use IIS Manager to configure handler mappings. After you have connected to an installation of IIS, you must choose at which level you want to configure mappings. You can configure mappings at the following levels:

- Web Server
- Web Sites
- Web Applications
- Virtual Directories
- Web Folders

Child items in the hierarchy automatically inherit handler mappings. For example, a child item automatically inherits the default handler mappings for a new Web application from the configuration of the parent Web site. Settings made at lower levels override the settings from higher levels. This enables a specific Web application to support a certain type of file content (such as ASP.NET pages) whereas other applications and the parent Web site might support only static content.

To view the handler mappings that are configured at a specific level, click the relevant object in the left pane of IIS Manager. Then, select Handler Mappings from the Features View in the center pane. Figure 6-14 shows the handler mappings that are defined for a Web site.

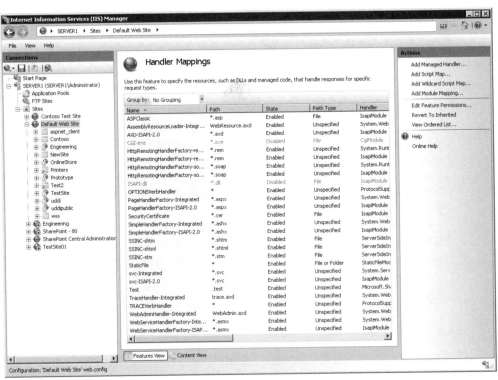

Figure 6-14   Viewing handler mappings for a Web site

The display includes information about all the handler mappings defined at the selected level. The name specifies information about the request handler itself. Examples include StaticFile and ASPClassic. Built-in handler mappings have default names, but administrators can provide names for new mappings when they are created. The Path column shows the specific request extensions for which the handler will be used.

The State column specifies whether the handler is enabled or disabled. If the handler is disabled, requests that match the mapping will not be processed. The Handler column specifies details about the program that is to be called. Finally, the Entry Type specifies whether the handler mapping is inherited from a parent object or is Local (defined directly for this object).

You can use the Group By drop-down list to view handler mappings based on different criteria. The Entry Type shows which settings have been inherited from parent objects and which handlers are configured directly for the selected object. The State grouping shows which handler mappings are enabled and which are disabled. These view options make it easy to determine the security attack surface for each component of the Web server.

Removing Handler Mappings

To secure your Web content, it is a good idea to remove any request handlers that you know will not be required when running in production. To remove a handler mapping, click it, and then select the *Remove* command from the Actions pane. After a handler is removed, requests for the types of content that it handled will not be processed. For example, Figure 6-15 shows the result that is returned to a local Web browser when the StaticFile request handler has been removed for the Web application. In this case, the request file (default.htm) is present in the Web application folder. However, because no request handler is available for the .htm file extension, the request cannot be processed. To the requester, it appears that the file does not exist.

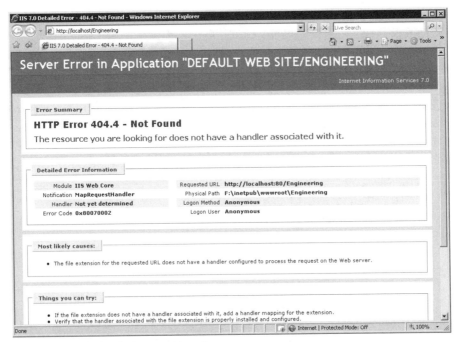

Figure 6-15   A detailed request handler error page

Managing Handler Inheritance

The inheritance feature of handler mapping settings can simplify the administration of servers significantly that host many Web sites and Web applications. In general, configure handler mappings at the highest applicable level. For example, if you are sure that none of the Web applications in a specific Web site will need to respond to the .soap file extension, you can remove this handler mapping at the level of the Web site. As mentioned earlier, to increase security, minimize the numbers and types of handlers that are enabled.

By default, it is possible for lower-level objects on the Web server to override handler mapping settings from parent objects. In some cases, you might want to prevent some types of requests from being processed on the entire server, regardless of settings for Web sites and Web applications. You do this by locking the configuration of the request handler. To lock the configuration, click the Web server object in IIS Manager, and then double-click Handler Mappings. Select the handler mapping you wish to lock, and then click the *Lock* command in the Actions pane.

It is also possible to restore the handler mappings settings to their default values. To do this, click the *Revert To Inherited* command in the Actions pane in IIS Manager. Performing this action will restore mappings from the parent object, but it will also result in the loss of any locally defined handler mappings.

Adding Handler Mappings

The architecture of IIS enables systems administrators to add new handler mappings based on specific needs. For example, if you want to provide support for a type of file that has a .mypage extension, you can add a handler for this path type. Additionally, Web developers can create their own programs to manage new types of requests.

To add a handler mapping, select the appropriate object, and then double-click Handler Mappings in the Features View in IIS Manager. The Actions pane contains several options for adding new types of request handlers. They are:

- **Add Managed Handler**   A managed handler processes requests based on a .NET-based code library. The Type setting enables you to choose from the existing .NET code modules registered on the local server, as shown in Figure 6-16. These types of options all belong to the *System.Web* namespace.

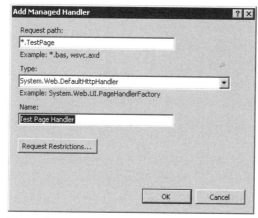

Figure 6-16   Adding a manager handler for a Web site

- **Add Script Map**   Scripting mappings are used to send request processing to a Dynamic Link Library (DLL) or executable (.exe) file type. These types of programs are designed to process request information and generate a response for IIS to send back to the end user.

- **Add Wildcard Script Map**   Wildcard script mappings are used to specify a default handler for types of documents that are not managed by other handlers. The Executable path option points to either a .dll or an .exe file designed to handle requests.

- **Add Module Mapping**   Modules are programs designed to integrate with the IIS request processing pipeline. They can provide a wide range of functions and are included with the default and optional role services that are part of the Web Server (IIS) role. Examples include the *FastCGIModule*, for processing scripts based on the Common Gateway Interface (CGI) specification, and *StaticCompressionModule*, which compresses static HTML content to reduce bandwidth usage. In addition to specifying the module that will be used for processing, administrators can define an optional executable or .dll file that will be used when processing requests, as shown in Figure 6-17.

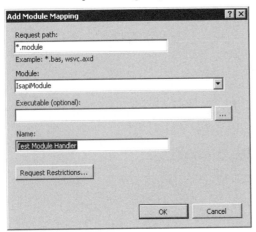

Figure 6-17   Adding a module mapping to a Web application

When you add a new request handler, you will be prompted to provide information about the request path. You can use wildcards, or you can specify a list of specific files. Examples include *.mypage (for responding to a request for any file with this extension) and Config.mypage (for responding to requests for this specific filename). You use the Name setting to help other developers and administrators identify the purpose of the handler mapping.

Configuring Request Restrictions

In addition to specifying the paths and filenames to which specific request handlers will be mapped, you can further secure IIS through request restrictions. To see the available options, click Request Restrictions in the dialog box when you are adding a mapping. Three tabs organize the request restrictions options: Mapping, Verbs, and Access.

You can use the Mapping tab to specify additional details related to whether files, folders, or both will be included in the mapping. The default setting is for the handler to handle requests automatically for both files and folders. You can choose either files or folders to limit whether the handler will respond to default documents or explicit file requests.

You can use the Verbs tab, shown in Figure 6-18, to specify which HTTP request verbs the handler will respond to. Although the most common types of verbs are GET and POST, some applications might use other verbs (such as HEAD) to request other details from the Web server. By default, all verb types will be sent to the request handler. If you want to use different handlers for different verbs, or if you want the handler mapping to apply only to specific types of requests, you can specify this by using the One Of The Following Verbs option.

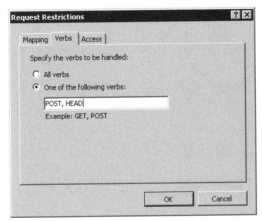

Figure 6-18 Viewing Verb Request Restrictions options for a handler mapping

Finally, the Access tab specifies the access permissions that will be granted to the request handler. To improve security, minimize the types of access the handler will have. The default setting is Script, which is acceptable for most types of executable handlers. Other options include None, Read, Write, and Execute.

Configuring Feature Permissions

Feature permissions specify which types of actions a request handler can take. You can configure these options by double-clicking Handler Mappings and clicking Edit Feature Permissions in the Actions pane, as shown in Figure 6-19.

Figure 6-19 Configuring Feature Permissions for a request handler

The three permission options are:

- **Read**   Enables the handler to read files that are stored within the file system.
- **Script**   Enables the handler to perform basic scripting-related tasks on the server.
- **Execute**   Enables the handler to run executable program code (such as .dll or .exe) files on the computer when processing a request. For Execute to be enabled, Script permissions must also be assigned.

By default, the Read and Script feature permissions are enabled for new handler mappings.

Quick Check

1. What steps must you take to enable users to manage IIS remotely, using the IIS Manager console?
2. What are two ways by which you can control which users can administer IIS remotely?

Quick Check Answers

1. To enable remote management, you must add the IIS Management Service role service and enable Management Service.
2. The IIS Management Service can authenticate users using Windows Authentication or IIS Manager credentials.

PRACTICE Managing IIS Security Settings

This practice will walk you through the steps required to manage security for a computer running Windows Server 2008 that has the Web Server (IIS) role installed. Specifically, you'll learn how to enable remote administration and the effects of configuring handler mappings to increase security. The steps assume that you have already installed the Web Server (IIS) role, using the default options on Server2.contoso.com, and that you are familiar with the process of adding role services.

▶ **Exercise 1 Configure and Manage Remote Administration**

In this exercise, you will use the IIS Management Service features to enable a user to connect to the computer. First, you will need to install the IIS Management Service role service. Then, you will create a new user based on IIS Manager credentials and configure permissions to access the Default Web Site. Finally, you will connect to IIS, using the new user account to verify that the permissions and feature delegation settings are in effect. The final steps can be performed locally on Server2, or you can use another computer, running either Windows Vista or

Windows Server 2008, that has the IIS 7.0 Manager console installed. The steps assume that you will perform the tasks locally on Server2.

1. Log on to Server2 as a user who has Administrator permissions.

2. Using Server Manager, add the IIS Management Service role service to the Web Server (IIS) server role. When you are finished, close Server Manager.

3. Open IIS Manager and connect to the local server (Server 2).

4. Click the server object in the left pane, and then double-click the Management Service icon in Features View.

5. On the Management Service page, you should see a message stating that the service has not been started. This is necessary to make configuration changes. Select the Enable Remote Connections option.

6. In the Identity Credentials section, choose Windows Credentials Or IIS Manager Credentials. This will enable you to create IIS Manager users later. Leave all other settings at their default values. Note that Management Service will respond on port 8172 by default.

7. Start Management Server by clicking Start in the Actions pane. Note that you are unable to modify settings while the service is running.

8. Return to Features View by clicking the Back button in the top toolbar.

9. Double-click IIS Manager Users to view a list of users who have been allowed to access the system. Note that, by default, there will be no users in the list.

10. Click Add User in the Actions pane to create a new IIS Manager user. Use the username WebAdmin01 and the password 1w3b!admin. (Always use strong passwords.) Click OK to create the new user and verify that it appears in the list of IIS Manager Users.

11. In the left pane of IIS Manager, click the Default Web Site object. Then, click IIS Manager Permissions in the Management section of the Features View.

12. Click the Allow User action. For the type of user, select IIS Manager, and then type **WebAdmin01** in the textbox.

    Note that you can also use the Select button to select from all the users who have been defined on the server.

13. Click OK.

14. In IIS Manager, click the Server2 object, and then double-click Feature Delegation in the Management section of Features View. In the Group By drop-down list, select Delegation. Note which features are set to Read Only in the list. In later steps, you will attempt to change SSL Settings to verify that feature delegation is working.

15. In IIS Manager, click the Start Page item in the left pane. In the center pane, click the Connect To A Site link.

16. For Server Name, type **Server2.contoso.com**. For Site Name, type **Default Web Site**. Click Next.

17. For Username, type **WebAdmin01** and type **1w3b!admin** for Password. Click Next.

18. For the name of the connection, type **Default Web Site – Test** to specify that this is a test connection. Click Finish.

     Once the connection is complete, you will see a new item called Default Web Site – Test in the left pane of IIS Manager. You can click this connection to administer the site, just as you would with the default local connection. However, note that the new connection shows only the contents of Default Web Site. You will have only the permissions that have been assigned to the WebAdmin01 user.

19. To verify the feature delegation settings, click the SSL Settings item in the IIS section of the Features View.

     Note the message stating that the feature is set to Read Only in the Actions pane. Also, verify that you are unable to make changes to these settings.

20. Optionally, you can remove the new connection in IIS Manager by right-clicking it and selecting Remove Connection.

21. When you are finished, close IIS Manager.

▶ **Exercise 2 Manage Handler Mappings**

In this practice exercise, you will learn how to configure and manage handler mappings for a Web application. Initially, you will verify that content is being presented correctly to Web users. Then, you will disable a request handler mapping and verify that the content is no longer accessible. Finally, you will revert the handler mappings to their inherited settings to restore access to the content.

1. Log on to Server2 as a user who has Administrator permissions.

2. Using Windows Explorer, navigate to the *%SystemDrive%*\Inetpub\Wwwroot folder. Make a copy of the Iisstart.htm file and name it **Iisstart.test**.

    Note that you might need to disable the Hide Extensions For Well Known File Types option on the View tab of the Folder Options dialog box by selecting Folder And Search Options on the Organize menu.

3. When you are finished, close Windows Explorer.

4. Open IIS Manager and connect to the local server.

5. In the left pane of IIS Manager, select Default Web Site. In the Actions pane, click the *Browse *:80(http)* command. This will launch Internet Explorer and connect to the default content for the site. Note that the default document (in this case, Iisstart.htm) is displayed and that the page contains a .png image type.

6. In Internet Explorer, modify the URL to request the iisstart.test page. An example of the full URL would be *http://Server1/iisstart.test*.

   Note that, although the file exists, you will receive an HTTP Error 404.3. The error states that no handler is available to process the request.

7. When you are finished, close Internet Explorer.

8. In IIS Manager, double-click the Handler Mappings item. You will see a list of all the default handlers that have been registered on the system.

9. Click the Add Module Mapping link to create a new mapping. For Request Path, type ***.test**. For Module, select StaticFileModule. For Name, type **Test Page Handler**. Leave the other settings at their default values, and then click OK to create the mappings.

   This will enable the Web server to process files that have the .test extension.

10. Open Internet Explorer and navigate to the Iisstart.test page, using the same URL you used in step 5.

    Note that this time, you will see a blank page and that an error message does not appear. This indicates that the new handler mapping you created is functioning properly.

11. Close Internet Explorer.

12. In IIS Manager, return to the Handler Mappings section for Default Web Site, and then click Revert To Inherited in the Actions pane. Click Yes to confirm the changes.

    This will restore the default handler mappings and will remove the Test Handler Mapping that you created in a previous step.

13. When you are finished, close IIS Manager.

Lesson Summary

- When implementing IIS security, consider the overall goals of implementing defense-in-depth best practices and reducing the server's attack surface.

- IIS 7 uses consistent built-in user and group accounts for managing security.

- You can enable remote management of IIS by adding the IIS Management Service role service.

- You can manage remote management capabilities by creating users, assigning permissions, and configuring feature delegation.

- Request handler mappings determine which types of content IIS will allow for a particular component in the hierarchy.

Lesson Review

You can use the following questions to test your knowledge of the information in Lesson 1, "Configuring IIS Security." The questions are also available on the companion CD if you prefer to review them in electronic form.

NOTE   Answers

Answers to these questions and explanations of why each answer choice is correct or incorrect are located in the "Answers" section at the end of the book.

---

1. You are a systems administrator responsible for securing a Windows Server 2008 Web server. You have created a new Web site called Contoso Intranet that will contain seven Web applications. One of the application developers has told you that her Web application requires a new request handler that is processed using a .NET library her team created. How can you meet these requirements while also maximizing security for the server?

   A. Add a new managed handler to the Contoso Intranet Web site.

   B. Add a new managed handler for the specific Web application that requires it.

   C. Add a new module mapping to the Contoso Intranet Web site.

   D. Add a new module mapping for the specific Web application that requires it.

2. You are a systems administrator responsible for managing a Windows Server 2008 Web server. Recently, your organization set up a new IIS Web site that will be accessed by users outside of your organizations. Consultants should be able to connect to this Web site, using IIS Manager. Your organization's security policy prevents you from creating domain accounts or local user accounts for these users. You attempt to use the IIS Manager Permissions feature for the Web site. However, when you click Allow User, you are able to select only Windows users. How can you resolve this problem?

   A. Verify that Management Service has been started.

   B. Reconfigure the file system permissions for the root folder of the Web site.

   C. Reconfigure Management Service to enable Windows And IIS Manager Credentials.

   D. Verify the Authentication settings for the Web site.

Lesson 2: Controlling Access to Web Services

Web servers commonly are deployed in a wide variety of configurations. Some servers provide content that should be directly accessible to the public through the Internet. Others contain Web application content that should be available only to a limited set of users. Web server administration must have the ability to define which users can connect to a Web service. After users have proven their identity, rules must be in place for determining which content is available to them.

In this lesson, you'll learn about how you can configure authentication and authorization for protecting Web content in IIS. Due to the many security standards and approaches for Web services, it is important to understand how to select the most appropriate one for a given scenario. You will also learn how you can use features such as IP Address And Domain Restrictions and .NET Trust Levels to further secure your Web services.

After this lesson, you will be able to:

- Describe the authentication options available for IIS Web services.
- Configure authentication options for a Web server, Web site, or Web application.
- Implement and manage Authorization Rules to limit access to specific Web content.
- Configure server certificates and enable Secure Sockets Layer (SSL) functionality for an IIS server.
- Create and manage IP Address And Domain Restrictions settings to limit access to an IIS Web server.
- Configure .NET Trust Levels based on the needs of specific Web applications.

Estimated lesson time: 75 minutes

Managing IIS Authentication

Authentication refers to the process by which a user or computer proves its identity for security purposes. The most familiar method is through a logon or username and an associated password. When working with Web servers such as IIS, authentication settings and options determine how users will provide their credentials to access content stored on the Web server. IIS provides numerous methods for securing content. By default, content stored in new Web sites, Web applications, and virtual directories will allow access to anonymous users. This means that users will not be required to provide any authentication information to retrieve the data. In this section, you'll learn about the authentication modes supported by IIS and how you can configure them.

Understanding Anonymous Authentication

For many types of Web servers, users should be able to access at least a default page or some content without being required to provide authentication information. When you enable the Web Server (IIS) role by using default options, anonymous authentication is enabled for the Default Web Site and its associated Web content. Anonymous authentication is designed to provide access to content that should be available to all users who can connect to the Web server. An example is the default IIS Web page for Default Web Site. When IIS receives a request for content, it automatically uses a specific identity to attempt to complete the request. By default, anonymous authentication uses the IUSR built-in account. (See Figure 6-20.) As long as this user account has permission to access the content (based on NTFS permissions), the request will be processed automatically.

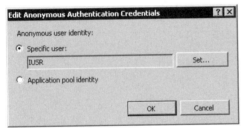

Figure 6-20   Editing settings for anonymous authentication credentials

It is also possible to use the *Set* command to provide a username and password for a different account. This is useful when you plan to use different NTFS permissions for different Web content. Finally, there is an option to use the Application Pool Identity. This setting instructs IIS to use the same credentials that are applied to the application pool used by the Web site or Web application.

If all the content on the Web server should be available to all users, then no further authentication configuration is required. More commonly, however, you will want to restrict access to at least some content on the server. For example, an intranet server might include a Web application or virtual directory that is intended for only members of the Human Resources department. To restrict access to content, you can use NTFS permissions. If the credentials that are configured for the anonymous authentication option are insufficient to access the content, it will not be returned to the user automatically. Generally, enable one of the other available authentication methods so that authorized users can access the content.

NOTE   Simplifying content protection

On all Web servers, some content exists that should not be accessible to any users. Examples include contents of system folders (such as the Windows system folder) and application source code stored within Web content folders. You can use Deny NTFS permissions to ensure that users cannot use anonymous credentials to access this content. If you are using multiple accounts for anonymous authentication of different content, it is best to create a group that contains these accounts. You can then deny permission to the group to simplify administration.

Understanding Forms Authentication

A common security approach used by Web developers is to use standard HTTP forms to transmit logon information. Forms authentication uses an HTTP 302 (Login/Redirect) response to redirect users to a logon page. Generally, the logon page will provide users with locations to enter a logon name and their password. When this information is submitted back to the logon page, it is validated. Assuming that the credentials are accepted, users are redirected to the content they originally requested. By default, form submissions send data in an unencrypted format. To secure the transmission of logon information, enable encryption through SSL or TLS.

Forms authentication is the most common approach used on the Internet because it does not have any specific Web browser requirements. Web developers typically will build their own logon pages. Logons are often validated against user account information stored in a relational database (for Internet sites) or against an Active Directory directory services domain.

The default settings for forms authentication are designed for use by ASP.NET Web applications. You can edit the settings of forms authentication to manage several settings. (See Figure 6-21.) The primary setting is the Login URL. This specifies the name of the Web page to which users will be sent when they attempt to access protected content.

Once the user has provided authentication information, cookies are sent from the Web browser to the Web server during each request. This enables the client to prove that it has authenticated with the Web server and is necessary because HTTP is a stateless protocol. The Cookie Settings section enables you to configure how cookies will be used by the site. The Mode options include:

- Do Not Use Cookies
- Use Cookies
- Auto Detect
- Use Device Profile

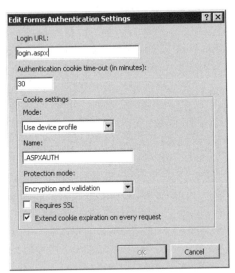

Figure 6-21   Configuring settings for forms authentication

The most appropriate option will be based on Web browser requirements (for example, whether your Web site requires users to enable support for cookies) and the requirements of the Web application or Web content.

Understanding Challenge-Based Authentication

Users who access secure Web sites on the Internet are familiar with the process of providing a username and password to access secured content or to perform actions such as placing online orders. IIS supports three methods of presenting a security challenge to users who are attempting to access Web content that has been secured using file system permissions. Each of these methods relies on sending an HTTP 401 Challenge—a standard method that prompts users to provide logon information. These three authentication methods are:

- **Basic authentication**   Basic authentication presents an authentication challenge to Web users through a standard method that is supported by all Web browsers. The main drawback to basic authentication is that information users provide is encoded but not encrypted. This means that, if the information is intercepted, the logon and password details can be obtained easily. To transfer basic authentication information securely, either ensure that your network connections are secure (for example, in a data center environment) or enable encryption using SSL or TLS.

- **Digest authentication**   Digest authentication relies on the HTTP 1.1 protocol to provide a secure method of transmitting logon credentials. It does this by using a Windows domain controller to authenticate the user. A potential drawback is that it requires clients' Web browsers to support HTTP 1.1. Current versions of most popular browsers support this method, so it is possible to use digest authentication for both Internet and intranet environments.

- **Windows authentication**   Windows authentication provides a secure and easy-to-administer authentication option. It relies on the use of either the NTLM or Kerberos authentication protocol to validate users' credentials against a Windows domain or local security database. Windows authentication is designed primarily for use in intranet environments, where clients and Web servers are members of the same domain. To simplify administration, administrators can use Active Directory domain accounts to control access to content.

One important consideration about these challenge-based authentication methods is their interaction with anonymous authentication. If you want to require users to provide logon information before accessing Web content, you must disable anonymous authentication. If anonymous authentication remains enabled, content that is not protected by using file system permissions will be made automatically available to users without requiring authentication. Another requirement to note is that you cannot enable both forms authentication and challenge-based authentication for the same content.

Understanding ASP.NET Impersonation

Impersonation is a security method by which an IIS Web request is processed using the security information provided by a specific user account or the user who is accessing the site. When ASP.NET impersonation is disabled (the default setting), the security context for processing requests is based on the account used by the Web application. When you enable impersonation, you can specify a user account for determining the security context. (See Figure 6-22.) To provide the username and password information, click the Set button.

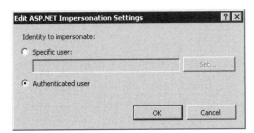

Figure 6-22   Configuring ASP.NET impersonation settings

Another option is to configure ASP.NET impersonation to the Authenticated User option. This setting specifies that the security permissions of a user who has been authenticated (using one of the other authentication options) will be used to provide access to content. This setting is useful when you want to use file system permissions that use specific users and groups to decide which content should be protected. When used in this way, it is most appropriate for environments that support relatively small numbers of users, such as department-level intranet Web servers.

Understanding Client Certificate Authentication

In addition to the other available types of authentication options, IIS provides support for using client certificates for validating the identity of a Web user. This method requires users to have security certificates installed on their computers. When a request is made for protected content, IIS automatically validates the identity of the client by querying the certificate information. There are three main modes by which client certificates can be used:

- **One-To-One mappings** In this configuration, the Web server must contain a copy of the client certificate used by every computer that will access restricted content. The server compares its copy of the certificate with the one that is presented by the client to validate requests.
- **Many-To-One mappings** It is often impractical to manage certificates for all possible Web users on the server. Although this method is slightly less secure, many-to-one mappings are based on the Web server performing authentication by using certain information found in the client certificate. A common example is validating the organization information in the certificate to ensure that the user is coming from a trusted company.
- **Active Directory mappings** Active Directory Certificate Services can simplify the creation and management of client certificates. To enable this method, organizations must first set up their own certificate-based infrastructure.

Because of the certificate requirements for client certificate authentication, this method is most often used in environments in which systems administrators have control over end users' computers. It is impractical to require certificates for publicly accessible Internet Web sites and applications.

Understanding Authentication Requirements

Handlers and modules manage IIS authentication. The specific authentication options available for a Web server are based on the Web Server (IIS) role services that are installed. The list of available role services includes:

- Basic Authentication
- Windows Authentication
- Digest Authentication

- Client Certificate Mapping Authentication
- IIS Client Certificate Mapping Authentication

To add or remove a security-related role service, open Server Manager, expand the Roles section, right-click Web Server (IIS), and then select either Add Role Services or Remove Role Services. (See Figure 6-23.) Because role services will affect the available authentication options for the entire Web server, determine the requirements of all the Web applications and Web content on your server.

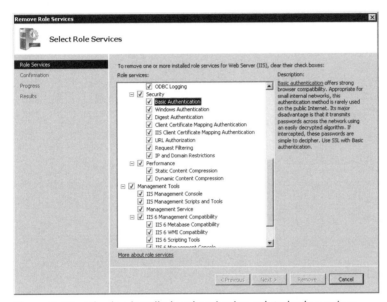

Figure 6-23   Viewing installed authentication-related role services

In addition to role service settings, each of the authentication methods has specific module requirements, as shown in Table 6-1. For more information about managing modules, see the "Managing Request Handlers" section discussed earlier in this chapter.

Table 6-1   IIS Authentication Methods and Their Requirements

Authentication Methods	Required Module(s)
Anonymous	AnonymousAuthModule
ASP.NET Impersonation	ManagedEngine
Basic	BasicAuthModule TokenCacheModule
Client Certificates	iisClientCertificateMappingModule

Table 6-1   IIS Authentication Methods and Their Requirements

Authentication Methods	Required Module(s)
Client Certificates (Active Directory Mapping)	CertificateMappingAuthenticationModule
Digest	DigestAuthModule
Forms	FormsAuthenticationModule
Windows	WindowsAuthenticationModule

Configuring Authentication Settings

IIS enables you to define configuration settings, using the Web object hierarchy. Authentication settings can be configured for objects at the following levels:

- Web server
- Web sites
- Web applications
- Virtual directories
- Physical folders and individual files

Authentication settings that are defined at higher levels (such as for a Web application) will be used automatically for lower-level objects. This method makes it easier to manage settings for multiple Web sites, Web applications, and their related content.

To configure authentication settings using IIS Manager, select the appropriate object in the left pane, and then double-click Authentication in Features View. Figure 6-24 shows the default authentication options for the Default Web Site object.

The default display shows a complete list of the available authentication options, grouped by the response type used. Each method can be enabled or disabled by selecting the item and using the Enable or Disable commands in the Actions pane. In addition, some authentication options provide additional commands for managing settings. By default, when you enable or disable an authentication option, the setting will apply to all lower-level objects and content in the IIS hierarchy. You can override this behavior by explicitly enabling or disabling authentication methods at lower levels.

To verify your authentication-related settings, you should always test access to content by using a Web browser. In some cases, it might be necessary to use a second computer to ensure that authentication is working properly. For example, if you are already connected to a computer running Windows Server 2008 as a member of the administrators group and you want to test Windows Authentication, you should attempt to connect from another computer in the environment. This will help prevent automatic authentication from affecting your test results.

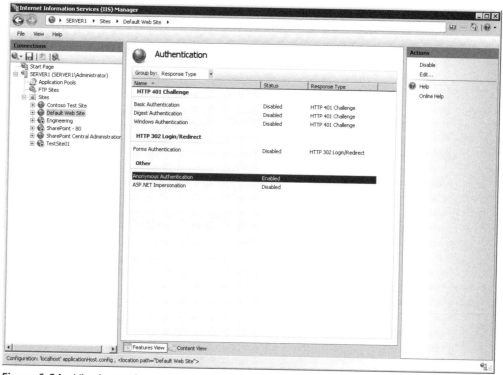

Figure 6-24   Viewing authentication options for Default Web Site, using IIS Manager

Managing URL Authorization Rules

Authorization is a method by which systems administrators can determine which resources and content are available to specific users. Authorization relies on authentication to validate the identity of a user. Once the identity has been proven, authorization rules determine which actions a user or computer can perform. IIS provides methods of securing different types of content using URL-based authorization. Because Web content is generally requested using a URL that includes a full path to the content being requested, you can configure authorization settings easily, using IIS Manager.

Creating URL Authorization Rules

To enable URL authorization, the UrlAuthorizationModule must be enabled. Authorization rules can be configured at the level of the Web server for specific Web sites, for specific Web applications, and for specific files (based on a complete URL path). URL authorization rules use inheritance so that lower-level objects inherit authorization settings from their parent objects (unless they are specifically overridden).

To configure authorization settings, select the appropriate object in the left pane of IIS Manager, and then select Authorization Rules in Features View. Figure 6-25 shows an example of multiple rules configured for a Web site.

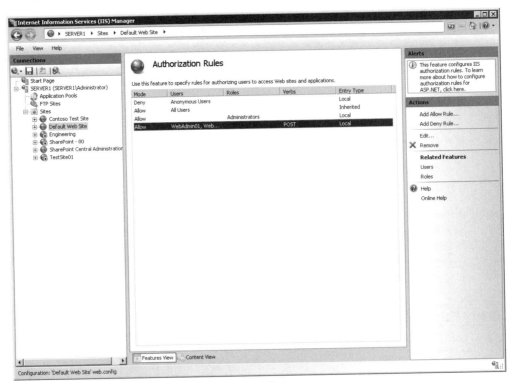

Figure 6-25   Viewing authorization rules for a Web site

There are two types of rules: Allow and Deny. You can create new rules by using the *Add Allow Rule* and *Add Deny Rule* commands in the Actions pane. The available options for both types of rules are the same. (See Figure 6-26.) When creating a new rule, the main setting is to determine to which users the rule applies. The options are:

- All Users
- All Anonymous Users
- Specific Roles Or User Groups
- Specific Users

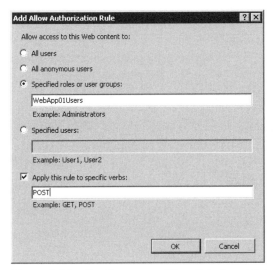

Figure 6-26   Creating a new Allow Rule for a Web application

When you choose to specify users or groups to which the rule applies, you can type the appropriate names in a command-separated list. The specific users and groups are defined using .NET role providers. This is a standard feature that is available to ASP.NET Web developers. Developers can create their own roles and user accounts and can define permissions within their applications. Generally, information about users and roles is stored in a relational database or relies on a directory service such as Active Directory.

In addition to user and role selections, you can further configure an authorization rule based on specific HTTP verbs. For example, if you want to apply a rule only for *POST* commands (which are typically used to send information from a Web browser to a Web server), add only the POST verb to the rule.

Managing Rule Inheritance

As mentioned earlier in this section, authorization rules are inherited automatically by lower-level objects. This is useful when your Web site and Web content is organized hierarchically based on intended users or groups. The Entry Type column shows whether a rule has been inherited from a higher level or whether it has been defined locally. IIS Manager automatically will prevent you from creating duplicate rules. You can remove rules at any level, including both Inherited and Local entry types.

Configuring Server Certificates

One of the many challenges related to security is that of verifying the identity of a Web server and, once you are reasonably sure that the server can be trusted, you need to protect communications between the Web client and the Web server. On many networks, and especially on the Internet, providing secure communications for sensitive data is a key concern. Server certificates are designed to provide added security for Web services. IIS provides built-in support for creating and managing server certificates and for enabling encrypted communications. In this section, you'll learn how to configure and enable these options.

Understanding Server Certificates

Server certificates are a method by which a Web server can prove its identity to the clients that are attempting to access it. The general approach to provide this functionality is by a hierarchy of trust authorities. The party that issues a server certificate is known as a Certificate Authority (CA). On the Internet, numerous third-party organizations are available for validating servers and generating certificates. Assuming that users trust these third parties, they should also be able to extend the trust to validated Web sites. Organizations can also serve as their own CA for internal servers. This enables systems administrators to validate and approve new server deployments by using a secure mechanism.

The general process for obtaining a server certificate involves three major steps:

- **Generating a certificate request** The request is created on a Web server, which produces a text file containing the information about the request in an encrypted format. The certificate request identifies the Web server uniquely.
- **Submitting the certificate request to a CA** The certificate request is submitted to a CA (generally by using a secure Web site or e-mail). The CA then verifies the information in the request and creates a trusted server certificate.
- **Obtaining and installing a certificate on the Web server** The CA returns a certificate to the requester, usually in the form of a small text file. This file can then be imported into the Web server configuration to enable secure communications.

NOTE Client certificates vs. server certificates

Certificate-based technology can be used with a Web server by several methods. Use client-based certificates to verify access to a Web server by validating clients. In this case, the client holds a certificate that the server can validate. You learned about this method earlier in this lesson. Server-side certificates are installed on Web server computers to prove their identity to Web clients and to enable encrypted communications. Client-side certificates are generally used in intranet or extranet environments, while server-side certificates are common for securing all types of Web servers.

Creating an Internet Certificate Request

Use IIS Manager to obtain a certificate for use on an IIS Web server. To begin the process, connect to a Web server running Windows Server 2008 and select Server Certificates in Features View. (See Figure 6-27.) Note that certificate requests are generated at the level of the Web server and not for other objects such as Web sites or Web applications.

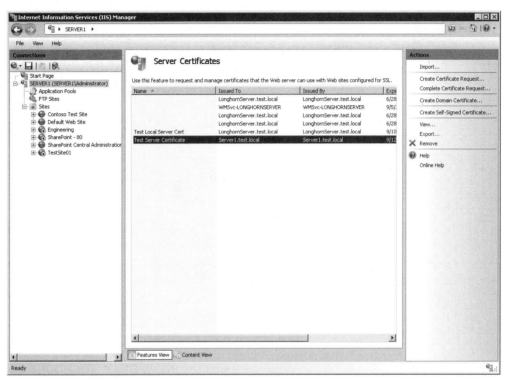

Figure 6-27   Viewing Server Certificate options for an IIS Web server

Depending on the configuration of the local server, some certificates might already be included in the default configuration. The Actions pane provides commands for creating new certificates.

To begin the certificate request process, click Create Certificate Request. As shown in Figure 6-28, you will be required to provide information about the requesting organization. This information will be used by the CA to determine whether to issue the certificate. Therefore, it is important for information to be exact. For example, the Organization field should include the complete legal name of the requesting company. The Common Name field generally defines the domain name that will be used with the certificate.

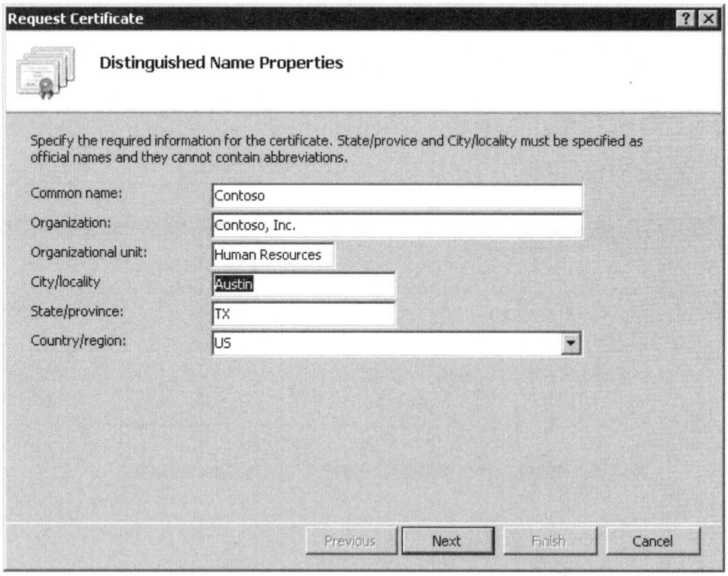

Figure 6-28   The Distinguished Name Properties page

The second step of the certificate request process requires you to choose the cryptographic method that will be used to secure the certificate request. (See Figure 6-29.) The Cryptographic Service Provider setting should use a method that is accepted by the certificate authority. (The default option of Microsoft RSA SChannel Cryptographic Provider is accepted by most third-party CAs.) The Bit Length setting indicates the strength of the encryption. Larger values take more time to process (due to computational overhead) but provide added security.

The final step of the process involves storing the certificate request to a file. Here you can provide a fully qualified path and file name into which the request will be stored. The request itself will be stored in a text file that contains encrypted information.

The next step of the process involves submitting the certificate request to a CA. Generally, the issuer's Web site will request that you either upload the certificate request or copy and paste the contents into a secure Web site. The issuer will also require additional information such as details about your organization and payment information.

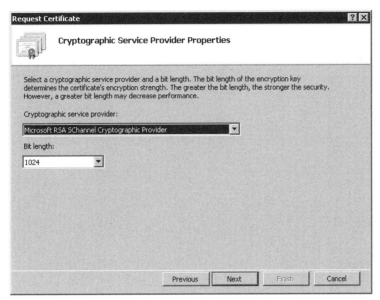

Figure 6-29   The Cryptographic Service Provider Properties page

Completing an Internet Certificate Request

The amount of time a public third-party CA can take to process a request will vary. Once the request has been processed and approved, the CA will send a response by e-mail or through its Web site. You can then store this response in a text file and provide it to IIS to complete the process. To do this, select the appropriate request in the Server Certificates feature view, and then click the *Complete Certificate Request* command in the Actions pane. You will be asked to specify the path and file name of the response along with a friendly name for administration purposes. (See Figure 6-30.) The convention is to use a file name with a .cer extension for the response; however, any type of standard text file will work.

Figure 6-30   Completing the certificate request process

Assuming that the certificate request matches the response, the certificate will be imported into the configuration of IIS and ready for use.

Creating Other Certificate Types

In addition to the standard certificate request process, you can use two other commands to create certificates. These commands are also available in the Actions pane in the properties of the Server Certificates feature. The Create Domain Certificate option generates a request to an internal certificate authority. This is used commonly in organizations that have their own certificate services infrastructure. Instead of sending the request to a third-party CA, the request is designed to be sent to an internal server. Figure 6-31 shows the available options. The Specify Online Certificate Authority text box accepts the path and name of an internal CA server. The Friendly Name can be used to identify the purpose of the certificate.

MORE INFO   **Active Directory Certificate Services**

Windows Server 2008 includes the Active Directory Certificate Services server role that allows administrators to create their own certificate-based security infrastructure. The details of implementing these services are outside the scope of this book and Exam 70-643. For more information about configuring certificate services, see Microsoft TechNet Active Directory Certificate Services at *http://technet2.microsoft.com/windowsserver2008/en/servermanager/activedirectorycertificateservices .mspx*.

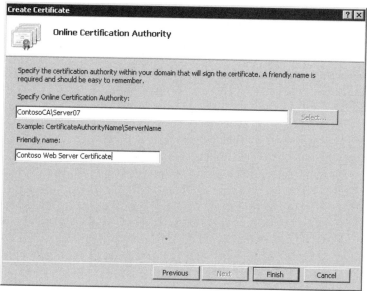

Figure 6-31   Specifying Online Certificate Authority settings for a Domain Certificate

Creating a Self-Signed Certificate

The certificate creation and management process can require several steps and usually requires an added cost for obtaining a certificate from a trusted third-party CA. Although these steps are necessary to ensure security in a production environment, an easier method is preferable for development and test environments. Self-signed certificates can test certificate functionality by creating a local certificate. By avoiding the CA process, it is easy to create these certificates, using the *Create Self-Signed Certificate* command in the Actions pane. Figure 6-32 shows the dialog box.

Unlike other certificate types, it is not necessary to provide organizational information for the certificate. This is because the certificate itself is created immediately on the local computer. The primary drawback of self-signed certificates is that users who access the Web server using a secure connection will receive a warning that the certificate has not been issued by a third party. (See Figure 6-33.) While this is generally not a problem in test environments, it prevents the use of self-signed certificates for production Web servers.

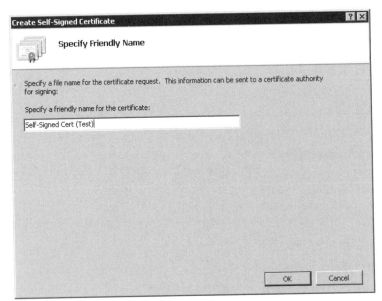

Figure 6-32   Creating a self-signed certificate

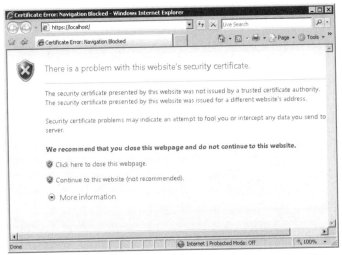

Figure 6-33   Viewing a certificate-related error when accessing a server that is using a self-signed certificate

Viewing Certificate Details

The contents of a server certificate include several details and properties. To view this information, double-click an item in the Server Certificates list for a Web server. The Certificate dialog box, shown in Figure 6-34, provides information about the server certificate. The General tab displays details about the issuer of the certificate. For Internet-based certificates, this will be the name of the trusted third party that issued it. Additionally, certificates have a range of valid dates.

Figure 6-34 Viewing general information for a server certificate

The Details tab displays additional properties of the certificate, including the encryption method. The Certification Path tab shows the entire trust hierarchy for the certificate. In environments that have multiple levels of CAs, this is useful for tracking all the trust relationships that are used. For the certificate to be considered valid, all the levels must be trusted.

Web users are also able to view security certificate details. This is useful for validating the identity of a Web server or organization. In Internet Explorer, users can right-click a Web page and select Properties. The General tab shows a button for viewing the certificate's status and other details. (See Figure 6-35.)

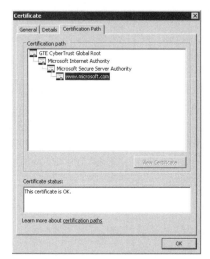

Figure 6-35   Viewing certificate information for a public Web site, using Internet Explorer

Importing and Exporting Certificates

Once a certificate has been installed on a Web server, you might need to export it to a file. You can do this using IIS Manager by right-clicking the certificate and choosing the *Export* command. You can then provide an export location and file name for the file along with a password to protect the certificate from being installed by unauthorized users. (See Figure 6-36.) By default, exported certificate files use the .pfx extension. However, you can use any other extension. The contents of the exported certificate are encrypted and protected, using the password you provide.

Figure 6-36   Exporting a server certificate, using IIS Manager

To import a certificate, click the *Import* command in the Actions pane. You will be prompted to provide the file system location of the exported certificate file along with the password to open it. Additionally, you can choose whether you want to allow the certificate to be exported in the future.

Enabling Secure Sockets Layer

Once you have added a server certificate to an IIS Web server, you can enable connections, using SSL. SSL-based connections rely on certificates to validate the identity of the Web server. Once the identity has been proven, users can create a secure connection, using the HTTP Secure (HTTPS) protocol. By default, HTTPS connections use TCP port 443 for communications. To modify the details or to enable HTTPS for a Web site, you must configure the site bindings for a Web site. (For complete details about configuring site bindings, see Chapter 5.)

You can also require SSL-enabled connections for specific Web sites by using IIS Manager. To do this, select a Web site, a Web application, or a folder, and then click SSL Settings in the Features view. Figure 6-37 shows the available options. The check boxes enable you to specify whether SSL is required to access this content. If the option is enabled, standard HTTP connections will not be enabled. Optionally, you can specify whether client certificates will be ignored, accepted, or required.

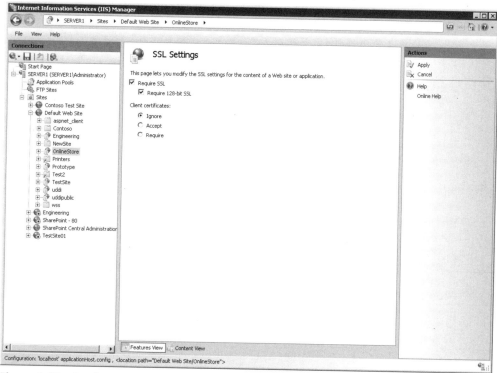

Figure 6-37   Configuring SSL settings for a Web application

Overall, server certificates and SSL provide a standard method of protecting Web-based connections and Web server content. Support for server certificates and SSL is often expected for all types of Web servers that contain sensitive information.

Configuring IP Address and Domain Restrictions

Although some Web servers are configured to provide public access to all content, it's also common to need to restrict access to only specific groups of users. By default, IIS is configured to accept requests on all connections based on site binding settings such as IP address and TCP port. Systems administrators can further restrict access to Web sites by responding only to requests that originate from specific IP addresses or domains using IIS Manager.

The first step is to select the level at which you want to assign the restrictions. The IPv4 Address And Domain Restrictions feature is available at the server, site, Web application, virtual directory, and folder level. In general, assign restrictions at the highest level for which the settings will apply. For example, if all the Web applications in a particular site should respond to requests only from a single domain, configure the request settings at the site level. By default, IIS does not include any restrictions. To configure request settings, select the appropriate object in the left pane of IIS Manager, and then double-click IPv4 Address And Domain Restrictions in Features View. Figure 6-38 provides an example of the settings.

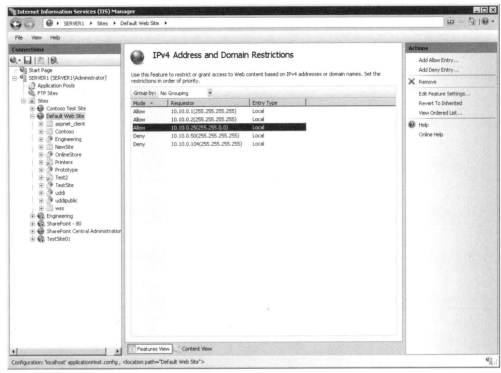

Figure 6-38   Configuring IPv4 Address And Domain Restrictions for a Web site

Adding Allow and Deny Entries

There are two main types of entries you can add to the IPv4 Address And Domain Restrictions configuration. Allow entries specify which IP addresses can access Web content; Deny entries define which addresses cannot access the content. When configuring IP address restrictions, you can specify either a single IP address or a range of IP addresses. (See Figure 6-39.) When specifying a range, you can enter the initial IP address and the subnet mask. This will determine the range of addresses that will be allowed or denied. It is possible to exclude specific addresses or ranges by using additional allow or deny rules. Overall, however, try to keep the configuration simple to make administration and management easier.

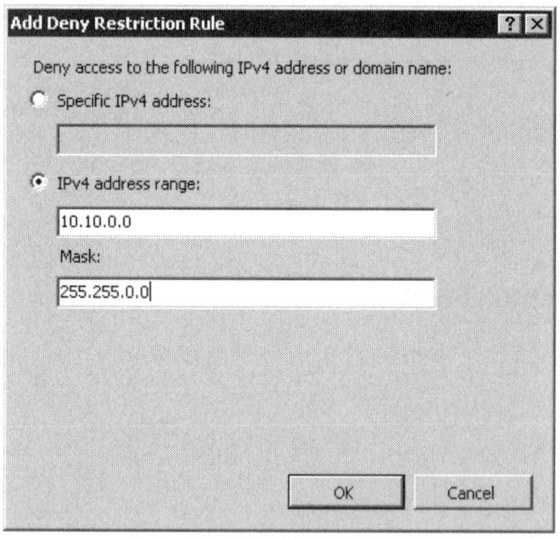

Figure 6-39   Adding a Deny entry IP address restriction for a Web site

The single address option is useful if only a few users require access to the site or if only a few other servers require access to the content. This is common in environments that support distributed server-side Web applications that are not designed for direct user access. IP address ranges are more appropriate when groups of users and computers should have access to the environment. For example, if all the users in the Human Resources department are located on the same subnet, that subnet can be allowed while other subnets are denied.

When evaluating connection rules, IIS will evaluate all allow and deny rules to determine whether an address has access. Deny rules will take precedence over allow rules. If users are denied access to a site, they will see a screen similar to the one shown in Figure 6-40.

An additional setting defines the default behavior for any IP addresses that are not explicitly added to the Allow or Deny list. By default, IIS will allow access automatically from these addresses. To change the setting, click Edit Feature Settings in the Actions pane, and choose Deny for the Access For Unspecified Clients setting. (See Figure 6-41.)

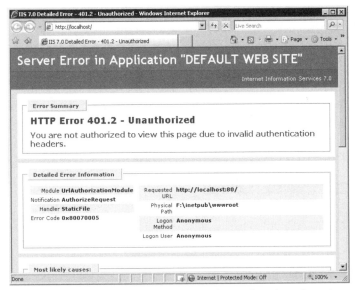

Figure 6-40   An error message returned to a client based on site restriction settings

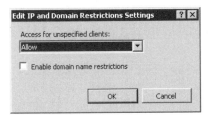

Figure 6-41   Configuring feature settings for IPv4 Address And Domain Restrictions

Adding Domain Restrictions

Managing access to Web services by using IP addresses is useful when the list of incoming clients is well known. This is typical of intranet and internal network environments where network administrators can configure and manage IP address ranges. In other types of Web server scenarios—such as public Web servers or extranets—managing IP address ranges can be time-consuming and impractical.

An alternative to using IP address–based restrictions is specifying allow and deny settings, using domain name restrictions. This method depends on a Domain Name System (DNS) reverse lookup operation. Whenever a user attempts to connect to IIS, the Web server will perform a reverse DNS lookup to resolve the requester's IP address to a domain name. IIS will then use the domain name to determine whether the user should have access. Domain-based restrictions are disabled by default because this feature can decrease server performance significantly. Every incoming request needs to be resolved, adding overhead to request processing. Additionally, this can place significant load on the DNS server infrastructure. From a management standpoint, however, this feature sometimes can be useful (especially in low-volume scenarios).

To enable domain name restrictions, select the IPv4 Address And Domain Restrictions feature for a portion of the Web site, and then click Edit Feature Settings in the Actions pane. As shown in Figure 6-41, you can check the Enable Domain Name Restrictions check box to enable this feature. Figure 6-42 shows the confirmation warning when you enable this feature.

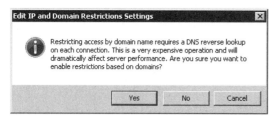

Figure 6-42   Viewing a warning when enabling domain name restrictions

Once you have enabled domain name restrictions, you can use the *Add Allow Entry* and *Add Deny Entry* commands to configure the rules. As shown in Figure 6-43, the dialog boxes include an additional setting for Domain Name.

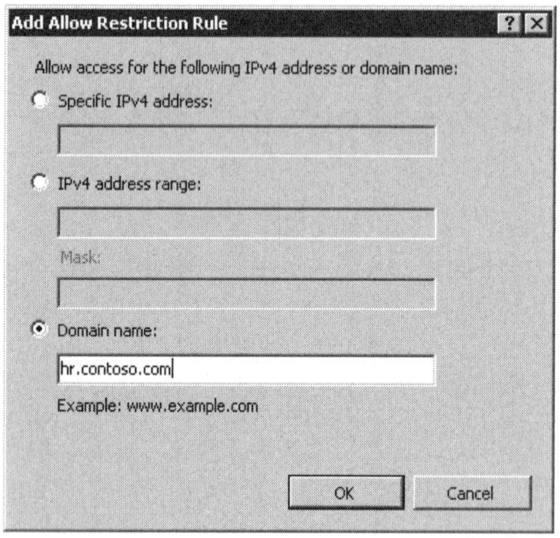

Figure 6-43   Adding a domain name restriction to a Web site

Exam Tip   IP address and domain restrictions can enhance the overall security of IIS, but they're not a replacement for carefully managing authentication and authorization settings. Use these restrictions when you can limit the source of incoming requests to a relatively small group of users and computers. Overall, you should use IP address and domain restriction settings as part of a complete Web server security strategy.

As mentioned earlier, the default behavior for allow and deny entries is for these restrictions to flow from parent objects to child objects. If you have made explicit changes to the settings for an object such as a Web application, you can use the *Revert To Inherited* command in the Actions pane to remove settings at that level. The effective settings will then be based on the parent hierarchy.

Configuring .NET Trust Levels

The .NET Framework technology provides Web developers with a strong set of features for implementing applications. The functionality includes Web applications (based on the ASP.NET platform) as well as other managed code features. It is relatively simple to create .NET applications that can perform a wide array of operations on a computer. From a security standpoint, however, it is important to restrict the permissions that are granted to a .NET application. Malicious or defective code can cause problems ranging from unauthorized access to data to the accidental deletion of content.

To help systems administrators manage permissions on production servers better, IIS supports Code Access Security (CAS) policy. CAS policies can be used to determine which operations are available to .NET-based application code. There are two main types of configuration. The full trust option provides ASP.NET application code with all permissions on the computer. For compatibility reasons, this is the default setting for applications that are based on the .NET Framework 1.0, 1.1, and 2.0.

Understanding Partial Trust Levels

The other CAS policy option is partial trust, which limits the actions .NET applications can perform. These options are available to applications that are built using .NET Framework 1.1 and .NET Framework 2.0. The goal with partial trust is to enable only the permissions that are necessary for a specific Web application.

Trust levels can be configured at different levels in the Web server object hierarchy. These levels include:

- Web server
- Web sites

- Web applications
- Virtual directories and physical folders

As with other security-related settings, trust levels that are defined at parent levels automatically apply to child objects unless they are specifically overridden. In general, define .NET Trust Level settings at the highest relevant setting. For example, if none of the Web applications in a Web site should have full permissions, you can configure these settings at the site level. You can then manage exceptions by assigning the necessary .NET Trust Level settings for specific Web applications or folders.

Understanding .NET Trust Levels

The .NET Framework contains many features and operations that potentially can cause security issues on a Web server. To provide a simpler method of configuring and applying trust settings, IIS includes five built-in levels that can be applied to IIS objects. The specific settings for each level are defined within various .config files. (For more information about using configuration files, see Chapter 5.) It is also possible to view and modify the settings in these files by using an XML editor or text editor. Table 6-2 lists the levels and their effects.

Table 6-2   .NET Trust Levels and Their Descriptions

.NET Trust Level	.Config File Name	Description	Restricted Actions
Full (internal)	N/A	Provides full permissions to an ASP.NET application	N/A
High	Web_hightrust. config	Provides access to most actions on the server and is designed for well-trusted and well-tested Web applications	<ul><li>Calling unmanaged code</li><li>Calling serviced components</li><li>Writing to the event log</li><li>Accessing message queuing services</li><li>Accessing ODBC, OLEDB, and Oracle data sources</li></ul>
Medium	Web_medium trust.config	Provides additional restrictions for Web applications that should not need to access the file system or registry	<ul><li>Accessing files outside of the application's directory</li><li>Accessing the registry</li><li>Making network or Web Service calls</li></ul>

Table 6-2   .NET Trust Levels and Their Descriptions

.NET Trust Level	.Config File Name	Description	Restricted Actions
Low	Web_lowtrust. config	Further restricts application capabilities	■ Writing to the file system ■ Calling the *Assert* method (a method that is often used for testing application code)
Minimal	Web_minimal trust.config	Allows only execute permissions and prevents access to other resources on the computer	Performing actions that require permissions greater than Execute

Exam Tip   When preparing for Exam 70-643, familiarize yourself with the purpose of each .NET trust level. Rather than memorizing specific restrictions, however, keep in mind which types of operations are considered the most risky. The levels are cumulative, from a standpoint of restrictions. For example, the Low level adds further restrictions to the Medium level and the levels above it. On the exam, be sure to understand a Web application's requirements before deciding which trust level is most appropriate.

The default setting is Full (internal), which provides the best compatibility but also the greatest security risk. Whenever possible, lower the .NET Trust Levels to ensure that application code is being run with minimal permissions. Often, this will involve interactions with Web developers to determine requirements and perform complete testing at various security levels.

Configuring .NET Trust Levels

To configure .NET Trust Levels using IIS Manager, select the object for which you want to assign the settings, and then double-click .NET Trust Levels from Features View. (See Figure 6-44.) To change the setting, select the appropriate level from the drop-down list, and click Apply. Once the trust level is set, it will apply to all ASP.NET applications running at the selected level as well as any child objects unless the settings are explicitly overridden.

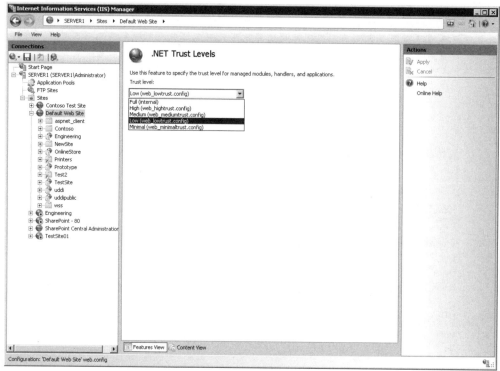

Figure 6-44   Viewing .NET Trust Levels options for a Web site

---

Quick Check

1. How can you manage which content is available to users without requiring any authentication?

2. What are the requirements for enabling SSL on an IIS Web server that will be accessible from the Internet?

3. How can you restrict access to an IIS Web application to only a limited set of computers?

> **Quick Check Answers**
> 1. Assuming that anonymous authentication is enabled, IIS will use NTFS file system permissions settings to determine which content requires credentials to be accessible.
> 2. To provide SSL security for Internet-based connections, obtain a security certificate from a trusted third-party issuer and install the certificate on the Web server. You will then be able to enable SSL through an HTTPS site binding.
> 3. You can use IP address restrictions to specify which computers should have access to an IIS Web server. Other options are also possible, including the use of client certificates.

PRACTICE Securing Web Servers and Web Content

In these exercises, you will apply the information you learned about ways to add security to specific Web content. The steps assume that you have installed the Web Server (IIS) role using the default settings and that you are familiar with the process of adding role services.

▶ **Exercise 1 Manage and Test Authentication Settings**

In this exercise, you will configure and verify the effects of various authentication settings.

1. Log on to Server2 as a user with Administrator permissions.
2. Using Server Manager, add the following role services to the Web Server (IIS) role:
   - ❑ Basic Authentication
   - ❑ Windows Authentication
   - ❑ Digest Authentication
   - ❑ URL Authorization
   - ❑ IP and Domain Restrictions
3. When you are finished, close Server Manager.
4. Open IIS Manager and select Default Web Site in the left pane. Double-click Authentication in Features View. Note that the default settings specify that only anonymous authentication is enabled.
5. Click Default Web Site, and then click Browse *:80 (http) in the Actions pane. Verify that the default IIS start page is displayed. Keep the Web browser open but return to IIS Manager.

6. Again, double-click Authentication in Features View. Select Windows Authentication, and then click Enable in the Actions pane.

7. Return to Internet Explorer and refresh the Web page.

   Note that you are not prompted to provide authentication information. This is because anonymous authentication is still enabled for the site.

8. Return to IIS Manager, select anonymous authentication, and then click Disable in the Actions pane.

9. Return to Internet Explorer and notice that this time you are prompted to provide logon information to access the site. Enter your username and password, and then click OK to verify that the site loads. Optionally, you can provide invalid logon information (such as a user account that does not exist) to see that you will be unable to access the site. When you are finished, close Internet Explorer.

10. To restore the original authentication settings, return to IIS Manager. Disable Windows Authentication and enable anonymous authentication.

11. When you are finished, close IIS Manager.

▶ **Exercise 2 Configure Server Certificates**

In this exercise, you will create a self-signed security certificate for Server2.contoso.com. You will then require SSL to access Default Web Site and test the settings, using Internet Explorer.

1. Log on to Server2 as a user with Administrator permissions on the computer.

2. Open IIS Manager and select the server object in the left pane.

3. Double-click Server Certificates in the IIS section of Features View.

   Note that, depending on which roles and role services have been installed on the local server, there might already be some certificates available on the server.

4. Click Create Self-Signed Certificate in the Actions pane.

5. For the name of the certificate, type **Test Local SSL Certificate**, and then click OK.

   You should now see the new certificate in the Server Certificates view of IIS Manager.

6. To view the properties of the new certificate, right-click it, and select View.

   Note details such as the issuer (which is the name of the server) and the dates for which the certificate is valid. (New certificates expire in one year.) The Certification Path tab will show only the certificate itself, signifying that it has not been issued by a trusted Certificate Authority (CA). For this reason, the certificate is not suited for access by users on public networks such as the Internet.

7. Click OK when you are finished.

8. In IIS Manager, right-click the Default Web Site object, and select Edit Bindings. Select the HTTPS binding type, and then click Edit. In the SSL Certificate list, select Test Local SSL Certificate. Click OK to save the settings, and then click Close.

9. Double-click SSL Settings in Features View. Enable the Require SSL option, and then click Apply.

10. Click the Back button to return to Features View for Default Web Site. In the Actions pane, choose *Browse *:80(http)*. This will launch Internet Explorer and attempt to connect to the site, using a non-SSL (HTTP) connection. Note that you receive an error stating, "The page you are trying to access is secure with Secure Sockets Layer (SSL)." Close Internet Explorer.

11. In IIS Manager, click Browse *:443 (https) in the Actions pane.

    Note that, this time, you receive a warning stating that there is a problem with the Web site's security certificate. This is because a self-signed certificate was not issued by a trusted CA.

12. To access the site anyway, click Continue To This Website.

    Note that the address bar turns red, and a Certificate Error message appears. The site content is, however, accessible.

13. When you are finished, close Internet Explorer.

14. In IIS Manager, double-click the SSL Settings feature for Default Web Site, and disable the Require SSL option. Click Apply in the Actions pane to save the setting.

15. When you are finished, close IIS Manager.

Lesson Summary

- Anonymous authentication provides access to site content without requiring users to provide credentials.

- Forms Authentication is useful for public Web sites and applications that manage their own security.

- URL authorization rules can determine which users or groups have access to which Web site content.

- Web server administrators can use Internet server certificates to enable encrypted connections through SSL over the Internet.

- Administrators can create self-signed server certificates for testing and development purposes.

- You can use IP Address And Domain Restrictions to restrict access to Web content.

- .NET Trust Levels restrict the permissions that managed code will have on a Web server.

Lesson Review

You can use the following questions to test your knowledge of the information in Lesson 2, "Controlling Access to Web Services." The questions are also available on the companion CD if you prefer to review them in electronic form.

NOTE   Answers

Answers to these questions and explanations of why each answer choice is correct or incorrect are located in the "Answers" section at the end of the book.

---

1. You are an IIS Web server administrator implementing authentication settings for a new Web site. According to the requirements for the Human Resources Web site, users should be prompted for authentication information when they attempt to access the site. The site will be accessed only by users who have accounts in your organization's Active Directory domain. You have already configured the file system permissions for the content based on the appropriate settings. You also want to maximize security of the site. Which two actions should you take to meet these requirements?

    A.   Enable Windows authentication.

    B.   Enable basic authentication.

    C.   Disable anonymous authentication.

    D.   Enable anonymous authentication.

2. You are a systems administrator troubleshooting a problem with accessing a Web server running Windows Server 2008. Previously, another administrator created and installed a server certificate on the computer. Users report that they are able to connect to the site using HTTP but that they receive a warning in Internet Explorer when trying to connect by HTTPS. You want to enable users to connect using both HTTP and HTTPS. You attempt to access the site by using an instance of Internet Explorer on the server itself, and you receive the same warning message for HTTPS connections. How can you resolve this issue?

    A.   Change the site binding for the Web site to enable connections on port 443.

    B.   Change the SSL settings for the Web site to enable the Require SSL option.

    C.   Obtain and install an Internet Certificate on the Web server.

    D.   Export and reimport the existing security certificate.

    E.   Reconfigure clients' firewall settings to enable traffic on port 443.

Chapter Review

To further practice and reinforce the skills you learned in this chapter, you can perform the following tasks:

- Review the chapter summary.
- Review the list of key terms introduced in this chapter.
- Complete the case scenarios. These scenarios set up real-world situations involving the topics of this chapter and ask you to create a solution.
- Complete the suggested practices.
- Take a practice test.

Chapter Summary

- Web server administrators should focus on implementing defense in depth and reducing the attack surface of IIS by using features such as request handler mappings.
- IIS allows for managing remote administration by configuring users, permissions, and feature delegation fot the Management Service.
- Server administrators can control access to the Web server by using authentication settings, URL authorization rules, server certificates, and IP Address And Domain Restrictions.

Key Terms

Do you know what these key terms mean? You can check your answers by looking up the terms in the glossary at the end of the book.

- ASP.NET impersonation
- attack surface
- Certificate Authority (CA)
- Client Certificate Authentication
- defense in depth
- domain restrictions (IIS)
- feature delegation (IIS)
- handler mappings (IIS)
- IIS Manager credentials
- Internet certificate request (IIS)

- IP address restrictions (IIS)
- IIS Management Service
- modules (IIS)
- .NET Trust Levels
- request handlers
- self-signed certificate
- server certificates
- URL authorization rules

Case Scenarios

In these case scenarios, you will apply the information that you have learned about securing IIS.

Case Scenario 1: Configuring Remote Management for IIS

You are a systems administrator responsible for managing four Web servers running Windows Server 2008. You would like to use a single instance of IIS Manager to connect to all the servers. Additionally, three other systems administrators need to manage the servers. One of these administrators is a consultant, and she does not have a Windows domain or local user account. You would like to create a username and password for her that is limited to managing IIS. You want all administrators other than you to be able to view but not change settings for the Default Document and Directory Browsing features.

1. What is the easiest method of managing settings for all the Web servers using IIS Manager?
2. How can you set up a username and password for a remote systems administrator?
3. How can you prevent the other users from modifying the Default Document and Directory Browsing features when using IIS Manager?

Case Scenario 2: Increasing Web Site Security

You are a systems administrator responsible for implementing and managing security for a production Web server running Windows Server 2008. The server is accessible from the Internet and contains eight Web sites. Each site contains at least one Web application. A Web application named Customer Database contains an ASP.NET 2.0 Web application that needs to access a remote database server. Another Web site named Service Desk contains static content, most of which should be available to all users. However, there is a folder called Admin that should be available only to specific users. Finally, you have a new requirement for an application named Contoso Central that specifies that all connections should use an encrypted connection.

1. Which .NET trust level should you configure for the Customer Database application?

2. How can you configure security for the Admin folder within the Service Desk application?

3. How can you require encryption security for connections to the Contoso Central application?

Suggested Practices

To help you successfully master the exam objectives presented in this chapter, complete the following tasks.

Implement Web Server Security

The practice items in this section will enable you to apply the methods you have learned to secure IIS-based Web servers, Web sites, and Web applications.

- **Practice 1**   Create a new Web site, using IIS Manager. The content of the Web site can contain copies of the Iisstart.htm file or other HTML files that you have available. Place some of the files within folders and create scenarios in which you want to protect content. Apply file system permissions, authentication settings, and URL authorization rules to ensure that only certain users can access the site. For example, create a new subfolder within a Web application called SecureDocuments. Place the appropriate limitations to ensure that users must provide credentials to access the content. Also, test the effects of changing handler mappings. For example, remove the StaticFile handler mapping for a Web site and test the effects, using Internet Explorer. You can also add your own custom handler mappings for new file types (such as files that have a .secure extension).

- **Practice 2**   Add the IIS Management Service role service to a Web server running Windows Server 2008. Practice using a variety of security features to support Web server administrators with different levels of restrictions. Options to test include:
  - ❑ Creating IIS Manager users.
  - ❑ Assigning IIS Manager Permissions settings to control which Web sites and Web applications administrators can access.
  - ❑ Assigning permissions to non-administrator users who have Windows accounts.
  - ❑ Creating IP address restrictions to control which computers can administer IIS.
  - ❑ Using feature delegation to control which settings can be modified by using IIS Manager.

To test settings most efficiently, it is recommended that you use a remote computer running Windows Vista or Windows Server 2008 that has IIS 7.0 Manager installed.

- ■ **Practice 3** View the following webcasts and resources for more information about IIS:
    - ❑ The Webcast entitled "Secure, Simplified Web Publishing Using Internet Information Services 7.0 (Level 300)" by Robert McMurray, available on the companion CD in the Webcasts folder. Alternatively, you can find this Webcast by visiting *http://msevents.microsoft.com* and searching for event ID 1032352159.
    - ❑ The Webcast entitled "Securing and Tuning Internet Information Services 7.0 (Level 300)" by Nazim Lala, available on the companion CD in the Webcasts folder. Alternatively, you can find this Webcast by visiting *http://msevents.microsoft.com* and searching for event ID 1032352141.
    - ❑ The Microsoft Internet Information Services Web site at *http://www.microsoft.com/iis*
    - ❑ The IIS.Net Web site at *http://www.iis.net*
    - ❑ IIS 7 Webcasts at *http://www.iis.net/default.aspx?tabid=2&subtabid=24*
    - ❑ IIS 7 Virtual Lab sat *http://virtuallabs.iis.net*

Take a Practice Test

The practice tests on this book's companion CD offer many options. For example, you can test yourself on just one exam objective, or you can test yourself on all the 70-643 certification exam content. You can set up the test so that it closely simulates the experience of taking a certification exam, or you can set it up in study mode so that you can look at the correct answers and explanations after you answer each question.

MORE INFO   Practice tests

For details about all the practice test options available, see the "How to Use the Practice Tests" section in this book's introduction.

Chapter 7
Configuring FTP and SMTP Services

The Internet Information Services (IIS) platform includes capabilities for sharing information by using several protocols. The File Transfer Protocol (FTP) provides a standard method by which computers can transfer files and other types of data among them. It is commonly used on both internal networks and the Internet to upload and download content. The Simple Mail Transfer Protocol (SMTP) is a standard method for transmitting e-mail messages. It is often used by Web applications to send notifications and communications to users' e-mail addresses.

In this chapter, you will learn how to configure these services in Windows Server 2008. In Lesson 1, "Configuring FTP," you will learn how to install and configure FTP functionality. In Lesson 2, "Configuring SMTP," you will learn how to install and configure the SMTP service.

Exam objectives in this chapter:
- Configuring a Web Services Infrastructure
  - Configure a File Transfer Protocol (FTP) server.
  - Configure Simple Mail Transfer Protocol (SMTP).

Lessons in this chapter:

Before You Begin

To complete the lessons in this chapter, you should have:

- A solid understanding of IIS configuration basics, including how to add the Web Server (IIS) server role and optional role services. This information is covered in Chapter 5, "Installing and Configuring Web Applications."
- Installed the Web Server (IIS) server role on Server2.contoso.com, using the default installation options for this server role. If you have created additional Web sites or Web applications in previous exercises, you may leave them configured on this server.

Lesson 1: Configuring FTP

Windows Server 2008 supports two versions of FTP servers. The FTP Publishing Service included with Windows Server 2008 provides the same functionality that was available with IIS 6.0 in Microsoft Windows Server 2003. This version is referred to as FTP 6. You can also download and install a new version of the product called FTP 7. Both versions provide features for setting up FTP sites that enable users to upload and download files easily. FTP 7 also provides enhanced security and administration features. In this lesson, you will learn about how to set up both versions of FTP on a computer running Windows Server 2008.

Exam Tip   At the time of this writing, Microsoft is planning to include coverage of FTP 6 in the initial version of Exam 70-643. Over time, as the exams are revised, you can expect to see questions about FTP 7 on the exam. Although the basic features and functionality are similar between the two versions, FTP 7 provides many new capabilities and uses, for administration, the version of IIS Manager in Windows Server 2008.

Real World

Anil Desai

In working as an IT consultant, I often see server and service configurations that seem to be set up haphazardly and without an understanding of security or other best practices. In some cases, systems administrators are faced with numerous priorities and don't have enough time to set up these services correctly. In other cases, they lack the knowledge to understand the implications. Regardless of the cause, the issue is the same: services are often deployed insecurely.

When you're responsible for deploying new features and services that provide additional functionality, it's important to consider the possible security ramifications of the changes. Implementing an FTP server is a good example. FTP sites provide a method by which users can upload and download data from your network. Especially when providing access through the Internet or external networks, it's important to ensure that only authorized users have access to the server. Configuration options such as authentication methods, encrypted connections, authorization settings, and user home directories can help ensure that a new FTP site does not lead to security breaches. (You'll learn about these features in Lesson 1.)

Be sure to take the time to understand the security implications of setting up network services such as FTP servers. A good rule of thumb is that if you don't have the time or experience to deploy the server securely, it's probably better not to deploy it at all.

> **After this lesson, you will be able to:**
> - Install and configure the FTP Publishing Service in Windows Server 2008.
> - Create and configure a new FTP site, using FTP 6.
> - Administer FTP 7 using IIS Manager.
> - Configure FTP site bindings for an IIS 7 Web site.
> - Manage FTP 7 settings, including SSL settings, authentication, authorization, and user isolation.
> - Use FTP client software to connect to and test an FTP site.
>
> **Estimated lesson time: 60 minutes**

Installing the FTP Publishing Service

The FTP Publishing Service (FTP 6) is included as an optional role service for the Web Server (IIS) server role. You can add the role to the server by using Server Manager. The first method is to select the FTP Publishing Service role service when adding the Web Server (IIS) server role to the computer. If you have already installed the Web Server (IIS) server role, you can use the Add Role Services command to add the necessary item. (See Figure 7-1.)

Using FTP 6

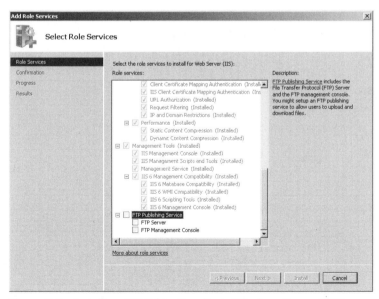

Figure 7-1   Installing FTP 6 functionality in Windows Server 2008

The FTP Publishing Service includes two role services. FTP Server is a system service that provides access to FTP sites. The FTP Management Console is used to create and manage FTP sites, using IIS 6.0 Manager.

Removing the FTP Publishing Service

If you no longer require the server to provide access through FTP, you can remove the FTP Publishing Service. Also, if you are planning to install FTP 7, it is recommended that you first remove the FTP Publishing Service from the computer. This will help prevent potential port conflicts or other configuration compatibility issues.

You can remove the FTP Publishing Service by using Server Manager. In the left pane, expand Roles, right-click Web Server (IIS), and then select Remove Role Services. Remove the FTP Publishing Services and its optional components to disable FTP publishing functionality on the server. Note that the contents of your FTP file system folders will not be deleted or modified during this process.

Configuring FTP Sites by Using IIS 6.0 Manager

You can manage the FTP Server component by using IIS 6.0 Manager, which can be launched from the Administrative Tools program group. To view the configuration of the local server, expand the server object and the FTP Sites folder. By default, the FTP Publishing Service installs an FTP site called Default FTP Site. (See Figure 7-2.)

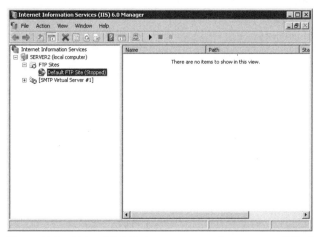

Figure 7-2   Using IIS 6.0 Manager to configure a new FTP site

In this section, you will learn how to use IIS 6.0 Manager to create new FTP sites and to manage FTP site configuration settings.

Creating a New FTP Site

You can create multiple FTP sites that respond on different ports and IP addresses. To create a new FTP site in IIS 6.0 Manager, right-click the FTP Sites folder, point to New, and then click FTP Site. This will launch the FTP Site Creation Wizard. The first page of the wizard (after the Welcome page) asks you to provide a description value for the site. This is simply a descriptive name that will help you identify the name of the site for administration purposes.

The IP Address And Port Settings page (shown in Figure 7-3) enables you to specify on which IP addresses and TCP port the server will respond. The default configuration is for the server to respond to requests on all unassigned IP addresses by using the default port of 21. Each FTP site on the server must have a unique combination of IP address and port assignments to run simultaneously.

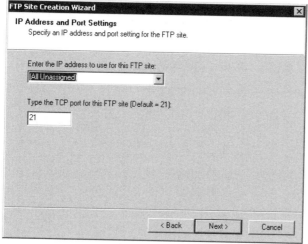

Figure 7-3   Configuring IP Address And Port Settings options for a new FTP site

The FTP User Isolation page enables you to specify which content users will be able to access. (See Figure 7-4.) The options are:

- **Do Not Isolate Users**   This setting enables all users to access all contents on the FTP site, including folders created by other users.
- **Isolate Users**   Each user will be automatically placed in a folder that matches his or her logon name. This option prevents users from accessing other folders or directories on the FTP server.
- **Isolate Users Using Active Directory**   This setting enables FTP home directory and isolation settings to be defined within Active Directory directory services. For users to log on

to the server, they must have Active Directory domain accounts, and the specified user folder path must exist.

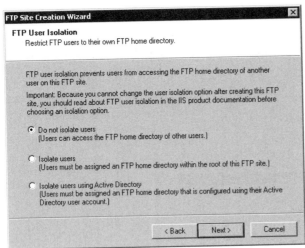

Figure 7-4   Configuring FTP User Isolation settings for a new FTP site

The FTP Site Home Directory page provides the root file system folder location for the FTP site. Typically, each new FTP site will have its own unique root folder. Default FTP Site is mapped to the *%SystemDrive%*\Inetpub\Ftproot folder.

The FTP Site Access Permissions page of the FTP Site Creation Wizard enables you to specify whether users will be able to read, write, or both read and write files to the server. Read-only configurations are common for allowing users to download but not upload data. Write permissions are required to add files to the site. It is also possible to provide only Write permissions if the site is intended to allow users to upload files but not view or download them.

When you click Finish on the FTP Site Creation Wizard, a new FTP site will be created. You can then manage this site and its settings, using IIS 6.0 Manager. FTP sites that are configured using the FTP Publishing Service can be started, stopped, and paused independently. When an FTP site is stopped, it will not allow incoming connections.

Configuring FTP Site Properties

To configure settings for an FTP site, right-click the site object in IIS 6.0 Manager and select Properties. You can change the IP address and TCP port properties for the site on the FTP Site tab. (See Figure 7-5.) To make these changes effective, you will need to restart the FTP site.

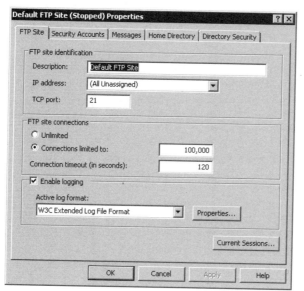

Figure 7-5   Viewing FTP Site settings in IIS 6.0 Manager

The FTP Site Connections section enables you to specify connection-related limits. The default settings are to allow up to 100,000 connections and for inactive connections to time out after 120 seconds. If you want to limit the amount of bandwidth and resources that specific sites use within the FTP publishing service, you can configure them here.

IMPORTANT   Connection limits

FTP servers, especially those accessible from the Internet, are often targets for unauthorized usage attempts. Users will sometimes connect to an insecure FTP server to provide others access to their own uploaded content. Settings such as a limit on the number of connections can help ensure that the site is being used only by authorized users. For example, if you are expecting only a few occasional users to access the site, lower the default limit. Although connection limits should not be used in place of security methods, they can help avoid certain types of misuse.

In the Enable Logging section, click the Properties button to display the Logging Properties dialog box. This enables you to specify when new log files are created and where they are stored. (See Figure 7-6.) You can also specify which information is collected by using the properties on the Advanced tab. Adding more information to the log files will increase log file size but can provide more details about the site. Log files are plaintext files and can be opened in a text editor such as Windows Notepad.

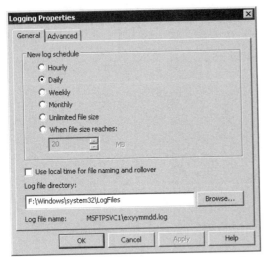

Figure 7-6   Configuring Logging Properties for an FTP site

The Current Sessions button on the FTP Site tab enables you to view which users are currently connected to the server. This information can be helpful for troubleshooting potential performance issues and for tracking how the site is being used at a given time.

Configuring Security Accounts

When users connect to an FTP server by using anonymous credentials, the FTP publishing service uses the permissions assigned to a specific account to process upload and download requests. By default, the IUSR_*MachineName* (where *MachineName* is the name of the local computer) validates permissions. The Security Accounts tab enables you to specify a different username and password (as shown in Figure 7-7). The Allow Only Anonymous Connections option specifies that all users to the site will be restricted to the permissions granted to the account you have specified, regardless of whether they have provided valid Windows logon credentials.

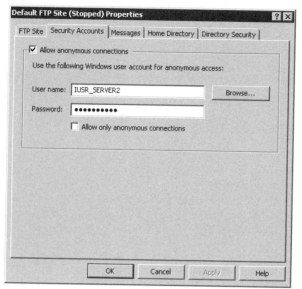

Figure 7-7   Configuring Security Accounts settings for an FTP site

Defining FTP Server Messages

The Messages tab enables you to provide text that will be displayed to the user. The banner displays before the user logs on to the FTP site. You can provide information about the site and contact information for site administrators here. (See Figure 7-8.) The Welcome message is sent after the user has successfully authenticated to the server. The Exit message displays when the user is terminating his or her connection, and the Maximum Connections message displays when the FTP server has reached the connection limit defined on the FTP Site tab.

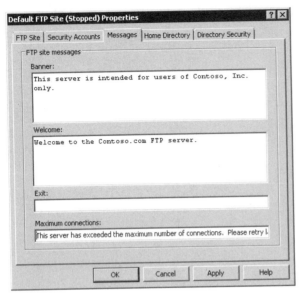

Figure 7-8   Configuring FTP site messages

Configuring Home Directory Options

The Home Directory tab enables you to specify the file system location of the FTP site's root directory. (See Figure 7-9.) The default option, A Directory Located On This Computer, enables you to enter the path to a local folder. You can also choose whether you want to allow read, write, or read and write permissions and whether visits to this folder should be logged. The Directory Listing Style affects the format of file lists that are returned to the FTP client.

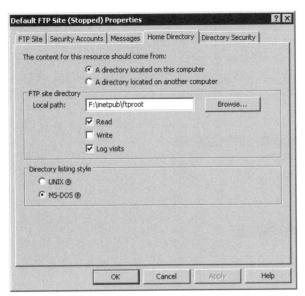

Figure 7-9   Configuring Home Directory settings for an FTP site

It is also possible to use a home directory located on another computer. A common reason for enabling this option is to enable multiple FTP servers to provide access to the same content. When you select A Directory Located On Another Computer, you can provide a Universal Naming Convention (UNC) network path to the content (for example, \\Server1\FTPData\). The Connect As button enables you to specify the username and password credentials to be used to access the content. (See Figure 7-10.) The default option is to use the authenticated user's credentials to validate access to the data. You can also designate a dedicated account for testing and validating permissions regardless of the user's credentials.

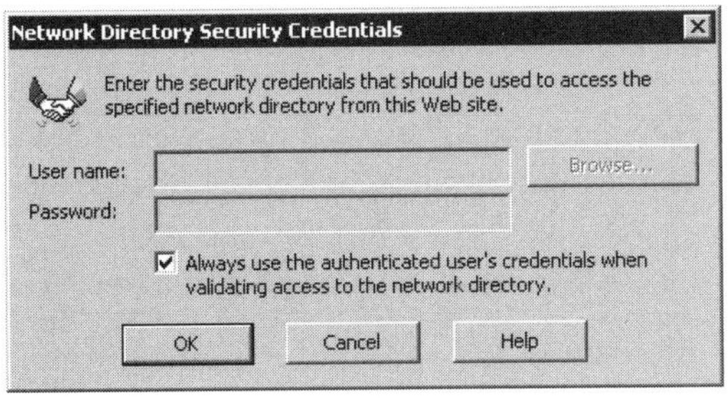

Figure 7-10   Setting Network Directory Security Credentials for an FTP Site

Managing Directory Security Settings

You can restrict access to an FTP site based on IPv4 address information. These settings are available on the Directory Security tab. (See Figure 7-11.) By default, all computers will be able to access the site. You can change the setting by adding new entries for specific computers or groups of computers and by changing the default setting to either Granted Access or Denied Access.

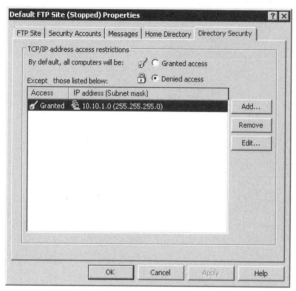

Figure 7-11   Configuring Directory Security settings for an FTP site

Installing and Managing FTP 7

Microsoft has provided an updated version of FTP services for use with Windows Server 2008. To enable FTP 7, you must manually download and install the Microsoft FTP Publishing Service for IIS 7.0. You can obtain the necessary files and installation instructions by accessing the Downloads section of the Microsoft Internet Information Services (IIS) Web site at *http://www.iis.net/downloads/*. Avoid running both FTP 6 and FTP 7 on the same computer at the same time because this might cause conflicts with site and port configurations. To avoid these problems, remove FTP 6 from the computer prior to installing FTP 7, as described earlier in this lesson.

The primary administration tool for FTP 7 is IIS Manager. Systems administrators can use IIS Manager to configure both HTTP and FTP services, using the same administrative interface.

Once you have downloaded and installed FTP 7, you can launch IIS Manager to configure server settings. Figure 7-12 shows the available FTP-related options for Default Web Site.

Figure 7-12   Viewing FTP options for Default Web Site in IIS Manager

Managing FTP Sites

After you have installed and configured FTP 7, you can use IIS Manager to create and configure FTP sites. In this section, you will learn how to create new FTP sites and how to add FTP functionality to an existing Web site.

Creating a New FTP Site

You can create new FTP sites to support different groups of users or to provide access to different sets of files. To create a new FTP site, right-click either the server object or the Sites folder in the left pane of IIS Manager, and then select Add FTP Site. This will start the Add FTP Site Wizard. The first page prompts you for information about the name of the site. (See Figure 7-13.) This name will be used for administration purposes, so you should choose a descriptive name if you plan to host multiple FTP sites on the same server. The Physical Path setting enables you to specify the root folder for the FTP site. You can choose any existing folder path, but many installations will use a subfolder within the *%SystemDrive%*\Inetpub folder.

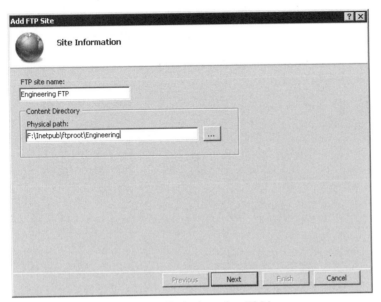

Figure 7-13   Adding a new FTP site by using IIS Manager

On the second page of the process, you can specify the binding and SSL settings for the new FTP site. (See Figure 7-14.) The binding settings include the following options:

■ **IP Address**   The default setting is for the FTP site to respond to all incoming requests on any network adapter or IP address on the server. If the computer is configured with multiple network adapters or multiple IP addresses on the same adapter, you can choose a specific address, using the drop-down list.

■ **Port**   This is the TCP port on which the FTP site will respond. By convention, the default port for FTP communications is port 21. If you choose a different port, FTP users will be required to configure their FTP client software to connect by using the server's port number.

■ **Virtual Host**   Administrators can create multiple Web sites that respond on the same IP address and port through virtual host names. These names rely on Domain Name System (DNS) entries to determine to which site users will connect. Users can also include the virtual host name as part of their logon name to specify to which site they want to log on.

- **Start FTP Site Automatically**   When this option is enabled, the FTP site will start automatically and whenever the computer is rebooted or the FTP service is restarted. If you plan to start the FTP site manually whenever it is required, disable this option.

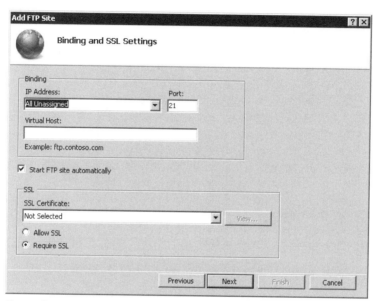

Figure 7-14   Configuring Binding And SSL Settings for a new FTP site

You can also select an SSL Certificate and whether to allow or require Secure Socket Layer (SSL) connections for this FTP site. You will learn more about these options later in this section.

On the Authentication And Authorization Information page, you specify how security will be managed for the new FTP site. (See Figure 7-15.)

When you click the Finish button, the new FTP site will be created and added to the left pane of IIS Manager. When you select the FTP Site object, you can use the commands in the Actions pane to start, restart, or stop the FTP site. You will also see a list of all the configuration options for the FTP site in the center pane of IIS Manager. (See Figure 7-16.)

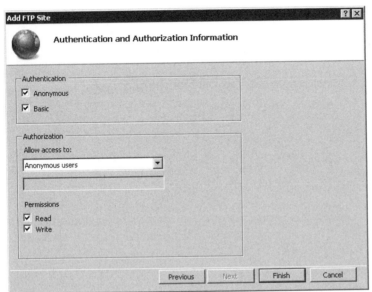

Figure 7-15   Configuring Authentication And Authorization Information settings for a new FTP site

Figure 7-16   Viewing FTP-related options in IIS Manager

Understanding FTP 7 Configuration Files

All configuration settings for FTP 7 sites are stored in the XML-based .config files. You can view and edit these settings, using a text editor. Server-level settings for both Web sites and FTP sites are stored within the ApplicationHost.config file. For more information about using these configuration files and for performing configuration backups, see Chapter 5.

Creating Virtual Directories

You can easily organize content through physical folders within an FTP site. For example, you can create a folder hierarchy for different types of applications and data. In some cases, however, you will want to provide access to content that is not located within the FTP root folder. To do this, you can create virtual directories. Virtual directories are pointers to folder locations and can be nested within other virtual directories or physical folders. Assuming that users have the appropriate permissions, they will see the virtual directory as if it were a physical folder. All upload and download operations, however, will be directed to the physical folder. Virtual directories are useful when you want some content to be shared between multiple physical sites or when you do not want to move or copy the data to the FTP root folder.

To create a new virtual directory, right-click the parent object in the left pane of IIS Manager and select Add Virtual Directory. This will launch the Add Virtual Directory dialog box. (See Figure 7-17.) Site Name and Path information shows you details about the location in which the new virtual directory will be created. Alias is the name of the folder as users of the site will see it. The Physical Path setting specifies the full physical location of the content that you want to make available.

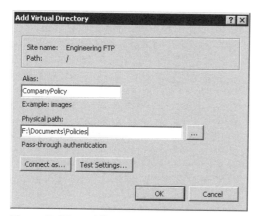

Figure 7-17 Adding a new virtual directory to an FTP site

By default, virtual directories will use Pass-Through Authentication for determining whether users have permissions to access the content. This means that the user account used during logon must have permissions on the content folder. You can change this behavior by clicking Connect As and selecting the Specific User option. You will then be able to provide a username and password for a specific account. When the Specific User account option is enabled, all requests for information stored in the physical path you specify will be performed using that user's security context.

Configuring Advanced FTP Site Properties

In addition to the standard properties available in Features View of IIS Manager, you can also configure Advanced Settings options. To access these settings, click Advanced Settings in the Actions pane. Figure 7-18 shows the available options and their default values.

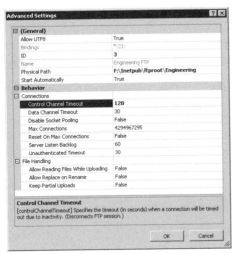

Figure 7-18   Configuring Advanced Settings for an FTP site

The Behavior section includes options for fine-tuning the settings of the FTP site. The Connections section enables you to control data channel timeouts (in seconds) as well as a maximum number of connections. These settings can be helpful for managing performance on busy Web and FTP servers. The File Handling section provides options for dealing with partial uploads and allowing a session to perform actions while uploading data.

Managing FTP Site Bindings

FTP 7 provides a simplified method for Web site administrators to manage their content by using FTP. In previous versions of FTP, administrators were required to configure a new site or virtual directories manually for accessing Web site content. You can now add a new FTP site binding to a Web site to provide access automatically to FTP clients. This is useful when you want to allow remote administrators and Web developers to access or modify the contents of specific Web sites.

To add a new FTP binding, select a Web site in IIS Manager, and then click Bindings. Click the Add button to create a new site binding. (See Figure 7-19.)

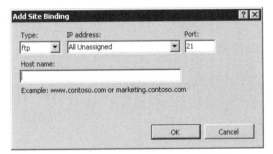

Figure 7-19   Adding a new FTP site binding to an existing Web site

In the Add Site Binding dialog box, you will be able to change the Type setting to FTP. You can then enter IP address, port, and host name information for determining how users will be able to access the FTP site. After you have added an FTP binding, you will see a grouping for FTP-related commands in Features View of IIS Manager. You can use these features to modify the settings of the FTP site binding in the same way as you would for a standalone Web site. You will also see a new Manage FTP Site section in the Actions pane. An FTP site that is part of a Web site can be started, stopped, and restarted independently of the Web site.

IMPORTANT   FTP port numbers and security

Changing the port from the default setting of port 21 can add a little extra security to an FTP server configuration. Casual intruders will often attempt to connect to this port to find unprotected FTP servers. In general, however, the idea of "security through obscurity" is not the best solution. Simply making an FTP server harder to find will not address the most important security issues. Always remember to use other security features such as firewall settings, authentication settings, and authorization rules in conjunction with site bindings.

Managing FTP User Security

Users can upload and download sensitive data through FTP servers, and you can choose from several methods to control which individuals have access to specific content. In this section, you will learn about authentication, authorization, and user isolation settings.

Configuring Authentication Options

You can use Authentication settings for an FTP site to determine how users can access the content stored on the site. There are several built-in methods for managing authentication. To configure these settings in IIS Manager, select the FTP site object, and then double-click FTP Authentication in Features View. Figure 7-20 shows an example of authentication options. You can enable or disable various authentication options, using the Actions pane. The Edit command in the Actions pane enables you to specify additional details for the selected authentication method.

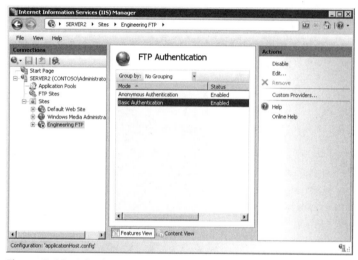

Figure 7-20   Viewing FTP Authentication settings for an FTP site

Anonymous Authentication allows all users that connect to the site to access content regardless of the credentials they provide. Use this option when you plan to make the content available to all visitors to the FTP site or when you are using other security methods to restrict access to the site. When an FTP user makes a request to read or write data, Anonymous Authentication will use a specified user account to validate permissions. The default setting is to use the built-in IUSR account for this purpose. You can assign a specific Windows account by clicking the Edit command in the Actions pane. You can then provide a specific user identity for use by Anonymous Authentication. (See Figure 7-21.)

Basic Authentication requires visitors to the Web site to provide credentials for a valid Windows user account. The account can be a local Windows username and password or can belong to an Active Directory domain if the server is a member of a domain. It is important to remember that, by default, credentials sent to the FTP server are sent in clear text. This can present a security risk, especially for FTP connections that are made over the Internet. You will use Basic

Authentication primarily when you want to restrict FTP-based access to content based on user credentials.

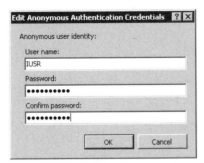

Figure 7-21   Modifying Anonymous Authentication Credentials settings

You can also choose from two other authentication methods by selecting the Custom Providers command in the Actions pane. IIS Manager Authentication (IISManagerAuth) configures the Web site to accept credentials for an IIS Manager User. This method is useful when you want to restrict access to the FTP site to specific users who do not have Windows accounts on the local FTP server. The IIS Management role service must be installed and enabled before you can use this authentication method. For more information about creating and managing IIS Manager Users, see Chapter 6, "Managing Web Server Security." Like Basic Authentication credentials, the username and password information is sent in clear text between the FTP client and the FTP server.

ASP.NET Authentication (AspNetAuth) relies on the .NET user management framework for authentication. It is useful when you have created an ASP.NET Web site that validates user credentials. It is common for Web applications to use credentials data stored in a database to validate access and permissions to the site.

Defining FTP Authorization Rules

You can use FTP Authorization rules to determine which users have access to specific content within the FTP site. Authorization rules can be defined at the level of the FTP site or for specific logical or virtual folders. These capabilities provide you with the flexibility to implement granular authorization rules based on the type of content that should be available to users. There are two types of authorization rules: Allow Rules and Deny Rules. By default, a new FTP site will not have any predefined authorization rules. You can use the commands in the Actions pane to create new rules. Figure 7-22 shows the available options when creating a new rule.

Figure 7-22   Adding an Allow FTP Authorization rule

Allow and Deny rules can apply to the following types of users:

- All Users
- All Anonymous Users
- Specified Roles Or User Groups
- Specified Users

After you select to which users or groups the rule will apply, you can select whether the user will have read, write, or read and write permissions.

Configuring FTP User Isolation Options

When you are managing access permissions and settings for an FTP server, a common requirement is to provide individual users with their own folders and directories. Users should be able to upload and download files from their own folders but should be prevented from accessing those that belong to other users. The FTP User Isolation feature enables you to configure these settings. To modify the settings, select an FTP site in IIS Manager, and then open the FTP User Isolation feature. (See Figure 7-23.)

The default selection for user isolation settings is FTP Root Directory. This option configures the server to start users in the FTP root directory, as you defined when you created the FTP site. This setting is most appropriate when you want all users to be able to access the same content. You can then use authorization rules to define permissions further on specific folders.

The User Name Directory option specifies that every user will have his or her own starting folder based on the username that was provided. If the user-specific folder name does not exist, the user will be placed in the root directory of the FTP site. Remember that this default folder setting is not designed as a security mechanism (at least when used by itself). If your FTP site is configured to allow anonymous authentication, you can create a folder called Default for these users.

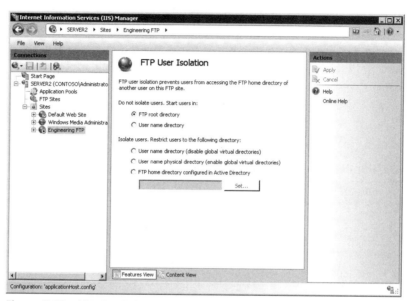

Figure 7-23   Viewing FTP User Isolation options

Exam Tip   You can manage FTP security settings through various features, including Authentication, Authorization, and IPv4 Address And Domain Restrictions. When you are implementing security for an FTP site, keep in mind that the best solution will likely involve using these features together to meet your goals. For example, you can use FTP User Isolation settings to determine which files and content users will have access to. You can then use FTP Authorization Rules settings to restrict access to specific content. Keep this in mind when you're working with FTP server security on production servers and when you're taking Exam 70-643.

The remaining three options enable isolation for FTP users. You can use them to restrict access to specific folders within the FTP site. The User Name Directory (Disable Global Virtual Directories) option will place users within a designated home directory based on the user account that was used for logon. The user will be unable to navigate to the parent folder and, therefore, will be prevented from accessing other folders. The user will not be able to see any global virtual directories defined for the FTP site. You can enable users to access these directories by choosing the User Name Physical Directory (Enable Global Virtual Directories) option.

To support FTP user isolation settings, you will need to create the appropriate folder structure for your users. The folder location for each user can be a physical or virtual directory on the server. The path to the folder is based on several variables:

- **FTPRoot** The root folder for the FTP site.
- **UserName** The name of the authenticated user as provided by the client during the logon process.
- **UserDomain** The name of the Windows domain used to validate credentials. This will be the name of the local FTP server or, if the server is a member of a domain, the name of the Active Directory domain.

The specific folder path you create is based on the authentication settings for the site and the type of user who is attempting to access the content. Table 7-1 provides a list of the default locations for each type of user account.

Table 7-1   Default FTP Folder Locations For User Accounts

FTP User Account Type	Home Directory Folder Location
Anonymous Users	%FTPRoot%\LocalUser\Public
Local Windows Accounts	%FTPRoot%\LocalUser\%UserName%
Domain Windows Accounts	%FTPRoot%\%UserDomain%\%UserName%
IIS Manager or ASP.NET User Accounts	%FTPRoot%\LocalUser\%UserName%

The final FTP user isolation option is FTP Home Directory Configured In Active Directory. You can use this method to define users' FTP folders within Active Directory, using the FTPRoot and FTPDir variables. These properties exist in Active Directory domains that are running Windows Server 2003 or later. (You can add the properties manually for Windows 2000 Server–based domains.) The Set button enables you to specify the credentials that will be used to connect to Active Directory. When a user logs on to the FTP Server, the FTP server will attempt to obtain these properties for the user. If the properties exist and the folder path is valid, the user will be placed in that folder. Otherwise, the user will be prevented from accessing the server.

NOTE   Creating user accounts by scripting

Creating individual folders for many user accounts at a time can seem like a time-consuming and tedious task at first. Fortunately, this is an ideal job for scripting. You can obtain a list of user accounts by using a variety of methods, including VBScript and Microsoft Windows PowerShell. You can then use this information to execute commands that create the necessary folders. For more information about scripting, visit the Microsoft TechNet Script Center at *http://www.microsoft.com /technet/scriptcenter*.

Configuring IIS Manager Permissions

In many environments, it is common to have multiple administrators who must be able to connect to and administer FTP sites and their contents. For example, a Web and FTP hosting provider might have separate administrators for each FTP site. You can allow other users to access the site by using the IIS Manager Permissions feature. The Allow User command enables you to add a new user who is defined within IIS Manager or who is based on a Windows account. Authorized users can then use IIS Manager on their computers to connect to an FTP 7 server. For more information about configuring IIS Manager Permissions settings, see Chapter 6.

Configuring FTP Network Security

FTP 7 provides numerous methods for ensuring that only authorized users can access an FTP site. In this section, you'll learn about using SSL, firewall settings, and IP address restrictions to control access to FTP sites.

Configuring FTP SSL Settings

By default, all control channel and data channel communications between an FTP server and client are sent in clear text. This is a serious security issue, especially when providing FTP access over the Internet. For example, if packets are intercepted during the authentication process, username and password information can be collected and used to access the site.

Administrators can encrypt communications between an FTP 7 server and an FTP client by using the FTP over SSL (commonly referred to as FTP/S or FTPS) standard. To modify these settings, select the appropriate FTP site in IIS Manager and double-click the FTP SSL Settings feature. (See Figure 7-24.)

The first setting enables you to specify which SSL certificate will be used by the FTP site. For more information about creating or obtaining SSL certificates, see Chapter 6. The SSL Policy section provides three options. Allow SSL Connections specifies that users may use SSL connections, but they can also connect to the server using an unencrypted connection. Require SSL Connections forces all users to use SSL and prevents unencrypted connections, and the Custom option enables you to specify different rules for the Control Channel and Data Channel. (See Figure 7-25.) You can use these options to minimize the performance overhead of implementing encryption. For example, by requiring encryption only for credentials, you can prevent usernames and passwords from being sent in clear text and still allow other control commands and data transfer to occur without encryption.

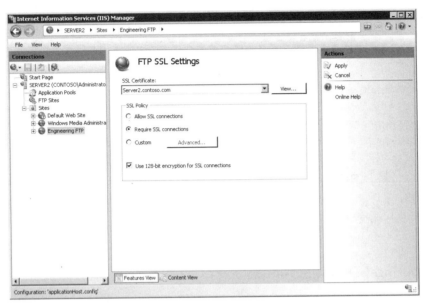

Figure 7-24   Configuring FTP SSL settings, using IIS Manager

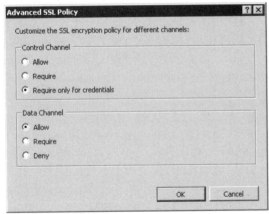

Figure 7-25   Configuring an advanced SSL policy for an FTP site

By default, the FTP SSL functionality will use a 40-bit encryption key strength. This reduces the CPU performance overhead while still maintaining adequate security for most scenarios. You can enable the Use 128-Bit Encryption For SSL Connections option to increase the strength of the encryption (at the expense of performance).

NOTE FTP security standards

The Secure Shell (SSH) standard can also be used to secure FTP communications. The combination of these technologies is sometimes referred to as Secure FTP or SFTP. The use of SSH-based security is not supported in Windows Server 2008 and FTP 7, but you might see this option in other FTP server software or in FTP client connection options.

Users typically will configure their SSL settings in their FTP client software. When they attempt to create a new connection, they will see a message that enables them to view and accept the SSL certificate that is installed for the FTP server.

Managing FTP Firewall Options

To access an FTP server, firewalls must allow network traffic to be passed for both the control channel and the data channel. When users connect to a Web server, the initial connection is made using the port provided in the address. (The default is port 21 if none is provided.) However, for sending data channel information such as directory listings and files, the FTP server can respond using a range of port numbers. If these ports are not allowed across the firewall, users will be unable to use the full functionality of the site.

NOTE Troubleshooting common FTP connection issues

A common FTP connection issue is related to accessing an FTP server from across a firewall. Users might report that they are able to connect to the FTP server and provide their authentication credentials. However, when they attempt to perform an action (such as listing the contents of a directory), they do not receive a response. This is a classic case of an issue with a firewall that is restricting data channel communications. One option for resolving this issue is to enable passive FTP connections on the FTP client. Another option is to reconfigure the firewall. Keep these symptoms in mind when you are troubleshooting FTP connection issues.

You can avoid this problem through the FTP Firewall Support feature in IIS Manager. (See Figure 7-26.) FTP 7 supports passive-mode FTP connections to specify the ports on which the FTP server will respond to requests. The Data Channel Port Range setting enables you to specify the range of ports that will be used for sending responses to clients. You should use ports between 1,024 and 65,535. The External IP Address Of Firewall setting enables the FTP server to determine from where packets are being sent. This is useful for supporting SSL encryption scenarios.

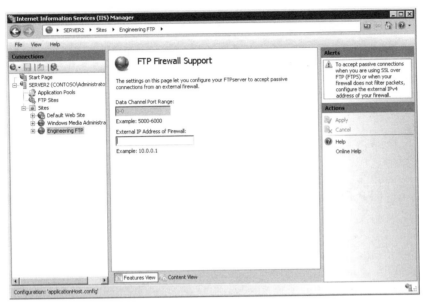

Figure 7-26 Configuring FTP firewall support options

Exam Tip Use the settings in the FTP Firewall Support feature to configure how the FTP site responds to FTP commands and requests. It does not make any changes directly to the Windows Server 2008 firewall configuration or to any other devices on the network. The terminology can sometimes be confusing. When you're taking Exam 70-643, remember to configure FTP Firewall Support settings to work in conjunction with firewall settings and that you might have to change your firewall's configuration manually to meet the requirements.

Implementing IP Address and Domain Restrictions

You can increase the security of an FTP server by limiting from which network addresses specific FTP sites or folders can be accessed. To manage these settings, select an FTP site or folder in IIS Manager, and then select the FTP IPv4 Address And Domain Restrictions feature. The Actions pane provides two commands for managing rules: Add Allow Entry and Add Deny Entry. IP address-based rules enable you to specify either a single IP address or a range of IP addresses that is defined using a subnet mask. (See Figure 7-27.)

Use the Edit Feature Settings command in the Actions pane to specify the default action for IP addresses that do not match any of the existing rules. The default setting, Allow, specifies that these IP addresses will be allowed to connect. You can restrict access to only those clients that match Allow Entries by selecting the Deny option.

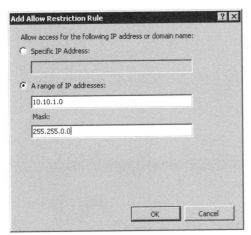

Figure 7-27   Adding a new IP address restriction rule for an FTP site

You can enable domain name restrictions through the Edit Feature Settings dialog box also. Domain name restrictions are based on DNS domain names (such as extranet.contoso.com). Although they can be easier to manage than specific IP address rules, the drawback is that domain name restrictions can reduce performance significantly. This is because rules are evaluated based on performing a reverse DNS lookup operation, which can be time-consuming and can create significant load on the DNS infrastructure.

IPv4 Address And Domain Restrictions settings are automatically inherited by child objects. For example, restrictions defined at the level of an FTP site will automatically apply to all the folders that are part of that site. You can override this behavior by creating explicit rules for specific folders and virtual directories. You can also use the Revert To Parent command in the Actions pane to remove any specific settings.

Managing FTP Site Settings

FTP 7 includes features for monitoring users and for improving the user experience. In this section, you will learn about these configuration options and how you can monitor FTP site usage.

Monitoring FTP Current Sessions

You can use the FTP Current Sessions feature for an FTP site to view which users are currently connected to the server. (See Figure 7-28.) The details that are shown include:

- User Name
- Client IP Address

- Session Start Time
- Current Command
- Previous Command
- Command Start Time
- Bytes Sent
- Bytes Received
- Session ID

Figure 7-28   Viewing a list of current sessions, using IIS Manager

Managing FTP Messages

You can use the FTP Messages feature to define text-based messages sent to clients. The specific types of text you can define are:

- **Banner**   This is the information that is presented initially when a user connects to the FTP site.
- **Welcome**   This message is displayed after a user has successfully authenticated to the FTP site.
- **Exit**   This message is displayed after the user chooses to end his or her connection and is sent just prior to closing the connection.
- **Maximum Connections**   This message is displayed when the FTP server has reached its maximum number of connections, and the user is unable to access the site.

FTP messages often include warnings related to the intended use of the site and can provide contact information for administrators of the site. (See Figure 7-29.)

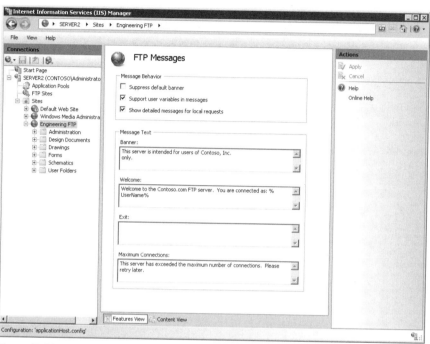

Figure 7-29   Configuring FTP messages settings for an FTP site

You can prevent the default banner from being sent to the user by using the Message Behavior section. This is useful when you do not want to disclose details about the purpose or function of the site until users are authenticated. The Support User Variables In Messages option enables you to use the following string values in your messages:

- BytesReceived
- BytesSent
- SessionID
- SiteName
- UserName

When the variable name is surrounded by percent symbols (for example, *%UserName%*), the FTP server will automatically replace the information with the appropriate value.

Configuring FTP Logging

FTP 7 can automatically create log files that keep track of the activity of the FTP site. By default, information is stored to text files stored in the *%SystemDrive%*\Inetpub\Logs\LogFiles folder. Separate folders are created for each FTP site created on the local machine. You can use the FTP Logging option to modify the log file settings.

The Select W3C Fields command enables you to specify which types of information are tracked for each command or request sent to the FTP server. Figure 7-30 shows the default options, which are designed to provide a balance between providing detailed information and reducing performance overhead and log file size.

Figure 7-30   Selecting which fields are included in FTP log files

You can use the Log File Rollover section to specify when new log files will be created. You can also enable the Use Local Time For File Naming And Rollover option if you are managing FTP servers in multiple time zones. The View Logs command in the Actions pane will open the folder that contains the FTP log files. The files themselves are text documents that contain comma-separated values. They can be viewed in Windows Notepad or by using third-party log analysis software. In general, it is a good idea to review FTP server logs regularly to detect any unauthorized activity or unexpected usage patterns.

Configuring Directory Browsing

One of the most commonly used commands sent by FTP clients is to request a directory listing. Most FTP client software programs will automatically execute a *LIST* command whenever the user changes the current working folder. You can configure these options by selecting the FTP Directory Browsing feature after selecting a site in IIS Manager. (See Figure 7-31.) The

Directory Listing Style options enable you to specify whether information should be returned in MS-DOS (the default style) or UNIX style. The setting specifies how information is presented to an FTP client. Most FTP clients are able to handle both formats.

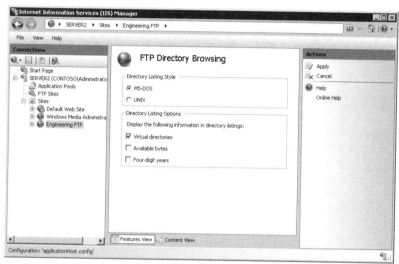

Figure 7-31   Configuring FTP Directory Browsing settings

You can use the Directory Listing Options section to specify which types of information are included in the directory listing. The Virtual Directories option specifies whether the names of virtual directories will be returned to the user. If you want to hide virtual directories from users, disable this option. The Available Bytes option returns the amount of remaining disk space for the FTP site. If disk quotas are enabled, the remaining space will be based on how much storage space is left for the currently connected user. Enabling Four-Digit Years will return all year information in four characters rather than in two.

Using FTP Client Software

Users can use several types of FTP client options for connecting to an FTP server. Windows operating systems include the FTP command-line utility that provides basic text-based functionality for connecting to an FTP server. This is useful for performing simple operations and for testing Web site functionality. You can also place FTP commands within a batch file to automate common operations such as transferring backup files to a remote server.

In addition, you can use an FTP-capable Web browser, such as Windows Internet Explorer, to connect to an FTP site. (See Figure 7-32.) The standard syntax for the URL is *ftp://ServerName.* You can provide logon information and port details in the URL by using the following syntax:

ftp://UserName:Password:ServerName:Port/Path

FTP URLs are helpful for providing quick access to files from Web sites. It is important to note that, by default, all communications will occur using a clear text connection. Therefore, you should generally use FTP URLs only for FTP sites that are intended for use by anonymous users.

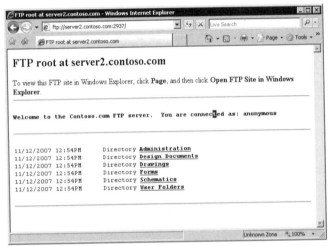

Figure 7-32   Connecting to an FTP site by using Internet Explorer 7

You can also use Windows Explorer to provide graphical access to an FTP site. (See Figure 7-33.) This method gives you the benefits of using familiar commands and functions such as drag-and-drop operations. To connect, simply enter the FTP URL in the Address bar of Windows Explorer. You can also use the Open FTP Site In Windows Explorer command from the Page menu of Internet Explorer 7 if you have already connected to an FTP site. Although some file and folder management features are limited, this is a useful method by which even nontechnical users can access FTP-based content.

Finally, there are numerous third-party FTP client software packages. You can find them by doing a Web search for "ftp client software." These products often provide advanced features such as the ability to script common operations and automated methods for keeping multiple folders synchronized with the same content.

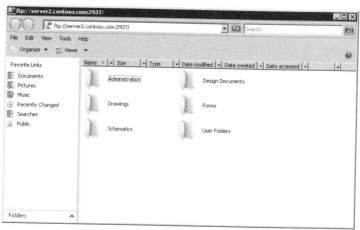

Figure 7-33   Using Windows Explorer to access an FTP site

Quick Check

1. When using FTP 7, what is the easiest way to prevent a particular group of users from accessing a specific folder that is part of your FTP site?
2. How can you ensure that credentials sent for an Internet-accessible FTP site using Basic Authentication are encrypted during transmission?

Quick Check Answers

1. FTP Authorization Rules can be used to set specific permissions on a portion of an FTP site.
2. Enable FTP Over SSL (FTPS) for the FTP site using FTP 7. The process involves obtaining a server SSL certificate and then requiring SSL for at least the passing of credentials on the server.

PRACTICE Configuring and Testing FTP

In this practice, you will learn about the process of setting up an FTP site by using both FTP 6 and FTP 7. You will then connect to the new site by using the FTP command-line utility.

▶ **Exercise 1 Use FTP 6 to Create a New Web Site**

In this exercise, you will create a new Web site by using FTP 6. You will begin by enabling FTP 6. The steps assume that you have already installed the Web Server (IIS) server role, using the default options, and that you have not yet installed the FTP Publishing Service role service.

1. Log on to Server2 as a user with Administrator permissions.

2. Open Server Manager. Expand the Roles section, right-click the Web Server (IIS) server role, and then select Add Role Services.

3. On the Select Role Services page, select FTP Publishing Service. Note that this will automatically install the FTP Server and FTP Management Console role services as well. Click Next to continue.

4. On the Confirm Installation Selections page, verify the selections, and then click Install to begin the installation process. When the installation is complete, click Finish.

5. In Server Manager, note that the FTP Publishing Service is installed for the Web Server (IIS) Server role. Close Server Manager.

6. To configure the FTP server, launch Internet Information Services (IIS) 6.0 Manager from the Administrative Tools program group.

7. Expand the node for Server2, and then expand the FTP Sites folder. Note that the Default FTP Site object exists but has not been automatically started.

8. Right-click the Default FTP Site object, and then click Properties. Note the settings on the FTP Site tab.
   The default settings are for the FTP site to respond on all unassigned IP addresses by using TCP port 21.

9. Click the Home Directory tab to view the file system location for the FTP site's root directory.
   The default file system location is *%SystemDrive%*\Inetpub\Ftproot. The default permissions are to allow only Read access to the contents of this folder.

10. When you are finished, click OK to close the Default FTP Site Properties dialog box.

11. Next, you will create some sample files for testing the FTP functionality. Using Windows Explorer, open the root directory for the FTP site and create a new folder called FTPContents. Within this folder, create a new text file called TestFile.txt. Close Windows Explorer.

12. In IIS 6.0 Manager, right-click the Default FTP Site object, and then click Start. This will start Default FTP Site.
    Next, you will use the FTP command-line utility to verify the configuration of the FTP site.

13. Open a command prompt by selecting Command Prompt from the Start menu. Type **FTP Server2** to connect to the local FTP server.
    Note that you do not need to provide a port number because the server is bound to the default port, TCP port 21.

14. At the User prompt, type the name of your Windows user account. Then, type your password when prompted. At the FTP prompt, type **dir** and press Enter to retrieve a list of files located in the root folder for Default FTP Site. You should see the FTPContents folder that you created in step 10.

15. Type **cd FTPContents** to change the active folder. Type **dir** to view a list of files. Type **get TestFile.txt** to download a copy of the test file you created earlier to the local working folder.

16. When you are finished, type **quit** to exit the FTP prompt. Then, close the command prompt window.

17. When you are finished, close the IIS 6.0 Manager utility.

▶ **Exercise 2 Use FTP 7 to Add an FTP Site Binding**

In this exercise, you will create a new FTP site binding for Default Web Site, using FTP 7 and IIS Manager. Before you begin this exercise, you must first remove FTP 6 if it is installed on Server2.contoso.com. Then, download and install the FTP 7 package from *http://www.iis.net /downloads.*

1. Log on to Server2 as a user who has Administrator permissions.

2. Open IIS Manager and connect to the local server.

3. Right-click the Default Web Site object in the left pane and select Edit Bindings. In the Site Bindings dialog box, click Add.

4. In the Add Site Binding dialog box, select FTP for the Type setting. Use the default IP Address setting of All Unassigned and the default port or port 21. Leave the Host Name section blank, and then click OK to add the site binding.

5. Verify that a new site binding for the FTP protocol on port 21 has been created. Click close on the Site Bindings dialog box.

6. To view the FTP-related options for the Default Web Site, click Refresh on the View menu in IIS Manager.

   You will now see an FTP section along with options for configuring FTP settings. The Actions pane also includes commands for managing the FTP site.

7. In the Actions pane, click Advanced Settings in the Manage FTP Site section. Note that the Physical Path setting is mapped to the root directory for the Default Web Site (*%SystemDrive%*\Inetpub\Wwwroot). Click OK to continue.

8. In Features View of IIS Manager, double-click FTP Authentication. Note that, by default, no authentication options are enabled. Enable the Basic Authentication and Anonymous Authentication options by selecting them and then clicking the Enable command in the Actions pane.

9. Click the Back button or the Default Web Site object to return to Features View.

10. Open the FTP SSL Settings feature. Note that, by default, the server is configured to Require SSL Connections. For the purpose of this practice exercise, change the setting to Allow SSL Connections. Note that you could optionally choose an SSL certificate from the drop-down list. Click Apply to save the settings.

11. Next, you will use the FTP command-line utility to test access to the FTP site. Open a command prompt by selecting this command from the Start menu. Type **FTP Server2** to connect to the local FTP server. Note that you do not need to provide a port number because the server is bound to the default port, port 21.

12. At the User prompt, enter the name of your Windows user account and enter your password when prompted. At the FTP prompt, type **dir** and press Enter to retrieve the list of files located in the root folder for Default Web Site. Optionally, you can use the *GET* and *PUT* commands to download and upload files. When you are finished, type **quit** to exit the FTP prompt. Close the command prompt window.

13. When you are finished, close IIS Manager.

Lesson Summary

- To host FTP sites by using FTP 6, you must add the FTP Publishing Service role service to the Web Server (IIS) server role.
- You can use IIS 6.0 Manager to create and manage settings for FTP 6 sites.
- You must download and install a separate package to use FTP 7 in Windows Server 2008.
- FTP 7 provides numerous improvements over FTP 6, including support for SSL-encrypted connections, simplified configuration by using IIS Manager, and the ability to create an FTP binding for a Web site easily.

Lesson Review

You can use the following questions to test your knowledge of the information in Lesson 1, "Configuring FTP." The questions are also available on the companion CD if you prefer to review them in electronic form.

NOTE   Answers

Answers to these questions and explanations of why each answer choice is correct or incorrect are located in the "Answers" section at the end of the book.

---

1. You are a Windows Server 2008 systems administrator responsible for configuring FTP Publishing Service for use by members of your organization's engineering department. The name of the server is FTPServer01. Several users have reported that they are able to access most files through the FTP site, but they cannot access the contents of the Drawings folder. You have verified that these users' Windows accounts have the correct file system permissions for this folder. You want to minimize the permissions granted to all the users. Which of the following changes should you make to enable users to access this folder?

    A. Change the permissions for the IUSR_FTPServer01 account on the Drawings folder.

    B. Create new TCP/IP Address Restrictions entries for the users who cannot access the Drawings folder.

    C. Disable the Allow Only Anonymous Connections option.

    D. Add the users to the local Administrators group on FTPServer02.

2. You are a systems administrator who has recently installed and configured FTP 7 on a computer running Windows Server 2008. You have enabled the FTP Over SSL (FTPS) option for the server by obtaining an SSL certificate from a trusted third-party issuer. Recently, the usage of the FTP site has increased, and users are complaining about slow download performance. You want to configure SSL settings to encrypt only credentials and commands but not file-related information. You also want to optimize encryption performance. Which of the following settings changes should you make? (Choose two. Each correct answer presents part of a complete solution.)

    A. Select the Allow SSL Connections SSL Policy option.

    B. Disable the Use 128-bit Encryption For SSL Connections Option.

    C. Select the Require SSL Connections SSL Policy option.

    D. Select the Custom SSL Policy option.

Lesson 2: Configuring SMTP

The Simple Mail Transfer Protocol (SMTP) feature in Windows Server 2008 enables you to relay e-mail messages. The SMTP standard provides a consistent method by which servers can send messages. It can be used for internal e-mail traffic or for communicating across the Internet. Individuals and applications often use SMTP functionality to send notifications and other information. In this lesson, you will learn how to enable and configure the SMTP Server feature in Windows Server 2008.

After this lesson, you will be able to:

- Enable the SMTP Server feature in Windows Server 2008.
- Create a new SMTP virtual server.
- Configure IP address and port settings for an SMTP virtual server.
- Secure SMTP services by configuring authentication settings for inbound and outbound connections.
- Test SMTP services by using an e-mail client application.

Estimated lesson time: 45 minutes

Installing the SMTP Server Feature

The Windows Server 2008 SMTP Server feature enables you to support many applications and network connections to send large volumes of messages. For example, a Web application can use SMTP to send e-mail notifications to users. The SMTP standard is designed to send e-mails that a messaging server such as Microsoft Exchange Server can receive. Messages can also be stored in a file system location, so they can be accessed by other applications. Users typically receive these messages by connecting to their mailbox on the messaging server by using a protocol such as the Post Office Protocol (POP).

You can install the SMTP Server feature on a computer running Windows Server 2008 by using Server Manager. To do this, right-click the Features object and select Add Features. The SMTP Server has several dependencies. (See Figure 7-34.)

You can also remove the SMTP Server feature by using Server Manager. To do this, right-click the Features object, and select Remove Features. When you remove the SMTP server, you will no longer be able to use the server to transmit or relay e-mail messages.

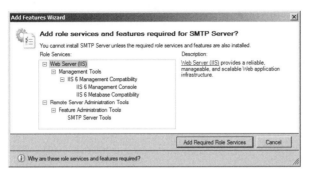

Figure 7-34   Viewing dependencies of the SMTP Server feature

Configuring SMTP Services

Once you have installed the SMTP Server feature on a computer running Windows Server 2008, you can use IIS 6.0 Manager to configure SMTP settings. To do this, open IIS 6.0 Manager, and expand the server object. A default site called SMTP Virtual Server #1 is included automatically when you add the SMTP Server feature.

Creating a New SMTP Virtual Server

You can use the New SMTP Virtual Server Wizard to create a new SMTP virtual server in Windows Server 2008. Each virtual server has its own set of configuration settings and can be managed independently. To begin the process of creating a new SMTP virtual server by using IIS 6.0 Manager, right-click the server object, point to New, and then click SMTP Virtual Server. The first page of the wizard asks you to provide a name for the virtual server. You should use a descriptive name that indicates the purpose of the virtual server because this setting will identify different servers in the IIS 6.0 Manager user interface.

On the Select IP Address page, select on which network connections the SMTP server will be available. If the server has multiple physical network adapters or multiple IP addresses, you can choose a specific one from the drop-down list. This is useful when you want to limit access to the SMTP server for security reasons. For example, if one or more IP addresses are accessible from the Internet, you might not want the server to respond on that address. The default IP address setting is All Unassigned, which specifies that the SMTP virtual server will respond on any IP address that is configured for the server.

Another reason to change the IP address is that no two SMTP virtual servers can run concurrently if they have the same IP address and port assignment. The default port for SMTP connections is port 25. If you attempt to create a new SMTP virtual server that has the same combination of IP address and port number, you will see the error message shown in Figure

7-35. In this case, you can continue to create the server, but you will have to modify its settings later before you can start it.

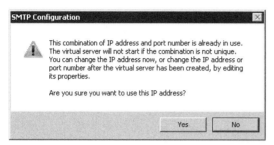

Figure 7-35   Viewing a warning about the SMTP configuration

On the Select Home Directory page, specify the file system location that will serve as the root for the SMTP virtual server. (See Figure 7-36.) Message files and other data will be stored in this location.

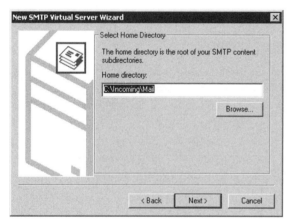

Figure 7-36   Configuring the home directory location for a new SMTP virtual server

The Default Domain page is where you specify the fully qualified domain name for which this SMTP virtual server will be responsible. Generally, you will use a DNS domain name such as hr.contoso.com. When you finish the New SMTP Virtual Server Wizard, the new server will appear in IIS 6.0 Manager. You can then access the properties of the server to make additional configuration changes.

Configuring General SMTP Server Settings

To access the configuration settings for an SMTP virtual server, right-click it in IIS 6.0 Manager, and then select Properties. The General tab includes details that specify the network connection settings for the SMTP server. (See Figure 7-37.) You can select an IP Address or All Unassigned from the drop-down list, or you can use the Advanced button to configure multiple bindings.

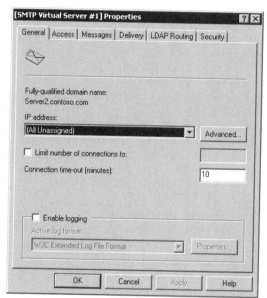

Figure 7-37   Configuring general settings for an SMTP virtual server

The Advanced option also enables you to change the port number on which the SMTP server can be accessed. On the General tab, you can limit the number of connections and set connection timeouts. Configuring these limits can help manage performance for busy SMTP servers. You can also use the Enable Logging option to store information about messages that are transmitted using this SMTP virtual server. The Properties button gives you options for determining the storage location of the log files. On the Advanced tab, you can specify which types of information will be included in the log file. You can view Log files by using a standard text editor such as Windows Notepad. On busy SMTP servers, enabling logging can decrease performance and increase disk space usage.

Securing Access to an SMTP Virtual Server

To prevent unwanted use of SMTP virtual servers, it is important to configure access rules for sending messages by SMTP. A large portion of unsolicited commercial e-mail (spam) is sent through SMTP relays that are unprotected. You can manage rules for using the SMTP virtual server through the properties on the Access tab. (See Figure 7-38.)

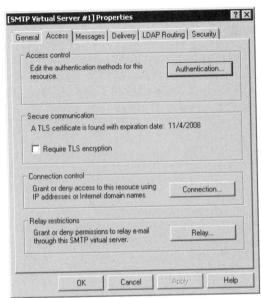

Figure 7-38 Configuring Access settings for an SMTP virtual server

You can use the Authentication settings to determine how potential users of the SMTP virtual server must pass their credentials to the service. Figure 7-39 shows the available options. The default setting is Anonymous Access, which specifies that no credentials are required to connect to the SMTP virtual server. This option is useful when you are using other methods (such as firewalls or trusted network connections) to prevent unauthorized access to the server.

The Basic Authentication option requires a username and password to be sent to the SMTP virtual server. By default, these logon credentials are transmitted using clear text and are, therefore, susceptible to being intercepted. You can also enable Transport Layer Security (TLS) to enable encryption for sent messages. TLS uses a certificate-based approach to create the encrypted connection. Integrated Windows Authentication relies on standard Windows accounts to verify credentials to access the system. This method is most appropriate for applications that will be used by a single Windows account or when all potential users of the SMTP server have Active Directory domain accounts.

Figure 7-39   Managing authentication options for an SMTP virtual server

In addition to configuring authentication settings, you can also restrict access to an SMTP virtual server based on IP addresses or domain names. This can help ensure that only authorized network clients are able to use SMTP services. To add these restrictions, click the Connection button on the Access tab of the properties of the SMTP virtual server. You will be able to choose the default behavior for connection attempts.

The Only The List Below option means that only computers that match the entry rules you have configured will be able to use the server. This is most appropriate when all the expected client computers are part of one or a few networks. The All Except The List Below option means that the rules you add are for computers that are not allowed to use the SMTP virtual server. Click the Add button to create new configuration rules. (See Figure 7-40.) You can configure restrictions by specifying a single IP address or an IP address range.

You can also use the DNS Lookup command to find a specific IP address based on a domain name. The Domain option instructs the SMTP server to perform a DNS reverse lookup operation when a computer attempts to connect. This method attempts to resolve the IP address of the incoming connection to a DNS name. Enabling this option can reduce performance due to the overhead of performing many DNS queries.

The final set of Access control options are relay restrictions. SMTP relaying occurs when a message is sent with both to and from addresses that are not part of the virtual server's domain. Relaying is a common method by which large spammers are able to use unprotected SMTP virtual servers to send unsolicited mail. The Relay Restrictions option enables you to specify which computers can relay messages through the SMTP server. (See Figure 7-41.) The default settings are for all users and computers to be allowed to relay messages as long as they are able to authenticate. You can use the Add command to define which IP addresses, domain names, or both will be allowed to relay messages.

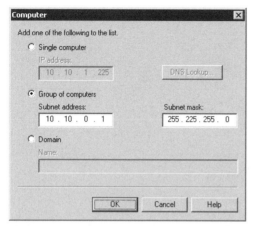

Figure 7-40   Creating a new Connection Control rule for an SMTP virtual server

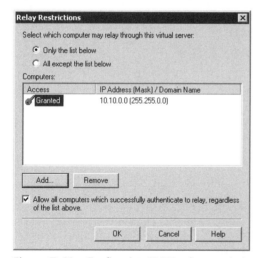

Figure 7-41   Configuring SMTP relay restrictions

NOTE   **Helping reduce spam**

Apart from the benefits of reducing load on unprotected networks, there are other good reasons to protect your SMTP virtual server from unauthorized access. Many anti-spam utilities will maintain a list of known unprotected SMTP servers and will add them to a blocklist. All messages sent through this SMTP relay might be marked as spam, making it difficult for your users and applications to communicate with individuals outside your organization. When you're setting up a new SMTP virtual server, be sure to take the time to secure the configuration. It is also important to review SMTP server configuration and log files regularly to find potential unauthorized use of the server.

Configuring Messages Options

The Messages tab of the properties of an SMTP virtual server enables you to configure limitations on messages that are sent through the server. (See Figure 7-42.) The first two options enable you to specify the maximum size of a message (including attachments) as well as the maximum amount of data that can be sent through one connection to the server. You can also limit the number of messages sent per connection and to limit the number of recipients to whom they can be sent. These methods all help reduce unwanted access to the server and helps preserve resources such as network bandwidth.

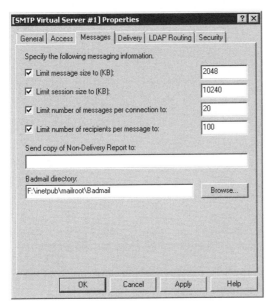

Figure 7-42   Configuring messages settings for an SMTP virtual server

The most common reasons for messaging failures include incorrect addresses or domain names entered by the sending user. The Send Copy Of Non-Delivery Report To option enables you to specify an e-mail address to which undeliverable mail will be forwarded. The Badmail Directory setting specifies the path to the folder into which these messages will be sent. You can review these messages or files to detect undeliverable mail.

Defining Delivery Properties

When communicating on the Internet, network routing issues and server failures can cause service outages. The SMTP standard was designed with reliability in mind. SMTP servers automatically store a copy of messages while they are trying to send them to their intended destination. If the destination server is unavailable, the SMTP server will attempt to retry the operation. You can manage the details of this behavior through the properties of the Delivery tab. (See Figure 7-43.) The Outbound rules define the intervals at which the server will attempt to retry the transmission of a message if a failure occurs.

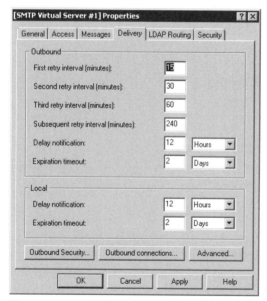

Figure 7-43   Default settings for the Delivery properties of an SMTP virtual server

You can also configure the Delay Notification and Expiration Timeout options for both the Outbound and Local settings to determine when resending of a message should end.

It is common for SMTP servers to send messages through other SMTP servers before they reach their final destination. Administrators can configure their SMTP servers to require authentication before they will relay a message. The Outbound Security command on the Delivery tab enables you to specify the authentication information to be used when connecting to another SMTP server. The Outbound Connections settings specify limits on the number of connections to other SMTP servers and how long they will remain active.

The Advanced command provides additional options for managing how messages are processed by the SMTP virtual server. The options include:

- **Maximum Hop Count**   When messages are forwarded to an SMTP server, the message itself includes a hop count to record the number of times it has been forwarded. When a message has exceeded the maximum hop count setting, it will be considered nondeliverable.

- **Masquerade Domain**   This setting instructs the SMTP server automatically to rewrite the domain of the From address used for outbound messages. You can use this setting when you want to ensure that outgoing messages have a consistent domain name.

- **Fully Qualified Domain Name**   This setting specifies the DNS address of the SMTP virtual server, based on Address (A) and Mail Exchanger (MX) records. In general, each SMTP server for a domain should have a unique fully qualified domain name that includes the server name (for example, Server01.mail.contoso.com).

- **Smart Host**   When a server name or IP address is defined for the Smart Host setting, all messages from this SMTP virtual server will be routed through the specified server. This option is commonly used when multiple internal servers should route their messages through a specific SMTP server that has access to the Internet. Using a smart host configuration can save bandwidth and increase security because only specific servers will require access to external networks. The Attempt Direct Delivery Before Sending To Smart Host option instructs the local SMTP server to attempt to connect directly to the destination SMTP server. If this operation fails, the message will be forwarded to the designated smart host.

- **Perform Reverse DNS Lookup On Incoming Messages**   This setting instructs the SMTP server to perform a DNS reverse lookup to verify that the user's domain matches the IP address in the message header. By enabling this option, you can reduce or prevent unauthorized usage of the SMTP server by messages that use inconsistent header information.

Enabling LDAP Routing

The Lightweight Directory Access Protocol (LDAP) is the primary standard by which directory services software can communicate with each other. Examples of LDAP-compliant directory services are Active Directory and Exchange Server. You can enable the LDAP Routing tab to configure an SMTP virtual server to use LDAP queries to resolve to and from addresses in mail messages. The configuration options specify to which type of LDAP system the SMTP server will be connecting and the address of the server. Other details include authentication information for connecting to and querying the LDAP server.

Managing Security Permissions

You can define which Windows users may manage SMTP Virtual Server settings by using the Security tab. (See Figure 7-44.) The list defines which users should be considered operators. Operators have permissions to change the configuration of the SMTP virtual server. By default, this includes the Administrators group and the Local Service and Network Service built-in accounts. You can click the Add button to include additional users or groups on the list of operators.

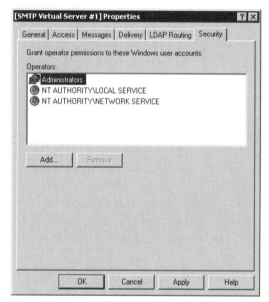

Figure 7-44   Configuring security settings for an SMTP virtual server

Monitoring SMTP Virtual Servers

There are several ways to monitor your SMTP virtual servers once they are properly configured. IIS 6.0 Manager provides the Current Sessions item to view all current connections to the SMTP server. If you are experiencing delays in message transmissions or performance problems on the server, you can use this information to determine the source of messaging traffic.

You can also monitor many Windows Performance Monitor counters that are part of the SMTP Server object. Some useful counters for monitoring SMTP server usage include:

- % Recipients Local
- % Recipients Remote
- Inbound Connections Current
- Message Bytes Total
- Messages Delivered/sec
- Messages Sent/sec
- Outbound Connections Total
- Total Connection Errors

In addition to monitoring usage of the server, you should check periodically for undeliverable messages. By default, these messages will be stored within the root folder that was defined for the SMTP server. The default SMTP Virtual Server #1 uses the *%SystemDrive%\Inetpub\Mailroot* folder. With this folder are several subfolders that can include message details:

- **Badmail**   Messages that are undeliverable due to addressing or security issues
- **Drop**   Storage of all incoming SMTP messages
- **Pickup**   Storage of messages that are waiting to be processed by another program or service
- **Queue**   Messages that are awaiting delivery

Additionally, if you have configured undeliverable messages to be forwarded to a specific account, you should review those messages periodically.

Using an SMTP Virtual Server

SMTP virtual servers can be accessed in several ways. Systems administrators can use the Telnet command-line utility to connect to an SMTP server directly and send commands or create messages. In general use, however, the most typical sources of SMTP messages are end-user applications and Web applications.

Using Telnet

You can connect to an SMTP server directly by using the *Telnet* command. The Telnet Client is an optional Windows Server 2008 feature that can be added to the computer. Once you have added this feature to the computer, you can use the Telnet command from a command prompt to connect to an SMTP virtual server. You can then type manual commands to carry out actions such as sending a new message. Generally, Telnet is used only for diagnostic and troubleshooting purposes. End users will most likely rely upon user-friendly applications to send and receive e-mail messages.

MORE INFO   Troubleshooting with Telnet

For more information about troubleshooting SMTP by using Telnet, see the Microsoft Help and Support article entitled "How To Test SMTP Services Manually in Windows Server 2003" at *http:// support.microsoft.com/kb/323350/*.

Using a Client Messaging Application

For end users, the most common method of sending e-mail messages is through a client e-mail application. Examples include Microsoft Outlook, Windows Mail (which is included with the Windows Vista operating system), and Outlook Express (which is included with Windows XP). The specific setup instructions for these applications will vary, but users will generally need the following information to configure their SMTP servers properly:

- SMTP server address or hostname
- SMTP server port
- SMTP authentication information (if authentication is required)

Configuring SMTP Settings for ASP.NET

A common requirement for many Web applications is the ability to send e-mail messages to users. To complete this task, the Web application requires information about an available SMTP server. You can configure these settings for an ASP.NET application that is running on IIS 7 by using IIS Manager. To do this, select the applicable Web server, Web site, or Web application in the left pane, and then open the SMTP E-Mail setting. (See Figure 7-45.)

Exam Tip   Don't confuse the SMTP e-mail settings in IIS Manager for IIS 7 and the SMTP virtual server settings that are accessible through IIS 6.0 Manager. The IIS 7 settings are used simply to provide information for use by Web applications and will not make any configuration changes to the SMTP virtual server. You will need to use the IIS 6.0 Manager to modify settings and permission for the SMTP Server service.

Web applications can be built to query this information whenever a new e-mail message needs to be sent, thereby reducing deployment configuration. The available options include E-Mail Address, which is the address that will be used in the From field for the message. The SMTP Server and Port settings define details for connecting to an available SMTP virtual server. The Authentication settings can be provided if the SMTP server requires credentials to be passed. Finally, the Store E-Mail In Pickup Directory option is an alternative to forwarding messages to an SMTP server. When you choose this option, outbound messages will be stored as individual files within the folder you have specified.

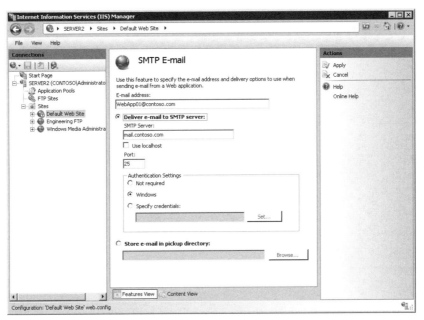

Figure 7-45   Configuring SMTP e-mail settings for an IIS 7 Web site

---

Quick Check

1. Which setting should you change to enable SMTP users to send large attachments by using an SMTP virtual server?
2. How can you configure an SMTP virtual server so that only a single Web server can send messages to it?

Quick Check Answers

1. The properties on the Messages tab enables you to configure the limits for message size in kilobytes.
2. You can enable the Connection options in the Access tab of the properties of the SMTP virtual server. You should modify the settings to allow only the IP address(es) of the Web server.

PRACTICE Configuring and Testing SMTP Services

This practice will help you practice the process of enabling SMTP services in Windows Server 2008.

▶ **Exercise 1 Create a New SMTP Virtual Server**

In this exercise, you will create a new SMTP virtual server by using IIS 6.0 Manager. The steps assume that you have not yet installed the SMTP Server feature.

1. Log on to Server2.contoso.com as a user with Administrator permissions.
2. Open Server Manager. Right-click Features, and select Add Features.
3. Select the SMTP Server and Telnet Client features, and then click Next to continue.
4. On the Confirm Installation Selections page, click Install to begin the feature installation process. When the installation process has finished, click Close.
5. Close Server Manager. Launch IIS 6.0 Manager from the Administrative Tools program group.
6. Expand the Server2 (Local Computer) object, and note that a default object, SMTP Virtual Server #1, has already been created.
7. Right-click the Server2 object, and select New Virtual Server.
8. For the Name setting, type **Contoso SMTP**. Click Next.
9. For the Select IP Address setting, keep the default setting, and then click Next. Read the warning message, and then click Yes to continue.
    You will resolve this conflict in later steps.
10. Using Windows Explorer, create a new folder named **Mail** in the root of your system drive. For the home directory, select the path to this folder (for example, C:\Mail).
11. In the Domain step, type **mail.contoso.com**, and then click Finish. Note that a new SMTP virtual server named Contoso SMTP appears in the left pane of IIS 6.0 Manager.
12. Right-click the Contoso SMTP object, and select properties.
13. On the General tab, click Advanced to open the list of IP address and port number settings for the SMTP virtual server. Select the (All Unassigned) entry in the list, and then click Edit.
14. Change the TCP Port setting to 2525, and then click OK. This will resolve the conflict with the default SMTP Virtual Server. Click OK three times to close the dialog boxes and save the settings.
15. In IIS 6.0 Manager, right-click the Contoso SMTP virtual server object, and select Start.

16. After you have completed the steps of this practice exercise, you can use an e-mail client to connect to the SMTP server and send a message. You can attempt to send a message to a known bad e-mail address (such as Recipient@mail.test) to verify the behavior of the SMTP server.

17. When you are finished, close IIS 6.0 Manager. You can optionally uninstall the SMTP server if you no longer need it on Server2.

Lesson Summary

- You can enable the SMTP Server feature by using Server Manager in Windows Server 2008.
- Each SMTP virtual server must be configured to use a unique IP address and port combination.
- You can configure authentication to require users to provide credentials to use an SMTP virtual server.
- You can use Relay Restrictions settings to reduce unsolicited commercial e-mail messages.
- You can test the configuration of an SMTP virtual server by using a client e-mail application.

Lesson Review

You can use the following questions to test your knowledge of the information in Lesson 2, "Configuring SMTP." The questions are also available on the companion CD if you prefer to review them in electronic form.

NOTE Answers

Answers to these questions and explanations of why each answer choice is correct or incorrect are located in the "Answers" section at the end of the book.

---

1. You are a systems administrator responsible for configuring a Windows Server 2008 SMTP server. Your organization is currently using the default SMTP virtual server for sending order notifications from a single Web application called ContosoOrderManagement. Recently, you have noticed that a large number of messages have been sent to the SMTP virtual server from other computers and users. Which two methods can you use to prevent unauthorized access to the SMTP server? (Choose two. Each correct answer presents a complete solution.)

    A. Enable Basic Authentication.

    B. Configure a smart host for use by the SMTP virtual server.

    C. Add Connection Control entries to limit which IP addresses can use the SMTP server.

    D. Modify settings on the Security tab of the properties of the SMTP virtual server.

2. You are a systems administrator responsible for managing a Windows Server 2008 SMTP server. Recently, users have complained that a Web application running on the same server is experiencing performance problems at specific times of the day. You suspect that the problem might be related to load placed on the SMTP Server service. Which of the following methods should you use to monitor the performance of an SMTP virtual server over time?

    A. The Current Sessions section of IIS 6.0 Manager

    B. SMTP Server counters collected by Performance Monitor

    C. Windows Event Viewer: Application Log

    D. Windows Event Viewer: System Log

    E. The contents of the Badmail folder for the SMTP virtual server

Chapter Review

To further practice and reinforce the skills you learned in this chapter, you can perform the following tasks:

- Review the chapter summary.
- Review the list of key terms introduced in this chapter.
- Complete the case scenarios. These scenarios set up real-world situations involving the topics of this chapter and ask you to create a solution.
- Complete the suggested practices.
- Take a practice test.

Chapter Summary

- Windows Server 2008 includes FTP Publishing Service (FTP 6) to enable users to upload and download files.
- You can download and install FTP 7 in Windows Server 2008 to provide new features such as integration with Web site bindings, administration using IIS manager, and support for FTP Over SSL (FTPS).
- The SMTP service enables Windows Server 2008 to route e-mail messages securely to other servers or users.

Key Terms

Do you know what these key terms mean? You can check your answers by looking up the terms in the glossary at the end of the book.

- File Transfer Protocol (FTP)
- FTP client
- FTP server
- FTP Over SSL
- FTP user isolation
- masquerade domain
- relay restrictions
- Simple Mail Transfer Protocol (SMTP)
- smart host
- SMTP virtual server

Case Scenarios

In these case scenarios, you will apply what you have learned about configuring FTP and SMTP services in Windows Server 2008.

Case Scenario 1: Implementing a Secure FTP Site

You are a systems administrator responsible for enabling Web developers to manage their Web applications on a test server. Some of these users are consultants who do not have accounts in your organization's Active Directory domain. You want to ensure that they are able to access and modify content for specific Web sites. You also want to minimize the administrative effort required to set up this configuration. Your organization's security policies state that logon credentials such as usernames and passwords should never be sent unencrypted.

1. Which version of the FTP server should you use?
2. How can you ensure that logon credentials are encrypted during transmission?
3. What is the easiest method of providing FTP-based access to existing Web sites?

Case Scenario 2: Configuring an SMTP Virtual Server

You are a systems administrator responsible for securing an SMTP virtual server in Windows Server 2008. The server on which the SMTP virtual server resides currently has two physical network adapters that are attached to separate networks. Your security requirements require the SMTP server to respond on only one of these IP addresses and only to requests on port 8937. Users and applications that require access to the SMTP server must be required to provide credentials. Recently, users have complained that they are unable to send attachments that are over 2MB in size. You want to allow attachments of up to 10MB in size to be sent through the server.

1. How should you configure the SMTP virtual server to respond only to specific network requests?
2. How can you configure the server to require credentials for sending SMTP messages?
3. How can you change the maximum allowable message size?

Suggested Practices

To help you successfully master the exam objectives presented in this chapter, complete the following tasks.

Work with FTP and SMTP Services

The practices in this section will enable you to practice the process of creating and managing FTP and SMTP services in Windows Server 2008.

- **Practice 1** In this practice, you will work with new features in FTP 7 for Windows Server 2008.

  1. Download and install the FTP 7 package for Windows Server 2008 from *http://www.iis.net/downloads*.

  2. Using IIS Manager, create a new FTP site binding for the Default Web Site object.

  3. Configure different FTP User Isolation settings and use an FTP client application to test their effects. Pay attention to the default folder location based on each setting and which folders are accessible to the users.

  4. Enable FTP Over SSL (FTPS) by creating a self-signed SSL certificate. Use an FTPS-compatible FTP client application to test the functionality.

- **Practice 2** In this practice, you will test and configure SMTP Services in Windows Server 2008.

  1. Install the SMTP Server feature in Windows Server 2008.

  2. Modify the settings of the default SMTP virtual server to require basic authentication to send messages.

  3. Test the SMTP server configuration by sending an e-mail through the SMTP server, using a client application such as Windows Mail, Outlook, or Outlook Express.

  4. Attempt to send a test e-mail message to an e-mail address that is incorrectly formatted or does not exist. Inspect the SMTP server's Badmail folder to attempt to find the message. Also, test whether you receive a nondeliverable failure e-mail message.

Take a Practice Test

The practice tests on this book's companion CD offer many options. For example, you can test yourself on just one exam objective, or you can test yourself on all the 70-643 certification exam content. You can set up the test so that it closely simulates the experience of taking a certification exam, or you can set it up in study mode so that you can look at the correct answers and explanations after you answer each question.

MORE INFO Practice tests

For details about all the practice test options available, see the "How to Use the Practice Tests" section in this book's introduction.

Chapter 8
Configuring Windows Media Services

Many organizations need to deliver a rich digital media experience efficiently to users. Audio and video files are often available to employees and to external users to communicate important information better. For example, an organization can store archived versions of company meetings and other presentations on an intranet server for later review. Some businesses provide audio and video content to their users as part of their business model. Users have come to expect a seamless experience that provides both live and on-demand access to various types of media. However, the process of sending media information over network connections and the Internet can create significant strains on network bandwidth and can tax server resources.

Windows Server 2008 provides features for efficiently streaming media to users over a public or private network. In this chapter, you will learn how to install and configure the Streaming Media Services server role and how you can configure Windows Media Services to provide access to different types of content. You will also learn about ways you can protect digital content through Digital Rights Management (DRM).

MORE INFO Obtaining Windows Media Services

The Windows Media Services server role is available as a downloadable add-on for Windows Server 2008. For more information on obtaining the product, see the Windows Media Servers Web site at *http://www.microsoft.com/windows/windowsmedia/forpros/server/server.aspx*.

Exam objectives in this chapter:
- Configuring Network Application Services
  - Configure Windows Media server.
  - Configure Digital Rights Management (DRM).

Lesson in this chapter:
-

Before You Begin

To complete the lessons in this chapter, you should have installed and configured the Web Server (IIS) server role on Server2.contoso.com.

Lesson 1: Configuring Windows Media Services

The Streaming Media Services server role in Windows Server 2008 provides a wide variety of features for managing and presenting audio and video content to users. It also includes administrative tools and configuration options for meeting many business and technical requirements. In this lesson, you will learn how to enable and configure the Windows Media Server service. You will also learn about methods of improving scalability, performance, security, and reliability.

> **After this lesson, you will be able to:**
> - Install the Streaming Media Services server role on a computer running Windows Server 2008.
> - Configure Streaming Media Services settings, using the Windows Media Services administrative tool.
> - Create publishing points for delivering broadcast and on-demand audio and video content to users.
> - Configure authentication and authorization security settings to protect access to content.
> - Enable cache/proxy features to increase performance and reliability of Windows Media server services.
> - Describe how you can implement Digital Rights Management (DRM) to protect intellectual property.
>
> **Estimated lesson time: 60 minutes**

Understanding Media Services

The technical requirements for providing access to audio and video media can differ significantly from requirements for other types of content. The Web Server (IIS) server role can provide access to many types of files to your users. For example, you can enable users to download Windows Media Audio (.wma) and Windows Media Video (.wmv) files by providing them with the appropriate URL and access permissions. The drawback of this approach, however, is that users typically will need to download an entire file before they can start using it. The need to wait for a complete file download offers a poor end-user experience. Many users will choose not to wait for the media due to this inconvenience. Whenever users request large video and audio files, Web servers attempt to send the information as quickly as possible. This reduces the performance of the server for other users of the server and limits overall scalability. The download process can also waste significant resources if users decide they do not want the entire file.

All these issues are reasons for using a specialized service for serving media content. The primary purpose of the Streaming Media Services server role in Windows Server 2008 is to provide access to both live and on-demand audio and video content over standard communications protocols such as those used on the Internet. Media can be made available in an intranet scenario or to users over a publicly accessible Web site. In many cases, a Web application will include links that help users easily locate and launch the content they need. Usually, the content can begin playing within seconds, and the media server can throttle network bandwidth automatically based on the client's connection speed and the desired quality. You can also use DRM to protect the content provided to users.

Delivering Live vs. Prerecorded Content

Users can use Windows Media Services to access two main types of content. Live broadcasts typically are used for events such as sportscasts, music concerts, and company meetings. The original source for live broadcasts is usually a server or camera that supports the Windows Media Encoder standard. This type of content starts at a specific time, and all users will receive the same audio or video content. Because the data is being sent as it is generated, users are unable to pause, fast-forward, or replay the content during the live event. Live broadcasts can, however, be archived so that users can access them on demand at a later time.

Prerecorded content is available to users on demand. Examples include access to a library of training videos, music videos, television shows, or other content that is available upon request. When users request content, Streaming Media Services starts sending it immediately. As soon as the client computer's media player has buffered enough of the data stream, the playback can begin. The buffering process often takes only a few seconds, so playback usually begins very quickly. Content developers can also create Web pages that include an embedded media player to provide easy access to content and associated information. Additionally, users can stop, pause, fast-forward, or rewind the playback when accessing on-demand content.

Understanding Unicast vs. Multicast Streaming

An important goal for providing access to streamed audio and video content is to reduce network bandwidth requirements. Both clients and servers often have limitations that can reduce scalability and can reduce the number of users who can access media. Windows Media Services provides two methods of sending data to clients.

Unicast streaming is based on a direct one-to-one connection between client computers and the media server. This is the most appropriate approach for scenarios in which users should be given the ability to start playing any content on demand. Because the content is sent individually to each client, users can pause, replay, or fast-forward content in their media player. The primary drawback of the unicast approach is that it can consume a significant amount of network bandwidth.

With multicast streaming, many clients can subscribe simultaneously to the same stream from a server. Server bandwidth requirements are minimized because the information is sent only once. As long as the network infrastructure supports multicast routing and distribution, clients can then receive the content without requiring a direct connection to the server. Multicast streaming is most appropriate for delivering live, broadcast-based media because users will be unable to control the playback of the stream. Multicast streaming is also well suited for internal corporate networks where administrators can ensure that the infrastructure supports it.

Comparing Data Transfer Protocols

Content providers must design their streaming media services to ensure accessibility and performance. Windows Media Services supports different protocols based on client and network capabilities. The Real-Time Streaming Protocol (RTSP) provides an efficient method to send audio and video content to computers that are running Windows Media Player 9 or later. RTSP can use the User Datagram Protocol (UDP, referred to as RTSPU), if it is supported by the client and network. If UDP is not supported, RTSP can use TCP (RTSPT). The default TCP port for connections is 554, but you can change this setting to support specific firewall requirements.

Windows Media Services can also stream information, using the HTTP protocol to support clients or networks that do not support RTSP. By default, data is sent on HTTP port 80, but the port can be changed to avoid conflicts with the Web Server (IIS) server role. To simplify the connection process, Windows Media Services provides a feature called automatic protocol rollover. This feature can determine the most appropriate connection type automatically for a particular media player client and send data using that method.

Installing Streaming Media Services

Windows Media Services is an optional role server that must be downloaded and installed from Microsoft. You can find the appropriate download package by browsing to *http://www.microsoft.com/downloads* and searching for Windows Media Services for Windows Server 2008. The site will provide information about installing the Streaming Media Services server role using Server Manager. To begin the process, open Server Manager, right-click Roles, and select Add Roles. The Streaming Media Services role will appear in the list. (See Figure 8-1.)

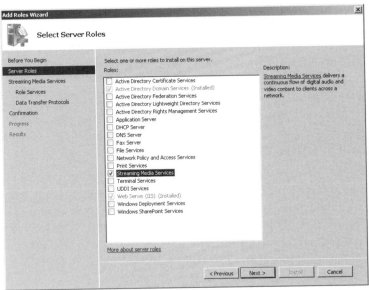

Figure 8-1   Adding the Streaming Media Services server role by using Server Manager

The Streaming Media Services Role includes the following role services:

- **Windows Media Server**   This option installs the basic Windows Media Services service and the Windows Media Services console. You must select this option to be able to stream audio and video to clients from the local server.

- **Web-Based Administration**   Windows Media Services also includes an optional Web-based configuration and management Web site that provides the same functionality as the default Windows Media Services console. This component requires the Web Server (IIS) server role to be enabled on the local computer.

- **Logging Agent**   This component works with Web servers to capture information about audio and video streams. It requires the Web Server (IIS) server role. If you install it on the same computer as the Windows Media Services role service, you will need to change the HTTP port the Default Web Site or the Logging Agent uses to avoid a binding conflict.

The Select Data Transfer Protocols page provides options for which protocols will be enabled by default. If you have previously installed the Web Server (IIS) server role and have a Web server that is bound to HTTP port 80, you will be unable to select the Hypertext Transfer Protocol (HTTP) option. (See Figure 8-2.) You will be able to reconfigure and enable HTTP after the role addition process has completed.

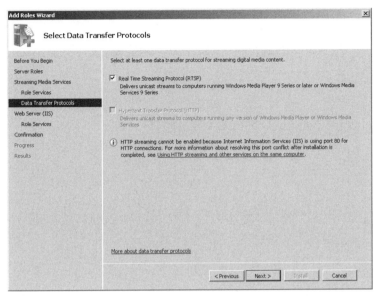

Figure 8-2 Configuring data transfer protocol settings for the Streaming Media Service server role

In addition to these role services, the Windows Media Services console provides features for testing access to content by using Windows Media Player. To make Windows Media Player available for use, you must install the Desktop Experience feature, using Server Manager. This feature is optional, however, and is not necessary if you do not plan to test media streaming on the local computer running Windows Server 2008.

After you have installed the Streaming Media Services server role on the computer, you can use Server Manager to view additional details. To do this, expand the *Roles* object and select Streaming Media Services. (See Figure 8-3.) Any errors that have been written to the Windows event logs are displayed in the Events section. The Resources And Support section provides numerous recommendations related to the configuration and deployment of streaming media.

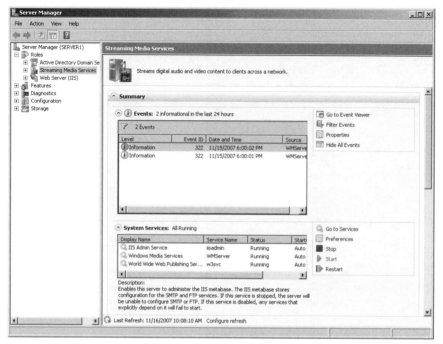

Figure 8-3   Viewing information about Streaming Media Services in Server Manager

Using Windows Media Services Management Tools

Windows Media Services has two main administrative tools. You can launch the Windows Media Services console by selecting Windows Media Services from the Administrative Tools program group. (See Figure 8-4.)

If you have chosen to install the Web-Based Administration option, you can also configure Windows Media Services by using a Web browser. The default port for the Windows Media Administration Web site is HTTP port 8080. You can start, stop, and reconfigure the Web site, using IIS Manager. (See Figure 8-5.)

Figure 8-4   Using the Windows Media Services console

Figure 8-5   Viewing the Windows Media Administration Site by using IIS Manager

Once you have started the site, you can access it by launching Windows Media Services (Web) from the Administrative Tools program group or by navigating to its URL directly. The default site bindings do not include an SSL-enabled site binding, so you will receive the warning shown in Figure 8-6. For more information about configuring and enabling Secure Sockets Layer (SSL) for a Web site, see Chapter 6, "Managing Web Server Security." You can also continue to the Windows Media Services administration Web site without using an SSL connection.

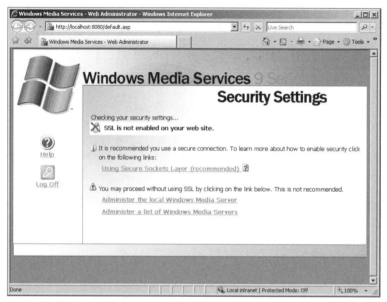

Figure 8-6   Viewing a Windows Media Services Security Settings warning

The Windows Media Services Administration Web site, as shown in Figure 8-7, has been designed to resemble the Windows Media Services console. All the same features and functions are available using this site. The Web pages are configured to refresh automatically at regular intervals to ensure that current information is displayed. In general, the administration Web site is more convenient for performing remote management features.

The remainder of the screens and instructions in this lesson will focus on using the Windows Media Services console. However, most of the same steps can be completed using the Windows Media Services Administration Web site.

Figure 8-7   Viewing the Windows Media Services Administration Web site

Managing Publishing Points

Publishing points are used to define the locations and types of content available to users of Windows Media Services. When you install the Streaming Media Services role, a default publishing point named <Default> (on-demand) is created automatically. The root file system location for this folder is *%SystemDrive%*\Wmpub\Wmroot. This location contains a set of default media files, including sample Windows Media Video (.wmv) video files, playlists, and image files.

Creating a New Publishing Point

When you want to provide access to new content, you can create a new publishing point, using the Windows Media Services console. To start the process, right-click the Publishing Points object on the left side of the console, and then select the *Add Publishing Point (Wizard)* command. On the Welcome page, click Next. The Publishing Point Name page of the Add Publishing Point Wizard will ask you to provide a name for the new publishing point. (See Figure 8-8.) This name should be brief but also descriptive because it will be used as part of the URL used by clients to connect to content.

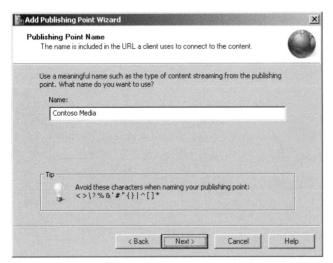

Figure 8-8   Providing a name for a new publishing point

The Content Type page of the wizard will prompt you to specify the type of content that will be made available through this publishing point. (See Figure 8-9.) The options are:

- Encoder (A Live Stream)
- Playlist (A Mix Of Files And/Or Live Streams That You Can Combine Into A Continuous Stream)
- One File (Useful For A Broadcast Of An Archived File)
- Files (Digital Media Or Playlists) In A Directory (Useful For Providing Access For On-Demand Playback Through A Single Publishing Point)

The Publishing Point Type page enables you to create either a Broadcast Publishing Point or an On-Demand Publishing Point. (See Figure 8-10.) Based on the option you chose on the previous page, one of the options might be unavailable.

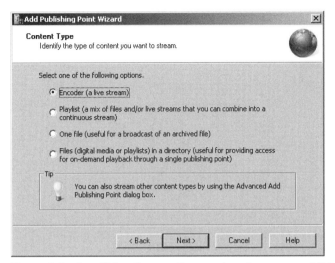

Figure 8-9   Specifying Content Type settings for a new publishing point

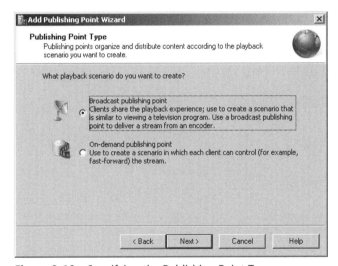

Figure 8-10   Specifying the Publishing Point Type

The Delivery Options For Broadcast Publishing Points page enables you to specify whether you want to use Unicast or Multicast communications. (See Figure 8-11.) The default setting is Unicast, which is the most compatible approach but which also uses the most bandwidth. For networks that support multicast, you can choose the Multicast option. When you select Multicast, you also can enable Unicast rollover, a feature that provides unicast transmissions to clients that cannot access the multicast stream.

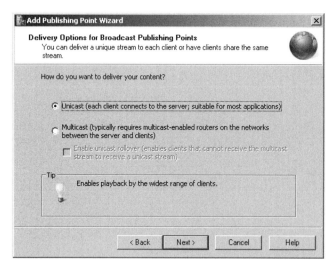

Figure 8-11   Selecting the unicast or multicast delivery option

When you are creating a publishing point that provides access to files, you will be presented with the Directory Location page. (See Figure 8-12.) The Location Of Directory setting specifies the root folder in which media content is located. You should plan to store all the audio and video files you want to make available within this folder.

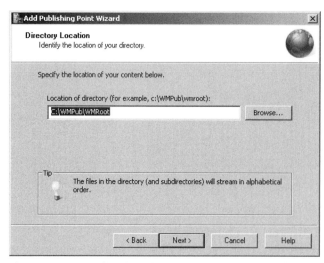

Figure 8-12   Configuring Directory Location settings for a new publishing point

The Enable Access To Directory Content Using Wildcards option enables users to access any of the files directly that are stored in this location. They can do this by manually modifying the URL if they know the name of the file to retrieve. Enabling this option is useful when you have a large number of files to which you want to link directly. However, if you want to ensure that users can access only the files you make available, using links on a Web site, disable this option.

The Content Playback page provides options related to how playlists will be created and managed for on-demand content. The two options are:

- Loop (Content Plays Continuously)
- Shuffle (Content Plays Randomly)

If you have chosen to create an on-demand publishing point that is based on a live feed, the Encoder URL page will prompt you to provide the URL of the encoder that will provide the media content. (See Figure 8-13.) The URL should include the full path and port number to a server that is running a Windows Media Services–based encoder.

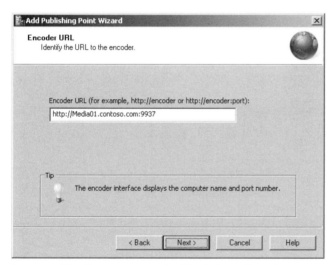

Figure 8-13   Providing encoder URL information when creating a broadcast publishing point

The Unicast Logging page of the Add Publishing Point Wizard enables you to set the collection and storage of usage statistics for Unicast users of the publishing point.

The Publishing Point Summary page provides a list of the selections you have made in previous steps. (See Figure 8-14.)

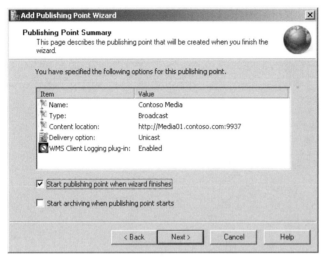

Figure 8-14   Viewing a summary of publishing point settings

The final page of the wizard contains important information about the URL that will be used to access the publishing point. (See Figure 8-15.) At this point, you will also be able to choose from various files that will help make your content accessible to users. You will learn more about these options later in this section.

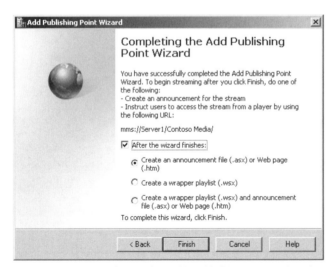

Figure 8-15   Completing the Add Publishing Point Wizard

Administering Publishing Points

You can manage the status of publishing points, using the Windows Media Services console. To manage the status of a publishing point and to perform other administrative functions, right-click the appropriate object. The available commands include:

- Start
- Stop
- Allow New Connections
- Deny New Connections
- Duplicate
- Rename
- Remove

Individual publishing points can be started and stopped individually. You can also use the *Duplicate* command to create a new publishing point (with a new name and URL) based on the settings of an existing one. Denying new connections effectively makes the contents of the publishing point inaccessible to new users but continues to send streamed information to users who have already connected. The *Stop* command ends all streams for the publishing point by disconnecting any active users.

Monitoring Publishing Points

The Monitor tab of a publishing point provides an overview of current connections and statistics related to the content currently being served. (See Figure 8-16.) By default, the display is configured to refresh automatically every three seconds. You can use the Reset All Counters command (icons located at the bottom of the tab) to reset all cumulative-value counters to their initial values.

The View Performance Monitor command opens a new window that displays relevant Windows Performance Monitor counters for the publishing point. As with the full Performance Monitor application, you can use the commands on the toolbar to add values or to customize the display. For example, you can add counters related to the Processor, Memory, and Network Interface objects to collect more details about the overall performance of the server.

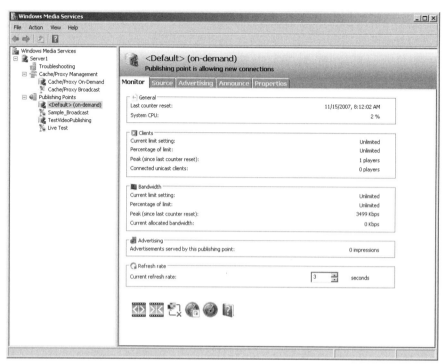

Figure 8-16 Monitoring activity for a publishing point by using the Windows Media Services console

Configuring Source Settings

Every publishing point must have source information to specify which media files will be available to users. As you learned in the previous section, you can specify the default information when you create a new publishing point by using the Add Publishing Point Wizard. You can also use the Windows Media Services console to make changes to the source settings. To do this, select a publishing point, and then click the Source tab. (See Figure 8-17.)

The options and details on this page will vary based on the type of publishing point you have created. For example, a publishing point that provides access to live broadcast video will have information about the URL of the streaming source whereas on-demand publishing points will include playlist and file location information. The Source settings provide an easy way to modify the type of content that is accessible to users without having to create a new publishing point. You can highlight a video and click the Test Stream button to access the media automatically by using Windows Media Player directly or by launching Windows Internet Explorer to play the content.

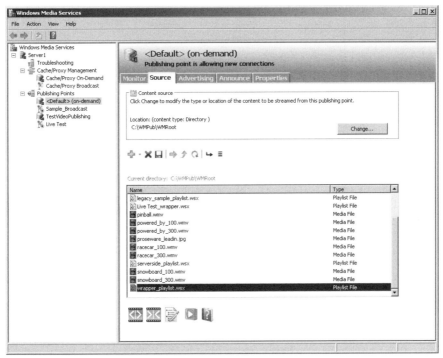

Figure 8-17   Configuring Source settings for an on-demand publishing point

Creating Announcements

After you have prepared a new publishing point for the Windows Media Services server, you will need a method to make the content available to users. The Windows Media Services console enables you to create announcements, which are a method of creating links and playlists for the content you want to make available. The last step of the Add Publishing Point Wizard enables you to create the relevant types of announcements automatically. The options include:

- Create An Announcement File (.asx) Or Web Page (.htm)
- Create A Wrapper Playlist (.wsx)
- Create A Wrapper Playlist (.wsx) And Announcement File (.asx) Or Web Page (.htm)

Depending on which option you select, you will be presented with one or more wizard options. You can also view and modify the announcement settings for an existing publishing point by selecting it in the Windows Media Services console and clicking the Announce tab. (See Figure 8-18.)

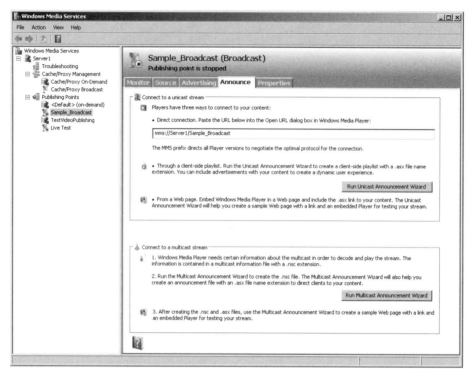

Figure 8-18   Viewing Announce settings for a publishing point

You can use announcements information in your own Web pages (for example, by creating a tag that links directly to a publishing point), or you can provide links to the playlist files or wrappers themselves.

Using the Create Wrapper Wizard

The Create Wrapper Wizard enables you to create a wrapper playlist that includes media files and advertisements. (See Figure 8-19.)

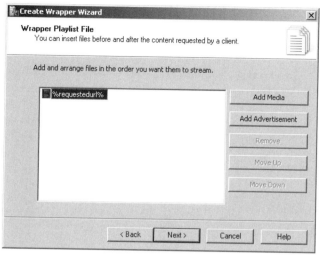

Figure 8-19   Using the Create Wrapper Wizard

Click the Add Media button to add new files or other types of content. (See Figure 8-20.) The data can come from other publishing points and can include a mix of on-demand and live encoder-based content. After you have selected the appropriate option, you'll be prompted for the location in which the .wsx file should be stored. Generally, you should place the file within the publishing point's root folder so it will be accessible to users. You can also copy or move the file to another location such as the root folder of a Web site.

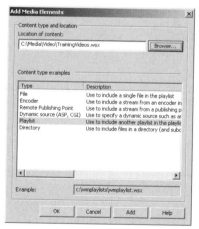

Figure 8-20   Adding media to a Wrapper playlist

Using the Unicast Announcement Wizard

If you have selected to deliver streaming content by using the unicast method, you can use the Unicast Announcement Wizard to configure the appropriate options. By default, unicast URLs are prefixed with the mms content type (for example, *mms://Server2.contoso.com/Media*). Client media players such as Windows Media Player are automatically associated with this URL type, so the content can start playback automatically when the user clicks an appropriate hyperlink in a Web page. The Save Announcement Options page of the wizard enables you to specify the location into which the Announcement file (.asx) will be saved. (See Figure 8-21.) The default location is within the root folder of the Web Server (IIS) server role's Default Web Site object.

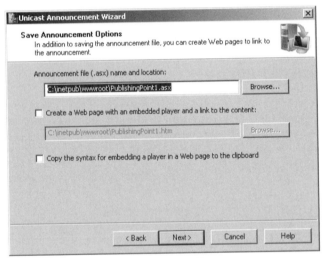

Figure 8-21 Saving announcement files

You can also use this page to create an HTML Web page that includes an embedded player and a link to the content. This method provides a simplified way for Web developers to see the HTML and media player tags they need to include in their own code. Later, you can load the Web page directly in Internet Explorer. If you have Windows Media player installed, you can then test the announcement by playing the video. (See Figure 8-22.) If you plan to place the link to the media within an existing Web page, you can use the Copy The Syntax For Embedding A Player In A Web Page To The Clipboard option.

Figure 8-22   Viewing an announcement Web page created using the Unicast Announcement Wizard

The Edit Announcement Metadata page enables you to specify details related to the title and author of the content as well as copyright details. This information will be sent to users' media player applications automatically.

To verify the settings you have selected, you can use the buttons in the Test Unicast Announcement window. This window is launched automatically after you have completed the Unicast Announcement Wizard. (See Figure 8-23.) The first Test button will provide direct access to the playlist and should open Windows Media Player and start playing the content. The Test Web Page With Embedded Player option Test button will launch Internet Explorer and load the test Web page (if one was created).

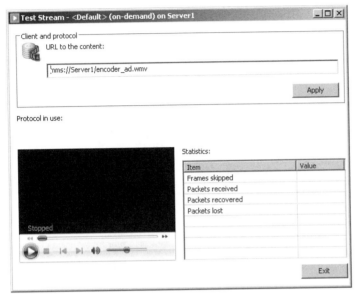

Figure 8-23 Testing announcements in the Windows Media Services Administration application

Using the Multicast Announcement Wizard

When configuring publishing points that support multicast broadcasting of media streams, you can use the Multicast Announcement Wizard to create the necessary files. The Specify Files To Create page enables you to select the method by which you will provide links to a multicast stream. (See Figure 8-24.)

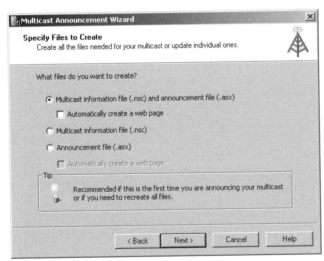

Figure 8-24 Creating a multicast announcement

The default option, Multicast Information File (.nsc) And Announcement File (.asx) creates all the necessary files to provide access to the content. You can also create or re-create the .nsc or .asx files individually. The Automatically Create A Web Page option generates an HTML file that includes a link to the multicast content.

The Stream Formats page enables you to define which streams will be made available through the announcement. You can provide access to different streams located on various publishing points either on the same server or on another Windows Media Services server. Click the Add button to access the Add Stream Formats dialog box. (See Figure 8-25.) The Location Of Content setting can point directly to an audio or video file, or it can specify the location of a live media encoder. You can also link to a stream from another publishing point. When you click Next to continue, the Multicast Announcement Wizard automatically will attempt to verify the links to the content that you specified.

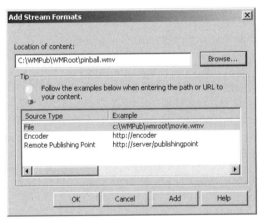

Figure 8-25   Adding stream formats by using the Multicast Announcement Wizard

The Save Multicast Announcement Files page lists the physical path locations into which the selected files will be stored. (See Figure 8-26.) The default location is the root folder for Default Web Site, created when you install the Web Server (IIS) server role. However, you can change the location to make the announcements available from another Web site.

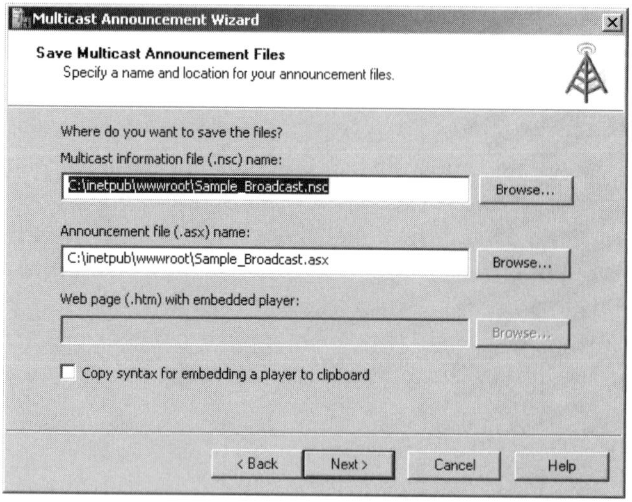

Figure 8-26   Choosing file system locations for multicast announcement files

An announcement can point to a Web server location or a network share for the actual .nsc file that stores the multicast information. You can choose the option in the Specify URL To Multicast Information File page. (See Figure 8-27.) If you are using a shared network location, the Windows Media Services service account must have permissions to read the file. The Network Share option is useful when you want to centralize the creation and management of multicast information files.

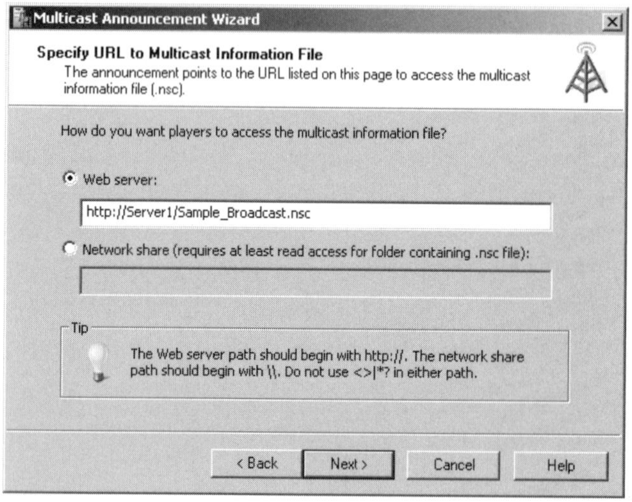

Figure 8-27   Specifying the location of multicast information files

Because multicast streams are designed for providing access to live content, the audio or video stream is not available for replay automatically. You can use the Yes option on the Archive Content page to create an archived video file automatically that can later be accessed after the live stream has concluded.

After you have finished the steps of the Multicast Announcement Wizard, you can test the files and settings that were generated as you did with the Unicast Announcement Wizard. For example, you can load the Web page that contains an embedded player link for the live webcast. You should note, however, that if a live stream has not started from the encoder link you specified, you will not yet be able to view any of the media.

Configuring Publishing Point Properties

Windows Media Services uses a plug-in–based architecture to configure the features and options available for each publishing point. To access these settings, select a publishing point using the Windows Media Services console, and then select the Properties tab. Figure 8-28 shows an overview of the available options.

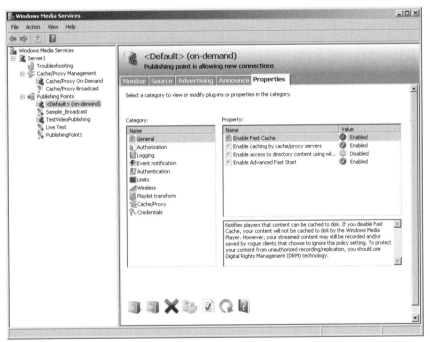

Figure 8-28   Viewing properties for an on-demand publishing point

The specific list of categories and their default property settings will vary based on the decisions you made when you created the publishing point.

For example, the Limits category provides numerous options for managing bandwidth and performance. The options include:

- Limit Player Connections
- Limit Outgoing Distribution Connections
- Limit Aggregate Player Bandwidth (Kbps)
- Limit Aggregate Outgoing Distribution Bandwidth (Kbps)
- Limit Bandwidth Per Player Connection (Kbps)
- Limit Bandwidth Per Outgoing Distribution Connection (Kbps)
- Limit Fast Start Bandwidth Per Player Connection (Kbps)
- Limit Fast Cache Content Delivery Rate

These settings are useful for managing network usage, especially when many Windows Media Services components might be competing for the same resources or when many publishing points are running on the same server. You will learn more about other properties settings related to security later in this lesson.

Managing Advertising Settings

For many content providers, audio and video advertisements are a significant source of revenue. You can use the Windows Media Services console to create and manage advertisements automatically. To view and modify settings, select a publishing point, and then click the Advertising tab. (See Figure 8-29.)

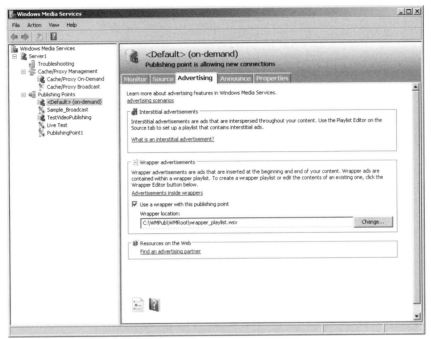

Figure 8-29 Configuring Advertising settings for a publishing point

It is possible to include advertisements manually by including the relevant files within a playlist. However, this process can be tedious and time-consuming, especially when users can access many audio and video files from the same publishing point. There are three primary methods of presenting advertising.

- **Banner ads**   Many Web pages that link to video or audio content can include advertisements on the source Web page. For example, the center of the screen might show a video broadcast while the surrounding areas of the page include relevant static image banner ads. This method does not require any special configuration in Windows Media Services.

- **Wrapper ads**   A typical requirement for many organizations is the ability to play a specific audio or video clip automatically before or after any streaming media is accessed. For example, a news video service might want to include a brief splash video whenever a user accesses their media. Wrapper ads point to a playlist that includes this information. These ads will also play automatically for live broadcasts, so they ensure that users who join a stream that has already started will also see the ads.

- **Interstitial ads**   These ads are presented at various times during the steaming of specific content. For example, an online television broadcaster might include a new advertisement after every four on-demand videos are played. You can define manually which ads are shown by modifying playlist settings on the Source tab of the properties of the publishing point. You can also edit playlists manually to achieve the same result.

The Advertising tab also provides a link to the Windows Media Partner Center. Companies listed here are able to provide services such as centralized advertisement distribution and DRM.

Configuring Security for Windows Media Services

As with other types of network-accessible content, it is important to ensure that only authorized users have access to streamed audio and video. Some organizations provide content only to paid or registered users and want to prevent others from using network bandwidth. Unauthorized individuals must also be prevented from directly linking to content or downloading and redistributing media files. Windows Media Services provides several methods for securing Streaming Media Services. Default security settings can be defined at the server level. These settings will apply automatically to all publishing points on the server. However, you can also override the settings for each individual publishing point. In this section, you will learn about authentication, authorization, and permissions settings that are available within the Properties tab of a publishing point.

Configuring Authentication Options

By default, new publishing points will inherit the security-related settings that are defined at the server level. You can define specific settings for different types of content by accessing the Authentication category on the Properties tab of a publishing point. (See Figure 8-30.)

You can authenticate users by one of three methods. WMS Anonymous User Authentication specifies that Windows Media Services should not prompt users for credentials. However, when this option is enabled, users will be able to access content designated only to the user account that has NTFS file system permissions. The default user account is the WMUS_*servername* account, which is automatically created when you install the Streaming Media Services server role. To change the account setting, double-click the WMS Anonymous User Authentication plug-in and provide the appropriate username and password. Anonymous authentication is useful when you want all the users of the media server to have access to the same set of content.

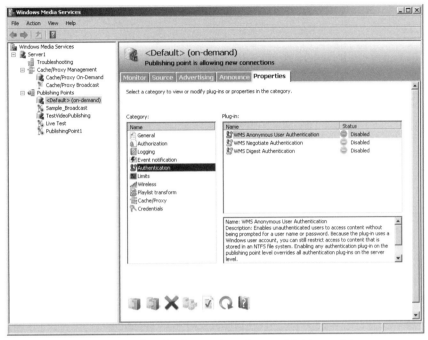

Figure 8-30   Viewing Authentication settings for a publishing point

WMS Negotiate Authentication uses either NTLM or Kerberos-based methods to determine the identity of the incoming user. This method is useful if you want to restrict access to users who have accounts on the local server or within an Active Directory directory services domain. When users attempt to access content, their Windows credentials will be used to determine whether they have permission to access the requested files.

The WMS Digest Authentication option is used primarily to support Internet users. It relies on the HTTP protocol to request and receive credentials over the network. For security, it does not send the actual password but a hash that can be used to validate the user's identity.

Configuring Authorization Options

The Authorization properties for a Windows Media Services server or a publishing point specify how permissions will be checked before users have access to content. There are three available options. (See Figure 8-31.) WMS NTFS ACL Authorization uses NTFS file system permissions to determine whether a user has access to files. If only anonymous authentication is enabled, then the designated anonymous user account must have at least permissions to the content. Otherwise, when user credentials are supplied, the user's effective permissions are checked before a stream is sent.

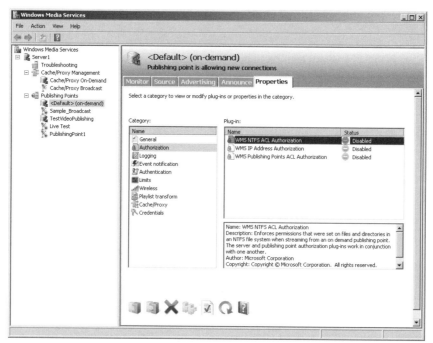

Figure 8-31   Viewing Authorization options for a publishing point

Some Windows Media Services installations are intended for use by only a certain group of computers. For example, an organization might provide company meeting videos that require all users to connect to the organization's local area network (LAN) to obtain access to the content. Administrators can use the WMS IP Address Authorization plug-in to specify which IP addresses will be able to access content. (See Figure 8-32.) Default settings can be configured to automatically allow or deny connections that are not explicitly listed.

You can use the WMS Publishing Points ACL Authorization plug-in to configure which users and groups have access to the publishing point. (See Figure 8-33.) To access content, users must have at least Read permissions. By default, the Everyone group has these permissions to the content. Users and groups can also be granted Write and Create permission to modify the contents of the publishing point.

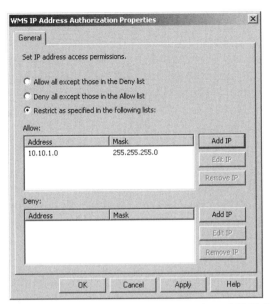

Figure 8-32   Configuring properties for WMS IP Address Authorization

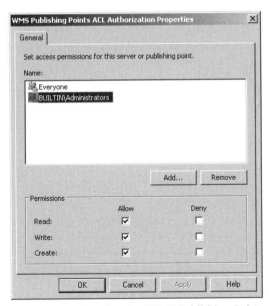

Figure 8-33   Configuring WMS Publishing Points ACL Authorization settings

Using Web Server Permissions

Another method of securing access to streamed audio and video content does not directly involve Windows Media Services. You can use permissions and security options that are available with the Web Server (IIS) server role to secure links and other content that might be accessible to users. For example, you might expose links and playlists for video content only to registered users who are connecting using a secure SSL connection. For more information on configuring security for IIS, see Chapter 6.

Enabling Cache/Proxy Features

Managing network bandwidth and server resources when supporting large numbers of users can be difficult when using only a single Windows Media Services server. The server itself can often become a bottleneck and can lead to performance problems for clients. Additionally, the failure of the server can result in a loss of access to audio and video data. To address these issues, you can use the Windows Media Services Cache/Proxy features.

Caching and proxying are methods by which Windows Media Services can relay streamed information from one publishing point to users who need it. Caching refers to when a Windows Media Services copies content from the origin server and stores it locally. The caching server is responsible for obtaining the data from the source and sending it directly to the client. A proxy configuration is used to have multiple computers that are running Windows Media Services send requests to other streaming media servers. Figure 8-34 provides an example of a typical server configuration.

In this diagram, the origin server is providing access directly only to the distribution servers. The distribution servers, in turn, can then send streamed information to the clients that require it. This reduces the network and processing load on the primary Windows Media Services server and enables users to connect to servers located optimally based on their network configuration.

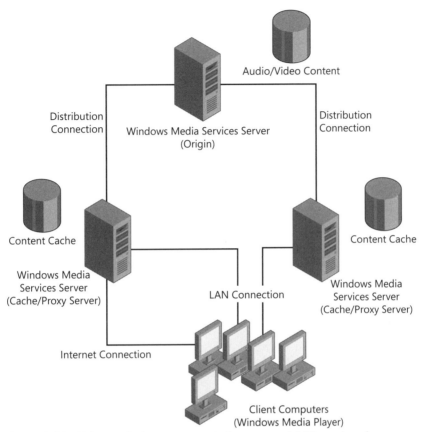

Figure 8-34   Using cache/proxy servers to increase scalability and performance

Enabling Cache/Proxy Settings

By default, Cache/Proxy Management is disabled for new Streaming Media Services installations. To enable this feature for a server, open the Windows Media Services console, and select the server object. Then, select the Properties tab and the Cache/Proxy Management category. Right-click the WMS Cache Proxy plug-in, and select Enable. You can also double-click the WMS Cache Proxy plug-in to access configuration options for the cache and proxy features.

The General tab enables you to select which protocol is preferred for streaming media between an origin server and the cache/proxy server. The default setting is to use whichever protocol the client has requested.

Exam Tip   When considering the features of Windows Media Services, a single server can serve multiple roles. For example, it can provide access to both on-demand and live broadcast publishing points while it is also proxying requests and caching content for other servers. For the sake of simplicity, this lesson refers to "source servers" and "proxy/cache servers." Depending on your network design or requirements presented on the exam, you might want to configure the same server with all these functions.

Configuring Caching Settings

The Cache tab enables you to specify storage space locations and limits. (See Figure 8-35.) A proxy/cache server will attempt to store as much information as possible to reduce load on the origin server. The default settings do not include any limits on caching, but if you are caching data for a large amount of content, it is recommended that you set some limits.

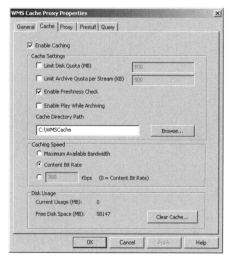

Figure 8-35   Configuring cache settings for a Windows Media server

The Caching Speed section specifies how quickly data will be pulled from the origin server. If you select Maximum Available Bandwidth, the proxy/cache server will attempt to transfer content from the origin server as quickly as possible and will then cache it locally. The Content Bit Rate option specifies that data will be transferred from the origin server at the same rate as the bandwidth of the file. This option is useful if there are many caching servers that are accessing the same origin server.

The Prestuff tab provides options related to populating the proxy/cache server's media cache, even when users are not requesting content. (See Figure 8-36.) It is useful when you want to populate server content initially before it goes into production (when the load will be significantly higher). The first option is to pull the information from a stream. This option requires the full URL to a publishing point that is located on the origin server. You can also limit the amount of bandwidth consumed for the prestuff operation.

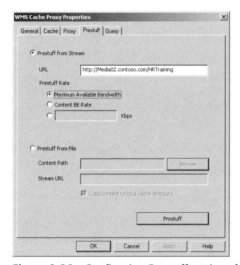

Figure 8-36   Configuring Prestuff settings for a caching server

To reduce network load when transferring large amounts of data, you can also load the prestuff data from a file. The Content Path setting can be a local file system location or a network path. The Stream URL validates the files from an existing publishing point. To start the prestuff operation, click the Prestuff button.

MORE INFO   **Testing your Windows Media Services infrastructure**

When you are planning to stream media to a large number of users, it helps to generate a sample load to test your Windows Media Services infrastructure. Microsoft has provided the Windows Media Load Simulator for Windows Media Services 9 Series as a free tool for generating load and simulating user activity. You can find this and other downloads on the Windows Media Services 9 Series Tools and Add-ins page at *http://www.microsoft.com/windows/windowsmedia/forpros/serve/tools.aspx.*

Configuring Proxy Settings

A Windows Media Services server can also proxy requests from clients to reduce the load on the origin server. The Proxy tab includes settings for three modes of proxy options. They are:

- **Proxy**   This is the default proxy functionality in which the server presents content to clients. The server appears to the client as the same computer as the origin Windows Media Services server.
- **Proxy Redirect**   This option specifies that client requests should be redirected to another proxy server located on the network. It is most often used in load-balancing configurations when you want to redirect all users to a specific server that has available content.
- **Reverse Proxy**   A reverse proxy redirects incoming requests to a specific publishing point. The reverse proxy server verifies authentication for the user and then requests the content from the origin server.

Overall, by using proxy servers, you can increase the scalability of a Windows Media Services server content distribution point.

Configuring Cache/Proxy Settings for Publishing Points

After you have enabled and configured Cache/Proxy Management settings on the appropriate servers, you can use Windows Media Services to configure caching settings. To do this, select a publishing point, and then click the Properties tab. The Cache/Proxy category will include properties for determining how information can be cached. For broadcast-based publication points, the available setting is the Stream Splitting Expiration. This represents the amount of time the content can be accessed before it must communicate with the origin server to check for content updates. The Cache Expiration property has the same effect for on-demand publishing points. The default setting for both is 86,400 seconds (24 hours).

Monitoring Proxy/Cache Servers

The Windows Media Services console includes two objects within the Cache/Proxy Management section. These objects are used for monitoring the current performance and usage of proxy services. The Cache/Proxy On-Demand and Cache/Proxy Broadcast sections show information based on the type of publication point on the origin server. You can manage these settings independently. For example, you can deny new connections for on-demand content while still allowing new clients to access broadcast streams. The Monitor tab provides performance statistics and configuration information. (See Figure 8-37.)

You can also configure settings for both types of cache/proxy points on the Properties tab. As with publishing points, you can configure categories such as Authorization, Authentication, and Limits.

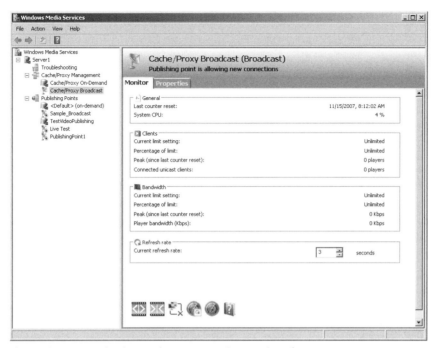

Figure 8-37 Monitoring cache/proxy settings and performance

Protecting Media by Using DRM

Organizations that provide valuable content to their users need to ensure that the information is used as it was intended. For example, if a user is able to save a copy of a video file on her computer, she should be restricted from sending it to other users or posting it on a Web site without the permission of the content provider. Digital Rights Management (DRM) enables content providers and content authors to limit the distribution of their information. You can protect content by several methods.

Using a Third-Party DRM Partner

Windows Media Services provides an extensible architecture that enables you to add plug-ins easily to provide DRM functionality. These plug-ins are available from third-party organizations that specialize in content protection. For more information about these organizations, visit the Microsoft Windows Media DRM Partners Web site at *http://www.microsoft.com/windows /windowsmedia/forpros/drm/9series/providers.aspx.*

Using Active Directory Rights Management Services

Windows Server 2008 includes a server role called Active Directory Rights Management Services (AD RMS). This server role allows a computer running Windows Server 2008 to issue licenses for creating and protecting content such as media files and documents. To use this infrastructure, content creation applications must be compatible with RMS. Compatible applications include Microsoft Office System 2003 and Microsoft Office 2007. You can also use RMS features through Internet Explorer. For more information about AD RMS, search for Active Directory Rights Management on the Microsoft TechNet Web site at *http://technet.microsoft.com*.

Other Content Protection Methods

There are also other methods of protecting digital audio and video content. For example, you can implement Web-based authentication and authorization to ensure that only registered users are permitted to access the content. You can also use network security devices such as firewalls to prevent direct access to content files. Overall, the goal of DRM involves several components that must be configured to ensure that only authorized users can access and use content.

Quick Check

1. Which type of publishing point should you create if you want to enable users to select and stream items from a large library of audio and video files?
2. How can you increase the scalability of a Windows Media Services publishing point that is experiencing network-related bottlenecks frequently?

Quick Check Answers

1. An on-demand publishing point will enable users to request the media they wish to access at any time and will allow them to fast-forward, pause, and replay the content.
2. Configure additional Streaming Media Services servers as cache/proxy servers to reduce the load on the origin server.

PRACTICE Configuring the Windows Media Services Server Role

In this practice, you will install and configure the Streaming Media Services server role on a computer running Windows Server 2008. You must complete the steps in Exercise 1 before you start the steps in Exercise 2.

▶ **Exercise 1 Install the Streaming Media Services Server Role**

In this exercise, you will use Server Manager to add the Streaming Media Services server role to Server2.contoso.com. The steps assume that you have already downloaded and installed the necessary Windows Media Services update package as described in the "Installing Streaming Media Services" section of this lesson. You should also have installed the Web Server (IIS) server role on the local computer. If you have not already done so, you will be prompted to add the necessary role and role services during the installation process.

1. Log on to Server2 as a user who has Administrator permissions.

2. Open Server Manager, right-click the Roles object, and select Add Roles. Click Next if the Before You Begin page is shown.

3. On the Select Server Roles page, select Streaming Media Services. Click Next to continue.

4. Read the Introduction To Streaming Media Services content, and then click Next to continue.

    Note that you can also access more details about configuring this server role by clicking the links in the Description section.

5. On the Select Role Services page, select all three role services: Windows Media Server, Web-Based Administration, and Logging Agent. Click Next to continue.

6. On the Select Data Transfer Protocols page, leave the default settings. Note that you will be unable to add the HTTP protocol if an existing Web site is already bound to HTTP port 80 on the local server. Click Next to continue.

7. If prompted, follow the instructions required to add the necessary components of the Web Server (IIS) server role. For more information about this role and its associated role services, see Chapter 5 "Installing and Configuring Web Applications."

8. Verify the summary of options you have selected, and then click Install to begin the installation process. When the installation finishes, click Close.

9. In Server Manager, expand the Roles object and select Streaming Media Services. Note the Events, System Services, Role Services, and Resources And Support information that is available. When you are finished, close Server Manager.

10. Launch Windows Media Services from the Administrative Tools program group. The console will automatically connect to the local Windows Media Services service. You can expand the server object to view the default configuration of the server. When you are finished, close the Windows Media Services console.

11. Open Windows Explorer, and browse to the *%SystemDrive%*\Wmpub folder. Note the default content located here. The wmroot folder contains sample files that you can use for testing purposes.

12. When you are finished, close Windows Explorer, and log off the server.

▶ **Exercise 2 Create and Test a New Publishing Point**

In this exercise, you will create a new Windows Media Services publishing point. The publishing point will provide on-demand access to several of the sample media files that were included with the default Streaming Media Services server role. You will then test access to content by connecting to a video file, using Internet Explorer. To perform the test, you must have installed the Windows Desktop Experience feature on the local computer.

1. Log on to Server2 as a user with Administrator permissions.

2. Open Windows Explorer and create a copy of the wmroot folder within the *%SystemDrive%*\Wmpub folder. Rename the copied folder to **ContosoVideos**. This folder will serve as the root folder for a new publishing point. When you are finished, close Windows Explorer.

3. Open the Windows Media Services console from the Administrator Tools program group.

4. Expand the Server2 object, right-click Publishing Points, and select Add Publishing Point (Wizard).

5. Click Next to begin the Add Publishing Point Wizard.

6. For the Publishing Point Name, type **ContosoVideos**. Click Next.

7. For the Content Type, select Files (Digital Media Or Playlists), and then click Next.

8. For the Publishing Point Type, select On-Demand Publishing Point.

   This will enable users to access any of the available videos (assuming that they have the appropriate permissions) and to control playback while they are receiving the stream. Click Next.

9. On the Directory Location page, select the path to the folder that you created in step 2. Select the Enable Access To Directory Content Using Wildcards option. This will enable users to type the name of a video manually to access it directly from the server. Click Next.

10. On the Content Playback page, leave the default option selection, and then click Next.

11. On the Unicast Logging page, leave the default option selection, and then click Next.

12. Verify the details on the Publishing Point Summary page, and then click Next to continue.

13. On the final step of the Add Publishing Point Wizard, keep the default options selected, and then click Finish.

14. The Unicast Announcement Wizard will open automatically after the publishing point is created. Click Next to start the wizard.

15. On the On-Demand Directory page, click the Browse button to select the serverside_playlist.wsx file in the folder that you created in step 2. Click Next.

16. On the Access The Content page, note the URL that you can use to access the content. You will use this in a later step to test the announcement. Click Next.

17. On the Save Announcement Options page, keep the default path. This is the location of Default Web Site, installed with the Web Server (IIS) server role. Also, select the option to create a Web page, and use the default setting. Click Next to continue.

18. On the Edit Announcement Metadata page, type **Contoso Training** for the title. Click Next.

19. On the final page of the Unicast Announcement Wizard, verify that the Test Files When This Wizard Finishes option is selected, and then click Finish.

20. In the Test Unicast Announcement dialog box, click the first Test button to test the Announcement directly. This should launch Windows Media Player and automatically start playing the video from the publishing point. When the video is finished, close Windows Media Player.

21. In the Test Unicast Announcement dialog box, click the second Test button to access a Web page that contains an embedded browser. Verify that the video plays properly, and then close Internet Explorer.

22. When you are finished, click the Exit button in the Test Unicast Announcement dialog box. Then, close the Windows Media Services console.

Lesson Summary

- Windows Media Services is designed to provide users with access to live and on-demand audio and video streams.

- The Streaming Media Services server role includes MMC-based and Web-based administrative tools.

- Multicast streaming can reduce bandwidth requirements on networks that support it.

- You can create multiple publishing points on a Windows Media Services server to provide access to different types of content.

- Cache/proxy servers can improve the performance and scalability of Windows Media Services servers.

- You can secure access to publishing points by using Authorization and Authentication plug-in settings.

■ Digital Rights Management (DRM) technology enables content producers to protect their intellectual property by retaining control of when and how the media is used.

Lesson Review

You can use the following questions to test your knowledge of the information in Lesson 1, "Configuring Windows Media Services." The questions are also available on the companion CD if you prefer to review them in electronic form.

NOTE Answers

Answers to these questions and explanations of why each answer choice is correct or incorrect are located in the "Answers" section at the end of the book.

---

1. You are a Windows Server 2008 systems administrator responsible for configuring the Streaming Media Services server role. Your organization would like to make numerous human resources training videos available for access by its employees. Employees should be able to pause and fast-forward content as needed. You also want to ensure that users can access the content only while they are connected to your company's LAN. Which actions should you take? (Choose two. Each correct answer presents part of the complete solution.)

   A. Create a new broadcast publishing point.

   B. Create a new on-demand publishing point.

   C. Enable WMS IP Address Authorization for the publishing point.

   D. Enable WMS Negotiate Authentication for the publishing point.

   E. Enable WMS NTFS ACL Authorization for the publishing point.

2. You are a Windows Media Services administrator responsible for configuring the Streaming Media Services server role for access by the public over the Internet. You currently have 200 large video files in a folder that is used by four publishing points on the server. You want to provide users with access to only 100 files, which are training videos. You have created a new on-demand publishing point that uses the folder containing the videos as its root folder. You also want to minimize the amount of storage space used on the server. Users should be able to access any of the 100 training videos on demand without providing credentials. Which of the following actions should you take?

   A. Run the Unicast Announcement Wizard to create an HTML page that provides access to the content.

   B. Enable WMS NTFS ACL Authorization for the Web site and set up the appropriate file system permissions.

    C. Copy the training videos to another folder and modify the root folder of the publishing point.

    D. Disable WMS Anonymous Authentication for the publishing point.

    E. Create a new Wrapper Playlist that includes only the training videos.

3. You are a Windows Server 2008 systems administrator responsible for providing access to a large volume of video files to registered users of your organization's public Web site. All the video files are located within the D:\Public\Videos folder. Content producers often create and modify these videos. Recently, users have complained that they are experiencing poor performance when accessing videos during busy times. During these times, the Windows Media Services server that hosts the content is experiencing high CPU and network bandwidth use. You want to minimize the administrative time and effort required to increase performance. Which of the following actions should you take to resolve the problem?

    A. Copy the training videos to another folder on the Windows Media Services server.

    B. Install the Streaming Media Services server role on additional servers, and configure them as caching servers.

    C. Install the Streaming Media Services server role on additional servers, and configure them as proxy servers.

    D. Enable the Limit Outgoing Distribution Connections option in the properties of the publishing point.

Chapter Review

To further practice and reinforce the skills you learned in this chapter, you can perform the following tasks:

- Review the chapter summary.
- Review the list of key terms introduced in this chapter.
- Complete the case scenarios. These scenarios set up real-world situations involving the topics of this chapter and ask you to create a solution.
- Complete the suggested practices.
- Take a practice test.

Chapter Summary

- Streaming Media Services in Windows Server 2008 provides a scalable method of delivery of on-demand and broadcast audio and video content to users.
- A Windows Media Services server can host many publishing points to provide access to different types of content.
- You can configure cache and proxy servers to improve the performance of Windows Media Services server installations.

Key Terms

Do you know what these key terms mean? You can check your answers by looking up the terms in the glossary at the end of the book.

- Active Directory Rights Management Services (AD RMS)
- Digital Rights Management (DRM)
- interstitial advertisements
- publishing points
- Real-Time Streaming Protocol (RTSP)
- Streaming Media Services (server role)
- Windows Media Load Simulator 9 Series utility
- Windows Media server announcements
- Windows Media server broadcast
- Windows Media server cache/proxy server
- Windows Media server playlist

- Windows Media server plug-ins
- Windows Media Services
- Windows Media Services multicast
- Windows Media Services unicast
- wrapper playlist advertisements

Case Scenarios

In the following case scenarios, you will apply what you've learned in this chapter. You can find answers to these questions in the "Answers" section at the end of this book.

Case Scenario 1: Protecting Streaming Media Content

You are a Windows Server 2008 systems administrator who works for a company that provides IT training services. Your company has recently decided to make training videos avaialble to registered students who are actively enrolled in a specific course. Users should have access only to training videos related to the classes for which they are currently enrolled. Students are given Windows user accounts within your organization's training Active Directory domain. They should be able to access any of the videos at any time and should be able to control the playback. Your training company would like to display a brief splash introduction before the playback of every video.

1. Which type of publishing point should you create to provide access to the media?
2. How can you restrict students' access to only the training videos that are relevant to them?
3. What is the easiest method of implementing the introduction to each video?

Case Scenario 2: Improving Windows Media Services Performance and Scalability

Your organization provides access to streamed audio content to paid users over the Internet. You have configured a single computer running Windows Server 2008 with the Streaming Media Services server role. Initially, this server was able to meet users' demands. However, recently, several thousand additional users have registered for the service, and some are reporting slow playback or other performance problems during certain times of the day. For security and management reasons, you want to avoid manually moving or copying the audio content from the current Windows Media Services server. Your organization also plans to provide access to a live music concert within the next month and would like to support as many client connections as possible.

1. Which type of publishing point should you create for the live music event?
2. How can you reduce the bandwidth requirements for the live event without including additional Windows Media Services servers?
3. How can you configure additional Windows Media Services servers to improve scalability?

Suggested Practices

To help you successfully master the exam objectives presented in this chapter, complete the following tasks.

Configure Windows Media Services

The items in this section will enable you to practice configuring and managing the Streaming Media Services role in Windows Server 2008 and help you learn about creating new publishing points on a Windows Media Services server.

- **Practice 1**   Create an on-demand publishing point and provide access to a playlist that includes multiple audio and video files. (You can use the sample media files included with the Streaming Media Services server role if you do not have access to other files.)

  Configure one of the videos to play automatically by creating a wrapper advertisement before any content is sent to users.

  Using a Web browser, start playback of content to verify that it is accessible. If you have multiple computers available, attempt to access the video from them simultaneously to test the effects of multiple concurrent connections.

  Access the publishing point's Monitor tab to view statistics and details related to the content playback.

- **Practice 2**   Install the Streaming Media Services server role on two computers running Windows Server 2008. Configure one of the servers with an on-demand publishing point.

  Use the Windows Media Load Simulator utility to test the performance and scalability of your Windows Media Services server. Attempt to simulate a large number of connections and use the Monitor tab in the properties of the publishing point to view access statistics.

  Configure the second Windows Media Services server as a cache/proxy server for the publishing point you created on the first Windows Media Services server.

  Repeat the Windows Media Load Simulator tests to measure performance and to see from which server the content is being served.

  Optionally, configure Limits settings in the properties of the publishing point, and measure the effects on the Windows Media Load Simulator tests.

Take a Practice Test

The practice tests on this book's companion CD offer many options. For example, you can test yourself on just one exam objective, or you can test yourself on all the 70-643 certification exam content. You can set up the test so that it closely simulates the experience of taking a certification exam, or you can set it up in study mode so that you can look at the correct answers and explanations after you answer each question.

MORE INFO   Practice tests

For details about all the practice test options available, see the "How to Use the Practice Tests" section in this book's introduction.

Chapter 9

Configuring Windows SharePoint Services

One of the many ways a server operating system can help users meet their goals is through collaboration support. Microsoft Windows SharePoint Services (WSS) has been designed to provide users with a way to share, modify, and discuss a wide variety of content. It provides features for centrally creating common types of information, including announcements, tasks, and reminders. Application developers can also use WSS as a platform for their own Web-based programs.

The Windows Server 2008 operating system supports Windows SharePoint Services as a server role that can be deployed quickly and easily into a production environment. In this chapter, you'll learn about configuring WSS. Details include setting up and managing new SharePoint sites and managing operations for a SharePoint server.

Exam objectives in this chapter:
- Configuring Network Application Services
  - ❏ Configure Microsoft Windows SharePoint Services server options.
  - ❏ Configure Windows SharePoint Services e-mail integration.

Lessons in this chapter:

Before You Begin

To complete the lesson in this chapter, you must have:

- Added the Web Server (IIS) server role to Server2.contoso.com, using the default options. For more information on installing this role, see Chapter 5, "Installing and Configuring Web Applications."

Lesson 1: Configuring and Managing Windows SharePoint Services

The primary purpose of WSS is to provide an environment in which users can collaborate by sharing information and documents. Organizations can use WSS as the basis for a company intranet Web site or to facilitate information sharing within and between teams and departments. The Web-based user interface is designed to be quick and easy to learn and offers simple browser-based access from throughout the organization. Many applications, such as those in the Microsoft Office suite, provide integration with WSS for managing and editing documents. WSS is also a platform that developers can use to write their own Web-based applications based on specific business needs.

Because WSS is a platform that enables a wide range of usage scenarios, it is important to configure various options and settings after installation. After you have installed the Windows SharePoint Services server role, you can make several configuration changes, using the SharePoint Central Administration Web site. In this lesson, you'll learn about the options and features that are available and how they should be used.

MORE INFO   Installing Windows SharePoint Services

At the time of this writing, Microsoft has not yet finalized the installation and configuration process for Windows SharePoint Services 3.0 on Windows Server 2008. WSS is not included as a default server role in Windows Server 2008 and must be downloaded and installed separately. Some portions of this chapter include assumptions based on the expected behavior of WSS 3.0. Be aware, however, that some changes might be made prior to the final release of the operating system. When practicing for Exam 70-643, remember that the exam objectives focus on configuring WSS based on requirements rather than on installation of the product. For more information about downloading and installing Windows SharePoint Services on Windows Server 2008, visit the Microsoft TechNet Windows SharePoint Services TechCenter at *http://technet.microsoft.com/en-us /windowsserver/sharepoint/default.aspx*.

After this lesson, you will be able to:
- Explain the purpose of Windows SharePoint Services (WSS).
- Describe the difference between a standalone deployment and a server farm deployment of WSS.
- Complete WSS configuration tasks, using the SharePoint Central Administration Web site.
- Manage WSS operations settings related to security, e-mail, and logging.
- Perform backup and recovery operations for SharePoint sites.
- Deploy and configure new SharePoint sites.
- Manage Web application settings for SharePoint sites.

Estimated lesson time: 60 minutes

Understanding Windows SharePoint Services

Windows Server 2008 includes support for Windows SharePoint Services (WSS) 3.0. Users interact with WSS, using Web sites that are hosted using Internet Information Services (IIS). Although IT professionals are usually responsible for setting up the initial server configuration, knowledgeable users can maintain content and information on WSS sites. For example, a department or group within the organization can create its own portal site or team workspace for communicating with others. Specific features and types of information that can be hosted include:

- Announcements
- Shared documents
- Calendars
- Tasks
- Discussions
- Links
- Contact information

Figure 9-1 shows an overview of the user interface of WSS.

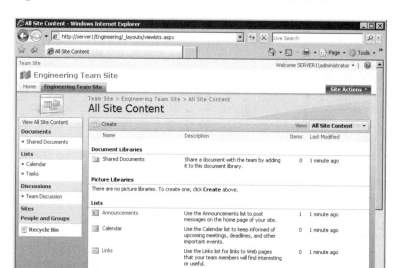

Figure 9-1 Accessing a Windows SharePoint Services team site by using a Web browser

Users can manage all this information directly, and it can be secured through security permissions. Users can use e-mail to receive notifications of content changes and to get information into and out of WSS. Presence-awareness features can also help distributed teams keep in touch by using instant messaging and other applications. WSS has also been designed as an extensible platform that can be used by applications developers to create new functionality. Overall, these features and capabilities offer an easy way for teams and departments to share information and collaborate.

MORE INFO Other SharePoint Services products

Windows SharePoint Services 3.0 (the same version that is included with Windows Server 2008) is also available as a free download for the Microsoft Windows Server 2003 SP1 platform. In addition, Microsoft offers a full-feature, server-side collaboration product called Microsoft Office SharePoint Server 2007. SharePoint Server 2007 provides additional features such as support for user profiles, single sign-on, personal sites, and many other features. For more information about these technologies, see *http://www.microsoft.com/sharepoint/default.mspx*.

Understanding WSS Deployment Options

WSS has been designed to support a broad variety of scenarios. From a systems administration standpoint, it's important to balance the ease of deployment against other features such as scalability. To meet different needs, WSS has two main types of deployment options: a standalone configuration and a server farm configuration. Both options are available when adding the Windows SharePoint Services server role. In this section, you'll learn about these different ways of deploying SharePoint.

Deploying WSS in a Standalone Configuration

The simplest method of getting up and running with WSS is to use a single server configuration. In the standalone deployment option, WSS is designed to use a single server that hosts all necessary components and services on the local computer.

The primary method of interacting with WSS is by using a Web browser. IIS is required to host the primary WSS user site and the SharePoint Central Administration Web site. The architecture of WSS requires the .NET Framework 3.0 feature to be installed on the computer. For data storage, the standalone configuration uses Windows Internal Database. This database has been designed to store operating system–related data including WSS content. The database itself is based on the Microsoft SQL Server technology.

By running all these services on the same computer, you can complete the setup and deployment process very quickly. Other than the server roles and features that are added automatically, there are no additional system requirements or necessary configuration steps. You perform additional setup using the SharePoint Central Administration Web site.

The primary drawback to a standalone configuration, however, is that a standalone configuration does not support multiple servers for scalability in larger environments.

Deploying WSS in a Server Farm Configuration

In many organizations, collaboration features become an important part of the infrastructure. Because WSS provides many useful features, scalability is an important consideration. The architecture of WSS enables systems administrators to divide the front-end functionality (the user and administration Web sites) from the back-end data storage (the WSS database). This deployment option is known as a *server farm configuration*.

In a server farm, multiple WSS front-end servers can connect to a back-end database server that hosts copies of all documents, settings, and related data. This helps organizations increase performance and provide access in a variety of scenarios. For example, it allows for creating an extranet scenario that third-party users and organizations (such as business partners or consulting partners) can use. In addition, remote offices might choose to have their own WSS servers for performance and accessibility reasons.

The basic system requirements are identical to those of adding the Windows SharePoint Services in a standalone configuration, with the exception of the Windows Internal Database. To deploy into a server farm configuration, a SharePoint database must already exist on a computer running either Microsoft SQL Server 2000 or SQL Server 2005. Although this process adds additional steps to the overall setup process, it enables organizations to have database administrators (DBAs) set up the databases and to use existing SQL Server installations for hosting the database.

The standard setup process is first to install and configure the required databases on a computer running SQL Server. Depending on the security and performance requirements for the deployment, SQL Server may be installed and configured on one of the computers that is running WSS. The next step is to add the Windows SharePoint Services server role to all the WSS front-end servers. Although additional servers can be added later, it is best to add the role to all the servers that will be part of the initial deployment. The SharePoint Central Administration Web site will be installed and configured on the first server that is to be part of the server farm.

Exam Tip   When preparing for Exam 70-643, it is important for you to understand the technical differences between a standalone and a server farm deployment of Windows SharePoint Services. A server farm configuration includes additional dependencies and requirements such as access to SQL Server. If you are not familiar with using SQL Server, focus on the setup and configuration steps for a standalone WSS deployment. Other than the initial setup, all the remaining configuration steps are similar.

Overall, the server farm deployment option is a more advanced configuration of WSS and requires additional planning and coordination.

Using the SharePoint Products and Technologies Configuration Wizard

Once the initial front-end WSS server roles have been added, administrators can use the SharePoint Products And Technologies Configuration Wizard to configure server options further. The configuration process performs the steps required to set up the WSS database and Web servers. (See Figure 9-2.) You can also use the wizard to repair an installation of WSS if the site is inaccessible or has encountered errors. When working in a server farm configuration, details include specifying the location and logon information for the database server that will be used for the server farm.

Figure 9-2   Using the SharePoint Products And Technologies Configuration Wizard

MORE INFO   **WSS and Windows Web Server 2008**

Although you can install and use WSS on Windows Web Server 2008, the license terms for this operating system restrict you to creating only public Internet sites. Therefore, you cannot use Web edition to create portals or team sites for use in intranet or extranet environments. In addition, you cannot deploy a standalone configuration of WSS by using this edition. For more information about editions, see the Microsoft Windows Server 2008 Web site at *http://www.microsoft.com /windowsserver2008/default.mspx*.

Verifying the WSS Installation

Once you have completed the installation of the Windows SharePoint Services (WSS) role, you can use Server Manager and Windows Internet Explorer to verify settings. In this section, you will learn how to ensure that the site is accessible.

Verify Server Roles and Settings

To get an overview of information about the Windows SharePoint Services server role, open Server Manager, expand the Roles section, and then click Windows SharePoint Services. As shown in Figure 9-3, you will be able to see various details about the status of WSS.

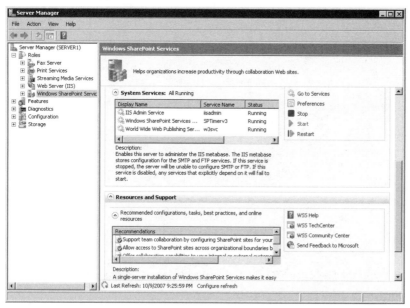

Figure 9-3 Using Server Manager to view information about the Windows SharePoint Services server role

The Events section shows event log information that is relevant to WSS. Review this information periodically to detect any configuration details or operational errors that might require attention.

The System Services section shows the main services related to WSS. If you are running in a single server installation, you will see several services. (See Table 9-1.) Optionally, you can start or stop particular services as needed.

Table 9-1   WSS System Services and Their Descriptions

Display Name	Service Name	Description
IIS Admin Service	iisadmin	Used to store and manage configuration information related to SMTP-related and FTP-related settings.
Windows SharePoint Services Timer	SPTimerv3	Used to perform scheduled tasks and to send notifications that are configured in the SharePoint Central Administration Web site. If the service is stopped, scheduled tasks and notifications will fail.

Table 9-1 WSS System Services and Their Descriptions

Display Name	Service Name	Description
World Wide Web Publishing Service	W3SVC	The HTTP server component of IIS that enables the SharePoint Web sites to accept connections and process requests. If this service is stopped, users and administrators will be unable to connect to the WSS, using a Web browser.

The Resources And Support section in Server Manager provides additional helpful information about configuring settings for WSS.

Verifying WSS Web Sites

As mentioned earlier in this lesson, when the Windows SharePoint Services server role is added to the computer, the installation process creates two new IIS Web sites. They are:

- **SharePoint – 80**   This is the primary Web site users of WSS will access with their Web browser. (See Figure 9-4.) It is created to respond on port 80 by default. Once the site has been created, users can use *http://ServerName* to access WSS.

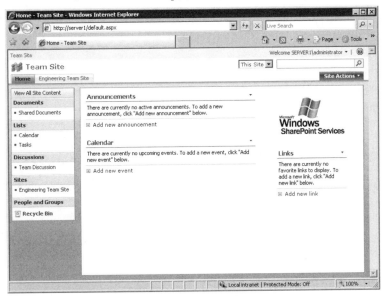

Figure 9-4   Accessing the SharePoint Web site

■ **SharePoint Central Administration v3** This Web site is designed to enable SharePoint administrators to configure WSS-related options. Examples include e-mail settings, user permissions, and settings for individual SharePoint sites.

Note that the server role installation process automatically will stop any other IIS site that is configured to use port 80 on the local server. This is necessary because IIS does not allow multiple sites to be running concurrently on the same HTTP port without the use of unique host headers. If the local server is hosting another Web site or Web application, consider changing its port settings to ensure that users will still be able to access it. For more information about configuring IIS, see Chapter 5.

Quick Check

1. What are the role and feature dependencies for installing Windows SharePoint Services in standalone (single server) configuration mode?
2. What are the advantages of installing Windows SharePoint Services in a server farm configuration?

Quick Check Answers

1. WSS requires the .NET Framework 3.0 feature, the Web Server (IIS) role, the Windows Process Activation Service feature, and the Windows Internal Database feature.
2. A server farm configuration enables multiple WSS Web servers to connect to back-end database servers. This helps increase scalability for larger deployments or for supporting extranet scenarios.

Using the SharePoint Central Administration Web Site

The primary systems administration tool for WSS is the SharePoint Central Administration Web site. If you have added the Windows SharePoint Services server role using the default options, you can access this site by opening a browser and navigating to *http://ServerName:PortNumber*. The site includes sections for managing the configuration of the server and for performing important tasks such as creating new sites for access by users.

Completing Administrator Tasks

The first time you connect to the site, you will be presented with a list of administrator tasks. The default items are ranked based on a suggested priority value of each task. They are:

- READ FIRST – Click this link for deployment instructions.
- Incoming e-mail settings.
- Outgoing e-mail settings.
- Create SharePoint sites.
- Configure workflow settings.
- Central Administration application pool account should be unique.
- Diagnostic logging settings.
- Add antivirus protection.

It is recommended that you complete these steps before allowing users to connect to the SharePoint Web site. To view more details about each task, click the link. As shown in Figure 9-5, you will be able to see additional details related to configuration options.

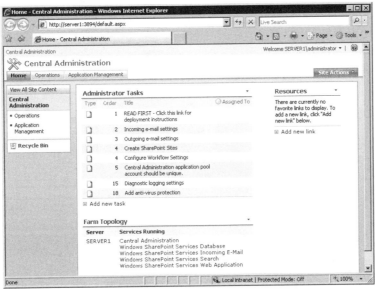

Figure 9-5 Viewing details about an administrator task in the SharePoint Central Administration Web site

Once you have completed a task, you can delete it so it no longer appears in the list. Note that the Action setting in some items provides a link that will take you directly to the appropriate configuration pages. You can also navigate to the pages manually.

Navigating the Central Administration Web Site

Although the Administrator Tasks list provides a quick overview of the most common operations performed as part of the deployment process, the SharePoint Central Administration Web site contains many additional options. The Web site is divided into two main areas. The first area is the Operations tab, which includes settings and tasks related to configuring and managing WSS. (See Figure 9-6.)

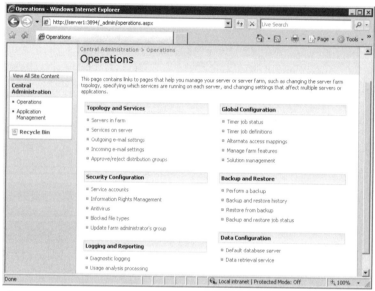

Figure 9-6   Viewing Operations items in the SharePoint Central Administration Web Site

The specific areas and their purposes are:

- **Topology and Services**   Defines the configuration of a server farm and manages e-mail–related settings
- **Security Configuration**   Manages service accounts, antivirus settings, and other security-related settings
- **Logging and Reporting**   Enables administrators to enable logging for troubleshooting and for monitoring site usage statistics
- **Global Configuration**   Settings related to scheduled jobs, managing solutions, and Web site mappings for the WSS Web site
- **Backup and Restore**   Provides the ability to perform backups, restore from backups, and monitor the status of backup jobs
- **Data Configuration**   Enables administrators to specify connection information for the database server that will be used by WSS

The second area of the SharePoint Central Administration Web site is the Application Management tab. (See Figure 9-7.)

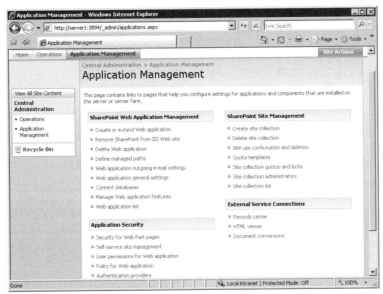

Figure 9-7   Viewing the Application Management tab on the SharePoint Central Administration Web site

These settings are related to the creation and management of SharePoint Web Applications. The areas include:

- **SharePoint Web Application Management**   Enables creation of new Web applications or configuration of other application-specific settings
- **Application Security**   Enables configuration of security settings, including permissions and authentication methods for a Web application
- **Workflow Management**   Enables configuration of workflow feature settings
- **SharePoint Site Management**   Tasks related to creating, deleting, and managing collections of SharePoint sites
- **External Service Connections**   Provides options related to the HTML Viewer, to Document Conversions, and to the Records Center

Although some of these options might appear similar to those on the Operations tab, it is important to note that tasks on the Application Management tab relate to specific WSS sites (rather than to the WSS server as a whole). You'll learn more about configuring many of these settings throughout the remainder of this lesson.

Exam Tip A good way to learn about the types of configuration options available in the Share-Point Central Administration Web site is to click each link. Many sections provide explanatory text and additional details that can help you determine which options are relevant to your deployment. It will also help prepare you for Exam 70-643 by familiarizing you with options for each setting.

Managing SharePoint Operations Settings

Once WSS is up and running, users can perform many content-related tasks by themselves. Before you enable users to access the site, however, there are some administrative settings you will want to review or change. In this section, you'll learn about the most important features and settings related to managing a WSS-enabled server.

Managing Security Settings

An important aspect of security is ensuring that applications and services run under the minimal permission they require to meet business and technical requirements. When you add the Windows SharePoint Services server role to the computer, several services are added to the local server. Each service uses a default account. The default settings for a standalone configuration are shown in Table 9-2.

Table 9-2 Windows SharePoint Services Default Account Settings

Service Name	Default Account	Startup Type
Windows SharePoint Services Administration	Local System	Manual
Windows SharePoint Services Search	Local Service	Manual
Windows SharePoint Services Timer	Network Service	Automatic
Windows SharePoint Services Tracing	Local Service	Automatic
Windows SharePoint Services VSS Writer	Local System	Manual

You can change the service account settings by using the Services console, but the preferred method is to configure settings within the SharePoint Central Administration Web site. Figure 9-8 shows the Service Accounts task and the available options. By default, each SharePoint site is configured in its own application pool. (For more information about IIS application pools, see Chapter 5.) You can change the security settings for each site by assigning it to a built-in account (such as Network Service or Local Service) or by providing a username and password. Specific local or domain accounts might be required, for example, if you require the site to have access to other servers in the environment.

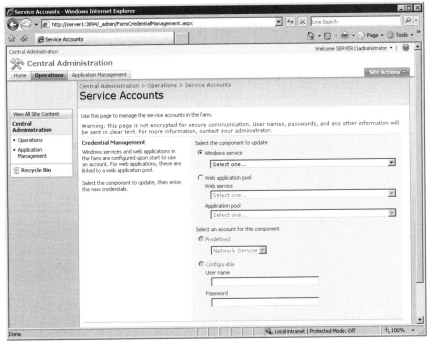

Figure 9-8   Managing Service Account settings in the SharePoint Central Administration Web site

One of the potential risks related to collaboration in network environments is the possibility of users uploading unwanted files or files that are infected with viruses. Although WSS does not include a built-in antivirus program, it is possible to use a third-party application to scan files automatically as they are transferred to and from the SharePoint site.

In addition, you can improve security by configuring the Blocked File Types option. (See Figure 9-9.) These restrictions help ensure that only valid types of files are uploaded. For example, many common script formats (such as VBScript) are blocked by default. Although it is possible for users to change file extensions, these settings help prevent users from downloading and automatically executing these types of files.

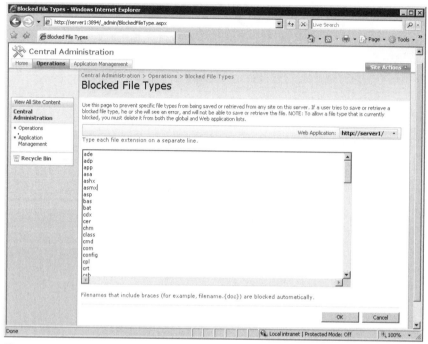

Figure 9-9   Configuring Blocked File Types by using the SharePoint Central Administration Web site

Configuring E-Mail Settings

WSS uses standard SMTP-based e-mail to send notifications and to send and receive messages. Although you are given the opportunity to provide e-mail server and address information during the Windows SharePoint Services server role installation process, you can leave the information blank. You might also need to change the settings after WSS has been installed, due to changes in your network environment. The Outgoing E-Mail Settings link on the Operations tab enables you to add or change these details. (See Figure 9-10.)

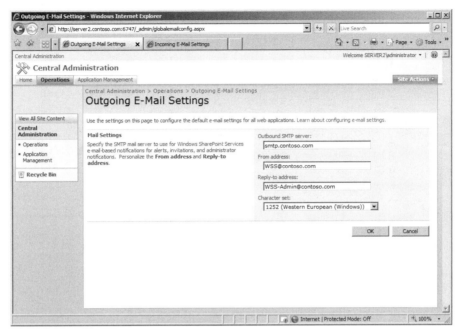

Figure 9-10   Configuring outgoing settings for WSS

In addition to sending e-mail, WSS also enables you to receive e-mail from users. By default, this feature is disabled. To enable it, click the Incoming E-Mail Settings link. Figure 9-11 shows the available options.

There are two main methods by which you can configure e-mail settings. The Automatic mode uses settings that you have defined in the outgoing e-mail settings page. (Specifically, it uses the SMTP server that you have defined.) If you have not defined this setting or if you do not want to use an SMTP server, you can choose the Advanced option. This setting requires you to specify a file system location in which new messages will be stored. You can also specify whether you wish to use the Directory Management Service for allowing access to e-mail distribution groups. For more information about configuring SMTP server settings, see Chapter 7, "Configuring FTP and SMTP Services." If you are running in an Active Directory directory services environment, this is a useful feature for identifying incoming messages.

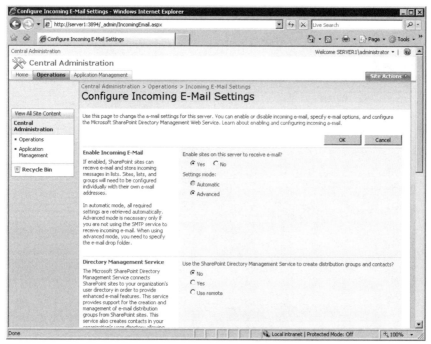

Figure 9-11   Configuring incoming e-mail settings for WSS

After you have enabled incoming e-mail for a WSS server, you can configure document libraries to accept incoming messages. To do this, access a SharePoint site, and open a document
library. On the Settings menu, click Document Library Settings, and then select the Incoming
E-Mail Settings link in the Communications section. The Incoming E-Mail Settings: Shared
Documents page provides settings for enabling e-mail and configuring how attachments will
be handled. (See Figure 9-12.)

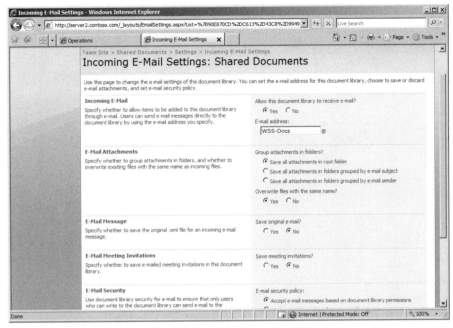

Figure 9-12   Configuring incoming e-mail settings for WSS

Managing Settings for Logging

Systems administrators are responsible for ensuring that WSS can take advantage of built-in logging and reporting functionality. The Diagnostic Logging page (shown in Figure 9-13) provides options for how and when events are recorded. By default, the collection or error reports are enabled. These reports are created automatically when serious WSS-related errors occur. Examples include hardware failures, missing critical files, or software configuration issues.

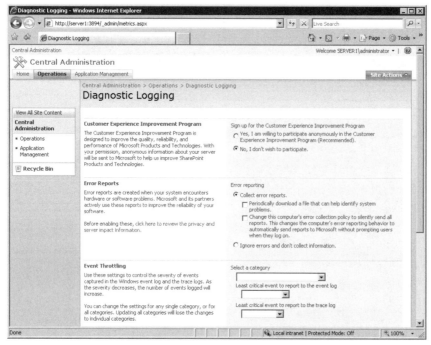

Figure 9-13   Managing Diagnostic Logging settings, using the SharePoint Central Administration Web site

Because busy SharePoint sites can generate a large number of events, the Event Throttling section enables you to specify which types of information are recorded. The category list displays the many types of events that can be monitored. These range from database-related messages to details from specific Web controls. You can change settings for one or all of the categories. Errors can be reported to the Windows event log (which can be accessed using the Event Viewer application or Server Manager), or they can be stored to trace log files.

The Least Critical Event To Report To The Event Log option includes the following options:

- None
- Error
- Warning
- Audit Failure
- Audit Success
- Information

The Least Critical Event To Report To The Trace Log option provides the following options:

- None
- Unexpected
- Monitorable
- High
- Medium
- Verbose

Although the default settings are useful for logging the most important issues, these settings can be helpful when troubleshooting specific problems. For example, if you suspect that there is a potential reliability issue with the Backup And Restore category, you can configure detailed logging to address those events. Finally, the Trace Log section enables you to specify how many log files will be created and how many should be retained. This helps achieve a balance between disk space use and manageability of the log files. The default file system location for the log files is *%Program Files%*\Common Files\Microsoft Shared\Web Server Extensions\12\Logs.

Enabling Usage Analysis Processing

A useful feature for systems administrators is the ability to monitor the usage of SharePoint sites. Details can help determine whether performance is adequate, or changes to the configuration might be required. For performance reasons, the Usage Analysis Processing feature is disabled by default. As shown in Figure 9-14, you can enable logging and configure the Log File Location setting based on the level of monitoring you require.

In addition to storing usage information, WSS provides the ability to process usage-related information automatically at particular points in time. Users who have the necessary permissions can view site usage reports from within specific SharePoint sites.

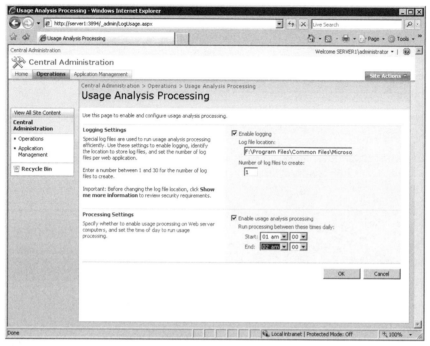

Figure 9-14   Configuring Usage Analysis Processing in the SharePoint Central Administration Web site

Viewing Timer Job Definitions

WSS uses either the Windows Internal Database (for standalone configurations) or a SQL Server database (for server farm configurations) to store data. The data stored in these databases must be maintained over time to ensure that unnecessary information is removed and to maintain overall performance. You can view details about scheduled jobs by using the Timer Job Definitions link on the Operations tab. (See Figure 9-15.) You can click individual jobs to enable or disable them if necessary.

To view a history of when jobs were executed, click the Time Job Status link. This page will show the title of each job that has been executed and includes the time the job started and whether it succeeded or failed. It is a good idea to review this information regularly to detect any potential problems.

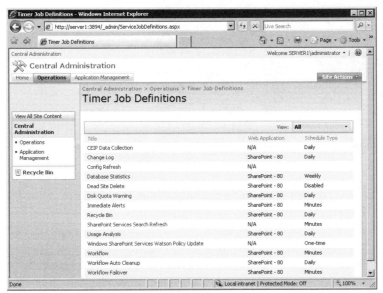

Figure 9-15   Viewing Timer Job Definitions in the SharePoint Central Administration Web site

Managing WSS Using *stsadm*

Although using the SharePoint Central Administration Web site is an intuitive and user-friendly way to manage configuration settings, it can be time-consuming to perform common operations on many WSS servers. To help automate the task, WSS includes the *stsadm.exe* command-line utility. Use this command to perform common tasks such as creating or deleting SharePoint sites or performing backups. You can use the -help switch to get more details about the syntax and operations the command can perform. Figure 9-16 shows a portion of the command usage.

Figure 9-16   Viewing help information for the *stsadm* command-line utility

By default, the *stsadm* command-line utility can be found in the folder *%ProgramFiles%*\Common Files\Microsoft Shared\Web Server Extensions\12\BIN.

Exam Tip   It might seem strange that the primary command-line utility for administering Windows SharePoint Services (WSS) is called *stsadm*. The reason for this is that earlier versions of WSS were known as SharePoint Team Services (STS). When taking the exam, remembering this fact can help you recall the purpose of this command-line utility.

Overall, *stsadm* is most useful when you need to perform the same or similar tasks on multiple computers running WSS, or if you need to script commonly performed operations. It is also useful when you do not have Web-based access to the SharePoint Central Administration Web site.

Understanding Backup and Recovery for WSS

Because users in your organization will likely depend on the data stored in SharePoint, it's important to ensure that the content and configuration is protected. The primary reason for performing backups is to prevent against data loss due to hardware failures, accidental modifications, or other issues that might arise. In this section, you'll learn about ways in which you can back up and restore SharePoint data.

Creating SharePoint Backups

The SharePoint Central Administration Web site includes features for creating and scheduling backups. To start the process, from the Operations tab, click Perform A Backup. The first step of the process requires you to select which information should be stored in the backup set. (See Figure 9-17.)

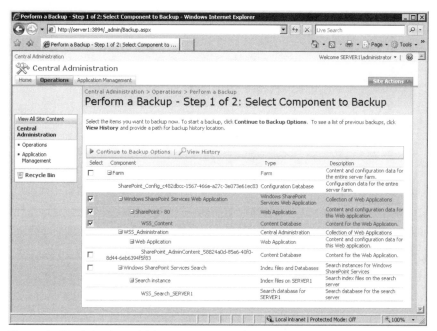

Figure 9-17   Selecting which components to be included in a backup

WSS includes many components, each of which can be included in the backup set. If you are backing up a relatively small WSS deployment or you want to ensure that all configuration and user data is protected, click the check box at the Farm level. This will select all the other components automatically. In other situations, you might want to back up only a specific site or collection of settings. You can do this by selecting only the appropriate options. Click Continue To Backup Options to specify further details.

The Start Backup page (shown in Figure 9-18) provides options for storing the backup content. The Type Of Backup section offers two options. Full backups include a copy of the latest data for all the selected components. The size of the backup will be based on the amount of content that is included on the SharePoint site. (An estimate is provided at the bottom of the screen.)

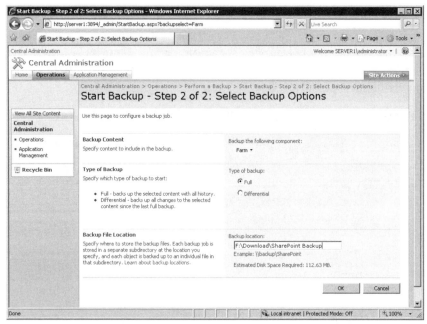

Figure 9-18 Selecting backup-related options in the Perform A Backup task

The other option is to create a differential backup. This backup will store only the data that has changed since the last full backup was performed. Although the backup storage space and resource overhead is less for a differential backup, note that you will need access to the Full and Differential backups to perform a complete restore of the WSS system.

The final setting is to specify a location for the backup. You can enter a local file system path or provide a network path to a shared folder location. To protect against permanent data loss due to storage hardware failures, backup files should be stored on another computer in the environment.

Once you have selected the appropriate options, you can click OK to schedule the backup process. The job will use the built-in timer feature in WSS to start the process as quickly as possible. Backups are performed without any downtime for the site, although users might notice a decrease in SharePoint system performance. The Backup And Restore Status page will show the progress of the job along with any additional details. The page will refresh periodically until the job is complete.

Restoring Windows SharePoint Services

There are several reasons you might need to perform a restore of SharePoint data. In some cases, a hardware failure or file system corruption might result in an unusable site, or important documents or other content might have been deleted or incorrectly modified. You can start the process by clicking the Restore From Backup link in the Operations tab. There are four steps to performing a restore operation.

- **Step 1: Select Backup Location**   This text box enables you to type the path of the local or network file system location in which the backup was stored. The default value is the path used for the last backup operation.
- **Step 2: Select Backup To Restore**   Based on the path provided in Step 1, WSS will find the backups that are stored in the location specified. If the appropriate backup is found, you can select it, and then click the Continue Restore Process link. Otherwise, you can choose Change Directory to specify a different location.
- **Step 3: Select Component To Restore**   This page will enable you to select one or more components to restore to the WSS server. The list of components will be based on which components were included in the original backup. (See Figure 9-19.) Select the appropriate items, and then click Continue Restore Process.
- **Step 4: Select Restore Options**   On this screen, you'll be able to specify the type of restore operation you wish to perform.

Figure 9-19   Specifying which components to restore

There are two options for performing the restore. The Same Configuration option is useful when you want to replace all the current components with those stored in the backup. Note that this option will result in the loss of any changes that have been made to the selected components since the time the backup was created.

The other option, New Configuration, enables you to specify an alternate configuration to which the data will be restored. This option is useful for making a new copy of the site from the backup. It is also a safer option because it will not affect the current SharePoint site. The available options will vary based on the selections you made when you created the backup. Details include the URL and Web application name for the SharePoint site. You can also choose the database server (or the Windows Internal Database if it has been installed), along with the database name and storage location. When you are ready to perform the restore operation, click OK.

Viewing Backup and Restore History

To verify that backups have been properly performed, you can click the Backup And Restore History link on the Operations tab. Figure 9-20 shows the available information. Details are displayed for the date and time of each job, the contents of the backup, the backup type, and the location of the backup files. It is also possible to start a restore process by selecting a backup and clicking Continue Restore Process.

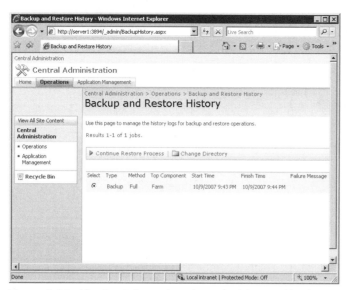

Figure 9-20   Viewing information about the history of backup and restore operations

Deploying and Configuring SharePoint Sites

Because WSS enables you to create many SharePoint sites on the same server, it is important to decide how to divide up content and users. In general, try to limit the purpose and number of users for each type of site. When a single site is used for numerous types of activity and by a wide variety of users, it can become difficult for people to find what they're looking for quickly. Further, organizing the content can become very difficult and time-consuming. In this section, you'll learn about ways in which you can create and manage sites.

Understanding Subsites and Site Collections

A *site collection* is a set of related SharePoint sites that share many settings. For example, all the sites within a site collection share the same navigation bars. This makes it easy for users to access sites within the collection without having to go to a different URL. In addition, details related to content types, search functionality, and security groups are common to all sites in the collection.

There are two main approaches to creating additional sites in WSS. Overall, it is best to add multiple sites to a single site collection if the content of each site is related and the technical requirements are similar. The other option is to create a new top-level SharePoint site in a new site collection. This approach is best used when the requirements for the new site differ significantly from settings in existing site collections. Sites in different site collections can have different configuration settings for security permissions. Other details such as search scope and quotas can be managed independently for different site collections. From operations and management standpoints, different site collections can be managed independently. Larger organizations can divide systems administration responsibilities for WSS by using multiple site collections. Also, these sites can be backed up and restored separately, enabling you to make backups more manageable.

Real World

Anil Desai

All too often, we IT professionals focus on technology rather than on how it will be used to benefit users. When deciding to deploy a product such as Windows SharePoint Services, it's important first to consider how it will be used in the production environment. The process of creating a new SharePoint site is simple, but understanding the best implementation approach can take significantly more time and effort. In some cases, it might be appropriate to just deploy a new site, allow users to access it, and see how it evolves on its own. In most cases, however, a little planning and forethought can ensure a successful deployment.

An important aspect of successful IT application and service deployments is involving affected users in the decision process. You need to understand the true objectives of employees throughout the organization. A good initial question is, "What problems are you trying to solve?" WSS has many powerful features that enable document sharing and collaboration. However, what users ask for is not always what they really want or need. Individuals might ask for a SharePoint site to be created when a similar one already exists, or they might try to use a single site to serve multiple purposes. Other considerations include the security requirements, the number of users who will use the site actively, and the volume of data expected to be hosted. You can combine this information to determine the best way to make WSS available to users. Having well-defined requirements also helps you verify whether the deployment was successful.

Take time to understand the needs and anticipated benefits of SharePoint (or of just about any IT technology, for that matter) for users. For more information and examples, see the Planning Worksheets for Windows SharePoint Services 3.0 page on Microsoft TechNet by searching for "SharePoint planning worksheets" at *http://technet.microsoft.com*.

Creating Site Collections

You can use the SharePoint Central Administration Web site to manage site collections, Web sites, and their related settings. The SharePoint Site Management section enables you to create or delete site collections. The Create Site Collection link, available from the Application Management tab, shows the options that are available. (See Figure 9-21.)

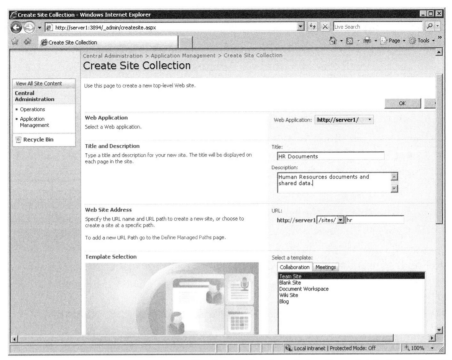

Figure 9-21   Creating a new site collection in the SharePoint Central Administration Web site

The required information includes:

- **Web Application**   This drop-down list includes all the Web applications that have been created in the SharePoint environment. If you have not yet created additional Web applications, only the default server URL will be shown.

- **Title and Description**   Use this information to identify the site collection. The title will be shown to users and administrators, and the description should include details about the purpose and intended usage of the site collection. In some cases, site collections might be based on the organizational units, such as for the Marketing or Human Resources department.

- **Web Site Address**   Each Web site created in WSS must have a unique URL. By default, a default URL path called /sites is available. The text box enables you to specify the browser link that will be used to access the site. Because users will need to type this address, in general, use an abbreviation of the site name and avoid characters such as spaces or other punctuation.

- **Template Selection**   Each new SharePoint site collection can be based on a specific template. The default templates are organized into two main categories: Collaboration and

Meetings. You can click each option to read a brief description of the purpose of the site. Later in this lesson, you'll learn how to add new templates to the server.

- **Primary Site Collection Administrator and Secondary Site Collection Administrator**   In relatively small SharePoint environments, a single systems administrator might be responsible for managing multiple sites and site collections. These sections enable you to specify which users will have permissions to manage the site collection. You can click the Browse icon to view a list of accounts available on either the local computer or the domain (if the computer is a member of a domain).

- **Quota Template**   This section enables you to select a quota template that will restrict the storage space available for the site collection. You will learn more about quota templates later in this section.

The contents and layout of the site will be based on the application template that you selected. Figure 9-22 shows an example of using the Basic Meeting Workspace template when you create a new site collection. When you click OK, WSS will perform the tasks required to create a new site collection. The resulting message will display the URL of the new top-level site. To verify that the site has been set up properly, either click the link or copy and paste it into a new browser window.

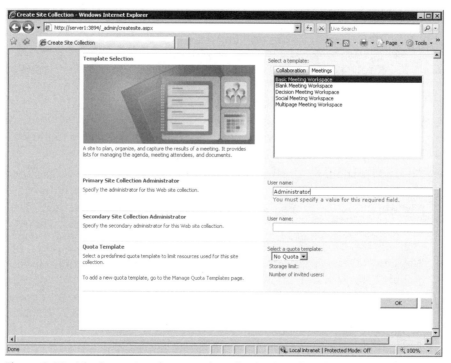

Figure 9-22   Viewing settings for a new site collection based on the Basic Meeting Workspace template

To view a list of all the site collections defined on a WSS server, click the Site Collection list on the Application Management tab. Details related to the administrator(s) for the site, along with the title and description, are available.

Defining Quota Templates

If you have experience with managing data storage, such as the contents of a file server or Microsoft Exchange Server, you know that users can consume large amounts of disk space quickly. WSS is no exception because users often upload many large documents to their sites. To help manage resource usage, you can create quota templates. These templates can then be assigned to specific SharePoint site collections. By default, no quota templates are included in the WSS configuration. Click the Quota Templates link on the Application Management to create a new one. Figure 9-23 shows the available options.

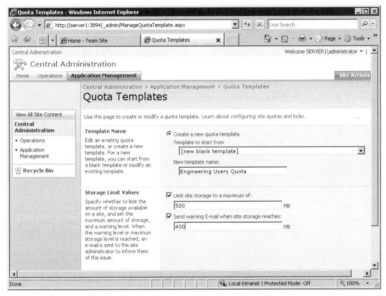

Figure 9-23   Defining a new quota template in the SharePoint Central Administration Web site

The first setting is to provide a name for the new quota template. You can edit the settings for any existing quota templates or provide a name for a new one. The name should be a description of the purpose of the template (for example, Engineering Dept. Quota). The Storage Limit Values section enables you to configure two restrictions. The Limit Site Storage To A Maximum Of field enables you to specify the maximum amount of content storage space that should be available for the site (in megabytes). When this limit is exceeded, users will be unable to add new content. The second option enables sending a warning e-mail notification to the site administrator when the site has reached a certain amount of storage space usage.

To attach a quota template to a site, click the Site Collection Quotas And Locks link on the Application Management tab. (See Figure 9-24.) This page allows you to choose a site collection and then specify storage-related options. The Site Lock Information section enables you to specify limitations on content storage for the site. The options include:

- Not Locked
- Adding Content Prevented
- Read-only (Blocks Additions, Updates, And Deletions)
- No Access

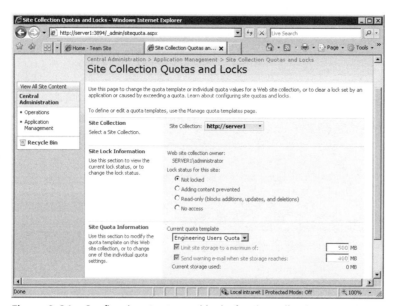

Figure 9-24 Configuring quotas and locks for site collections

These options are useful when you no longer want to enable users to modify the contents of a SharePoint site, but you want them to be able to view existing data. The Site Quota Information section enables you to select a quota template or to use the Individual Quota option to define specific settings for this site collection. The primary benefit of using a quota template is that the storage limitations can be modified centrally for numerous site collections without having to edit the settings of each one.

Configuring Site Settings

In addition to the basic details that you can provide when creating a new SharePoint site or site collection, there are numerous settings that can be managed for the content of the site itself. To access these settings, first navigate to the site you want to administer. All sites have a Site Actions drop-down menu in the top-right section of the screen. The Site Settings command enables you to view a large number of options. (See Figure 9-25.)

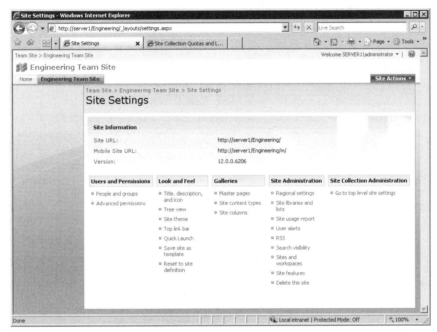

Figure 9-25 Viewing a list of site settings

They are organized into the following groups:

- Users And Permissions
- Look And Feel
- Galleries
- Site Administration
- Site Collection Administration

In some cases, systems administrators might be responsible for making changes and managing the site. However, users with basic SharePoint experience (and the necessary permissions) also can administer details based on their organization's requirements.

Managing Web Applications

Web applications are used to manage the front-end SharePoint sites to which users connect. By default, the Windows SharePoint Services server role includes two built-in Web applications: The SharePoint – 80 site and the SharePoint Central Administration v3 site. You can create new Web applications by using the Create Or Extend Web Application command on the Share-Point Central Administration Web site's Application Management tab. The Create A New Web Application page enables you to specify the details for a new Web site and a new database. (See Figure 9-26.)

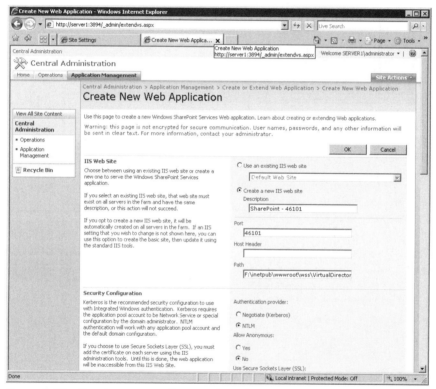

Figure 9-26   Creating or extending a Web application

You can also extend an existing Web application. Use this page to provide multiple Web sites that connect to the same back-end database storage system. One scenario that can require this is an extranet configuration. In this setup, multiple URLs are used: one for internal company users and another for users who might access the site from the Internet. Although the content they will see will be the same, systems administrators can create different configuration settings for an externally accessible Web site. For example, the site can run on a different port, and security settings for accessing the site can be managed separately.

The Web Application List link, on the Application Management tab, will take you to a list of existing Web applications defined for the WSS installation. Two other links on the Application Management tab enable you to remove Web applications. You can use the Delete Web Application link to remove the entire application for the WSS installation. You can delete the content databases for the Web application, delete the associated Web site, or both.

If you want to remove only the Web site, use the Remove SharePoint From IIS Web Site link. This will remove the Web application from the WSS configuration. You can delete the associated IIS Web site as well.

Configuring General Settings for Web Applications

Systems administrators can configure many settings individually for each Web application. The Web Application General Settings link shows the available options. (See Figure 9-27.) Once you select which Web application you want to modify, the available options include:

- Default Time Zone
- Default Quota Template
- Person Name Smart Tag And Presence Settings
- Maximum Upload Size
- Alerts
- RSS Settings
- Blog API Settings
- Web Page Security Validation
- Send User Name And Password In E-Mail
- Backward-Compatible Event Handlers
- Change Log
- Recycle Bin

Some initial settings are based on server-level configuration settings, and others use the WSS new Web application defaults. It is a good idea to review these options for each new Web application that you create. Details such as the time zone for the Web application might vary, especially in geographically distributed organizations or for smaller team sites.

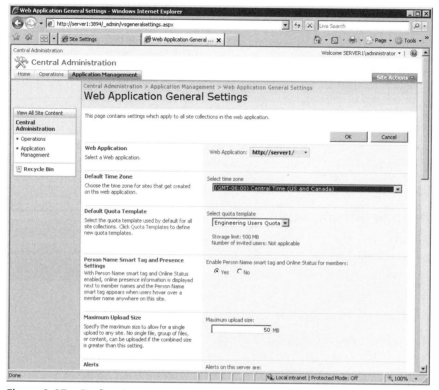

Figure 9-27   Configuring general settings for Web applications

Defining Managed Paths

Earlier in this lesson, you learned about how you can define sites and site collections. Managed paths enable you to specify how WSS responds to certain Web requests. To access the settings, click Define Managed Paths on the Application Management tab. (See Figure 9-28.)

By default, WSS includes two managed paths. The (root) path is the default location accessed when a user navigates to the default Web site on port 80. The sites path includes a base URL that can include multiple additional sites and Web applications. You can add a new path if you want to create a URL namespace for a collection of new Web applications. This is useful when you have a large number of Web applications, and you want to simplify the URLs used to access them.

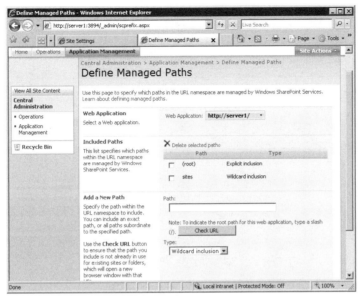

Figure 9-28   Defining managed paths for Web applications

Configuring Web Application Permissions

Because organizations often store sensitive information on SharePoint Web sites, managing security settings is an important concern. Administrators can restrict access and control permissions to the site in several ways. The configuration pages can be accessed in the Application Security section of the Application Management tab.

The User Permissions For Web Application page (shown in Figure 9-29) includes many options. The actual permissions are not granted to specific users. Instead, the settings here pertain to which permissions may be granted to users by administrators of the Web application. The permissions are divided into three groups:

- **List Permissions**   These permissions apply to SharePoint controls that enable adding or removing data. Examples include Announcements, News, and Discussion components. The available permissions include the ability to add, edit, delete, and view items.
- **Site Permissions**   Use these permissions to determine which features and operations can be performed by administrators of a SharePoint Web application. Examples include the ability to manage permissions for other users, add and customize pages, and view site usage information.

■ **Personal Permissions**   Users of SharePoint-based Web sites can create their own customized views of components known as Web Parts. Users can add, remove, and rearrange these parts based on personal preferences. These permissions determine whether users can create and manage personal views.

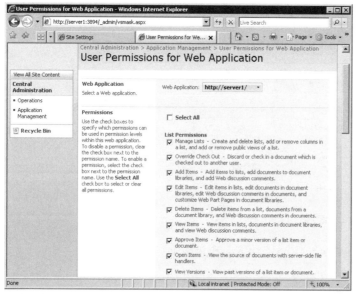

Figure 9-29   Configuring user permissions for a Web application

Managing Authentication Settings

A critical aspect of overall SharePoint security is ensuring that only authorized users can access specific sites. The Edit Authentication page, available by clicking Authentication Providers on the Application Management tab and then clicking a provider, enables you to specify how the authentication process occurs. (See Figure 9-30.) Security settings can be defined separately for each Web application defined within WSS.

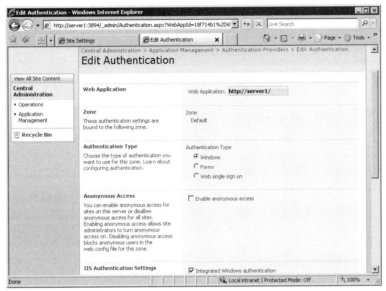

Figure 9-30   Managing authentication settings in the SharePoint Central Administration Web site

There are three primary options for the Authentication Type setting.

- **Windows**   This method takes advantage of the standard Windows authentication method. This is the best solution if the primary users of the site will be employees who have accounts either on the local computer or within an Active Directory domain. Apart from using strong security protocols (such as Kerberos), authenticated users might not need to enter a username and password to access the site.

- **Forms**   Forms-based authentication requires users to provide a valid username and password to log on to the site. This setting is most appropriate when Windows-based authentication is not possible. For example, if external business partners or Internet users need access to the SharePoint site, Forms authentication is a viable option.

- **Web Single Sign-On**   The Web Single Sign-On (SSO) is a standard mechanism by which users can be authenticated against a Web service. It is useful when Windows-based authentication is not possible. This is a simplified access method for users who frequently need to access numerous Web-based systems and applications. Windows Server 2008 Active Directory Federation Services (ADFS) can be used to provide SSO-based services.

Additional details can be specified, including the option to allow anonymous access to a SharePoint site. This option is useful for sites that contain information that should be available to the public or to all users within an organization. Overall, the ability to choose from among several authentication options helps administrators ensure that their SharePoint sites are secure while still maintaining accessibility for users outside of the organization.

Enabling Self-Service Site Management

In smaller and less dynamic environments, it can make sense for systems administrators to be responsible for creating new sites. In larger environments, however, a better management approach can be to allow users to create their own sites. The Self-Service Site Management settings page, accessible from the Application Management tab, includes settings for enabling users to create their own SharePoint sites. The default setting is for this feature to be disabled for new Web applications.

Installing Application Templates

Although the default site provides much useful functionality, there are numerous ways the architecture of SharePoint can be enhanced to meet specific needs. To help organizations achieve a wide variety of goals, Microsoft has developed a set of free Application Templates for use with WSS. Examples include:

- Discussion Database
- Classroom Management
- Employee Training Scheduling and Materials
- Request for Proposal
- Call Center
- Event Planning
- Help Desk
- IT Team Workspace
- Sales Lead Pipeline

Two main types of templates are available. Site Admin Templates can be installed within a specific SharePoint site by users who have the necessary permissions. Server Admin Templates are installed at the level of the server and require systems administrators to make them available for Web applications and sites. For more details and to download the templates, see the Microsoft SharePoint Products and Technologies Templates Web site at *http://www.microsoft.com/sharepoint/templates.mspx*. The download package includes details about how to install the templates on a WSS server.

Quick Check

1. Which option should you choose to create a new SharePoint site that shares the same navigation and security options as an existing site?
2. How can you limit the amount of storage for several SharePoint sites?

Quick Check Answers

1. You should create a new site within the same site collection as the original. This will allow you automatically to use the same navigation and security settings for the new site.
2. The easiest method of enforcing storage limitations is to create a quota template and assign it to the relevant site collection(s). It is also possible to specify individual quota settings for each site collection.

PRACTICE Configuring and Managing Windows SharePoint Services

In this practice, you will look at the process of configuring WSS settings and using the backup and restore features that are part of the SharePoint Central Administration Web site. The steps in these exercises assume that you have installed the Windows SharePoint Services server role and all required dependencies in a standalone server configuration on the local computer. Because the steps in the exercises require you to make configuration changes, you should perform them on a test computer that users in your environment do not rely on.

▶ **Exercise 1 Configure WSS Sites and Site Collections**

In this exercise, you will walk through the steps required to create a new SharePoint Services site. You will then verify the site by connecting to it using Internet Explorer.

1. Log on to Server2 as a user with Administrator permissions on the computer.
2. Open the SharePoint 3.0 Central Administration Web site by clicking the SharePoint 3.0 Central Administration icon in the Administrative Tools program group.
3. When prompted, provide the credentials you used to log on to the server in step 1. You will now see the Central Administration Web site in Internet Explorer.
4. On the Home tab, make a note of the suggested Administrator tasks. You can later return to this page to carry out configuration steps that are not covered in this exercise.
5. Click the Application Management tab at the top of the page. Click the Create Or Extend Web Application link in the SharePoint Web Application Management section.
6. On the Create Or Extend Web Application page, select Create A New Web Application.

7. On the Create New Web Application page, choose the default settings for the IIS Web Site section. Note that the Central Administration Web Site has automatically created a description and port number. It has also chosen a Path setting based on the location of existing Web content.

8. In the Application Pool section, select Create A New Application Pool. Change the security account information to Predefined and choose Network Service.

9. View the other available options, including the Security Configuration and Database Name And Authentication settings. In this practice exercise, you will use the default settings for these options.

10. In the Search Server section, choose Server2. To begin the site creation process, click the OK button. The site creation process might take several minutes, depending on the performance and other activity on the server.

11. When the process has completed, you will see the Application Created page. Click the Create Site Collection page to begin the process of creating a new site collection.

12. On the Create Site Collection page, type **Contoso Meetings** for the Title.

13. In the Template Selection section, select the Meetings tab, and then select the Decision Meeting Workspace item in the list.

14. For the User Name setting in the Primary Site Collection Administration section, type the username you used to log on to the server in step 1.

15. To begin the creation of the site collection, click OK.

16. The Top-Level Site Successfully Created page provides you with the URL that you can use to access the new site. Click this link to access the site, and type your authentication credentials when prompted.

17. Note that you will now be able to access a new SharePoint site titled Contoso Meetings. The default site includes numerous elements, including an Agenda, Objectives, and Document Library sections. Optionally, you can create new items and upload files to augment practice working with the site. Also, note the URL for the new site if you plan to revisit it later.

18. When you are finished, close Internet Explorer and log off Server2.

▶ **Exercise 2   Back Up and Restore a Windows SharePoint Site**

In this exercise, you will create a backup of your WSS server configuration on the local computer. You will then restore the Contoso Meetings SharePoint site that you created in Exercise 1. The specific steps assume that you have completed Exercise 1. Further, because content and configuration settings will be overwritten during the restore process, it is highly recommended that you perform this exercise on a test server.

1. Log on to Server2 as a user who has Administrator permissions on the computer.

2. Using Windows Explorer, create a new folder into which you will store the backup. The folder can be located on any volume on the server. Make a note of the full path to this folder because you will be using it in later steps.

3. Open the SharePoint 3.0 Central Administration Web site by clicking the SharePoint 3.0 Central Administration icon in the Administrative Tools program group.

4. When prompted, provide the credentials you used to log on to the server in step 1. You will now see the Central Administration Web site in Internet Explorer.

5. Click the Operations task. Click the Perform A Backup link in the Backup And Restore section.

6. In the Select Component To Backup step, select the top-level component entitled Farm. Note that this will automatically include all the content for the entire server, including all SharePoint sites. Click Continue To Backup Options.

7. On the Select Backup Options page, leave the default settings for the Backup Content and Type Of Backup sections. For the Backup File Location, provide the full path to the new folder that you created in step 2. Note that the information includes an estimate of the amount of required disk space to store the backup. Click OK to continue.

8. The backup will begin automatically. To view the status of the backup, click Refresh. The screen will also automatically refresh every few seconds. Wait until the screen shows that the backup process Phase shows that the process has completed.

9. To begin the process of restoring a SharePoint site, click the Operations take in the Central Administration Web site. Click Restore From Backup in the Backup And Restore section.

10. The Backup File Location should automatically have the path of the folder you created in step 2. If it is not correct, manually enter this path. Click OK to continue.

11. On the Select Backup To Restore page, select the backup that you created. If multiple backups are present, you can recognize the backup based on the Start Time and Finish Time of the process. Click Continue Restore Process.

12. On the Select Component To Restore page, select the new SharePoint site that you created in Exercise 1. You can identify it based on the name and port number. Note that the Content Database for the site is also selected automatically. Click Continue Restore Process.

13. On the Select Restore Options page, select Same Configuration in the Restore Options section. Press OK when you receive a warning about overwriting the existing site. Note that you could also restore the site to another database if you wanted to make a copy of it without overwriting the current version. Click OK to continue.

14. The restore process will begin automatically. You can click the Refresh button to view the progress of the operation. When the Phase shows that the restore has been completed, the entire contents of the Contoso Meetings SharePoint site should be restored to the server. Optionally, you can verify that the site is accessible by opening an instance of Internet Explorer and connecting the site's URL.

15. When you are finished, close all open browser windows, and then log off Server2.

Lesson Summary

- WSS can be deployed in a standalone configuration or as part of a server farm.
- The SharePoint Central Administration Web site provides a location for managing sites, site collections, and related configuration settings.
- After installing WSS, verify or update settings related to e-mail, logging, and usage analysis.
- The *Stsadm.exe* command-line utility can be used to perform common administration tasks without using the SharePoint Central Administration Web site.
- You can create multiple subsites and site collections to segment SharePoint content based on users' needs.
- Quota templates enable you to specify the maximum amount of storage that a site collection can use.
- You can configure SharePoint to use several authentication mechanisms.
- You can install application templates to add task-specific features to new SharePoint sites and Web applications.

Lesson Review

You can use the following questions to test your knowledge of the information in Lesson 1, "Configuring and Managing Windows SharePoint Services." The questions are also available on the companion CD if you prefer to review them in electronic form.

NOTE   Answers

Answers to these questions and explanations of why each answer choice is correct or incorrect are located in the "Answers" section at the end of the book.

---

1. You are a systems administrator in charge of adding the Windows SharePoint Services (WSS) server role on a computer running Windows Server 2008. You have completed the initial installation process for the server but have not yet added any roles or features to the installation. Based on your technical requirements, you have decided to install WSS in a server farm configuration. Which of the following is not a dependency of the WSS server role? (Choose all that apply.)

    A. Windows Internal Database role service

    B. Windows Process Activation role service

    C. Microsoft .NET Framework 3.0

    D. Web Server (IIS) role

    E. File Server role

2. You are a systems administrator responsible for deploying Windows SharePoint Services (WSS) for access by users from an external business partner. You have installed the appropriate server role and have verified that the SharePoint Web site loads properly from the local server computer. All options are using their installation default values. External users report that they cannot log on to the site. Which of the following changes should you make to resolve the problem?

    A. Create a new site within an existing site collection for the external users.

    B. Create a new site collection for the external users.

    C. Change the authentication mode for the Web application to Forms authentication.

    D. Modify the User Permissions For Web Applications settings.

    E. Modify the Quota Template settings for the default Web application.

Chapter Review

To further practice and reinforce the skills you learned in this chapter, you can perform the following tasks:

- Review the chapter summary.
- Review the list of key terms introduced in this chapter.
- Complete the case scenarios. These scenarios set up real-world situations involving the topics of this chapter and ask you to create a solution.
- Complete the suggested practices.
- Take a practice test.

Chapter Summary

- Windows SharePoint Services includes a default Web site and the SharePoint Central Administration Web site.
- Windows SharePoint Services can be deployed in a standalone configuration or in a server farm configuration.
- Administrators can create and manage sites, site collections, and Web applications, using the SharePoint Central Administration Web site.
- Web applications can have their own security and authentication settings, based on the needs of the organization.

Key Terms

Do you know what these key terms mean? You can check your answers by looking up the terms in the glossary at the end of the book.

- application templates (Windows SharePoint Services)
- Quota templates (Windows SharePoint Services)
- Server Farm Configuration (Windows SharePoint Services)
- SharePoint Central Administration Web site
- site collection (Windows SharePoint Services)
- standalone server configuration (Windows SharePoint Services)
- stsadm

- Web application (Windows SharePoint Services)
- Windows Internal Database
- Windows SharePoint Services (WSS)

Case Scenarios

The following case scenarios will help you determine the best way to deploy Windows Share-Point Services based on different organizational and technical requirements.

Case Scenario 1: Deploying Windows SharePoint Services

You are a systems administrator responsible for enabling Windows SharePoint Services on seven computers running Windows Server 2008. Your organization plans to use a single back-end database for storing the site configuration data and contents. On six of the servers, you will need to create several site collections and Web applications.

1. Which deployment option should you use when installing the Windows SharePoint Services server role on the computers?
2. How can you automate the process of creating the site collections and Web applications?

Case Scenario 2: Managing Windows SharePoint Services

You are a systems administrator responsible for managing an existing Windows SharePoint Services (WSS) server. The server has been configured with several site collections and sites. The WSS server is part of an Active Directory domain, and all the users have individual accounts. Users have been able to access the site for several months but have reported several problems. Users of some SharePoint Web applications note that they are always required to provide username and password information when connecting to certain sites. Also, in the past, the WSS server has become unavailable when the computer ran out of available disk space. Finally, some users would like to be able to create their own sites without requiring the involvement of the IT department.

1. How should you configure the authentication settings to meet users' requirements?
2. How can you prevent future disk storage issues from occurring on the WSS server?
3. What is the easiest method of enabling users to create their own SharePoint sites?

Suggested Practices

To help you successfully master the exam objectives presented in this chapter, complete the following tasks.

Implement and Manage Windows SharePoint Services

The practice items in this section will enable you to practice the process of setting up and managing WSS.

- **Practice 1**   Create a new site collection, using the SharePoint Central Administration Web site. Choose one of the built-in application templates to configure the default content. Add a second site to the same site collection and note the changes to the navigation bar. Download and install new application templates from Microsoft. Create a new site that uses one of the new templates and test the included functionality, using a Web browser.

- **Practice 2**   On a test WSS server, practice the process of creating and restoring configuration information from backups. First, restore the configuration settings over an existing site and verify that the contents have reverted to the earlier version. Then, use the backup and restore process to create a second copy of a SharePoint site collection by restoring it with different site information.

- **Practice 3**   Access additional information on the companion CD or at the following URLs. Specific topics include:

  - Windows SharePoint Services TechCenter: *http://technet.microsoft.com/en-us/windowsserver/sharepoint/default.aspx*
  - Microsoft TechNet Virtual Labs: SharePoint Products and Technologies: *http://technet.microsoft.com/en-us/bb512933.aspx*
  - Microsoft Office Windows SharePoint Services technology Home Page: *http://office.microsoft.com/en-us/sharepointtechnology*

Take a Practice Test

The practice tests on this book's companion CD offer many options. For example, you can test yourself on just one exam objective, or you can test yourself on all the 70-643 certification exam content. You can set up the test so that it closely simulates the experience of taking a certification exam, or you can set it up in study mode so that you can look at the correct answers and explanations after you answer each question.

MORE INFO **Practice tests**

For details about all the practice test options available, see the "How to Use the Practice Tests" section in this book's introduction.

Answers

Chapter 1: Lesson Review Answers

Lesson 1

1. **Correct Answer: C**

    A. **Incorrect:** Windows PE is used to boot from a CD to service a hard disk.

    B. **Incorrect:** The ImageX utility captures, modifies, and applies WIM images.

    C. **Correct:** Sysprep prepares a Windows installation to be imaged by removing all unique system information from the Windows installation, for example, by resetting security IDs (SIDs), clearing system restore points, and deleting event logs.

    D. **Incorrect:** Windows System Image Manager (SIM) is the tool used to create unattended Windows Setup answer files.

Lesson 2

1. **Correct Answer: C**

    A. **Incorrect:** The image store is found in the *Path*\RemoteInstall folder on your WDS server and is used to contain and manage boot and install images used for deployment.

    B. **Incorrect:** WDS includes a TFTP server that can respond to a PXE-enabled client computer so that the client can download the WDS client to display the boot menu and begin the installation.

    C. **Correct:** Although Windows SIM is useful for creating answer files for performing unattended installations using WDS, it is not a part of WDS—Windows SIM is included as part of the Windows AIK.

    D. **Incorrect:** WDS includes a PXE server that can respond to BOOTP requests from PXE-enabled client computers and provide these computers with the location of the WDS client, which is needed to start the installation process.

2. **Correct Answers: A and C**

    A. **Correct:** FAT32 volumes are not supported by Windows DS.

    B. **Incorrect:** PXE Server Initial Settings are irrelevant to this scenario. In fact, the settings you've chosen for this are the least restrictive settings you can choose.

C. **Correct:** Only the Boot.wim file found on Windows Server 2008 or Windows Vista integrated with Service Pack 1 media enable you to take advantage of the enhancements found in the new Windows Server 2008 version of WDS. The Boot.wim file on the Windows Vista RTM media supports only an earlier version of Windows DS.

D. **Incorrect:** You're mixing up boot and install images.

Lesson 3

1. **Correct Answer: D**

   A. **Incorrect:** Both Virtual Server and Windows Server Hyper-V support network load balancing.

   B. **Incorrect:** Both Virtual Server and Hyper-V provide the ability to assign a host processor to a virtual machine.

   C. **Incorrect:** All three Microsoft virtualization technologies allow 64-bit host support.

   D. **Correct:** Only Hyper-V supports 64-bit guests.

2. **Correct Answer: D**

   A. **Incorrect:** Assisted physical-to-virtual migration is not a feature of Virtual PC.

   B. **Incorrect:** Assisted physical-to-virtual migration is not a feature of Virtual Server.

   C. **Incorrect:** Assisted physical-to-virtual migration is not a feature of Hyper-V.

   D. **Correct:** The Virtual Server Migration Toolkit is a free, downloadable tool that simplifies physical-to-virtual (P2V) migration.

Lesson 4

1. **Correct Answer: C**

   A. **Incorrect:** A total of 25 computers need to request activation before Windows Vista clients can be successfully activated. The branch office meets this requirement, but it also meets the requirement for Windows Server 2008 activation.

   B. **Incorrect:** A total of five computers need to request activation before Windows Server 2008 can be successfully activated through a KMS host. The branch office meets this requirement, but it also meets the requirement for Windows Vista activation.

C. **Correct:** KMS licensing is available for both client types. For Windows Vista clients to be activated through KMS, the KMS host needs to receive activation requests from 25 computers. For Windows Server 2008 installations to be activated, the KMS host needs to receive activation requests from five computers. The branch office meets these requirements.

D. **Incorrect:** The branch office network meets the requirements for KMS licensing for both operating systems.

2. **Correct Answer: B**

A. **Incorrect:** Without Internet access, MAK-independent activation would require activating each computer by telephone. This process would be very time-consuming and inefficient.

B. **Correct:** MAK proxy activation provides the most efficient way to activate fewer than 25 computers that are running Windows Vista and that have no Internet access. In MAK proxy activation, you use an XML file to gather installation IDs from the clients to be activated. You then obtain confirmation IDs from Microsoft on a computer that can connect to the Internet, and these confirmation IDs are used to activate the computers.

C. **Incorrect:** You cannot use KMS licensing or activation in this scenario because there are not enough computers on the research subnet to support a KMS host.

D. **Incorrect:** You cannot perform retail key activation because the question states that volume licenses have been obtained for the 15 client computers.

Chapter 1: Case Scenario Answers

Case Scenario 1: Deploying Servers

1. System Center Configuration Manager 2007.

2. You should use virtualization (either Virtual Server or Hyper-V) to consolidate the servers running Windows NT and Linux applications. This option reduces the costs of running the servers and the number of servers you will need to purchase for Windows Server 2008 deployment.

Case Scenario 2: Creating an Activation Infrastructure

1. At the Headquarters site, you should use KMS licensing and activation for all computers except those on the research subnet. For the computers on the isolated research subnet, you should use MAK proxy activation.
2. At the Binghamton site, you should use KMS licensing and a locally installed KMS host.
3. At the Syracuse site, you should use MAK licensing.

Chapter 2: Lesson Review Answers

Lesson 1

1. **Correct Answer: B**
    A. **Incorrect:** No disks will appear in Disk Management unless the vendor solution includes the VDS hardware provider. Even then, they will appear only once LUNs have been created and assigned to the server.
    B. **Correct:** VDS is an API that exposes disk subsystems and SAN hardware to administrative tools in Windows. For built-in storage management tools such as Storage Manager for SANs to connect to disk enclosures produced by independent hardware vendors, the hardware must include a software interface to VDS. This interface is known as the VDS hardware provider.
    C. **Incorrect:** If the vendor software can be used to connect to the disk subsystem, then the iSCSI connection to the device is already established. In addition, iSCSI Initiator in Windows will not see the device unless the vendor solution includes the VDS hardware provider.
    D. **Incorrect:** If the vendor software can be used to connect to the disk subsystem, then the connection to the device is already established. Configuring an iSNS server will not enable the physical discovery of the device. To enable physical discovery of the device, the vendor solution needs to include the VDS hardware provider.

2. **Correct Answer: D**
    A. **Incorrect:** A simple volume would use only one of the three disks, and it would not offer the highest read or write performance.
    B. **Incorrect:** A spanned volume could use the maximum space on all three disks, but it would not offer the highest read or write performance.

   C.   **Incorrect:** A mirrored volume would use the space equivalent of just one disk. In addition, a mirrored volume would not offer the highest read or write performance.

   D.   **Correct:** A striped volume would use the total space available on all three disks. In addition, a striped volume offers the best read and write performance of any volume type.

   E.   **Incorrect:** A RAID-5 volume would use the space equivalent of two out of the three disks. In addition, although a RAID-5 volume offers excellent read performance, it would also offer relatively poor write performance.

Lesson 2

1.   **Correct Answer: B**

   A.   **Incorrect:** A more powerful server might be able to meet the performance requirements of the Web site in the short term, but if traffic is expected to grow for many years, this solution does not provide the best way to meet that demand in the long term.

   B.   **Correct:** An NLB cluster (Web farm) would enable you to meet the performance demands of the Web site in the short term and in the long term. As traffic to the Web site increases, you merely need to add additional servers to meet the increased demand.

   C.   **Incorrect:** A failover cluster would not enable a Web site to sustain an increased workload. A failover cluster merely enables one server to take over for another if that second server fails.

   D.   **Incorrect:** Round-robin might be adequate for some small deployments, but it is not the best solution in the long term. In the long term, you do not want Web clients to be directed to failed or busy Web servers, and you want to be able to control the workload distribution better than round-robin allows.

2.   **Correct Answer: B**

   A.   **Incorrect:** You don't want to choose the node majority quorum configuration because this option is best suited for failover clusters with an odd number of nodes.

   B.   **Correct:** Node and disk majority is the most suitable quorum configuration for failover clusters that have an even number of nodes and plentiful shared storage options.

C. **Incorrect:** Node and file share majority is the most suitable quorum configuration for a failover cluster that has an even number of nodes but that does not have access to a share volume that can be used for a witness disk.

D. **Incorrect:** The No Majority: Disk Only quorum configuration is not generally recommended. It can be used in testing environments or in special circumstances for which no other quorum configuration is suitable.

Chapter 2: Case Scenario Answers

Case Scenario 1: Designing Storage

1. You should choose an iSCSI-based SAN because this option provides excellent performance while enabling you to draw upon the networking expertise of the IT staff.

2. You should look for vendor solutions that include a hardware provider for VDS.

Case Scenario 2: Designing High Availability

1. You should configure an NLB cluster to host IIS and the Web application. This option would maximize performance by load balancing the client requests among servers. In addition, an NLB cluster minimizes downtime by redirecting requests away from inactive servers.

2. You should choose a failover cluster to host the back-end database. Because the data must always be internally consistent, the database needs to reside on a single storage solution. The failover cluster will also minimize downtime by providing failover service if the database server fails.

Chapter 3: Lesson Review Answers

Lesson 1

1. **Correct Answers: A and C**

   A. **Correct:** This command configures a local Server Core installation of Windows Server 2008 to accept Remote Desktop connections.

   B. **Incorrect:** This command configures a local Server Core installation of Windows Server 2008 to block Remote Desktop connections.

C. **Correct:** This command configures a local Server Core installation of Windows Server 2008 to accept Remote Desktop connections from clients running Windows XP or earlier versions of Windows.

D. **Incorrect:** This command configures a local Server Core installation of Windows Server 2008 to block Remote Desktop connections from clients running Windows XP or earlier versions of Windows.

2. **Correct Answer: D**

   A. **Incorrect:** Remote Desktop for Administration is the unlicensed version of Terminal Services that allows only two concurrent desktop sessions. Two sessions are not enough to support 75 consultants working in the field. In addition, if you were to use Remote Desktop for Administration, you would not need to purchase any licenses.

   B. **Incorrect:** Remote Desktop for Administration is the unlicensed version of Terminal Services that allows only two concurrent desktop sessions. Two sessions are not enough to support 75 consultants working in the field.

   C. **Incorrect:** You need to install Terminal Services on the application server so that more than two users can connect to it simultaneously. However, it is advisable to use per-user CALs because the number of devices exceeds the number of users.

   D. **Correct:** You need to install Terminal Services on the application server so that more than two users can connect to it simultaneously. In addition, although you would have to purchase only 75 per-user CALs, you would have to purchase many more per device TS CALs because of the large number of computers from which consultants might connect. Purchasing per-user CALs is, therefore, the best option in this case.

Lesson 2

1. **Correct Answer: B**

   A. **Incorrect:** TS Session Broker keeps track of user sessions in a farm and is responsible for reconnecting users to disconnected RDP sessions. For the Terminal Services Session Broker service to keep track of the sessions on each farm member, each member server needs to be added to the Session Directory Computers local group on the Session Broker server. In this scenario, the Session Broker server is TSLB1.

   B. **Correct:** For users to be able to reconnect disconnected RDP sessions in a Terminal Services server farm, each member server needs to be added to the Session Directory Computers local group on the Session Broker server. In this scenario, the Session Broker server is TSLB1.

    C. **Incorrect:** This option ensures that only some of the client requests for TSFARM1 will be directed to TSLB6. It does not enable the Terminal Services Session Broker service to reconnect to disconnected sessions.

    D. **Incorrect:** This option ensures that users can connect to TSLB6 only by specifying the server directly. It does not enable users who connect through the farm name TSFARM1 to reconnect to disconnected RDP sessions.

2. **Correct Answer: D**

    A. **Incorrect:** This option would prevent Terminal Services clients from printing to printers local to the client. It would not configure a fallback printer driver for Terminal Services clients.

    B. **Incorrect:** This option would change the default printer within a Terminal Services session to a printer local to TS1. It would not configure a fallback printer driver for Terminal Services clients.

    C. **Incorrect:** This policy setting improves printing consistency for Terminal Services clients, but it does not configure a fallback printer driver.

    D. **Correct:** To configure a printer driver fallback, you must configure this policy setting in Group Policy.

Chapter 3: Case Scenario Answers

Case Scenario 1: Choosing a TS Licensing Strategy

1. Yes, you should install Terminal Services because you need to support many simultaneous connections. You should choose per-user CALs because there are fewer users than devices that connect to TS1.

2. No, you do not need to install Terminal Services on TS2 because there is no stated need for more than two concurrent desktop sessions. You can merely enable the Remote Desktop feature on the server instead. You do not need to purchase any client access licenses for Remote Desktop.

Case Scenario 2: Troubleshooting a Terminal Services Installation

1. On the General tab of the RDP-Tcp Properties dialog box on App3, clear the check box to allow connections only from computers running Remote Desktop with Network Level Authentication.

2. On the Sessions tab of the RDP-Tcp Properties dialog box on App1, set the End A Disconnected Session setting to Never.

Chapter 4: Lesson Review Answers

Lesson 1

1. **Correct Answer: B**

   A. **Incorrect:** Mandatory profiles are incompatible with the stated requirement that users be able to save their own data.

   B. **Correct:** By implementing disk quotas, you can ensure that the size of the user profiles does not exhaust the storage capacity of the disk.

   C. **Incorrect:** Roaming user profiles by themselves will not solve the problem. You would need to store the profiles in a separate location with more storage capacity.

   D. **Incorrect:** Profiles for Terminal Services users are stored on the remote terminal server, not on the local computer. Assigning disk quotas to each user's local disks will not address the problem.

2. **Correct Answer: A**

   A. **Correct:** Use the *Rwinsta* or *Reset session* command to delete a user session on a terminal server. Deleting the disconnected, idle sessions will free up server resources for active sessions.

   B. **Incorrect:** The *Tdiscon* command disconnects user sessions that are currently connected. You want to delete disconnected sessions, not disconnect active ones.

   C. **Incorrect:** The *Tskill* command ends an individual process on a terminal server. It does not end user sessions in general.

   D. **Incorrect:** The *Tscon* command connects to a disconnected session. It does not end user sessions.

Lesson 2

1. **Correct Answer: C**

   A. **Incorrect:** TCP port 25 is used for SMTP traffic. This port is not needed to communicate with TS Gateway.

   B. **Incorrect:** TCP port 3389 is used for direct RDP connections without TS Gateway. You want clients to communicate through TS Gateway.

   C. **Correct:** TCP port 443 is the port used for SSL. TS Gateway communicates with clients over SSL.

   D. **Incorrect:** TCP port 80 is used for HTTP traffic. You would need to leave this port open for a client to communicate with a Web server hosted behind your company firewall.

2. **Correct Answer: D**

   A. **Incorrect:** If you enable HTTPS–HTTP bridging, you will not be using ISA Server as an SSL endpoint for TS Gateway connections. Communications with TS Gateway will be sent unencrypted through HTTP.

   B. **Incorrect:** It is necessary to open TCP port 443 on ISA Server so that external clients can initiate connections to it. However, opening this port will not ensure that ISA Server can communicate with TS Gateway.

   C. **Incorrect:** You need to export the TS Gateway certificate to ISA Server, not the other way around.

   D. **Correct:** When ISA Server is deployed between external TS clients and an internal TS gateway, ISA Server acts as a client to TS Gateway. For this reason, the TS Gateway certificate used for SSL must be installed on the computer running ISA Server.

Lesson 3

1. **Correct Answer: B**

   A. **Incorrect:** This command is used to enable or disable logons from client sessions on a terminal server. It will not ensure that an installed application will support multiple users.

   B. **Correct:** Use the *chguser /install* command before installing an application to create .ini files for the application in the system directory. This ensures that when users run the application, they will all be able to save personal settings for the application. After installation, use the *chguser /execute* command.

   C. **Incorrect:** This command displays a list of all the terminal servers on the network. You cannot use it to ensure that an installed application will support multiple users.

   D. **Incorrect:** This command launches the Terminal Services client, Remote Desktop Connection (Mstsc.exe). You cannot use this command to ensure that an installed application will support multiple users.

2. **Correct Answers: A and B**

   A. **Correct:** The new TS Web Access site will list the RemoteApp program and point to its new location.

   B. **Correct:** After the RemoteApp program is migrated, the old RDP file can no longer be used. You need to re-create the file and distribute the file to users.

   C.   **Incorrect:** You can modify some settings in an RDP file, but you cannot modify the
        location of the RemoteApp program to which it is pointing. If you move an appli-
        cation, you need to re-create any associated RDP file.

   D.   **Incorrect:** You can change the server name in Terminal Server Settings, but this
        step is performed primarily when the local server belongs to a server farm.
        Changing the name of the server will not enable users to connect to the moved
        application.

Chapter 4: Case Scenario Answers

Case Scenario 1: Managing TS Sessions

   1. You can use the Query session command to find his session ID. You can use the Rwinsta
       or Reset session command to end (delete) his session.

   2. You can use the Remote Control feature to take over her user session and then show her
       how to use the application.

Case Scenario 2: Publishing Applications

   1. You should use Group Policy to publish the RemoteApp program to their desktops. You
       could achieve this with either an RDP file or an MSI file.

   2. Use TS RemoteApp Manager to add App1 to the list of RemoteApp programs and then
       to create a Windows Installer package of the application. Configure the MSI file to install
       a shortcut to the RemoteApp program in the Start menu and to launch the program
       whenever a file with the associated extension is opened. Deploy the MSI file by using
       Group Policy.

   3. Deploy a TS Gateway server in your company's perimeter network. Use TS RemoteApp
       Manager to create an RDP file for App1 that specifies the TS Gateway server. Distribute
       the RDP file to remote users.

Chapter 5: Lesson Review Answers

Lesson 1

1. **Correct Answer: B**

   A. **Incorrect:** The HTTP Errors role service is used to send custom error pages to users. Because the server does not appear to be responding, this is unlikely to resolve the problem.

   B. **Correct:** The most likely cause of the problem is that the World Wide Web Publishing Service has been stopped. You can verify the status of the service (and view any related events) by using Server Manager.

   C. **Incorrect:** Because multiple users are having problems accessing the site, it is most likely that the problem is related to a server-side issue.

   D. **Incorrect:** The HTTP Logging role server will enable you to collect information about requests to the Web site. However, because the Web server is not responding to requests, adding this role service will not resolve the problem.

   E. **Incorrect:** The IIS Admin Service is required to make configuration changes to the Web server. However, even if this service is stopped, the Web server should still be able to respond to user requests.

Lesson 2

1. **Correct Answers: A and D**

   A. **Correct:** Because both applications must be accessible by using the standard HTTP port, they must be contained within the same Web site.

   B. **Incorrect:** IIS does not allow multiple Web sites to share the same site-binding settings; therefore, you cannot start multiple Web sites that bind to HTTP port 80.

   C. **Incorrect:** Assigning both Web applications to the same application pool will not prevent problems in one Web application from affecting the other.

   D. **Correct:** By using separate application pools, each Web application will run, using isolated processes. This helps protect against potential performance and reliability problems.

2. **Correct Answer: D**

    A. **Incorrect:** The process of re-creating the Web sites can be time-consuming, and it will be difficult to ensure that all settings have been restored to the correct options.

    B. **Incorrect:** Manually adding settings to the ApplicationHost.config file can be time-consuming and risky.

    C. **Incorrect:** Because no manual backups of the IIS configuration have been made, you cannot use AppCmd to restore a backup.

    D. **Correct:** Because each Web site includes numerous additional settings, and because no additional changes have been made to the server, the quickest method of restoring the sites is to restore the IIS configuration by copying an automatic backup of the ApplicationHost.config file to the working location.

Chapter 5: Case Scenario Answers

Case Scenario 1: IIS Web Server Administration

1. The IIS Shared Configuration feature enables multiple Web servers to use the same configuration files. To do this, export the configuration from one of the servers and configure them all to use the same settings file.

2. You should include all the Web site content folders (including their Web.config files). The backup should also include the *%SystemDrive%*\Inetpub\History folder because this location contains previous versions of configuration files.

3. You can use the AppCmd.exe utility to create and restore manual backups of the IIS configuration. Making a manual backup is recommended before you make configuration changes to the server. Alternatively, you can restore previous versions of the ApplicationHost.config over the working version to revert to an earlier configuration of the server.

Case Scenario 2: Managing Multiple Web Sites

1. By adding each Web application to a separate application pool, memory and processing errors can be contained to minimize negative effects.

2. You can modify the site bindings for each Web site to include a different host name value. Users will be redirected automatically to the appropriate site based on this information.

3. By adding the IIS 6 Management Compatibility role service, you can provide access to the IIS 6.0 metabase and other features. If the ASP.NET application requires access to the classic pipeline mode, you can create or change the settings for its application pool.

Chapter 6: Lesson Review Answers

Lesson 1

1. **Correct Answer: B**
   A. **Incorrect:** Adding the handler to the entire Web site will make it available to all Web applications and potentially can decrease security.
   B. **Correct:** A managed handler enables you to call a .NET library to process the request. To reduce the attack surface of IIS, make this handler available only to the one Web application that requires it.
   C. **Incorrect:** Module mappings are not designed to provide access to .NET libraries.
   D. **Incorrect:** Module mappings are not designed to provide access to .NET libraries.

2. **Correct Answer: C**
   A. **Incorrect:** IIS Manager enables you to configure user permissions for Web sites even when Management Service has been stopped.
   B. **Incorrect:** File system permissions will not affect whether IIS Manager users can be added to a Web site.
   C. **Correct:** To add IIS Manager users to the Web site, Management Service must be configured to accept IIS Manager credentials.
   D. **Incorrect:** Authentication settings apply only to users attempting to access Web content by using a Web browser or other applications. These settings do not affect remote IIS Manager user settings or connections.

Lesson 2

1. **Correct Answers: A and C**
   A. **Correct:** Windows authentication is designed to enable users with Windows domain or local user accounts to authenticate to the server.
   B. **Incorrect:** Basic authentication is a less secure option than Windows authentication because all required users have Windows accounts.

C. **Correct:** Anonymous authentication must be disabled for users to be prompted to provide credentials when accessing the site.

D. **Incorrect:** If anonymous authentication is enabled, users will be able to access the site without presenting credentials.

2. **Correct Answer: C**

A. **Incorrect:** The site appears to be accepting connections on port 443 because users are receiving a warning message rather than an error.

B. **Incorrect:** The requirements specify that users should be able to connect using both HTTP and HTTPS; therefore, you should not require SSL to access the site.

C. **Correct:** The warning that users are receiving is because the server certificate is not issued by a trusted third party. It is likely that a self-signed certificate was installed earlier. You can resolve the issue by generating an Internet Certificate Request, obtaining a certificate, and then registering it on the server.

D. **Incorrect:** Because the server certificate appears to be installed properly, exporting and re-importing it will not solve the problem.

E. **Incorrect:** Because users are receiving a warning message when attempting to connect to the Web site, firewall issues are not preventing the connection.

Chapter 6: Case Scenario Answers

Case Scenario 1: Configuring Remote Management for IIS

1. Assuming that you have the necessary permissions, you can create multiple connections (one for each server) within IIS Manager. Optionally, you can provide different credentials for each connection.

2. The most secure option is to enable IIS Manager credentials for the Management Service and to create a new IIS Manager user account for the administrator.

3. Feature delegation settings determine which settings IIS Manager administrators can view or modify. Set the Default Document and Directory Browsing settings to Read Only to prevent administrators from making modifications.

Case Scenario 2: Increasing Web Site Security

1. Because the Web application must be able to connect to a remote database server, you must select the High (Web_hightrust.config) .NET trust level. This setting should be assigned at the level of the Web application.

2. First use file system permissions to restrict access to the content to only the approved users. You can then use authorization rules to manage which users can access the content.

3. You must first obtain and install an Internet Security Certificate on the Web server. Then you can enable SSL connections, using the site bindings settings. Finally, to require encryption, use the SSL Settings feature for the Web application.

Chapter 7: Lesson Review Answers

Lesson 1

1. **Correct Answer: C**
    A. **Incorrect:** The IUSR_*MachineName* account is used to validate permissions for anonymous connections to the FTP server. Because the users have Windows accounts and permissions, these settings will not affect access to the Drawings folder.
    B. **Incorrect:** TCP/IP Address Restrictions are used to configure access to the FTP server based on IP addresses or DNS names. These settings will not prevent access to specific folders.
    C. **Correct:** The most likely cause of the problem is that all connections are being treated as anonymous. To enable the FTP server to verify permissions based on the user's Windows account, disable this option.
    D. **Incorrect:** Adding the users to the local Administrators group would provide them with unnecessary permissions on the server.

2. **Correct Answers: B and D**
    A. **Incorrect:** Allowing SSL connections will not require all users to enable encryption. Therefore, this option does not meet the requirement to encrypt credentials and commands.
    B. **Correct:** Disabling 128-bit encryption will instruct the FTP site to use 40-bit encryption for transfers. This will increase FTP server performance while still encrypting data.

C. **Incorrect:** The Require SSL Connections policy encrypts all communications between the FTP client and the FTP site.

D. **Correct:** The Custom SSL Policy option enables administrators to set Control Channel and Data Channel settings independently.

Lesson 2

1. **Correct Answers: A and C**

   A. **Correct:** By requiring Basic Authentication, all users or applications will need to provide credentials to use the SMTP virtual server.

   B. **Incorrect:** A smart host setting will force the SMTP virtual server to route all new mail messages through a specified server. This will not directly prevent unauthorized access to the server.

   C. **Correct:** Connection Control rules can be used to define which computers or IP addresses can use the SMTP virtual server.

   D. **Incorrect:** The Security tab is used to determine which users are operators of the SMTP server. This will not directly prevent unauthorized users from sending messages.

2. **Correct Answer: B**

   A. **Incorrect:** The Current Sessions section shows only which users and applications are accessing the server at a specific point in time. It does not provide a good method of monitoring performance over time.

   B. **Correct:** Performance counters that are part of the SMTP Server object can provide details about how many messages are sent and received by the server over time. You can also correlate these statistics with other information such as CPU, memory, and network usage.

   C. **Incorrect:** The Windows Event logs will not contain performance-related statistics for the SMTP Server service.

   D. **Incorrect:** The Windows Event logs will not contain performance-related statistics for the SMTP Server service.

   E. **Incorrect:** Messages that are undeliverable are stored in the Badmail folder, but the performance problems are not necessarily caused by undeliverable messages.

Chapter 7: Case Scenario Answers

Case Scenario 1: Implementing a Secure FTP Site

1. To support the security and Web integration requirements, download and install FTP 7.
2. Obtain a server certificate for the FTP server, and then enable the FTP Over SSL (FTPS) option by using IIS Manager.
3. You can use IIS Manager to add a new FTP site binding to an existing Web site. This will automatically configure the root directory for the site.

Case Scenario 2: Configuring an SMTP Virtual Server

1. You can use the settings on the General tab of the SMTP virtual server to specify the IP addresses and port numbers to which the server will respond.
2. On the Access tab of the properties of the SMTP virtual server, enable the Basic Authentication option.
3. The Limit Message Size option on the Messages tab enables you to specify the maximum size of a single SMTP message.

Chapter 8: Lesson Review Answers

Lesson 1

1. **Correct Answers: B and C**
    A. **Incorrect:** Users will not be able to fast-forward media that is streamed from a broadcast publishing point.
    B. **Correct:** Users can access an on-demand publishing point to select which videos they want to view and can control the playback.
    C. **Correct:** WMS IP Address Authorization settings can allow only computers that are part of the specified LAN to connect to the server.
    D. **Incorrect:** WMS Negotiate Authentication is designed for authenticating users based on Windows accounts, but it will not prevent clients from accessing content from locations other than the LAN.
    E. **Incorrect:** WMS NTFS ACL Authorization verifies users' Windows accounts to determine whether they have access to content, but it will not limit the network locations from which streamed media can be accessed.

2. **Correct Answer: B**

   A. **Incorrect:** The Unicast Announcement Wizard will not prevent users from accessing specific content from the publishing point.

   B. **Correct:** You can use NTFS permissions to determine which content will be available using the publishing point. You can configure the WMS NTFS ACL Authorization plug-in to specify the user account that should be used.

   C. **Incorrect:** Copying the training videos will increase storage space requirements and is not necessary to meet the requirements.

   D. **Incorrect:** Disabling WMS Anonymous Authentication will require users to provide authentication credentials to access the content.

   E. **Incorrect:** Providing users with access to the Wrapper Playlist will not enable users to choose which videos they want to watch.

3. **Correct Answer: B**

   A. **Incorrect:** Copying the training videos will make it more difficult to manage updates and revisions to the content and will use additional disk space on the server.

   B. **Correct:** Caching servers will automatically obtain and store copies of the video content from the origin server and will make streams available to users.

   C. **Incorrect:** Proxy servers are used to redirect client requests to other servers. They can increase performance, but they will not improve scalability as much as caching servers.

   D. **Incorrect:** Limiting distribution connections will not increase scalability directly for supporting client connections.

Chapter 8: Case Scenario Answers

Case Scenario 1: Protecting Streaming Media Content

1. You should create a single publishing point that provides access to video files on demand. This will enable users to select which videos they want to view and pause or fast-forward the content during playback.

2. Because the users have Active Directory accounts, you should enable WMS NTFS ACL Authorization. For ease of administration, you can place students in groups based on their class enrollments. You can then apply file system permissions to specify which files are accessible to which users.

3. You can use wrapper advertisements to play a video clip automatically before the play-back of specific videos. This is the easiest method because it does not involve the manual creation of individual playlists.

Case Scenario 2: Improving Windows Media Services Performance and Scalability

1. A broadcast publishing point is most suitable for live events because it can obtain information directly from a Windows Media Services live encoder stream.

2. For networks that support it, multicast broadcasts can significantly reduce the bandwidth requirements for the origin server. Users who cannot access the multicast stream can fall back on using the unicast method.

3. Adding cache/proxy Windows Media Services servers can greatly improve performance while enabling content to remain on the origin server.

Chapter 9: Lesson Review Answers

Lesson 1

1. **Correct Answers: A and E**

    A. **Correct:** Unlike a standalone (single server) WSS installation, a server farm installation does not require the installation of the Windows Internal Database role service. All content and configuration information will be stored in a dedicated SQL Server database.

    B. **Incorrect:** The Windows Process Activation role service is required to host the SharePoint Web sites.

    C. **Incorrect:** WSS requires .NET Framework 3.0 for it to run.

    D. **Incorrect:** The Web Server (IIS) server role is required to host the SharePoint user and administration Web sites.

    E. **Correct:** The File Server role is not a requirement for a server running WSS.

2. **Correct Answer: C**

    A. **Incorrect:** It is not necessary to create a new site to provide access to the default SharePoint site.

    B. **Incorrect:** It is not necessary to create a new site collection to provide access to the default SharePoint site.

C. **Correct:** The default authentication option for the default SharePoint site is Windows authentication. To connect, users require access to logon information for the local domain. External users who do not have local domain accounts will not be able to access the site unless you change the authentication mode to Forms.

D. **Incorrect:** User permissions settings apply only to operations that can be performed after a user is connected to the SharePoint site. They do not prevent users from connecting to the site itself.

E. **Incorrect:** Quota Templates affect only the maximum amount of storage allowed for a site collection and will not prevent users from connecting to the site.

Chapter 9: Case Scenario Answers

Case Scenario 1: Deploying Windows SharePoint Services

1. Because a single back-end database server will be used to store content, you should deploy the servers by using the server farm configuration option. You can use the SharePoint Products And Technologies Configuration Wizard later to configure database access settings.

2. You can use the Stsadm.exe command-line utility to perform tasks such as creating new sites without using the SharePoint Central Administration Web site. The commands can be placed in a script file to simplify the setup process.

Case Scenario 2: Managing Windows SharePoint Services

1. Because the site's users are all part of the same Active Directory domain, Windows authentication will enable them to connect to WSS without requiring additional authentication information.

2. Quota templates can be created and assigned to specific site collections to limit the amount of disk space used by each site. You can also configure e-mail warnings to be sent if specific sites are approaching their limits.

3. The SharePoint Self-Service Site Management feature enables users to create their own SharePoint sites. You can enable this option on the Application Management tab of the SharePoint Central Administration Web site.

Glossary

Active Directory Rights Management Services (AD RMS) A Windows Server 2008 server role that enables a computer to issue certificates and permissions for creating and editing contents of documents and media files.

AppCmd.exe A command-line utility for managing IIS 7.0 configuration settings and for performing tasks such as configuration backup and restore operations.

ApplicationHost.config file The primary settings that store server-level configuration details for IIS. The file is based on an XML format that can be edited manually.

application pools (IIS) A method by which multiple Web sites can run using separate worker processes in IIS. Application pools minimize the possibility of Web sites and Web applications adversely affecting other sites and applications.

application templates (Windows SharePoint Services) Downloadable SharePoint site templates that can be installed for use by new sites. Application templates are usually task-specific or organization-specific.

ASP.NET Microsoft Web application development technology, based on the Microsoft .NET Framework. ASP.NET applications are supported by IIS.

ASP.NET impersonation An IIS security method that enables ASP.NET applications to run under a specific security context or the security context of the authenticated user.

attack surface A term that refers to the overall potential security liability of a server or service. The attack surface for a Web server, for example, can be reduced by disabling unnecessary features and services.

block-based Direct or unformatted as opposed to file-based. Block-based access provides fast and direct access to the data needed by operating systems and applications.

boot image A WIM file you can use to boot a bare-metal computer. The Windows Vista and Windows Server 2008 product DVDs are able to boot the computer by using versions of a boot image named Boot.wim.

capture image A special boot image used to boot a master computer and upload an image of that computer to WDS.

certificate A digital document that provides proof of identity and a key for encryption.

Certificate Authority (CA) An organization or service that generates server certificates. Trusted third-party organizations can issue certificates for Web servers accessed by using the Internet.

Client Certificate Authentication A method by which security certificates are installed on client computers and are verified by a Web server to confirm the identity of the user or computer.

cluster A general term that represents any group of servers that act as one. Despite some similarities, Network Load Balancing (NLB) clusters and failover clusters serve very different purposes.

console session On a terminal server, the session of the user who is logged on locally and who has current access to the desktop.

defense in depth A security approach that involves the implementation of multiple layers of security to protect sensitive data such as Web server content.

Digital Rights Management (DRM) Technology that enables content producers to prevent unauthorized use of their intellectual property.

discover image A boot image you can use to enable a bare-metal computer that is not PXE-enabled to locate a WDS server and download a boot menu and image.

domain restrictions A method by which systems administrators can restrict which users can connect to a Web server based on the DNS domain of the client computer.

feature delegation A method of limiting which configuration settings users can view or change when they connect to a Web server, using IIS Manager.

File Transfer Protocol (FTP) A standard protocol for transferring files among computers.

FTP client Software that enables users to connect to an FTP server to upload and download files. Examples include the FTP command-line utility in Windows and FTP features in Internet Explorer.

FTP Over SSL (FTPS) A secure implementation of the FTP protocol that enables server administrators to require or allow encryption of data and control channel information.

FTP server A computer that is configured to enable users to access, upload, and download files.

FTP user isolation Settings that determine the default folders and to which folders FTP users will have access.

guest (child) operating system The operating system of a virtual machine.

handler mappings (IIS) Configuration settings that specify which types of content requests are handled by which request handlers.

home folder The default location in which a user's files are saved.

host (parent) operating system The base operating system installed on a computer in which virtualization technology is being used.

HTTPS HTTP-over-SSL. A commonly used method to encrypt Web traffic.

Hypertext Transfer Protocol (HTTP) The primary protocol used for communicating between Web browsers and Web servers. By default, HTTP uses TCP port 80 for communications.

Hypertext Transfer Protocol Secure (HTTPS) A secure version of the HTTP protocol that enables using Secure Sockets Layer (SSL) and certificates. By default, HTTPS uses TCP port 443 for communications.

hypervisor A small layer of software that is installed beneath a parent operating system and that grants the parent and all guests equal access to hardware resources (such as the CPU).

IIS Manager The primary graphical management tool for configuring IIS.

IIS Manager credentials An authentication method that enables Web server administrators to define user accounts and passwords to enable remote users to manage IIS.

IIS Management Service A role service for providing remote IIS management to users of the Web Server (IIS) role.

install image An image of a Windows Vista or Windows Server 2008 installation that you can deploy onto a computer.

Install mode A mode of Terminal Services that is used to install applications for multiple users.

Internet certificate request (IIS) A request for a server certificate generated on a Web server that will be publicly accessible. The request is sent to a Certificate Authority (CA), which can then generate a server certificate for installation on the computer.

Internet Information Services (IIS) The Web server platform that is included with Windows Server 2008. IIS provides support for HTTP, FTP, SMTP, and other communications protocols. It also supports a wide variety of Web development languages and platforms.

interstitial advertisements Audio or video advertisements that are designed to play back at periodic intervals when users are accessing content.

IP address restrictions (IIS) A method by which systems administrators can restrict which users can connect to a Web server, based on IP address information.

iSCSI initiator A software agent that initiates a connection to an iSCSI device on behalf of a computer.

iSCSI target A hardware device with a SCSI interface connected to a computer through an iSCSI adapter and cabling.

Key Management Service (KMS) A service and volume licensing option based on a KMS key. In KMS, clients automatically discover a locally installed KMS host and activate themselves without user intervention.

masquerade domain, SMTP An SMTP domain name option that rewrites the domain information for all messages sent through an SMTP virtual server.

modules (IIS) Web server code designed to provide additional functionality or capabilities for Web services. Modules can be added, removed, and disabled using the IIS Manager utility.

Multiple Acess Key (MAK) A volume-license key that can be activated a specific number of times.

.NET trust levels IIS configuration settings that determine the Code Access Security (CAS) rules applied to an application based on the .NET Framework.

Network Level Authentication (NLA) A feature of RDP 6.0 that enables user authentication to occur before a connection to a remote computer is established.

parity Error-checking information based on the evenness (0) or oddness (1) of values. Parity data is used to provide fault tolerance in a RAID-5 volume.

partition style The basic structure of a disk that defines how partitions are created and used. By far the most common partition style is Master Boot Record (MBR).

Printer Redirection A feature that enables a Terminal Services client to print to printers local to the client in a Terminal Services session.

publish (an application)   Make an application available remotely.

publishing points   A Windows Media server endpoint that provides access to either on-demand or broadcast-based content. A single Windows Media Services server can host numerous publishing points.

quorum configuration   In a failover cluster, the chosen rules that determine the number of failures the cluster can sustain before the cluster stops running.

Quota templates (Windows SharePoint Services)   Settings that control the maximum amount of storage space that can be used by a site collection. Quota templates can be created and managed by using the SharePoint Central Administration Web site.

Real-Time Streaming Protocol (RTSP)   A streaming protocol used by Windows Media Services with compatible players (such as Windows Media Player Series 9 or later). RTSP can function over UDP (RTSPU) or TCP (RTSPT).

relay restrictions, SMTP   SMTP security settings that specify which users or computers can send messages that are neither from nor to the SMTP domain. Implementing relay restrictions can help reduce the number of unwanted e-mail messages sent through an SMTP server.

Remote Desktop for Administration (RDA)   A mode of Terminal Services that does not require the installation of the Terminal Services server role or the purchase of any TS CALs. Also called Remote Desktop, this feature allows only two concurrent desktop sessions on the local server, including the console session. This feature is disabled by default.

Remote Desktop Protocol (RDP)   The protocol that enables the transport of a desktop session from one computer to another in the Terminal Services and Remote Desktop features.

request handlers   Programs that are designed to accept incoming IIS requests and generate a response. Request handlers can be enabled or disabled based on the specific needs of Web applications.

round-robin DNS   A simple method used to distribute client requests for one server among a group of servers.

SAN fabric   The hardware devices that connect servers and storage in a storage area network (SAN).

Secure Sockets Layer (SSL)   A security protocol designed to provide encryption and authentication capabilities for Web servers and Web browsers. SSL is a predecessor to the Transport Layer Security (TLS) protocol.

self-signed certificate   A security certificate a computer issues to itself, created on a server for development and testing purposes. A self-signed certificate does not provide proof of identity, but it still can be used for encryption. Self-signed certificates do not require the involvement of a Certificate Authority (CA).

server certificates   A method by which Web servers can provide their identity to Web users. Server certificates are obtained from a Certificate Authority (CA).

Server Farm Configuration (Windows SharePoint Services)   A Windows SharePoint Services deployment option that enables multiple front-end Web servers to access back-end database servers for performance, scalability, and reliability improvements.

SharePoint Central Administration Web site   The default management Web site for Windows SharePoint Services. It enables features for completion operations and application management tasks.

Simple Mail Transfer Protocol (SMTP)   An Internet standard for sending text-based messages among computers by using the TCP/IP protocol.

site bindings   Information that specifies to which types of requests an IIS Web site should respond. The site binding includes a protocol type, IP address settings, port numbers, and, optionally, a host name.

site collection (Windows SharePoint Services)   A group of SharePoint sites that share the same navigation and configuration settings. Multiple site collections can be created to allow different options.

smart host, SMTP   An SMTP virtual server configuration option that specifies that all outbound messages should be forwarded to a specific SMTP server rather than being sent directly. The use of smart hosts can increase performance and security.

SSL   Secure Sockets Layer. A method that is used to encrypt network traffic and that relies on digital certificates.

standalone server configuration (Windows SharePoint Services)   A Windows SharePoint Services deployment option that includes all the necessary components on the same server.

Streaming Media Services (server role)   An optional, downloadable Windows Server 2008 server role that includes Windows Media Services, sample content, and administrative tools and features.

stsadm.exe   A command-line utility for configuring and managing Windows SharePoint Services.

Terminal Services client access license (TS CAL)   Licenses you must purchase either for every user or for every device that connects to Terminal Services in Windows Server 2008. Without TS CALs, Terminal Services ceases to operate after 120 days.

Terminal Services connection   An open window displaying a logon session on a computer running Terminal Services.

Terminal Services connection authorization policy (TS CAP)   This type of policy is applied to a TS Gateway server and restricts client access to the gateway from external sources.

Terminal Services Gateway (TS Gateway)   A feature in Windows Server 2008 that enables authorized users on the Internet to connect to a terminal server on a private network.

Terminal Services RemoteApp (TS RemoteApp)   A feature of Terminal Services in Windows Server 2008 that enables a user to run a program installed on a remote server as if that program were installed. locally.

Terminal Services resource authorization policy (TS RAP)   This type of policy is applied to a TS Gateway server and is used to restrict access to Terminal Services resources in an organization.

Terminal Services session   A continuous period during which a user is logged on to a computer running Terminal Services.

Terminal Services Session Broker (TS Session Broker)   An optional component of Terminal Services that enables a computer to keep track of all user sessions in a terminal server farm. One benefit of TS Session Broker is that users who are accidentally disconnected from sessions on a server farm can be reconnected to the same session on the correct server.

Terminal Services Web Access (TS Web Access)   A Terminal Services component that enables a user to access RemoteApp programs and remote desktops through a Web page.

Transport Layer Security (TLS)   A security protocol that provides encryption and authentication capabilities for network connections.

URL authorization rules   IIS server settings that define which content is available to which users based on the path of the URL request.

user profile   The collection of data that comprises a user's individual environment, including individual files, application settings, and desktop configuration.

virtual server, SMTP   A specific instance of an SMTP server that is designed to respond to requests for a particular domain, IP address, and port number. SMTP virtual servers can be independently started and stopped.

Web application (Windows SharePoint Services)   A SharePoint Web site that provides functionality for a team or portion of the organization. Web applications can be created to serve the needs of different groups of users.

Web farm   An NLB cluster used to answer client requests for a Web site or group of Web sites.

Web Server (IIS) server role   A Windows Server 2008 server role that provides support for Web sites and Web applications. This role installs IIS 7.0 and allows administrators to enable a wide array of additional role services.

Web server farms   Groups of Web servers that work together to provide increased capacity, scalability, performance, and reliability. Generally, the servers within a farm will share the same content and configuration settings.

Web.config files   Configuring files that can be created within IIS Web applications and Web sites. These files can contain settings that override details specified in the ApplicationHost.config file.

WIM file   A file that contains one or more images in the native Windows Imaging format.

Windows Internal Database   A built-in database engine used by Windows Server 2008 for storing internal information. Windows SharePoint Services and other operating system features can store their data within this database.

Windows Media Load Simulator 9 Series utility   A free utility provided by Microsoft for simulating client load and activity on Windows Media servers.

Windows Media server announcements   A method by which content providers can include links to content available on their servers. Options include creating a Web page or special announcement files that users can connect to directly.

Windows Media server broadcast   A method of sending streamed audio or video to many users at once. Broadcasts are most commonly used for live events and in conjunction with a streaming media encoder.

Windows Media server cache/proxy server   A Windows Media server configuration that enables servers to manage client connections and to store copies of streamed content to increase performance and scalability.

Windows Media server playlist   A file that contains a list of audio and video media scheduled for playback.

Windows Media server plug-ins   A method by which Microsoft and third-party providers can extend the functionality of a Windows Media server. Plug-ins are available for managing authentication, authorization, and performance.

Windows Media Services   A server service that provides access to broadcast-based and on-demand audio and video content.

Windows Media Services multicast   A streaming media delivery method that involves many clients connecting to a single outbound stream from Windows Media Services.

Windows Media Services unicast   A streaming media delivery method that involves point-to-point connections between a Windows Media Services server and client computers.

Windows PowerShell   A Microsoft scripting environment and programming language. Windows PowerShell enables users to create scripts using object-based programming techniques.

Windows SharePoint Services (WSS)   A server role that enables users to access SharePoint sites for collaboration, document management, and communications functionality. WSS provides a Web-based administration interface for accessing content and for administration.

Windows System Resource Manager (WSRM)   A Windows Server 2008 utility that enables resource management. Administrators can define processor and memory priorities for applications and services that are running on their servers.

witness disk   In a failover cluster, a disk that contains a copy of the cluster configuration database. The availability of a witness disk is sometimes used to determine whether a cluster should run.

wrapper playlist advertisements   Audio or video advertisements that are designed to play before or after a client requests access to on-demand media.

Appendix
Windows Server 2008 Deployment

The following sections provide supplemental information about deploying Windows Server 2008. Although the purpose of this material is to provide assistance with real-world deployments, the information provided in this appendix will also be beneficial to you on the 70-643 exam.

The deployment technologies used to deploy Windows Server 2008 range from simple manual installs from the product DVD to unattended deployment by using the Windows Automated Installation Kit (Windows AIK), from using Microsoft Windows Deployment Services (WDS) to using Microsoft System Center Configuration Manager 2007. The technology you choose should reflect the size of your organization and your needs for automation in the deployment process.

Understanding Windows Deployment Technologies

Before you choose a tool or platform for deploying your servers, you need to ask yourself a few key questions:

- Will my deployment be high-volume or low-volume? That is, do I need to deploy a lot of servers or only a few? Using a high-volume deployment technology to install a handful of servers means you'll need to spend a lot of time at the outset learning how to use these technologies. High-volume deployment technologies can also have high purchase and licensing costs. Alternatively, using a low-volume deployment technology to install a thousand servers can take an excessive amount of time and involve a lot of repetition—you're likely to get bored going through the installation steps over and over again, and boredom can lead to inattention, which can cause mistakes.

- Is time an important constraint for your deployment? If you have lots of time on your hands, or an assistant with too much time, you can easily perform or delegate the task of manually installing a dozen servers. If time is limited however, then learning how to create answer files to perform unattended installations can be a big benefit to your organization.

- What degree of customization is required for the servers you plan to deploy? If all your servers will be deployed on identical hardware and will run the same server roles, then performing an unattended, image-based deployment can save you much time and effort. However, if each server has unique hardware requirements and a different set of roles, then some combination of manual and unattended install might be more appropriate to your situation.

The point of these questions is that you must choose the right tool for the job when it comes to deployment. Using an expensive, complex, difficult-to-learn platform such as System Center Configuration Manager is really only appropriate for large enterprises that have the time, budget, and staff to make proper use of the platform's capabilities and features. So before you choose a deployment technology, ask yourself the preceding questions to determine which technology best suits your needs.

Let's look now at the different technologies and platforms available for deploying Windows Server 2008.

Manual Installs

You can install from media by inserting a Windows Server 2008 product DVD in your server's DVD drive, copy the contents of this DVD to a share on your network and run Setup.exe remotely after booting your system from a previous operating system installed on the system, or boot from a Windows Preinstallation Environment (Windows PE) CD.

Windows AIK

The Windows AIK provides both corporate administrators and original equipment manufacturers (OEMs) with a set of tools and documentation for performing unattended installs of Windows Server 2008, Windows Vista, and some earlier versions of Microsoft Windows, including Windows XP and Microsoft Windows Server 2003.

IMPORTANT   Windows AIK versions

You must use the latest version of the Windows AIK if you want to deploy Windows Server 2008, using this technology. Windows AIK 1.1 is the latest version at time of writing and is capable of deploying both Windows Server 2008 and Windows Vista integrated with Service Pack 1.

Windows Deployment Services

WDS is a suite of components that replaces Remote Installation Services (RIS), a deployment technology first included as part of Windows 2000 Server. Windows Server 2008 includes a WDS server role you can add to servers by using Server Manager, and WDS provides a server-based, image-based deployment technology suitable for mid-sized companies that need to automate the deployment of workstations, servers, or both.

Microsoft Deployment

Microsoft Deployment is the most recent version of the Microsoft Solution Accelerator for Business Desktop Deployment (BDD). Microsoft Solution Accelerators provide end-to-end solutions for efficient planning, building, testing, and deploying of Microsoft platforms and products. Microsoft Deployment is a best-practices set of comprehensive guidance and tools from Microsoft for optimally deploying Windows servers, Windows clients, and Microsoft Office 2007. Microsoft Deployment is targeted mainly at the small to mid-sized business environment and contains tools, scripts, templates, and documentation that allow administrators to plan deployments, test for application compatibility issues and mitigate them, customize and package applications for deployment, and automate image-based desktop deployment. Microsoft Deployment does all this by providing a central workbench application that integrates the operation of the following tools:

- Windows AIK
- Application Compatibility Toolkit
- User State Migration Tool
- WDS

Microsoft Deployment also supports integration with Microsoft System Center Configuration Manager 2007 and provides for automated server role definition using Windows Server 2008 Server Manager.

Microsoft System Center Configuration Manager 2007

Microsoft System Center Configuration Manager 2007 is the latest release of Microsoft Systems Management Server (SMS) and uses policy-based automation to manage the full deployment, update, and extension life cycle for servers, clients, and handheld devices across physical, virtual, distributed, or mobile systems. Configuration Manager is an enterprise-class platform that is part of the Microsoft System Center family of products that includes Microsoft System Center Operations Manager 2007, Microsoft System Center Data Protection Manager (DPM) 2007, Microsoft System Center Virtual Machine Manager 2007, and other products designed to help enterprise IT departments manage their IT resources and life cycles.

MORE INFO   System Center Configuration Manager 2007

Using System Center Configuration Manager to deploy Windows Server 2008 is beyond the scope of this book. For more information about Configuration Manager and the System Center family of products, see *http://www.microsoft.com/systemcenter/*.

Quick Check

- Which deployment technology integrates tools, templates, scripts, and documentation to provide an end-to-end tool for deploying desktop and server versions of Windows for small to mid-sized business environments?

Quick Check Answer

- Microsoft Deployment

Understanding the Windows AIK

As mentioned previously, the Windows AIK is a set of tools for deploying the latest version of Windows. The following tools are either included with or provided by the Windows AIK:

- **Windows System Image Manager (Windows SIM)**   Enables you to create answer files (unattend.xml) and distribution shares for performing unattended installation of Windows

- **Windows Preinstallation Environment (Windows PE)**   Enables you to boot bare-metal systems to deploy Windows on them

- **ImageX**   Enables you to capture, modify, and apply file-based images for rapid deployment

In addition to these tools, installing the Windows AIK also provides:

- Windows Recovery Environment (Windows RE) tools for building diagnostic and recovery solutions based on Windows PE.

- Additional command-line tools such as Pkgmgr.exe, PEImg.exe, and others. These tools are discussed in later sections of this appendix.

- Documentation in the form of Windows Help (.chm) files.

MORE INFO   Built-in tools

Some built-in operating system tools can be useful for deployment. Examples of such tools include DiskPart, BCDEdit, and others. This is discussed further in the next section and in the Command-Line Tools Technical Reference section of the Windows Automated Installation Kit (Windows AIK) User's Guide.

To implement actual deployment, however, the Windows AIK tools listed here aren't enough. Instead, these tools need to interact with other Windows technologies and components, including the following:

- **Windows Setup** The program that installs Windows on a bare-metal system or upgrades previous versions of Windows
- **Windows Image (.wim) file** A single compressed file used to duplicate a Windows installation onto a disk volume
- **Windows Deployment Services (Windows DS or WDS) (optional)** Used to install Windows Server 2008 and Windows Vista or Windows Server 2008 remotely without the need of visiting each destination computer

Figure A-1 shows the architecture of the Windows Server 2008 and Windows Vista deployment platforms.

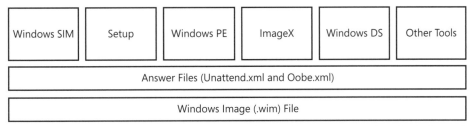

Figure A-1 Deployment platform architecture for Windows Server 2008 and Windows Vista

NOTE Supported Windows versions

Most of what is described in this book concerning Windows Server 2008 deployment also holds true for Windows Vista desktop deployment because, using Windows AIK 1.1, you can install both Windows Server 2008 and Windows Vista. Unless indicated otherwise, any reference to installing Windows Server 2008 or to installing Windows applies to Windows Vista as well. However, the main focus of the deployment appendixes of this book is deploying Windows Server 2008, not Windows Vista.

Comparing Deployment Tools for Different Windows Versions

Table A-1 provides a quick (but not exhaustive) comparison between the various tools and technologies used for deploying Windows Server 2008 and Windows Vista and the deployment tools used for the previous Windows versions of Windows Server 2003 and Windows XP Professional. If you are familiar with all the various tools used for deploying Windows Server 2003 and Windows XP, this table will provide a quick way of updating your deployment skills to support Windows Server 2008 and Windows Vista deployments. In addition, you can find more information concerning them in the Windows Automated Installation Kit (Windows AIK) User's Guide.

Table A-1 Comparison of Deployment Tools and Technologies for Windows XP /
Windows Server 2003 and Windows Vista / Windows Server 2008

Windows Server 2003 and Windows XP	Windows Server 2008 and Windows Vista
Answer File Tools and Settings	
Setup Manager	Windows SIM
Plaintext answer files	XML answer files
Multiple answer files Unattend.txt Winnt.sif Winborn.ini Oobeinfo.ini Sysprep.inf	Only two answer files Unattend.xml (or Autounattend.xml) Oobe.xml (used primarily for Vista)
Cmdlines.txt	RunSynchronous
[GUIRunOnce] section	FirstLogonCommands
OEM folders	Data image (though OEM is still supported using configuration sets)
Windows PE Versions	
Windows PE 1.0	Windows PE 2.0
Disk Imaging Tools	
Must use third-party tools	ImageX
Windows Setup	
Winnt.exe and Winnt32.exe	Setup.exe
Adding Device Drivers	
OEMPnPDriverPath	Package Manager
Adding Language Support	
MUI files	Language packs

The sections that follow examine the various Windows AIK tools in more detail and the enhancements made to these tools in Windows AIK 1.1.

Understanding Windows SIM and Answer Files

Windows System Image Manager (SIM) is the tool you use to create and manage answer files, which are used to perform unattended installs of Windows. Windows SIM provides a graphical user interface for creating new answer files and customizing the settings to be used for installing Windows (Figure A-2).

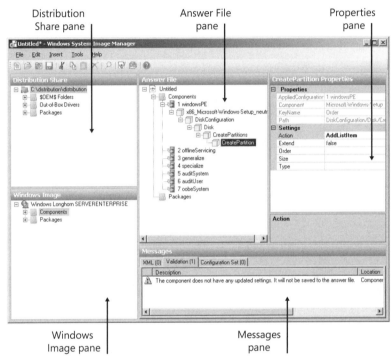

Distribution Share pane   Answer File pane   Properties pane

Windows Image pane   Messages pane

Figure A-2   The Windows SIM interface

The five panes of the Windows SIM shown in the figure are:

- **Distribution Share**   Shows the currently open distribution share folder and its subfolders. This pane enables you to select, create, explore, and close distribution share folders as well as add items from the open distribution share folder to your answer file. Distribution shares are discussed further later on in this section.

- **Windows Image**   Shows the currently open Windows Image (.wim) file and the components and packages it makes available for installation. You usually open a .wim file before you create an answer file to perform an unattended installation of Windows. More information about .wim files is available later in this section.
- **Answer File**   Shows the different configuration passes used by Windows Setup and any answer file settings you have added for processing during each pass.
- **Properties**   Shows the properties you can configure for the answer file setting currently selected in the Answer File pane.
- **Messages**   Displays informational messages about the correctness of XML syntax for an answer file, the validity of its settings for the version of Windows you want to install, and other types of messages.

Using Windows SIM, you can do the following:

- Create a new answer file and configure settings for components and packages so that these settings are processed during a particular configuration pass.
- Edit the settings in an existing answer file.
- Add third-party drivers, applications, and other packages to an answer file.
- Validate an answer file to ensure that it is syntactically correct and its settings are applicable for the version of Windows being deployed.
- Create a distribution share for performing an unattended install of Windows over the network.
- Create a configuration set for performing an unattended install of Windows when a network is not available.

In Windows SIM terminology, a **component** is a part of the Windows operating system that specifies the files, resources, and settings for a specific feature of Windows or some part of a feature. Many components include unattended installation settings that can be used for customizing the way they are configured during a Windows installation. In contrast, a **package** is a group of files that can be used to modify some feature of Windows. The types of packages available can include service packs, security updates, language packs, and hotfixes. Packages can also include unattended installation settings that can be used for customizing the way they are configured during a Windows installation.

When you configure an unattended installation setting for a component or package, you also choose the configuration pass during which this setting will be processed. A **configuration pass** is a phase of Windows installation, and Windows Server 2008 Setup includes seven configuration passes that can be used during an installation. Different portions of Windows are installed during different configuration passes, and you can even specify that an unattended installation setting be processed in more than one configuration pass if needed.

A **distribution share** is a set of folders for storing third-party drivers, applications, and packages issued by Microsoft such as software updates and service packs. Distribution shares are optional and can be created and managed on the technician's computer by using Windows SIM, although you can also create distribution shares manually if you prefer. In contrast, a **configuration set** is a self-contained file and folder structure that contains only the files that are needed to control the installation process. Basically, a configuration set is a smaller version of a distribution share, and it can either be stored on a network share or copied to removable media for installation of Windows without a network. The files in a configuration set contain the same information as the distribution share but have been converted to binary form.

Distribution shares or configuration sets, together with answer files, can be used to perform unattended installs of Windows over the network onto bare-metal systems. Figure A-3 shows the folder structure created when you use Windows SIM to create a new distribution share.

Figure A-3   Folder structure for a distribution share

The subfolders of a distribution share have the following purposes:

■ **OEM folders**   Contain files used to brand custom applications, add them, or both to your installation of Windows. This is an earlier deployment technology that is still supported in Windows Server 2008, but the preferred approach to add new files and resources to Windows installations is to use data images. A **data image** is an additional .wim file that contains applications, files, or other resources to supplement the main .wim file used to install Windows itself. For more information about .wim files, see later in this section.

■ **Out-of-Box Drivers folder**   Contains additional device drivers you want to install during Windows Setup.

■ **Packages folder**   Contains software updates for Windows such as service packs, language packs, security updates, and other types of updates. Packages must be imported into this folder by using Windows SIM, and once you've imported the package, you can add it to your installation by using Windows SIM and configure any settings available for the package.

Device Drivers and Windows Setup

Sometimes, to install Windows successfully, you will need additional device drivers, and it's important to understand the difference between the types of device drivers and how they can be added to a Windows installation:

- **In-box drivers**   These are generally .inf-based drivers that are included with Windows itself. Another type of in-box driver, however, is one that is installed by using a Windows Installer (.msi) file, and this type of driver is added using the same method by which applications are added to an installation.

- **Out-of-box drivers**   These are additional .inf-based drivers you add to Windows Setup by using the Windows SIM. Out-of-box drivers must be located in the Out-of-Box Drivers folder of your distribution share, and they are typically processed during the auditSystem configuration pass of Setup. If your out-of-box drivers are boot-critical drivers, however—drivers needed to boot the system itself successfully—then these drivers must be added to the windowsPE configuration pass instead by configuring the Windows-PnpCustomizationsWinPE component, using Windows SIM.

The answer files you create by using Windows SIM are XML files that contain definitions and values for the different settings you configure for your unattended installation of Windows. Answer files are usually named one of the following:

- **Unattend.xml**   An answer file used for most types of unattended installs of Windows Server 2008. Unattend.xml is a single XML answer file that controls almost all phases of the unattended install process. By way of comparison, previous versions of Windows such as Windows Server 2003 and Windows XP Professional used multiple types of answer files to control different phases of the installation process.

- **Autounattend.xml**   An answer file used for unattended installs of Windows using the DVD-boot method. To boot from the Windows Server 2008 product DVD and perform an unattended install, you copy your Autounattend.xml answer file to the root of a floppy disk or USB flash device. This is similar (but not identical to) how you used a Winnt.sif file to perform boot-from-CD installations of previous versions of Windows.

To see what an XML answer file looks like, examine the different sections of the autounattend_sample.xml file found in the *%ProgramFiles%*\Windows AIK\Samples folder:

```
<?xml version="1.0" encoding="utf-8"?>
<unattend xmlns="urn:schemas-microsoft-com:unattend">
    <settings pass="Windows PE">
        <component name="Microsoft-Windows-Setup" processorArchitecture="x86"
publicKeyToken="31bf3856ad364e35" language="neutral" versionScope="nonSxS"
xmlns:wcm="http://schemas.microsoft.com/WMIConfig/2002/State"
xmlns:xsi="http://www.w3.org/2001/XMLSchema-instance">
```

After this header information, which specifies things such as the configuration pass during which the settings that follow are processed (Windows PE), the component being installed (Microsoft-Windows-Setup), and the architecture of the system on which Windows is being deployed (x86), the disk partition and formatting scheme is specified:

```
<DiskConfiguration>
    <Disk>
        <CreatePartitions>
            <CreatePartition wcm:action="add">
                <Order>1</Order>
                <Size>20000</Size>
                <Type>Primary</Type>
            </CreatePartition>
        </CreatePartitions>
        <ModifyPartitions>
            <ModifyPartition wcm:action="add">
                <Active>true</Active>
                <Extend>false</Extend>
                <Format>NTFS</Format>
                <Label>OS_Install</Label>
                <Letter>C</Letter>
                <Order>1</Order>
                <PartitionID>1</PartitionID>
            </ModifyPartition>
        </ModifyPartitions>
        <DiskID>0</DiskID>
        <WillWipeDisk>true</WillWipeDisk>
    </Disk>
    <WillShowUI>OnError</WillShowUI>
</DiskConfiguration>
```

The next section specifies the product key to be used for the install and accepts the End-User Licensing Agreement (EULA).

```
<UserData>
    <ProductKey>
        <Key>&lt;productkey&gt;</Key>
        <WillShowUI>OnError</WillShowUI>
    </ProductKey>
    <AcceptEula>true</AcceptEula>
</UserData>
```

The section that follows tells Setup to install Windows on the partition created earlier:

```
<ImageInstall>
    <OSImage>
        <InstallTo>
            <DiskID>0</DiskID>
            <PartitionID>1</PartitionID>
        </InstallTo>
        <WillShowUI>OnError</WillShowUI>
    </OSImage>
</ImageInstall>
</component>
```

Settings for another component are now specified. These settings indicate that the language to be used during Setup is U.S. English.

```
<component name="Microsoft-Windows-International-Core-WinPE"
processorArchitecture="x86" publicKeyToken="31bf3856ad364e35"
language="neutral" versionScope="nonSxS"
xmlns:wcm="http://schemas.microsoft.com/WMIConfig/2002/State"
xmlns:xsi="http://www.w3.org/2001/XMLSchema-instance">
        <SetupUILanguage>
            <UILanguage>en-us</UILanguage>
        </SetupUILanguage>
        <InputLocale>0409:00000409</InputLocale>
        <SystemLocale>en-us</SystemLocale>
        <UILanguage>en-us</UILanguage>
        <UserLocale>en-US</UserLocale>
    </component>
</settings>
```

The next section contains settings that are to be processed during the oobeSystem configuration pass, which are applied during the first-boot experience for end users. These settings indicate that Sysprep is to be run in audit mode to reseal the system before delivery to the customer:

```
<settings pass="oobeSystem">
    <component name="Microsoft-Windows-Deployment">
```

```
processorArchitecture="x86" publicKeyToken="31bf3856ad364e35"
language="neutral" versionScope="nonSxS"
xmlns:wcm="http://schemas.microsoft.com/WMIConfig/2002/State"
xmlns:xsi="http://www.w3.org/2001/XMLSchema-instance">
        <Reseal>
            <Mode>Audit</Mode>
        </Reseal>
    </component>
  </settings>
```

The final section, which follows, contains settings to be processed during the specialize configuration pass, in which machine-specific information for the image is applied. An original equipment manufacturer (OEM) might use this section to indicate the make and model of the system and provide telephone support information for end users. Corporate users might use this section to specify contact information for department heads or URLs for support of Web sites on the company intranet.

```
  <settings pass="specialize">
    <component name="Microsoft-Windows-Shell-Setup"
processorArchitecture="x86" publicKeyToken="31bf3856ad364e35"
language="neutral" versionScope="nonSxS"
xmlns:wcm="http://schemas.microsoft.com/WMIConfig/2002/State"
xmlns:xsi="http://www.w3.org/2001/XMLSchema-instance">
        <OEMInformation>
            <Manufacturer>&lt;manufacturer&gt;</Manufacturer>
            <Model>&lt;model&gt;</Model>
            <SupportHours>&lt;support hours&gt;</SupportHours>
            <SupportPhone>&lt;support phone&gt;</SupportPhone>
        </OEMInformation>
    </component>
  </settings>

  <cpi:offlineImage cpi:source="catalog:c:/dan/install_windows vista
ultimate.clg" xmlns:cpi="urn:schemas-microsoft-com:cpi" />
</unattend>
```

MORE INFO   Windows SIM and Answer Files

Additional information about the Windows SIM can be found in the Deployment Tools Technical Reference section of the WAIK.chm Help File in the Windows AIK. Detailed information about individual answer file settings can be found in the Unattended Windows Setup Reference in the Windows AIK.

Quick Check

1. How is an Autounattend.xml file similar to a Winnt.sif file?
2. How are these two files different?

Quick Check Answers

1. Both are text files that can be used for performing unattended install-from-media installations of Windows.
2. Winnt.sif is an earlier technology used for installing Windows 2000, Windows XP, and Windows Server 2003. Autounattend.xml is used for installing Windows Vista and Windows Server 2008. Another difference is that Autounattend.xml uses XML syntax whereas Winnt.sif consists of section headers, parameters, and values for those parameters.

Understanding Windows PE

Windows Preinstallation Environment (Windows PE) is a minimal version of Windows based on the Windows Vista kernel (which is identical to the Windows Server 2008 kernel) that can be used for deployment and troubleshooting purposes. Specifically, you can use Windows PE to:

- Boot a bare-metal system to install Windows on it. (See Figure A-4.) Using Windows PE, you can boot the system, partition and format the hard drives, and connect to a distribution share on the network to copy down disk images and install Windows on the system in either attended or unattended mode as desired.
- Troubleshoot a system on which Windows is already installed but not functioning properly. Using Windows PE, you can launch Windows RE and run built-in diagnostic and troubleshooting tools. You can also use Windows PE to build a customized recovery solution for automatically recovering or rebuilding computers running Windows.

In addition to these uses, Windows PE also runs each time you install Windows Server 2008 on a system. The graphic tools displayed during setup are actually running within the Windows PE environment.

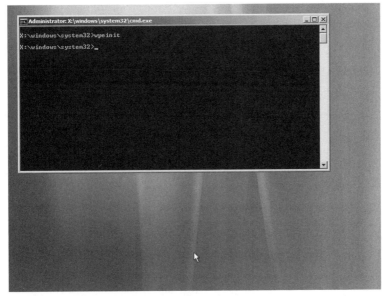

Figure A-4 The Windows PE command shell

As can be seen from Figure A-4, Windows PE presents you with a command-prompt interface from which you can run various built-in tools useful for installation or troubleshooting purposes. The following tools are available from the Windows PE prompt.

NOTE What's the X drive?

The X drive in Windows PE is a RAM disk (a writable volume in memory) used when Windows PE is booted from read-only media such as a CD or DVD, a USB key, or a WDS image. By default, Windows PE allocates 32 MB for this RAM disk, but you can customize the size of the RAM drive by using the PEImg.exe utility. See the section titled "Understanding Windows AIK 1.1 Enhancements" later in this section for more information.

- **Boot Configuration Data**   This tool can be used to edit the boot configuration data (BCD) store, which describes boot applications and boot application settings. The BCD store in Windows Vista and Windows Server 2003 replaces the Boot.ini used by earlier versions of Windows.

- **Bootsect**   This tool can be used to restore the boot sector on your computer by updating the master boot code for hard-disk partitions to alternate between BOOTMGR and NTLDR. The tool replaces the FixFAT and FixNTFS tools used in earlier versions of Windows.

- **DiskPart**   This tool can be used to manage disks, partitions, and volumes both interactively from a command prompt and in automated mode, using scripts.

- **Drvload**   This tool can be used for adding out-of-box drivers to a booted Windows PE image, using one or more driver .inf files as its inputs.

- **Oscdimg.exe**   This tool can be used for creating an image (.iso) file of a customized 32-bit or 64-bit version of Windows PE, which you can then burn onto CD media to create a bootable Windows PE CD.

- **PEImg.exe**   This tool can be used to create or modify a Windows PE image, for example, by importing a package, installing a driver, and so on.

- **Winpeshl.ini**   This tool can be used to customize the default shell for Windows PE to enable you to run your own shell application instead of the default Windows PE command prompt.

- **Wpeinit.exe**   This tool is used to initialize Windows PE every time Windows PE boots.

MORE INFO   Windows PE tools

For more information about the Windows PE command-line tools, see the section titled "Windows PE Tools Technical Reference" in the Windows Preinstallation Environment (Windows PE) User's Guide of the Windows AIK.

Windows PE was originally designed as a way of initiating Windows Setup on bare-metal systems without using MS-DOS network boot floppies. The first version of Windows PE was based on the Windows XP kernel and was called Windows PE 1.0. When Windows Vista was released, a new version called Windows PE 2.0 was also released and was based on the newer Windows Vista kernel.

NOTE   Limitations of Windows PE

Windows PE has a number of limitations, which means that it is not intended as an operating system for daily use. For example, Windows PE automatically stops working after 72 hours and reboots, and you can't remove this limitation. Also, any changes made to the Windows PE registry are lost upon reboot (unless you make the changes when Windows PE is offline). Additionally, Windows PE does not support the .NET Framework, the common language runtime (CLR), or applications packaged as Windows Installer (.msi) files. Finally, Windows PE supports only a subset of Win32 APIs, which limits the applications that can be run on it.

Limitations of MS-DOS Boot Floppies

For many years, real-world administrators used MS-DOS boot floppies to boot bare-metal hardware to perform unattended network installs of Windows operating systems. There are a number of reasons why this practice is on the way out. For example, MS-DOS has:

- Minimal native networking support.
- No support for the NTFS file system.
- No support for 32-bit or 64-bit Windows device drivers.

Because of these limitations—and the difficulty of even finding MS-DOS nowadays or people who know how to customize it—Microsoft developed Windows PE as a new tool for booting computers that have no installed operating system. By way of contrast with MS-DOS boot floppies, Windows PE has:

- Support for NTFS 5.x, including support for creating and managing dynamic volumes.
- Support for TCP/IP networking, including a file-sharing client.
- Support for 32-bit or 64-bit device drivers, depending on the version of Windows PE.
- Support for booting from CD or DVD media, USB flash devices, and WDS used remotely.

To use Windows PE, you typically use the tools included with the Windows AIK to create a Windows PE build environment and convert it into an .iso file containing the ready-to-run Windows PE operating system. If needed, you can also customize your Windows PE build environment by adding additional tools to it. Then, you use third-party CD-burning software to burn your .iso file to CD media, and the result is a bootable Windows PE CD you can use to launch the installation process on bare-metal hardware.

Understanding ImageX and the .wim File Format

Imagex.exe is a command-line tool that enables you to manage Windows Imaging (.wim) files to perform image-based deployment of Windows onto bare-metal hardware. In the past, many system administrators deployed earlier versions of Windows by using third-party disk-imaging software. Such software typically used sector-based imaging to copy or "clone" Windows installation disks on a sector-by-sector basis to newly formatted volumes on disks in target systems. ImageX is designed to provide greater flexibility than sector-based imaging; to speed deployment by reducing the size of the image; and to enable offline servicing of images by adding, removing, or deleting files from the image.

ImageX works together with three other Windows imaging technologies, as shown in Figure A-5.

- **Windows Imaging (.wim) files** These are collections of image files that contain one or more Windows operating systems and their components and added packages. WIM is a compressed, file-based disk image format first introduced with Windows Vista.
- **WIM File System Filter** This enables you to browse and edit the contents of a .wim file to perform offline servicing on it after mounting the file to a directory.
- **WIM API set** These APIs provide the underlying capabilities for the WIM FS Filter driver and the ImageX command. The APIs also enable third-party independent software vendors (ISVs) to develop deployment tools compatible with WIM.

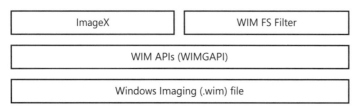

Figure A-5   The ImageX architecture

To use ImageX, you typically type the command with one of its command options plus additional information as needed. For example, typing the **imagex /capture image_path image_file "name"** command will capture the *image_path* volume image from a drive to *image_file.wim* with name *name*.

Following are high-level descriptions of each ImageX command option. For the detailed syntax of these command options, type **imagex /?** at the Windows PE Tools Command Prompt on a computer on which the Windows AIK has been installed.

- **/append** Appends a volume image to an existing.wim file
- **/apply** Applies a volume image to a specified drive
- **/capture** Captures a volume image from a drive to a new .wim file
- **/delete** Deletes the specified volume image from a .wim file with multiple volume images
- **/dir** Displays a list of the files and folders within a specified volume image
- **/export** Exports a copy of the specified .wim file to another .wim file
- **/info** Returns the total file size, the image index number, the directory count, file count, description, and other stored XML descriptions for the specified .wim file

- **/split**   Splits an existing .wim file into multiple read-only .wim files
- **/mount**   Mounts a .wim file with read-only permission to a specified directory, enabling you to view but not modify all the information contained in the directory
- **/mountrw**   Mounts a .wim file with read/write permission to a specified directory, enabling you to view and modify all the information contained in the directory
- **/unmount**   Unmounts the mounted image from a specified directory

Understanding Sysprep

Sysprep.exe is a deployment tool that has several important uses. Specifically, you can use Sysprep to:

- Remove all system-specific information from a Windows installation so that you can capture an image from it using ImageX and then deploy the image on other bare-metal systems.
- Configure a Windows installation to boot into Audit mode so you can install third-party device drivers and applications and test the functionality of the system before capturing an image from it.
- Configure a Windows installation to boot to Windows Welcome the next time the computer is started. This is typically done just before delivering the computer to the end user or customer.
- Reset Windows Product Activation up to three times.

CAUTION   Using Sysprep

You should use Sysprep only on new, clean installations of Windows. You should not use Sysprep on existing Windows installations, and you can't use it on in-place-upgrade installations.

The general syntax of the Sysprep command is as follows:

sysprep.exe [/oobe | /audit] [/generalize] [/reboot | /shutdown | /quit] [/quiet] [/unattend:answerfile]

Following are high-level descriptions of each Sysprep command option.

- **/audit**   Restarts the computer into audit mode so you can add additional drivers or applications to Windows and test the installation before delivering it to the user.
- **/generalize**   Prepares the Windows installation for imaging by removing all unique system information from the Windows installation, which means resetting Security IDs (SIDs), clearing system restore points, and deleting event logs. The specialize configuration pass then runs the next time the system is booted, which means new SIDs

are created and the Windows activation clock is reset (provided the clock has not already been reset the maximum three times allowed).

- **/oobe** Restarts a computer running Windows into Windows Welcome mode to enable users to customize their Windows installations by creating user accounts, naming the computer, and performing other tasks. Any answer file settings specified in the oobeSystem configuration pass are processed immediately before Windows Welcome starts.

- **/reboot** Restarts the computer—use this option when auditing the computer and for verifying that your OOBE customizations work properly.

- **/shutdown** Shuts down the computer once Sysprep has finished its work.

- **/quiet** Runs Sysprep without displaying any onscreen confirmation messages. This is useful when you need to automate Sysprep.

- **/quit** Closes Sysprep after running the commands you specified.

- **/unattend:answerfile** Applies settings contained in the specified answer file to Windows during unattended installation.

In addition to running Sysprep from the command line or from scripts, you can also select certain Sysprep options from the UI by typing **%systemroot%\system32\sysprep\sysprep** with no parameters following it, which opens the dialog box shown in Figure A-6.

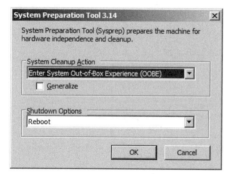

Figure A-6   Sysprep Preparation dialog box

Although Sysprep is generally useful for preparing Windows installations for image capture, there are some limitations for its use with Windows Server 2008. Specifically, the following installed server roles *cannot* be resealed using sysprep /generalize for preparing them for imaging:

- All Active Directory server roles, including AD CS, AD DS, AD FS, AD LDS, and AD RMS
- DNS Server
- Fax Server
- File Services

- Network Policy and Access Services
- Print Services
- UDDI Services role
- Windows Deployment Services
- Windows SharePoint Services

For any of the roles listed, you must install the particular role after installation is finished for the role to work properly. In addition, the following role-related limitations also apply to using Sysprep:

- The Web Server (IIS) role does not support Sysprep with encrypted credentials in the applicationhost.config file.
- The Terminal Services role does not support Sysprep when the master Windows image is joined to a domain.

Understanding Windows AIK 1.1 Enhancements

Windows AIK 1.1 includes a number of enhancements for performing image-based deployments over the initial version of Windows AIK 1.0 that was released with Windows Vista. Some of the more important enhancements include:

- The ability to deploy Windows Vista, Windows Vista integrated with Service Pack 1, and Windows Server 2008.
- The ability to automate adding server roles, role services, and features during the final stages of Windows Setup.
- The ability to deploy 64-bit versions of Windows from a 32-bit preinstallation environment.
- The ability to apply Windows images to Unified Extended Firmware Interface (UEFI)–enabled computers.
- Extensible Firmware Interface (EFI) support for 64-bit and installation to iSCSI disks from media.
- IA64 support for Windows SIM to enable you to mount a .wim file from IA64 media.
- Additional answer file settings supported only by Windows Server 2008 and not by Windows Vista. These include settings to specify the type of install (Windows Server 2008 or Windows Server 2008 Server Core), disable Internet Explorer Enhanced Security Configuration (IE-ESC), specify the administrator password, enable autologon using the administrator account, disable the Initial Configuration Tasks screen from running, and disable Server Manager and other server-only settings from running.
- Enhancements to Windows PE, including the ability to configure the size of the RAM disk (X: drive) by using the *PEImg /scratchspace size* command where *size* can be 32, 64,

128, 256, or 512 MB; an updated Oscdimg.exe utility that includes new command options and support for larger images; support for booting directly from the hard disk instead of from the RAM disk; and an IA64 version of Windows PE.

- Support for a virtual floppy drive to install Windows using retail media.

- A new tool called PostReflect.exe that can be used to reflect all boot-critical drivers out of the driver store in an offline Windows image, allowing the image to be deployed to various hardware configurations.

- A set of schema definitions that enable you to add tasks, links, and branding items to the OOBE of Windows installations.

Understanding Preinstallation Terminology

The term *preinstallation* refers to the process of planning, preparing, customizing, deploying, and maintaining Windows operating system images for use in image-based deployment. A Windows image is a single compressed file that contains a collection of files and folders that can be used to duplicate a Windows installation onto a disk volume. To understand how to plan and implement the preinstallation process, you need to understand the following terminology:

- **Technician computer**   This is the computer on which you install Windows System Image Manager (Windows SIM) and on which your configuration sets and the distribution share are typically also found.

- **Master installation**   This is the customized installation of Windows that you plan to duplicate onto one or more destination computers.

- **Master computer**   This is the assembled computer that contains your master installation.

- **Base image**   This is a collection of files and folders (sometimes compressed into a single file) that have been captured from a master installation and which contain the base operating system plus any additional configurations and files you specify.

- **Destination computer**   This is any computer on which you preinstall Windows, either by running Windows Setup on the computer or by copying a master installation onto it.

Understanding the Preinstallation Process

The preinstallation process for deployment of Windows Server 2008 and Windows Vista using image-based deployment is a life-cycle process that involves the following six phases. (See Figure A-7.)

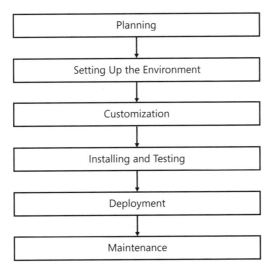

Figure A-7   The preinstallation process

1. Planning

   This phase involves choosing the deployment method and tools that best serve your needs.

2. Setting up the environment

   This phase involves designating your technician computer and installing Windows SIM on the computer. This phase also involves creating your lab environment so you can test your installations before deploying them on your production network.

3. Customization

   This phase involves creating your answer file, using Windows SIM so you can use this file to customize your installations.

4. Installation and testing

   This phase involves creating your master installation and testing it to make sure everything works as designed.

5. Deployment

   This phase involves capturing a Windows image from your master installation and deploying the image onto your destination computers, using the method appropriate to your environment.

6. Maintenance

   This phase involves modifying your captured images to add additional device drivers, software updates, service packs, and third-party applications as needed.

Understanding the Different Deployment Methods

The most basic way of differentiating deployment methods is by whether they are designed for high-volume, mid-volume, or low-volume deployment:

- **High-volume deployment**   This is typically a desktop computing scenario for large enterprises where you must deploy hundreds or thousands of computers, which are running Windows Vista, quickly and easily. (The main scenario in which large numbers of computers running Windows Server 2008 might need to be deployed is for large data center environments.) The typical approach used for high-volume deployment is called "install from image" and involves creating a master installation, capturing its image, and deploying the image to destination computers from a network share.

- **Medium-volume deployment**   This is typically a desktop or server computing scenario for small to mid-sized business environments where you must deploy, quickly and easily, a few dozen computers running Windows Vista or a handful of computers running Windows Server 2008 but without the overhead involved in capturing and maintaining a library of Windows images. The typical approach used for medium-volume deployment is called "install from configuration set" and involves booting your destination computers from a floppy disk or USB flash device and then running Windows Setup from a network share.

- **Low-volume deployment**   This scenario is typical for small office and home office environments where administrative skills are limited and only a few systems need to be deployed or for small to mid-sized business environments where administrative resources are limited and only a few servers need to be deployed. The typical approach used for low-volume deployment is called "install from DVD."

Table A-2 compares and contrasts each of the three deployment methods described.

Table A-2   Comparison of Deployment Methods

Method	Volume	Speed	Network Required
Install from image	High	Fast	Yes
Install from configuration set	Medium	Slow	Optional
Install from DVD	Low	Slow	No

The following section examines each of these three deployment methods in more detail.

Using the Install from DVD Method

Figure A-8 illustrates the basic install from DVD method of deploying Windows, which is typically used for low-volume deployments of desktop or server computers in small office and home office environments or for deploying servers in small to mid-sized environments where administrative resources are limited.

In this method, you use Windows SIM on a technician computer to create an answer file named Autounattend.xml. You then boot the destination computer by using the product DVD with that answer file on a floppy or USB flash device.

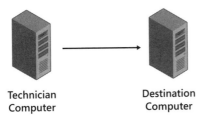

Technician   Destination
Computer   Computer

Figure A-8   The install from DVD method of deploying Windows

Another use for this method is for building your master installation so you can then deploy Windows by using the install from image installation method. For example, to build a master installation using this method, replace "destination computer" with "master computer" in the preceding diagram.

The steps involved in deploying Windows by using the install from DVD method are as follows:

1. Using Windows SIM on your technician computer, create and configure an answer file and save it using the file name Autounattend.xml. Validate your answer file, and then copy the answer file you created to a floppy disk, USB flash device, or other removable media device.

2. Insert the Windows product DVD into your destination computer's DVD drive. Also insert a floppy disk or USB flash device containing your answer file into your destination computer. Be sure that your destination computer's BIOS is configured to boot from DVD.

3. Turn on the destination computer. When Windows Setup starts, it will search for an answer file named Autounattend.xml. If it finds this file, it will use the customizations specified in the file during setup.

4. When setup is finished running and the destination computer reboots, you can either deploy the computer as is onto the network or make additional customizations, run *sysprep /generalize /shutdown*, and deploy the computer onto the network, depending on your needs.

Using the Install from Configuration Set Method

Figure A-9 illustrates the basic install from configuration set method of deploying Windows, which is typically used for medium-volume deployments of desktop or server computers in small to mid-sized environments.

In this method, you use Windows SIM on the technician computer to create an answer file followed by a configuration set. You then copy the configuration set to a network share (or onto portable media). Finally, you boot the destination computer by using Windows PE and connect to the network share to install Windows from the configuration set.

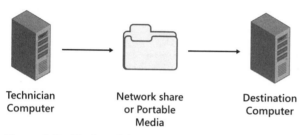

Technician
Computer

Network share
or Portable
Media

Destination
Computer

Figure A-9   The install from configuration set method of deploying Windows

The steps involved in deploying Windows by using the install from configuration set method vary depending on whether you store your configuration set on a network share or on removable media.

Install from Configuration Set Method Using Removable Media

To deploy Windows by using the install from configuration method when your configuration set is stored on removable media, do the following:

1. Using Windows SIM on your technician computer, create and configure an answer file and save it using the file name Autounattend.xml.

2. Using Windows SIM again, create a distribution share folder on your technician computer. If needed, add additional device drivers and third-party applications to your distribution share and customize your answer file accordingly. Validate your answer file.

3. Using Windows SIM once more, create a configuration set that gathers into one location all the resource files that you specified in your answer file.

4. Copy your configuration set to removable media, for example, to a USB flash device.

5. Insert the Windows product DVD into your destination computer's DVD drive. Also insert the removable media, or point to the network share, containing your configuration set into your destination computer. Be sure that your destination computer's BIOS is configured to boot from DVD.

6. Turn on the destination computer. When Windows Setup starts, it will search for an answer file named Autounattend.xml. If it finds this file, it will use the customizations specified in the file during setup.

7. When setup is finished running and the destination computer reboots, you can either deploy the computer as is onto the network or make additional customizations, run *sysprep /generalize /shutdown*, and deploy the computer onto the network, depending on your needs.

Install from Configuration Set Method Using a Network Share

To deploy Windows using the install from configuration method when your configuration set is stored on a network share, do the following:

1. Using Windows SIM on your technician computer, create and configure an answer file and save it, using the file name Autounattend.xml.

2. Using Windows SIM again, create a distribution share folder on your technician computer. If needed, add additional device drivers and third-party applications to your distribution share and customize your answer file accordingly. Validate your answer file.

3. Using Windows SIM once more, create a configuration set that gathers into one location all the resource files that you specified in your answer file.

4. Create a share on your network and create two subfolders beneath it, one for the Windows source files and one for the files of your configuration set. For example, create the following folder structure:

   ```
   \\sharename\source
   \\sharename\confsets
   ```

5. Copy the Windows installation files from the \source folder on your product DVD to the \source subfolder of your network share.

6. Copy your configuration set files to the \confsets subfolder of your network share.

7. Boot your destination computer, using bootable Windows PE media. Once the Windows PE command prompt window appears, connect to your network share by mapping a drive, using a command such as the following:

   ```
   net use y: \\sharename
   ```

   You might need to specify credentials to connect. If so, be sure to specify these credentials in the form *computer_name\username*.

8. Once connected to the network share, run Windows Setup, referencing the answer file contained in your configuration set by using a command such as the following:

   ```
   y:\source\setup.exe /unattend:y:\confsets\autounattend.xml.
   ```

9. When setup is finished running and the destination computer reboots, you can either deploy the computer as is onto the network or make additional customizations, run *sysprep /generalize /shutdown*, and deploy the computer onto the network, depending on your needs.

Quick Check

- When performing an install of Windows Server 2008 without a network, when should you use the install from configuration set method of deploying Windows instead of the simpler install from DVD method?

Quick Check Answer

- Use the install from configuration set method if you need to perform an install without a network, which requires additional device drivers or third-party applications as part of your installation.

Using the Install from Image Method

Figure A-10 illustrates the basic install from image method of deploying Windows, which is typically used for high-volume deployments of desktop computers in enterprise environments and of servers in data center environments.

In this method, you use Windows SIM on the technician computer to create an answer file and, optionally, a distribution set. You then build a master installation on the master computer and then prepare that computer for imaging by using Sysprep. Next, you use ImageX from Windows PE to capture an image of the master computer and upload it to a network distribution share. Finally, you boot the destination computer in Windows PE, format the hard drive by using Diskpart.exe, and connect to the distribution share to apply the image.

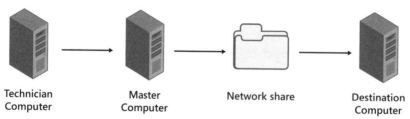

Technician Computer   Master Computer   Network share   Destination Computer

Figure A-10 The install from image method of deploying Windows

The steps involved in deploying Windows by using the install from image method vary depending on whether you apply the captured image of your master installation onto your destination computer by using ImageX or Windows Setup.

Install from Image Method Using ImageX

To deploy Windows using the install from image method by using ImageX, do the following:

1. Use either the install from DVD or install from configuration set method to create your master installation of Windows. Customize your installation as needed and test it thoroughly before proceeding further.

2. Use the *sysprep /generalize /shutdown* command to prepare your master installation by removing machine-specific information from it such as SIDs.

3. Boot your master computer, using bootable Windows PE media. Make sure your Windows PE media includes the *ImageX* command.

4. From your Windows PE command prompt, use the *imagex /capture* command to capture a Windows image from your master installation.

5. Use the *net use* command to map a drive to connect to your network share. (You might need to provide credentials to do this.) Use the *copy* command to copy your captured .wim file to your network share.

6. Boot your destination computer, using bootable Windows PE media.

7. Use the *diskpart* command from your Windows PE command prompt to partition and format the hard drive of your destination computer. Note that you can also automate this step by scripting diskpart actions.

8. Use the *net use* command from your Windows PE command prompt to map a drive to connect to the network share where the captured image of your master installation is stored.

9. Use the *imagex /apply* command from your Windows PE command prompt to apply the image of your master installation onto your destination computer's hard drive.

Install from Image Method Using Windows Setup

To deploy Windows using the install from image method, using Windows Setup, do the following:

1. Use either the install from DVD or install from configuration set method to create your master installation of Windows. Customize your installation as needed and test it thoroughly before proceeding further.

2. Use the *sysprep /generalize /shutdown* command to prepare your master installation by removing machine-specific information from it such as SIDs.

3. Boot your master computer, using bootable Windows PE media. Make sure your Windows PE media includes the *ImageX* command.

4. From your Windows PE command prompt, use the *imagex /capture* command to capture a Windows image from your master installation. Make sure you name your captured image as Install.wim—this is needed for this method to work.

5. Use the *net use* command to map a drive to connect to your network share. (You might need to provide credentials to do this.) Use the *copy* command to copy your captured .wim file to your network share.

6. Using Windows SIM on your technician computer, open the .wim file you captured from your master installation. Create and configure an answer file and save it, using the file name Unattend.xml. Validate your answer file and then copy it to the network share where your captured master image (Install.wim) is stored.

7. Boot your destination computer, using bootable Windows PE media.

8. Use the *net use* command from your Windows PE command prompt to map a drive to connect to the network share where the captured image of your master installation and Unattend.xml answer file are stored.

9. Start Windows Setup, referencing the answer file stored together with the captured image of your master installation, for example, by using this command:

   y:\setup.exe /unattend:unattend.xml.

Other Types of Image-Based Deployment

In addition to deploying a captured image of a master installation by using *imagex /apply* or Setup.exe, you can use two other methods for performing image-based deployment of Windows:

- You can use Windows Deployment Services (WDS), which enables you to start Windows PE remotely so that you don't have to visit your destination computers manually to partition and format their drives and launch the installation process.

- You can use a third-party Preboot Execution Environment (PXE) server, copy your Windows PE source files to your PXE server, and configure your PXE server boot configuration to use Windows PE.

For more information concerning the second method, see the Windows Automated Installation Kit (Windows AIK) User's Guide in the Windows AIK.

Understanding Windows Setup

Finally, before you can actually start creating answer files and use them for automated deployment of Windows, using the methods described previously, you need to understand how Windows Setup works. Windows Setup is key to the deployment process, for both clean installs and upgrades. Windows Setup (Setup.exe) is a program that starts the installation, gathers the information necessary to perform the installation (either by prompting the user directly or by reading settings from a supplied answer file), installs and configures Windows, reboots the computer as needed, and displays the Out Of Box Experience (OOBE) or Windows Welcome. In a clean install of Windows, Setup.exe begins by booting to Windows PE to configure the disk and copy the Windows image to the disk.

Windows Setup takes place in a series of configuration passes. A **configuration pass** is a phase of Windows Setup during which the settings specified in an answer file can be applied for unattended installation of Windows. There are seven configuration passes supported by Windows Setup, but not all of these passes are used in a typical install of Windows.

The seven sections that follow describe the different configuration passes and are followed by a section explaining how these various passes are used during a typical install from image deployment of Windows. The order in which the passes are described corresponds to the order in which these passes appear in an answer file. (See Figure A-11.)

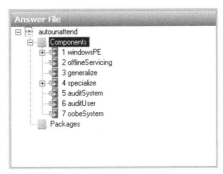

Figure A-11   Configuration passes for Windows Setup as displayed in an answer file

Understanding the windowsPE Configuration Pass

The windowsPE configuration pass is used to configure settings that are specific to Windows PE. Examples of such settings include the location where log files are saved, the display resolution of Windows PE, and so on.

The windowsPE pass is also used for configuring settings that are specific to the installation. Examples of such settings include the following:

- How the hard disk should be partitioned and formatted
- Which image of Windows should be installed (for example, Enterprise Edition or Standard Edition, full or Server Core)
- The product key to be used for the installation
- Language and locale settings to be used for the installation

Understanding the offlineServicing Configuration Pass

The offlineServicing pass is used when you want to apply answer file settings to an offline Windows image. Examples of what you might add to an offline image include:

- Language packs.
- Software updates.
- Additional driver packages.
- Service packs.

Understanding the generalize Configuration Pass

Unlike the windowsPE and offlineServicing passes, the generalize pass never runs as part of normal Windows Setup. Instead, this pass runs only when you use the *sysprep /generalize* command to reseal a Windows installation by removing all machine-specific information such as SIDs, log files, and so on. The system then shuts down immediately after the generalize pass is finished, and the system is then ready for image capture and deployment to other systems. Finally, if the generalize pass runs like this, then the next time the system starts, the specialize pass runs immediately on the system.

Understanding the specialize Configuration Pass

The specialize pass is used to configure machine-specific information for the installation. This can include such information as:

- Time zone.
- Locale and language settings.
- Network settings.
- Domain information.
- URL for department home page.

The specialize pass is always used in conjunction with the generalize pass and is never run as part of normal Windows Setup. When a system has been resealed using the *syspresp /generalize* command, the next time the system is started, the specialize pass immediately runs. In other words, what the generalize pass takes away from the system, the specialize pass restores.

Understanding the auditSystem Configuration Pass

The auditSystem pass runs in the context of audit mode, and for this mode to run, the *sysprep /audit* command must have been run on the system. The auditSystem pass is typically used for installing additional device drivers and software updates to a reference image that contains only a minimal set of device drivers. After the auditSystem pass runs, the auditUser pass then runs on the system, and neither of these passes can run during normal Windows Setup.

Understanding the auditUser Configuration Pass

The auditUser pass runs immediately after the auditSystem pass on a system that has had the *sysprep /audit* command run on it. The auditUser pass is typically used to execute additional commands for running scripts or applications on the system. These commands can be run using either the RunSynchronous or the RunAsynchronous answer file setting.

Understanding the oobeSystem Configuration Pass

Finally, the oobeSystem pass configures settings that are applied during the Out Of Box Experience (OOBE) portion of Windows Setup. For computers running Windows Vista, this means during the Windows Welcome phase of Setup.

Configuration Passes Used During an Install from Image Deployment

To conclude this section, you will learn how these various configuration passes are used during a typical install from image deployment, specifically an install from image method that uses ImageX to capture an image of a master computer and apply that image to a destination computer. Table A-3 summarizes the various steps that occur during this type of deployment and indicates which configuration passes are used during each step where appropriate.

Table A-3   **Configuration Passes During an Install from Image Deployment Using ImageX**

Deployment Step	Configuration Passes
Create a master installation, using the install from DVD method with Autounattend.xml answer file.	windowsPE offlineServicing oobeSystem
Use sysprep /generalize /oobe to reseal the master installation to prepare it for imaging.	generalize
Start the master computer from bootable Windows PE media and capture a Windows image from the computer, using ImageX.	windowsPE
Start the destination computer from bootable Windows PE media and apply the previously captured master image.	windowsPE
Restart the destination computer from its installed image.	specialize oobeSystem

Upgrading to Windows Server 2008

The objective of this section is to familiarize you with upgrading previous versions of Windows Server operating systems to Windows Server 2008. The section highlights several important things to consider before deciding upon upgrading instead of clean installs and lists preparatory steps to perform before starting an upgrade. The supported upgrade paths and system requirements for Windows Server 2008 are also explained. Finally, the section explains how to use various setup logs for troubleshooting purposes when a clean install or upgrade fails.

Upgrading a system from Windows Server 2003 to Windows Server 2008 is a very different process from performing a clean install on a new bare-metal system that has no operating system. When you perform a clean install, you can automate the install process, using Windows AIK and other deployment technologies; alternatively, upgrades need to be manually performed and require careful planning.

Before you upgrade your existing servers from Windows Server 2003 to Windows Server 2008, you need to ask yourself several questions:

- Are the applications currently running on the server compatible with the new version of Windows? The last thing you want to do is upgrade your servers only to discover that your third-party (or even Microsoft) applications running on them no longer work properly and cannot support the operational needs of your business. To ensure that your current applications are compatible with Windows Server 2008, download the latest version of the Microsoft Application Compatibility Toolkit (ACT) from the Microsoft

Download Center at *http://www.microsoft.com/downloads* and carefully test your applications for compatibility with the new platform.

- Is the hardware of your existing servers capable of running Windows Server 2008? Be sure to review the hardware requirements for Windows Server 2008 in Table A-4 later in this section and consider carefully whether it makes sense to upgrade your existing servers or purchase new hardware and do clean installs instead. In addition, you need to check that Windows Server 2008 device drivers are available for any mass storage devices on your existing server systems; otherwise, you won't be able to upgrade them. Visit the Windows Server Catalog at *http://www.windowsservercatalog.com* to verify that the hardware devices on your servers support the new operating system. In addition, be aware that Windows Server 2008 supports only systems that use the hardware requirements for Windows Server 2008 ACPI, and you cannot specify a custom hardware abstraction layer (HAL) file when installing Windows Server 2008.

- Have your backed up your servers? You should back up both the configuration of your servers and any data stored on your servers before you upgrade them to the new version of Windows. You should also back up any role-specific data from your servers, for example, by backing up the DHCP database from your DHCP servers.

- Do the current server roles installed on your servers support upgrading to Windows Server 2008? Not all server roles support upgrading, and some roles might be easier to upgrade than others. Be sure to visit the Windows Server 2008 TechCenter at *http://technet.microsoft.com/en-us/windowsserver/2008/* for the latest information concerning upgrading different server roles.

In addition to general upgrade considerations like the preceding ones, you need to perform some specific tasks before upgrading a Windows Server 2003 system to Windows Server 2008:

- Run diagnostics on your server's memory and hard drives to make sure there are no problems that could corrupt the installation.

- Disable any virus protection software running on the server because such software can sometimes interfere with the installation process.

- Disconnect any UPS device connected to your server because such devices can sometimes cause issues with the hardware detection process used by Windows Setup.

Finally, you also need to be aware of the supported upgrade paths from earlier Windows Server operating systems to Windows Server 2008. This is discussed later, in the section titled "Supported Upgrade Paths to Windows Server 2008."

Performing Side-by-Side Upgrades

One way of using existing server hardware while keeping your options open in case the upgrade process goes wrong is to perform a side-by-side upgrade. In this scenario, you would install Windows Server 2008 onto a separate partition from where your Windows Server 2003 installation is located. For example, if Windows Server 2003 is installed on your C drive, you can create a second partition called D and then launch Windows Setup from within Windows Server 2003 to install Windows Server 2008 on D drive.

Although this approach is really a form of clean install and not an upgrade, it enables you to reuse your existing server hardware while maintaining the ability to access your previous version of Windows in case the upgrade causes problems. In addition, you could use this approach to migrate your server settings gradually from Windows Server 2003 to Windows Server 2008 on the same system.

System Requirements for Windows Server 2008

Before you upgrade an existing server system to Windows Server 2008, make sure it meets the system requirements shown in Table A-4:

Table A-4   System Requirements for Windows Server 2008

Component	Requirement
Processor	Minimum: 1 GHz (x86 processor) or 1.4 GHz (x64 processor). Recommended: 2 GHz or faster. Note: An Intel Itanium 2 processor is required for Windows Server 2008 for Itanium-based systems.
Memory	Minimum: 512 MB RAM Recommended: 2 GB RAM or greater Maximum (32-bit systems): 4 GB (Standard Edition) or 64 GB (Enterprise Edition and Datacenter Edition) Maximum (64-bit systems): 32 GB (Standard Edition) or 2 TB (Enterprise Edition, Datacenter Edition, and Itanium-based systems)
Available Disk Space	Minimum: 10 GB. Recommended: 40 GB or greater. Note: Computers with more than 16 GB of RAM will require more disk space for paging, hibernation, and dump files.
Drive	DVD-ROM drive

Table A-4   System Requirements for Windows Server 2008

Component	Requirement
Display and Peripherals	Super VGA (800 x 600) or higher-resolution monitor Keyboard Microsoft mouse or compatible pointing device

Supported Upgrade Paths to Windows Server 2008

Before you consider upgrading systems from earlier Windows Server versions to Windows Server 2008, you also need to be aware of the supported upgrade paths. Table A-5 summarizes the upgrade paths that are supported.

Table A-5   Supported Upgrade Paths to Windows Server 2008

If you are running . . .	You can upgrade to . . .
Microsoft Windows Server 2003 R2 Standard Edition Microsoft Windows Server 2003 operating systems with Service Pack 1 (SP1) Standard Edition Microsoft Windows Server 2003 operating systems with Service Pack 2 (SP2) Standard Edition	Full installation of Windows Server 2008 Standard Edition Full installation of Windows Server 2008 Enterprise Edition
Microsoft Windows Server 2003 R2 Enterprise Edition Microsoft Windows Server 2003 operating systems with Service Pack 1 (SP1) Enterprise Edition Microsoft Windows Server 2003 operating systems with Service Pack 2 (SP2) Enterprise Edition	Full installation of Windows Server 2008 Enterprise Edition
Microsoft Windows Server 2003 R2 Datacenter Edition Microsoft Windows Server 2003 with Service Pack 1 (SP1) Datacenter Edition Microsoft Windows Server 2003 with Service Pack 2 (SP2) Datacenter Edition	Full installation of Windows Server 2008 Datacenter Edition

Here are some additional notes concerning the upgrade matrix for Windows Server 2008:

- You cannot upgrade from Windows 2000 Server to Windows Server 2008.
- You cannot upgrade from Windows NT 4.0 Server to Windows Server 2008.
- You cannot upgrade across architectures. For example, you cannot upgrade a 32-bit version of Windows Server 2003 to a 64-bit version of Windows Server 2008, and neither can you upgrade a 64-bit version of Windows Server 2003 to a 32-bit version of Windows Server 2008.
- You cannot upgrade Windows Server 2003 Web Edition to any edition of Windows Server 2008.

- You cannot upgrade any Itanium (IA64) edition of Windows Server 2003 to any edition of Windows Server 2008.

- You cannot upgrade the RTM release of any version of Windows Server 2003 to Windows Server 2008. In other words, you must apply at least Service Pack 1 to Windows Server 2003 before you can upgrade it to Windows Server 2008.

- You cannot upgrade any edition of Windows Server 2003 to a Windows Server Core installation of Windows Server 2008. In other words, you can upgrade only to full installations of Windows Server 2008—Server Core installations require a clean install.

Quick Check

1. Why should you disconnect any UPS device attached to your server before upgrading it?
2. How can you check whether a mass storage device supports upgrading to Windows Server 2008?

Quick Check Answers

1. The UPS device can interfere with the hardware detection process used during setup.
2. Visit the Windows Server Catalog at *http://www.windowsservercatalog.com* to verify whether the device supports Windows Server 2008.

Troubleshooting Installation Issues

Whether you perform a clean install of Windows Server 2008 or upgrade from Windows Server 2003, sometimes things go wrong during a deployment. It's important to know what troubleshooting steps you can perform when situations like this arise, and the following are some tips in this regard.

Setup Log Files

If an installation failed for an unknown reason, a good place to start is with reviewing the setup logs. Two log files in particular are often useful for troubleshooting installation problems:

- **setupact.log**   This log file contains information about the *setup actions* that occurred during the installation process.
- **setuperr.log**   This log file contains information about any *setup errors* that were generated during the installation process.

Where these log files can be found can depend on during which phase of the setup process they were generated. Typically, this can mean that these log files are found in one of the following directories:

■ **C:\$WINDOWS.~BT\Sources\Panther**   The setup log files are stored in this location during the windowsPE configuration pass of Windows Setup. The logs can also be found in the X:\$WINDOWS.~BT\Sources\Panther directory on the Windows PE RAM disk—that is, in memory.

■ **C:\Windows\Panther**   The online configuration phase is the first boot phase of Windows Setup and begins when the "Please wait a moment while Windows prepares to start for the first time," message is displayed. During the online configuration phase, basic hardware support is installed, and if you are performing an upgrade installation, data and programs are also migrated during this phase. The setup log files are also stored in this location during the oobeSystem configuration pass.

Note that in the preceding examples, C drive is either the partition on which Windows Server 2008 is being installed or the partition that contains the previous operating system being upgraded. If the system uses an Itanium (IA64) hardware architecture, the log files might also be located on another hard drive, depending on the amount of disk space available during setup.

Driver Problems

A common issue in failed installs is problems with device drivers. Some examples of driver-related setup problems include the following:

■ Installing an unsigned device driver during setup can render an x64 installation of Windows Server 2008 unbootable. A workaround for this is to press F8 during the boot process and select Disable Driver Signature Enforcement from the Advanced Boot Options menu, but the best solution is to obtain a digitally signed version of the driver causing the issue.

■ If setup cannot detect a removable boot device during an upgrade installation, setup might fail with a blue screen after the first restart. If you need to load a device driver for a boot device during setup, store the driver on removable media such as a floppy disk, USB flash device, CD media, or DVD media. The driver should be located either in the root directory of the media or in one of the following subfolders:

  ❑ \Sources for x86-based systems

  ❑ \AMD64 for x64-based systems

  ❑ \IA64 for Itanium-based systems

Installing Server Core

A new feature of Windows Server 2008 is the Windows Server Core installation option, which enables you to install a stripped-down version of Windows Server 2008 that, compared to the full installation option, has fewer hardware requirements, is more secure, and is easier to maintain. IT administrators will welcome Server Core as a new platform for running critical network services such as DHCP and DNS.

Although the tools for deploying Server Core are the same as those for deploying the full version of Windows Server 2008, there are some differences in how these tools are used, especially for automating post-installation tasks such as performing the initial configuration of the server and adding server roles and features.

Understanding Windows Server Core

With previous versions of Windows server operating systems such as Windows Server 2003, installing the operating system also installed binaries for features that were often not required in many networking environments. For example, a server that isn't being used as an application server doesn't really need the .NET Framework and CLR installed on it. Similarly, a headless server that is managed remotely doesn't really need the Windows Explorer desktop shell or various GUI-dependent elements such as Themes or the Search window. In fact, the problem with installing the binaries for such features is that they can increase the maintenance requirements for the server. For example, if the .NET Framework is installed on your server, any software updates released by Microsoft for this feature must be applied to your server— even if you are not actually using this feature. Otherwise, you risk leaving your server unprotected if you fail to apply patches to unused features like this. Another reason installing unneeded features on a server is a bad idea is because each feature has its own resource needs in terms of memory, processor, and disk requirements.

Because of these issues, Microsoft has created two separate installation options for Windows Server 2008: full and Server Core. The full installation option installs the binaries for all features onto your system. By contrast, the new Server Core option installs only a subset of these binaries that are required to support a limited set of server roles, role services, and features. By providing only a minimal environment for running a limited set of server roles and features, the new Server Core installation option can help reduce both the hardware and maintenance needs for your server. Specifically, the Server Core installation option provides the following benefits:

- **Greater stability and performance**   Server Core supports running only a limited number of server roles, which means fewer services running on your server. Having fewer services means more stability and better performance.

- **Smaller attack surface**   Because fewer network services are running on a computer running Server Core, the attack surface of the computer is smaller as well. By eliminating binaries for unneeded services from your system and reducing the number of running services required, Server Core can be a more secure platform than the full installation option.

- **Less maintenance required**   If a role or feature is not available on Server Core, the binaries for that role or feature are not even present on the system. Therefore, when a software update is released for a role or feature not present, you don't even need to apply it to your system. In fact, Microsoft estimates that Server Core needs only about 40 percent of the software updates that earlier versions of Windows Server required.

- **Smaller disk requirements**   Because many binaries included in the full installation option are not needed in Server Core, the Server Core option has much smaller disk requirements than the full installation option (about 1.5GB compared to approximately 5.9GB for a full installation). In addition, Server Core can also run more efficiently than the full option on systems having a limited amount of RAM.

Availability and System Requirements for Server Core

Server Core is available as an installation option for both the 32-bit and 64-bit versions of these Windows Server 2008 SKUs:

- Windows Server 2008 Standard Edition
- Windows Server 2008 Enterprise Edition
- Windows Server 2008 Datacenter Edition

Table A-6 shows the minimum and recommended system requirements for installing the Server Core option of Windows Server 2008.

Table A-6   Minimum and Recommended System Requirements for Server Core

Component	Requirement
Processor	Minimum: 1GHz. Recommended: 2GHz. Optimal: 3GHz or faster. Note that an Intel Itanium 2 processor is required for Windows Server 2008 for Itanium-based systems.
Memory	Minimum: 512MB RAM Recommended: 1GB RAM Optimal: 1GB RAM (Server Core installation) or more Maximum (32-bit systems): 4GB (Standard) or 64GB (Enterprise Edition and Datacenter Edition) Maximum (64-bit systems): 32GB (Standard Edition) or 2TB (Enterprise Edition, Datacenter Edition, and Itanium-based systems)

Table A-6   Minimum and Recommended System Requirements for Server Core

Component	Requirement
Hard Disk	Minimum: 8GB. Recommended: 10GB (Server Core installation). Optimal: 40GB (Server Core installation) or more. Note that computers with more than 16GB of RAM will require more disk space for paging, hibernation, and dump files. In addition, although Server Core has an initial disk requirement of about 1.5GB, a partition of at least 10GB is recommended to accommodate updates, hotfixes, temporary files, and other future changes.
Drive	DVD-ROM drive
Display	Super VGA (800 × 600) or higher-resolution monitor
Other	Keyboard and Microsoft mouse or compatible pointing device

What's in Server Core

Server Core is intended mainly for dedicated servers running one or more critical server roles. For example, you might use Server Core for a dedicated DHCP server, DNS server, domain controller, and so on. Because the goal behind the design of Server Core is to keep its requirements and attack surface at a minimum, only a subset of the server roles available on the full installation of Windows Server 2008 are available in Server Core. Specifically, the following server roles are the only roles available for a Server Core installation:

- Active Directory Domain Services (AD DS)
- Active Directory Lightweight Directory Services (AD LDS)
- DHCP Server
- DNS Server
- File Services
- Print Services
- Web Server (IIS)
- Hyper-V

Another role that can be installed on Server Core is Streaming Media Services. This role is not available in Windows Server 2008, however, but is instead available as an out-of-band (OOB) download that can be accessed from a link in Microsoft Knowledge Base article 934518 (*http://support.microsoft.com/kb/934518*).

Note that the mere fact of a server role being available for installation on Server Core does not mean that all role services associated with that role can be installed. For instance, although

IIS7 (the Web Server [IIS] role) can be installed on Server Core, the .NET Framework cannot be, and as a result, ASP.NET, a component of IIS7, also cannot be installed. Furthermore, because Server Core has no GUI shell, you cannot install the IIS7 management tools on a computer running Server Core.

Server Core also supports only a subset of the features available on a full installation of Windows Server 2008. Recall that a *role* is a specific function that your server performs on a network. Roles are supported by one or more *role services*, which provide different kinds of functionality to each role. Alternatively, a *feature* is an optional component you can install to provide added functionality to your server. Features sometimes provide support for one or more roles, whereas at other times, features provide other stand-alone functionality to the server. The only features that can be installed on a computer running Server Core are the following:

- Bitlocker Drive Encryption
- Failover Clustering
- Multipath IO
- Network Load Balancing
- Removable Storage
- Simple Network Management Protocol (SNMP)
- Subsystem for UNIX-based applications
- Telnet client
- Windows Internet Name Service (WINS)
- Windows Server Backup

Note that some of these features require special hardware for them to provide their functionality to the server. For example, the Bitlocker Drive Encryption feature requires hardware that supports Trusted Platform Module (TPM) 1.2 or higher, including a Trusted Computing Group (TCG)–compliant BIOS. Bitlocker also requires two NTFS disk partitions—one for the system volume and one for the operating system volume. In addition, some features are not available for every edition of Windows Server 2008. For example, the Failover Clustering feature is not supported in Standard Edition, only in Enterprise Edition and Datacenter Edition.

As far as GUI tools are concerned, only a handful of such applications are supported in Server Core. Table A-7 summarizes these available tools along with a brief explanation of why they are included. In addition, note that some of the functionality in these tools doesn't work. For example, if you select Help from the menu in Notepad, no Help file opens because the Help engine for running .chm files is not present in Server Core.

Table A-7   TGUI Tools Available in Server Core

Tool	Reason for Inclusion
Command Prompt (cmd.exe)	Used for administering Server Core from the local console
Notepad (notepad.exe)	Used for viewing log files, editing configuration files, and so on
Registry Editor (regedit.exe)	Used for viewing and modifying the Registry
System Information (msinfo32.exe)	Used for viewing system information
Task Manager	Used for managing processes and for starting new command prompt windows
Windows Installer (msiexec.exe)	Used for interpreting Windows Installer (.msi) packages and installing applications
Microsoft Support Diagnostic Tool (msdt.exe)	Used to collect system information and send it to support engineers when working with Microsoft Product Support Services (PSS) to troubleshoot a problem

What's Not in Server Core

If you're planning server deployment, you also need to know what's not available in Server Core; otherwise, you might have to reinstall the full installation option to get the roles or features you need. The following roles are *not* available in Server Core:

- Active Directory Certificate Services (AD CS)
- Active Directory Federation Services (AD FS)
- Active Directory Rights Management Services (AD RMS)
- Application Server
- Fax Server
- Network Policy and Access Services
- Terminal Services
- UDDI Services
- Windows Deployment Services
- Windows SharePoint Services

This means, for instance, that you can't deploy a computer running Server Core as the root Certificate Authority (CA) for your organization's Public Key Infrastructure (PKI) solution, and you can't deploy a terminal server running Server Core to provide centralized application services for your users.

Actually, the second statement bears some further investigation, namely, that Server Core in general is not intended as a platform for running network applications. For instance, not only can you not install the Terminal Services role on Server Core, you also can't install applications such as the 2007 Microsoft Office System or Microsoft Visual Studio on Server Core. The reason an application such as Office or Visual Studio can't run on Server Core is because most of the GUI functionality has been removed from Server Core to reduce the system's requirements and minimize its attack surface. This means no Windows Explorer and, therefore, no Explorer dialog boxes such as Open or Save As are available. Further, because applications such as Office have many dependencies with such dialog boxes, such applications can usually not be installed on Server Core—or if they can be installed (by using application compatibility shims), their functionality might be constrained.

NOTE   Remote Desktop

Although the Terminal Services role is not supported on a Server Core installation, Server Core does support Remote Desktop connections from other computers for purposes of remotely managing the computer running Server Core. (Note that a Remote Desktop connection to a Server Core installation does not make any graphical tools available on the remote server.)

The list of features that are not supported by Server Core is even longer than the list of unsupported roles:

- BITS Server Extensions
- Connection Manager Administration Kit
- Desktop Experience
- Group Policy Management
- Internet Printing Client
- Internet Storage Name Server
- LPR Port Monitor
- Message Queuing
- Microsoft .NET Framework 3.0 Features
- Peer Name Resolution Protocol
- Quality Windows Audio Video Experience
- Remote Assistance
- Remote Differential Compression
- Remote Server Administration Tools
- RPC Over HTTP Proxy
- Services For NFS

- Simple TCP/IP Services
- SMTP Server
- Storage Manager for SANs
- Telnet Server
- TFTP Client
- Windows Internal Database
- Windows PowerShell
- Windows Process Activation Service
- Windows Recovery Disc
- Windows System Resource Manager
- Wireless LAN Service

For some of these features, it's obvious why they can't be installed on Server Core. For example, you can't install the Desktop Experience feature on Server Core because Server Core has no desktop! And you can't install the Remote Server Administration Tools (RSAT) on Server Core because these tools are Microsoft Management Console (MMC) tools that run in windows, and with no desktop, there can't be any windows! For some features, however, it might seem mysterious why they can't be installed on Server Core. The reason usually has to do with some hidden dependency that prevents the feature from working given the limited set of operating system binaries available on Server Core. To understand this better, you will examine the architecture of both Server Core and the full installation of Windows Server 2008 in the next section.

Finally, although the list of GUI tools available in Server Core might seem small (see Table A-7), the list of GUI tools that aren't present in Server Core is quite large. Here's a quick but far from comprehensive list of GUI tools that are *not* available in Server Core:

- The Windows desktop shell (Explorer.exe)
- The .NET Framework and CLR
- The Microsoft Management Console (Mmc.exe) and its various snap-ins
- Most of the applets found in Control Panel
- Internet Explorer
- Windows Media Player
- Windows Mail

The absence of many of these tools in Server Core can have additional consequences. For example:

- No Internet Explorer means no HTML rendering engine, which means you can't view HTML Help in Server Core. So if you need help concerning some feature of Windows Server 2008, you have to look up Help on a full installation of the product.

- No MMC or snap-ins means it can be difficult to administer a computer running Server Core locally because all you have is the command prompt. This means that if you want to manage a computer running Server Core, using MMC tools, you need to do it remotely—MMCs can't be run locally.

- No desktop shell means no taskbar, which means no system tray and, therefore, no balloon notifications. So, for example, if you lose network connectivity on your computer running Server Core, or your password expires, or an application needs activation, you won't see a balloon informing you of the problem.

- No .NET Framework means you can't run any managed code on a computer running Server Core. In particular, this also means you can't run Windows PowerShell scripts locally. You can, however, run PowerShell scripts remotely against computers running Server Core if the scripts use Windows Management Instrumentation (WMI) because Server Core does include many (but not all) of the WMI providers included in the full installation.

- Very few Control Panel applets—only the Regional and Language Options (Intl.cpl) and Date and Time (Timedate.cpl) applets are included in Server Core—means that configuring a computer running Server Core is not as simple a task as it can be on a full installation. The answer to this is to use scripts to automate configuration tasks on computers running Server Core or to use unattended installs that also perform any post-installation configuration tasks that are needed.

NOTE   Shell DLLs

Although Server Core does not include Explorer.exe, it does include Shell32.dll and Shlwapi.dll.

Quick Check

1. Why is Task Manager necessary on Server Core?
2. Why is Notepad available on Server Core?

> **Quick Check Answers**
> 1. If you close the Server Core command shell, you can open a new one by using Task Manager to start a new instance of cmd.exe.
> 2. Notepad can be used for viewing log files, writing scripts, and many other useful actions on Server Core.

Architecture of a Full Installation of Windows Server 2008

Figure A-12 shows the architecture of a full installation of Windows Server 2008. This architecture includes components that are common to all installations (both full and Server Core) and components that are available in the full installation only.

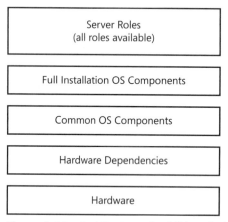

Figure A-12   Architecture of a full installation of Windows Server 2008

The operating system components that are common between Server Core and the full installation include such things as remote procedure call (RPC) functionality, the networking stack, security features, Component-Based Servicing (CBS), Package Manager (Pkgmgr.exe), OCSetup.exe, and others. The full installation of Windows Server 2008 adds a number of additional components to these, including the .NET Framework, the CLR, the Windows desktop shell, and so on. The different roles that can run on the full installation use these various operating system components to do their jobs.

Architecture of a Server Core Installation of Windows Server 2008

At first glance, the architecture for Server Core looks very similar to that of the full installation. (See Figure A-13.)

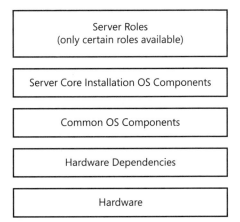

Figure A-13   Architecture of a Server Core installation of Windows Server 2008

The key difference is in the layer above the common OS components, where Server Core contains a different set of operating system components that are not found in the full installation. Examples of Server Core OS components that are exclusive to Server Core include OCList.exe, SCRegEdit.wsf, and others. You can take away several key ideas by comparing these two architectures, including:

- The architecture of Windows Server 2008 is a *modular* architecture that is built upon layers of functionality, starting at the bottom with the hardware the operating system is running on and ending on top with the server roles that provide critical services to users and computers on your network.

- Both the full installation and the Server Core installation are built upon a smaller set of *core* operating system components. Each installation option (full or Server Core) then adds its own unique set of additional operating system components to these core components to support the functional needs of the particular installation option.

What should also be apparent from comparing Figure A-12 and Figure A-13 is that Server Core is not a version or edition of Windows Server 2008 but rather an installation *option*. This means, for instance, that if a particular binary exists on both the full installation and Server Core installation of Windows Server 2008, it's the *same* binary on both of these installation options. That is, there isn't a Server Core kernel versus a full installation kernel–both installation options use the same kernel. The same is not true of different editions, however: the kernel in Standard Edition is not identical to the kernel in Enterprise Edition or Datacenter Edition. If the same kernel were used in different editions, the editions couldn't have different levels of symmetric multiprocessing (SMP) support as, in fact, they do.

Deploying Server Core

Because Server Core is simply an installation option of Windows Server 2008, you can deploy Server Core by using any of the following methods:

- Install from DVD method (either manual or unattended install)
- Install from configuration set method, using either removable media or a network share
- Install from image method, using either ImageX or Windows Setup

In addition, you can deploy Server Core by using other Windows deployment technologies such as WDS, Microsoft Deployment, or System Center Configuration Manager.

Upgrades Not Supported

The only type of installation you can perform with Server Core is a clean install; that is, you must deploy Server Core onto a bare-metal system (or install it onto a second partition of an existing Windows Server system, although multiboot installations are not recommended in production environments). In other words, you cannot perform an upgrade installation of Server Core. In particular:

- You cannot upgrade any previous version of Windows Server to Windows Server 2008 Server Core.
- You cannot upgrade from a full installation of Windows Server 2008 to the Server Core installation option.
- You cannot upgrade a Server Core installation to the full installation option of Windows Server 2008.

The bottom line for deploying Server Core, then, is: clean installs only—no upgrades.

Device Drivers and Server Core

An important consideration when deploying Server Core is that this installation option has a more limited set of in-box device drivers than the full installation option has. Again, the reason for having fewer in-box drivers in Server Core is to minimize the size of a Server Core installation by reducing the disk requirements of the installation. Specifically, Server Core includes only in-box drivers for the following types of device classes:

- Storage devices
- Standard VGA video
- Network adapters

The drivers included in Server Core for these different device classes are the identical drivers included in the full installation for these classes. Note also that Server Core also includes the

Plug and Play subsystem found in the full installation of Windows Server 2008. This enables Server Core to install available in-box drivers silently for any hardware devices of these three classes that are detected during the installation process.

▶ **Exercise Examining Server Core**

In this exercise, you will examine an installation of Server Core. In particular, you will examine which GUI tools are available from the command prompt to configure your Server Core installation.

For this exercise, you can use the Core1 server whose setup was described in this book's introduction. However, you can use any Server Core installation. Before beginning the exercise, log on as an administrator.

1. Type **notepad** at the Server Core command prompt to open Notepad.

2. Select File, and then Open from the Notepad menu.

    Notice that Notepad in Server Core uses the old Windows 3.1 version of the Open dialog box.

3. Select Help, and then View Help from the Notepad menu.

    Notice that nothing happens. Server Core doesn't support Windows Help as an application.

4. Close Notepad and type **regedit** at the Server Core command prompt to open Registry Editor.

5. Close Registry Editor and type **control timedate.cpl** at the command prompt.

    The Date And Time applet from Control Panel is displayed, enabling you to configure the date and time on your server.

6. Close the Date And Time applet and type **control sysdm.cpl** at the command prompt.

    Doing this does not open the System applet from Control Panel. Rather, it throws an error saying, "Windows cannot find 'SystemPropertiesComputerName.exe'. Make sure you typed the name correctly, and then try again."

    On a Server Core installation, you must configure your computer name and domain membership using other methods.

7. Click OK to close the error message, and then type the following two commands:

    ```
    net start > services.txt
    notepad services.txt
    ```

    The first command displays a list of all Windows services currently running on the system and saves the list to the file *%USERPROFILE%*\Services.txt. The second command then opens the Services.txt file and displays it in Notepad.

Notice that 40 services are running by default on a Server Core installation that has no additional roles or features installed on it.

8. Close Notepad. Then, close your Server Core command prompt by clicking Close (the X at the top right of the window). You now have a completely blank screen.

   You can you get your command prompt back by pressing CTRL+ALT+DEL (right ALT+DEL in Virtual PC) and then selecting the Start Task Manager option. When Task Manager appears, select the Applications tab and click the New Task button.

9. Type **cmd.exe** in the Create New Task dialog box and click OK. Your Server Core command prompt reappears, and you can close Task Manager.

   Notice how the new command prompt differs from the old one: the default Server Core command prompt has *%USERPROFILE%* as its current directory. The new command prompt you opened using Task Manager has *%WINDIR%\System32* as its current directory.

   You can change the current directory back to *%USERPROFILE%* by typing **cd %userprofile%** at the new command prompt.

10. Type **ipconfig** at the command prompt. You should have an IP address dynamically assigned to your Server Core installation by the DHCP server on your network.

11. Type **msinfo32** at the command prompt. The System Information tool opens and displays hardware and software information concerning your system. Expand the System Summary node to display the subnodes under the Software Environment node and select the Print Jobs node. The right-side pane displays an error message that says, "Cannot access the Windows Management Instrumentation software. Windows Management Instrumentation files may be moved or missing."

   This error message essentially indicates that some WMI providers are not available on Server Core.

12. Shut down Core1 by typing the command **shutdown /s /t 0**.

Performing Post-Deployment Tasks

Once you've installed either the Server Core or full installation option of Windows Server 2008 on a system, you still need to perform a number of configuration tasks before you can use your server in your production environment. These configuration tasks can range from setting the time zone to installing and configuring roles, role services, and features on your server. Many of these tasks can be automated, and the objective of this section is to familiarize you with the various ways you can perform post-installation tasks during Windows Server 2008 deployments. The methods covered here include configuring servers manually, using both GUI tools and the command line, and configuring them automatically by using answer files.

Understanding Post-Installation Tasks

Once you've successfully installed Windows Server 2008 on a system, you're not finished; you still need to configure your installation and install the roles and features your server will need so it can perform its function on your network. Post-installation tasks can be performed in a variety of ways on Windows Server 2008, including:

- Locally using the GUI tools available on the server for administering it.
- Locally from the command-line (including using batch scripts).
- Remotely using the Remote Server Administration Tools (RSAT), Terminal Services, Group Policy, WMI or PowerShell scripts, or the Windows Remote Shell (WinRS).

The difficulty here is that not all configuration tasks can be performed using every type of tool, so sometimes you need to know the right tool for the job because other tools might not do. In addition, some configuration tasks are performed differently on Server Core installations because of the limited number of binaries available on this installation. Again, it's a matter of knowing the right tool for the job, and the task of an IT administrator is to know which tool can be used for which purpose on which installation option.

Finally, the post-installation tasks themselves can be broadly classified into two categories:

- Initial configuration tasks such as configuring networking settings, configuring the time zone, enabling Remote Desktop, activating your installation, and other tasks that usually must be performed on all servers being deployed on your network
- Adding roles and features to your server so it can perform some specific function on your network or have some type of functionality you can use on it

Look at some of the various ways you can perform these kinds of tasks on both Server Core and full installations of Windows Server 2008. For simplicity, configuring the full installation option will be covered first because this will enable you to highlight how configuring Server Core is different.

Performing Initial Configuration Tasks on a Full Installation

The simplest way of performing initial configuration tasks on a full installation of Windows Server 2008 is to log on to the server for the first time and use the Initial Configuration Tasks screen, shown in Figure A-14.

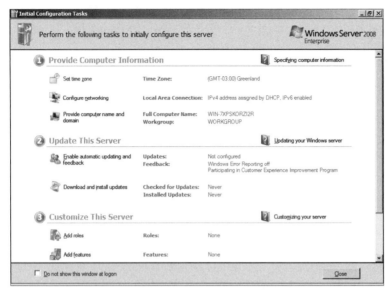

Figure A-14 The Initial Configuration Tasks screen on the full installation of Windows Server 2008

Using the Initial Configuration Tasks screen enables you to perform the following tasks, which are common for all servers being deployed on your network:

- Setting the password for the local Administrator account
- Configuring TCP/IP networking settings on your server
- Changing the name of your computer
- Joining your server to a domain
- Enabling automatic updating of your server by using Windows Update
- Downloading and installing any available updates by using Windows Update
- Enabling Windows Error Reporting for the Customer Experience Improvement Program
- Enabling Remote Desktop on your server
- Enabling the Windows Firewall on your server

NOTE The *Oobe* command opens Initial Configuration Tasks

If you selected the Do Not Show This Window Again At Logon check box in the Initial Configuration Tasks screen, you can execute the Oobe.exe command from the Run box, the Start Search box, or a command prompt to load the screen again.

In addition to providing you with a simple way of performing these tasks, the Initial Configuration Tasks screen also enables you to launch the Add Roles Wizard and Add Features Wizard to install additional roles or features on your server.

The simplest way of performing these tasks on a full installation of Windows Server 2008 is to log on locally to your server after Setup is finished and perform each of the preceding tasks manually as needed. Some of these tasks can also be automated, however, as part of the installation process itself. For example, the password for the local Administrator account can be configured using the following answer file setting:

Microsoft-Windows-Shell-Setup\UserAccounts\AdministratorPassword

Similarly, the time zone can be specified during installation by configuring the Microsoft-Windows-Shell-Setup setting in your answer file. (See Figure A-15.)

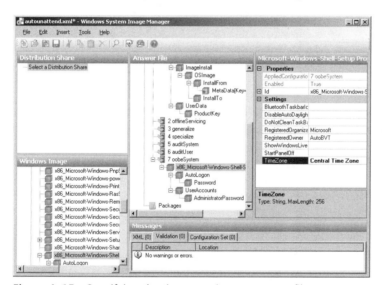

Figure A-15   Specifying the time zone in your answer file

If you want to enable Remote Desktop on your server during installation, you can do this by configuring the following answer file setting:

Microsoft-Windows-TerminalServices-LocalSessionManager

To do this, add this setting to the offlineServicing pass section of your answer file and then use Windows SIM to configure the fDenyTSConnections setting so it has the Boolean value of *False*. (See Figure A-16.)

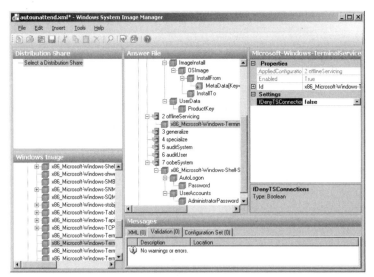

Figure A-16 Enabling Remote Desktop using an answer file

Once Remote Desktop has been enabled on a server, it's easy to continue performing the other initial configuration tasks remotely because you can use Remote Desktop Connection from another computer and access the desktop of your server remotely. Note that, by default, when you enable Remote Desktop using the Microsoft-Windows-TerminalServices-LocalSession-Manager answer file setting like this, users attempting to connect remotely to your server will be authenticated according to the Allow Connections Only From Computers Running Remote Desktop With Network Level Authentication option.

This is the most secure form of authentication for Remote Desktop connections and requires that the computer doing the connecting be running Windows Vista or Windows Server 2008 (or have the optional Remote Desktop Connection 6.1 software downloaded and installed on a computer running Windows XP). For greater flexibility, you might allow remote connections to use the less secure Allow Connections From Computers Running Any Version Of Remote Desktop authentication option.

To configure this form of authentication in your answer file, add the Microsoft-Windows-TerminalServices-RDP-WinStationExtensions setting to the specialize pass section of your answer file and use Windows SIM to configure UserAuthentication to have a value of zero.

Performing Initial Configuration Tasks on Server Core

Performing initial configuration tasks on a Server Core installation is very different from performing it on a full installation of Windows Server 2008. The main reason for this is because Server Core has no desktop, so tools such as the Initial Configuration Tasks screen can't be displayed or used on this installation option. All the initial configuration tasks that can be performed on the full installation of Windows Server 2008 can also be performed on Server Core, but to do so requires a good understanding of certain Windows command-line tools and a script or two as well. Now you will look at how to configure a new Server Core installation, using only the command shell.

Configuring the Local Administrator Password

On a Server Core installation, you can set the local administrator password from the command line by typing the following command:

```
net user administrator *
```

Type your new password twice, and the password for the account is changed. There are other useful tasks you can perform on a Server Core installation by using the *net* commands. For example, you can add a user to the local Administrators group, using the following command:

```
net localgroup Administrators /add domain\username
```

In this example, *domain\username* are the domain and username for the user you are adding to the local Administrators group on the server. You can also remove a user from the local Administrators group by typing the following:

```
net localgroup Administrators /delete domain\username
```

This also works with other local groups if you change Administrators to the name of the other group you want to add members to or remove members from. You can also create a new local user account in the built-in Users local group by typing the following command:

```
net user username * /add
```

Configuring TCP/IP Networking Settings

By default, DHCP is enabled on a Server Core installation so it can obtain an IP address dynamically from a DHCP server on the network (if there is one). Servers typically have statically assigned IP addresses, however, and you can use the *Netsh.exe* command to configure static IP address settings on a Server Core installation, using only the command line.

Before you try to configure a static address, however, view a list of your server's current adapters and connections. To do this, type the following command:

```
netsh interface ipv4 show interfaces
```

Make a note of the interface number displayed in the IDX column of the output from this *netsh* command for your correct network interface, which is typically Local Area Connection. You need to do this because this number is required for the other *netsh* commands that follow.

To assign the IP addresses to the desired interface, type the following:

```
netsh interface ipv4 set address name=ID source=static IP SM DG
```

In this example, *ID* stands for the interface (IDX) number for the interface, *IP* is the static IP address that is being set, *SM* is the subnet mask used by the IP address, and *DG* is the default gateway.

If you assign your server a static address, you also need to assign it a static DNS server address. To do this, use the following command:

```
netsh interface ipv4 add dnsserver name=ID address=DNSIP index=1
```

In this example, *ID* is the interface (IDX) number for the interface, and *DNSIP* is the IP address of your DNS server. You can repeat this command to add additional backup DNS servers, but be sure to increment the index number each time you do this.

If you decide later to re-enable DHCP on your server, you can do this by typing the following:

```
netsh interface ipv4 set address name=ID source=dhcp
```

Changing the Server Name

To change the server name of your Server Core installation before joining it to a domain, type the Netdom.exe command as follows:

```
netdom renamecomputer %computername% /NewName:NEWNAME
```

To verify the name change, you can simply type **hostname** at the command prompt. Alternatively, you can type **set** and examine the contents of the *%COMPUTERNAME%* environment variable, or you can type **echo %COMPUTERNAME%** to display the name of the computer.

NOTE Changing the computer name

Changing the name of your server requires a reboot before the change can take effect.

If your server is already joined to a domain, you need to use the following command instead if you want to change its name:

```
netdom renamecomputer %computername% /NewName:NEWNAME /userd:domain\username /passwordd:*
```

Joining a Domain

You can also use Netdom.exe to join your server to a domain or remove it from a domain. To join the server to a domain, use the following command:

```
netdom join NAME /domain:DOMAIN /userd:ADMINUSER /passwordd:*
```

In this example, *NAME* is the name of the server, *DOMAIN* is the name of the domain the server is joining, and *ADMINUSER* is a domain administrator account.

Likewise, you can remove the server from a domain by typing the following:

```
netdom remove NAME /domain:DOMAIN /userd:ADMINUSER /passwordd:*
```

NOTE **Joining or leaving a domain**

Joining or leaving a domain requires a reboot before the change can take effect.

Enabling Automatic Updates

The Scregedit.wsf script can be used to configure a number of aspects of a Server Core installation, including:

- Enabling automatic updates.
- Enabling Remote Desktop.
- Allowing Remote Desktop clients on previous versions of Windows to connect to a server running a Server Core installation.
- Configuring DNS SRV record weight and priority.
- Managing IPSec Monitor remotely.

Exam Tip   Become familiar with the different command-line options of scregedit.wsf. To view a list of available options, type **cscript %systemroot%\system32\scregedit.wsf /?** at the Server Core command prompt. You can also type **cscript %systemroot%\system32\scregedit.wsf /cli** to display a "cheat sheet" of various commands you can perform to configure a Server Core installation.

To use Scregedit.wsf to enable Automatic Updates on a Server Core installation, type the following:

```
cscript %systemroot%\system32\scregedit.wsf /AU 4
```

If you later want to disable Automatic Updates, use the following:

```
cscript %systemroot%\system32\scregedit.wsf /AU 1
```

NOTE   Configuring Automatic Updates

If you need to configure other settings for Automatic Updates, it's best to use Group Policy to configure them.

Enabling Remote Desktop

The Scregedit.wsf script is also used for configuring Remote Desktop on a Server Core installation. For example, to enable the server to accept Remote Desktop connections, type the following command:

```
cscript %systemroot%\system32\scregedit.wsf /ar 0
```

If you later need to disable Remote Desktop on the server, you can do this by typing the following:

```
cscript %systemroot%\system32\scregedit.wsf /ar 1
```

If you want to allow previous versions of Remote Desktop Connection to connect to your Server Core installation, you need first to disable the default enhanced security level for Remote Desktop by typing the following:

```
cscript %systemroot%\system32\scregedit.wsf /cs 0
```

Finally, if you want to view the current Remote Desktop configuration on your server, type the following:

```
cscript %systemroot%\system32\scregedit.wsf /ar /v
```

Enabling Windows Error Reporting

A different command-line tool is used to enable and configure Windows Error Reporting (WER) on your server, namely ServerWEROptin.exe. The syntax for this tool is as follows:

```
C:\Windows\System32>serverweroptin /?
ServerWerOptin /h[elp] | /q[uery] | /s[ummary] | /de[tailed] | /d[isable]
```

```
Description:

This tool allows you to enable Windows Error Reporting to automatically send
descriptions of problems on this server to Microsoft. For more information on
Windows Error Reporting, refer to the privacy statement at
http://go.microsoft.com/fwlink/?linkid=50163

Parameter list:
/query     Displays Windows Error Reporting opt-in status.
/summary   Automatically send summary reports with Windows Error Reporting.
/detailed  Automatically send detailed reports with Windows Error Reporting.
/disable   Disable Windows Error Reporting.
/help      Displays parameters and syntax for this command.

Examples:
ServerWerOptin /query
ServerWerOptin /summary
```

For example, from this information, you can see that if you want to send detailed WER reports to Microsoft automatically, you must use the following command:

serverweroptin /detailed

Enabling Windows Firewall

Enabling Windows Firewall on a Server Core installation is a bit tricky from the command line because it uses the advfirewall context of the *netsh* command, and there are many options for this context. So instead of configuring firewall profiles and rules individually, using *netsh advfirewall* commands, it's better if you simply enable remote firewall management for all firewall profiles by typing the following:

netsh advfirewall set allprofiles settings remotemanagement enable

Once you've done this, you can then use Group Policy Management from an administrative workstation running Windows Vista or from a server that has the full installation option of Windows Server 2008 installed. The Windows Firewall With Advanced Security snap-in for Group Policy Editor then provides a simple way of remotely configuring Windows Firewall on computers running Windows Vista or Windows Server 2008 (including Server Core installations).

Automating Initial Configuration Tasks

Finally, you can use on a Server Core installation the same answer file settings you use for automating some of the initial configuration tasks you need to perform on a full installation of Windows Server 2008. Again, just as with the full installation option, not all initial configuration tasks can be performed by using answer files on Server Core.

Installing Roles and Features on a Full Installation

Once the initial configuration tasks are performed on your server, you can install roles and features on it to enable it to function as intended on your network. For example, you might want to install the DHCP Server role on your server so it can lease IP addresses to client computers that need them.

Installing roles and features can be done several ways on a full installation of Windows Server 2008, specifically:

- By launching the Add Roles Wizard or the Add Features Wizard from the appropriate link on the Initial Configuration Tasks screen.
- By launching the Add Roles Wizard or Add Features Wizard by right-clicking the appropriate node in Server Manager.
- By using the ServerManagerCmd.exe command-line tool.

All three of these approaches can be used for manually installing roles and features and for uninstalling them. To automate the installation of roles and features, however, you must use *ServerManagerCmd.exe* together with an answer file, as will be demonstrated shortly.

Manually Installing Roles and Features by Using the Wizards

Roles and features can be added manually using the Add Roles Wizard and Add Features Wizard. For example, to add the DHCP Server role to your server, you can click the Add Roles link in the Customize This Server section of the Initial Configuration Tasks screen. As you proceed through the steps of the wizard, you are typically prompted to provide additional information needed for configuring the role you are installing. (See Figure A-17.)

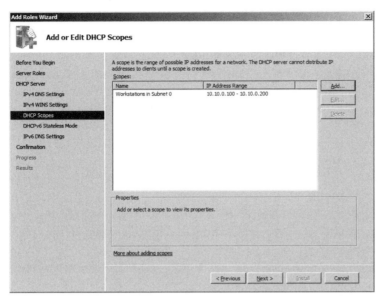

Figure A-17   Installing the DHCP Server role, using the Add Roles Wizard

Manually Installing Roles and Features by Using *ServerManagerCmd.exe*

Roles and features can also be added manually from the command line by using the *Server-ManagerCmd.exe* command. *ServerManagerCmd.exe* is a powerful tool for both installing and removing roles and features and for previewing which components would be installed if you decide to add a particular role or feature to your server. *ServerManagerCmd.exe* can take the following top-level parameters:

- **-query [<query.xml>]**   Displays a list of all roles, role services, and features installed and available for installation on the server. If you want the query results saved to an XML file, specify an XML file to replace query.xml.
- **-inputPath <answer.xml>**   Installs or removes the roles, role services, and features specified in the answer file, an XML file represented by <answer.xml>.
- **-install <name>**   Installs the role, role service, or feature specified by <name>.
- **-remove <name>**   Removes the role, role service, or feature specified by <name>.

The <name> parameter specifies the role or feature you want to install or remove by using *Server-ManagerCmd.exe*. For example, the <name> parameter for the DHCP Server role is simply DHCP whereas the <name> parameter for the Active Directory Domain Services (AD DS) role is ADDS-Domain-Controller. The <name> parameter is not case-sensitive.

Here are a few examples of how you can use *ServerManagerCmd.exe* to perform common role-related and feature-related tasks:

- **servermanagercmd –install Web-Server –whatif** Analyzes which specific roles, role services, and features would be installed as part of installing the Web Server (IIS) role. This command compares the list of roles, role services, and features that are part of the Web-server role with the list of roles, role services, and features that are already installed on the server. Only the roles, role services, and features that are currently not installed are then identified as applicable for installation on the server. The main purpose of the **–whatif** parameter is to help you understand the full list of actions that will be performed with a *ServerManagerCmd.exe* command but without actually making any changes to your server.

- **servermanagercmd –install Web-Server** Does the same as the previous command but without the **–whatif** parameter, which means that it actually installs the Web Server (IIS) role on the server.

- **servermanagercmd –remove Web-Server** Removes the Web Server (IIS) role from the server, assuming that this role has already been installed on the server. If any other roles and features that depend on the Web Server (IIS) role are currently installed (such as Windows SharePoint Services), these roles will also be removed from the server.

- **servermanagercmd –remove Web-Server –resultPath *results*.xml** Does the same as the previous command, but the addition of the **–resultPath** parameter means that *ServerManagerCmd.exe* will save the results of the removal operation as an XML file that can be analyzed later or programmatically parsed.

- **servermanagercmd –install Terminal-Services –restart** Installs the Terminal Services role on the server. Because installing this role requires a reboot, the *–restart* parameter can be used to restart the machine automatically after the role has been installed. If *–restart* is not used, you will need to restart the computer manually to complete the installation of this role.

- **servermanagercmd –inputPath *input*.xml** Enables you to install or remove multiple roles, role services, and features by using a single *ServerManagerCmd.exe* command. This can be a more expedient way of adding or removing roles and features than by using multiple *–install* or *–remove* commands. You can specify as many items as you like in your input.xml file. A typical *input.xml* file might look like this:

```xml
<?xml version="1.0" encoding="utf-8" ?>
<ServerManagerConfiguration Action="Install"
  xmlns="http://schemas.microsoft.com/sdm/Windows/ServerManager/Configuration
  /2007/1" xmlns:xs="http://www.w3.org/2001/XMLSchema">

    <Feature Id="NLB"                   InstallAllSubFeatures="true"/>
    <Feature Id="Desktop-Experience"    InstallAllSubFeatures="true"/>
```

```
        <Feature Id="NET-Framework"              InstallAllSubFeatures="true"/>
        <Feature Id="WSRM"                       InstallAllSubFeatures="true"/>
        <Feature Id="Wireless-Networking"        InstallAllSubFeatures="true"/>
        <Feature Id="Backup"                     InstallAllSubFeatures="true"/>
        <Feature Id="WINS-Server"                InstallAllSubFeatures="true"/>
        <Feature Id="Remote-Assistance"          InstallAllSubFeatures="true"/>
        <Feature Id="Simple-TCPIP"               InstallAllSubFeatures="true"/>
        <Feature Id="Telnet-Client"              InstallAllSubFeatures="true"/>
        <Feature Id="Telnet-Server"              InstallAllSubFeatures="true"/>
        <Feature Id="Subsystem-UNIX-Apps"        InstallAllSubFeatures="true"/>
        <Feature Id="RPC-over-HTTP-Proxy"        InstallAllSubFeatures="true"/>
        <Feature Id="SMTP-Server"                InstallAllSubFeatures="true"/>
        <Feature Id="LPR-Port-Monitor"           InstallAllSubFeatures="true"/>
        <Feature Id="Storage-Mgr-SANs"           InstallAllSubFeatures="true"/>
        <Feature Id="BITS"                       InstallAllSubFeatures="true"/>
        <Feature Id="MSMQ"/>
        <Feature Id="MSMQ-Services"/>
        <Feature Id="MSMQ-DCOM"/>
        <Feature Id="WPAS"                       InstallAllSubFeatures="true"/>
        <Feature Id="Windows-Internal-DB"        InstallAllSubFeatures="true"/>
        <Feature Id="BitLocker"                  InstallAllSubFeatures="true"/>
        <Feature Id="Multipath-IO"               InstallAllSubFeatures="true"/>
        <Feature Id="ISNS"                       InstallAllSubFeatures="true"/>
        <Feature Id="Removable-Storage"          InstallAllSubFeatures="true"/>
        <Feature Id="TFTP-Client"                InstallAllSubFeatures="true"/>
        <Feature Id="SNMP-Service"               InstallAllSubFeatures="true"/>
        <Feature Id="Internet-Print-Client"      InstallAllSubFeatures="true"/>
        <Feature Id="PNRP"                       InstallAllSubFeatures="true"/>
        <Feature Id="CMAK"                       InstallAllSubFeatures="true"/>

    </ServerManagerConfiguration>
```

NOTE *ServerManagerCmd.exe* Help

For help with the syntax of *ServerManagerCmd.exe*, type **ServerManagerCmd.exe –help** at a command prompt.

Automating the Installation of Roles and Features

You can also automate the installation of roles and features on your server by using *ServerManagerCmd.exe* in conjunction with your Autounattend.xml or Unattend.xml answer file. The key to doing this is to add the Microsoft-Windows-Shell-Setup\FirstLogonCommands component to the oobeSystem configuration pass section of your answer file. (See Figure A-18.)

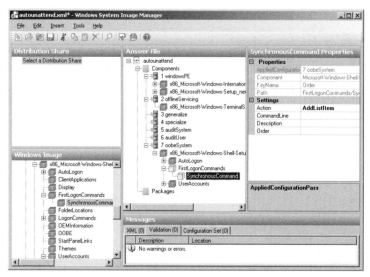

Figure A-18   Configuring the Microsoft-Windows-Shell-Setup\FirstLogonCommands section of the oobeSystem pass for an answer file

The FirstLogonCommands setting specifies any commands you need to run the first time a user logs on to the computer. In other words, FirstLogonCommands are run after logon but prior to showing the desktop. These commands are run only once and are silently elevated provided the logged-on user has administrative privileges. (Elevation is not needed on Server Core because this installation option does not support User Account Control.) Such elevation is needed because running commands to configure your server or add roles or features typically requires either editing the registry or launching Windows Setup with FirstLogonCommands specified in an answer file. FirstLogonCommands also launches all its commands synchronously, which means that it launches the next command only after the previous command has finished doing its job.

To use the FirstLogonCommands setting to run a command during the oobeSystem configuration pass of setup, you need to configure the following three values for your command:

- **CommandLine**   Specifies the path to the command to execute
- **Description**   Describes the command to be run
- **Order**   Specifies the order in which the command is run

If you need to run several commands during the oobeSystem pass, simply add multiple First-LogonCommands sections to your answer file and specify a different Order number for each command. For example, Figure A-19 shows three commands being executed synchronously (one after the other) during the oobeSystem pass of setup, with the second command installing the DHCP Server role using its default settings.

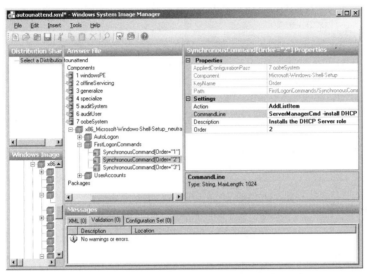

Figure A-19   Running multiple commands during the oobeSystem configuration pass of setup

Note that in addition to using FirstLogonCommands as described, you must also use the Microsoft-Windows-Shell-Setup\Autologon and Microsoft-Windows-Shell-Setup\Autologon \Password settings in your answer file so that the installation of roles and features can be performed in unattended fashion.

NOTE   FirstLogonCommands vs. [GUIRunOnce]

FirstLogonCommands replaces the [GUIRunOnce] section used in Unattend.txt answer files on previous versions of Windows.

Quick Check

1. Why do you have to configure autologon settings in your answer file if you plan on automating initial configuration tasks by using the FirstLogonCommands answer file setting?

2. How can you use ServerManagerCmd.exe to install multiple roles and features using a single command?

Quick Check Answers

1. If no autologon is configured, the FirstLogonCommands won't be run as part of the oobeSystem pass of setup.

2. Use the *servermanagercmd –inputPath input.xml* command to do this.

Installing Roles and Features on Server Core

Installing roles and features on a Server Core installation must be done differently than on a full installation. This is because Server Core supports neither the Add Roles Wizard or Add Features Wizard nor the *ServerManagerCmd.exe* command. Instead, roles and features can be added and removed from Server Core by using the following OC (Optional Component) command-line tools:

- **OCList.exe**   Used to list the server roles, role services, and features that are available for installation and their installed state (either Installed or Not Installed). This utility is available on a Server Core installation only and is not available on a full installation.

- **OCSsetup.exe**   Used to install or uninstall server roles, role services, and features. This utility is available on both the full and Server Core installations.

To install a role or feature on a Server Core installation, start by typing **oclist** at the command prompt. This displays the current install state for optional roles and features and displays the package name needed to install each particular role or feature. (See Figure A-20.)

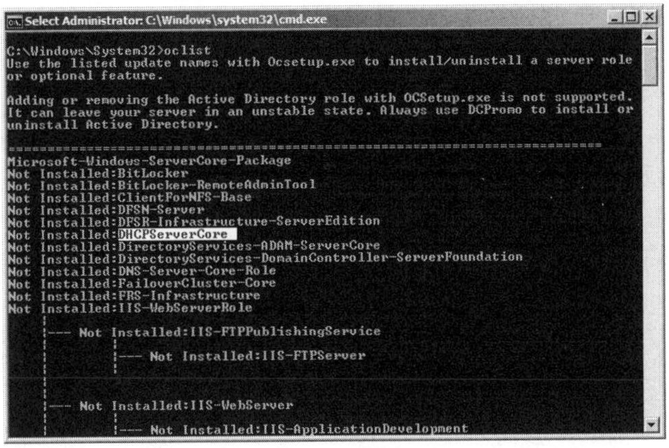

Figure A-20 Results of running *OCList.exe* on Server Core

From this figure, you can see that the package name for the DHCP Server role is DHCPServer-Core. Knowing this, you can then install this role on your server by typing the following command:

```
start /w ocsetup DHCPServerCore
```

There are two things to note when using the *OCSetup.exe* command like this:

- The syntax for *OCSetup.exe* is case-sensitive, so you must type the package name exactly as displayed by the *OCList.exe* command used earlier. Failing to do this can cause installation of the specified role or service to fail.

- Although the *start /w* portion of the command is not required, its use is recommended. This is because, depending on the component being installed, *OClist.exe* might actually misreport the role or feature as not being installed because it is still in the process of installing the component. The *start /w* portion of the command prevents this type of misreporting. Specifically, the */w* (WAIT) argument is used together with *start* to start the specified application (that is, *OCSetup.exe*) and wait for the application to terminate before returning to the command prompt.

OCSetup.exe operates by providing a wrapper for the command-line interface of Package Manager (*PkgMgr.exe*), which is the Windows tool that is used for installing and removing packages and for enabling and disabling features. Package Manager (*PkgMgr.exe*) is called by *OCSetup.exe*. During a normal installation of Windows (either manual or unattended), Package Manager is called by Windows Setup and runs transparently in the background. Package Manager can also be used for unattended installation of hotfixes or other software updates, and it can be used for enabling or disabling Windows features and for servicing an offline Windows image.

OCSetup.exe can take the following command-line parameters:

- **/log:file**   Specifies a nondefault log file location.
- **/norestart**   Specifies that the computer is not rebooted even if required after the component has been installed.
- **/passive**   Uses unattended mode. Progress only is displayed.
- **/quiet**   Uses quiet mode. No user interaction is displayed.
- **/unattendfile:*file***   Uses the specified file, which contains overrides or additions to default configuration settings. (Implies passive mode.)
- **/uninstall**   Uninstalls the specified component.
- **/x: *parameter***   Specifies additional configuration parameters to be applied when installing the component.

For additional information concerning this syntax, type **ocsetup /help** at a command prompt.

NOTE   Using *PkgMgr.exe* instead of *OCSetup.exe*

Although *OCSetup.exe* is the preferred way of installing roles and services on Server Core, you can also use Package Manager to do this. For example, the following command will install all available IIS7 components on Server Core:

```
start /w pkgmgr /iu:IIS-WebServerRole;IIS-WebServer;IIS-CommonHttpFeatures;IIS-
StaticContent;IIS-DefaultDocument;IIS-DirectoryBrowsing;IIS-HttpErrors;IIS-HttpRedirect;IIS-
ApplicationDevelopment;IIS-ASP;IIS-CGI;IIS-ISAPIExtensions;IIS-ISAPIFilter;IIS-
ServerSideIncludes;IIS-HealthAndDiagnostics;IIS-HttpLogging;IIS-LoggingLibraries;IIS-
RequestMonitor;IIS-HttpTracing;IIS-CustomLogging;IIS-ODBCLogging;IIS-Security;IIS-
BasicAuthentication;IIS-WindowsAuthentication;IIS-DigestAuthentication;IIS-
ClientCertificateMappingAuthentication;IIS-IISCertificateMappingAuthentication;IIS-
URLAuthorization;IIS-RequestFiltering;IIS-IPSecurity;IIS-Performance;IIS-
HttpCompressionStatic;IIS-HttpCompressionDynamic;IIS-WebServerManagementTools;IIS-
ManagementScriptingTools;IIS-IIS6ManagementCompatibility;IIS-Metabase;IIS-
WMICompatibility;IIS-LegacyScripts;IIS-FTPPublishingService;IIS-FTPServer;WAS-
WindowsActivationService;WAS-ProcessModel.
```

Automating the Installation of Roles and Features

You can automate the installation of roles and features on Server Core by combining *OCSetup.exe* with the FirstLogonCommands settings in your answer file. This is done basically the same way as using *ServerManagerCmd.exe* together with FirstLogonCommands as discussed earlier.

Index

W

Prepare for Certification with Self-Paced Training Kits

Official Exam Prep Guides—
Plus Practice Tests

Ace your preparation for the skills measured by the MCP exams—and on the job. With official *Self-Paced Training Kits* from Microsoft, you'll work at your own pace through a system of lessons, hands-on exercises, troubleshooting labs, and review questions. Then test yourself with the Readiness Review Suite on CD, which provides hundreds of challenging questions for in-depth self-assessment and practice.

- **MCSE Self-Paced Training Kit (Exams 70-290, 70-291, 70-293, 70-294): Microsoft® Windows Server™ 2003 Core Requirements.** 4-Volume Boxed Set. ISBN: 0-7356-1953-0. (Individual volumes are available separately.)

- **MCSA/MCSE Self-Paced Training Kit (Exam 70-270): Installing, Configuring, and Administering Microsoft Windows® XP Professional, Second Edition.** ISBN: 0-7356-2152-7.

- **MCSE Self-Paced Training Kit (Exam 70-298): Designing Security for a Microsoft Windows Server 2003 Network.** ISBN: 0-7356-1969-7.

- **MCSA/MCSE Self-Paced Training Kit (Exam 70-350): Implementing Microsoft Internet Security and Acceleration Server 2004.** ISBN: 0-7356-2169-1.

- **MCSA/MCSE Self-Paced Training Kit (Exam 70-284): Implementing and Managing Microsoft Exchange Server 2003.** ISBN: 0-7356-1899-2.

For more information about Microsoft Press® books, visit: **www.microsoft.com/mspress**

For more information about learning tools such as online assessments, e-learning, and certification, visit:
www.microsoft.com/mspress *and* **www.microsoft.com/learning**

Windows Server 2008— Resources for Administrators

Windows Server 2008 Resource Kit— Your Definitive Resource!

Windows Server® 2008 Resource Kit

Microsoft® MVPs with Microsoft Windows Server Team

ISBN 9780735623613

Your definitive reference for deployment and operations—from the experts who know the technology best. Get in-depth technical information on Active Directory®, Windows PowerShell™ scripting, advanced administration, networking and network access protection, security administration, IIS, and other critical topics—plus an essential toolkit of resources on CD.

Also available as single volumes

Windows Server 2008 Security Resource Kit

Jesper M. Johansson et al. with Microsoft Security Team

ISBN 9780735625044

Windows Server 2008 Networking and Network Access Protection (NAP)

Joseph Davies, Tony Northrup, Microsoft Networking Team

ISBN 9780735624221

Windows Server 2008 Active Directory Resource Kit

Stan Reimer et al. with Microsoft Active Directory Team

ISBN 9780735625150

Windows® Administration Resource Kit: Productivity Solutions for IT Professionals

Dan Holme

ISBN 9780735624313

Windows Powershell Scripting Guide

Ed Wilson

ISBN 9780735622791

Internet Information Services (IIS) 7.0 Resource Kit

Mike Volodarsky et al. with Microsoft IIS Team

ISBN 9780735624412

See our complete line of books at: **microsoft.com/mspress**

System Requirements

We recommend that you use a single test workstation, test server, or staging server with Microsoft Virtual PC to complete the exercises in each practice. The following are the minimum system requirements your computer needs to meet for you to complete the practice exercises in this book. For more information, see the Introduction.

Hardware Requirements (Virtual PC)

The practice setup instructions in the book assume that you are using Virtual PC 2007 or later, which you can download for free at *http://www.microsoft.com/downloads*. Alternatively, you can use other virtualization software, such as Virtual Server 2005 R2 or Hyper-V. If you are not using virtualization software, see the "Hardware Requirement (Physical)" section that follows.

The following hardware is required to complete the practice exercises if you are using virtualization software:

- Personal computer with 1-GHz or faster processor.
- 2.0 GB of RAM or more is recommended if you are using Windows Vista or Windows Server 2008 as the host operating system to support a virtual environment.
- 80 GB of available hard disk space.
- DVD-ROM drive.
- Internet connectivity.

Hardware Requirements (Physical)

The following hardware is required to complete the practice exercises if you are using physical computers instead of virtualization software:

- Three personal computers, each with a 1-GHz or faster processor, at least 512 MB of RAM, a network card, a video card, and a DVD-ROM drive.
- The following storage requirements:
  - ❑ Computer 1 (Server1) must have one attached hard disk with a storage capacity of at least 20 GB.
  - ❑ Computer 2 (Server2) must have at least two and preferably three attached hard disks. Each hard disk should have a storage capacity of at least 15 GB.

- ❏ Computer 3 (Core1) must have one attached hard disk with a storage capacity of at least 5 GB.
- ❏ All hard disks must be freshly formatted. (No software should be installed.)
- All three computers must be physically connected to each other and to the Internet.
- The network adapter on Computer 2 (Server2) must be PXE-boot compatible.
- If your network does not already include an Internet gateway, Computer 1 (Server1) needs a second network adapter so that it can act as the Internet gateway for the other two computers.
- The test network that includes these computers should be isolated from your production network. (For example, your test network cannot already include a DHCP server that automatically assigns addresses to computers.)

Software Requirements

The following software is required to complete the practice exercises:

- If you are using Virtual PC 2007 or later to create the practice in a virtual environment, the physical host computer must already be running a Windows operating system and have network drivers installed. At the time of this writing, Virtual PC 2007 is officially supported on Windows Vista Business, Windows Vista Enterprise, Windows Vista Ultimate, Windows XP Professional, and Windows XP Tablet PC Edition. You can check the Virtual PC Web site at *http://www.microsoft.com/windows/products/winfamily/virtualpc/default.mspx* for updated information about which operating systems can run Virtual PC.
- Windows Server 2008. You can download an evaluation edition of Windows Server 2008 at the Microsoft Download Center at *http://www.microsoft.com/downloads*. Note that you must use a 32-bit version of Windows Server 2008 within Virtual PC.
- The Windows Automated Installation Toolkit (WAIK). You can download the WAIK at the Microsoft Download Center at *http://www.microsoft.com/downloads*.
- If you are *not* using virtualization software, you need software that allows you to handle .iso and .img files. This software needs to perform either or both of the following functions:
  - ❏ Burn .iso and .img files to CDs or DVDs. (This solution also requires CD/DVD recording hardware).
  - ❏ Mount .iso and .img files as virtual CD or DVD drives on your computer.

What do you think of this book?

We want to hear from you!

Do you have a few minutes to participate in a brief online survey?

Microsoft is interested in hearing your feedback so we can continually improve our books and learning resources for you.

To participate in our survey, please visit:

www.microsoft.com/learning/booksurvey/

...and enter this book's ISBN-10 or ISBN-13 number (located above barcode on back cover*). As a thank-you to survey participants in the United States and Canada, each month we'll randomly select five respondents to win one of five $100 gift certificates from a leading online merchant. At the conclusion of the survey, you can enter the drawing by providing your e-mail address, which will be used for prize notification only.

Thanks in advance for your input. Your opinion counts!

* Where to find the ISBN on back cover

ISBN-13: 000-0-0000-0000-0
ISBN-10: 0-0000-0000-0

0 00000 00000

Example only. Each book has unique ISBN.

Microsoft®
Press